D1546332

REALITY, REPRESENTATION, AND PROJECTION

MIND ASSOCIATION OCCASIONAL SERIES

This series is to consist of occasional volumes of original papers on predefined themes. The Mind Association will nominate an editor or editors for each collection, and may co-operate with other bodies in promoting conferences or other scholarly activities in connection with the preparation of particular volumes.

Publications Officer: M. A. Stewart
Secretary: P. J. Clark

REALITY, REPRESENTATION, AND PROJECTION

Edited by
John Haldane
Crispin Wright

New York   Oxford
OXFORD UNIVERSITY PRESS
1993

Oxford University Press

Oxford   New York   Toronto
Delhi   Bombay   Calcutta   Madras   Karachi
Kuala Lumpur   Singapore   Hong Kong   Tokyo
Nairobi   Dar es Salaam   Cape Town
Melbourne   Auckland   Madrid

and associated companies in
Berlin   Ibadan

Copyright © 1993 by The Mind Association

Published by Oxford University Press, Inc.
200 Madison Avenue, New York, New York 10016

Oxford is a registered trademark of Oxford University Press

All rights reserved. No part of this publication may be reproduced,
stored in a retrieval system, or transmitted, in any form or by any means,
electronic, mechanical, photocopying, recording, or otherwise,
without the prior permission of Oxford University Press.

Library of Congress Cataloging-in-Publication Data
Reality, representation, and projection / edited by John Haldane and
Crispin Wright.
p.   cm.—(Mind Association occasional series)
Includes bibliographical references and index.
ISBN 0-19-507878-0
1. Realism.   2. Reality.   3. Representation (Philosophy)
4. Objectivity.   I. Haldane, John.   II. Wright, Crispin, 1942–
III. Series.
B835.R35   1993   149'.2—dc20   92-39896

2 4 6 8 9 7 5 3 1

Printed in the United States of America
on acid-free paper

To the memory of Ian McFetridge

Acknowledgements

The papers published here all originated in, or continue discussions which took place at an International Conference held at the University of St Andrews in April 1988. Funds for the original conference were provided by a variety of sources. The Department of Logic and Metaphysics at St Andrews is fortunate to be the beneficiary of a trust fund instituted by the late Anne Wright, daughter of J. N. Wright, Professor of Logic and Metaphysics at St Andrews from 1936 to 1966. The Trust generates a sum specifically for the holding of conferences on subjects in Logic and Metaphysics every three years, and provided the core of our funding on this occasion. Additional generous support was provided by the Mind Association, *The Philosophical Quarterly*, the British Academy, and the University of St Andrews. We are grateful to all these institutions for their support. We would also like to express our thanks to our fellow contributors for their excellent essays. The decision to invite them to extend their discussions where it seemed appropriate was naturally a somewhat risky one and we greatly appreciate the patience shown by both them and our publishers during the rather lengthy time it has taken us to organize a final version of the collection. Our thanks to the St Andrews Philosophy Departments' secretaries, Janet Kirk, Anne Cameron, and Kyle Galloway for their assistance both with the organization of the conference and the preparation of the typescript of this collection. The delay notwithstanding, the result of everyone's efforts has been, we believe, to produce a volume which will deservedly become a major focus of discussion in the ongoing debates about realism.

Contents

Notes on Contributors

SIMON BLACKBURN is Edna J. Koury Distinguished Professor of Philosophy at the University of North Carolina, Chapel Hill. He has published in the areas of metaphysics, philosophy of language, and metaethics. He was editor of *Mind* (1985–91), and is the author of *Spreading the Word* (1984) and *Essays in Quasi-Realism* (1993).

JOHN CAMPBELL is Fellow and Tutor at New College, Oxford. He has published on metaphysics and the philosophy of psychology. His book *Self-Consciousness and Spatiotemporal Thought* is forthcoming from MIT Press.

EDWARD CRAIG is Fellow of Churchill College and Reader in Modern Philosophy at the University of Cambridge and a Fellow of the British Academy. His publications include *The Mind of God and the Works of Man* (1987) and *Knowledge and the State of Nature* (1990). He was editor of *Ratio* (1988–92), and is now Chief Editor of *The Routledge Encyclopaedia of Philosophy*.

JOHN HALDANE is Reader in Moral Philosophy at the University of St Andrews. He has published in history of philosophy, philosophy of mind, and social philosophy. He co-edited (with Roger Scruton) Ian McFetridge, *Logical Necessity and Other Essays* (1990) and is an editor of *The Routledge Encyclopaedia of Philosophy*.

BOB HALE is Reader in Logic and Metaphysics at the University of St Andrews. He has published in philosophy of language and philosophy of mathematics and is the author of *Abstract Objects* (1989).

MARK JOHNSTON is Professor of Philosophy at Princeton. His main areas of interest are philosophy of mind and metaphysics, in which he has published a number of influential papers.

IAN McFETRIDGE was Lecturer in Philosophy at Birkbeck College, University of London until his death in 1988. His philosophical papers are collected in *Logical Necessity and Other Essays* (1990).

CHRISTOPHER PEACOCKE is Waynflete Professor of Metaphysical Philosophy in the University of Oxford and a Fellow of the British Academy. He is the author of *Holistic Explanation: Action, Space and Interpretation* (1979), *Sense and Content* (1983), *Thoughts: An Essay on Content* (1986) and *A Study of Concepts* (1992).

PETER RAILTON is Professor of Philosophy at the University of Michigan at Ann Arbor. His interests include, in addition to metaethics, normative ethics and the philosophy of science, and he has authored a number of influential essays in these fields.

JOHN SKORUPSKI is Professor of Moral Philosophy at the University of St Andrews. He is the author of *Symbol and Theory* (1976), *John Stuart Mill* (1989) and *English-Language Philosophy 1750–1945* (1993).

MICHAEL SMITH is Reader in Philosophy at Monash University, Australia. He has published principally on issues in moral psychology and ethical theory.

DAVID WIGGINS is Professor of Philosophy at Birkbeck College, University of London and a Fellow of the British Academy. His publications include *Identity and Spatio-Temporal Continuity* (1967), *Sameness and Substance* (1980) and *Needs, Values, Truth* (1987, 1992).

MICHAEL WILLIAMS is Professor of Philosophy at Northwestern University. His primary area of research is epistemology, in particular the nature of scepticism, to which he has contributed two monographs: *Groundless Belief* (1977) and *Unnatural Doubts* (1991).

CRISPIN WRIGHT is Professor of Logic and Metaphysics at the University of St Andrews, Nelson Professor of Philosophy at the University of Michigan, Ann Arbor, and a Fellow of the British Academy. His main publications are *Wittgenstein on the Foundation of Mathematics* (1980), *Frege's Conception of Numbers as Objects* (1983), *Realism, Meaning and Truth* (1987) and *Truth and Objectivity* (1992).

REALITY, REPRESENTATION, AND PROJECTION

Introduction

John Haldane and Crispin Wright

In the last twenty-five or so years, analytical philosophy has revived many of the traditional metaphysical concerns which, during its first half century, it found reason to bury. During this renaissance no cluster of issues has loomed larger than those very general questions concerning the relationship of mind and world which are debated by realism, of various stripes, and its various forms of opponent. The essays published here cover a wide conspectus of the issues about realism which have been of greatest concern in recent discussion.

One effect of the scale and intensity of contemporary philosophical work in this area has been that if there ever was a consensus of understanding about 'realism' as a philosophical term of art, that consensus has fallen away. The essays that follow bear witness to this diversity of understanding. But disagreements about how realism ought to be understood suggest a deeper consensus about a less theoretical and more intuitive viewpoint; what is controversial is its most effective philosophical elucidation. We believe, then, that it is still possible, and may be useful, to say something not too contentious about the meaning of the term 'realism' and to locate the concerns of the following essays within a single broad design.

A fair characterization of an 'intuitive' realism about, for instance, the external world would be that it is a fusion of two kinds of idea, the one evincing a certain deference, the other a degree of self-assurance. The deferential kind of thought concerns the *independence* of the external world; for example, that it exists independently of us, that it is as it is independently of the concepts in terms of which we think about it, and that it is as it is independently of the beliefs about it which we do, will, or under the most favourable circumstances would form. (Naturally, someone may quite consistently be drawn only to some of these thoughts.) A full-fledged deference will have it that human thought about the external world is, as it were, at best a *map*. Maps can represent better or less well the terrain which they concern. But nothing about that terrain will depend for its existence, or character on the institution of cartography, or on the conventions and techniques employed therein.

The self-assured component in realism is, by contrast, the idea that, while such fit as there may be between our thought and the world is determined

3

independently of human cognition, we are nevertheless capable, at least in favourable circumstances, of forming concepts suitable for the depiction of the real character of the world and, often, of knowing the truth about it as thereby described. Not merely is there a good measure of fit between the external world and our thoughts about it, but we are capable of knowing that this is so, or at least of justifiably taking it to be so. The external world is, as it were, there for us to engage with, our proper cognitive territory.

Applied to the external world, these ideas are apt to seem little more than common sense. But versions of the two kinds of thought are available, naturally, not just for discourse about the external world but for all the regions of discourse—theoretical science, mathematics, aesthetics, ethics, politics, literary criticism, and so on—in which the expression of opinion, argument, inference, and persuasion have a place. And the two kinds of thought have rather different degrees of attraction as the region of discourse varies. Self-assurance weakens, for instance, when we enter more abstruse branches of physical theory, or engage in the most fundamental kind of scientific cosmological speculation. And deference tends to diminish when we are concerned, for instance, with judgements about what is funny, or revolting; and anyway *ought* to diminish, so many philosophers have argued, in the case of discourse concerning secondary qualities of material objects, or in the case of moral, aesthetic, and certain other kinds of evaluative discourse.

In any event, the combination of deference and self-assurance is potentially open to two directions of attack, naturally labelled as *sceptical* and *idealistic*, respectively. A sceptical attack will challenge the element of self-assurance: taking issue either with the truth of the claim that our cognitive powers are adequate in the way we self-assuredly believe them to be, or with our right to make that claim. Much recent work, epitomized by Thomas Nagel's remark that 'Scepticism . . . is only a problem because of the realist claims of objectivity' (*The View from Nowhere*, p. 71), has argued that a vulnerability to sceptical challenge is implicit in deference itself. The idea that our thought in some area is, at best, a mere reflection of wholly independent, autonomous states of affairs cannot but give rise, it is supposed, to imponderable questions concerning the warrant, if any, for taking such thought to be largely successful. The notion that there is an intrinsic connection between realism and scepticism, that scepticism flows out of only the most natural and minimal realist preconceptions about and aspirations for our thought, provides the focus of attention for the contributions to this volume of Michael Williams and Edward Craig. Williams contends that there *is* a route from realism to scepticism, but that it is not as usually perceived. In particular, the concession that truth has no intrinsic connection with the availability of evidence—the distinctive thesis of Dummettian realism, about which more later—gives no particular succour to the sceptic. The realism which sceptical arguments do exploit is rather a special *epistemological* realism: the idea that justificatory relations constitute, as it were, natural kinds whose instantiation is altogether independent of context and human purposes. This realism, Williams contends, so far from being a common-sense premise at the service of sceptical paradox, is actually a highly theoretical assumption which we can and must avoid. In reply, Edward Craig argues that an emphasis on the context-sensitivity of standards of justification is unavailing against the most nagging forms of sceptical doubt, which are best seen as arising quite naturally at the limit of a process of 'objectivization'—the process in which ordinary practical pressures dictate a recourse to more and more exigent tests for our beliefs. Yet there is a singularity in allowing those pressures to take us so far: for *practical* pressures cannot demand the wholly impractical standard implicit in the sceptical challenge. The proper conclusion, Craig contends, is that our ordinary concepts of knowledge and justification neither determinately sustain nor determinately exclude sceptical doubt.

In contrast with the sceptical direction, an idealistic attack on realism will challenge one or more aspects of the way in which the idea of *independence* features in deferential thought. More radically, it may challenge the very idea that the discourse in question is geared to the expression of thoughts whose aim is to reflect some kind of independent reality. The idealist tradition in philosophy, for all the criticism and caricature meted out to it over the years, has proved strikingly durable—sufficiently so to encourage the belief that there are insights for which it is striving but for which philosophy has yet to find definitive means of expression.

Post-war Anglo-American philosophy, of an idealist—or as we shall henceforward say, *anti-realist*—inclination has been dominated by three quite distinct paradigms. The first is that developed in Michael Dummett's work, though it draws, as he has emphasized, both on the ideas of the logical positivists and on the philosophy of language of the later Wittgenstein, and exhibits important points of affinity with the more recent neo-pragmatist writings of Hilary Putnam. In Dummett's view the most fruitful formulation of the dispute between realist and anti-realist lies within the theory of meaning, being focused on the question: what is the proper theoretical description of an understanding of the declarative sentences of a contested area of discourse? Dummett proposes that for the realist such an understanding should consist in possessing an idea of what it is for any particular sentence to be, respectively, true or false, independently of any capacity we may have to verify it as true or false, or to gather relevant evidence either way. Dummett's anti-realist, by contrast, takes it to be a central lesson of Wittgenstein's later philosophy, crystallized in the slogan that meaning is use, that understanding a sentence cannot consist in any conception which is underdetermined by the thinker's manifest capacities. Rather, it must devolve into the essentially practical ability to *use* the sentence in appropriate ways in response to conditions whose obtaining we can recognize; centrally, these conditions are ones whose obtaining justifies the assertion or denial of the sentence.

Some critics, even if willing to allow that Dummett's debate concerns a fundamental issue in the philosophy of language, have questioned its connection with any natural or intuitive understanding of the term 'realism'. But the connection is easy to see. To allow that the meaning of statements in a certain discourse is fixed, as Dummett's realist suggests, by assigning them conditions of potentially evidence-transcendent truth is to grant that, depending upon the world, the truth or falsity of such statements may be settled beyond our ken. So Dummett's realist is committed to a distinction between what confers acceptability on such a statement, in the light of whatever standards inform the discourse to which it belongs, and what makes it actually true. Realism as Dummett understands it is consequently one natural semantical preparation for the idea that our thoughts aim to reflect a reality whose character is independent of us. Dummettian anti-realism, by contrast, whether maintained for reasons local to a particular discourse or on the very general grounds characteristic of Dummett's own exposition, contends that no satisfactory theory of meaning can lay the semantical groundwork which realism demands.

These ideas provide the stage setting for three of the exchanges which follow. John Haldane and Ian McFetridge focus on the question of how the discussion of Dummettian realism relates to the extensive investigation of positions taking the title of 'realism' which loomed so large in philosophical debates in the mediaeval period and in the seventeenth and eighteenth centuries. The symposiasts note that Dummett's formulation of the issue marks a historical shift in the idea of what cognition most fundamentally is, from the mediaeval paradigm of an intellectual grasp of, or perception-like interaction with objects of an appropriate sort, to the contemporary conception that it is first and foremost a matter of believing and saying the true, of acquiring, for the right kind of reason, states of appropriate propositional content. Thus the question arises: may not important issues about realism be better formulated in terms of the earlier, 'object'-directed cognitive paradigm? And if so, may it not be that the Dummettian debate passes them by?

In their different ways, Haldane and McFetridge both return positive answers to these questions. Haldane's discussion involves a sympathetic treatment of certain mediaeval ideas about the relationship between concepts and properties—ideas which he then brings into exchange with claims presented by contemporary authors such as Wright and Putnam—and of the Thomist claim that in cognition the thinker becomes, to the extent that one and the same ontological principle determines the nature of both his thought and its object, *identical* with that of which he thinks. McFetridge casts doubt on something usually viewed as a strong point in global Dummettian anti-realism: that, in contrast to the logical positivists who held that meaningfulness is bounded by verifiability, the Dummettian anti-realist's claim need concern only the *truth-aptitude* of evidence-transcendent statements and need not involve questioning their *assertoric content*. McFetridge argues, to the contrary, that if the anti-realist accepts anything broadly resembling our ordinary theory of the world and of our place in it, he must insist that there can be no statement—not even a 'homophonic' statement—of the assertoric content of the statements which he finds problematical.

The Dummettian anti-realist may be regarded either as recommending that we drop the notion of truth altogether from the semantics of a contested discourse, replacing it with, for instance, proof, or verification or warranted assertibility, or as proposing that we retain truth-conditional semantics but with the proviso that truth is now thought of as an essentially evidentially constrained notion, so that the principle of bivalence (that a statement is determinately either true or false) is no longer acceptable for discourse where evidence cannot always be guaranteed to be available. The conception of truth as essentially evidentially constrained provides the starting point for the essays by Crispin Wright and Mark Johnston. Wright makes a case that the notions of truth, of truth-aptitude, and of a genuine statement, are essentially formal ones, and hence carry no substantial metaphysical implications. In particular, truth is intrinsically neither evidentially constrained nor not. The issue between the Dummettian realist and his opponent is thus best viewed as focused on the question whether the truth predicate in the contested discourse may defensibly be viewed as having a further feature—freedom from evidential constraint— whose possession goes some way to vindicating intuitive realist imagery. And this, Wright contends, rather than the specific issue about evidence-transcendence, should be the paradigm for all realist/anti-realist debates. If the Dummettian debate fails satisfactorily to capture realist and anti-realist intuitions with respect to such matters as value and the aesthetic, the crucial question is consequently, what *other* features are there, besides (freedom from) evidential constraint, such that the fact that a truth predicate in a particular discourse has or lacks them may justify an intuitively realist or anti-realist outlook? A number of such features are identified in Wright's paper, which thus offers a framework for a measure of re-integration in the contemporary debates.

Mark Johnston presents a critique of the verificationist component in the recent writings of philosophers working in the tradition of American pragmatism, with arguments of Goodman, Rorty, and Putnam all coming in for detailed scrutiny. His most general criticisms, if successful, have the wider implication that truth cannot coherently be viewed as evidentially constrained at all. These criticisms, together with those developed in the course of McFetridge's contribution, add up to a case which proponents of Dummettian anti-realism will surely feel the need to answer. But Johnston contends that insofar as realism stands opposed to pragmatism, the pragmatist has no need or reason to go verificationist. Rather, the clear-headed pragmatist will maintain a view not about truth but about the notion of a global theory's being acceptable. That view will be that the notion of a theory's being acceptable is a 'response-dependent' one.

A perception of the importance of the idea of response- or judgement-dependent concepts in the debates about realism has been growing over the last few years. Johnston's statement of one possible direction of development of the idea, to the service of the above contention about pragmatism, is more explicit that can be found elsewhere in his publications to date and will, in conjunction with the concluding section of Wright's essay, on the latter's related idea of order of determination, provide a useful focus for further work. Wright and Johnston did indeed continue their exchange on this issue, and at one point we planned to include further material by Johnston on the position he styles 'Conceptual Protagoreanism', together with an extended discussion by Wright, 'Order of Determination, Response Dependence, and the Euthyphro Contrast', of his own and Johnston's approaches and some additional commentary by

Johnston. In the event, various considerations, including those of space and balance, dictated the omission of this material, but it is very much to be hoped that it will find other outlets in the near future.

One of the most fascinating aspects of the Dummettian debate is its bearing on the foundations of logic—specifically on the question of the adequacy of classical logic and on more general issues concerning the justifiability of entrenched logical practice and the kinds of grounds on which it might coherently be argued to need revision. It is to these questions that the contributions by John Skorupski and Christopher Peacocke are devoted. Both writers are agreed that learning such lessons of Wittgenstein's later philosophy of language as are summarized in the slogan that meaning is use ought to encourage neither the imposition of an evidential constraint on the notion of truth nor the idea that meaning can fully adequately be explained in terms of assertibility conditions. Consequently, in the view of both authors, the traditional semantical foundation for classical logic goes unchallenged by those Wittgensteinian ideas. But this very general point of agreement stands in contrast to many points of difference. Skorupski holds that while truth is not any kind of construct out of assertibility, and the meaning of a sentence in general is determined by its truth-condition, this truth-condition is constituted out of twin, primitive contributions from the assertibility conditions of the sentence and its inferential powers. In consequence, and in contrast with the classical account, the inferential powers of a sentence may not be explained by or viewed as consequent upon its truth-conditions. There is therefore no space for the idea that the inferential powers assigned to a sentence in standard, reflective deductive practice could clash with its truth-condition; and no space, Skorupski maintains, for a *justification* of deductive practice. Against this, Peacocke deploys the 'commitment' model of meaning familiar from others of his recent writings, and the contrast between sense-determining and sense-resultant principles concerning a particular concept, in order to reject the suggestion that the inferential powers of a sentence may always be thought of as a primitive component in the determination of its truth-conditions. A space for certain kinds of issue concerning justification of inferential practice is consequently reopened. Peacocke goes on to explore a number of sensitive questions concerning the relation between the meaning of the logical constants and the rules of inference which govern them. He argues in particular for the superiority of his realist, commitment model of understanding in explaining and licensing the very natural thought that the universally closed undecidable sentence constructed in the course of Gödel's first incompleteness theorem for arithmetic may informally be recognized to be true; and he defends the contention that there is no abrasion between (the acceptable components in) Wittgenstein's later thought about rules and the claim that deductive practice is open to substantial justification.

Considered as a global thesis, Dummettian anti-realism denies that in anything justifiably regarded as representational discourse, we can intelligibly make semantic provision for the depiction of states of affairs whose obtaining, or not, is in principle beyond our detection. It is clear, but too seldom recognized, that it is consistent with this view that some of our discourse is genuinely representational, and concerns states of affairs which, on at least some proper understandings of the term, are independent of us. In shifting, for example, to a broadly intuitionistic conception of number theory, we do not immediately foreclose on the idea that the series of natural numbers constitutes a real object of mathematical investigation, which it is harmless and correct to think of the number-theoretician as exploring. In this respect, the second anti-realist paradigm prominent in modern philosophy amounts to a much more radical view than the Dummettian one. According to this second kind of anti-realism, the Dummettian realist may well have matters more or less right as far as the *semantics* of the contested discourse is concerned. The fundamental error presupposed by ordinary realist thought about say ethics, or mathematics, is not semantical at all but one of *metaphysical superstition*. Such is the view adopted by, for instance, John Mackie about ethics and Hartry Field about pure mathematics. For Field, the semantics of mathematical statements may well prepare them to receive potentially proof-transcendent truth-values, conferred by the intrinsic properties of the pure mathematical realm. The trouble is: there *is* no such realm—there just are no structures of abstract mathematical entities of the kind which a face-value construal of the singular terms and quantifiers of number theory, analysis, and set theory, etc., would call for. The conviction that we attain to truth in pure mathematics is simply a great mistake; there is nothing out there to make our pure mathematical statements true.

Mackie's view of ethics is broadly similar. According to Mackie, our ordinary understanding of moral discourse requires the existence of moral properties with something like the objectivity and autonomy possessed by the primary qualities of material objects dealt with by physical science. But he argues that when we look in detail at the demands which moral discourse places on the entities with which it putatively deals, we find that they are unsatisfiable—or at least that the belief that they are satisfied is totally without justification. As before, the conclusion is that ordinary moral thought is guilty of a sweeping, systematic mistake: *semantically* it is indeed representational thought, true or not according to whether certain properties apply or fail to apply in the world. But there are no such properties: reality is simply devoid of all features and states of affairs which it would take thought of distinctively moral content to represent.

It is this second paradigm of debate between realist and anti-realist—the debate between the realist and the *irrealist* (or error-theorist)—which provides the backcloth for the contributions of Michael Smith, John Campbell, Peter Railton, and David Wiggins. Michael Smith's paper fixes directly on John Mackie's error theory of moral discourse, and the charge levelled against it by writers such as John McDowell that Mackie fails to find real moral properties in the world only because he works with too denuded a conception of the world, overlooking in particular the possibility of an apt comparison between moral qualities and what Locke called the *secondary* qualities of material objects. Smith's contention is that certain important aspects of ordinary moral argument go unrecognized in the comparison with secondary qualities, and that these, together with certain constitutive platitudes governing our conception of moral value, powerfully support a *rationalistic* conception of moral qualities and their epistemology. But if a broadly rationalistic account provides the best reconstruction of our actual concept of moral value, there is an immediate 'Mackiean' question whether anything real answers to that concept. If, as many moral theorists accept, there are simply no moral norms which are binding on any rational, reflective subject, Mackie may after all have been right in the contention that there are no real moral qualities, even if unpersuasive in the grounds he advanced for it.

McDowell's response to Mackie presupposes, of course, a realism about secondary qualities, secured on McDowell's account by treating them as dispositions to generate certain distinctive subjective affects. John Campbell's contribution focuses on colour and the assumptions about it which structure the debate between Mackie and McDowell. The basic argument for an irrealist view of colour is that whereas fundamental physical science has no use for colour properties in the formulation of its laws and its descriptions of the fundamental physical characteristics of things, the phenomenology of ordinary colour vision is as of objects which possess mind-independent colour properties. In McDowell's view, this phenomenology is quite coherent with the conception of colours as dispositions to produce colour experience in us, and such dispositions should surely rank as real enough properties, even if not mind-independent ones. Campbell rejects McDowell's account. He argues for a conception of colour which agrees with McDowell's in rejecting the idea implicit in Mackie's discussion, that only the mind-independent qualities ultimately recognized by theoretical science are real; but he contends, in contrast to McDowell, that colours *are* nevertheless mind-independent properties of objects, which ground, rather than are to be identified with dispositions of objects to produce experiences of colour, and yet which are just as they are perceived, at least in favourable circumstances, to be—properties whose real nature is transparent to us in colour experience. In his response, Michael Smith queries whether this difficult yet attractive set of features can indeed be combined by any coherent philosophy of colour.

The extended exchange between Peter Railton and David Wiggins involves a double contribution from each author, and covers a very broad sweep of issues in contemporary ethical theory. But its central focus is on whether those features in moral discourse which, Railton suggests, most commonly motivate the view that there are no real facts for it to describe—which he identifies respectively as the 'queerness' of moral facts, the obduracy of moral disagreement, and, most importantly, the normative (intrinsically directive or reason-giving) character of moral judgement—whether these features might be assuaged or accommodated by some form of ethical naturalism. Railton canvasses the prospects in these respects of a *substantive naturalism*: a naturalism which holds that moral properties are indeed identical with certain natural properties, the kind of properties that can 'pull their weight' in empirical science, but for which the identities in question are not analytic but a posteriori, so comparable in that respect to the identification of water with H_2O. Wiggins, however, argues that even this form of non-analytic naturalism is likely to succumb to Moore's 'open-question' argument, when that much misunderstood consideration is given its fullest development, and contends that the best hope for a proper explanation of the normativity of moral judgement lies elsewhere, with a position that would have been much more congenial to Moore, according to which moral properties are non-natural and *sui generis* but, properly understood, in no way 'queer'. Indeed, Wiggins identifies a way of thinking which he terms 'explanatory or Humean naturalism' (Railton calls this 'methodological naturalism') within which an advocate of the open-question argument might yet allow that, in this sense, moral discourse concerns *natural* qualities and relations. This explanatory naturalism, unlike the views Moore opposed, is thus not in the business of identifying the 'real' empirical nature of the extensions of moral predicates, and Wiggins' suggestive, if admittedly inconclusive, development of Moore's argument proposes that, inasmuch as it reflects a different kind of interest in the world, no non-evaluative predicate can be guaranteed to keep track of the extension of any evaluative one.

The last of the three currently dominant anti-realist paradigms disputes something which the other two grant: that the declarative sentences of the contested discourse equip us for the expression of genuinely representational thoughts. The fundamental error of the realist, according to an anti-realist of this third kind, is one susceptible to a broadly Wittgensteinian diagnosis: the error of being misled by merely superficial 'grammatical' similarities between different regions of discourse, so that we are deceived into thinking that they are in the business of doing the same essential thing: *stating facts*, expressing representational thoughts 'which may be about houses, pains, good or evil, or anything else you please' (*Investigations* 304). On this view, what needs to be recognized is that a discourse may have all the overt trappings of genuine assertion, expression of belief, etc., yet in reality not be in the business of making statements, genuinely true or false, at all.

Modern anti-realist writers in this non-cognitivist tradition about ethics include, of course, A. J. Ayer and R. M. Hare, and more recently, Simon Blackburn and Allan Gibbard. Over-simplifying slightly, for each of these authors the fundamental role of ethical 'assertion' is not to state facts but to express moral attitudes and (thereby) to prescribe or caution against certain specific forms of conduct. A somewhat similar idea surfaces in the philosophy of science in various forms of theoretical instrumentalism, in the idea of laws as 'inference tickets', and in the view of theoretical statements as metaphor, associated with such writers as Mary Hesse. In each case, high level theoretical statements, despite their apparent meaningfulness and apparently assertoric syntax, are denied any truth-evaluable content. And of course similar ideas are found also in the philosophy of mathematics, in the writings of thinkers as otherwise disparate as Hilbert and the later Wittgenstein.

Simon Blackburn's sophisticated attempts to delineate the form and elaborate the detail of a competitive expressivist—in Blackburn's preferred term, 'quasi-realist'—account of moral discourse have been conspicuous in recent work in this tradition. The quasi-realist programme for a discourse consists in seeking to explain and justify the 'assertoric surface' withouty invocation of the idea that it is genuinely factual; to 'earn the right' to speak with the realist, as it were, without accepting his metaphysics. In his contribution to the present volume Bob Hale addresses a key question of detail for any such programme: that concerning the analysis and treatment of conditionals with putatively non-factual—he focuses specifically on the case of moral—antecedents. Hale makes a powerful case for a simple but potentially lethal dilemma of quite general importance: if the dominant operator in such a conditional is taken to be, as its surface grammar suggests, the conditional itself, then, Hale argues, there is no hope for a genuinely *expressive* analysis of the moral clause in the antecedent. If, on the other hand, the dominant operator is taken to be some sort of expression of attitude, then there is no hope of disclosing a *logical*, as opposed to a *moral*, failing in one who accepts the premises but rejects the conclusion of, say, a *modus ponens* or *modus tollens* inference in which such a conditional features as the major premise. If this is right, then expressivism about moral discourse can find no place for the idea that it is subject to the ordinary canons of logic. In his reply, besides pursuing the issues concerning conditionals raised by Hale, Simon Blackburn takes the opportunity to respond to a criticism of Wright's—roughly, that to earn the right to 'speak with the realist' is to divest of content the original contention that moral discourse, for example, is not genuinely assertoric—and provides a usefully clarified and deepened statement of the quasi-realist programme. Bob Hale briefly responds.

I

REALISM: THE HISTORICAL AND CONTEMPORARY DEBATES

1

Mind–World Identity Theory and the Anti-Realist Challenge

John Haldane

I

Most, and perhaps even all, philosophical problems have a history, and upon examination it usually turns out that the history involved is a long one. It is a familiar feature of philosophy, as contrasted with empirical studies, that often a contemporary problem can be better understood by looking at what earlier writers have had to say about it or about a related issue. In this discussion, then, I wish to offer an example of 'philosophizing historically' which I hope may be of interest for the light it sheds upon a little known and rarely discussed aspect of the work of Thomas Aquinas and upon a now familiar and much discussed family of theses in contemporary philosophy of language and epistemology.

II

Realism and *anti-realism* are titles beneath which a remarkably wide range of philosophical views has been presented. In the present discussion, however, I shall be concerned principally with two areas in which claims falling under these headings have been proposed and disputed: viz., *ontology* and *epistemology*. Firstly, then, let *ontological realism* be the thesis that there is a world, independent of thought and language. Secondly, and relatedly, let

This essay is a revised version of a paper written in 1987 and given to a conference on *Realism and Reason* held at the University of St Andrews in 1988. On that occasion a related paper was delivered by the late Ian McFetridge. The text of the latter paper together with additional material appears as 'Realism and Anti-Realism in a Historical Context', Chapter 2 in the present volume, and (under the same title) as Chapter 7 in Ian McFetridge, *Logical Necessity and Other Essays*, J. Haldane and R. Scruton (eds.). Any revisions made to the present text since 1988 are not in parts which were the subject of discussion by McFetridge.

epistemological realism be the view that in thought we may have knowledge of this mind-independent reality and that in utterance we may speak truly of it. The relevant versions of *anti-realism* are now to be understood as involving the denial of part or all of one or other (or both) of these theses.

The two affirmative doctrines admit of strong and weak interpretations. Regarding ontological realism, for example, one might maintain, in nominalist fashion, that while the *existence* of the world is independent of us, such *structure* (of, for example, substances, events, processes, properties, and relations) as we seem to find there is in fact of our own creation. With respect to epistemological realism it might be supposed either that knowledge and linguistic reference are essentially indirect, involving some kind of inference from the content of intentional states, and mediation via intervening intensional entities, respectively; or else, that cognition and meaning are constituted by direct, unmediated relations between subject and world.[1]

Concerning the relations between ontological and epistemological realism, it is clear enough that the latter presupposes the former in some or other version of it apt to the content of the version of epistemological realism being advanced, but clear also that there is no converse relation of dependence between them. This said, however, ontological realism is not likely to be held in conjunction with the denial of epistemological realism. If the latter is false it is quite obscure what reason there could be for maintaining the former. In reply someone might perhaps suggest a transcendental argument for the ontological thesis. But, given the denial of the claim that the world is available to us in thought, and by way of our linguistic representation of it, I can envisage no plausible reasoning taking one from the occurrence of *immanent* thought and utterance to the existence of *transcendent* reality via the supposed necessity of the latter for the former. Certainly no such argument could be constructed given the rejection of both strong and weak versions of epistemological realism; and from the attack on Cartesian representationalism launched by Thomas Reid and subsequent writers—a theory which appears to deny only the strong variant of epistemological realism and to advocate a weaker doctrine of cognition via intermediate signs—we have learnt that the representationalist claim that these latter signify elements of an external world is simply an unwarranted, question-begging assumption. Without such signification, however, weak epistemological realism collapses, leaving only epistemological (or 'subjective') idealism, i.e. (sceptical) anti-realism.[2] Accordingly, anyone disposed to reject strong epistemological realism had better be careful if he is also antagonistic towards ontological idealism. For without some credible version of the former, ontological realism is left unsupported and thereby vulnerable to the excising cut of Ockham's razor.

III

A question of immediate interest which arises from the foregoing is this: is the epistemological realist committed to any further claims which bring him into conflict with contemporary *semantic* anti-realism? This latter view, as it has been developed in the writings of Michael Dummett, Crispin Wright, Hilary Putnam, and others, is concerned with the notions of *truth, meaning,* and *understanding.* In essence this kind of anti-realism consists in the rejection of theories of linguistic meaning which identify semantic comprehension with understanding of the truth-conditions of statements where these conditions may transcend the recognitional capacities of speakers of the language. For Putnam the point at issue is, in the first instance, the determination of reference,[3] but there is general agreement among the authors mentioned that what is problematic about realist accounts of meaning is their common attachment to a notion of truth as objective conformity between, on the one hand, statements (and unuttered thoughts) and, on the other, objects and features in an independent, pre-structured world.

One way in which adherence to this realist conception of truth may reveal itself is in the now familiar claim that the world may be determinately thus and so in ways which are characterizable in thought and language but which may transcend even our very best efforts, in the most favourable circumstances (even 'in the limit'), to describe its structure. Equivalently, such a realism envisages the possibility of an empirically ideal theory, supported by total available evidence and satisfying all theoretical constraints, none the less proving to be false. The anti-realist takes this to be senseless. On his account the meaning of a statement is indeed intimately related to the types of conditions under which it would be appropriate to assert it, but these cannot coherently be taken to be such as might forever transcend a speaker's capacity to recognize their obtaining, which is what realist semantics is supposed to require. Realism's picture of objective truth as an external relation holding between thoughts (and words) and the things they represent excludes any epistemic limit—what the subject does *or could ever* know is not to the point.[4] And if this picture is unintelligible, then so too is the idea that truth could transcend its recognition by even the most favoured investigator. Anti-realism, by contrast, insists that truth and epistemology go hand in hand. This is not simply the truistic claim that one cannot know that *p* unless *p* is true, but the more radical assertion that having the idea of *p* as being such as may be true, and hence understanding the very idea of *p*, depend upon the possibility of its being known that *p*.

It is clear enough that these claims stand in direct opposition to a view of meaning as being given by possibly recognition-transcendent truth-conditions. It is equally clear that such a view presupposes a conception of objective truth. Consequently, it can easily seem that semantic anti-realism and epistemological and ontological realism are at odds. That is to say, it may appear that either indirectly (by challenging the former and so leaving the latter vulnerable to Ockham's razor) or directly (by a frontal attack on the very coherence of ontological realism) semantic anti-realism yields something like old style idealism. It *may* be that this is so. However, it is not at all certain, I think, that what the semantic anti-realist denies is anything that the advocate of ontological and epistemological realism, even in their strong versions, is *necessarily* bound to claim. For it is not obvious that these, even together with the idea of an objective truth-predicate, commit the realist to a conception of truth as being *in principle* recognition-transcendent.

IV

If the latter is correct, and epistemological realism is compatible with semantic anti-realism as it has been characterized above, that is surely a fact worth knowing about and reflecting upon. For it may help to show how realism is both possible and plausible while also serving to bring into clearer focus the proper targets of the modern anti-realist attack. Here I aim to do no more than outline what I believe to be a not incredible form of realism and to offer a suggestion about how, if one were to accept it, familiar anti-realist challenges might then best be conceived.

Introducing his own work on these topics, Crispin Wright remarks that 'it is open to question whether modern anti-realism actually takes issue with realism on any point which marks a realist/idealist divide'.[5] To see why this question deserves to be pressed one first needs to consider something of the opposition between realism and idealism.

In contradiction to scepticism the proponent of epistemological realism holds that we have the capacity to reflect (something of) the structure of the world in the structure of thought. That is to say, we actually possess (some) *adequate concepts*. In addition, such a realist also maintains that this conceptual capacity is sometimes appropriately exercised in respect of objects and features in extra-mental reality. This is to say that we can form *true beliefs*. The position of the idealist with respect to these claims is succinctly stated in the same section of the work by Crispin Wright from which I quoted above. Writing on behalf of the idealist, he observes:

> It is an error to think of our investigations as confronting an objective array of states of affairs which are altogether independent of our modes of conceiving and investigative enterprises. No truth is altogether 'not of our making'. Rather reality is—on one version—a reification of our own conceptual and cognitive nature with no more claim to autonomy than a mirror image. There is, accordingly, no possibility of states of affairs which outstrip our capacities for knowledge, still less transcend our understanding.[6]

In the light of his remark about the possible relationship between 'modern anti-realism' and idealism, this way of expressing the idealist view is interesting, for it looks pretty similar to what many commentators have taken the modern anti-realist to be claiming. This is not to suggest that Wright is unaware of the need to show how, if at all, these views actually differ. Much of his recent work, including that from which I have quoted, is precisely concerned with the task of distinguishing anti-realism from other views and with analysing the several elements out of which it is composed. This said, however, if anti-realism, at least as Wright conceives of it, does not coincide with idealism or fall on the same side of the divide between it and realism, then this needs to be made quite clear, for at least two reasons. First, as I remarked, it is a quite widely entertained and not utterly foolish thought that contemporary semantic anti-realism is, or is on the way to being, a version of idealism—be it of a linguistic sort.[7] This estimate *may* rest on confusion and *may* be entirely without substance, but if so these facts need to be demonstrated, particularly since, as Wright also acknowledges, some anti-realist arguments appear to be perfectly general in their application. This is true, for example, of those focusing upon the conditions of acquiring and manifesting semantic understanding, and of others deriving from the Wittgensteinian rule-following considerations. Second, if a version of realism can be made out which is clearly opposed to both scepticism and idealism, but which is also modest to the extent of disavowing recognition-transcendent truth and restricting meaning to conceptual capacity (and restricting the latter to cognitive ability), the question will arise: what remains for anti-realism to be *anti* with respect to? Perhaps the same arguments may then be redirected against *ultra-realism*, but at that point the modest realist is very likely to be an ally in the attack.

V

The next task, then, is to outline a theory which combines the features of the strong versions of ontological and epistemological realism but which is not committed to a notion of truth as extending beyond the full power of cognition to recognize it. It is at this point that I want to introduce Aquinas, who makes claims about the nature of the world, the process of cognition, the semantics of natural language, and the character of truth which suggest just such a theory.

The title 'realism' is sometimes employed by commentators in describing Aquinas' philosophical thought, usually in reference to his views on metaphysics and about perception and knowledge. In connection with the former issue this epithet is used to distinguish his position from that of nominalists such as Ockham, and in regard to the latter it is intended to mark a contrast with representationalism and phenomenalism. On both scores, I think, there is little doubt that Aquinas is a realist, though the details of his positive views remain somewhat obscure and such of them as are clear often strike contemporary philosophers as simply bizarre. For present purposes it is not necessary to devote space to problems associated with Thomist exegesis and I shall simply offer what I take to be the general character of his positions so far as these bear upon the current topic.

On the issue of ontological structure, Aquinas follows Aristotle in rejecting Platonic ultra-realism (*universalia ante res*) in favour of a theory of natural kinds. Each individual, or primary substance, has an essential nature (*quidditas*) which determines its organizational structure and characteristic powers. While these natures, or '*substantial forms*', are numerically distinct, they fall into classes in virtue of being qualitatively (or formally) identical. Thus, for example, since Peter and Paul are different individuals they have numerically diverse natures—the form-of-Peter and the form-of-Paul, respectively. Nonetheless, these individual forms are of the same general type, viz., *humanity*. This common nature is instantiated by these and by all other men and women, but there is nothing general in the various individuals themselves, for humanity *qua* universal only exists intentionally, in thought, as abstracted from various of its instances. By positing regular mind-independent structures within it, and thereby rejecting nominalism, this view aims to show how systematic study of the world is possible—but without having recourse to the ontological extravagance of Platonism.

There is good reason to be reticent in following those commentators who describe Aquinas' position as being simply a version of Aristotle's moderate realism (*universalia in rebus*), since his denial that there is anything universal (save in the mind) tells against this reading. None the less, it is clear enough that he believes there is an external world with a pre-existing structure of individuals grouped into natural classes. Moreover, he employs the familiar Aristotelian taxonomy of *substance* and *attribute*, and *essence* and *accident*, so as to show that there is an order of priority between the various natural groupings and that certain of these, viz., those composed of individuals exhibiting common (or, as might now be said, 'qualitatively identical') substantial forms, are ontologically fundamental.

Although it is nowadays barely known outside of neo-scholastic circles, Thomist epistemology has much to commend it to contemporary philosophers. In particular its anti-foundationalist and anti-representationalist aspects should appeal. However, it is also likely to prove puzzling, and perhaps even ultimately unintelligible on account of the central and much repeated claim that cognition involves *the identity of known and knower*.[8] As before, I shall not take space here to pursue any exegetical debates over the fine details of Aquinas' thought. Suffice it to say that this identity thesis is intended to serve two central explanatory roles: first, to indicate how world-intending thoughts are possible; and second, to show how they engage directly with objects and features within it. In regard to the latter point Aquinas is explicit in his rejection of the view that cognition involves intermediate representations. He writes as follows:

> Some have held that our cognitive faculties know only what is experienced within them, for instance that the senses perceive only the impressions made on the organs. According to this opinion the intellect thinks only of what is experienced within it, i.e. the species [ideas] received in it. Thus again according to this opinion, these species are *what* is thought of [*quod intelligitur*].
>
> The opinion however, is obviously false . . . because the things of which we think are the same as the objects of science [i.e. real objects and properties] . . . we must say, therefore, that species stand in relation to the intellect *as that by which* the intellect thinks [or has understanding] [*quo intelligit intellectus*].[9]

Here and elsewhere, Aquinas is not denying that conceptual contents may sometimes be the objects of thought nor that the intellect may be directed not outwards towards the environment but inwards upon its own operations. Indeed, he often remarks upon the reflexive character of cognition and upon the potential for self-awareness in its acts.[10] However, he also insists that reflection is secondary to the principal cognitive activity which is aimed at mind-independent reality:

> No one perceives that he thinks save from this: that he thinks of something, because he must first know something before he knows that he knows; and the consequence is that the mind comes to know itself through that of which it thinks or senses.[11]

Elsewhere, Aquinas comments: 'The first things known are things outside the mind to which the intellect is first directed in thought.'[12]

In the Thomist scheme concepts invest thoughts with their intentional contents, just as properties provide particulars with their characters. For Descartes and for most subsequent Cartesians the process of thinking is in itself neutral, or devoid of sense, and content is only acquired by way of the mind becoming directed upon mental objects; that is to say, thinking is conceived of as a contentless medium of pure awareness and the intentional individuation of distinct (types) of thoughts is achieved by reference to whatever phenomena are seen through this medium.[13] For Aquinas, by contrast, different (types) of thoughts differ intrinsically—being informed by and expressing distinct concepts, what in scholastic vocabulary are termed *species expressae*. The primary manner in which *species* feature in cognition, therefore, is as determinants of the character of mental activity, thereby directing it towards classes of real (or possible) objects. For example, a thought informed by the concept *Cat* has '*catness*' as its content. It is (intentionally) about *catness* and serves to direct the subject's mind towards this nature including, in appropriate circumstances, real instances of it. Singular reference may then be secured either (for the most part contingently) by 'descriptive fit'—where the conceptual content is uniquely satisfied—or else by the involvement of causal or contextual relations between an object exemplifying a given kind or kinds, and the subject whose mental activity manifests an appropriate conceptual character.[14]

So far as concerns the issue of epistemological realism there are two important features of the Thomist theory of cognition. First, the insistence that the intellect engages directly with reality and not with some *tertium quid* intervening between them (concepts being the *means* and, apart from in reflection, not the *objects* of thought). And second, the striking claim that the forms or natures which give structure to the world, and the concepts which give 'shape' to thought, are one and the same. Thus, a cat and an idea of a cat differ not in their nature, that is *catness* in both cases, but in the modes of exemplification of this nature. Felix instantiates (or better, from the point of view of avoiding Platonism, actualizes a case of) felinity *in esse naturale*, and my thinking of him actualizes the very same form (*qua* universal) *in esse intentionale*.

Notwithstanding its initial strangeness, I do not believe that the difficulties which may stand in the way of accepting Aquinas' theory are insurmountable. Whatever may be the case about this, however, the cognitive identity thesis has clear advantages over theories of thought which regard thinking as consisting in the mind's engagement with some type of mental representations—usually either words or images, or both. In addition to supporting epistemological realism, Aquinas provides what these familiar alternatives notoriously lack, viz., an *explanation* of how it could be that thoughts are essentially related to their objects. The intrinsic character of a mental act is formally identical with that of the extra-mental entities to which it is directed. Thus, the claim of identity between subject and object of cognition:

> Knower and known are one principle of activity inasmuch as one reality results from them both, *viz.*, the mind in act [i.e. actually thinking]. I say that one reality is the result, because therein the mind is conjoined with its object;[15]

and elsewhere Aquinas explains that

> The intelligible species [concept] is a similitude of a thing's essential nature, and is in some fashion the very essence and nature of it but existing intentionally and not physically.[16]

This account of the relation between thought and world as involving the literal conformity of the mind to the formal structure of nature gives a precise meaning to the idea of truth as correspondence between the content of a judgement and a state of affairs. Aquinas is explicit in his descriptions both of the nature of this relation and of its subjective term, that is, an *asserted proposition.*

> Truth is defined by the conformity of mind and thing. Accordingly to know this conformity is to know truth ... the mind [can come to know of] its own conformity with an intelligible entity [i.e., a form instantiated *in esse naturale*] not by remaining simply with the apprehension of this nature but by proceeding to evoke an affirmation or denial [i.e. an asserted proposition], for truth is only known and articulated when the intellect judges that something corresponds to [its content].[17]

Earlier, I remarked that Aquinas believes that common natures only exist as universal when abstracted from particular cases. This claim may be of doubtful coherence and risks collapse into a version of conceptualism not very different from the view of Ockham, or from those versions of nominalism favoured by Goodman and Putnam. Given other things he says, however, Aquinas is more plausibly interpreted as advancing a type of moderate realism similar, but not identical, to that of Aristotle. I suspect, that this interpretation is only intelligible if one discounts the suggestion that generality is nowhere to be found outside of thought.[18] Certainly, one may do well to accept the thesis that there are individual natures, for example, the *humanity-of-Peter* as an entity numerically distinct from the *humanity-of-Paul*, but this claim seems to entail that there are also common forms. For what are to be found in Peter and Paul (or more precisely, and less Platonistically, what Peter and Paul are) are different individual *cases* of the same *general* thing, viz. humanity.

Whatever the correct interpretation of Aquinas on this issue, it is important to note that the *species* which inform cognitive activity, and which are the mental counterparts of the species that determine the natures of particular things and thus are responsible for the structure of the world, come to be exemplified intentionally as a result of subjects' causal relations with their environment. As Aquinas has it: 'the intellect is receptive; it is, as it were, modulated and measured by things'.[19] However, the sense in which this 'modulation' of the mind by the world is causal is not properly captured by the idea of an *efficient* cause. Rather it incorporates what in Aristotelian vocabulary would be characterized as *formal* causation. This fact is significant so far as it concerns the appropriate response to Putnam's criticism of causal theorists' replies to his model-theoretic argument against realism.[20]

The extent to which Aquinas' view of the genesis of cognitive *species* commits him to abstractionism has been the subject of some dispute. Peter Geach has argued—to my mind somewhat implausibly and unnecessarily[21]— that Aquinas held no such doctrine. Later I shall return briefly to an aspect of the issue to show that whatever may be his position on abstraction Aquinas certainly does not attribute to our minds an occult capacity for directly grasping the essential natures of things. Unfortunately, some writers have supposed otherwise and on that account they have dismissed Thomist epistemology as hopelessly esoteric.

To conclude this section of exposition, however, it is necessary to give some brief account of Aquinas' theory of meaning. This stands in the tradition deriving from the remarks of Aristotle that spoken and written words are signs of 'passions in [i.e. modifications of] the soul'—a tradition the influence of which is easily detected even in writers of the modern period such as Locke who make a point of stating their opposition to the theories of the Aristotelian schoolmen.[22] Any suggestion to the effect that linguistic meaning is given by association with mental entities is now likely to prompt familiar objections involving the requirement that meaning be public and the claim that an *ideational* theory is unable to satisfy this condition.[23] Such objections are well taken with respect to any proposal which holds that the meaning of a term is given by its reference and that the immediate referents of all terms are mental objects. However, they fail to engage with the view presented by Aquinas. What St Thomas proposes is that utterances express the same intentional contents as inform mental acts. Save for such special circumstances as reflection words are no more about concepts than are thoughts turned toward them. In both cases concepts provide the *senses* of judgements, thereby directing the latter on to their referents.

As before, Aquinas maintains a strong version of epistemological realism and regards language as a means by which we may (re)present the world both to others and to ourselves.

> [Man] is naturally a social animal, and hence one man's thoughts should be made known to another through language. ... Furthermore if men were restricted to sense perception which concerns only what is present it would be enough for them to make noises such as animals. However man ... is aware not only of the present but also of the future and of what is distant. To express this understanding it is necessary to use writing.[24]

Unlike the signalling of animals, speech acts can have abstract and general significance, but these semantic properties are not intrinsic to them as sounds and marks. Rather, they derive from logically (though not necessarily temporally) prior, naturally meaningful, intentional states and processes. It is to the credit of Aquinas that unlike some recent writers he sees that if a regress of content-bestowing items is to be avoided then mental acts must not themselves be regarded as literally linguistic or pictorial representations. They must be such as not to require an interpretation through the assignment of semantic values but somehow be intrinsically significant. This is explained by the theory of concepts as abstracted general natures existing *in esse intentionale*. The exercise of a concept in thought or language *is* the actualization of something intrinsically intentional.[25]

For all that thoughts cannot *be* words, however, it is natural to characterize them in linguistic terms given their role in bestowing content upon utterance, and given also the expressive function of language. Accordingly, Aquinas sometimes writes of an idea or *conceptus* as a mental word (*verbum mentis*):

> That which is conceived by the intellect is called an interior word for it is the interior word that is signified by the spoken word, for the exterior word does not signify the intellect itself, nor the intelligible form, nor the art of thinking itself, but the concept of the intellect *by means of which it signifies the thing*: as when I say 'man', or 'man is an animal'.[26] (my emphasis)

VI

So much then for Thomist metaphysics and cognitive psychology. Whatever uncertainty may remain concerning the nature of his views it should now be clear that Aquinas advocates strong versions of both epistemological and ontological realism as these were characterized earlier (in section II). Next, therefore, I wish to consider whether there is anything in the essential content of these doctrines that renders them vulnerable to the main challenges presented by modern anti-realism.

The epistemological realist attributes truth to thoughts, or to their linguistic expression, when the content of these is appropriately related to the world and the subject possessed of this content articulates it in judgement. For a variety of reasons, having to do with the structured character of thought and language, their generality and non-extensionality and the possibility of reference failure, for example, the realist should already be disposed to the view that judgement involves concepts as at least partial constituents of content. As was seen, this need not involve any appeal to mental representations as *objects* mediating between subject and world and thus poses no threat to realism. However, the question arises: how are concepts able to reflect the structure of reality? For how can something on the side of thought be essentially such as to relate the thinker to something outside the mind? Epistemological realism appears to require that the following both be true:

(1) The world is ontologically independent of thought.
(2) Concepts and what they represent are intrinsically related.

However, to the extent that one favours (1) it seems necessary to qualify or abandon (2), and vice versa.

In resolution of this tension the realist may now avail himself of the general view of concepts suggested by Aquinas, and claim that they are the mental counterparts of extra-mental features acquired by the subject through his encounter with the world. The presupposed ontological realism implies that the existence of properties in nature is independent of and prior to the existence of concepts in mind, but the epistemological thesis has it that the reverse is not true. Indeed, it is the dependence of concepts on extra-mental features that explains their intrinsic connection with the world thereby making (re)presentation possible. Following the scholastics one might say that concepts are *natural signs* of their extensions in virtue of the isomorphism of their intensions and the character of the corresponding natures and properties. In saying this, however, it is once again important to note that this relation of signification is not ontologically reducible to that of merely efficient causation.

Hence, (1) and (2) may be harmonized so as to preserve the essence of realism, while demonstrating that (2), which initially appeared to compromise it, is in fact necessary for the claim that thought is able to engage with an independent world. Moreover, the realist can now be happy to endorse a thesis somewhat similar to the parallelism of thought and object proposed by Wright on behalf of the idealist. Unlike the earlier suggestion, however, the direction of dependence between intellect and world is now reversed. Yet, like the idealist, the realist in question rejects the coherence of general scepticism (or epistemological anti-realism) by closing the gap between mind and reality, but without prejudice to the ontological independence of the latter. Thus he may speak as follows:

> It is an error to think of reality as being confronted by investigators whose cognitive capacities are altogether independent of the structure of the world. No thought is altogether of our making. Rather cognition is a conceptualization of objective features, with no more claim to autonomy than a mirror image. There is, accordingly, no possibility of our capacities for knowledge outstripping the structure of encountered states of affairs.

The image which suggests itself is of meaning, conceptual capacity and cognitive ability as developing in parallel and growing out of the world as the regions of it through which the subject passes are conceptualized. This account is undoubtedly realist, but it is not obviously committed to a conception of truth-conditions as possibly recognition-transcendent. Hereabouts, of course, there lie pitfalls into which even the wary may unwittingly stumble. The notions of recognition and, relatedly, of evidential availability are themselves problematic and give rise to such contentious questions as whether in memory one is directly related to past events or only to present representations. In addition, the idea of the structure of states of affairs involves realism about structuring principles. For all that, however, the following two claims are in harmony with the version of realism outlined above. First, there can be no more to meaning than belongs to conceptual capacity and this in turn is restricted to recognitional ability. Second, it is not possible that, even in ideal cognitive conditions, the structure of reality may elude our conceptual powers.

The justification of the former thesis is simply that—to adapt an ancient tag—'there is nothing on the lip that was not first (or simultaneously, and *ipso facto*) in the intellect and nothing in the latter that was not first in the senses'. And the support for the latter claim derives from the idea introduced earlier, that mental reference is only possible because of the possession by subjects of cognitive features (concepts) that correspond in point of natural similarity (that is formal identity) to properties of things in the world. An implication of this account is that thought and reality are related somewhat in the manner of reflected image and object of reflection. This state of affairs suggests two complementary descriptions, viz., that thought is *intrinsically representational* and that the world is *intrinsically intelligible*. In sum, that which is required for epistemological realism, that is the mind's capacity to reflect the structure of reality, seems also to encourage the idea that no part of the latter is, in principle, outwith possible cognition, that is 'descriptive conceptualization'. (It is, of course, quite another matter whether every particular is *de re* thinkable, and failure to distinguish these issues has sometimes made certain anti-realist arguments appear more telling than in fact they are.) Accordingly, the realist I have described has no necessary reason to advance a view of truth as essentially recognition-transcendent even 'in the limit', and he has some reason to regard such a view as mysterious and perhaps even incoherent.

Earlier I stressed the importance of the question of what exactly the advocate of epistemological realism is committed to which renders him vulnerable to philosophical objections, and I suggested that this deserves further consideration than it has received to date. My impression is of a tendency on the part of some participants in the current dispute between realism and anti-realism to conflate ontological and epistemological issues. For why should someone wish to argue, in defence of a thesis termed *realism*, that we can conceive of the obtaining of states of affairs which in principle we are incapable of ever recognizing, unless he also supposed that inability to do so entails their non-existence? To assume this, however, is to be immodest to a startling degree. It supposes that the whole world is only there if it is wholly available, where the criterion for 'availability' means available to *our* cognitive powers.

Proper modesty, by contrast, encourages us to accept that our conceptual and recognitional capacities go hand in hand and hence that (at the level of *types* of situations) what we cannot recognize to be the case we cannot think to be the case either. These admissions, however, have no ontological implication unless of course some connecting premise involving ontological relativity is introduced. Immodesty links reality with our present capacities in such a way as to require that we can conceive what we cannot know. It is not immodest, however, to suggest that thought (and utterance)—whether ours in idealized circumstances or that of a less restricted intellect—may be such that there is no state of affairs of which it cannot form a conception. For what gives reason to suppose that this may be so is the idea that the world is intrinsically intelligible, that no part of it is such as cannot be reflected in thought.[27] This idea should also serve as a corrective to exaggerated claims about our present competence, since one can only reflect that before which one stands, that is, what is accessible to experience or extractable by intelligent interpretation. To repeat, however, none of this taken by itself implies any ontological claim about the extent of reality. Suitably re-interpreted, the saying 'out of sight, out of mind' might be thought to encapsulate the anti-realist theses about meaning and understanding. Yet, so long as it remains free of any association with talk of 'out of being', the realist who adopts the structure of the Thomist scheme need not disagree.

VII

Earlier I remarked that for Hilary Putnam the main route into anti-realism is via considerations concerning the determination of reference, and at this point I wish to observe how elements of Aquinas' theory may be employed in response to such considerations.

As is familiar, Putnam presents these arguments in both informal and formal versions—the latter being an adaptation of a permutation argument in set theory (involving the Skolem-Löwenheim theorem) which is then applied to the task of providing a semantic interpretation for a language organized in the form of a theory. For all that this formal argument may be thought to achieve a precision lacking in its informal relations the general character of the presuppositions of Putnam's general reasoning is perhaps more easily appreciable in the latter.[28] Briefly, and in rough, the idea is as follows. In considering the nature of language and of its relation to the world, semantic theorists (including Putnam) failed to attend to the 'epistemological position' of the philosopher himself. They too readily assumed that in some or another way 'meanings' connected speakers with the external world. Certainly there was disagreement about the form of this supposed connection and in particular there was (and remains) a debate between *descriptivists* who argue that the referents of our words are determined by the senses with which we invest them, and *extensionalists* who hold that, on the contrary, the meaning of terms is partly or wholly a function of their referents—with this dependence usually being viewed as involving causal connections between world and speakers. However, notwithstanding this important dispute, most semantic theorists have been at one in supposing that whatever the main direction of movement between speaker and reality the two are in direct intercourse.

This philosophical claim is now rejected by Putnam as involving a 'naïve realism'. For while it may be acceptable in ordinary speech to describe words as 'referring to' wholly independent objects and as 'characterizing' features, as if our access to the latter were unproblematic, this proves incoherent once one becomes at all metaphysically sophisticated. The elementary, naïve conception pictures us as putting words into a correspondence with the world. In fact, all we have are two sets of *representations*: 'word representations' and 'world representations', and we cannot break through these to secure a direct link between thought and language and what lies beyond them.

One response to this worry might be to argue that given sufficient content, and operational and theoretical constraints, the system of representations will prescribe a unique interpretation. Thus, even if there remains some kind of gap between language and what it represents we can none the less be assured that the two stand in a determinate relation of correspondence. However, the familiar implication of solipsistic cognitive psychology, and the less familiar result of the model-theoretic and informal permutation arguments, is that *whatever content* is assumed and *whatever constraints* are imposed no such unique interpretation is forthcoming. With respect to the former, the point is just that the world could be more or less any old way no matter what the character of our thought; and as regards the latter, the conclusion is that however theory is constrained, providing that it is consistent, there will be infinitely many satisfaction relations between it and the world it is taken to represent—provided that the world is not too sparsely populated.

At this point an objector is likely to recall Putnam's own earlier work on reference and observe that it argued for a direct relation between language and reality, that is, not one of descriptive fit between a representation and that which it depicts, but one of causal interaction. Here, however, Putnam now offers two replies: first, the earlier claim was not, as was generally supposed, that there *is* such a phenomenon as direct reference (metaphysically construed, for example as by Kripke[29]) but only that our referential intentions and practices are not as the descriptivist characterizes them; but second, and in this context more importantly, an appeal to a causal theory to fix the correct satisfaction relation fails because it is simply a further addition to theory, to the body of representations, and like the original the new set stands in indefinitely many correspondence relations to the world. The same reply is then extended to any other constraint the semanticist might try to impose—'*It's just more theory!*'.

The anti-realist conclusion which Putnam draws from this argument is that the idea of there being a single, determinate, correspondence relation between language and world, the obtaining of which constitutes objective truth, is an illusion. Rather, the concept of truth is properly an *epistemological* one whose field of operation is not in the space between representation and world but within our theorizing. It is a measure of justification for the assertion of certain claims where that justification is given by reference to an ideal theory. Accordingly Putnam writes:

> A statement is true, in my view, if it would be justified under epistemically ideal conditions . . . the two key claims of such an idealization theory of truth are: (1) that truth is independent of justification here and now, but not independent of *all* possibility of justification. To claim that a statement is true is to claim it could be justified; (2) that truth is expected to be stable, or 'convergent'; if either a statement *or* its negation could be justified, even if conditions were as ideal as one could hope to make them, there is no sense in thinking of the statement as having a truth value.[30]

And elsewhere he draws a related conclusion about the idea of the world as awaiting our putting language into a unique correspondence with it:

> 'Objects' do not exist independently of our conceptual schemes. *We* cut up the world into objects when we introduce one or another possible scheme of description.[31]

Putnam's arguments invite and deserve extensive commentary.[32] Here, however, my purposes are strictly limited and they will best be achieved by observing a further line of reply which Putnam considers very briefly only to dismiss it as unfit for modern minds. He imagines an objector claiming that the most his argument establishes is that no constraints imposed on the side of theory—no additional representations, or formal conditions on systems of them—will fix reference if this is not already determinate. But that leaves open the possibility of constraints imposed not from *within* as part of theory, but from *without* as non-epistemological restrictions on theorizing. And this possibility may be realized if the world itself plays a significant role in the formation of our thoughts. Putnam's dismissal of this suggestion (in a version presented by David Lewis[33]) takes the form of identifying it with mediaeval doctrines of essentialism and of occult essence-intuiting epistemology:

> T[he] idea that the 'non-psychological' fixes reference—i.e. that *nature itself* determines what our words stand for—is totally unintelligible. At bottom to think that a sign relation is *built into nature* is to revert to mediaeval essentialism, to the idea that there are 'self-identifying' 'objects' and 'species' out there[34]

and later he comments:

> the mediaevals (and the rationalists) thought the mind had an intellectual intuition (*intellektuelle Anschauung*) a sort of perception that would enable it to perceive essences, substantial forms or whatever. But there is no such faculty. 'Nothing is in the mind that was not first in the senses *except the mind itself*' as Kant put it, quoting Leibniz.
>   Again, no one but a few relics challenge *this* conclusion.[35]

I am not especially concerned to escape the charge of being a relic (in the sense of a surviving trace of an earlier way of thinking), but I think it is proper to show that Putnam misrepresents the view of at least some of those he opposes. Fairness demands this, but more importantly the objection he ridicules suggests a more appealing solution to the problem he has set than his way of characterizing it may permit one to appreciate. If the world is structured independently of our conception of it, and if that structure can impress itself upon us, then there are non-theoretical constraints upon the content of thought. Not any scheme of classification will be as good as any other. For all that several may be operationally and theoretically satisfactory, not all will correspond to the structure of similarities and differences inherent in the world.

While allowing this possibility and agreeing that it would make constraints available which escape the 'just more theory' reply, one might nevertheless suppose that it is a more extravagant solution than is necessary to block

Putnam's path to anti-realism. For one might reasonably enter an objection at a much earlier stage of his argument, viz., at the point where he seems to claim that the belief that we have direct access to the world must be rejected as naïve realism. For if this is accepted then it is not clear how any response could be adequate. I agree with such an objection and see no good reason for favouring even a sophisticated version of representationalism over direct realism as one's fundamental epistemology. However, I also think that, whether by accident or design, Putnam's connecting epistemological realism with realism about classes of natural objects is especially apt. For the connection, as I see it, is that while one may avoid idealism by insisting that thought is non-solipsistic and 'extends' into the world, one is not thereby altogether free of one form of anti-realism, viz., conceptual relativism. Only the claim that thoughts are shaped by concepts which reflect the general structure of reality is sufficient for full-blooded realism, and that claim presupposes that the world is divided into kinds of things independently of the organizing tendency of thought.

This latter idea is certainly to be found among the schoolmen but it neither originated with them nor perished with their demise. Of course, like any other substantial philosophical theory it is open to challenge but it can hardly be described as unintelligible. In fact, Putnam's charges of unintelligibility or incoherence seem in part to result from a conflation in his responses to writers such as Devitt, Glymour, and Lewis.[36] In claiming that the world determines the semantic values of expressions one might have in mind either the view I have been urging, that is that the world has a formal structure within which particulars are determined to be *what* they are (for example, cats, oak trees, etc.) by certain substantial forms or organizing principles, or else one may be thinking of the nowadays more familiar idea that chains of causal interaction originating in objects account for the fact that certain patterns of thought and speech are *about* those objects. The latter view is compatible with a nominalist ontology—one, for example, within which there are only individual entities and relations. Interpreted as such, however, this second view faces a real difficulty in meeting Putnam's argument, for it cannot give sense to the idea that one of the multitude of actual causal relations holding between a given object and a (token) singular term or predicate, say, is privileged in being a *semantic* relation. If one moves simply to (efficient) causation and regards this as something like an energy trail leading from one object to another then the problem arises that there are too many such trails (and too many objects) for a supposedly privileged relation to be determined by causation (however *that* relation is itself nominalistically individuated). One can of course elect to single out one among the multitude of trails and accord special status to it, but to do so is in effect to adopt Putnam's own view that reference is determined by language-users and not by the world—*we say what our words mean*. This collapse is unavoidable, I think, if one tries to ground realism upon a physicalist and nominalist foundation. I am in agreement with Putnam, therefore, that *scientific realism* construed in this way is incoherent. But *physicalistic nominalism* is the only view against which whose intelligibility he actually presents an argument. In a recent review of the model-theoretic proof and of responses to it Putnam writes as follows:

> The upshot is this: if the realist wants to be a metaphysical realist ... then he must insist that it is something other than operational and theoretical constraints that singles out the right reference relation. But this, I argued is an incoherent idea.
>
> ... the model-theoretic argument shows that for any physicalistic relation you like (satisfying the operational and theoretical constraints) there is another which does just as well. If someone says, 'Well, one of these is just intrinsically identical with reference; it is the essence of reference that, say, a term T refers to whatever has the same number of chromons as that token of T has gluons' we would not be able to say 'you are inconsistent', for the speaker would not have contradicted himself; but we would feel that we had received nothing but scholastic-sounding noises as an answer to our puzzlement.[37]

While I am confident that this response is well directed against authors such as Devitt, I am somewhat doubtful of its force against Lewis—if indeed he is even an intended target of *this* 'anti-causalist' line of reply.[38] Certainly it does not engage as argument with the Thomist proposal. One might say, indeed, that what is wrong with the scientific causal-realist response is that it *fails* to make the right 'scholastic-sounding noises'. As was seen earlier, however, it is clear that Putnam also regards the direct appeal to 'forms' as just so much mediaeval mystery (and in fact I think he means to place Lewis in this camp rather than with Devitt and Glymour). Unlike the response to causal realism, however, reported mystification is not an *argument*. And if a case is proposed which invokes the idea that natural structuring principles are *entia non grata* on account of being metaphysical rather than physical entities, this sits ill with Putnam's own principled stand against scientism. As he rightly insists, neither all forms of explanation nor every type of entity are reducible to those postulated by physical theory.[39] Moreover, in holding that substantial (and accidental) forms are metaphysical items I am not claiming that they are supra-empirical Platonic *eide*. On the contrary, they are structuring principles (and characterizing features) immanent within nature; and they are what one is acquainted with in judging that the objects before one are cats and dogs, say, or again (in second intention) in judging that cats and dogs are animals. In the Thomist scheme which I am proposing, to be a cat is to be a substance of a certain kind; but in saying this it is not being assumed that the catness of an object is something imperceptible lying beneath or behind its sensible features—something detectable only by an occult form of intuition ('*intellektuelle Anschauung*'). Certainly if I see something which is a cat and properly take it to be such then it is true that I do not *see* its catness in the sense that I *see* its colour, or *feel* the softness of its fur. My perception of its nature is an intellectual act involving the exercise of a sortal concept, but it is an act whose object is the individual substance: the cat, and not a mysterious imperceptible essence residing within it. Of course, one might still argue that if the charge of epistemological occultism is to be refuted then the perception of a thing's nature must be reducible to experience of its sensible properties. To demand that, however, would be to lapse back into a form of empiricism which authors such as Putnam have rightly been concerned to discredit.

There are, though, other reasons why the idea that through experience we may discern the essential natures or forms of particular things has seemed to be flawed. For example, some critics regard philosophers like Aquinas as being deceived about the power of cognition. Even Peter Geach, who is otherwise sympathetic to Aquinas' philosophy, argues that 'he greatly exaggerates the ease and certainty of this knowledge [of the specific nature of material substances]'.[40] Such assessments, however, rest upon a conception of the scholastics' view which is not only ill-formed but creates a puzzling impression of them as committed to an obviously feeble epistemology. It is illuminating, therefore, to discover Aquinas, one of the authors of the 'form-grasping' theory, writing of 'the deficiency which every day we experience in our knowledge of things. For we are ignorant of many of the properties of sensible things',[41] and elsewhere he indicates how we may pass from such ignorance to a grasp of the *intima rei*, the essential nature of a thing:

> [We proceed as it were] through certain doors. This is the manner of human apprehension which passes from effects and properties to knowledge of a thing's essence, and since in doing this there must be a certain discourse, human apprehension is termed interpretation [*ratio*] although it leads to understanding [*intellectus*], in that the enquiry brings one to the essence of a thing.[42]

This and other similar passages provide evidence that Aquinas, at least, is not guilty of the charges brought against scholastic epistemology of introducing occult powers of intuition. They also confirm his appreciation that no easy solution to the problem of locating the joints in nature is available to us. We must proceed through the experimental method, working from salient patterns discerned in the things around us to the (usually underlying) source of these in the constitution of those things. As Aquinas writes elsewhere:

> essential differences are not known to us; we indicate them through the accidental differences that flow from the essential differences, as we refer to a cause through its effect.[43]

But these difficulties, though epistemological, are not philosophical. Not only is there no claim of an occult intuitive faculty but the assumption on which Aquinas works is precisely that quoted by Putnam, viz., that all knowledge comes through experience. What is asserted in opposition to Putnam's view, however, is that in experience we are directly acquainted with a world structured thus and so independently of our conception of it, that is, the two realist theses with which I began. These may be controversial but they are not, I think, less plausible than the assumptions from which Putnam and others derive their anti-realism, and, as I tried to show earlier, while they commit the realist to a conception of truth as an objective relation of conformity between thought and world they do not *require* him to suppose that truth so conceived is *in principle* possibly recognition-transcendent.

VIII

In the preceding sections I have been concerned to set out some of the elements of a philosophical theory in which the conceptual structure of our thinking is securely connected to the ontological structure of the world. The character of this connection is of such an order, viz., *formal or structural equivalence*, as to warrant the title '*mind–world identity*' in a description of the theory within which it features.[44] For according to this account the relationship between a thought of an *F* and a naturally existing *F* is *internal*. Such a characterization might seem to invite an idealist interpretation, but to construe this form of internality idealistically would be a mistake. It is certainly true that the relationship between thought and world is a non-contingent one. However, this is not on account of the latter being a product of the former, but rather because thought is constituted by the world. In a fuller articulation of the Thomist view of cognition it would be necessary to consider what picture of mind best accords with it. Suffice it to note, however, that for Aquinas himself the intellect (that is the intellectual *aspect* of mind) is not to be regarded as a pre-existing cognitive mechanism but as a capacity to be informed by the structuring principles of the world. It is, so to say, 'not a something but not a nothing either'—in this case being a *potentiality* for the reception of form.

The idea of an internal connection between thoughts and objects, conceived of as numerically distinct entities, may still seem problematic. Anyone disposed to regard it as such may find it instructive to consider the relationship between two or more instances of a natural kind. Presuming ontological realism, the relationship of co-specific class-membership is not a contingent affair. Certainly, it is a contingent matter whether there are no cats, one cat or many cats, but the relationship between one cat and another is an internal one, unlike that between a cat and a rose. In the context of epistemological concerns this point emerges in the fact that there is a body of knowledge derivable from study of one member of a natural kind which is non-inductively applicable to others.

In appealing to the relationship between instances of a kind I am adverting to a phenomenon which is so close to that proposed in the Thomist scheme that the term *analogy* is (though strictly accurate) almost misleading. For if one holds that the relationship between the conceptual structure of a judgement and the sortal structure of the natural situation it concerns is one of formal identity, then this is pretty much akin to the relationship between two natural situations of the same kind—the only difference residing in the mode of being of the structuring principles. Doubtless this response will not be acceptable to one who denies that there are any such principles as forms, natures, or universals existing independently of human classifications. But it is worth noting that if this is the ground upon which the contest between realism and anti-realism is to be conducted then what looked to be in some important sense a new challenge turns out to be none other than a repetition of old style (that is Ockhamist) nominalism. Even so, perhaps something of the contemporary discussion would remain distinctive inasmuch as recent anti-realisms have focused on the idea of *truth* and charged realism with being committed to a recognition–transcendent view of this, complaining that such a view is demonstrably incoherent. I have not addressed this complaint since the version of realism which I have been discussing is not as such committed to transcendent truth. It can happily allow that the idea of truth is tied to that of conceivability which is in turn connected to that of existence, while rejecting the suggestion that the latter is epistemologically constrained. 'To be is to be conceivable' need not be accorded a subject-dependent interpretation and it is not given one in the variety of realism discussed above.

Suppose, then, that one were to adopt some version of the *mind–world identity theory*. How from that perspective might recent anti-realist challenges then be regarded? In part, of course, they would have to be viewed as misconceived in their attack. But they need not, and should not, be regarded as entirely inappropriate. One legitimate target might be the sort of realist who wishes to reject any form of internal connection between thought and world, and who is therefore willing to countenance the possibility that we are not only in error about the environment but that our concepts bear no adequate relationship to the general structure of the world. This form of realism (which includes Thomas Nagel among its advocates[45]) is in *some* respects like that associated with Plato. Both seem to insist upon the unconditional transcendence of reality over our natural means of coming to know about the world.[46] Unlike Plato, however, the contemporary ultra-realist sees no way, and no need, to identify any other form of cognition adequate to conceive the structure of this transcendent realm. Setting aside the question of whether these are good or bad reasons for such a view, it is clear that the cost of defending it is very considerable: it has no way of responding to even the most radical (or non-pragmatically self-refuting) versions of scepticism. The anti-realist regards such a cost as so great as to be unbearable. In this judgement he and the moderate realist may be united. Moreover, they may also agree that a major source of the difficulty lies in the ultra-realist's conception of thought. If beyond that point the alliance then dissolves, the moderate may nevertheless still see some merit in his former ally's continuing objection to even his own non-sceptical realism. But if he is to maintain the integrity of his position then the moderate realist will have to offer some other account of his erstwhile associate's persistent challenges.

Happily, an account is available of what lends anti-realism such plausibility as it sometimes seems to possess. This is that it represents a demand that any claim to knowledge about some given realm of objects, properties, or relations be substantiated by demonstrating how it is possible that we could have any adequate conception or true beliefs concerning things of that sort. Such an interpretation focuses not on any blanket challenge but on the case by case demand for an account of how realism in respect of a given class of judgements is intelligible. So conceived these challenges are welcome. Not just because they counter any tendency to easy and unjustified presumption, but because in forcing the would-be realist to consider how it might be possible to conceive of some supposed feature of the world, it is likely to move him to produce interesting philosophy concerning both *that which is*, and how *that which is* is knowable and known. As such challenges are pressed and taken up it will not be surprising if realists, of the sort with which I am happy to identify myself, find themselves following Aquinas in investigating the idea of *analogy* as a way of understanding. As with realism, we might do worse than to begin the investigation by looking at what St Thomas himself had to say on this issue; but here I shall end, not even beginning to take up that task.[47]

Notes

1. Here the further possibility may suggest itself, that there is a single basic relation, viz., mental reference, upon which other semantic connections depend. See Aristotle, *De Interpretatione* 16a 2–6, and, for a recent statement of a view of this sort, John Searle, *Intentionality.*

2. The attack begins with Reid's *An Inquiry into the Human Mind on the Principles of Common Sense*, T. Duggan (ed.). For a commentary connecting Reid's realism with that of Aquinas and arguing the case for both against contemporary representationalism, see J. Haldane, 'Reid, Scholasticism and Current Philosophy of Mind', in M. Dalgarno and E. Matthews (eds.), *The Philosophy of Thomas Reid.*

3. The issue, that is, of what determines the semantic value of singular terms and of predicates; see H. Putnam, *Reason, Truth and History*, ch. 2.

4. As Wright states the point: '[This kind of realism involves the idea that] truth values are, so to speak, ground out on the interface between language and reality. . . . Whether [a] thought [expressed by a particular sentence] is true depends only on which thought it is and germane features of the world. At [no] point [do] human judgment or response come into the picture', 'Realism, Anti-Realism, Irrealism, Quasi-Realism', in P. French, T. Uehling, Jr., and H. Wettstein (eds.), *Midwest Studies in Philosophy* 12, p. 28.

5. See Crispin Wright, *Realism, Meaning and Truth*, p. 3.

6. Ibid., p. 2.

7. This issue arises, for example, in connection with Wittgenstein's views about the basis for correctness in the use of statements, which appear to locate it in nothing other than natural reactive dispositions. See, for example, *On Certainty.* It is then not unproblematic to sustain the idea that these reactions are elicited by a world structured thus and so independently of them, since it is part of this picture that the very idea of the world (like every other idea) is itself a product of our immediate responses. A similar response is likely to be evoked by examination of Putnam's version of metaphysical anti-realism: transcendental idealism is an unstable position.

8. The charge of unintelligibility is made by Roderick Chisholm in 'Theory of Knowledge in America', *The Foundations of Knowing*, pp. 177–8; but his discussion is directed towards the account presented by Jacques Maritain in *The Degrees of Knowledge*, and I believe that Maritain's is not an adequate, or accurate, treatment of the identity doctrine as entertained by Aristotle in respect of sensory cognition and as generalized to all cognitive acts by Aquinas. For relevant exegesis and discussion see J. Haldane, 'Brentano's Problem', *Grazer Philosophische Studien* 35.

9. *Summa Theologiae*, Ia, q.85, a.2.

10. Ibid.

11. *De Veritate*, q.10, a.8.

12. *De Potentia*, q.7, a.9.

13. For a recent influential contribution in this tradition see J. Fodor, *Representations*, pp. 26 ff.

14. For some further discussion of this issue see: J. Haldane, 'Aquinas on Sense-Perception', *Philosophical Review* 92, and 'Brentano's Problem'. My representation of the nature of singular reference involves a non-standard though, I believe, faithful interpretation of Aquinas. The more usual claim is that thoughts individuate singulars via association with sensory images of their objects, by means of 'turning to images', *conversio ad phantasmata*. For a non-scholastic discussion of this see P. Geach, *Mental Acts*, p. 65. My account regards the involvement of conscious sensory imagination as being but one way in which extra-conceptual contexts feature.

15. *De Veritate*, q.8, a.6.

16. Ibid., a.4.

17. *Summa Theologiae*, Ia, q.16, a.2.

18. I now find myself less confident about this issue than I once used to be, but the present occasion does not allow for discussion of the matter. Suffice it to say that Aquinas seems to think that a nature is not as such, or 'in itself', either particular or general, but rather particular-in-nature and general-in-the-mind. Unfamiliar and odd though it sounds this thought may not be incoherent.

19. *De Veritate*, q.1, a.2.

20. See Section VII below and nn. 28 and following for references.

21. The question of the *plausibility* of Geach's claim, that Aquinas was opposed to abstractionism, is largely a matter for scholarly exegesis. I remark that this disavowal of abstractionism may not be *necessary* since I have doubts about the cogency of Geach's general argument against abstraction. For some discussion of this issue see J. Haldane, 'Chesterton's Philosophy of Education', *Philosophy* 65, sec. IV.

22. *An Essay Concerning Human Understanding*, P. H. Nidditch (ed.), I, i, 7, see also III, viii, 2.

23. For a clear statement of the objections discussed in connection with Locke see J. Bennett, *Locke, Berkeley, Hume, Central Themes*.

24. *Sententia libri Peri Hermeneias*, Lectio 2.

25. For a defence of intrinsically intentional mental acts against challenges presented by Putnam in *Reason, Truth and History* and elsewhere, see J. Haldane, 'Putnam on Intentionality', *Philosophy and Phenomenological Research* 52.

26. *De Potentia*, I, q.9, a.5.

27. Here perhaps one may find *an* interpretation of Parmenides' report that 'the same thing exists for thinking and for being', see G. Kirk and J. Raven, *The Presocratic Philosophers*, p. 269.

28. See chs. 2 and 4 in *Reason, Truth and History*, and 'Reference and Truth' and 'Why There Isn't a Ready-Made World', in H. Putnam, *Realism and Reason, Philosophical Papers*, Vol. 3.

29. On this point see Putnam, 'Why There Isn't a Ready-Made World'.

30. *Realism and Reason*, p. 85.

31. *Reason, Truth and History*, p. 52.

32. A small contribution to which is offered in Haldane, 'Putnam on Intentionality'.

33. See David Lewis, 'Putnam's Paradox', *Australasian Journal of Philosophy* 62.

34. *Realism and Reason*, p. xii.

35. *Realism and Reason*, p. 209.

36. In addition to the article by Lewis cited above see Michael Devitt, *Realism and Truth*, and Clark Glymour, 'Conceptual Scheming or Confessions of a Metaphysical Realist', *Synthese* 51. For Putnam's replies see 'Is the Causal Structure of the Physical

Itself Something Physical?', in P. French, T. Uehling, Jr., and H. Wettstein (eds.), *Midwest Studies in Philosophy* 9, and 'Model Theory and the Factuality of Semantics', in A. George (ed.), *Reflections on Chomsky.*

37. 'Model Theory and the Factuality of Semantics', pp. 215–16.

38. I say 'something doubtful' because I am not sure how Lewis hopes to combine his belief in universals, and in the possibility of our being influenced by them, with his physicalism. I sense a contradiction here but I am not in a position to offer a proof. Relevant to the matter is Lewis' discussion of epistemology in connection with his modal realism: see D. Lewis, *On the Plurality of Worlds*, pp. 108–15.

39. In this regard see especially *The Many Faces of Realism* and *Representation and Reality.*

40. *Mental Acts*, p. 131.

41. *Summa Contra Gentiles*, I, 3.

42. *Scriptum Super Libros Sententiarum*, III, d.35, q.2, a.2, sol. 1. See also *Summa Theologiae*, II, IIae, q.8, a.1.

43. *De Entia et Essentia*, 5.

44. In fact this view may have counterparts in contemporary metaphysics. See, for example, George Bealer, *Quality and Concept*, ch. 8 'Qualities and Concepts', who offers a theory according to which 'the primary bearers of truth (i.e., thoughts) are built up ultimately from the primary constituents of reality', pp. 187–8; and John McDowell, 'Scheme-Content Dualism, Experience and Subjectivity', who in connection with Wittgenstein remarks that 'We are [to stand] firm on the idea that the structure of elements that constitutes a thought (a Thought itself, in Fregean usage), and the structure of elements that constitutes something that is the case, can be the very same thing'.

45. Thomas Nagel, *The View From Nowhere*, ch. VI.

46. I hesitate actually to ascribe such a view to Plato, notwithstanding that such ascriptions are familiar, because I judge the matter to be a complicated one.

47. Were one to want to do so, some useful places to begin might be *De Veritate*, q.2, a.11; *Scriptum Super Libros Sententiarum*, I, d.19, q.5, a.2; and *Summa Contra Gentiles*, c. xxxii–xxxiv.

2

Realism and Anti-Realism in a Historical Context

Ian McFetridge

I

John Haldane's essay raises a special case of a general question.[1] To what extent do contemporary discussions of, and attacks on, realism, engage with various historical positions which we might wish to place beneath that heading? Are certain traditional realist positions under attack from contemporary *semantic* anti-realism? No, replies Haldane, for there is a position—Aquinas—which embraces distinctively realist theses in ontology and epistemology, but which *need not* be committed to a central target of (at any rate some versions of) such anti-realism: that the truth conditions of sentences can be such as to transcend all possibility of verification. In characterizing Aquinas as a realist, despite his alleged rejection of such a notion of truth, Haldane is implicitly rejecting Dummettian claims as to how realism should be formulated. I wish to look at aspects of these claims and at a certain historical thesis which Dummett has enunciated. Part of my aim will be to suggest certain initial difficulties in applying the Dummettian characterization of realism (or anti-realism) to some earlier views one might naturally regard as 'realist' (or anti-realist). So I agree with Haldane's conclusion that there is some question as to whether Dummett's attacks on realism engage with certain historical positions.

In connection with this I want to explore a number of strands in, or forms of, realism and their inter-connections. For, I shall suggest, there is some unclarity concerning the point or points in realism on which the new anti-realism focuses—an unclarity, therefore, concerning the positive views of contemporary anti-realists. A further aim will be to provide some historical

[This essay has been composed of material drawn from three sources: a paper titled 'Realisms and Anti-Realisms', written largely in 1977 and amended in 1982, and again at some more recent date—a caveat added then reads 'Descendants will be either/or more historical/more up-to-date'; a paper titled: 'Realism in a Historical Context', delivered in reply to mine at the conference on *Realism and Reason* held at the University of St Andrews in March 1988; and correspondence of 9 June 1987. (J.H.)]

39

allusions which may then at least partially justify Dummett's claim to be discussing, in a new guise, an ancient dispute in metaphysics.

Dummett has repeatedly urged that disputes about realism with respect to a particular segment of reality should best be seen as raising questions about the appropriate notion of truth for sentences which have that segment of reality as their subject-matter. So seen, he further argues, disputes about realism, and about particular realisms, will concern the kind of meaning possessed by sentences in general, or by particular classes of sentences. A central issue, and a number of important sub-issues, in metaphysics will devolve to the theory of meaning.

In the course of developing these views, Dummett and others have made a number of historical remarks. A central one has been that though the approach to the issues is new, the issues themselves are old ones: though the conception of realism came into sharp focus only with Frege, there had been many realists before him. Crispin Wright remarks that 'Dummett's interpretation of realism, and the kind of general anti-realist criticism of it which he presents, are put forward by way of a recommended *Übersicht* on a significant class of disputes in traditional and modern philosophy.'[2] These, however, are large and vague claims. What are the adequacy conditions on recommending an *Übersicht*? How many, and which, debates should be illuminated? In the present context it seems appropriate to begin by raising some rather general questions about how we are to apply Dummett's characterization of realism to positions formulated independently of his overall characterization.

Both Dummett's and Wright's remarks suggest that the *Übersicht* is meant to cast light on historically occupied positions earlier than the analytical tradition, that is, prior to Frege. It is notable, though, that when Dummett relates his *Übersicht* to the *details* of positions occupied and arguments deployed prior to, and independently of, his own suggested formulations, the positions he discusses are almost invariably within the analytical tradition. Realist and opposed views of the material world are exemplified in debates, beginning in the 1930s, between phenomenalists and their opponents; issues about mental states inspired by the search—largely stimulated by Wittgenstein's *Philosophical Investigations*—to formulate a satisfactory position in the philosophy of mind between (so-called) Cartesianism and behaviourism. Now a feature of these historical debates is that they were already largely conducted within the presupposition which Dummett claims to be the hallmark of analytical philosophy and which it owes, in his view, to Frege, viz., that the prime task of philosophy is the analysis of thought, and that it is only by the analysis of *language* that we can analyse thought. Characteristic of the debate on phenomenalism were such questions as: is a sense-datum language possible? Can sentences about material objects be translated into such a language? Of the debate in the philosophy of mind: how do words for mental states acquire a meaning? Do they function differently in first- and third-person ascriptions? Applying the Dummettian *Übersicht* to such positions and debates can therefore be relatively straightforward. It will consist in relating the particular accounts offered of the meaning of the sentences descriptive of the disputed area to the general positions about meaning which Dummett holds to be characteristic of realism and anti-realism.

II

I wish, though, to raise some questions concerning how the *Übersicht* is to be applied to earlier philosophical positions not formulated within the presuppositions of the analytical tradition. We may begin, then, by asking: is realism, as characterized by Dummett, *essentially* a doctrine concerning the correct conception of a theory of meaning for a language, or for particular fragments of a language? Or, alternatively, does it consist of one or more doctrines which though, in Dummett's view, they *should* be debated via questions concerning the nature of a theory of meaning, can at least be stated independently of answers to such questions? Dummett often suggests the former. A fairly recent case is in *The Interpretation of Frege's Philosophy*. He suggests there that 'full-fledged realism' should consist in 'the adoption, for the statements in question ... of a truth-conditional theory of meaning taking as its base a completely unmodified classical two-valued semantics'[3]—a conception of the theory of meaning which we owe to Frege.

But if realism just *is* that, then it is hard to see how to ask pointfully if such historical figures as Descartes, Berkeley, or Kant were or were not *realists*, either globally or locally. They may have had views about meaning, but they certainly had no explicit conception, realist or otherwise, of a theory of meaning in the sense here intended, viz., a systematic description of what is involved in understanding a language.

Perhaps, then, we ought to take the second option noted above, that is, to conceive of realism as some doctrine or doctrines which, though they *can* be seen to flow from a certain 'realist' conception of theories of meaning, can at least be formulated independently of that conception—of bivalence, say, or the possibility of verification-transcendent truth. The question would then be whether, consistently with their explicit metaphysical, or epistemological doctrines, particular earlier philosophers could or could not have adopted these allegedly distinctively realist theses; of whether their positions commit them to realist theses. And it is in fact in these terms that Dummett generally couches his remarks concerning the classification, in terms of his *Übersicht*, of such philosophers as Berkeley or Kant as realists or otherwise. For example, Dummett suggests that when considering Berkeley's final position, with the role assigned to God therein, he ought probably to be classified as a sophisticated realist; though concentrating merely on the phenomenalist-reductionist strand in his thought one might be inclined to view him as an anti-realist about the sensible world. Dummett does not spell out the reasoning underlying these attributions, but in the light of his discussion of phenomenalism elsewhere the point would be that without God, Berkeley is not, but with God he is, entitled to assert the Principle of Bivalence for statements about the sensible world.[4] This application of the Dummettian *Übersicht* requires then that we can detach from a realist conception of a theory of meaning a thesis—here Bivalence— which can be taken as distinctive of realism, and ask, concerning a historical philosopher, whether his conception of a certain segment of reality would or would not allow him, or would require him, to embrace that thesis.

A number of critics of Dummett, however, have suggested that what is crucial in his semantic characterization of realism, and in his exposition of what he sees as its serious difficulties, is not Bivalence but rather a commitment to a notion of truth under which a statement can be true even if we lack the ability to determine that it is. Again, it seems that if we are to apply such a characterization to pre-Fregean philosophers, we must, detach this claim from the further one that such a notion of truth can be used as the central notion of a theory of meaning. This done, it would then seem very natural to characterize Locke, for example, as an arch-realist concerning many aspects of reality. Book IV of the *Essay* abounds with expressions of the thought that contingent, but in many cases irremovable, limitations on our cognitive capacities can debar us from knowing, or even having a conception of, aspects of reality of which, nevertheless, his overall view of reality, in particular his corpuscularianism, compels him to acknowledge the existence. He not only acknowledges that how things are may transcend our ability to determine how things are; he has a picture of the nature of reality, and of our modes of acquiring that knowledge of it, which provides an *explanation* of why reality can outstrip our capacities for knowledge. A clear example is provided by claims about the necessary 'connexions and repugnancies' between the qualities and powers of substances:

> Because the active and passive powers of bodies, and their ways of operating, consisting in a texture and motion of parts which we cannot by any means come to discover; it is but in very few cases we can be able to perceive their dependence on, or repugnance to any of those *ideas* which make our complex one of that sort of things. I have here instanced in the corpuscularian hypotheses, as that which is thought to go furthest in an intelligible explication of those qualities of bodies; and I fear the weakness of human understanding is scarce able to substitute another, which will afford us a fuller and clearer discovery of the necessary connexion and co-existence of the powers which are to be observed united in several sorts of them. This at least is certain, that, whichever hypothesis be clearest and truest ... our knowledge concerning corporal substances will be very little advanced by any of them, till we are made to see what qualities and powers of bodies have a *necessary* connexion or repugnancy one with another, which in the present state of philosophy I think we know but to a very small degree: and I doubt whether, with those faculties we have, we shall ever be able to carry our general knowledge ... in this part much further.[5]

It would be natural to think that this position is realism in Dummett's sense concerning necessary connexions and repugnancies between qualities and powers. For it seems precisely to be the claim that these (alleged) aspects of reality can transcend what we can know, even what we could have evidence for. Locke here, unlike Aquinas on Haldane's account, *appears* to derive from his ontology and epistemology a position vulnerable to attacks from contemporary 'semantic' anti-realism. But one may ask whether in fact Locke's position is so vulnerable. Is Locke here committed to a doctrine about truth which cannot resist the pressure of the kinds of criticisms developed by Dummett and others?

It might seem obvious that he is. Locke's conception of reality, in part derived from contemporary science and his conception of how we can have (what he would call) knowledge, clearly commits him to instances of the following schema:

I   It could be that (*p* although we could not know that *p*).

Indeed, allowing for the unLockean terminology, he would seem also to be committed to instances of:

II   It could be that (*p* although we could have no evidence that *p*).

The particular object-language instances of these schemata do not involve the concept of truth. But to derive from them a commitment to the view that truth can transcend the possibility of verification seems merely to require the acceptability of semantic ascent, licensed by the equivalence, in some sense, of *S* and '*S* is true'. Deploying that, we have Locke committed to many instances of:

III   It could be that (*S* is true although we could not know, or have evidence that, *S* is true).

This commitment obviously derives directly from Locke's view of reality and our epistemic relation to it. The question which arises, therefore, is whether the derivability, in this way of instances of III constitutes a commitment to what the Dummettian *Übersicht* would call realism?

There is, I think, at least some reason for doubting that it does. Suppose that III did express something which could be undermined in Dummettian style by considerations concerning what acceptable account can be given of the meaning of the sentences (*S*) involved. This would require that instances of III could be acceptable (true) only under an unacceptable account of the meaning of *S*; but could be seen to be unacceptable (false) when this was replaced by an acceptable account of the meaning of *S*. This can only be so, however, if the applicability or otherwise of the notion of truth involved in III to a sentence *S* depends on what *S* means—that is, on what account of the meaning of *S* is acceptable. It might appear that the claim that this is so is the merest platitude. As Crispin Wright puts it: 'truth-values cannot be settled unilaterally, as it were, by the world alone but are a function simultaneously of the meanings of the statements to which they attach'.[6] Whether or not *S* is true in certain circumstances must surely depend on what *S* means. Hence issues about the applicability of the concept of truth and the properties it can legitimately be taken to possess must be, in part, answerable to questions about what account of the meanings of the sentences to which it applies is acceptable.

However, it is just the apparent platitude elaborated by Wright which should be questioned in the context of assessing the applicability of the Dummettian *Übersicht* to a pre-Fregean philosophical position such as that held by Locke. For to accept it is to prevent semantic ascent from being an innocent way of deriving semantically-expressed theses about the relation of reality to us and our powers of cognition from their object-language correlates. Consider such minimal anti-realist claims as that the existence of Venus is independent of our existence; that is, that Venus would have existed even if we had not. Does this commit its holder to the semantic claim that the truth of the sentence 'Venus exists' is independent of our existence? If it does, then the notion of truth deployed in it cannot be subject to the platitude that its applicability to a sentence depends on facts about what meaning (and hence that *a* meaning) has been conferred upon it by us. If the notion of truth here did conform to the alleged platitude, what would then be the falsehood, viz., that the truth of that sentence was independent of our existence, could not be a consequence of the minimal anti-idealist claim that Venus' existence was likewise independent. It seems here that, if the object-language claim has the semantic one as its consequence, then the notion of truth in the latter must no more involve commitments about what S means, or the conditions of S meaning what it does, than the object-language sentence S itself does.

The question, then, is whether there is any such innocent notion of truth, and the answer is surely that there is, viz., that identified by Quine as a device of disquotation, a means of semantic descent. Wishing to assert each of an infinite set of sentences (for example, all the instances of a logical schema) I am debarred from doing it straightforwardly. I need a device for infinite conjunction. Saying 'each of these sentences is true' provides me with such a device. But it would not serve that purpose if, in deploying it, I was undertaking commitments concerning the meaning attached to the instances of the schema, the sentences to which I am applying the notion, commitments not undertaken by the piecemeal assertion of particular instances.

We can suggest now that if Locke, say, is committed to there being verification-transcendent truths—instances of III—simply by his commitment to object-language instances of I and II, then the notion of truth involved in the former should be seen as purely disquotational. It no more involves him in commitments about the kind of meaning possessed by the sentences in question than he is so involved by their unquoted deployment in I and II. In particular, then, he would seem not to be committed to the central target of Dummettian anti-realism: that our grasp of the meanings of sentences is constituted by knowing under what—possibly verification-transcendent—conditions they would be true. If this is so, then mere commitment to III is not enough to constitute realism as characterized in Dummett's *Übersicht*.

III

Related to the question whether Locke's position on necessary connexions and repugnancies between qualities and powers is realist in *Dummett's* special sense, is the issue of the general tenability of Lockean realism, and other historical views which Dummett claims can be placed within the class of philosophical positions against which he has mounted an anti-realist challenge. Here, I wish to distinguish two kinds of philosophical position which deserve the name realism.[7] I shall call them *subject-matter realism* and *realism with respect to representations*.

Subject-matter realism is expressed in a loose array of thoughts about reality and our place in it. At its most abstract, it consists in the vague thought that how things are in the world is not, in general, dependent on the existence of, or facts about, human beings or other subjects of experience. In particular, how things are in the world is, in general, independent of facts about the cognitive states and capacities of human beings or subjects of experience—independent not merely of the *actual* states of such beings but also of any *possible* states of such beings.

The filling out of such a doctrine at any stage in the history of philosophy will be conditioned by the then current paradigm of a cognitive state and its concomitant notion of how things are in the world—its notion of the 'object' of such a state. Thus, for the bulk of seventeenth- and eighteenth-century epistemology, the model cognitive state was that of *perception* (perceiving *things* rather than perceiving *that*); and the associated notion of how things are was the rather specialized one of an object's existing. In such a framework, subject-matter realism will typically take the form of the thought that the existence of an object is not, in general, dependent on its being the object of any actual (or possible) perceptual state of any human or other conscious subject. Subject-matter anti-realism will accordingly be the denial of that thought. (Clearly weaker and stronger denials are possible.[8]) *Idealism*, if we are going to be strict, is then that special version of anti-realism which emerges in the present framework when, as typically in the seventeenth and eighteenth centuries, its ground for denying this version of realism starts from the thought that the only possible objects of perception are entities—*ideas*—the existence of which is dependent on their being objects of perception.

In post-Fregean analytical philosophy, the paradigm cognitive state is, rather, propositional knowledge, knowledge that p: and the concomitant notion of how things are in the world is the notion of such and such's being the case.[9] For us, then, subject-matter realism will typically take the form of the thought that something's being the case is not, in general, dependent on any human being's (or other knowing subject's) knowing, or being capable of knowing that it is the case. An adherent of subject-matter realism will thus be prepared to assent to numerous instances of the schema:

(SR) It could be that p even though no human being or knowing subject knows, or could know, p.

The *global* subject-matter anti-realist will, quite generally, deny this. That is, he will commit himself to accepting all instances of the schema:

(SAR) If p, then it could be known (by a human being or subject of experience) that p.

Neither realist nor anti-realists of the present kind need be global. They may accept or reject instances of (SR) involving only a limited range of substitutions for '*p*'. Again, the nature of the dispute, be it local or global, can be highly sensitive to the interpretation of the modality 'could be known' in (SR), and to the limitations, if any, to be imposed on the knowing subjects alluded to therein. These matters have been extensively discussed, again most notably by Dummett and Wright. But for the purposes of this paper these issues can largely be ignored; though I shall later make some comments about one form of selective anti-realism—anti-realism with respect to the subject-matter of mathematics.

I wish now to consider one interpretation of the realist schema which appears to put certain instances of it in a very strong position, and hence puts the corresponding *global* anti-realism in a very weak position.

Subject-matter realists are prepared to assert instances of: *it could be that* p *although no human being or knowing subject could know that* p. Consider the claim as one about the capacities of knowledge possessed by human beings, given how they and the world actually are. Then the resulting version of realism would seem to be, for many substitutions for '*p*', an expression of a number of modal facts which form part of, or are grounded in, our common sense-cum-scientific view of the world. They are, in Strawson's phrase—'parts of what it is now fashionable to call our general *theory* of the world'.[10]

We know enough about the natural world, ourselves, and, most importantly, our means of acquiring knowledge of the natural world, to render many instances of the above schema, as currently interpreted, overwhelmingly plausible. We know enough, that is, to know that nothing about the world, or ourselves, guarantees that we must, in general, have the capacity to determine how things are in the world. Thus, to take the vexed example of the past, we know that knowledge of it can be acquired only if the past state of affairs has left sufficient, and sufficiently cognitively transparent, causal descendants which are now, or will become, accessible to us. And we know that such causal descendants are, given how the world is, sadly vulnerable to irrecoverable elimination. We know, therefore, that it is perfectly possible that, for example, the Venerable Bede should have died on such-and-such a day even though things are now such that nothing remains on the basis of which we could determine this. Thus the discovery, which we could well make (perhaps have made) that we shall never gain sufficient information to determine that he did die on such-and-such a day is quite insufficient—as it would not be on the anti-realist conception—to establish that he did *not* die on that day. (And the point can be extended to other cases anti-realists tend to insist on.)

In general, then, we have knowledge of the world and of our own modes of cognitive access to it which enables us to see, in many cases, not merely that the realist possibility of epistemic inaccessibility is an abstract philosophical possibility, but also how and why it is repeatedly realized.

Given the entrenchment of what I am calling subject-matter realism in our view—our theory—of the world and ourselves, it seems to be *reductio ad absurdum* of any philosophy if it ends up simply denying such cases of (SR). This is not to say that they cannot be denied: but to deny them could not be a merely philosophical enterprise. Rather, they could only be denied by one who was prepared and able to reconstruct our current common sense-cum-scientific accounts of the world which serve to explain why, and hence justify the claim that, the present version of realism is, in many cases, true.

Returning to Berkeley, in the present perspective he may be seen as a model subject-matter anti-realist, a model rarely followed. The realism Berkeley opposed held that, in general, the existence of an object was not dependent on it being an object of actual or possible perception. Now as was seen above in connection with Locke, one scientific underpinning of that realism, in the seventeenth century, was an account of the world, and of our perception of it, in which a crucial role was assigned to essentially imperceptible corpuscular constituents of the material world. And Berkeley, quite correctly, saw himself as committed to denying not merely certain 'philosophical' claims of his realist opponents but also the above component of contemporary science.

IV

I have so far hardly related the doctrine I am calling subject-matter anti-realism to the views of contemporary anti-realists. Deliberately so: for as we shall later see, there is considerable unclarity—and not, I think, merely on my part—concerning whether or not their views do reject what I am calling subject-matter realism. But that Dummett does seem disposed to reject it, while misunderstanding its underpinnings, emerges in his response to similar thoughts expressed by Strawson. Reflecting on Dummett's approach to anti-realism, Strawson wrote:

> Certainly the route *into* the areas is comparatively new: the new anti-realism starts from certain views on mathematical truth and mathematical discourse and seeks to generalise them to the extent of advancing counterpart views on discourse concerning the natural world. ... There is a certain initial air of paradox about this approach; for I suppose that part at least of the appeal of anti-realist views about pure mathematics lay precisely in the *contrast* between the content of that science and the subject-matters of history, geography, natural science and ordinary chat; that it lay precisely in the view that the notion of a realm of facts waiting to be explored, some parts of which might, indeed would, remain undisclosed or be irrecoverably lost sight of, (a matter of speculation or uncertain inference)—that any such notion was quite improperly imported into mathematics from its natural home, viz. the natural world.[11]

After quoting this passage in the Preface to his *Truth and Other Enigmas*, Dummett seeks to 'dispel this air of paradox' by, in effect, repeating several of the arguments of his 'The Philosophical Basis of Intuitionist Logic', reprinted in the same volume. I can best approach Dummett's response to Strawson, and suggest that it involves a misunderstanding on Dummett's part, by first rehearsing the relevant issues and arguments of that paper.

In the first part of the essay Dummett was concerned with two kinds of issues arising between Platonists and intuitionists in the philosophy of mathematics. The first concerns the status of mathematical *objects*, the intuitionist maintaining that they are 'mental constructions'. The dispute is one concerning realism about the subject-matter of mathematics conducted within a framework like that of seventeenth- and eighteenth-century epistemology. The issue is whether the existence of mathematical objects is or is not dependent on their being the objects or actual or possible human cognitive states. The second issue concerns the nature of mathematical *truth*, and the role it has to play, if any, in an account of our grasp of the meaning of mathematical statements. The Platonist holds that to understand a mathematical statement is to grasp under what conditions it would be true, where it is held that a mathematical statement can be true quite independently of whether or not we could, by means of a proof, determine that it was. The intuitionist holds, rather, that:

> the notion of *truth*, considered as a feature which each mathematical statement
> either determinately possesses or determinately lacks, independently of our
> means of recognizing its truth-value, cannot be the central notion for a theory
> of the meanings of mathematical statement.[12]

The Platonist, on the second issue, would appear to be committed to realism with respect to the subject-matter of mathematics, as expressed in the twentieth-century framework. He would seem to be prepared to assert mathematical instances of: it could be that *p* even though we could not know that *p*. And the intuitionist would appear, on Dummett's account of the matter, to reject this for the mathematical case: to hold, that is, that for mathematical *p*: if *p*, then it could be known (via a proof) that *p*.

Now at one stage Dummett raises the question whether we can settle the second dispute between the Platonist and the intuitionist by settling the first: can we find grounds for accepting one of the opposed views of the *objects* of mathematics, and *thereby* find grounds for the corresponding (as it seems) view of mathematical *truth*? And Dummett argues, to my mind convincingly, that such an attempt would fail on two counts. Firstly, there may be no way of explicating the metaphors involved in the opposing pictures of mathematical objects except via their apparent expression in divergent views of mathematical truth. Secondly, and more importantly, there is no valid move from the Platonist view of mathematical objects to the Platonist view of mathematical truth, nor from the intuitionists' view of mathematical objects to their view of mathematical truth. For, he claims, both the following positions are internally consistent: (i) mathematical objects are 'mind-independent' but there are no undiscoverable mathematical truths; (ii) mathematics treats of 'mental constructions', but there could be truths about these which we are incapable of determining. (One might be encouraged to think that the latter position is consistent by asking the question: was Berkeley, by his view of the status of sensible objects, committed to the view that all questions concerning them were (humanly) decidable?)

Let us return now to Strawson and to Dummett's comments on his suggestion. Strawson, remember, found it paradoxical that we were to be moved to a global anti-realism by considerations first mooted in the philosophy of mathematics; for what, in his view, made mathematical anti-realism at least prima-facie attractive was some contrast between the subject-matter of mathematics and those areas of thought and discourse which treat of the natural world. And Dummett, in his comments, regards Strawson as having in mind the contrast between the natural world as composed of objects which are 'external' and 'mind-independent'; and mathematics as treating either of no objects at all, or of objects which are not external or mind-independent. Dummett then repeats the arguments from 'The Philosophical Basis of Intuitionistic Logic' that one cannot move from doctrines about the status of certain objects to doctrines about the status, with respect to verifiability, of truths concerning them. In particular, then, realism concerning the subject-matters of history, geography, etc. cannot be defended simply on the basis that these disciplines deal with 'external' objects.

But it should be evident that Strawson was not appealing simply to that idea. His claim concerning the natural world, which makes realism with respect to it compelling, is that we have sufficient knowledge of the natural world, and our modes of access to it, to see how and why some parts of it, as he puts it, 'might, indeed would, remain undisclosed or be irrecoverably lost sight of'. He then suggests that, at the very least, we have difficulties in importing such ideas into our thoughts about mathematics and its subject-matter.

Strawson says little concerning *why* we have such difficulties. I shall conclude this section by saying a little about this—about why, if I am right in seeing such ideas as underpinning realism about the natural world, there is such a strong pull in the direction of mathematical anti-realism. I wish to challenge Dummett's thought that such selective anti-realism can spring only from irredeemably metaphorical, and argumentatively inefficacious, views about the difference between mathematical and natural objects.

The rather simple points which I wish to make can be summed up as follows: (1) we have no account of principled mathematical ignorance, no account, that is, of why mathematical instances of (SR) might be true; (2) this is because we are inclined, in various ways, to think Platonistically about mathematics.

Let me first spell out these thoughts in the context of the 'Platonist' position in the philosophy of mathematics. This is the view, mentioned above, concerning the subject-matter of mathematics, which holds that it treats of certain *abstract objects*, objects which are neither mental nor physical, lack spatio-temporal location, are causally inert and (hence) are not possible objects of sensory perception. The attractions, or otherwise, of such a view are not here my concern.[13] I wish rather to point out how difficult it is for such a view to explain how or why a mathematical instance of the realist schema (SR) should be true.

Two preliminary points: firstly, many see Platonism in mathematics as conducive to, even as entailing, subject-matter realism concerning mathematics, in the twentieth-century sense captured in (SR). (As we have seen, though Dummett denies, with plausibility, the entailment.) But they are right to this extent: Platonism does leave room for the abstract possibility of unknowable mathematical truths. It does not entail, in any obvious way, *anti*-realism with respect to the subject-matter of mathematics. For if mathematical propositions owe their truth to how things stand in some mind-independent abstract realm, there is no obvious reason to believe that all such truths must be knowable by us. But, as I claimed above, in the case of propositions about the natural world, we have much more than the mere abstract possibility of unknowable truths. It is this *more* that, I claim, Platonism in mathematics has difficulty in providing.

The second point is this. In contemporary philosophy of mathematics the first (and usually the only) epistemological thought which people have when confronted with the ontological doctrine of Platonism is how difficult, on such a view, it is to account for mathematical *knowledge* (at least in the context of some popular current accounts of knowledge).[14] For example, adherents to causal theories of knowledge ask: how can there be knowledge of truths concerning a causally inert subject-matter? It is commonly held that were ontological Platonism true, we should be doomed to *universal* mathematical ignorance. How then can I claim that Platonism makes it difficult to understand the possibility of principled mathematical ignorance, of undiscovered mathematical truths?

The answer is quite easy. We clearly *do* have mathematical knowledge. If Platonism is not finally to be ruled out of court it is going to have to come up with an epistemology explaining how, compatibly with its ontology, *some* mathematical knowledge is possible. But then, I suggest, it will have difficulties in giving a theory of ignorance in any way analogous to that which science-cum-common sense gives us for the natural world. Given a Platonist account of our epistemic 'access' to the abstract realm of mathematics, what account could be forthcoming of how portions of this abstract realm might be, or be rendered, inaccessible to the knowledge-yielding capacity it has discerned? In the case of sensory perception—our fundamental epistemic access to the natural world—we can see at once at least three ways a portion of that world might be epistemologically inaccessible—in virtue of its spatial remoteness, its temporal remoteness, or its size in relation to our perceptual capacities. But none of these can apply literally to a non-spatio-temporal reality. It is hard to see how to begin to develop any plausible analogues for a faculty allegedly giving us access to the abstract.

I have sketched a contrast between the natural world and the subject-matter of mathematics on a Platonist account of the latter. It is worth stressing that, banal though these thoughts have been, they have pointed in the opposite direction to a common thought—namely, that the Platonist by over-assimilating mathematics to (for example) geography, makes subject-matter realism far too easy. I have left open the question whether, on other views of mathematics, one might 'import' into our thinking about mathematics the ideas Strawson and I see as crucial to subject-matter realism concerning the natural world.

Focusing directly on the epistemology of mathematics, our first thought is likely to be that the prime mode of mathematical knowledge is mathematical proof. (Proving things is, after all, what most mathematicians do most of the time.) We see again how hard it is to introduce analogues of our thoughts about the natural world. We tend to think Platonistically about *proofs*. To say of a mathematical proposition that it is provable is standardly taken to mean that *there is* a proof of it: and the '*there is*' is read Platonistically, that the truth of such a claim is independent of the existence, in the spatio-temporal realm, of a written, spoken, or thought token of the proof. We think of such writing, speaking, or thinking not as the bringing into existence of the proof but as the discovery of it. Once again, we have no obvious way of spelling out the thought that though there might be (in the present sense) a proof of a mathematical proposition, we might be incapable of knowing the mathematical truth in question because something about us, or the proof, might render us incapable of discovering it. (Of course, on this conception, there are countless proofs that never will, as a matter of fact, get discovered: but such happenstance gives no account to the thought that there are mathematical truths which we are incapable of knowing.)

V

So far we have been discussing what I have labelled subject-matter realism, a doctrine summed up in the idea that how things are may transcend our capacity to know how things are. Such realism embodies a possibly pessimistic doctrine concerning human powers of knowledge as measured against the constituents of reality. My second strand of realism—realism with respect to representations— is rather an optimistic doctrine concerning human powers of representation as measured against the constituents of reality, viz. that human beings have the power to represent to themselves how things are in the world. Now this, taken on its own, need not be a doctrine that one would characterize as realism, for it can be founded on the idealist-sounding thought that the very notion of how things are in the world has to be cashed in terms of, and hence in principle could not transcend, how human beings are capable of representing to themselves how things are. But it takes on a realist tinge if we combine it with some version of subject-matter realism. For that, at its most abstract, said that how things are in the world is, in general, independent of our actual or possible cognitive states. The combined doctrines, therefore, entail that we have the capacity to represent to ourselves those aspects of how things are which are independent of, and can transcend, our cognitive powers to determine them. And it is (fleshings out of) this latter doctrine that I wish to label 'realism with respect to representations'.[15]

As with subject-matter realism, the form this doctrine *takes* at any stage in the history of philosophy will depend on the current view of the central form of representation. When, in the classical epistemology of the seventeenth and eighteenth centuries, the essential form of representation consisted of 'ideas', realism with respect to representations consisted in the view that we could represent to ourselves objects the existence of which were independent of their being objects of perceptual awareness (themselves typically conceived as constituted by 'ideas'.) Anti-realism with respect to representations, in this period, is the denial of this. Seen in these terms, two of Berkeley's most famous (or notorious) arguments are, in the first instance, arguments for anti-realism with respect to representations. The first rests on his thought that ideas can be like, hence (on a resemblance theory of representation) can represent, only ideas. The second is the argument which concludes that we cannot so much as conceive—that is represent to ourselves in the medium of ideas—a tree or other sensible object existing unperceived. For much twentieth-century philosophy, the prime medium of representation is linguistic. We represent to ourselves ways the world might be by producing sentences which we understand. And we succeed (even if, sometimes, unknowingly) in representing to ourselves how things actually *are* if we produce and understand sentences which are *true*. But since, by the first strand of realism, how things are in the world is, in general, independent of our capacity to determine how things are in the world, realism about representations emerges (in a doctrine familiar to readers of Dummett) as the view that we have the capacity to produce and understand sentences which can be true, independently of our capacity to determine that they are true. The realist with respect to representations, in the present framework, is not prepared to accept that, in general, for any sentence S which we understand, if S is true then we must be able to determine that it is.

I now wish to enquire into the relations between subject-matter realism and realism with respect to representations (in their contemporary forms). Since we have arrived at the present formulation of realism with respect to representations by *incorporating* subject-matter realism, the former trivially entails the latter. (Moreover, the former is a special case of the latter, with the particular subject-matter of the truth-value of sentences. So realism with respect to representations is incompatible with *global* subject-matter anti-realism.) The interesting question is the converse: does (global) subject-matter realism entail (global) realism with respect to representations? Prima facie the answer would seem to be 'no', for at least two reasons.

Firstly, subject-matter realism concerning (say) the natural world speaks of that world and our ability to know how things stand in it. In particular it says that how things do so stand can transcend our capacity to know. It seems to contain no materials entailing that we have the ability to represent to ourselves in language, those aspects of reality which can thus transend our cognitive powers. Indeed (given some premises about knowledge requiring the linguistic representation of what is known) we might argue for subject-matter realism concerning the natural world precisely on the grounds that we have *not* the ability to produce and understand sentences which can be undetectably true. So not merely does anti-realism with respect to representations seem *compatible* with the corresponding subject-matter realism, it might be a premiss in an argument in favour of the latter viewpoint.

Secondly, if subject-matter realism entailed the corresponding realism with respect to representations, there could be a valid argument, starting from the premiss that if a sentence which we understand is true then we could determine that it is, to the conclusion that we must be able, in general, to determine how things are in the world, that is how things are in the world cannot transcend our cognitive powers. But such a move—from a claim about the limits of the linguistically representable world to one about the limits of the world—would surely only seem remotely plausible given the further ('idealist') thought, alluded to above, that there could be no more to reality than how we, in sentences, were capable of representing reality to be.[16]

These thoughts concerning the derivability of subject-matter anti-realism from the corresponding anti-realism with respect to representations would seem to offer a welcome prospect for those who wish to espouse (as Dummett appears at times to do), in some areas at least,[17] anti-realism with respect to representations. For, as I argued above, to be committed, in such cases, to the corresponding subject-matter anti-realism would involve one in the onerous task of reconstructing or reconstruing[18] those empirical views which, I claimed, underpin such cases of subject-matter realism. If anti-realism with respect to representations did entail the corresponding subject-matter anti-realism, then the former could not remain a self-contained doctrine in the theory of meaning, revisionary, at most, of our logic.

VI

Despite these thoughts, I think a case can be made, not quite for the view that subject-matter realism *entails* realism with respect to representations (and hence that anti-realism with respect to representations would entail subject-matter anti-realism); but for this: one who is prepared to *assert* instances of the schema definitive of subject-matter realism ((SR) above) must (given two further assumptions) be prepared to accept the corresponding instances of realism with respect to representations, and hence must reject *global* anti-realism with respect to representations.

The subject-matter realist is not prepared to hold that, in general,

(AS) If p, then it could be known (by a human being or knowing subject) that p.

Suppose, then, that he is actually prepared to assert instances of the denial of this schema, instances of:

(SR) It could be that p even though no human being or knowing subject knows, or could know, that p.

Let S be a sentence substitution of which for 'p' in (SR) gives an instance he is prepared to assert. For definiteness let S be 'The Venerable Bede died on a Tuesday'. Now if the subject-matter realist believes that by uttering that instance of (SR) he can assert what he takes himself to be asserting this requires that he believes *inter alia* that:

(A) By uttering 'The Venerable Bede died on a Tuesday', he could assert that the Venerable Bede dies on a Tuesday.

Only thus, it would seem, could he think that by uttering 'It could be that the Venerable Bede died on a Tuesday', he could assert that it could be that the Venerable Bede dies on a Tuesday.

As was noted earlier it seems to be a general truth about truth that:

> (B)   By uttering '*S* is true' one can assert what one asserts when one assertively utters *S*.[19]

Putting these thoughts together, someone who is prepared to assert an actual instance of (SR) must believe that he could assert what he intended to assert by means of an instance in which '*p*' is replaced systematically by the relevant instance of '*S* is true'. That is, in the above case, he must be prepared to think he could assert the very same thing by, and hence be prepared to assert:

> It could be that 'The Venerable Bede died on a Tuesday' is true although no human being or knowing subject does or could know that 'The Venerable Bede died on a Tuesday' is true.

He must be prepared, that is, to accept that a sentence which he understands could be true even though it could not be known to be true. That is to say that he must accept at least one case of realism with respect to representations and *ipso facto* deny global anti-realism with respect to representations.

Contraposing, then, someone who accepts global anti-realism with respect to representations (that is who holds that, for any sentence which we can understand, if it is true it could be known to be true) seems debarred from accepting any instance of the above schema which is definitive of subject-matter realism. But then, it seems, he is committed to denying those common sense-cum-scientific views which (we argued) render many such instances overwhelmingly plausible. By this argument, then, global anti-realism with respect to representations seems committed to being massively revisionary of everyday thought and of science.

VII

Before I say what I think the anti-realist with respect to representations ought to say about all this, I wish to raise a preliminary question: is Dummett, when he presents arguments for what *he* calls anti-realism, within the context of the theory of meaning, espousing what *I* am calling anti-realism with respect to representations? Is he, that is, denying that a sentence could be true independently of our ability to determine that it is? Now it may be said that this is precisely what Dummett *is* denying (laying aside what I view as irrelevant entanglements with bivalence). For he typically states realism, expressed as a doctrine in the theory of meaning, in the following terms. In 'The Reality of the Past' realism is the view that:

> We have ... succeeded in ascribing to our statements a meaning of such a kind that their truth or falsity is, in general, independent of whether we know, or have any means of knowing, what truth-value they have.[20]

Again:

> The fundamental tenet of realism is that any sentence on which a fully specific sense has been conferred has a determinate truth-value independent of our actual capacity to decide what that truth-value is.[21]

It would seem, therefore, that the anti-realism which is opposed to this would be precisely the doctrine that, in general, the truth-value of a statement is *not* independent of our capacity to determine that truth-value. Hence, for all sentences *S* which we understand, if *S* is true then we can determine that *S* is true. And this is just the version of anti-realism with respect to representations which, in section VI, I argued led to a highly implausible version of subject-matter realism.

In fact matters are more complicated than this. If one searched the relevant texts for a statement of the doctrine which Dummett conceives the anti-realist as holding, in opposition to the realism he has defined, it is not—at least not always—the view that if *S* is true then we are capable of determining that it is. Rather one finds such things as the following:

> In the case of a sentence for which we have no effective means of deciding its truth-value, the state of affairs which has, in general, to obtain for it to be true is, by hypothesis one which we are not capable of recognizing as obtaining whenever it obtains. Hence a knowledge of what it is for that sentence to be true is a knowledge which cannot be fully manifested by a disposition to accept the sentence as established whenever we are capable of recognizing it as true: it is knowledge which cannot, in fact, be fully manifested by actual linguistic practice; and therefore it is a knowledge which could not have been acquired by acquiring a mastery of that practice. Rather, when we are concerned with sentences of this kind, we should regard an understanding of them as consisting in an ability to do just what we actually learn to do when we learn to use them, that is, in certain circumstances to recognize them as having been verified and in others as having been falsified. The truth- and falsity-conditions for any sentence hence should instead be taken as ones which we are capable of recognizing effectively whenever they obtain: it is in just this that the difference resides between the realist conception of truth and falsity and the alternative conception of verification and falsification.[22]

Or, more briefly,

> we could not possibly have come to understand what it would be for the statement to be true independently of that which we have learned to treat as establishing its truth.[23]

Let us concentrate for the moment on the second quotation. It could be seen as ambiguous. (Or rather, I shall force an ambiguity on it.) It could be seen as saying: we could not possibly have come to understand the conception that a statement might be true independently of what we learnt to treat as establishing its truth. That is, we cannot understand the idea that a statement might be true in a situation in which it could not be known to be true. This would be to say that we simply cannot understand the position which I have called realism with respect to representation, which would presumably entail that something had gone wrong if we attempted to embrace that position.

This, of course, is not the point Dummett intends to make. He does not think he cannot understand the position he seeks to oppose.[24] Rather, Dummett's characterization of anti-realism is supposed to have the following force: concerning any particular statement, we cannot have come to understand what it would be for that statement to be true in a situation in which we could not establish its truth. And *this* doctrine is not, as it stands by itself, incompatible with our realism with respect to representations—that, simply said, there can be statements which are true even though we could not know them to be true. The present Dummettian formulation of anti-realism, in conjunction with that, merely entails that, for such sentences, we cannot understand what it would be for them to be true. And in the preceding passage we saw Dummett arguing in precisely this way. That is, from the premiss that there are sentences the truth of which *can* transcend our powers of verification to the conclusion that we cannot, for such sentences, represent a speaker's knowledge of their meaning as an understanding of the conditions under which they would be true. Thus construed, Dummett's views in the theory of meaning—his denial of a truth-conditional theory of meaning and his replacement of it by one centring on verification and falsification—far from denying what I am calling realism with respect to representations, rest squarely upon that doctrine.

Though I think this position—acceptance of realism with respect to representations as a ground for rejecting a truth-conditional conception of meaning—is, at points, Dummett's, it is not, I think, consistently so. It is not too difficult, even in advance of consulting his writings, to see why this might be so. The present position combines the thought that while there are sentences of our language the truth-conditions of which transcend our abilities to determine whether or not they obtain, we cannot have acquired, nor can we manifest, any knowledge of what such truth-conditions are. We know that the sentences have verification-transcendent truth-conditions while not knowing what these might be. And this seems an unhappy thought.[25]

Presumably to avoid this unhappiness, we find Dummett, at other points, espousing anti-realism with respect to representations (and thereby depriving himself of his central argument against truth-conditional theories of meaning). In one place he writes as follows:

> The actual fact of our linguistic practice is that the only notions of truth and falsity which we have for such sentences are ones which do not entitle us to regard the sentence as determinately true or false independently of our knowledge. The truth of such a sentence can consist only in the occurrence of the sort of situation in which we have learned to recognize it as true or false.[26]

Hence if a sentence is true we could recognize it to be true. And the whole tenor of his writings makes it clear that the anti-realism with respect to representations he epouses is of a very strong form: he is talking of capacities for recognition which we actually possess and can manifest in our actual use of sentences in the position in the world in which we find ourselves. How then can he avoid the collapse, by the argument of VI, into an extreme, and absurd, version of subject-matter anti-realism?

VIII

I shall conclude by making a suggestion as to how Dummett might avoid this collapse—a suggestion which does render Dummett's anti-realist views in the theory of meaning in a sense consistent with subject-matter realism, though at the cost of rendering anti-realism in the theory of meaning an extremely bizarre doctrine.

As I remarked above, Dummett's anti-realism in the theory of meaning appears, in the first instance, to be based squarely upon what I called realism with respect to representations. Dummett's view was not the denial of that but was rather the doctrine that to understand a sentence was not, in general, to know under what conditions it would be *true*; or, still more vaguely put, that the meaning of a sentence is not, in general, given by its truth-conditions.

These slogans are vague. I think we can best get some grip on what they come to by outlining a conception of the role of a theory of sense for a language developed by McDowell.[27] The conception might be crudely and briefly stated along the following lines. A theory of sense for some language L must entail, for each indicative sentence of L, a theorem which can, initially, be represented schematically as follows: $S \ldots p$ where 'p' is to be replaced by a sentence of the metalanguage. The most basic requirement on the sentence replacing 'p' is that it can serve to specify the content of the propositional acts performed by speakers of L by means of utterances of S (and sentences related syntactically to S). That is, given information that the speaker, in uttering S (or an appropriately related non-indicative sentence), is asserting (commanding, asking, or whatever), then we must be able to use the sentence replacing 'p' in the theorem for S correctly to complete the description of his act as, say, asserting that p (asking whether p, and so on).

The kinds of theory of sense Dummett considers all conceive of the '$\ldots$' in the schematic form of such theorems as being filled to yield something syntactically of the sort: S is C iff p. The theorems can then be described, in a convenient shorthand, as stating the C-conditions of the (indicative) sentences of L. And we can, if we like, say that, on a given view of this kind, a speaker's understanding of a sentence S is constituted by his knowledge of the conditions under which S would be C.

Dummett's most general requirement on such a representation of speaker's knowledge is that it be capable of being fully manifested in his use of sentences. And he takes this to require that, where 'C' is the proposed filling in theorems of the above style, for any S:

If S is C then we can know it to be C.
If S is not C then we can know it not to be C.

And his initial objection to truth conditional theories of meaning, based precisely on realism with respect to representations, is that where '*C*' is read as 'is true', these conditions are not met. Sentences can be *unknowably* true and false.

But, as we saw at the end of section VII, Dummett does not consistently maintain this position. He seems also inclined to take the line of *rejecting* realism with respect to representations: that is, of holding that the above two requirements *are* met if '*C*' is read as 'true'. There is then no objection to representing speakers' semantic knowledge as knowledge of the truth-conditions of sentences, provided it is conceded, in accordance with *anti*-realism with respect to representations, that truth cannot out-run our powers of recognizing it.[28] How then, can Dummett avoid being committed to the very strong version of (global) subject-matter anti-realism noted at the end of section VII? We can spell out, in the present framework, the argument of VI, which tries to extract the commitment from anti-realism with respect to representations, as follows. If the sentence replacing '*p*' correctly gives the *C*-conditions of some sentence *S*; and if correctly giving the *C*-conditions of any sentence entails its being usable to give the content of acts of uttering it; and if (by the Dummettian requirement on '*C*') it cannot be the case that *C* (or not-*C*) without our being able to know that *C*, (or not-*C*), then it must be that (where '*p*' is replaced by the sentence *S* in question):

if *p*, then we can know that *p*
if not-*p*, then we can know that not-*p*.

To avoid global subject-matter anti-realism, there must be some substitutions for '*p*' for which these two latter claims fail. This then can *only be* because some substitutions fail to give the *C*-conditions of any sentence of the language in question. But it is presumed that giving the *C*-conditions of a sentence *S* is what is required to be usable to give the propositional content of utterances of *S*. There must be, therefore, some sentences '*p*' of the metalanguage (which can, of course, be the object-language *L*)—viz., those which yield true instances of the schema for subject-matter realism (SR)—which cannot be used to give the propositional content of any assertoric act performed by a sentence *S* of object-language *L*. For such a substitution for '*p*' it must be the case that we can never truly report the content of an act performed by uttering a sentence *S* as: asserting that *p*. And this holds even when the sentence replacing '*p*' is *S* itself.

Let us now return to the original version in section VI of the argument which claimed that acceptance (as common sense and science compel) of particular instances of subject-matter realism compelled acceptance of realism with respect to representations. A key premiss was the thought that by uttering the sentence the speaker did succeed in asserting that *p*, where *S* is, and '*p*' is replaced by, the very sentence substitution of which in the realist schema gave a truth attested by common sense and science. (The example used was: by uttering 'The Venerable Bede died on a Tuesday' one could assert that the Venerable Bede died on a Tuesday; where, in turn, in accord with subject-matter realism, that he did so die could unknowably be the case.) And it is this key premiss which the present version of anti-realism in the theory of meaning must deny, if it is not to collapse into global subject-matter anti-realism.

But if, in assertively uttering, say, 'The Venerable Bede died on a Tuesday', we are not asserting that the Venerable Bede died on a Tuesday, then *what* are we asserting? I think that if the present formal preservation of subject-matter realism is to be possible, the answer must be: nothing. For, on the present view, a sentence '*S*' can be used to give the content of an assertive use of 'The Venerable Bede died on a Tuesday' only if *S* has *C*-conditions which cannot obtain undetectably. But as the Venerable Bede could have died, undetectably, on a Tuesday, *no* sentence the *C*-conditions of which meet this Dummettian requirement can have the same content as, that is serve to report the assertoric act performed by the utterance of, 'The Venerable Bede died on a Tuesday'.

The position, then, is that the anti-realist with respect to representations can formally preserve subject-matter realism in this sense: he can utter, without contradicting anything he holds in the theory of meaning, instances of the realist schema (SR). But he can give no account of what, in uttering such instances, he is asserting. On this position we preserve our realist view of the world at the cost of depriving ourselves of any natural account of what, in uttering those sentences which purport to express that view, we are doing.

Notes

1. See J. Haldane, 'Mind–World Identity and the Anti-Realist Challenge', this volume.

2. C. Wright, *Realism, Meaning and Truth*, p. 9.

3. M. Dummett, *The Interpretation of Frege's Philosophy*, p. 441.

4. In Berkeley's position minus God, any statement about sensible objects must, if true, be true in virtue either of the actual perception, by finite spirits, of appropriate ideas: or; a relatively fitful theme, of the truth of certain subjunctive conditionals concerning what ideas would be perceived, under appropriate conditions, by finite spirits. But, at least on the assumption that such subjunctive conditionals cannot be barely true, this conception of physical reality gives no grounds for the view that for each statement concerning it, there is something in virtue of which it or its negation is true. Consequently, there are no grounds for asserting of each such statement that it is determinately true or false. Bivalence will fail for such statements. To the extent that Dummett wishes to view the acceptability of bivalence as the hallmark of realism, Berkeley emerges as an anti-realist about the sensible world. The thought would then be that this verdict might change when, in the full picture, God enters. Of course the detailed interpretation of the role of God in Berkeley's philosophy is controversial. But on any view, features of God—be it his perception of, or conception of, an idea-constituted physical realm, or his standing intention to produce appropriate ideas in appropriate circumstances—can be seen as massively extending the range of that in virtue of which statements about the sensible world can be true. The suggestion would be that it would at least be consistent for Berkeley to hold that the features of God in question extended that range sufficiently to render determinately true or false each of

the relevant statements concerning the sensible world; that is, on the present conception, to embrace realism with respect to that world.

5. Locke, *An Essay concerning Human Understanding*, A. S. Pringle-Pattison (ed.), IV, iii, 16.

6. C. Wright, *Realism, Meaning and Truth*, p. 5.

7. Distinguishing versions of realism and idealism is, of course, an old game which Kant, and many others, have played. I shall not try to relate *my* distinctions to those of other writers—particularly not to that of Kant. I increasingly feel that Kant's account of his distinction—between 'empirical' and 'transcendental' realisms and idealisms—is so intertwined with his whole philosophy that subsequent writers' appropriation of his terms rarely embodies more than a loose and unhelpful analogy with his deployment of them.

8. In this connection see Haldane's remarks about acceptance or rejection of the strong and weak versions of ontological and epistemological realism as he defines them in his essay: Haldane, 'Mind–World Identity', section II.

9. This notion is sometimes equated with that of the obtaining or existing of a state of affairs. I am inclined to resist any such equation, however, on grounds of suspicion of the ontology of states of affairs.

10. Strawson, 'Scruton and Wright on Anti-Realism Etc.', *Proceedings of the Aristotelian Society* 77.

11. Strawson, 'Scruton and Wright on Anti-Realism Etc.', pp. 17–18.

12. Dummett, 'The Philosophical Basis of Intutitionistic Logic', in Dummett, *Truth and Other Enigmas*, p. 225.

13. For both, see the extensive treatment in Crispin Wright, *Frege's Conception of Numbers as Objects*.

14. For discussion see e.g. Wright, *Frege's Conception of Numbers as Objects*, section xi.

15. In connection with this see Section II of Haldane's essay, this volume.

16. An awareness of the quite distinct positions here, but an apparent underplaying of the distinction, emerges in the following passage, where Crispin Wright is defending contemporary anti-realism from the charge of being a species of idealism. 'We do not ordinarily think of those aspects of reality which we are able conclusively to determine as any less *of* the world—or, at least, those of its features to which we can give intelligible expression.' 'Truth Conditions and Criteria', in Wright, *Realism, Meaning and Truth*, p. 55.

17. For example, in respect of sentences concerning the past, or other minds.

18. See Crispin Wright, 'Strawson on Anti-Realism', *Synthese* 40, pp. 289 f. and in his *Realism, Meaning and Truth*, pp. 76 f. It is interesting to contrast the quite different response of Dummett, *Truth and Other Enigmas*, pp. xxii ff.

19. See e.g. John McDowell, 'Truth, Conditions, Bivalence, and Verificationism', in G. Evans and J. McDowell (eds.), *Truth and Meaning*, p. 46; W. V. O. Quine, *Philosophy of Logic*, p. 12. There are indeed arguments, of the 'translation' sort, modelled on Church's objections to Carnap's account of assertion, which have been deployed against this thought. Despite these, it is hard to believe that there is not a notion of asserting (hypothesizing etc.) the same thing, in which, at least for one who understands *S* (and this is implicit throughout the above discussion), he can use '*S* is true' to asset etc. what he asserts etc. by means of *S*.

20. Dummett, *Truth and Other Enigmas*, p. 358.

21. Dummett, *Frege: The Philosophy of Language*, p. 466.

22. Ibid., p. 467.

23. Dummett, *Truth and Other Enigmas*, p. 362.

24. We might compare here, though, a familiar complaint about Kant's transcendental idealism: that, on his own principles, he ought not to have been able to give content to the transcendental realism by contrast with which his own position was, in part, defined.

25. Some evidence of this unease may be found in Wright's paper quoted above. Thus in one paragraph he begins by writing of sentences of which our '*standard conception* [my emphasis] of the truth conditions of the sentence is such that if actualized, they would not, or need not, be recognizably so' ('Truth Conditions and Criteria', p. 53). (And later he speaks of 'sentences whose truth conditions we *picture to ourselves* [my emphasis] as (possibly) verification-transcendent' (Ibid., p. 54).) But he goes on to say, of such sentences, that 'in cases like these there is not, or need not be anything in which this alleged knowledge (of truth conditions) can consist'. So we can have a 'conception' or a 'picture' of these verification-transcendent truth-conditions, but no 'knowledge'.

26. Dummett, *Frege: The Philosophy of Language*, p. 468.

27. See his 'Truth Conditions, Bivalence and Verificationism', especially pp. 42–7.

28. In writing later than any here considered, Dummett takes precisely this line, criticizing his own earlier formulations, see *Truth and Other Enigmas*, p. xxii. But in still later writings he seems to revert to the old way of putting it, which the Preface to *Truth and Other Enigmas* has rightly criticized. See e.g. *The Interpretation of Frege's Philosophy*, pp. 434–5. Earlier on p. 434 ibid. he also moves, between sentences, from formulations concerning subject-matter realisms, to formulations concerning realism with respect to representations.

3

Realism: The Contemporary Debate— W(h)ither Now?

Crispin Wright

I

The philosophical literature about realism displays as many disagreements about what is at issue as about which side of the fence to stand. A signal example is provided by the debates, conducted in almost complete insulation from each other, concerning realism as opposed by Dummettian *anti-realism*— the realism which believes in evidence-transcendent truth and the rest—and realism as opposed by *irrealism* or *projectivism*—the realism which believes in a face-value, 'fact-stating' construal of moral, aesthetic, or scientific-theoretical discourse. Is there any single issue which is the ultimate focus of both the debates, or are the respective 'realisms' alike in little but name?

There is a simple, if rather artificial way to unify the debates. Take it (i) that *truth is the stuff of realism*—the realist about a given region of discourse is someone who holds, simply, that its statements are apt to be true or false—and (ii) that the concept of *truth is, of itself, evidentially unconstrained*. That does not mean that, absurdly, the availability of evidence can never be an analytical consequence of the supposition that a particular type of statement is true; it requires only that, if that is so, it is a reflection not on the concept of truth but on the nature of the particular subject-matter.

With both these assumptions in place, Dummett's anti-realist becomes a species of irrealist. The line would be that there should be no complaint about a truth-conditional conception of meaning where genuinely factual statements are concerned; that, for the familiar anti-realist sorts of reason, there have to be epistemic constraints on truth if a truth-conditional conception of meaning

The text which follows is a lightly edited version of that presented at the St Andrews conference. The proposals announced here are pursued in considerably greater detail, and with many qualifications, in my Waynflete Lectures, *Truth and Objectivity*.

is to be sustained; and hence that, where the purported subject-matter of statements of a particular kind fails to impose appropriate such constraints—remembering that the notion of truth has, of itself, no such inbuilt constraints—an irrealist conception of them is imposed, and their content should be accounted for in some suitable, non-truth-conditional way.

One difficulty with this regimentation of the debates is that the non-truth-conditional semantic proposals made by Dummettian anti-realists typically treat as central such notions as proof, verification or warranted assertion, which seem to demand construal in terms of truth. What is a proof if not a demonstration of truth? When is an assertion warranted if not when it is reasonable to believe that what is asserted is true? What indeed, *is* an assertion if not a purported presentation of the truth? But the most basic problem with the proposal, it seems to me, is not its procrustean effects on Dummettian anti-realism but simply that it is doubtful, recent efforts not-withstanding,[1] whether irrealism is any longer a philosophically progressive programme. I do not propose to try to argue this in detail here. The general point is that when irrealism is taken as the anti-realist prototype, the inevitable effect is that the propriety of aspects of the *syntax* of disputed regions of discourse comes to be central to the debate. At least, this is the effect of the would-be conservative kind of irrealism which is not content—contrast the late John Mackie's view of ethics[2]—to hold the discourse in massive error. The would-be conservative irrealist has to attempt to construe the discourse as involving no genuine assertions, no claims of truth; and it is then an open question whether any alternative non-assertoric semantic construal can save all those aspects of the syntax of the discourse which seem to connect most intimately with truth-claiming. It seems to me that, on the contrary, the meaningfulness, ergo syntactic propriety, of the discourse should be agreed by all hands. What ought to be at issue is what *kind* of content it possesses.

Even if the irrealist can somehow save the syntax, the price paid may very well be to call into question whether ordinary canons of logical consistency, and ordinary constraints on the ascription of what appear to be propositional attitudes, continue to have any bearing. Such is one side effect of recent[3] irrealist construal of conditionals with moral antecedents. And again, it seems to me that it should be possible for the realist and anti-realist to agree at the outset that discourse about the moral, modal, or comic is subject to ordinary sentential logic; and that the ascription of propositional attitudes concerning the moral, modal, or comic is constrained accordingly.

The foregoing is no argument, only an expression of scepticism about the irrealist direction. I am sceptical whether it is the direction in which many of the influential anti-realist arguments about different subject-matters really point; I am certain that it cannot satisfactorily accommodate Dummettian anti-realism; doubtful of the propriety of the syntactic issues which con-servative irrealists are forced to take as central; and sceptical whether they can, anyway, ever win. But what other direction is there for anti-realism to take?

II

The proposal considered in effect took irrealism as the anti-realist prototype, and attempted to extend it to Dummettian anti-realism. I suggest we try to play matters the other way around. But not in the most immediate way. The suggestion is not, that is to say, that moral anti-realism should be a species of verificationism. Probably no moral realist, whether of secular or religious inspiration, would be comfortable with the notion that moral truth may essentially transcend human appraisal. The key thought is rather that, contrary to the considered proposal, truth is *not* the exclusive property of realism. The central thesis of Dummettian anti-realism is, or ought to be, the claim that truth is, of itself, essentially epistemically constrained. The exact statement of an appropriate constraint may be a matter of some difficulty but that does not now concern us. The crucial point is that the debate between the mathematical realist, for instance, and a Dummettian opponent is not about whether pure mathematical sentences should be thought of as candidates to be true or false; that is agreed on both sides. The question is rather *what* notion of truth informs pure mathematics, how the notion of pure mathematical truth is to be understood if the meaning of theses in pure mathematics is to be thought of as determined by reference to their truth-conditions.

The respect, then, in which the dispute between semantic realism and Dummettian anti-realism should be taken as prototypical is that the applicability of the truth-predicate among statements in the disputed class is not at issue. I am proposing that moral anti-realists, for instance, should grant that moral judgements are apt for truth and falsity, and hence unproblematically enjoy the sorts of combinatorial possibilities focused on by the *modus ponens* argument,[4] and are unproblematically constrained by ordinary notions of logical consistency and validity of inference. What is in dispute concerns, rather, what *else* is true of moral judgements.

Just now, and elsewhere, I have presented this proposal as though it involved dropping the idea that the notion of truth is uniform across different regions of discourse, with the essence of realism about a certain class of statements being the view that the notion of truth appropriate to them was appropriately 'substantial', in a sense or senses to be worked on.[5] But actually it is moot whether the idea of a possible variety of concepts of truth has to be part of the perspective I am recommending. Rather than regard the notion of truth as non-univocal, we can seek to draw relevant distinctions among the characteristics possessed by a single notion of truth as it applies to statements of different kinds. So although in what follows I may sometimes tend to talk in the former kind of way, it will be possible to represent the distinctions I shall draw as reflecting different realism-relevant characteristics of one notion of truth, characteristics which it sometimes possesses and sometimes lacks, rather than distinctions within the notion. And it may well be that, in the end, nothing of importance hangs on this contrast.

The suggestion I am making is apt to provoke a protest. How can we make the notion of truth be neutral ground? How can we think of a statement's truth except in terms of its corresponding to reality, fitting the facts, 'telling it like it is'? For, contrary to the impression given by old debates about truth—in which the 'correspondence theory' was opposed by coherentists, pragmatists, and so on—such phases incorporate no substantial theory of truth but connect with the predicate, 'is true', platitudinously. I think this thought is correct, but that it needs to be set in a proper perspective. The *representative* aspect of the concept of truth which these platitudinous connections highlight is one of its aspects. Another is its *normativity*: truth supplies a parameter of appraisal, is what our (sincere) assertions aim for. The thought that truth is the stuff of realism, and hence that the anti-realist has to contest its applicability to statements in a disputed class, sees the representative aspect as primary and the normative as a consequence of the representative: roughly, the thought is, it is because we *value* representation that we aim at truth. But that cannot be right. For if it were a question of placing a value upon something determined independently, then it should be possible to describe the patterns that would be assumed by the linguistic practice of people who were capable of the same sort of thoughts as we are, and had the same concept of truth, but placed no value on it. But there is no such conceivable practice. The normative aspect is essential to truth.

Equally, so is the representative; the platitudes ensure that. A notion which functioned normatively for a region of discourse—supplied a constraint to which speech acts within the region had to conform—would not be truth if its practitioners rejected such platitudes. What I am suggesting, however, is that the appropriateness of characterizing utterances of a particular kind as 'true' and 'false' does not await a *separate* justification of their representative fitness, so to speak, which can still be lacking even though the normativity of the truth-predicate and its platitudinous connections with representation are granted. We get the notion of truth off the ground, as it were, by establishing the currency of a norm of correct utterance whose connections with talk of correspondence, representation and their kind are taken to be platitudinous. There is no further question of the authenticity of that kind of talk; if there were, the connections would not be platitudinous.

An analogy may help. Elsewhere[6] I have argued that Frege's Platonism about numbers is best interpreted as based on the view that candidacy to refer to an object, properly so regarded, is a matter of syntax; that once it has been settled that a class of expressions function as singular terms by syntactic criteria, there is no further question about whether they succeed in objectual reference which can be raised by someone who is prepared to allow that appropriate contexts in which they so feature are true. What is here being proposed is a thesis of similar flavour concerning candidacy for truth itself. A significant sentence is a candidate for truth if it has the appropriate syntax. And having the appropriate syntax means, primarily, admitting of significant embedding within negation, the conditional, and other connectives, and within ascriptions of propositional attitude. That a class of sentences will sustain such embeddings is something we should expect if their use is appropriately constrained: if, that is, any particular use may be appraised and criticized for being based on ignorance or error, and if justification for a use can be better and worse. In particular we should expect indicative conditionals to have a role whenever the correct assertibility of a sentence is something about which we can, at least temporarily, be in ignorance but which can be, in various ways, of practical consequence for us. Likewise for propositional-attitude embeddings: the currency of notions of ignorance and error will provide a use for a potential contrast between any particular subject's attitude to a particular such statement and the attitude which, we suppose, it is proper to take. My claim is not, however, or not merely, that the kinds of syntactic potentialities described are to be expected in discourse which is subject to a constraint of correctness of the relevant kind—a constraint whose demonstrated violation demands withdrawal of an utterance and about whose satisfaction, in a particular case, there is use for the notions of ignorance, error, and improved assessment. It is that the operation of such a constraint has no expression *except* in such syntactic conditioning of a region of discourse; and that it is not a further, metaphysical step to regard its statements as candidates for truth and falsity.

These claims need much more fine-grained development and support than I am here in a position to offer. It is necessary to account, in particular, for the emergence of a contrast—operative in our discourse in so many areas and arguably implicit in the use of a genuine negation—between truth and assertibility; equivalently, the emergence of a distinction between finding fault with a claim and finding fault with its pedigree. A possible strategy of explanation might run like this. Once we have the notion of better and worse justification for particular statements, we can understand the notion of a statement's continuing to be justified no matter how much more information we may gather which is germane to its justifiability. Say that a statement is *superassertible*[7] if that is so. Now, there is no evident contrast between the normative functions of truth and assertibility as far as one's own, currently envisaged statements are concerned. The contrast concerns, rather, the use of statements, whether by oneself or others, on other occasions. And it is appraisals of other-occasion assertibility that are, perhaps surprisingly, the more demanding. I count as appraising the *truth* of what you said yesterday if I (competently) appraise its current assertibility today. But in order to appraise its yesterday-for-you assertibility, I need additionally to know something of your state of information yesterday. And this is an additional requirement, because if I fulfil it, I can hardly fail to be in a position to appraise the statement by the light of my own current state of information, which is all I have to do to appraise its truth. (Which is not to say that truth is current assertibility.) In contrast, I can be in a position to appraise the current assertibility of your statement without knowing anything about your state of information yesterday.

It seems plausible that this distinction is integral to the representative aspect of the notion of truth; the representative platitudes *would* be out of place if the distinction could not be drawn, since it should in general be no disqualification, in appraising the accuracy of a *representation*, to know little or nothing of the situation of others who have believed it accurate. But notice that the *shape* of the contrast just characterized is well enough explained if truth is actually *identified* with superassertibility, and the content of an assertion, subsequently appraised, taken to be a claim of its own superassertibility. So—in prospect anyway—the introduction of a notion of truth, contrasting with assertibility, does not have to be taken to reflect the operation of a parameter of appraisal quite different to assertibility. It may be that nothing in the uses to which the notion is put distinguishes it from superassertibility. It is, of course, important to what I am proposing whether or not this is so.[8]

I am making, to use a fashionable term, a *minimalist* claim about the notion of candidacy for truth; and suggesting that the irrealist version of anti-realism, issuing in instrumentalism in the philosophy of science, expressive theories of value, etc., is in error in exceeding this minimalism. But, as in the case of singular reference to abstract objects, candidacy is one thing and success is another. There, the suggestion was that reference is, as it were, imposed on a candidate singular term by its occurrence in appropriate true contexts. What is the corresponding condition on the success of a statement which is a candidate for truth? Here too, I am advocating minimalism. John Mackie, for one, might have accepted the overall drift of what I have been saying, but evidently felt that a further metaphysical issue, connecting with a *deep* possibility of misfit, still remains. Talking in all respects as if there are moral facts—saying things which are candidates for truth and whose truth would require the existence of moral facts—is one thing; but the real truth of such talk is quite another. And it is another thing *notwithstanding* the degree of discipline in principle which a governing notion of assertibility imposes on such talk. Moral realism, in Mackie's view, should be identified with the belief that some moral judgements are, in this deeper sense, *really* true—a belief which Mackie rejects.

However I do not think the foregoing considerations leave any option of such belief or disbelief. They provide, simply, no space for an account of the kind of metaphysical rift which would generate the truth of a kind of wide-scope negation of all our moral judgements. Moral statements have the relevant potentialities for embedding, and frequently sustain a complex range of justifying considerations, of differing degrees of strength. And if the line sketched above about superassertibility is correct, then the notion of truth for which they are thereby candidates is a very short abstraction from the notion of justification which governs our appraisal of any particular moral statement. It contains nothing to give sense to the idea of Mackie's rift. My claim, in other words, is not merely that it should not be controversial, between realism and its opponents, whether moral, aesthetic, and comic judgements, hypotheses of theoretical science, and theses of pure mathematics are candidates for truth; it is that, in addition, there is as much reason to think that some of them are true are there is reason to accept them by the standards which prevail in the ordinary appraisal of such statements. If anti-realism about a given region of discourse does not profitably channel itself into the conviction that no genuine, apt-to-be-true-or-false statements are made therein, neither should realism express itself as the thesis that some of these statements are genuinely true.

What then is the proper focus of debate? Have we not simply abrogated the resources for a debate—committed oursleves to *quietism*? I do not think so. I have emphasized the inseparability of the normative and representative aspects of the notion of truth; and I have suggested that the operation of a constraint upon an assertoric practice which is generated out of but, in the fashion described, contrasts with justified assertibility, and is expressed in the relevant kind of syntactic potentialities, suffices to justify the claim that we are there in the business of representation. That is because that claim is anodyne, has no more substance than the claim that we are there in the business of talking truth; and the latter essentially does no more than advert to the relevant features of the assertoric practice. So, I am suggesting, it is never *wrong*, in these circumstances, to endorse the platitudinous expressions of the representative aspect of truth—so long as one remembers that the connections *are* platitudinous, and that one succeeds in claiming no more, by dignifying a statement as 'fitting the facts', or 'corresponding to an aspect of reality', or whatever, than by claiming that it is true. The platitudinous equivalents embody, to repeat, no substantial theory, have no independent content—so far.

I therefore propose that we experiment with the idea that we may get an interesting and progressive exegesis of realist/anti-realist disputes in different areas by focusing on the question whether some kind of independent content and justification *can* be found for the notion of truth as representation or fit, or anyway for something somehow seriously dyadic, as it were— some consideration, perhaps, which forces a contrast between truth and superassertibility. Can we find a home, within this way of looking at the matter, for some of those considerations—concerning, for instance, evidence-transcendence, convergence of opinion, and best explanation of belief, to take just three—which have been regarded as pivotal in the various debates?

That will be the question for the following sections. I close this one by remarking that I personally take satisfaction in the dialectical situation which the strategy of interpretation which I have been outlining establishes. Anti-realism is now properly identified with the view that, with respect to a particular region of assertoric discourse, nothing further can be done to substantiate the representative aspect of the notion of truth beyond what is accomplished by the platitudinous connections with normativity. Anti-realism thus becomes the natural, initial position in any debate. It is the position from which we have to be shown that we ought to move. All the onus, everywhere, is on the realist.

III

To recap. The notion of truth which, I have been suggesting, is, as it were, neutral territory regulates any statement-making practice which displays the interlocking set of characteristics described; a practice, that is, which is disciplined by acknowledged standards of justification and justified criticism, which has the syntax to be subjugated to ordinary sentential logic, which sustains embeddings within propositional attitudes, and where ignorance and error are possible categories of explanation of aberrant performances by its practitioners. As suggested, however, these characteristics subtend an ideal of truth—call it *minimal truth*—which, while contrasting with context-relative assertibility, may be viewed as constructed out of it. Nothing is so far put into the notion to frustrate its construal *as* superassertibility; nothing to force us to think, for instance, of truth as conferred by factors other than those which determine proper practice within the region of discourse in question. The challenge to the realist to fill out the representative aspect of the notion of truth as applied to the disputed class of statements will be well met if some distance can be interposed at this point, between the determinants of truth and the determinants of those statements' proper use; or if, anyway, some appropriate distinction between the concepts of truth and superassertibility can somehow be disclosed.

Let us begin with the case of *evidence-transcendence*. It is a particularly straightforward case. It would be a decisive *coup* on the part of the realist if it could be shown that the notion of truth which informs our understanding of a disputed class of statements is intelligibly conceived as potentially transcending all possible evidence. Such a demonstration would precisely establish the residual content called for. For superassertibility *cannot* be evidence-transcendent: if there is a case to be made for accepting a particular statement which complies with the acknowledged standards and will endure through all attempts to improve or fault it, it has to be possible to gather (defeasible) grounds for saying so. By contrast, though, a victory for Dummett's anti-realist—a demonstration that only an evidentially constrained notion of truth can feature in an acceptable account of assertoric content—would not be decisive against the realist; the possibility would remain that realism might contrive to meet its explanatory obligations in some other way.

The case of *convergence* is less straightforward. The issue has typically been perceived as central in the debate about evaluative realism, with moral anti-realists, in particular, taking comfort from what they have perceived as unnegotiable diversity in basic moral standpoints. But, on the face of it, it is unclear why one who perceived the responsibilities of realism in the way I am recommending should think that realist capital can be made from demonstrating that truth satisfies a convergence constraint. The constraint, one assumes, will look something like:

Convergence[1]

> If a class of statements are apt to be true, then there will be a tendency, in suitable circumstances, for competent subjects to agree on the truth of members of that class.

Clearly, no realist will want to defend this who thinks that we can be shown to work with a potentially evidence-transcendent notion of truth for the statements in question. For if that could be shown, the realist case could not possibly be *strengthened* by any considerations about convergence. So better to suppose we are concerned with a class of statements—moral judgements perhaps—about which realism in Dummett's sense is not an attractive option. Then Convergence[1] imposes a substantial requirement only if minimal truth fails to satisfy it? But *can* minimal truth fail to satisfy it? And if it can, how exactly is something *realistic* added—something that somehow beefs up the representative aspect, or suggests the operation of factors independent of those which confer assertibility—by demonstration that convergence is satisfied in a particular type of case?

Convergence[1] is terribly weak. Its effect is merely that we are entitled to regard some at least of the given class of statements as true only if there is, or would be under favourable circumstances, some measure of consensus about their truth. But minimal truth is (undifferentiable from) a construction from a notion of assertibility which was to be associated with *acknowledged* standards of justification and criticism. Where such standards are acknowledged, consensus ought—at least sometimes—to be elicitable. So in order to give minimal truth a chance of failing, we need to strengthen the test.

How? Well, two points are salient. First, nothing in the apparatus of minimal truth requires that disagreements cannot occur in which neither disputant can justly be criticized. There are to be operational standards of proper assertibility, and criteria for the ascription of ignorance and error: but nothing was said which enjoined that, in any disagreement, at least one party would be convictable of improper assertion, or of ignorance or error, by those standards. Second, the intuition that convergence is important to the realist has it that (ignoring complications to do with vagueness) it should be a *global* property of the statements at issue—the thought, for instance, that something is shown about the (lack of) objectivity of the comic by the possibility of irreducibly divergent opinions about comedy is not assuaged at all by the reflection that there is, very probably, convergence about some—perhaps many—comic judgements. So it looks as though the intentions of those who have felt that convergence is important might be better reflected by something like:

Convergence[2]

The members of a certain class of statements are candidates for truth only if each of them will, under suitable circumstances, command a convergence of opinion on its truth, or falsity.

Is this a test which may be failed by statements of which minimal truth and falsity are predicable? Obviously it would, again, be applicable only for statements for which the possibility of evidence-transcendent truth had been ruled out. The intuition it is trying to reflect is that, in any region of discourse where we cannot provide that excuse—cannot explain how relevant aspects of the world may simply outstrip our cognitive powers, even in principle—we may think of ourselves as dealing in genuine fact only if we have a guarantee that no intractable disagreements will arise.

The question, then, is: when the statements in a particular class pass this test, does that indicate that the truth-predicate applicable to them has the kind of additional substance which, for instance, evidence-transcendence would also bestow on it? Not yet. For one thing, the test only offers a necessary condition. For another, a class of statements which fails it—judgements of comedy, may be—might command convergence in different possible circumstances. There might have been a universal sense of humour. Why would not this count as one of the relevant kind of 'suitable circumstances'—so that judgements about comedy could pass the test after all?

Clearly, the phrase 'in suitable circumstances' marks a place that has to be filled somehow or other; it would be futile to impose a condition of convergence *tout court*. But it must not, obviously, be allowed to mean anything equivalent to 'conditions actually conducive to the emergence of a consensus'. And when we begin to reflect on what it ought to mean, if a substantial test is to be conveyed in keeping with the original intuitions, we can see that the notion of convergence itself is actually inessential and that those who have thought it important have somewhat misformulated their requirement.

Think of a device—a camera, say—whose function is to produce a representation of a state of affairs. There is a platitudinous enough connection between the accuracy of any particular such representation and convergence: simply, a particular representation—photograph—is accurate (within the limits of the apparatus) only if other cameras of the same marque which function properly and are presented with the same input produce convergent representations (very similar photographs). It is thus a necessary condition of ascribing a representational function to a class of devices that divergent output be explicable, at least in principle, in terms either of divergent input or of less than perfect function. Similarly: the representative aspect of truth in some region of discourse is rightly conceived as more than the minimum imposed by the platitudes only if genuine divergences of opinion have to be explicable, at least in principle, in terms of some breach of ideal cognitive function. *Either* some material ignorance or error must be involved in the information at the disposal of one of the relevant parties *or* one of the parties must be guilty of misappraisal of the information at their disposal—of inferential error, or prejudicial over- or under-rating of data, or deployment of faulty background information, or whatever. Now, the 'suitable conditions' for convergence, mooted in the two principles formulated above, can hardly be meant to include anything other than circumstances suitable for *cognitive* functioning. *Suitable* circumstances, in the spirit of the proposal, are circumstances in which subjects have access to a sufficiency of information of some appropriate kind and are in a position, internally and externally, to respond to it in an appropriate way. But then, rather than impose a requirement of convergence, we might as well impose a requirement that *divergence* always be explicable by circumstances being less than suitable, in the sense just sketched. So what the convergence constraint is after, I suggest, is nothing other than what I have elsewhere called the *cognitive command* of truth: where truth has cognitive command with respect to a certain class of statements if and only if

Cognitive Command
> It is a priori that disagreements, when not attributable to vagueness, are ultimately explicable in terms of cognitive shortcomings; specifically, some material ignorance, material error, or prejudicial assessment.

And the connection of this idea with our concerns is, as noted, its link with the idea of representation. Where the truth-predicate lacks this feature, it will not be *wrong* to think of discourse as aimed at 'representing the facts'; but if statements satisfy the cognitive command condition, the imagery of representation draws additional substance from the analogy which may then be displayed with the products of other uncontroversially representational systems.

IV

Wiggins[9] formulates the convergence requirement as

> If x is true, then x will under favourable circumstances command convergence, and the best explanation of the existence of this convergence will require the actual truth of x.

Later[10] he further specifies the second part of that as

> we have the truth-relevant sort of convergence where *the statement of the best explanation of the agreement in the belief needs a premise to the effect that item t is indeed F, and the explanation would be simply invalidated by its absence.*

This actually introduces a distinct idea, which does not need to keep company with convergence. It is that when the beliefs which we express in a given region of discourse are rightly viewed as responses to, reflections of a reality 'out there', features of that reality ought to have an ineliminable part to play in any fully satisfactory explanation of our formation of those beliefs. The perceived importance of this idea coheres nicely with the re-direction I am recommending. For a genuine explanation has to advert to something *independent*, a cause or source of the phenomenon to be explained. So where the best account we can give of the epistemology of statements of a certain kind represents the beliefs which they enable us to express as the products of interaction with the states of affairs which they describe—or anyway essentially adverts, one way or another, to those states of affairs in explaining why we hold those beliefs—our conception of what it is for those statements to be true crucially exceeds the minimal conception. It is not open to us to think of the 'facts' to which such beliefs may correspond merely as things we are licensed harmlessly to talk about by way of spin-off from platitudinous links with the propriety of regarding them as candidates for truth, minimally conceived—not if a reference to such facts has to be made in any finally satisfactory explanation of why we form beliefs of that sort.

This third constraint—the constraint of *best explanation*—represents a sufficient condition for the propriety of a move away from minimalism (anti-realism). It is not obvious that it represents a necessary condition (it cannot do so unless its satisfaction is implicit in the satisfaction of any other condition which might suffice for such a move, which seems doubtful). But at least some of the literature which has pivoted around it seems to be proceeding on the assumption that it is something which a would-be realist about a certain region of discourse *has* to argue is satisfied. Harman,[11] for example, argues against moral realism on the ground that the best explanation of our moral responses to a particular action can dispense altogether with any reference to its moral status. The explanation can proceed entirely in terms of the non-evaluative properties of the act, and the features of our natures and moral upbringing which have resulted in a disposition, for example to deplore acts with such features. No *moral* facts need be cited; the explanation may be wholly contained within references to the 'natural' features of the act and the origins of the psychological conditions which sustain the effects upon us which those features work.

The question, however, is what we should look for from a 'best explanation' (or one which is good enough). One strand in Wiggins' attempted rebuttal of Harman's argument[12] is based on the thought that natural science will not actually be able to deliver the goods that Harman needs. I shall not engage that. A second and more important contention in Wiggins' discussion is to the effect that, insofar as there is a legitimate constraint here, it is one which ethics and mathematics, to take the two most widely disputed examples, may be seen, when it is properly conceived, to comply with. The impression to the contrary, in Wiggins' view, derives from a misplaced emphasis on causality, the belief that 'People think that p because p' is an acceptable claim only where the 'because' is causal.[13] Wiggins writes—remember that he intertwines the convergence and best-explanation constraints—as follows:

> there is at least one general way in which we might try to conceive of the prospects for moral judgements' commanding the sort of convergence that truth requires. This is by analogy with the way in which arithmetical judgements command it. There is an impressive consensus that $7 + 5 = 12$; and, when we rise above the individual level and look for the explanation of the whole consensus, only one explanation will measure up to the task. There is nothing else *to* think that 7 and 5 add up to. ... Since any other answer besides '12' will induce a contradiction in arithmetic, no wonder we agree. We believe that $7 + 5$ is 12 because $7 + 5$ *is* 12. We have no choice.[14]

Put on one side the question how the arithmetical case might illuminate the moral. The question is, does the acceptability, in the spirit which informs Wiggins' remarks, of 'We accept that 7 and 5 make 12 because they do' suffice to show that the citation of arithmetical truths should feature in the best explanation of our arithmetical beliefs. Well, if the 'because' is not causal, what is it? Reason-giving, presumably. But then it is an ellipsis to describe our reason for believing that $7 + 5 = 12$ as consisting in the fact that it is so. The reason is rather, what Wiggins adverts to, that we have *proof*, that we can, for instance, generate contradictions from '$7 + 5 \neq 12$'.

One immediate consequence is that it begins to seem less clear that there can be any uncontentious moral parallel. If the 'because' in

We think that wanton cruelty is wrong because it is

is likewise reason-giving, what exactly constitutes the reason (when unpacked)? What corresponds to proof? A second, more important reflection is that the reason, in the arithmetical case, is simply constituted by our recognition of a canonical form of *assertibility*—the availability of a proof. Whereas what we were looking for was something which would impose some distance or, anyway, somehow *distinguish* between truth and superassertibility. If the best-explanation test is to provide a basis for such a distinction, then Wiggins' remarks have no tendency to show that our arithmetical judgements pass the test.

If we so understand the best-explanation constraint that Wiggins is right, for the reasons he gives, to think that elementary arithmetical equalities satisfy it, no departure from arithmetical minimalism seems thereby justified. But that is a fair complaint only if the test may be interpreted, otherwise, in such a way that passing it *does* justify a departure from minimalism. Can it be?

I think it can, and that the analogy with abstract singular terms, viewed in what I see as Frege's way, is once again helpful. Dummett writes as follows about the referents of such abstract singular terms as numerals and expressions purportedly standing for sets:

> Pure abstract objects are no more than reflections of certain linguistic expressions, expressions which behave, by simple formal criteria, in a manner analogous to proper names of objects, but whose sense cannot be represented as consisting in our capacity to identify objects as their bearers.[15]

A Fregean will reject the last part of this thought, with its anti-Platonist overtones. But he must accept that there is something right about the spirit of this and similar remarks in Dummett's discussion. Abstract objects can, in general, impinge upon us only as the referents of understood abstract singular terms. There is no question of such an object influencing the thought of someone who does not know what it is, or producing other kinds of effects on our consciousness, or on our bodies, or on non-human objects of any kind. By contrast to the ordinary, 'robust' objects with which Dummett is tempted towards a disadvantageous comparison, abstract objects play a decidedly limited role. The Fregean—in effect, a minimalist about singular reference—finds no reason in that reflection to doubt the *reality* of reference to abstract objects. But the fact remains that there are reasons which force us to think of concrete objects as playing a role in the world quite independent of our thought and talk about them—reasons which impose what Dummett calls, I think unhappily, a 'realistic conception of reference' for concrete singular terms, and which simply have no counterparts for abstract objects.

Now let's transpose the passage I quoted from Dummett as follows

> The states of affairs which (merely) minimally true sentences represent are no more than reflections of those sentences, sentences which behave, by simple formal criteria, in a manner analogous to sentences which are apt to depict real states of affairs, but whose senses cannot be represented as consisting in our capacity to identify states of affairs necessary and sufficient for their truth.

Once again, the minimalist's response will be to reject the concluding part of the thought—the suggestion that understanding such a sentence does not really consist in grasping its truth-conditions, with its attendant irrealist overtones. But the parallel is striking. Like pure abstract objects, the states of affairs to which merely minimally true sentences correspond do not *do* anything except answer to the demands of our (true) thoughts.

We can now see some cause for sympathy with Wiggins' suggestion that an emphasis on causality may not provide the best way of explaining what the best-explanation constraint is after—that it is not most happily formulated as to the effect that states of affairs of the sort depicted by a given class of judgements should be mentioned in the best *causal* explanation of our making those judgements. However, the reservation about the causal emphasis ought to be, it seems to me, not that the constraint can be satisfied in cases where no causal relations obtain, but that causality is—if it is—a *consequence* of what is important, which should be characterized differently. And what is important for this particular constraint is that the states of affairs which we regard our judgements as reflecting enjoy a *width of cosmological role*, as it were, sufficient to force us to regard their role as truth-conferrers in more than minimal terms. They must therefore participate in other kinds of explanation besides those in which germane beliefs of ours are the explananda. There must be more things which are so *because* of the obtaining of such states of affairs than the formation in us of certain beliefs.

So far as I can see, this will always be so when best explanations of the appropriate kind are causal, since to play any kind of causal role at all is to play, at least potentially, a wide causal role: states of affairs apt to cause the formation of certain beliefs in us will also be essentially apt to cause other kinds of effects in items which do not form beliefs at all. Perhaps the constraint, properly developed, will be seen to have only causally active satisfiers, though it's notable that mathematics contributes to the explanation of other phenomena besides belief. (Why do these rectangular titles not cover, without remainder, this rectangular floor? Because there are a prime number of them.) But notably, to revert to the moral case, the unjustness of a particular act seems to have a role in explaining nothing other than people's *beliefs* that it is unjust; more accurately, anything else it might explain—like our sympathy for a victim or his chagrin—will, *qua* so explicable, be a consequence of such beliefs.[16]

In general, then, the suggestion is that an explanation of our belief that *p* in terms, *inter alia*, of the obtaining of the state of affairs that *p* counts as best (or good enough) for the purposes of a useful best-explanation test only if *other* kinds of things are also to be explained by, *inter alia*, the obtaining of that state of affairs. This is just a consequence of the simple reflection that good explanations involve disclosing some sort of underlying unity in phenomena of overt diversity. Finding acausal satisfiers of the constraint will require, naturally, scrutiny of apparently acausal forms of explanation. But it is worth noting, to conclude this section, that the range of causal satisfiers is, at least prima facie, wider than might as first be expected. In particular, ascriptions of Lockean *secondary qualities*—colours, tastes, sounds, smells, palpable textures, and so on—seem to pass the test. It is not a *conceptual* error to suppose that bulls are enraged by red rags, and colours do as a matter of fact figure in the explanation of the behaviour of bees and butterflies, of small children without language, and of certain purely physical phenomena. (What is the best explanation of the manifest colours on a photographic negative?) Sounds startle babies and animals, and activate reflexes like blinking. The smell of cheese in a trap may attract a mouse. A cat sits by a fire because it is warm. And so on. The effect of the constraint is not to create a club admitting only statements couched in the austere, primary quality vocabulary of physical science.

V

We have been trying to find a place for and, to some extent, refine constraints—evidence-transcendence, convergence, and best explanation—whose importance in the debates about realism has already been widely perceived. It is that which makes it possible to present the general reorientation which I have been recommending as a rationalization of existing debates. But it is otherwise with the fourth and final constraint which I shall discuss here. The importance of this has been less widely perceived, although the basic idea goes back to Plato[17] and it promises well for the exegesis of the old form of anti-realism illustrated by Locke's view of secondary qualities. The idea has a potential bearing on a number of issues of recent and contemporary concern, including the status of the self-ascription of 'folk-psychological' states, and the interpretation of Wittgenstein's ideas about rule-following.

The constraint is what I have called the *order-of-determination* constraint.[18] Intuitively, it marks the distinction between classes of statements about which our *best* opinions—opinions conceived by subjects and in circumstances which we think of as cognitively ideal for statements of that kind—(partially) *determine* the extension of the truth-predicate among them, and classes of statements our best opinions about which at most *reflect* an extension determined independently. A demonstration that a given class of statements comes in the latter category provides one, very direct way of distinguishing truth, as applied to them, from anything constructible out of assertibility, and so for enforcing a departure from minimalism. For a judgement is the deliverance of our *best* opinion, in the above sense, just in case it meets our highest standards of assertibility, and is therefore superassertible.

That explains the shape of a distinction which it would certainly be germane to draw, but it does not draw it. What should be the criteria for saying that a class of statements should be regarded in one way rather than the other? The matter is complicated, and I have no space to do more than sketch some initial moves here. We can usefully begin with the general form of what has come to be known as a *basic equation*:[19]

$$P \leftrightarrow \text{for any } S: \text{if conditions } C \text{ obtain, then } S \text{ believes that } P.$$

Here conditions C are to be thought of as concerning the *pedigree* of S's belief. They are to be such that any belief whether or not P which is generated under them is true. For particular choices of P there may, of course, be no such conditions. For instance, there are, plausibly, no conditions C such that, if S forms a belief about the Generalized Continuum Hypothesis under C, he will believe that the notorious Cantorian imponderable is true if and only if it is. Likewise if we believe, whether because accepting the underdetermination of all scientific theory by empirical data or for some other reason, that best scientific method is impotent to distinguish the total truth about the world from certain false accounts of it, then for suitable P selected from among the hypotheses in the 'total truth', there are, again, no appropriate C-conditions. So we put those cases on one side and concentrate on examples of P where we do believe, at least in principle, in the feasibility of such cognitively ideal conditions.

Consider, for any such P, the following rather trivial elaboration of the basic equation:

Whatever-it-takes

$P \leftrightarrow$ for any S: if S is a *suitable* subject, and operates in conditions which are *conducive* to the appraisal of P, and goes through a procedure *appropriate* to the appraisal of P, and goes through it *properly*, then S forms the belief that P.

This is trivial, of course, because the C-conditions are specified totally *insubstantially*; we are told no more than that S and the prevailing circumstances are to have whatever-it-takes for a successful appraisal of P. Just for that reason, granted only that there is some content to the idea that such conditions might obtain, the biconditional holds a priori. Now, the distinction we wish to draw begins to emerge, I suggest, when we ask: what is the effect on the status of such formulations when we replace these trivially formulated, whatever-it-takes C-conditions with *substantial* specifications of what it does take? In particular, can the a priority of such a basic equation survive such specifications? If it cannot, then that is just to say that any convergence between best opinion, when we give a substantial account of what makes opinion best, and truth is itself at most an a posteriori truth; accordingly, since the tie between best opinion, substantially accounted for, and superassertibility will not presumably be merely a posteriori, a distinction will be imposed between the concepts of truth and superassertibility, even if not between their extensions. By contrast, if the a priority of the basic equation survives substantial specification, then, subject to qualifications to emerge below, we have the makings of a case for regarding best opinion as playing an extension-determining role.

A possible exemplification of this rather abstract train of thought is provided by the contrasting situations of judgements of shape and of colour. Consider first the latter. What conditions do we need to impose on a subject S in order to ensure that it is true that something is red if and only if S believes that it is? Well, S has to be equipped to experience the object as red, and must suffer no internal impediment to the formation of the belief appropriate to that experiential content; and the background conditions must assist the exercise of these abilities. In more detail, and to a cut a longish story short, the following, it seems, is plausible:

Red

> x is red $\leftrightarrow$ for any S: if S knows which object x is, and knowingly observes it in plain view in suitable perceptual conditions; and is fully attentive to this observation; and is perceptually suitable and is prey to no other cognitive disfunction; and is free of doubt about the satisfaction of any of these conditions, then if S forms a belief about x's colour, that belief will be that x is red.

There are still two occurrences of 'suitable' which might make us wonder whether we yet have sufficient distance from the whatever-it-takes type of formulation. But we can effectively gloss them as follows: 'suitable perceptual conditions' can be conditions of lighting like those which actually normally obtain out-of-doors and out-of-shadow at noon on a cloudy summer's day (such conditions are actually *more* than suitable, though that does no harm). But 'normally', construed broadly statistically, is still required because the lighting conditions on such occasions are sometimes disrupted by solar eclipses, nuclear explosions, and so on. And more simply: 'perceptual suitability' involves nothing other than having perceptual capacities which fall within the range of statistical normality among actual human beings.

My suggestion is that, even when the C-conditions in the above basic equation are specified in this substantial, broadly statistical way, it still remains a priori true that their satisfaction ensures that correctness of S's belief about x's being red or not. That, by itself, need be of no significance for the order-of-determination constraint. But, I suggest, it becomes so when supplemented by the consideration that satisfaction of the C-conditions as glossed above is logically independent of any truths concerning the extension of colour predicates; and could, indeed, be appraised by someone who, because possessed only of monochromatic vision, for example, had no concept of colour at all. If this were not so, it would not be unquestionable—to express the matter cautiously—that the a priority of the connection between satisfaction of the C-conditions, S's believing that p, and its truth, makes a case for best opinion being extension-determining. But it is so, and no other suggestion comes to mind of what *else*, quite independently of human judgement, might be viewed as determining the extension of the truth-predicate among judgements of colour—some different kind of account of which the a priori connection illustrated would be a consequence. I therefore conjecture that judgements of colour *fail* the order-of-determination test: our best opinions about colour constrain, rather than reflect, the extension of colour predicates among the objects which they concern.

Contrast the situation of shape. Consider, for instance, the judgement that x is pear-shaped. (I choose a shape-property which, unlike, e.g., sphericity—if a sphere has to be perfect—is visually salient.) The following is a plausible start:

Pear-shaped

> *x* is pear-shaped ↔ for any *S*: if *S* knows which object *x* is, and knowingly observes it in plain view from a sufficient variety of positions in suitable perceptual conditions, and is fully attentive to these observations, and is perceptually suitable and is prey to no other cognitive disfunction, and is free of doubt about the satisfaction of any of these conditions—then if *S* forms a belief about *x*'s shape, that belief will be that *x* is pear-shaped.

No doubt this is not beyond objection. For instance, *S* might lack the concept, pear-shaped, and form a belief about *x*'s shape whose content featured some still cruder concept. But let us bypass that. The question is: is something a priori true in prospect involving only substantially specified *C*-conditions? Well, only if an appropriate gloss can be placed on the two occurrences of 'suitable' to distance them from whatever-it-takes construal. But when we try to envisage such a gloss, two apparent disanalogies emerge with the case of colour.

First, since multiple observations are essentially involved in any *best* opinion about three-dimensional shape, 'suitable perceptual conditions', however glossed, will count for nothing unless *x*'s *stability* in shape through the period of observation is somehow ensured. A dilemma ensues. Suppose that we elaborate the *C*-conditions, somehow or other, so as to have them logically entail that *x* is indeed stable in shape throughout *S*'s observations. Then, in contrast with the case of 'red', their satisfaction will not be independent of all matters concerning shape, but will imply that there is some particular shape which *x* has throughout. It will consequently be open to question—even if the resulting basic equation is fully substantial and holds a priori—whether a best opinion about *x*'s shape, characterized as an opinion meeting *these* *C*-conditions, may coherently be viewed as determining what the truth about *x*'s shape is. For if facts about *x*'s shape enter into the determination of whether or not *S*'s opinion is best, how can best opinion be regarded as determining what are the facts about *x*'s shape? Suppose, on the other hand, we so elaborate the *C*-conditions that the question of *x*'s stability in shape is logically independent of their satisfaction. Then it will not be true a priori that when the *C*-conditions are satisfied, *x* is indeed stable in shape. Consequently, since *x*'s stability in shape is, a priori, a precondition of *S*'s opinion being best, it follows that the basic equation will not now concern *best* opinion. And more: it seems impossible to understand how *Pear-shaped* could now be a priori—how satisfaction of these *C*-conditions could provide an a priori guarantee that *S* was operating under conditions which ensured the correctness of his judgement. For how could that be guaranteed if, for all anyone, including *S*, could a priori affirm to the contrary, *x*'s shape might be undergoing unnoticed changes? On each horn of the dilemma, then, a case will not have been made that best opinion is, in this instance, extension-determining.

The dilemma argues that the a priority of *Pear-shaped* can be conserved under substantial specification of its *C*-conditions only if the specification begs some independent determination of truth-value among judgements of the appropriate kind. Neither horn is conclusively developed. But it might seem that its suggested conclusion, that best opinions about shape are extension-reflecting, is premature in any case, since it depends on the assumption that a best opinion about shape is accessible to a subject working alone. For there is the alternative of spreading the responsibility for the judgement of *x*'s shape among a number of simultaneous observers. For instance, the extension of 'pear-shaped' might be constrained not by the best opinions of a single observer but by the overall drift of the not-quite-so-good opinions—not-quite-so-good because based on single observations—of a sufficient number of sufficiently variously positioned observers. And in this scenario, instability is not a consideration.

Enter the second disanalogy with colour. The fact is that it is not a priori true of our actual typical visual capacities and of the circumstances in which we typically consider that their exercise is at its most effective, that they are conjointly suitable for the reliable visual appraisal of shape.[20] We can make theoretical sense of worlds in which, even by beings with such capacities, reliable visual appraisal of shape would be impossible—because, for example, the paths assumed by photons were subject to massive gravitational distortion, or because the physics of light was entirely different. Likewise we can make good sense of the idea of sighted beings who, in a world like the one we actually inhabit, are relatively poorly endowed for the visual appraisal of shape. It is not an a priori truth that we as we actually are and our actual world come into neither of these categories. Perhaps it is something which humankind, in some sense, has always *held* a priori—started out without questioning, as it were; but that we have found no cause to question it is courtesy of eons of congenial experience. So even judgements based on collectively pooled impressions of shape must lack the requisite a priori guarantee: there are no conditions, specifiable in such a way that their satisfaction is logically independent of any truths concerning shape, of which it holds a priori that collectively pooled visual judgements made under them will furnish truthful syntheses about objects' shapes. So there is a case for saying that judgements of shape *pass* the order of determination test.

The principle governing the development of the disanalogy, as far as I have here taken it, is that best opinion may, at least prima facie, be regarded as constraining the extension of the truth-predicate among a given class of statements if we can substantially specify what makes an opinion best without presupposing that extension to be determined independently, and if it is then a priori that opinions which are formed when the specification is satisfied are correct. By contrast, there is a prima-facie case for regarding best opinion merely as at most extension-reflecting if these two constraints cannot simultaneously be met. I say both times a 'prima-facie case' because there probably are other ways of substantiating the order-of-determination test. The condition met in the case of colour—that satisfaction of the appropriate kind of C-conditions is *globally* independent of truth about colour—is a very demanding one, and invites the thought that less demanding conditions might yet subserve the direction of determination from best opinion to truth. One kind of possibility would be *mixed* cases: cases where best opinions have to bear some specified relation to a core of judgements of the appropriate kind whose truth is conceived as determined independently of their being the deliverances of best opinion, although outside this core best opinion is determinative rather than reflective. More generally, it ought not to matter if what qualifies an opinion as best can only be explained in a way that presupposes antecedent determination of the truth or falsity of certain judgements in the germane class, provided none of these are logically connected with the particular judgement in question—more generally, provided detailed specifications of the C-conditions can have some sort of overall predicative structure, as it were.

Whether these rather abstract possibilities are realized by any familiar class of judgements I am not sure. But at least one other kind of case is. It is the case where it is a priori that an opinion is best unless there is positive reason to think otherwise. Consider, for instance, avowals of psychological states—a self-ascription of an intention, say. Here the appropriate C-conditions would seem to be: a clear-headed appreciation of the content of the intention avowed: a lack of any material self-deception which might motivate one to believe that one had the intention in question when one did not; and, perhaps, the lack of any distracting or muddling influence—a drug or whatever—which might induce something of the phenomenology of intending while impairing the ability to form genuine intentions. But it seems a priori true that, subject to the provisos, I believe I have a certain intention only if I really do. Now, there is every cause to be sceptical whether one can specify what is involved in the satisfaction of these conditions—the absence of any material self-deception, for instance—in a fashion which presupposes no prior determination of facts about a subject's intentions and intention-related states. But it is open to us, nevertheless, to regard subjects' beliefs about their intentions as at least *provisionally* extension-determining precisely because the C-conditions in question are *positive presumptive*: rather than representing a hurdle which the opinion has to jump, as it were, before it can be taken seriously, they merely constitute the categories of criticism within which someone who would reject the opinion is obliged to make their case.[21]

VI

A major question for further work concerns the extent to which the four constraints focused on—evidence-transcendence, cognitive command, best explanation/cosmological width, and order-of-determination—are complementary or cut across each other. We have seen reason to think, for instance, that secondary qualities fail order-of-determination but pass best explanation. One might anticipate that elementary arithmetical equalities would pass cognitive command, but their situation with best explanation is not so clear. If in the end best explanation does turn out to be a requirement with only causal satisfiers, then arithmetic will presumably fail—at least on any view but the most far-fetched (lunatic) platonism. I would also anticipate that arithmetic will fail order-of-determination. But that is an expression of the conviction that platonism is untenable. For the essential epistemology of platonism is exactly the view that mathematical propositions *pass* the order-of-determination test—that proof in mathematics is a mere cognitive auxiliary whereby finite minds may bring their opinions into line with states of affairs constituted independently. Of course, that belief very naturally finds expression in the conviction that mathematical truth may be evidence (proof)-transcendent. One rather attractive prospect to have emerged from the preceding reflections is that there may be a way of appraising the root epistemology of platonism, which finds expression in the endorsement of evidence-transcendence, otherwise than by directly engaging the commitment to evidence-transcendence. For instance, the thesis that best mathematical opinion is wholly extension-reflecting may be forced to acknowledge certain quite definite commitments concerning the epistemic status of certain appropriate basic equations—or whatever supplants them in a better formulation of the distinction—and may therefore be criticizable without engaging the very large issues which evidence-transcendence raises. However, the evidence-transcendence and order-of-determination tests remain distinct: there is, of course, no space for the idea that statements may possess in principle indeterminable truth-values if those truth-values are precisely determined by our best opinions;[22] but statements may pass the order-of-determination test without allowing of evidence-transcendent truth-value—the judgement that x is pear-shaped is a plausible example.

I tentatively conclude that the four ideas on which I have focused are each available to motivate a departure from minimalism, and perhaps even allow a simple arrangement in order of strength. That, and the notification of other cruces besides these four, are among the issues for further study. There is a great deal that is unclear about this programme. But perhaps I have made it clear that it would be worth making it clear.

Notes

1. See for instance chapter 6 of Simon Blackburn, *Spreading the Word*. Compare his contribution in the present volume.

2. See Mackie, *Ethics—Inventing Right and Wrong*.

3. Cf. n. 1. Blackburn's proposal has the effect that one who accepts both
    (i)   Lying is wrong
and   (ii) If lying is wrong, getting others to lie is wrong,
but rejects (iii) Getting others to lie is wrong,
is guilty merely of a *moral* shortcoming. For further discussion see my Gareth Evans Memorial Lecture, 'Realism, Anti-realism, Irrealism, Quasi-realism', in P. French, T. Uehling Jr., and H. Wettstein (eds.), *Midwest Studies in Philosophy* 12.

4. See n. 3.

5. This is the line taken in 'Realism, Anti-realism, Irrealism, Quasi-realism'.

6. In Wright, *Frege's Conception of Numbers as Objects*.

7. Cf. my *Realism, Meaning and Truth*, ch. 9.

8. For more detail on this matter, see especially the first two Waynflete lectures.

9. D. Wiggins, *Needs, Values, Truth*, p. 147.

10. Ibid., p. 151.

11. G. Harman, *The Nature of Morality*, ch. 1.

12. Wiggins, *Needs, Values, Truth*, pp. 156 ff.

13. Ibid.; cf. Wiggins' remarks about Harman and Benacerraf at the foot of p. 153.

14. Ibid.

15. M. Dummett, *Frege: Philosophy of Language*, p. 505.

16. Matters are of course more complicated. For discussion of some of the complexities, see *Truth and Objectivity*, ch. 5.

17. To the *Euthyphro*, in fact. See *The Dialogues of Plato*, trans. B. Jowett, Vol. II, pp. 84–6.

18. See my 'Wittgenstein's Rule-Following Considerations and the Central Project of Theoretical Linguistics', in A. George (ed.), *Reflections on Chomsky*, pp. 246 ff.

19. So styled by Mark Johnston. There are well-known drawbacks, from which I here prescind, to using 'basic equations' as a framework for discussion of the contrast in which we are interested. But it would take us too far afield to go into them here. For some indications, see my 'Moral Values, Projection and Secondary Qualities', *Proceedings of the Aristotelian Society*, Supplementary Volume LXII, section IV, n. 26 and my 'Wittgenstein's Rule-Following Considerations and the Central Project of Theoretical Linguistics'. The matter was discussed in some detail in my circulated 'Notes on Basic Equations' to which Johnston refers below (this volume p. 122). See also the Appendix to chapter 3 of my *Truth and Objectivity*.

20. Of course, the two uses of 'actual' in that sentence may have the effect that it is a *necessary* truth that the capacities so specified are, in the circumstances so specified, up to the job. But necessity is one thing and a priority is another.

21. Perhaps the effect of that last point is that we can in effect express the relevant C-conditions in *second intension*: if no reason is available to doubt that . . . , then a subject intends that *P* if and only if they believe that they do. If that is right, then perhaps the case may be assimilated to colour after all. For some elaboration of the application of these ideas to intentional psychological states, see my 'Wittgenstein's Rule-Following Considerations and the Central Project of Theoretical Linguistics', section IV.

22. Unless any relevant opinion's being best is itself indeterminable.

4

Objectivity Refigured: Pragmatism Without Verificationism

Mark Johnston

Let us say that metaphysics in the pejorative sense is a confused conception of what legitimates our practices; confused because metaphysics in this sense is a series of pictures of the world as containing various independent demands for our practices, when the only real legitimation of those practices consists in showing their worthiness to survive on the testing ground of everyday life. Then metaphysics is not just a technical discourse within philosophy to which, since Kant, a technical apparatus of philosophical criticism has been opposed. It is endemic to our culture. So defined, metaphysics is the proper object of that practical criticism which asks whether the apparently legitimating stories which help sustain our practices really do legitimate, and whether the real explanations of our practices allow us to justify them. There then ought to be a critical philosophy which not only corrals the developed manifestations of metaphysics within philosophy but also serves the ends of practical criticism. Such a critical philosophy would be the content of anything that deserved the name of a progressive Pragmatism.

Alas, Pragmatism has now become so dissolved in Verificationist idioms that commanding a clear view of its prospects requires precipitating out the pragmatic insights from the heady Verificationist concoction.

The alliance between Pragmatism and Verificationism is not a wholly unnatural one. They both have a common enemy in a certain kind of Realist, a Metaphysical Realist, for want of a better name. To my taste, what is most distinctive about Metaphysical Realism comes out when set against the background of mediaeval natural theology, a theology according to which God is a being who created the world by realizing one of his own consistent and complete conceptions of how things might go. The world is then a divine artefact. The real structure of this divine artefact is therefore the structure that God represented to himself when he made the world. So God is, among other things, the solution to the problem about what makes one of the many alternative accounts of the world the account attributing the right structure to the world. The privileged cognitive task is therefore set in advance: it is to rethink God's thoughts, or equivalently, to come to know the real structure of the world. This real structure is constituted wholly independently of our cognitive activity.

Just as there is a certain kind of materialism which lives off the Cartesian legacy by taking over the Cartesian idea of the body as dumb matter, there is a certain kind of scientism which lives off the legacy of mediaeval theology by taking over the idea of the world's having a structure privileged independently of our cognitive activity, a structure which any able cognizer should want to know. Metaphysical Realism is the common element in scientism and mediaeval theology; it is at root the idea that there is a privileged structure constituted independently of our cognitive activity, a structure privileged in the sense that the most significant knowing is knowing that structure.

While Verificationism and Pragmatism both oppose this idea of an independent, privileged structure, they deserve different names because they are in fact opposed to different aspects of the idea. The Verificationist rejects the notion that what is the case is independent of our capacity to come to know or verify it. Charles Sanders Pierce and William James also rejected this notion, emphasizing that a difference in truth had to make a difference in experience. However, the role of this Verificationist element in their thought was mostly to underline their more basic claim that the standard of rightness for any cognitive response was the acid test of practice rather than any formal correspondence to independent archetypes. That is, both Pierce and James were most fundamentally opposed to the idea of a privileged structure which determines the cognitive task in advance and in a way that is independent of human interests. Compare William James in *The Meaning of Truth*.

> As I understand the pragmatist way of seeing things, it owes its being to the breakdown which the last fifty years have brought about in the older notions of scientific truth. [James is writing in 1903.] 'God geometrizes,' it used to be said; and it was believed that Euclid's elements literally reproduced this geometrizing. There is an eternal and unchangeable 'reason'; and its voice was supposed to reverberate in *Barbara* and *Celarent*. So also of the 'laws of nature', physical and chemical, so of natural history classifications—all were supposed to be exact and exclusive duplicates of pre-human archetypes buried in the structure of things, to which the spark of divinity hidden in our intellect enables us to penetrate. The anatomy of the world is logical, and its logic is that of the university professor, it was thought. Up to about 1850 almost everyone believed that sciences expressed truths that were exact copies of a definite code of non-human realities. But the enormously rapid multiplication of theories in these latter days has well-nigh upset the notion of any one of them being a more literally objective kind of thing than another. There are so many geometries, so many logics, so many physical and chemical hypotheses, so many classifications, each one of them good for so much and yet not good for everything, that the notion that even the truest formula may be a human device and not a literal transcript has dawned upon us.[1]

Notice that the pragmatist way of seeing things, as James presents it, is unlike Verificationism in directly opposing that scientism which represents itself as literally transcribing an independent, privileged structure. A Verificationist could consistently endorse a qualified version of the scientistic picture, urging only that the privileged structure be in principle accessible. (Indeed, the term 'positivism' is usually appropriated for a mixture of scientistic and verificationist ideas.) The Pragmatist is therefore a potentially deeper and more articulate critic of scientism. So why are Verificationist idioms so appealing to Pragmatists?

The answer emerges when we consider that the very idea of the *independence* of the privileged structure, the central idea on which the whole debate with the Metaphysical Realist turns, is in fact very obscure. What can it mean to deny that the world has a privileged structure that is independent of our cognitive activity? Verificationism at least has the virtue of giving this denial a clear sense. The structure of the world is what is the case. What is the case cannot outrun our capacity to verify it. That is the sense in which the structure of the world is not independent of our actual and potential cognitive activity. A Verificationist can make this point either by urging a conceptual connection between verification and meaning or by urging a conceptual connection between verification and truth. The first route involves suggesting that the meaning of sentences cannot transcend our capacity to verify or falsify them, the second that truth is just what we would come to accept under ideal epistemic conditions. The trouble is that these claims are not themselves coherent. It is worth seeing in detail why Pragmatism should eschew such Verificationist claims and what a Pragmatism minus Verificationism would look like. (The question of whether Pragmatism minus Verificationism is *really* a pragmatism is mostly terminological; the important issue is the philosophical interest of the resultant position.)

1. Pragmatism and the Theory of Truth

Though I shall have some occasion to discuss some work by Nelson Goodman and Richard Rorty, I shall first concentrate on the thought of the most ingenious contemporary advocate of Pragmatism, Hilary Putnam. In a developing series of important works Putnam offers to defend a so-called 'Internal' Realism against an allegedly metaphysical conception of truth and goes on to catalogue the philosophical ills resistance to which Metaphysical Realism allegedly lowers, for example the fact–value distinction, reductive physicalism, dichotomies between subjective and objective views of human reason.[2]

According to Internal Realism, truth is warranted assertibility with respect to the ideal limit of rational investigation. As Putnam writes, 'Truth is an idealization of rational acceptability.'[3] If T is the theory at the ideal limit of rational investigation, then T meets all operational constraints on theory construction. T correctly predicts all accepted observation sentences and it is complete, consistent, beautiful, simple, plausible, etc.[4] Putnam claims to be able to make no sense of the characteristic idea of the Metaphysical Realist—that the ideal theory T may nevertheless be false, may not correspond to the facts.

(Here I think we should balk. The Metaphysical Realist's characteristic claim should instead be that truth is *not* idealized rational acceptability, and hence in the context in which we are thinking of idealized rational acceptability in terms of the ideal theory *T*, truth is not truth-according-to-*T*.)

Putnam points out that we have a model-theoretic guarantee that since *T* is consistent it has a model in which its sentences are true. Putnam supposes that the Metaphysical Realist must denigrate this model as not representing the intended interpretation of *T*, so that truth in that model falls short of truth. But, Putnam observes, the Metaphysical Realist's constraints on some model's being the intended model are 'just more theory'. If the statement of these constraints is true then if it is added to *T*, the resulting theory will be consistent and so will have a model.[5]

This argument has just produced a stand-off with Putnam's opponents. They insist that simply having another model, however unintended, for the theory which is the union of *T* and the Metaphysical Realist's constraint on when a model is intended does not amount to the constraint's being observed.[6]

Although much has been written about this dialectical situation, no one to my knowledge has pointed out that the so-called Metaphysical Realist has an easy way of resisting the burden of specifying when a model is intended. He should instead say that whatever the constraints on intended models are, it is obvious that truth cannot be even co-extensive with truth-according-to-*T* unless every truth follows from *T*.[7] Therefore the claim to be considered is not simply the claim that *T* could be false (the claim on which the model-theoretic argument explicitly bears) but rather the claim that all and only the truths follow from *T*, so that truth just is warranted assertibility according to *T*.

There is nothing for it but to engage head on. Is truth warranted assertibility according to an ideal theory?

The objections to be developed can be organized around four motifs. Firstly, there cannot be *an* ideal theory but at most an ideal hierarchy of theories each getting more complete with respect to non-empirical truth. Secondly, if there is one such ideal hierarchy then there are many, with consequent embarrassing indeterminacies for the Internal Realist. Thirdly, if the Internal Realist tries to avoid such indeterminacies by strengthening the evidential base of an ideal theory he gives the game away. Fourthly, even if there were an equivalence between eventually holding up in an ideal sequence of theories and being true, then this equivalence would not hold a priori but as an empirical grace of fortune. Perhaps only the last two clusters of objections cut against Putnam's basic claim that truth is an idealization of rational acceptability. But the point of these later objections will emerge more clearly if they are given on the heels of objections which force us to make Internal Realism's basic claim about truth more precise.

As a matter of some simple metalogic it could not be true that something is true if and only if it follows from the ideal theory *T*.[8] For if this biconditional were true then given what the biconditional says the biconditional itself will follow from the ideal theory. But then there will be in the ideal theory a predicate provably equivalent to provability in the ideal theory. That is, if *T* is the ideal theory then

(1) T implies that for any sentence S, S is provable in T iff S is true.

Now the language of T will be rich enough to express arithmetic, otherwise many truths of physics will not appear in it. And T had better be axiomatizable, that is, there had better be a computation procedure for telling in a finite number of steps whether or not a given statement is an axiom of T. Indeed T had better be finitely axiomatizable. Why?

Return to the motivating picture behind Internal Realism: the rejection of an 'alienated' conception of truth—truth that could outrun even our idealized capacity to recognize it as such. If the axioms of T are not finite then there will be syntactic truths of the form 'S does not follow from the axioms of T' which we cannot in principle come to recognize. For if the axioms of T are infinite in number then although we can in principle enumerate any finite subset and, depending on the underlying logic,[9] tell that S does not follow from the subset, we can never know whether the finite subset which yields S is just around the corner. This is so no matter how many corners we have so far turned. The alienated conception of truth threatens to break out in the Internal Realist's own backyard.

So T had better be axiomatizable. T will be rich enough to include the weak arithmetic (Robinson's Arithmetic) which suffices to introduce Gödel's system of numbering arithmetic sentences so that those sentences can be understood as containing names for themselves. So we can form in the language of the ideal theory T the familiar Gödel sentence with the intuitive meaning of

(2)   I am not provable in T.

The Gödel sentence is either provable in T or it is not. Suppose it is not provable in T. Then given what the Gödel sentence says, the Gödel sentence is true, and so by (1) it is provable in T. So we have shown by *reductio* that the Gödel sentence is provable in T. But then, given what the Gödel sentence says, T proves a falsehood and so is not an ideal theory. This result is a by-product of the result attributed to Tarski—no consistent, axiomatizable, extension of arithmetic can contain its own truth-predicate.[10] The present point is that the most straightforward way to understand the Internal Realist's claim about truth and the ideal theory is at odds with Tarski's result.

Just as a matter of logic, an ideal theory is a chimera. The best we can have is an indefinitely extensible hierarchy of theories all of which are *empirically* ideal, a hierarchy such that each member of the hierarchy is better than its predecessor in containing more mathematical and philosophical truths. The hierarchy begins with an empirically ideal theory T^*. The Internal Realist's claim will now be that exactly if S is an *empirical* truth then S follows from T^*. The improvements on T^* which figure in the hierarchy are got by adding as axioms further a priori truths not provable in T^*.

The next problem is that T^*, *the* empirically ideal theory, is also a chimera. Much idealization is built into the characterization of T^*. For how far we *actually* get with theorizing and whether in fact we hit on any very good theories at all is a matter of luck, depending upon, among other things, human ingenuity and the timing of the heat death of the sun. When talking about theories truth-according-to-which might be candidates for empirical truth we are obviously then talking about what would happen if the theories we do have were indefinitely improved on the scores of empirical completeness, consistency with observations, breadth of observation base, simplicity, unity, elegance, etc. Given all these idealizations, there is no reason to believe and considerable reason to disbelieve that there will be a single theory best with respect to all these ways of improving our present theories.

Firstly, there may be no unity of theoretical virtue, with the consequence that improvements in one respect are essentially to be purchased at the cost of neglecting other theoretical virtues. Some think that baroque architecture is elegant. It achieves this elegance by being far from simple. It could be so with theoretical architecture. In any case, the unity of theoretical virtue is probably not an issue which can be settled a priori. One of the things we may discover as we continue to pursue better theories is whether or not the theoretical perfections are compatible in the highest degrees. If this is now an open question then no one has a right to propose

(3)   If S is an empirical truth then S follows from the empirically ideal theory T^*.

as an a priori claim about truth. It is at best a high level theoretical claim whose truth-value we are not yet in any very good position to evaluate.

Secondly, even given the unity of theoretical virtue, it may in principle be possible to do better and better by it, so that there is no ideal theory but rather a sequence of theories that get better and better. This is anyway what common sense suggests. Just to take the virtue of completeness, there is no good reason to believe that at some point we will know all the discoverable truths about Mozart's music and its relation to the history of composition, criticism, and performance. It is of the nature of human ingenuity that more and more truths not implied by the truths already known *can* be discovered about this sort of thing.

Thirdly, even if someone could come up with an a priori proof of the unity of theoretical virtue, and of its having a maximal degree, it would not follow that only one theory can exemplify the maximal degree of theoretical virtue. There is the familiar difficulty deriving from the underdetermination of theories by the empirical data. It may be that there is some empirical claim S and two highly virtuous theories T_1 and T_2 such that T_1 yields S and T_2 yields not-S. S holds up in all improvements of T_1. Not-S holds up in all improvements of T_2.[11] How are we to solve these three problems?

Let each empirically good theory T_i carry with it a hierarchy which begins from T_i and approaches mathematical and logical completeness. Let us say that S holds up in T_i just in case it follows from T_i or from some theory in the hierarchy of T_i. Then we say that S holds up in a sequence of improving theories just in case S holds up in some empirically good theory T_i in the sequence and in every subsequent member of the sequence. Now it seems that the Internal Realist can deal with all the difficulties raised so far if he formulates his a priori claim as

(4) S is true iff S holds up in all sequences of empirically improving theories.[12]

This account of truth only assumes that there is a partial ordering of empirically improving theories. So it can accommodate both the possibility of the disunity of theoretical virtue and the general phenomenon of empirical underdetermination. Happily, the account does not assume that the sequences of improving theories must terminate. So it does not imply that there are maximally good empirical theories. Finally, the account includes a device for handling the problem of logical and mathematical incompleteness.

The account which has it that (4) is a priori does of course assume the comparability or commensurability of the theoretical virtues, otherwise there would be no ordering and no sequences at all. Putting aside for the moment worries—legitimate worries I think—about incommensurability, there is a remaining difficulty which suggests that neither (4) nor any adequate improvement of it can be a definition or reductive account of truth.

Consider a sentence about an observable state of affairs, for example about the number of cakes on a particular tray at a specific time during a party held years ago. Since, as we may suppose, no one in fact counted the cakes or observed anything which would suffice to determine the number by inference, equally good theories taking into account all the observations which are ever in fact made could differ over this or each leave this undecided. And no improvements of good theories will have enough observations to settle it either way. But, madness aside, no one in fact would deny that the claim that there were then more than ten cakes on that tray is, vagueness aside, either true or false.[13] Yet the denial follows from this little story and (4).

If the Internal Realist is to avoid such implausible local failures of bivalence, then he must idealize still further, requiring that for a theory to be ideal it must have as its evidential base not only all actual observation statements but . . . . Well, just how does the Internal Realist fill this condition out? Not by allowing all possible observation statements or statements about observable states of affairs, for this will be a list of sentences and their negations, a very unpromising starting point for a good theory. Instead the Internal Realist needs to include along with the sentences actually accepted on the basis of observation the sentences about the observable but unobserved states of affairs which we *would* have accepted had we made the crucial observations we did not in fact make. The idealization in question can be vividly captured by the device of a ubiquitous observer. So the Internal Realist should now say that it is a priori that

(5) S is true iff S holds up in all sequences of empirically improving theories based on the observation sentences that would be accepted by a ubiquitous observer.

The obvious question is whether talk of a ubiquitous observer is just a way of smuggling in talk of truth. Before we press that question let us generalize the problem which led to talk of the ubiquitous observer.

Much that is not actually observable by us and so much that would be missed by a ubiquitous *observer* has physical effects which we could *detect* by extending our perceptual powers by means of instruments or the testimony of beings whose observational capacities outstrip our own. Consider the claim that more than half of the US hundred dollar notes presently in circulation are impregnated with minute amounts of cocaine. A 'minute amount' can be specified in such a way that it is impossible for either a human being or a ubiquitous observer with just the sensory capacities of human beings to observe the presence of the minute amount. Here, however, as with any statement about a state of affairs that is detectable in the sense of having physical effects that some extension of our observational powers could detect, local failures of bivalence are very hard to accept. Vagueness aside, it is very hard to believe that neither the claim that a particular hundred dollar bill has at least the specified minute amount of cocaine in it nor the negation of this claim is true. The Internal Realist can avoid such implausible truth-gaps only if he defines truth over improving empirical theories based on the beliefs of a ubiquitous detector, for example

(6)   *S* is true iff *S* holds up in all sequences of empirically improving theories based on the sentences accepted by a ubiquitous detector.

Unless something like this is advanced by the Internal Realist he will have to countenance a causal network filled with bizarre fact-gaps. Suppose you load a high-powered pistol with a bullet marked with an identifying scratch. You fire the pistol and you find the marked bullet lodged in the target. You have sufficient observational evidence to settle it that the bullet had some trajectory between your pistol and the target. But neither you nor the ubiquitous *observer* has any evidence as to the exact trajectory, for example whether the bullet swerved minutely or rotated minutely between you and the target. The bullet just goes too fast to see this. No one wants to say that the bullet had a trajectory but no specific trajectory. Bullet trajectories are of their natures specific things.[14] The bizarre result is avoided by considering as input to theory the beliefs of a ubiquitous detector who gets to use high-speed cameras and the like.

Despite the extreme idealizations we are here allowing the Internal Realist it is still far from clear that all of the problem of implausible local truth-gaps has gone away. The ubiquitous detector has an extended perceptual capacity incorporating anything that could be counted as an instrument for detecting facts. But if the beliefs generated by this extended perceptual capacity are akin to perceptual beliefs they will involve hypotheses, wagers on future developments and what could be considered tendentious classifications of the objects, events and states perceived. So it seems that there could be equally good ubiquitous detectors who because of different perceptual hypotheses, wagers, and tendentious yet tenable classifications yield different verdicts about the exact trajectory of your bullet. Bizarre fact-gaps threaten to open up once more.

Moreover, things are even worse with respect to the aim of analysing truth in epistemic terms. Something counts as a ubiquitous observer just in case it delivers a verdict on each eternal sentence, proposition, or belief about an observable state of affairs. Something counts as a ubiquitous detector just in case it delivers a verdict on each eternal sentence, proposition or belief about a detectable state of affairs. But when are sentences, propositions or beliefs (or whatever the primary bearers of truth are) *about* observable or *about* detectable states of affairs? The idea of a sentence's being about observable states of affairs is not the idea of a sentence's containing only observational predicates, where these are predicates whose content involves no theoretical idea. The sentence 'Alexander is recharging his car battery' is a sentence about an observable state of affairs. The idea of a sentence's being about observable states of affairs seems to be the idea that if the sentence were true then the causal consequences of its being true would include the sort of causal consequences which could trigger an observation.[15] The idea of a sentence's being about detectable states of affairs seems to be the idea that if the sentence were true the causal consequences of its being true would include the sort of causal consequences which could trigger a detection, that is, could be registered on an instrument which extended our observational capacities. *Mutatis mutandis* for propositions or beliefs about observable and detectable states of affairs respectively. The trouble is that we need the notion of truth in order to specify the notion of a ubiquitous observer or detector, in order then to say what truth is in terms of the verdicts of a ubiquitous observer or detector.

The Internal Realist must then abandon the hope of analysing truth in epistemic terms. There may however be something interesting left, namely a position which takes (6) to be a non-reductive but a priori biconditional which puts an epistemic constraint on (but does not define) truth. To show some consequences of (6) so construed let us say that

(7)   *S* is a strongly theoretical sentence iff *S* is not about a detectable state of affairs and *S* is not a sentence of logic or mathematics.

Now we have as an allegedly a priori biconditional got by restricting (6)

(8)   *S* is a true strongly theoretical sentence iff *S* is a strongly theoretical sentence and *S* holds up in all sequences of improving theories based on the sentences accepted by a ubiquitous detector.

The position which consists of the claim that (6) and hence (8) are, although circular, a priori is a very interesting one, telling us that truth, and in particular theoretical truth, cannot outrun what holds up in the sequence of improving theories which provide the theoretical bookkeeping for the detectable truths. If (6) and hence (8) were a priori, they could do an enormous amount of good work. They would not imply that strongly theoretical sentences are never true, but they would show that the reasonable attitude at any point in our epistemic development would be that one's strongly favoured theoretical sentences simply represent one's favoured style of theoretical bookkeeping of the detectable facts and will probably not be the only style of bookkeeping of these facts which holds up in all sequences of improving theories. This is a salutary observation for philosophers whose characteristic method of arguing for their philosophical positions is not by pointing to the detectable consequences of these positions but to their marginal theoretical advantages over alternative styles of theoretical bookkeeping. It is not that there cannot be philosophical truth, it is rather that the condition on there being philosophical truth is really quite strong. There is a very live worry that much of the philosophical content of many disputes in philosophical logic and analytic ontology will turn out merely to be a clash of roughly equally good styles of theoretical bookkeeping. (Of course, the live worry probably applies to (6) too.)

As well as this critical consequence of (8) there is an important consequence for a central issue in the philosophy of science. Bastiaan van Fraassen has sharply urged the question of by what right we think the theoretical virtues of elegance and simplicity have any correlation with theoretical truth, so that a theory having these virtues gives us a ground for thinking it true.[16] A very good question, even if one does not accept van Fraassen's own answer. Someone who believes (8) is a priori can answer the good question. Elegant and simple theoretical frameworks track the theoretical truth because the theoretical truth is connected a priori with the theoretical sentences we would accept and continue to accept, and it is a *pro tanto* reason to accept a framework of theoretical sentences that the framework is simple and elegant. We get a neat answer to van Fraassen's question where it bites *most*, that is, not with respect to sentences about unobserved but observable states of affairs, but with respect to the strongly theoretical sentences. We also have an explanation of why the attitude of working with a theoretical framework does not reasonably involve thinking it true. Given (6) and hence (8), thinking a framework of theoretical sentences is true is *very* incautious, involving as it does thinking that the framework will hold up in every sequence of improving theories.

If one likes these results of (6) and (8) being a priori then one had better find some other way of securing the results, for neither (6) nor (8) is a priori.

This final insult to the ambitions of the Internal Realist comes from a 'missing explanation' argument that can be given quite general application. If a sentence S about a detectable state of affairs holds up in all sequences of improving empirical theories based upon the deliverances of the ubiquitous detector then there would typically be an explanation of this along the following lines: S *is true; that is why* S *holds up in all sequences of improving empirical theories based upon the deliverances of the ubiquitous detector.* The explanation may be elaborated as follows. The detectable state of affairs that makes S true has a causal impact on what we observe or detect and in this way constrains our theorizing about matters. The ubiquitous detector comes under the causal influence of every detectable state of affairs. Improving theories based on the deliverances of such a detector will therefore be theories in which S holds. That is why in all sequences of improving theories based on such deliverances there comes a point at which S is recognized as a truth and continues to be so recognized. Conveying some such content would be the point of offering the explanation. The content concerns a causal relation between the state of affairs that obtains when S is true and the ubiquitous detector's accepting S as true.

However, if (6) is a priori then the sentence 'S holds up in all sequences of improving theories based on the sentences accepted by a ubiquitous detector *because S* is true' cannot convey such causal explanatory content. For if (6) is a priori then the alleged *explanandum* is a priori equivalent to the proffered *explanans*. There are no *explanations* of the form 'A because B' where 'A' and 'B' are equivalent as an a priori and necessary matter. We cannot explain Mary's being taller than Joseph in terms of Joseph's being shorter than Mary.

Nonetheless, as against all this, there might well be an explanation of why the ubiquitous detector believes that (say) Oswald did not act alone and hence of why all sequences of theories based on the detector's beliefs eventually converge upon the claim that Oswald did not act alone. The explanation would be that Oswald did not act alone. (The ubiquitous detector saw this and so believed it.) Some such causal explanations must be true if the ubiquitous detector detects at all. So (6) is not a priori, and we have no motive for thinking (8) a priori.[17]

All this applies just as directly in the case of Richard Rorty's claim that for a proposition to be true is just for it to be accepted by our cultural peers. My cultural peers believe the proposition that the moon is a satellite of the earth because it is testified to on all hands, and it is testified to on all hands because it is true, that is, because the moon is a satellite of the earth. We can abbreviate this causal explanation of the belief of my cultural peers as follows: my cultural peers believe the proposition that the moon is a satellite of the earth because the moon is a satellite of the earth. But we cannot endorse a claim about truth that implies that the *explanans* and the *explanandum* are not genuinely distinct. That is, if one persists with Rorty's claims about truth, or with the epistemic account of truth, one must reject such explanations and so reject a central belief we have about many of our other beliefs, namely that our having those beliefs is the result of having detected some facts, where this implies that these facts are part of the causal explanation of their detection by us and so are part of the causal explanation of our having the beliefs based upon those detections. That is to say that there is a conflict between various epistemic accounts of truth and the causal theory of detection which would be central to any naturalized epistemology of our beliefs. The missing explanation argument just points to this tension between such accounts of truth and the explanatory consequences of uncontroversial parts of an empirical theory of detection which is included in folk psychology and which in all probability will be underwritten by any naturalized epistemology which holds up in all sequences of improving theories. Given the view that a theory is empirically very strong if it rules out an antecedently well-confirmed empirical theory, we may put the problem for Rorty and Putnam this way—contrary to their own clear intentions, *they are, in offering their accounts of truth, putting forth a very strong empirical theory, that is, a theory at odds with a well-confirmed theory of detection.*

The same 'missing explanation' argument applies to Bruce Wilshire's attempt to defend certain remarks about the concept of truth which William James makes in *The Meaning of Truth*. Wilshire writes,

> I say there are 281 lemons on a tree and [it turns out that] there are just that many. But James's point is that what we *mean* by saying that I speak the truth is that if persons counted, 281 would be all they could consistently get.[18]

If this is James' point, it is mistaken. For it makes nonsense of the explanation of the fact that if persons counted the lemons on the tree, 281 would be all they could consistently get. The explanation is that there are 281 lemons on the tree, or equivalently (so long as we understand ourselves as here appending 'It is true' to a propositional name[19]) the explanation is that it is true that there are 281 lemons on the tree.

As this last example shows, the missing explanation argument does not depend on the assumption that there is an ideal epistemic condition for evaluating all propositions. Perhaps the ideal condition for enumerating the lemons, that is, careful counting, is incompatible with the ideal condition for evaluating claims about the beauty of the arrangement of the lemons on the tree. (We murder to dissect. Putnam himself emphasizes this problem in the Preface to his latest work, *Realism with a Human Face*.[20]) The missing explanation argument still goes through. For it begins with a quite specific explanation of why we would believe a given proposition in the conditions deemed ideal for evaluating that proposition, for example careful counting in the case of the proposition about the number of lemons.

To turn now to a less central point: some, because they think that the idea of facts constraining and hence partly explaining good theorizing only gets a purchase when we can talk of the causal consequences of those facts for perceivers and detectors, might think that there is nothing explanatory about citing the truth of a strongly theoretical claim as the reason why it would hold up in all sequences of improving theories. They would not endorse the crucial explanatory premise of the missing explanation argument as applied against the claim that (8) is a priori. Even if nothing more could be said, the position that (8) is a priori while (6) is not would be hard to motivate, involving as it does the claim that truth is not univocal across various fact-stating discourses.

Let us add a further consideration which suggests that (8), the restriction of (6) to strongly theoretical truth, is, like (6), not a priori.

Consider the Enigmas: entities essentially undetectable by us. There are those who would claim that the sentence 'There are entities essentially undetectable by us' is devoid of content because we could never in fact possess evidence which we would recognize to warrant or make probable the claim that there are Enigmas. They maintain that since the sentence could not be used in a warranted assertion it is devoid of content. But this argument depends on too strong a premise. There are very long sentences which we would never in fact employ in warranted assertions just because of their length. These sentences are contentful because they can be built up compositionally from a finite list of predicates, names, functors, etc. which do find a use in warranted assertions. So if there is a plausible constraint on contents then it had better allow that sentences can have a content in virtue of being built up from predicates, names, functors, etc. which figure in sentences which we can recognize to be made probable or warranted by certain kinds of evidence. The sentence 'There are entities essentially undetectable by us' is such a sentence. Accordingly, there is no good reason to deny it a content.

However this sentence is a strongly theoretical sentence. For it is not a sentence of logic or mathematics. And it is not a sentence whose truth involves the obtaining of a state of affairs with causal consequences which could be detected by any being who had all the (metaphysically) possible idealizations of our powers of detection.

Notice that it is not analytically false to suppose that there are Enigmas. It cannot be settled a priori whether there are or are not Enigmas. But if there were Enigmas then there could be no reason to think that there were and no good theory would say that there were. So the claim that there are Enigmas would not hold up in any sequence of improving theories, even if it were true. So it cannot be a priori that (8).

What might Enigmas be like? No one of course knows. But it is possible to fill out logically coherent scenarios which put some flesh on the formal observation that there is nothing logically or analytically incoherent about the supposition that there are Enigmas.

One (bleak) scenario is this. Materialism in some form is true about us. Although there are immaterial things we never interact with anything immaterial thanks to a causal caste system in which, as a metaphysically necessary matter, the immaterial interacts only with itself. Since the immaterial realm gives off no signals that might affect us or any instrument we could develop, no idealization which abstracts away from our contingent limitations on our powers of observation and detection would have us detecting the immaterial realm. The whole immaterial realm then would be enigmatic in the intended sense.

None of this is to say that we should care about whether there really are Enigmas and what they are like. Any question about the Enigmas is *practically* speaking empty. It would be good practical advice to care only about detectable truth, mathematical truth and the *accessible* theoretical truth, that is, the theoretical truth we could in principle have good reason to accept as such.

The characteristic mistake of the Anti-Realist and of the Internal Realist is to misrepresent the provenance of this kind of good advice. The advice comes not from the right account of the concepts of meaning and truth, but from common sense as it applies to cognitive labour.

2. Pragmatism and Theory-Independent Structure

In his recent work *Reality and Representation* Putnam explicitly distances himself from the epistemic *analysis* of truth.[21] He writes that in his earlier work *Reason, Truth and History* he was concerned only to emphasize the conceptual *inter*dependence of the notions of truth and ideal warrant. Of course, even this interdependence claim falls to the missing explanation argument. However, Putnam in that earlier work and in his recent *Many Faces of Realism* makes an interesting change of emphasis, no longer focusing on an issue about the notion of truth but on an issue about our classificatory activity.[22]

This second issue was always woven in with Putnam's claims about truth, even in the early paper 'Realism and Reason', which set out the contrast between Metaphysical and Internal Realism. There Metaphysical Realism is said to be the doctrine that there is

> a determinate relation between terms in [one's language] L and pieces (or sets of pieces) of the world. ... The world ... [is] independent of any particular representation we have of it ... truth is radically non-epistemic.[23]

The last condition suggests that the Metaphysical Realist is one who denies any epistemic condition on being true, as any straightforward correspondence theorist might. But what comes earlier suggests that the Metaphysical Realist has a peculiarly strong conception of correspondence, namely correspondence to pieces (or sets of pieces) of the world which are distinguished as objects of reference, and distinguished not just because the users of *L* have come to represent and refer to those objects in expressing their beliefs. How else could they be distinguished according to the Metaphysical Realist?

The answer to this question comes out most clearly in Putnam's recent work where the issue between the Internal Realist and the Metaphysical Realist is fundamentally an issue about concepts or schemes of description. There we are told that the Pragmatic Realist maintains that the world does not demand to be described in terms of one set of concepts or another. Nature has not its own preferred description.[24] The Metaphysical Realist is described as wedded to the idea that truth is correspondence to a pre-structured reality, and is attacked by means of an example which purports to show that although there can be alternative conceptual schemes, there is no dividing out an unconceptualized stuff which is described, cut up, or overlain by different conceptual schemes.[25] Kant is hailed as a precursor in the opposition to Metaphysical Realism: 'the first philosopher to reject the idea of truth as correspondence to a pre-structured reality'.[26]

There are still some unclarities here. For example the rejection of a pre-structured reality can sound like Idealism according to which the mind or the linguistic community makes up reality. And it is of course trivial that Nature has not its own preferred description since Nature has *no* biographical preferences. However, a long-standing issue is certainly being raised here, namely, are the only standards governing the choice of a scheme of concepts intended to describe nature the internal standards of theory choice or does following these standards lead us, albeit fallibly and only in the most favourable cases, to a scheme of description of nature which corresponds to theory-independent features of the world, features which even an internally ideal theory could get wrong? It is *because* the Metaphysical Realist takes the latter view that he characteristically denies that an internally ideal theory must be true and so is opposed to the identification of truth with truth according to the ideal theory.

Now we can see better what Putnam's concerns are. One fundamental issue between the Metaphysical and the Internal Realist is a modern-day variant of one traditional dispute over Universals, the dispute between still another class of Realists on the one hand and Nominalists on the other. I have in mind neither the dispute about whether there are properties (that I think is trivial) nor the dispute about whether properties are concepts, platonic universals, parts of objects, classes (a mixture of triviality and variant styles of theoretical bookkeeping) but the issue of whether our classificatory activity corresponds to any theory-independent structure in the world.

Is there really a debatable issue here? Who could really believe that quite generally the world's structure is dependent on our classificatory activity, so that the fact that the earth has a molten core is our doing? Putnam himself is more cautious, writing in the introduction to *Reason, Truth and History* 'My view is not a view in which the mind makes up the world. If one must use metaphorical language then let the metaphor be this: the mind and the world jointly make up the mind and the world.'[27] The metaphor is one of inter-dependence. But how are we to articulate the literal content of this metaphor or indeed the literal content of Richard Rorty's claim that neither philosophy nor science can develop a discourse which 'mirrors nature' or, to change the metaphor, a discourse in which the world 'demands' to be described, a discourse that would be the right discourse anyway, whether or not employing it answered to any human interests.[28]

Given the failure of both the epistemic analysis and the epistemic explication of truth it will follow that the literal content of these metaphors can only be somewhat jejune, at least relative to the heady rhetoric of some contemporary Pragmatists. Before we see that, let us turn to one contemporary Pragmatist who is certainly not offering a jejune thesis.

3. Pragmatism and Alternative, Conflicting Theories

In his *Of Mind and Other Matters*, Nelson Goodman writes 'What there is consists of what we make ... everything including individuals is an artefact' and 'We do not make stars as we make bricks, not all making is a matter of molding mud. The worldmaking mainly in question here is not with hands but with minds, or rather with languages or other symbols systems. Yet when I say that worlds are made, I mean it literally; and what I mean should be clear from what I have already said. Surely we make versions, and right versions make worlds.'[29] That Goodman means here to endorse a kind of Idealism becomes even clearer when in response to the obvious question 'If stars and constellations are made by making up cosmological theories, how can the stars have been there eons before all versions?' He answers:

> Plainly, through being made by a version that puts the stars much earlier than itself in space-time. As the physicist J. R. Wheeler writes: 'The universe does not exist "out there" independent of us. We are inescapably involved in bringing out that which appears to be happening. We are not only observers. We are participators in making [the] past as well as the present and the future.'[30]

The quotation of Wheeler not only serves to underwrite the extreme nature of Goodman's ontological claim but it points to the oddity of making that claim on the basis of the kinds of considerations Goodman invokes. As we shall see, Goodman is concerned with very general philosophical considerations about objectivity. No amount of well-placed scepticism about the sharpness or usefulness of the analytic/synthetic distinction serves to undermine the common-sense idea that you do not find out about the large scale structure of space–time or the conditions of quantum events occurring by means of such very general considerations. What if Wheeler and the authority of science had spoken differently? What if they came to speak differently? What then would be the status of Goodman's general considerations? It seems that if those considerations really do deliver the result about worldmaking we could tell the physicists in advance part of the truth about the large-scale causal structure of space–time.

Philosophical cosmology is not a promising research programme. There is no good proof of a detailed cosmological thesis from philosophical considerations. Indeed, when we look at Goodman's consideration in favour of his pivotal claim that one cannot distinguish world-versions and worlds we see that it crucially depends upon an epistemic explication of the notion of truth which we already have reason to doubt.

The sort of considerations moving Goodman are most powerful in the case in which we have two theories apparently about the same subject-matter, each apparently complete and closed to the other. They are each steadfastly assertible, that is, each continues to be assertible as more and more evidence comes in and as more and more collateral theorizing is done. The theories are not formally inconsistent. However because of our background beliefs we cannot take both theories to be true of the same reality. Here is an example, due to Catherine Elgin.[31] We have two particle theories T_1 and T_2. T_1 says there are P particles and these are causally responsible for all the detected facts about the strange actions of R particles. T_2 says there are Q particles and these are causally responsible for all the detected facts about the strange actions of R particles. T_1 characterizes P particles in such a way that given how T_2 characterizes Q particles it follows that no P particle is or overlaps with a Q particle. In fact things turn out so that P particles and Q particles are never detected. They remain *de facto* purely theoretical entities.

Now we cannot accept that T_1 and T_2 are simply true together. For although they are not inconsistent we find it just too implausible to believe in a pre-established harmony of the P causes and the Q causes over-determining every R event. Goodman's way out is to allow us to say that the T_1 theory is true of one world—the world which is as the T_1 version says, while the T_2 theory is true of another world—the world which is as the T_2 version says. To say there are two *worlds* can seem a quite extreme and unmotivated reaction. The less extreme reaction would be to say that even if all the evidence which actually comes in supports both T_1 and T_2, they cannot both be true.

To displace the less extreme reaction Goodman can now appeal to a crucial premise articulated in 'Notes On the Well-Made World'. There he writes:

> Obviously we cannot equate truth with acceptability, for we take truth to be constant while acceptability is transient. Even what is maximally acceptable at one moment may become unacceptable later. Nevertheless something may be done about relating truth to ultimate acceptability. Although we may seldom if ever know when acceptability that will never thereafter be lost has been or will be achieved, *such steadfast acceptability is a sufficient condition for truth.*[32] (My italics)

Given the italicized premiss and the plausible claim that T_1 and T_2 could each turn out to be steadfastly acceptable in the actual long run, the ordinary reaction of regarding at least one of T_1 and T_2 false is not available. For it follows that T_1 and T_2 are both true. However, given disbelief in massive and precisely matched causal overdetermination we cannot rest content with the conclusion that T_1 and T_2 are both true simpliciter. Goodman offers us a way out: T_1 is true of one world, T_2 is true of another.

One question is what it could possibly mean to say that there are the R-particles of the T_1-world, particles whose interactions are explained by P-particles, and there are the (different?) R-particles of the T_2-world, whose interactions are explained by the Q-particles. One way of understanding Goodman, perhaps not his preferred way, is to take him as observing that T_1 and T_2 (each consistent theories) have their own models which we could call the T_1-world and the T_2-world respectively. To this he adds the claim that there is no way of singling out a theory-independent world as the intended model that a theory aims to describe. So we are stuck with truth-in-a-model or truth-according-to-a-version. We may then impose further constraints to approximate something like truth fully-fledged. We can at least prefer theories which we believe to be steadfastly acceptable to those we believe not to be. However when we believe that a theory is steadfastly acceptable there is no good reason to withhold the honorific 'true' from it. But given what we are now meaning by 'true theory'—namely a consistent theory which will steadfastly hold up in the face of rational inquiry—there is no presumption that all true theories can be assimilated into a single, consistent, believable world picture. We then do better to say that a true theory is true-to-its-world, thereby collapsing the distinction between the theory and what makes the theory true. For the world of the theory is just the theory mirrored.

Two difficulties with this adventurous line of argument are worth highlighting here. First, there is a problem with the idea that there could be theories T_1 and T_2 each steadfastly assertible and yet together inconsistent with something we take either to be true or steadfastly assertible. The grounds for taking a theory to be acceptable are holistic, going beyond the direct evidence for the theory. So also with the grounds for withholding assent from a theory. That T_1, T_2 and the ban on massive and perfectly matching overdetermination of the activities of R-particles are inconsistent when taken together is an excellent reason for not regarding any of the triad steadfastly acceptable as things presently stand. One member of the triad may be recognized as steadfastly acceptable if another member gets discredited. However Goodman needs them all to be taken to be steadfastly acceptable if he is to resist the obvious reaction that at least one of T_1, T_2 and the denial of overdetermination is false.

The argument to multiple worlds or mutually acceptable conflicting versions also falters at another point: the appeal to the claim that being steadfastly acceptable is a sufficient condition for truth. What has happened to the common-sense idea that the limitations of our cognitive powers allow us to be stably deceived? The world is independent enough of the best cognitive reactions we *actually* have to allow that something may continually seem to us to be so without being so. Suppose we never had hit upon and never come to hit upon indeterministic phenomena. In that situation the thesis of physical determinism would be steadfastly acceptable yet false. Suppose alternatively that in our actual situation the thesis of determinism is true and yet the hidden variables which account for apparent indeterminacy remain forever hidden. Then the thesis of physical indeterminism will be steadfastly acceptable even though false.

However, it is insufficient to focus on these defects of a Goodmanian argument for various worlds. At the heart of Goodman's thesis is his own interpretation of a common theme of contemporary pragmatism, a theme echoed by Putnam and Rorty, namely that there is something bogus about the notion of truth as correspondence to an independent reality, as if the world 'demanded' description in a certain way, as if employing a certain description could be correct anyway independently of its serving interests. Still, it is quite obscure what this thesis or its denial could mean short of an account of the central notions of independence and of the world's providing an independent demand to be described such and so.

Since the issue of what owes its existence to what is a detailed empirical issue it is the worst kind of armchair science to suppose as part of a general account of objectivity that what there is and how it hangs together is existentially dependent upon our best theorizing. Nor is the notion of truth conceptually dependent upon the notion of our best theorizing. The central thesis of contemporary pragmatism is none the less that (in a sense of 'right' yet to be adequately explicated) the rightness of accepting a theory is in some sense dependent on our interests, activities, or reactions. Hence the *Metaphor of Nature's Toleration*: nature does not demand to be described in a certain way, having instead the grace to tolerate various descriptions. The import of the metaphor must be that the rightness of accepting a theory is at least conceptually interdependent with our finding it right to accept the theory. We cannot make sense of it being right to accept a theory even though we are not disposed to find it so at the idealized limit of rational enquiry.

So our problem is to give a content along these lines to the metaphor without relying upon an a priori connection between truth and the deliverances of theories at the ideal limit of rational inquiry. This would be to explicate a *Pragmatism without Internal Realism*, a Pragmatism still available even after the negative results of Section 1.

The solution to this problem goes by way of developing and applying the notion of response-dependence. Let me first set out the notion and discuss a tempting misapplication.

4. Response-Dependence

When does a concept F count as response-dependent? As a preliminary, we need to say what a concept is. For our purposes, talking about a concept F is just a way of talking about the core of a conception or cluster of beliefs *de dicto* about Fs. A belief *de dicto* about Fs is one which can be properly reported by using the predicate 'is F' in an oblique context. Certain beliefs *de dicto* about Fs will be relatively non-negotiable beliefs in that we would not know what talk of Fs amounted to if these beliefs turned out false. (Compare married bachelors, intransitive lengths, asymmetric identity relations.) The a priori conditions on the application of the concept F are the conditions which these relatively non-negotiable beliefs represent Fs as satisfying. The concept F is the concept G just when F and G have the same a priori conditions of application in the sense defined. So we can make good enough sense of talk of the concept F expressed by the predicate 'is F'. It is what is determined by the non-negotiable core of those beliefs which can be properly reported by using the predicate 'is F' in an oblique context. In saying all this we need not anywhere assume that the non-negotiable core is precisely bounded so that the a priori/empirical distinction is a sharp one.

We now introduce dispositional concepts. The concept F is a dispositional concept just in case there is an identity of the form

(9) The concept $F = $ the concept of the disposition to produce R in S under C,

where R is the manifestation of the disposition, S is the locus of the manifestation and C is the condition of manifestation. So the concept fragility is the concept of the disposition to break when struck, where the locus of the manifestation is the fragile thing itself.

Let us say then that the concept F is a response-dispositional concept when something of the form of (9) is true and (i) the manifestation R is some response of subjects which essentially and intrinsically involves some mental process (responses like sweating and digesting are therefore excluded), (ii) the locus S of the manifestation is some subject or group of subjects, and (iii) the conditions C of manifestation are some specified conditions under which the specified subjects can respond in the specified manner. Moreover, we shall require (iv) that the relevant identity does not hold simply on trivializing 'whatever it takes' specifications of either R or S or C.

Where R is some x-directed response of subjects S under conditions C, both the concept of the disposition of x to produce R in S under C and the concept of the disposition of subjects S to issue R in response to x under C will count as response-dispositional concepts.

Explicitly employing the dispositional idiom serves to distinguish response-dispositional concepts from those natural kind concepts introduced as concepts of the standard explanatory basis of some set of response-dispositions. Thus 'water' might be introduced to denote the stuff which has the standard explanatory basis of the dispositions to seem liquid, colourless, odourless, and tasteless. So understood, the concept water is not a response-dispositional concept. For so understood we are not acquainted with the nature of water by being acquainted with water's dispositions to seem liquid, colourless, odourless, and tasteless. On the natural kind account, in knowing those we know water's nature only by description, as it were. That is, we know it only as the stuff, whatever it is like in itself, which accounts for these response-dispositions.

Some concepts involve truth-functional or quantificational compounds of response-dispositional concepts. Thus the concept of a U.S. state or federal law's being constitutional is not the concept of the Supreme Court's being disposed to ultimately regard it as constitutional but rather the concept of the Supreme Court's *not* being disposed to ultimately regard it as *un*constitutional. (Being constitutional is the default condition.) So we introduce a more inclusive notion by saying that a concept is response-dependent just in case it is either a response-dispositional concept or a truth-functional or quantificational combination of concepts with at least one non-redundant element being a response-dispositional concept. Otherwise we shall say that the concept is a response-independent concept.

Obviously things have been set up so that one traditional distinction between primary and secondary quality concepts is just the distinction between response-independent and response-dependent concepts restricted to concepts of sensible qualities. So someone who alleges that

(10) The concept of being red = the concept of the disposition to look red to standard perceivers under standard conditions,

is claiming that the concept of being red is a response-dispositional concept of a sensible quality, that is, a secondary quality concept. So the following are also secondary quality accounts.

(11) The concept of being red = the concept of the disposition to look red to standard perceivers as they actually are under standard conditions as they actually are.

(12) The concept of being red for subjects S_i under conditions C_i = the concept of the disposition to look red to the S_is under condition C_i.

Talk of response-dispositions immediately provides useful consequences. As (11) indicates, it is not an objection to all secondary quality accounts of colour concepts to observe that in a possible world in which the standard perceivers saw things differently in the standard conditions of that world the colours of things need not be different from what they actually are; (11) allows just that. As (12) indicates, it is not an objection to all secondary quality accounts of colour concepts to observe that for many or all of the things we take to be coloured there are no standard perceivers or standard viewing conditions, so that the best we can do is talk about the relative colours; (12) allows just that.

Are many of our concepts response-dependent as they actually stand? I dub the thesis that they are the thesis of 'Descriptive Protogoreanism'.

Mostly on Plato's say so, Protagoras is supposed to have begun his book (entitled either *Truth* or *Knockouts*) with the claim that Man is the measure of things. He has consequently been cited as the precursor of an incoherent Relativism.[33] The famous slogan of Protagoras would however do as well as the slogan of a believer in widespread response-dependence. (So well that the collateral scholarly grounds for attributing the incoherent doctrine are worth examining again.) In any case, I propose to appropriate the term 'Descriptive Protagoreanism' for the position which has it that at least at the conceptual level, human response is the measure of most things, so that many or most concepts have built into them conditions on our dispositions to respond. If we set aside the formal or topic-neutral concepts of logic and semantics, a Descriptive Protagoreanism consistent with our results so far may claim that our topic-specific concepts are all of them response-dependent concepts.[34]

A philosophically interesting Protagoreanism might put forward conceptual identifications along the lines of (9) which would yield a priori claims like

(13)   *x* is a good state of affairs iff we are stably disposed to judge it so under conditions of increasing non-evaluative information and critical reflection.

(14)   *X*s cause *Y*s iff under conditions in which we wanted to bring about *Y*s and in which our abilities were not subject to the various sorts of contingent limitations from which we suffer we would be disposed to manipulate *X*s as a means of bringing about *Y*s.

(15)   One of us survives some process iff we are stably disposed to judge this so under conditions of increasing information and critical reflection.

(16)   *S* has attitude *A* with content *K* iff we are stably disposed to attribute this to *S* under improving interpretive conditions.

(17)   *A* is an act for which *S* is responsible iff we are disposed to hold *S* responsible for *A*.

Notice that in each of these cases the Descriptive Protagorean is not plausibly understood as offering an analysis of the philosophically interesting notions. After all, the righthand sides of these biconditionals, and of the concept identities they represent, employ overtly or covertly the notion on the lefthand side. For example, manipulating *X*s is causing them either to come into being or pass away or change in some identity-preserving way. So we have in each of these philosophically interesting examples the assertion of an *interdependence* between the philosophically interesting concept and the relevant concept of our disposition to respond. This circularity in the biconditionals and their related identities does not deprive them of interest. Circularity would be a vice if the Protagorean's aim were reductive definition. However the aim is instead to exhibit the kind of conceptual connection which shows how the facts about some matter, perhaps not overtly having to do with human response, do turn out none the less to implicate our responses in a certain way. Indeed, if the Protagorean is right, the facts in question cannot outrun our dispositions to respond in the relevant ways. *The limits of our responses measure the limits of these sorts of facts about things.* Since the Protagorean aims to give a detailed articulation of that thesis, circularity of the sort indicated would be a defect only if it made the biconditionals and their associated identities empty. But this is evidently not the case. The biconditionals are actually very strong claims.

Notice that a Descriptive Protagorean, despite his emphasis upon the critical role of human response in specifying the application conditions of a predicate '*F*' need not be a Non-Realist in any of the senses now current. He can deny the Pragmatist or Internal Realist claim that truth is response-dispositional. So, he can also deny the Anti-Realist claim that the meanings of statements employing the concept *F* are to be given in terms of the conditions of warranted assertibility of those statements. Moreover, thanks to the availability of response-dispositional accounts which rigidify on our actual responses under actual conditions, a Protagorean is in a position to deny the characteristic thesis of Empirical Idealism concerning *F*s, namely that *F*s would not exist or be the way they are but for our responses as they actually are. Finally, as is obvious, the Protagorean's claim about *F*s is at odds with both forms of so-called irrealism about *F*s. As against Non-Cognitivism concerning apparent statements about *F*s, Protagoreanism generates straightforward truth-conditions for statements about *F*s. And since it is evident how these disposition-involving truth-conditions can be satisfied, we here have a foil to Eliminativist denials that there are *F*s.

Thus Descriptive Protagoreanism, the claim that all topic-specific concepts are response-dependent, bids fair to be the best candidate for an appropriately qualified realism, the qualification being precisely the denial that the concepts in question are independent of concepts of subjects' responses under specified conditions. This independence of subjectivity is the hallmark of complete objectivity in one of its obvious senses.

Unfortunately, Descriptive Protagoreanism has itself to be severely qualified to be at all plausible. Firstly, only if fundamental reality were intrinsically mental could a set of concepts adequate for its description consist only of response-dependent concepts. Secondly, general reflections on the nature of concepts suggest that response-dispositional concepts are actually few and far between. Given our earlier story about concepts being abstractions from clusters or beliefs, we can explain what goes wrong with response-dispositional accounts of concepts of one sort, concepts associated with rich clusters of beliefs. Among the cluster of non-negotiable beliefs associated with such a concept *F* there are beliefs which serve to characterize the response-independent nature of *F*s and there are beliefs about which conditions help us to detect facts about *F*s. Given beliefs of both kinds we can readily conceive of there being *F*s which escape our capacities to detect or otherwise respond to them even under ideal conditions. In such cases response-dispositional accounts will fail. For in such cases we have beliefs that characterize Fs in terms independent of their actual and potential effects upon us. It will then be an empirical matter that the things so characterized are just those disposed to affect us in certain ways.

Another class of concepts, those that are or are akin to natural kind concepts, will resist a response-dispositional treatment for a different reason. For such a concept F we initially have a very austere set of associated non-negotiable beliefs, so austere that we possess no very good characterization of the nature of the property F. However we have a way of indicating the property F, perhaps in terms of the effects, including the effects on us, which it helps to explain. Moreover, we have a preferred methodology for investigating the nature of property F. So we might pick out the property F as the property which causally explains our dispositions to respond in a certain way. Here the property F is fixed upon or *indicated* via our dispositions to respond. It is not *characterized* as a disposition to make us respond in certain ways in certain circumstances. Instead, we hope that by applying the preferred methodology we will arrive at a characterization of the property which involves no essential reference to us. We have the shallow anthropocentricity that derives from picking out features by means of reference-fixing descriptions which mention our responses, not the deeper anthropocentricity that derives from the features' being adequately captured by response-dispositional concepts.

The problem for Descriptive Protagoreanism is that many scientifically interesting concepts are of this second sort, that is, they are or are akin to natural kind concepts, while many philosophically interesting concepts are of the first sort, that is, they are complex cluster concepts.

At least in the philosophical case, the Protagorean who is prepared to adopt a revisionary rather than a descriptive thesis has a characteristic strategy at his disposal. He can defend an error theory of the original response-independent concept F and then argue that a response-dependent surrogate for the concept captures the respectable core of the non-negotiable beliefs about Fs. Elsewhere I have argued that this is the plausible position to take about the concept of value and have set out the details of a response-dependent surrogate for our ordinary notion of value.[35]

A similar position is plausible in the case of colour. The intuitive idea of the colours is of a family of properties which would not only explain our experiences of colour but also be the bases of the various dispositions to look coloured. The colours naïvely understood are a family of response-independent properties. However, it is not that our response-independent conception of colour is a conception of a family of physical properties, *whatever they might be like*, which explain the dispositions of things to look coloured to us. We in fact have a battery of beliefs about the nature of the colours, beliefs evidently derived from the battery of similarity and difference relations which the colour appearances exhibit. On this conception, just as red *looks* more similar to yellow than it looks to green, red *is* more similar to yellow than it is to green. So also for all the difference and similarity relations found in the colour appearance solid. On this conception those relations hold among and are definitive of the colour properties. Moreover, just as an experience of a patch of uniform colour represents the uniform colour as dissective or such that every visible part of the surface of the patch has the same colour, so that pointillism and the revelations of the microscope are real surprises, so also on this conception, the colours are properties instantiated dissectively. For we arrive at the conception in question by taking the colour appearances completely and transparently to reveal the nature of the colours. Features of modes of presentation of the colours, higher-order properties such as similarity, difference, and dissectiveness are taken to be properties of the colour properties themselves.[36]

If, for the obvious reason, we call this the conception of colours as they naïvely seem to us to be, then given what we know about the physical world it follows that there are no colours as they naïvely seem to us to be. For a non-negotiable belief about colours is that if there are colours of external things then we have seen some of them. If a property has been seen then there must be a true causal explanation of some experience in terms of the object of the experience having the property. Barring a strange pre-established harmony between the colours as they naïvely seem to us to be and the microphysical and light dispositional properties of surfaces, no colour so conceived is implicated in the causal explanation of any of our experiences of the colours of things. Therefore even if there were properties whose natures corresponded to the colours as they naïvely seem to us to be they would never have been seen and so would not deserve the name of colours.

The case of colour is a kind of philosophical paradigm for a Revisionary Protagorean, that is, a philosopher who recognizes that our concepts are not many of them response-dependent as they stand and yet holds that they need to be replaced with response-dependent surrogates. The aspects of the case which he would hope to find replicated elsewhere are these

(A) When it comes to conceiving of what grounds and justifies our responses we are susceptible to a certain kind of error. We have a response-independent conception of the objects of those responses which includes a rich characterization of the objects to which we really have no right and which may be in fact satisfied by nothing.

(B) Such an error is often 'projective' in origin, that is, we arrive at the rich characterization as a result of taking our experience transparently to reveal the nature of what it presents.

(C) Such rich and projectively generated response-independent conceptions are shown to be erroneous when we ask for a detailed account of how we could be responding to things satisfying the conception.

(D) The question of realism versus irrealism turns on the extent to which adequate response-dependent surrogates can be found. Good surrogates are those that can serve a central core of the practical and theoretical ends to which the original concepts were put. When there are no such surrogates we may speak of a discourse that is vitiated by its metaphysical commitments.

On this view a discourse is therefore metaphysical in the pejorative sense when there is no adequate account of how the users of the discourse could be responding to the subject-matter of the discourse when the subject-matter is taken to instantiate the central concepts of the discourse. Colour discourse is not metaphysical in the pejorative sense. Literally intended Animist discourse about nature is pretty obviously metaphysical in the pejorative sense, there being no good response-dependent surrogates for nymphs, sylphs, and satyrs. The Protagorean's natural hope is that most philosophically interesting areas of discourse—talk of free will, of the passage of time, of causation, of correctly following a rule, of going through an inferential manipulation of content, of personal identity—are as they stand under real threat of being vitiated by their metaphysical commitments. Hence the programme of the Revisionary Protagorean, the programme of developing response-dependent surrogates for the central conceptions in these areas of discourse.

It must be granted to the Revisionary Protagorean that for each of these areas of discourse we can conjure up pictures of the subject-matter which are suspiciously related to features of our experience of the subject-matter and which if taken seriously make impossible any plausible account of how we could be responding to the subject-matter so conceived.

There is the picture of free agency as the undetermined initiation of action none the less somehow associated with human personalities otherwise under-stood as morasses of causal determination. Compare one's experience of one's own agency—vivid awareness of initiated action combined with little or no awareness of the causal determinants of that initiation.

There is the picture of the passage of time as involving reality growing at one end and diminishing at the other at the same unspecifiable rate, the view, as it is sometimes put, that the present alone is real. Compare our experience of the passage of time; the past we experience as gone, the future equally absent by being not yet.

There is the picture of causings as particular pushes and pulls in the world alongside the ordinary forces. Compare our experience of effort in bringing something about and of forces acting on our own bodies.

There is the picture of a subject's correctly following a rule which applies to a potentially infinite series of cases as his being guided by a demanding abstract entity—a content, rule or proposition that already some-how incorporates and dictates a specific response for each case. Compare the phenomenology of being guided by a rule, or better, as if by a commandment from God.

There is the associated picture of inference as causally *produced* by the contents manipulated in the inference and the more general picture of rational causation as content causation. Compare one's first experience of the remorselessness of a novel but valid train of inference. The contents of the premisses and the content of the rule seem to demand the conclusion's content.

There is the picture of value as 'the right road . . . the road such that everyone as a matter of logical necessity would have to take it or feel shame'.[37] Compare one's experience of the irresistibility of what one takes to be a great good.

There is the picture of the persistence of a person as involving the continued existence of, as Derek Parfit puts it, a 'separately existing entity' distinct from any body or brain, an entity whose survival could not but be an all or nothing matter, an entity simple enough to survive any amount of physical or psychological discontinuity. Here again the picture is plausibly taken to be the result of mistaking aspects of the first-person mode of presentation of oneself for aspects of oneself. From the inside, consciousness presents itself to its subject as complete and self-contained. That is, it is as if the continued existence of my consciousness has no external necessary conditions, in particular no physically necessary conditions. Taking this aspect of what it is like to be conscious to reveal the self-contained nature of being conscious it can seem an utter mystery how the continued existence of one's consciousness could depend upon anything, for example brain functioning, and equally mysterious how anything, for example brain functioning, could be sufficient for consciousness. Indeed the phenomenology of being a conscious subject over time is the phenomenology of being a self-contained constant while the objects of one's conscious experience and the psychological dispositions manifested in that experience vary, sometimes quite abruptly. Such phenomenology can encourage not only the idea that being a persisting conscious subject is independent of any external physical condition but also that no psychological continuity is in fact necessary for the persistence of the conscious subject that one is. Thus we arrive at the Bare Locus View: the view of a conscious subject as a thing capable of persisting through any amount of psychological or physical discontinuity and hence only tenuously related to any particular human body or human personality.

These concessions concerning our tendency to arrive at a metaphysical picture of some subject-matter having been made, let us now examine the claim of the Protagorean in his revisionist mode, viz., that response-dispositional surrogates are required for each of these metaphysically infected concepts. Are the ordinary concepts of free agency, the passage of time, of causation, of correctly following a rule, of going through an inferential manipulation of content, of personal identity just like the ordinary concept of colour in that the only tenable reconstruction of or surrogate for the ordinary concept is a response-dependent one?

On the face of it this seems far from plausible. What is perhaps less obvious is that there is a systematic position about the ordinary concepts which claims that the metaphysical pictures associated with those concepts do not represent central beliefs of the users of those concepts which guide the users in applying the concepts. The position has it that the metaphysical pictures are philosophical epiphenomena. Metaphysical pictures, although they emerge from the experience of ordinary concept users, do not guide ordinary practitioners in their everyday applications of the concepts and so do not represent the sort of central beliefs whose falsity would deprive the concepts of everyday application.

This position is best illustrated in the case of personal identity. While the consequences of the Bare Locus View do seem to be what we are describing when we describe our 'intuitions' about personal identity in certain bizarre cases, we give no thought to that view in our everyday reidentifications of ourselves and others. Those reidentifications are made in easy and offhand ways on the basis of physical appearance and, as a back-up, some gross psychological continuity. In making such identifications we never worry about what would be in fact a deep worry for us if we held the Bare Locus View. We never worry about ruling out the hypothesis that Bare Loci of consciousness have been replacing themselves behind the stage of the bodily and psychological continuities. Nor have we long ago assuaged that worry by decisively confirming that each Bare Loci is monogamous, that is, wedded to only one body throughout the body's life. We are not interested in the ways of Bare Loci. They are not what we are tracing when we trace ourselves and each other. The concept of personal identity, although associated with a metaphysical picture, is itself metaphysically austere.[38]

This thesis of Minimalism, that the concept in question carries no metaphysical commitments, was the thesis in the background in our discussion of truth. Some theorists have in effect run together the claim that truth is a response-independent notion with the metaphysical picture of a substantial correspondence relation between truthbearers and truthmakers. The truthmakers on this picture are entities the very existence of which is sufficient for all the truths. More, on this view, the truths, or at least a basic class of them which imply all the truths, are isomorphic to their truthmakers, thereby exhibiting a robust relation of correspondence. As we have seen, defending the response-independence of the notion of truth via the missing explanation argument nowhere essentially involves appeal to this robust relation of correspondence. The notion of truth is a Minimalist paradigm, at least in this sense: although in using the notion ordinary practitioners are thereby using a response-independent notion, it is none the less a metaphysically austere notion. Ordinary practitioners in aiming for truth are never aiming to secure the robust correspondence of the metaphysical picture; nor are they being lax about the real commitments of their practice.

I do not say that Minimalism is the last word for all of the concepts of philosophical interest, but it is the position which a Revisionary Protagorean must first overcome. And there are enough metaphysically austere response-independent notions to severely limit the successes of even the Revisionary Protagorean. Still, as we shall now see, one or two strategically placed successes may have quite general consequences.

5. Response-Dependence and Pragmatism

We have rejected Descriptive Protagoreanism and by implication the thesis that 'all qualities are secondary qualities', a thesis by which Putnam himself seems attracted in certain passages of *Reason, Truth and History*.[39] But one response-dependent account which can be defended as a revisionary reaction to metaphysical elements in the original concept is a response-dependent account of the concept of value.[40] And this is of considerable interest in refurbishing Pragmatism once Pragmatism has been stripped of its Verificationist garb.

To focus on a concrete response-dispositional proposal in the case of value, consider the following condition on the application of the predicate 'x is a valuable (or good) state of affairs', the most general predicate of commendation applicable to states of affairs

(18) x is a good or valuable state of affairs iff we are stably disposed to judge it so under conditions of increasing non-evaluative information and critical reflection.

Here the requirement that we are stably disposed to make the judgement of value is the requirement that (i) there be some state of non-evaluative information of ours about the issue which supports the judgement under conditions of critical reflection and (ii) any application of critical reflection to more inclusive states of non-evaluative information about the issue would also support the judgement. Information is here understood to be truth, including possibly evidence-transcendent truth.

Given (18) it will be the case that even if the predicate 'is true' has no interesting epistemic constraints which hold a priori, *the truth* about value, about which states of affairs are good states of affairs, will be epistemically constrained, in the sense that it cannot transcend our idealized capacity to judge that the states of affairs in question are valuable or worthy of valuing.

Turn now to the cluster of theses and attitudes gathered under the heading of Pragmatism. The central Verificationist thesis, the claim equating truth and ideal warrant, is a mistake. However this may be less important than it initially seems. Although the Pragmatism of John Dewey and William James is characteristically anti-metaphysical, it nowhere needs to claim that metaphysical statements, because neither verifiable nor falsifiable, are devoid of truth-value. It is enough that an interest in such unconstrained claims is just idle. Likewise, the emphasis John Dewey and William James placed on practical rationality even in high theoretical matters needs no theory of truth, let alone a Verificationist theory that explicates truth in terms of ideal warrant. The practical element in Pragmatism is best presented as a normative claim, the claim that our interest in the truth should always be a practically constrained interest, an interest restricted in principle to accessible truth (at least to this and probably to something more practically accessible). The relevant notion of in principle accessible truth *is* a response-dependent notion. It is the notion that might be specified thus

(19) S is accessibly true iff S is true and we are disposed to take it to be true under ideal epistemic conditions, i.e. under conditions in which we could survey any finite segment of any sequence of improving theories based on the deliverances of the ubiquitous detector.

The norm of restricting even your theoretical interests to the accessible truth has a powerful anti-speculative bite, at least as powerful as that of Verificationism. For much philosophical speculation in areas such as analytical ontology and philosophy of language looks like the articulation of various styles of high theoretical bookkeeping for the detectable facts. The history of philosophical systems provides little reason to think that one's own style of theoretical bookkeeping would eventually hold up in all sequences of improving theories. So even if one's philosophical system is true one could hardly believe it to be accessibly true in the sense of (19).

The Pragmatist norm has a clear justification: if you are interested in getting at the truth don't waste your time with truth which you can't in principle recognize as such. There is much about this justification which needs discussion since we can seldom know in advance what is in principle accessible as opposed to being merely hard to access. And it may be that any attempt to defend the Pragmatist norm will end up being a defence of something even more restrictive than the norm against aiming beyond the accessible truth. However, for present purposes the important thing to notice is that Internal Realism—the (mistaken) identification of truth with ideal warrant—would not make the justification for the Pragmatist norm any more compelling. The Pragmatist has so far lost nothing crucial in seeing the Verificationist lose a battle over truth.

What then of the metaphor which looms large in Contemporary Pragmatism, *The Metaphor of Nature's Toleration*, the idea that Nature does not *demand* to be theorized about or described in one specific way, so that the *rightness* of employing a theory and hence the scheme of description it embodies is not the solitary work of nature but is in some sense up to us?

The natural Verificationist construal of this idea is that the truth of any theory on offer is not independent of our capacity to verify the theory under ideal conditions, for example those conditions fixed by talk of the deliverances of a ubiquitous detector. Having rejected that account of dependence by rejecting the associated account of truth, what are we now to make of the metaphor?

What is the metaphor intended to rule out? Return to the root idea of Metaphysical Realism with which we began: the idea of a privileged set of truths constituted independently of human activity, a set of truths privileged in the sense that the most significant knowing is knowing those truths, so that the cognitive task is set in advance and in a way that is independent of human activity. The Verificationist emphasis makes it seem as if what is most objectionable here is the idea of a *set of truths* which could transcend anything revealed by the human activity of falsifying or verifying, however that activity is idealized. But I think that more antipathetic to the spirit of Pragmatism might be the idea that a set of truths could be *privileged* or *especially worth knowing* independently of any capacity of ours to come to recognize what is in our cognitive interest, the idea of *the* cognitive task being determined independently of such capacities. From that point of view, the core of the Metaphor of Nature's Toleration of various cognitive responses is the idea that the *rightness* of a cognitive response, such as accepting a theory, is not simply determined by the way nature is anyway, but is conceptually connected with certain facts about our capacity to recognize that the response is right.

One way of giving content to the idea that the rightness of accepting a theory for a given purpose is not the solitary work of nature is to claim that the notion of the rightness of accepting a theory for a given purpose is itself a response-dependent notion, a notion conceptually equivalent to the notion of our being disposed under ideal conditions to take it to be right to accept the theory in question for the given purpose. Hence, as a first approximation, the Metaphor of Nature's Toleration might be cashed out as the claim that (20) is a priori (and not as a result of a trivializing reading).

(20)   The act of accepting in some given situation and for some given purpose a theory T and the scheme of description T embodies is right iff we are stably disposed to judge the act right under conditions of increasing non-evaluative information and critical reflection.

Notice that if the very general notion of a state of affairs being a good or valuable state of affairs is a response-dependent notion, that is, if something like (18) is a priori and not as a result of a trivializing reading, then the notion of the goodness or, more idiomatically, the rightness of a choice of a specific means for a specific purpose will also be a response-dependent notion. For the catch-all category of states of affairs will include acts of choosing specific means for specific purposes.

Although we have here a direct argument that (20) is a priori and not merely as a result of a trivializing reading, the claim that (20) has this status may seem to not adequately capture the general thesis of Nature's Toleration. For when the purpose is knowing the truth at whatever cost to our other interests, facts about the way the world is, including facts about the subject-matter of the theory under consideration, are enough in themselves to settle the truth of the theory and hence to settle it that it is right to accept the theory given our purpose.

Suppose for example that the theory in question is a theory about the assassination of John F. Kennedy and the purpose in question is just the purpose of knowing the truth at whatever cost to our other interests. (The purpose that seems to have consumed so many professional critics of the Warren Commission.) Then we will be in a position stably to judge that it is right to accept the theory for the relevant purpose only when we have the non-evaluative information which settles the claims of the theory, that is, information about whether Oswald acted alone, how many bullets were fired, what motives the conspirators acted on, etc. If under critical conditions we are stably disposed to judge it right to accept the theory for the purpose of knowing the truth about the assassination this is only because under ideal critical conditions we would be provided with enough information to recognize that the theory is true. In such cases the rightness of accepting the theory may seem in no important sense up to us, we would merely *recognize* that it was right to accept the theory given that we knew enough to know that the theory is true. It follows directly from the fact that the theory is true that it is right to accept it for the purpose of knowing the truth.

Pragmatism is partly the reminder that even in theoretical matters we have more complex purposes than the purpose of simply knowing the truth (at whatever cost to our other interests). Hence Pragmatism's demand for practical upshot, even in high theoretical matters. Once we move away from a pure unadulterated interest in the truth at whatever cost (a *fiendish* curiosity?) a gap opens up between a theory's being true and its being right to accept the theory for certain purposes. The way the world non-evaluatively is cannot itself make it right to accept the theory for the practical purposes in question. There is the further evaluative question of whether the theory is a good means to our end. Whether that is so is in a certain way up to us. That is, it is a priori that

> (21) Fiendishly pure theoretical purposes aside, the act of accepting for some given purpose and in some given situation a theory T and the scheme of description T embodies is right iff we are stably disposed to find this act right under conditions of increasing non-evaluative information and critical reflection.

Although both (20) and (21) hold a priori, it is (21) that more clearly captures the residual truth in the Metaphor of Nature's Toleration. This is what the picture of a nature without independent demands comes to: the acceptability of a theory and the scheme of description it embodies is *up to us*, in the sense that it is a response-dependent matter. The irony is that this crucial thesis is entailed by the central thesis of an anti-Platonist metaethics, namely that the notion of value is response-dependent. It is not a thesis in ontology, philosophy of language, or naturalized (as opposed to normative) epistemology.

We can put the same point in another way. Consider the idea of an independent justifier of certain responses on the part of subjects, be they cognitive, emotional, volitional or sensory responses. A justifier is an independent justifier of our responses iff (i) it justifies those responses and (ii) it justifies those responses *anyway*, that is, independently of our being disposed to find them so justified under internally ideal conditions for considering the matter. In our terminology, its justifying those responses is a response-independent matter. Now we may understand the content of the Metaphor of Nature's Toleration as the claim that there are no independent justifiers of our cognitive responses. This should occasion no surprise. Given a response-dispositional account of value or rightness, there are no independent justifiers of any of our responses. (This denial seems to me a literal content fairly and usefully attached to the Nietzschean claim that God is dead.)

Once again, in order to defend this construal of the Metaphor against an obvious rejoinder, we have to fall back on a Pragmatist reminder. The obvious rejoinder is that since truth is not a response-dependent notion and since the truth of P is enough to justify the response of believing that P, there *are* independent justifiers of those cognitive responses which are acts of believing propositions. The Pragmatist reminder is that the rejoinder suppresses the full story. Even if P is true this may not justify or make right our coming to believe P. P may be a horrible, depressing, or despicable thing to believe or even to entertain. (I avoid examples for the obvious reason.) Of course, relative to a fiendish curiosity, an interest in the truth at whatever cost to our other interests, the truth of P justifies or makes right our coming to believe P. But firstly, a fiendish curiosity is hardly justified, and secondly and more importantly, even if it were justified this would be a response-dispositional matter, a matter of our being stably disposed to find it justified under conditions of increasing information and critical reflection. The rightness of a cognitive response cannot be assessed independently of assessing the place of that response in a whole network of legitimate human interest, and nothing just makes human interests legitimate *anyway*, that is, independently of our best-formed dispositions.

Along with the anti-speculative norm, the emphasis on practical upshot even in high theoretical matters, and the Metaphor of Nature's Toleration, Pragmatism is often taken to include the pluralist attitude. In politics this is the attitude which combines awareness of and tolerance towards the *range* of good lives and toward the institutions which help such lives along. In theoretical matters pluralism is the claim that for most purposes to which theories are put there are several equally good (or roughly equally good) theories, each with their own schemes of description of the relevant subject-matter. Whether or not this claim of Theoretical Pluralism is true it should now be evident that it can be true even if so-called Internal Realism is false.

For even if Theoretical Pluralism is true this would be no insult to the sensibilities of naïve Realism about truth properly construed. This is because our naïve Realist has contented himself with denying that the notion of truth is response-dependent. In denying this he nowhere need help himself to what he, being naïve, has no business believing in anyway, that is, a substantial relation of correspondence between truthbearers and truthmakers, an isomorphism of structure between propositions and facts, or a reductively characterized relation of reference between words and things. If eschewing such pictures of what truth *consists in* means that our naïve Realist does not deserve the name of Metaphysical Realist then all the better. This just shows that the defenders of epistemic accounts of truth have concentrated on rather easy targets and not to the *minimal* denials of their claims.

How does the foregoing bear on the issue that is central in Putnam's latest work—the claim that the world has no theory-independent structure? Let us say that a structure is a set of particulars, properties of any adicity had by the particulars, individually or severally, and kinds, both substance and phase-kinds, which the particulars exemplify. Then the world has a structure if there is a true theory which claims there are certain particulars, predicates various things of them, and represents those individuals as falling under kinds. The world has as many structures in this sense as there are true theories representing distinct structures. Probably none of these true theories implies that independently of our employing the predicates of the theory, the world lacks the structure attributed by the theory. In any case, it is not part of this liberal notion of the world's many structures that prior to our structuring activity the world was an amorphous blob. (Hence we avoid what Putnam calls the 'cookie-cutter' metaphor, a metaphor which Putnam convincingly rejects in *The Many Faces of Realism.*[41])

Notice however that endorsing the liberal notion of the world's structures does not imply that the world's having a particular structure cannot transcend our idealized capacity to recognize that it has that structure. Quite the contrary; since the truth of a theory can transcend our idealized capacity to recognize it as true, the fact that the world has the structure represented by the theory can transcend our idealized capacity to recognize it. For we recognize that the world has a particular structure by recognizing that some theory representing the structure is true.

So even on this rather liberal account of when the world has a structure it will not be a priori that

(22)   The world has structure K iff we are disposed to believe this at the limit of rational inquiry.

since it is not a priori that

(23)   A theory is true iff we are disposed to believe this at the limit of rational inquiry.

The structures of the world are independent of our cognitive activity however idealized, not only existentially independent but also conceptually independent, and in the strong sense indicated by the failure of (22) and the like when maintained as conceptual claims.

If we call the thesis that the world's having some structure is a response-dependent matter the thesis of Conceptual Idealism, on the grounds that the thesis is one of *conceptual* dependence between the notion of the world's having a structure and the notion of our being ideally disposed to accept that it does, then Conceptual Idealism falls with Internal Realism.

Our Pragmatism purified of Verificationism (or at least of a verificationism about meaning and truth) consists of four theses separately and collectively independent of Internal Realism:

(i)   the anti-speculative norm, which has it that it is idle to aim at inaccessible truth;

(ii)   the emphasis on practical upshot even in high theoretical matters;

(iii) the response-dependence of theoretical rightness, or equivalently the denial that there are independent justifiers of our responses, including our cognitive responses; and

(iv)   Theoretical Pluralism, the doctrine that for many purposes to which theories are put there are several equally good theories each with their own scheme of description, and such that there is nothing incoherent in supposing that each of these alternative theories might be true (given a liberal conception of the multiple structures the world exhibits).

A full defence of such a pragmatism would have to explain in detail why the 'missing explanation' argument which defeated Internal Realism does not cut deep against the doctrine that value and so theoretical rightness are response-dependent notions.[42] But perhaps we have done enough to strongly suggest that Internal Realism is as unnecessary as it is mistaken.

Appendix 1: The Euthyphro Argument

There is a generalization of the 'missing explanation' argument used against Internal Realism which shows that probably only those concepts which wear their response-dispositional character on their linguistic face—pleasing, shymaking, nauseating, etc.—are response-dispositional concepts. The archetype of this argument occurs in Plato's *Euthyphro*.[43] There Socrates objects to Euthyphro's definition of the pious as what the gods love. Socrates insists that rather than acts' being pious because they are loved by the gods, the gods love such acts because those acts are pious acts. It simply turns out that, thanks to their natures, the gods are very good detectors of piety which in fact they invariably love. There is, as we might put it, nothing a priori about this, as is shown by the fact that while certain empirical information is given by the remark 'The gods love pious acts because they are pious', the same empirical information is not given by the remark 'The gods love pious acts because they are the acts the gods love'. The latter remark is an explanatory solecism in that it does not describe any realizable pattern of causal dependence. Yet it comes from the former remark by substituting the expressions which Euthyphro alleges are a priori equivalent. Given the principle that substituting a priori equivalents into a statement that provides an explanation should not generate such explanatory solecisms we have a *reductio ad absurdum* of *Euthyphro*'s claim of a priori equivalence and hence a *reductio* of his definitional claim.

This (avowedly tarted-up) version of the argument from the Euthyphro is the characteristic bugbear of response-dispositional accounts. In each of the philosophically interesting examples of response-dispositional accounts given above ordinary intuition backs a remark of the form 'It cannot be that the concept of an F is either the concept of the disposition to prompt such and so responses or the concept of the disposition to issue such responses. For it is explanatory to say that it is because x is F that it has or we have the disposition.' That is, these claims are intuitive

(1) In the most fortunate case, a thing is disposed to look green to us because it is green.

(2) We are stably disposed to judge something valuable under conditions of increasing information and critical reflection because it is valuable.

(3) We are disposed to manipulate Xs to produce Ys under certain conditions because Xs cause Ys.

(4) We are stably disposed to judge that some person survived some process because that person did survive that process.

(5) We are under improving interpretive conditions stably disposed to attribute attitude A with content K to some person because that person has attitude A with content K.

(6) We are disposed to hold S responsible for A because S is responsible for A.

Each of statements (1)–(6) is an empirical statement claiming that what disposes us to detect or appropriately react to some fact under ideal conditions is the holding of the fact. In each case, the corresponding response-dispositional accounts imply that the *explanans* and *explanandum* are a priori equivalent. If we substitute into the 'because'-statements on the basis of the a priori equivalences implied by the various response-dispositional accounts, we derive explanatory solecisms like 'In the most fortunate case something is green because it is green'. Conclusion: the various response-dispositional accounts make mistaken claims about what is a priori.

That is, of course, not the end of the matter. There is room to insist that although an ordinary concept (or core conception) is as it stands response-independent, in some cases this is because the concept or core conception is in part the product of a kind of projective error which has incorporated empirically unsatisfiable or even flatly inconsistent conditions into the concept. This is a plausible position about colour concepts and about the concept of value.

Appendix 2: Complexities in the Notion of a Disposition[44]

The notion of a disposition contains some hidden complexity not widely appreciated. It may be useful to display some of this complexity. Consider—

Case 1. There might have been a ray emitted from the centre of green objects, a ray which acted directly on our visual cortices so that green objects always would look red to us in any viewing situations. But this would not be enough to make them surface green.

Case 2. There might have been a shy but powerfully intuitive chameleon which in the dark was green but also would intuit when it was about to be put in a viewing condition and would instantaneously blush bright red as a result. So although in the dark the chameleon is green it is not true of it in the dark that were it to be viewed it would look green. It would look bright red.

Case 3. There might be an object (I have one) which is surface green but never looks and never would look surface green because it also *radiates* orange light at such an intensity that the greenness is masked or obscured. It is none the less surface green even though it would never look so, as is shown by the fact that it *reflects* just the same kind of light that some other surface green things reflect.

These sorts of cases would constitute good objections to a dispositional account of colour if that account had to assert things like

(1)   It is a priori that x is red for S_i in C_i iff x would look red to S_i under C_i.

However to assume that is to assume that something's having a disposition to produce R in S under C is equivalent to the holding of the corresponding dispositional conditional: if the thing were to be in C it would produce R in S. That this is not so, that the relation between the holding of a disposition and the holding of its corresponding dispositional conditional is more complex, is shown by cases of just the sort given above.

Case 1* Mimicking.   A gold chalice is not fragile but an angel has taken a dislike to it because its garishness borders on sacrilege and so has decided to shatter it when it is dropped. Even although the gold chalice would shatter when dropped, this does not make it fragile because while this dispositional conditional is not bare, that is, its holding is *underwritten* (in a sense to be explained) by the laws and the way some things are intrinsically, its holding is not underwritten by the laws and the way the *chalice* is intrinsically. *Mutatis mutandis* for the ray-bedevilled green surface. Even though it would look red if viewed, this does not make the surface red. For although this dispositional conditional holds and is not bare, its holding is not underwritten by the laws and the way the *surface* is intrinsically. (An object gets called (surface) red because it has a red surface, not because something other than its surface has the disposition to look red.)

Case 2* Altering.   The glass cup is fragile but an angel has decided to make the cup hard if it begins to fall to the ground or if it is about to be hit by a hammer, etc. Even though the conditional corresponding to fragility does not hold, that is, the cup would not break if struck, the cup is fragile because in all the ways of deviating as little as possible from the way the world actually is, consistent with removing the interfering angel, the intrinsic nature of the cup and the laws underwrite the dispositional conditional—if the cup were struck it would break. *Mutatis mutandis* for the shy but intuitive chameleon.

Case 3* Masking.   Another glass cup is also fragile but packing companies have discovered that the breaking of glass involves three stages: first a few bonds break, then the glass deforms and then many bonds break, thereby shattering the glass. They find a support which when placed inside the glass cup prevents deformation so that the glass would not break when struck. Even though the cup would not break if struck, the cup is still fragile. For in all ways of deviating from the actual world as little as possible consistent with removing the support, the laws and the way the cup is intrinsically would underwrite the dispositional conditional—if the cup were struck it would break. *Mutatis mutandis* for the surface green thing which is also radiant orange due in part to its interior. In all the worlds as close as possible to the actual world, consistent with removing the radiator behind the surface, the laws and the way the surface is intrinsically underwrite the characteristic dispositional conditional for surface green—if the surface were inspected it would look surface green.

What then is it for the way x is intrinsically at a given time t to *underwrite* the characteristic conditional of the disposition to R in S under C—if x were in C at $t + d$ then x would R in S at $t + d + e$? Just this: (i) there are some near enough worlds in which x is in C at $t + d$ and (ii) in every such world w, the laws of w and some complete specification of what is intrinsically involved in x's being in C at $t + d$ entail a specification of a state of affairs which realizes x's R-ing in S at $t + d + e$.

What is it for the way x is intrinsically at a given time t to *underwrite* an 'unmasking conditional' of the disposition to R in S under C, a conditional of the form: if x were not to have extrinsic property M and x were to be in C at $t + d$ then x would R in S at $t + d + e$? Just this: (i) there are some near enough worlds in which x lacks M and is in C at $t + d$ and (ii) in every such world w, the laws of w and a specification of what is intrinsically involved in x being in C at $t + d$ entail a specification of a state of affairs which realizes x's R-ing in S at $t + d + e$.

We can now present in analytic form one notion of a disposition. At t, x has the disposition to R in S under C iff one of the following three cases hold.

The (possibly vacuous) case of the bare disposition

The characteristic conditional holds, that is, if x were in C it would R in S, but nothing is such that the way it is intrinsically at t underwrites the conditional.

The case of the constituted disposition that is not masked

The characteristic conditional holds and the way x is intrinsically at t underwrites the conditional. (The requirement of underwriting rules out mere mimicking of the disposition.)

The case of the masked, constituted disposition

The characteristic conditional does not hold and yet

(a) There is an extrinsic property M of x at t such that the unmasking conditional—if x were to lack M and were to be in C at $t + d$ then x would R in S—holds and the way x is intrinsically at t underwrites this conditional.

(b) Where R' is incompatible with R, there is no extrinsic property M' of x at t such that the conditional—if x were to lack M' and were to be in C at $t + d$ then x would R' in S at $t + d + e$—holds and is underwritten by the way x is intrinsically at t.

The intuitive idea behind the case of the masked, constituted disposition is that masking is having some extrinsic feature to prevent the thing from doing what it is otherwise disposed to do thanks to its intrinsic nature and the laws as they apply in the circumstances of manifestation.[45]

Appendix 3: On Two Distinctions

As it now stands, the distinction between response-dependent and response-independent concepts is a development of an idea presented in my seminar on ethics during the spring of 1986. I was fortunate enough to have Crispin Wright in attendance, and ever since then he and I have talked and corresponded about this and related distinctions. For his purposes Wright finds a different but in some ways parallel distinction useful. This is a distinction between extension-determination and extension-reflection. There are some important differences between the two distinctions, both at the level of formulation and of motivation.

In the seminar I employed what seemed then to be a relatively obvious way of pointing to a common structure among secondary quality or dispositional accounts of colour concepts and ideal-observer accounts of goodness and rightness. They were accounts of concepts for which a 'basic equation' of the form

> x is F iff a certain class of subjects S are disposed to produce response R under conditions C.

was a priori as a result of a reading which 'moved from right to left' in the sense of specifying who the subjects in question were, what the response in question was, and what the conditions of response were, all in a way which had no recourse to the concept F. Hence the metaphor of movement; the concept F was to be built up out of different concepts. Clearly such an idea of a right to left reading rules out the following interpretations of the subjects, conditions, and responses: the infallibly F-detecting subjects whoever they are, the infallibly F-detecting response whatever that is, the infallibly F-detecting conditions whatever they are. Crispin Wright's useful phrase here is that 'whatever it takes' interpretations are to be ruled out.

In the seminar I suggested that since in the cases of goodness and rightness a 'right to left' reading was defensible, such a reading focusing on the dispositions of subjects to approve would be hard to distinguish from a defensible projectivism about value, especially a projectivism like Simon Blackburn's which aimed ultimately to provide truth-conditions for evaluative remarks. (Related points against Blackburn's projectivism were also made by Michael Smith, from whose work on dispositional theories I have learnt much.) Partly as a way of making the point against Blackburn's projectivism, I called the 'right to left' reading of the basic equation the 'projective' reading.

Despite thinking that there was something of quite general application in the basic equation idea I hesitated to do anything with it in print. Firstly, as formulated, a projective reading was inevitably an analytically reductive reading and I took it that there were not too many defensible analytic reductions. Secondly, I did not know quite what to say about the relation between dispositions and conditionals.

Some months later Crispin Wright circulated a very useful discussion of basic equations—'Notes on Basic Equations'—in which he moved immediately to the cases in which the responses were beliefs involving the concept F in question on the lefthand side of the basic equation. He also proposed that we deal with cases like the chameleon by means of 'provisoed equations' of the form

> Under C, for all S, Fx iff S believes that Fx.

This condition is reminiscent of Rudolf Carnap's account of solubility—under conditions in which x is placed in water it dissolves iff it is soluble—about which there are familiar worries which may generalize to the provisoed equation. More importantly, allowing the concept F to figure in the specification of the response, although required in many cases, is always at odds with any metaphor of a directional reading. This point appears to undermine Wright's account of his own distinction.

Of his distinction, generated by what he calls the order of determination test, Wright remarks:

> Intuitively it [is] the distinction between classes of statements our best opinions about which—opinions conceived by subjects and in circumstances which we think of as cognitively ideal for statements of that kind—determine the extension of the truth predicate among them, and classes of statements our best opinions about which at most reflect an extension determined independently. ... What should be the criteria for saying that a class of statements should be regarded in one way rather than another? ... We can usefully begin with the general form of what Mark Johnston has styled a basic equation.
>
> P iff for any S: if conditions C obtain, then S believes that P.
>
> Here conditions C are to be thought of as concerning the pedigree of S's belief. They are to be such that any belief whether or not P which is generated under them is true.[46]

Wright then goes on to rule out a trivializing 'whatever-it-takes' reading of the C-conditions:

> Now the distinction we wish to draw begins to emerge, I suggest, when we ask: what is the effect on the status of such biconditionals when we replace these trivially formulated whatever it takes C-conditions with *substantial* specifications of what it does take? In particular, can the a priority of such a biconditional survive such specification? ... if the a priority of the biconditional survives substantial specification, then, subject to qualifications to emerge below, we have the makings of a case for regarding best opinion as playing an extension determining role.[47]

We now come to Wright's distinctive second requirement on a basic equation, the requirement which underlines his interest in the question of the order of the determination of the extensions of the concepts or propositions in question on the lefthand side of the basic equation.

The second requirement is:

> that satisfaction of the C-conditions ... is logically independent of any truths concerning the extension of [the predicates in question on the lefthand side] and could indeed be appraised by someone who [lacked the determinable concepts whose determinates are in question on the lefthand side].[48]

The idea here is this. Suppose that the proposition in question is the proposition Fa. Wright's intent is to pick out a class of cases where our opinion in certain circumstances C as to Fa determines the extension of the proposition Fa. Given that aim, it makes sense to require that in specifying C one not rely upon any concept, for example the concept F, whose extension is supposed to be determined by our opinion in C. And if the extension of any determinable is fixed in part by that of its determinates then one also wants to exclude from the specification of C the determinables of which F is a determinate.

By means of these conditions and one more:

> no other suggestion [is available] of what else might be viewed as determining the extension of the truth-predicate among [the relevant] judgements, some different kind of account of which the a priori connection illustrated would be a consequence.[49]

Wright intends to explicate a distinction on one side of which are meant to fall propositions (and concepts) whose extensions are determined by our best opinions about their being true (or applying).

Wright's distinction turns on the directional idea of determination. But how can the extension of the proposition P be determined by anyone's belief under specified circumstances that P? Surely only if the belief that P already has some extension already associated with it. For if the belief that P has no extension and so no mode of determining an extension associated with it then the belief that P will be devoid of content and so will not constrain anything at all.

As far as extension-determining goes there seem to be just two live options. Either P and 'believes that P' have their extensions determined together, in which case talk of *order* of determination is out of place, or talk of order is in place and the order in question is the order exhibited in a standard compositional semantics. The extensions of P is first specified and then as *a result* of that and the extension of the relational predicate 'believes that' being specified the extension of 'believes that P' is then determined. The motivating idea behind Wright's distinction, the idea that there could be an order of extension-determination in which the extension of P gets fixed as a result of a prior fixing of the extension of the belief that P, is yet to get a purchase.

Maybe the idea is this. Suppose you know the basic equation for P and you are told the extension of the predicate 'believes that P', that is, you are told who believes that P. You are also told under what conditions various people believe that P. Then you would be able to use this information and the basic equation to determine the extension of P, that is to determine whether P is true. If that is the motivating idea behind talk of order of determination then the same problem remains. Talk of order is still misplaced, for this account provides for no real asymmetry. For if you know the basic equation for P and you are told whether P is true then you can determine via the basic equation the extension of the predicate 'believes that P under conditions C'.

One would only get an asymmetry which would give talk of *order* a place if the basic equation in question represented a reductive definition analysing a complex content into semantically *simpler* constituents, as with the old idea of a projective reading. Then by assigning extensions to the simpler constituents one would thereby fix the extension of the complex content. But Wright's doxastic cases are obviously not such cases. The beliefs in question involve the very concept under discussion.

These doxastic cases, in which substantial a priori biconditionals which are *not* reductive hold, correspond to a subclass of the response-interdependent concepts. But there is no *order* here, just an a priori connection between a concept F and the concept of our best judgements about which things are F, evidencing a certain kind of interdependence between the concepts in question. If that is so then there is no motivation for Wright's distinctive second requirement that the concept F not figure in the specification of the ideal conditions C. For even if the concept F did so figure we *could* still have an interesting a priori connection between something's being F and our ideally taking it to be so.

To put it as a dilemma: either one should aim to characterize strict one-way response-dependence, in which case the concept F in question should be banished from the specification of the response as well as from the specification of the conditions of response, or one should abandon the idea of an order of determination and allow (but of course not require) the concept F to figure both in the specification of the response and in the specification of the ideal conditions of response.

To take the first horn of the dilemma would be to have a distinction on one side of which fell only those concepts which allowed for a reductive definition or analysis in terms of concepts of our responses. This would mean for example Naturalism ('the Naturalism that Moore despised *not* the Naturalism that Hume admired'[50]) in the account of value and an account of propositional content in terms that do not involve reference to content-bearing responses of ours. There are good reasons to believe that such reductive accounts have very dim prospects.[51]

The second horn of the dilemma thus seems to be the one to take. Taking it, dropping Wright's second requirement, and dealing neatly with the problems of masking, mimicking, and altering which will plague any simple conditional formulation leads to the response-dispositional concepts, including those concepts of dispositions to produce beliefs or judgements.

Taking the second horn requires thinking differently about the motivation for the distinction. None the less, perhaps there is something to be gained here. To take one example: in a subtle and compendious discussion of rule-following Paul Boghossian objects to Wright's 'judgement-dependent' account of meaning and mental content as follows:

> The idea [of judgement-dependence] is clearly appropriate in the case of facts about the chic or the fashionable; familiar, though less clearly appropriate, in connection with facts about color and sound; and, it would appear, impossible as a conception of facts about mental content. For it cannot be true that facts about content are constituted by our judgements about content: facts about content, constituted independently of the judgements are presupposed by the model itself.[52]

Surely this is a good objection to claiming content is judgement-dependent when the claim of judgement-dependence is that facts about content are *simply determined or constituted by* facts about the contents of our best judgements.

However the idioms of determination and constitution are only appropriate in the case of reductive, one-way response-dependence. So long as we have a case of response-interdependence, where we have to use the concept F in specifying the relevant response-disposition, talk of facts about Fs being constituted by or being mere projections of facts about response-dispositions is entirely out of place.

A response-interdependent account of meaning or content, say along the lines of (16) above, if it could be made to work, would not itself be an account of the ontology of meaning or content. It would imply that the truth about meaning and content cannot outrun our idealized dispositions to grasp that truth. This in its turn might rule out certain extreme Platonist conceptions of meaning. But precisely because of *inter*dependence there is no implication of content or meaning being constituted out of the contents of attitudes. Here as elsewhere it is the case of response-*inter*dependence which is of most philosophical interest.

This rather abstract expansion of the space of possible positions can have significant consequences for one's preferred account of particular concepts. Thus in the case of value Wright correctly rejects the idea that our evaluative responses *determine* the extensions of the evaluative concepts on the grounds that a substantive evaluative conception is required to pick out the relevant responders and responses. But from the perspective which emphasizes interdependence, Wright seems to be working with a restricted range of options when he takes this failure of determination to invalidate the analogy between values and secondary qualities.[53]

As against this, the secondary quality analogy is adequate if taken to be the assertion that both evaluative and secondary quality concepts are best reconstructed as response-dependent concepts, where we include the case of interdependence. Of course, an analogy at this level of generality has little to do with the perception-based epistemology of value which John McDowell, if I understand him, had in mind when he recently resurrected the analogy.[54] (For problems with both a perceptual and quasi-perceptual epistemology of value see my contribution to The Aristotelian Society Symposium on Dispositional Theories of Value.[55])[56]

Notes

1. W. James, *The Meaning of Truth: A Sequel to Pragmatism*.

2. H. Putnam, *Reason, Truth and History* and *The Many Faces of Realism*.

3. H. Putnam, *Reason, Truth and History*, p. 55.

4. H. Putnam, *Meaning and the Moral Sciences*, p. 125.

5. H. Putnam, 'Models and Reality', in *Realism and Reason: Philosophical Papers*, 3.

6. For example, see D. Lewis, 'Putnam's Paradox', *Australasian Journal of Philosophy* 62.

7. What if T has a model in which all and only the truths hold, even though T does not imply all the truths? Then the model in question is not fully specified by T, and the

model would be at least a good stand-in for the world for the purposes of saying what the Metaphysical Realist wants to say, i.e. that the true claims about the world go beyond what is true according to T.

8. A neat, accessible version of the relevant results of Gödel and Tarski is provided by J. R. Shoenfield, *Mathematical Logic*.

9. Of course if the underlying logic is like standard predicate logic in not having a negative decision procedure then there will be 'alienated' truths of the form 'S does not follow from T' just in virtue of the logic's lacking a full decision procedure.

10. A truth-predicate of a theory T_i is a predicate $B(x)$ such that for every sentence S in the language of T_i, T_i implies that (S iff $B(\langle S \rangle)$), where $\langle S \rangle$ is a numerical name of S. In the main text the argument focuses on a condition that entails that T contains its own truth-predicate.

11. As Bas Van Fraassen points out, someone prepared to go intuitionist in his interpretation of 'There are two theories . . .' may need an example of two such theories, or at least a way of generating them, in order to accept that this is a problem. In a longer version of the present essay I show how the intuitionist account of the existential quantifier is indefensible at least when generalized beyond the mathematical case. We get a series of paradoxical consequences beginning with a proof from logic alone that it is not the case that there are material objects that remain forever unconsidered. If you respond by saying that theories can be treated as mathematical objects, so that we do not need to generalize beyond the mathematical case, I am then at a loss as to why the Intuitionist's symbol '∃' should be interpreted as existential quantification. Existential quantification is a topic neutral notion, amounting to the same thing in mathematics and physics.

12. Talk of the a priori in what follows presupposes only that some post-Quinean notion of conceptual truth can be reconstructed. Compare Putnam, *Representation and Reality* 'The fact that a philosophically useful analytic/synthetic distinction cannot be drawn (because for one thing most of the things that a philosopher would say are conceptual truths have in one way or another empirical presuppositions) does not mean that the notion of a conceptual truth must be totally abandoned. It means, rather, that conceptual truth is a matter of degree' (p. 133). But doesn't this mean that the analytic/synthetic distinction is a matter of degree and indeed that some truths are maximally analytic?

13. May be 'madness' is too strong, 'evident implausibility' might be better. Compare Putnam 'I confess that I find this kind of anti-realism about the past a sure sign of a mistake wherever and whenever it occurs', p. 249 of 'James's Theory of Perception', in *Realism with a Human Face*.

14. Even if there are some things with unspecific trajectories, e.g. electrons, the point in the text about middle-sized objects is not affected. Even about the electrons, the point is that we do not and cannot discover the indeterminacy of their trajectories by meditating on an epistemic account of truth and the resultant fact-gaps.

15. That the idea of a sentence about the observable is not the idea of a sentence built up from observational vocabulary is well argued by Bas Van Fraassen in *The Scientific Image*, pp. 10–11, 13–19, 56–9, and 87–92.

16. Van Fraassen, *The Scientific Image*, pp. 1–19, 71–3, and 204–16.

17. Notice that the problem does not go away if one insists that the real explanation of why the sentence 'Oswald did not act alone' holds up is not because this sentence (on its standard English interpretation) is true, but because Oswald did not act alone. Since it is a priori and necessary that ['Oswald did not act alone' on its standard English interpretation is true iff Oswald did not act alone], we can substitute into the sentence

['"Oswald did not act alone" holds up because Oswald did not act alone'] and get the sentence ['"Oswald did not act alone" holds up because "Oswald did not act alone" on its standard English interpretation is true']. Again, this last sentence cannot convey the original information to the effect that as a causal consequence of Oswald's acting with others a ubiquitous detector would have observed this, and hence all theories based on the deliverances of a ubiquitous detector would have it that Oswald did not act alone. At least the sentence cannot convey this information if it is a priori and necessary that

> (6′) 'Oswald did not act alone' on its standard English interpretation is true iff 'Oswald did not act alone', so interpreted, holds up in all sequences of improving theories based on the deliverances of the ubiquitous detector.

18. Editorial introduction to *Williams James: The Essential Writings*, p. xliv.

19. Talk of propositions here need not depart from ordinary language in which believing that p and believing the proposition that p are equivalent, the latter being a pleonastic form. Propositions are just the denotata of 'that'-clauses, and the redundancy theory of truth is correct for propositions in the sense that it is a logical truth that for any p, the proposition that p is true iff p. On the so-called 'Pleonastic' account of propositions see Stephen Schiffer, *Remnants of Meaning* and my 'The End of the Theory of Meaning', *Mind and Language*, 3.

Could one escape that argument by saying that there is only a sentential notion of truth such that

> (i) 'There are 281 lemons' is true iff we counted we would count 281 lemons

is contingent? So that it is still coherent to claim that

> (ii) The causal explanation of why if we counted we would count 281 lemons is that there are 281 lemons.

This is only possible if (a) one has a principled argument against the coherence of the 'language-fixed' sentential notion introduced in n. 17; and (b) one is prepared to admit that the causal explanation of the fact that 'There are 281 lemons' is true is that there are 281 lemons. But it does not seem coherent to causally explain the truth of a sentence in terms of the state of affairs the sentence is about.

20. *Realism with a Human Face*, pp. v–vii.

21. *Reality and Representation*, p. 115.

22. *The Many Faces of Realism*, pp. 16–21.

23. 'Realism and Reason' in *Meaning and the Moral Sciences*, p. 125.

24. *The Many Faces of Realism*, p. 20, where we are told that the very idea of what objects there are makes no sense independently of a choice of concepts.

25. *The Many Faces of Realism*, pp. 16–25.

26. Ibid., p. 43.

27. *Reason, Truth and History*, p. xi.

28. Rorty, *Philosophy and the Mirror of Nature*, pp. 12–13, 210–11. and 392–3.

29. Goodman, *Of Mind and other Matters*, p. 31.

30. Ibid., p. 36.

31. Elgin has her own ingenious construal of the example.

32. 'Notes on the Well-Made World', p. 9. Compare Wright's notion of super-assertibility in his *Realism, Meaning and Truth*, pp. 295–309.

33. *Theaetetus*, 125a. Aristotle, Diogenes Laertius, and Sextus Empiricus all have fragmentary things to say about Protagoras but it is unclear how much of what they

have to say provides independent corroboration of the Platonic material. In *Outlines of Pyrrhonism* (1, 216–19) Sextus tells us that Protagoras 'accepts only what appears to each individual and therefore introduces the relative. . . . He also says that the *logoi* of all appearances lies in matter . . . but that men apprehend different things at different times, depending upon the differences in their make-up.'

Putnam in *Reason, Truth and History*, pp. 120–1, follows Plato in arguing that Protagoras' view is incoherent. But see the next note in which Protagoras and Putnam are found to exhibit a deeper harmony.

34. Putnam seems to favour an unrestricted form of Protagoreanism when he says in *Reason, Truth and History* that all properties might be secondary. See pp. 61–4.

35. 'Dispositional Theories of Value', *Proceedings of the Aristotelian Society*, Supplementary Volume LXII.

36. Compare John Campbell's account of colour in the present volume. For a more extensive discussion of the case of colour see my 'How to Speak of the Colors', *Philosophical Studies* 68.

37. This is a quotation from Ludwig Wittgenstein's 'Lecture on Ethics' published in *The Philosophical Review* 74 (1965). David Wiggins has some interesting remarks about this passage in his contribution to the present volume.

38. For more on this and an account of how the relevant projective error can influence our intuitions in bizarre cases, see my 'Human Beings', *Journal of Philosophy* 84, and 'Reasons and Reductionism', *Philosophical Review* 101.

39. Especially pp. 61–4.

40. The concept of value fits the paradigm exemplified in the case of colour, i.e. (A) through (D) hold in the case of value. For a defence of this see my 'Dispositional Theories of Value'.

41. *The Many Faces of Realism*, pp. 19 and 33–6.

42. See 'Dispositional Theories of Value', pp. 170–3, for part of the explanation. A crucial point is that although minimalism about our ordinary notion of truth is defensible, a corresponding Minimalism is not defensible when it comes to the ordinary idea of value or rightness.

43. *Euthyphro*, 108–18.

44. The views contained in this appendix were formulated some while ago and no longer represent my current thinking. It would not now be appearing save that due to a misunderstanding this version went to press and is discussed by Crispin Wright in *Truth and Objectivity*. For an alternative treatment of masking, mimicking, and altering, see Mark Johnston 'Dispositions: Predication with a Grain of Salt' (forthcoming).

45. Of necessity this account leaves out several refinements having to do with intrinsic masking, probabilistic dispositions, the role of the idea of proper functioning, and standardized dispositions. Since colours are best reconstructed as standardized dispositions something should be said about them. One advantage of bringing out some hidden complexity in the notion of a disposition is to reveal several parameters which context might vary. So, for example, if we have a small positively charged particle in the vicinity of a large positively charged ball, then consistent with the present account we may say that electromagnetically the particle has the disposition to move away from the ball, while gravitationally it has the disposition to move toward the ball. On the present account we are to think of the qualifiers as restricting the laws that figure in the underwriting derivations. So too redness is the standard disposition to look red, where the laws underwriting the conditional are those standardly involved in colour vision. Thus even a strange ray from the surface of a green object which acted directly

on the visual cortex to produce an experience as of a red object would not make the surface count as red.

Why not talk of explanation rather than underwriting? Mainly because of cases of actual and counterfactual 'veridical mimicking'. These are cases in which the thing has the disposition and the conditional holds but not causally because of the way the thing is intrinsically.

46. This volume pp. 77–78.

47. Ibid., p. 78.

48. Ibid., p. 79.

49. Ibid., p. 79.

50. This euphonious contrast is from David Wiggins, this volume, p. 301.

51. But see Peter Railton's contribution to the present volume.

52. P. Boghossian, 'The Rule Following Considerations', *Mind* 98, p. 547. See also *The Many Faces of Realism*, p. 15, where Putnam also objects to the metaphor of projection in the case of intentionality.

53. See Wright 'Moral Values, Projection and Secondary Qualities', *Proceedings of the Aristotelian Society*, Supplementary Volume LXII.

54. McDowell, 'Values and Secondary Qualities' in T. Honderich (ed.), *Morality and Objectivity*.

55. 'Dispositional Theories of Value.'

56. Much of this paper was the basis for three talks given at the Research School of Social Sciences at the Australian National University in August of 1989. I thank the Research School for the provision of an ideal working environment, and Andy Clarke, Martin Davies, Frank Jackson, Peter Menzies, Neil Tennant, and Michael Tooley for their helpful comments. Crispin Wright was kind enough to give extensive comments on several drafts. Thanks also to John Burgess, Catherine Elgin, Gil Harman, David Lewis, David Sosa, Sarah Stroud, Bas Van Fraassen, Jonathan Vogel, and Paul Boghossian. Research on this paper was supported by a grant from the State of New Jersey (The Governor's Fellowship in the Humanities).

II

REALISM AND LOGIC

5

Anti-Realism, Inference, and the Logical Constants

John Skorupski

I

Complex sentences, and the sentential operators by means of which they are formed, are of great importance in the debate about 'realist' and 'anti-realist' conceptions of meaning. It is on the anti-realist's ability to give an account of our understanding of complex sentences of various types that the most serious questions about the coherence of his position turn. This applies to tensed sentences and to those which describe psychological attitudes; most centrally, it applies to compound sentences formed by means of the truth-functional connectives, 'not', 'and', 'if... then', and 'or'.

Reflection on any of these types of complex sentence soon makes it clear that the content of a sentence S cannot be equated with the content of *It is assertible that S*. And it is only natural to see this as a major stumbling block for the anti-realist. After all, is not the essence of an anti-realist conception of meaning given by the thesis that a sentence's meaning or content is given in terms of its assertion conditions? Do not the pair S and *It is assertible that S* have the same assertion conditions and must they not therefore, on the anti-realist view, have the same content?

An obvious response to these questions is that the dictum 'meaning is given by assertion conditions' should be considered no more than convenient shorthand. For the basic thought behind anti-realism is that meaning is exhaustively constituted by use. But use encompasses inferential as well as assertoric practice. (It encompasses more of course: the linkage of inferential and assertoric practice to actions other than assertings, supposings, inferrings,

I thank all those at the St Andrews Conference who gave me comments on the first draft of this paper, particularly Paul Boghossian for his comments on the relation between EM, meaning-as-use, and rule-scepticism, Michael Williams on Wittgenstein and Crispin Wright on EM and ET. Christopher Peacocke's first response was valuable in clearing up misunderstandings between us and in other ways; and he showed great patience with my inability to meet deadlines.

and the like is essential to meaning; without those links our assertions and inferences would not properly be so called. However it is the relation between inferential and assertoric dispositions which will be our direct concern here.) It seems then that one ought to say that the meaning of a sentence is given by its assertion conditions *and its inferential power*; and *S* and *It is assertible that S* plainly differ in their inferential power.

II

'Anti-realism', in the current Dummettian sense, embraces two doctrines. I shall call them the epistemic conception of meaning (EM) and the epistemic conception of truth (ET). The first is the thesis that understanding the meaning of a sentence is constituted by grasping its assertion conditions—more fully, its assertion conditions and its inferential power. The second holds that truth is epistemically constrained. It equates truth with some concept of assertibility. Michael Dummett's anti-realist endorses both, and so does Crispin Wright's. But the connections are not obvious. I have argued elsewhere that Wittgensteinian considerations concerning meaning as use support the first thesis but in themselves provide no argument for the second.[1]

The point, if right, is central to the issue. For ET (as we shall see) seems to make it inevitable that the semantics of a sentence are given in terms of its assertion conditions; whereas EM, if divorceable from ET, leaves open the possibility that, in framing a semantic theory of sentence-contents, we may appeal to the concept of a truth-condition for a sentence—*without* identifying it with that of a condition under which assertion of the sentence is warranted. A position which in this way endorses EM without endorsing ET might, in other words, be able to recognize an independent role for the notion of a truth-condition in semantics, even while insisting, against the realist, that the notion is, philosophically speaking, derivative, not primitive. It will hold that our grasp of a sentence's truth-condition is constituted by our assertoric and inferential dispositions and cannot transcend them, but that that in itself does not force us to ET. Correspondingly it will not generate the philosophical critique of classical logic which is developed by Dummett's anti-realist.

These doctrines—that meaning is given by assertion conditions and inferential power, and that it is possible to divorce an epistemic conception of meaning from an epistemic conception of truth—are developed in what follows. In Sections III–V I discuss the need to divorce EM from ET and the possibility of doing so. I shall call the anti-realist who adopts EM while rejecting ET the 'EM theorist'. The EM theorist must give some account of compound sentences and in Sections VI–VII I consider what account he should give. I contrast his position with some of the arguments Dummett has presented for holding that anti-realism forces rejection of classical logic.

The distinction between EM and ET is in turn crucial for larger philosophical issues; concerning the relationship between anti-realism and idealism, and the tenability of an anti-realist defence of naturalism against Kantian critique. Sections VIII–IX explore whether there can be substantive a priori knowledge of the kind which the Kantian critique of naturalism requires, without the transcendental idealism which the Kantian thinks is presupposed by it. These epistemological issues lead us, in Section IX, to examine some aspects of Christopher Peacocke's recent work on the relation between what he calls 'acceptance conditions' and truth-conditions. Peacocke aims to show, for a range of concepts, how the acceptance conditions of contents in which those concepts feature determine the contents' truth-conditions; and in 'Understanding the Logical Constants' he applies this programme to the logical constants. In doing so he throws a sharply focused light on questions about our warrant for accepting logical principles, and about the relationship between understanding such a principle and having such a warrant—from an angle which will be congenial to anyone who believes that EM can and should be accepted without endorsement of ET.

Our discussion of Peacocke's approach will lead us into the question of the nature of realism. I have been assuming, in what I have just said, that the EM theorist's position is still a species of 'anti-realism'. This might well be questioned. Peacocke, for example, describes his account of the constants as realist precisely because it rejects ET; and the EM theorist rejects ET just as Peacocke does. I conclude in Section X by examining whether, and in what sense, someone who endorses EM while rejecting ET should still be regarded as rejecting a philosophical doctrine properly and significantly termed *realism*.

III

What relations hold between EM and ET? They may be thought to entail each other via the principle that to understand an assertoric sentence is to grasp what must be the case for it to be true—its truth-condition. What is asserted by the use of a sentence is that its truth-condition obtains. To assert that *p*, and to assert that it is true that *p*, is to make the same assertion.

The principle as I have stated it will immediately be denied by anyone who thinks that some assertions cannot be said to be true or false—for example moral or mathematical ones. But we can sidestep this issue. If these are genuine assertions they must in principle be liable to evaluation as being correct or otherwise, whether or not in practice we are able in particular cases so to evaluate them. The central function of assertions is to convey information and information conveyed must be assessable as correct or incorrect. So if one holds that truth is narrower than the generic concept of correctness (for reasons we will come to), one must still accept that the internal goal of assertion is *objective correctness*.

The principle then, put neutrally in respect of arguments about the extension of 'true', is that to understand an assertoric sentence is to grasp its correctness condition. Suppose now that we are given an independent argument for ET—where this is now understood broadly, as an epistemic reading of correctness of assertion. We can then argue to EM quite straightforwardly:

understanding meaning is grasping correctness conditions; correctness equates with assertibility, so understanding meaning is grasping assertion conditions. ET entails EM—more, it entails that the content of S is identical with the content of *It is assertible that S*. For if a sentence's content is given by what makes it correct, then assertion of the sentence is assertion that what makes it correct holds. And if 'what makes it correct' is understood epistemically—as 'what warrants assertion of the sentence'—we shall have to equate the contents of S and *It is assertible that S*.

There is, in contrast, no comparably straightforward argument from EM to ET. For suppose we are given an independent argument for EM. We might argue thus: if the meaning of a sentence is determined by assertion conditions, the content of an assertion of that sentence will be that its assertion conditions obtain. After all, what other feature of the sentence do we discern—on this view—in grasping its meaning? But since, by the uncontroversial principle, what is asserted is that the truth- (or correctness) condition obtains, this must equate with assertion conditions.

In this argument, however, the thesis that under EM the content of S must be identical with the content of *It is assertible that S* is a premiss, not a conclusion. It is supported only by the rhetorical question of the previous paragraph. Given the thesis, ET will follow from EM. But must the EM theorist accept it?

The rhetorical question has force, and the EM theorist must find a way of answering it if he wishes to avoid the thesis. In fact there is every reason for him to wish to avoid it, because it leads to disaster. For it is evident that, to take just one among many possible examples, *It is not the case that S* and *It is not the case that it is assertible that S* do not have the same assertion conditions. So even on a view which determines content by assertion conditions, S and *It is assertible that S* cannot make the same contribution to the content of complex sentences in which they are embedded.

The alternatives are (i) that S and *It is assertible that S* have different content or (ii) that matching complex sentences in which they appear have different content even though they themselves do not. (ii) must be rejected; this much compositionality is inevitable. We can draw two conclusions:

> S and *It is assertible that S* differ in content, even though they have the same assertion conditions;
>
> the doctrine that assertion conditions of complex sentences are functions of the assertion conditions of their constituents is false. (Call it the doctrine of assertion-functionality.)

IV

The defender of EM must find a way of coping with these points. But if he arrives at EM by means of ET then he cannot do so. This is the predicament of the 'ET theorist'. Since he gets to EM via ET, he is forced to equate understanding with grasp of assertion conditions alone. One might think of this as the intuitionistic, or perhaps, positivist, route to EM. I believe that it should be distinguished from the Wittgensteinian (or possibly pragmatist) route. The visibility of this latter approach is central to the issues and we must devote some space to elaborating it further.

Wittgensteinian or pragmatist lines of thought can lead us to EM quite independently of ET. The essential insight is encapsulated in the slogan that 'meaning is use':[2] there can be no more to the understanding of an expression than is constituted by the practice which embodies it. Practice means inferential as well as assertoric practice. What I understand by S is constituted (abstracting from the further constitutive link with action) by (i) what pairs, respectively of experimental input and existing beliefs, I recognize as rationalizing in some degree the addition of S to my beliefs and (ii) what further modifications in my beliefs I would recognize as rationalized if S were allowed in.

The suggestion then is that if we recognize that the meaning of a sentence is not just a matter of its assertion conditions, but of the role it plays in inference, we can accept that the meaning of S and *It is assertible that S* will differ—since their inferential powers differ. But is this not sleight of hand? Any information state that forces S must force *It is assertible that S*, and vice versa. And is not the basic concept for the EM theorist that of what is warranted in an information state? So how can *he* explain the difference in the inferential power of the two sentences? Is he not borrowing intuitions that he has no right to?

I have said that the internal goal of assertion is objective correctness, where this is a wider notion than that of truth. It ought to be uncontroversial that moral and mathematical assertions aim at objective correctness, but it is quite rightly not uncontroversial that they aim at truth. For truth involves the idea of an object ontologically independent of the knower, or more precisely, of his particular knowing, which interacts intelligibly with that knowing but can have facets other than those he knows. It is far from obvious that there could be any such objects in the moral or the mathematical realm.

That debate is about mathematical or moral 'realism', in one perfectly good sense of the term—we shall come back to its links with the general notion of philosophical realism in Section X. But whatever one may think about mathematical or moral truth, the arguably thinner notion of objective correctness which applies across the whole field of genuinely assertoric discourse at least requires this much: that there should be a distinction between whether the reasoner is (epistemically) *justified* in his assertion, and whether the assertion is itself *correct*. The two notions are distinct but tied together; where the latter, that of objective correctness, has no place, neither has the former, that of epistemic justificaton—the very notion of a rational warrant for assertion presupposes an ideal of correctness at which assertions aim; while the ideal of correctness is empty if we can never be warranted (if only provisionally) in holding ourselves to have attained it.

Where we regard a field of discourse as properly assertoric, rather than merely expressive or fictional, we must accept that the notion of objective correctness is in place. What puts that notion in play? In recognizing the field of discourse as assertoric, we accept that enlarged information states may produce successive sets of warranted assertions—which contain assertions not contained in a previous set, or do not contain assertions contained in a previous set. So an enlarged information state, while still warranting the assertion that *S* was indeed assertible in a previous information state, may no longer warrant the assertion then expressed by *S*, or may even force the conclusion that that assertion was incorrect.

If we further introduce the ontic notion of truth referred to three paragraphs ago, that is, the picture of a domain with which the knowing subject interacts, something more becomes intelligible; namely, that there should be truths which no knowing subject is, or in empirical fact *could be*, justified in asserting. For there must be concrete limitations on the interactions possible for *any* particular empirical knower. However even the notion of objective correctness, uninflated into truth, gives the EM theorist materials for distinguishing the inferential power of *S* and *It is assertible that S*, and their respective role in negations or conditionals—just because it compels a distinction between objectively correct and epistemically warranted assertions.

That in turn gives reason for rejecting the deducibility of *S* from *It is assertible that S*, and vice versa, since we require deductive inference to preserve correctness indefeasibly (that is, under all enlargements of information up to those which—granting empiricism about logic—force a change of logic). Inferences from *S* to *It is assertible that S* and vice versa can be guaranteed to preserve assertibility relative to a given information state, but they cannot be relied upon to preserve correctness—given that a warranted assertion may be defeated in an enlarged information state.

A weaker notion of inferability requires only that the inference should be correctness-preserving—not indefeasibly so. If the assertion of a conditional is the assertion that such an inferability relation holds, we shall not hold the assertor to be committed to the conditional's assertibility in every *possible* enlargement of his information state up to a change of logic. On the other hand he still does, in making the assertion, commit himself to something like its continuing assertibility in enlarged information states which will *in fact* ensue, or could *in fact* be achieved—or at least to its survival 'in the long run stable state'. The exact nature of this commitment is a delicate issue, which cannot be teased out further here. But certainly a state of evidence and argument which undermines all confidence in a proposition's assertibility in future information states must also undermine the present warrant for making it.

Consider then the conditional *If S then it is assertible that S*. The consequent is indexical. To assert the conditional, I would have to be confident that in any future state in which I shall be justified in asserting (what is now asserted by utterance of) *S*, I shall be justified in asserting what is *now* asserted by utterance of *It is assertible that S*. But *S* may not now be assertible; in which case, I shall never in future be justified in making the assertion presently made by utterance of *It is assertible that S*.

The position is more complicated with *If it is assertible that S then S*, given that holding *S* to be assertible involves some sort of commitment to the future assertibility of (what is now asserted by utterance of) *S*. But any account of this commitment must at least allow that I can be more confident of the future assertibility of the antecedent than of the consequent: we know that unexpected evidence can come in, and therefore cannot unrestrictedly assert conditionals of this form.

So the EM theorist, starting from the notions of a warranted assertion and its defeasibility, is led to recognize a notion of objective correctness distinct from warranted assertion. Let us now call that feature of sentences which determines their contribution to the meaning of sentences in which they are embedded their *semantic content*. Semantic content is what is captured by a semantic theory—by denotation rules for atoms and compositional rules by which these build up into conditions of correctness—*not* of justified assertion—for sentences. So the semantic content of a sentence is given by its correctness condition and is a function of the correctness conditions of its constituents. Semantic theory captures the structure of a language and semantic content is that feature of a sentence's meaning which it has in virtue of its structural place in the language.

In contrast we shall refer to what is understood when a sentence is understood as its *cognitive role*. Cognitive role is correlative with understanding, where understanding is constituted by appropriate assertoric and inferential dispositions.

Note that cognitive role is a normative notion: the cognitive role of a sentence is determined by when it is rightly assertible and what sound inferences it can appear in. The epistemic conception of meaning is a conception of cognitive role. A theory of semantic content for a particular language would systematically specify correctness conditions for sentences of the language—the EM theorist is not objecting to such a theory; he is engaged in a different, purely philosophical, project which is that of showing what it is for a sentence to have semantic content by showing how content is determined by cognitive role.

V

There being nothing to constitute understanding beyond assertoric and inferential practice (linked to action), one might think it a truism that cognitive role is the primary notion of meaning in terms of which semantic content must be understood. But cognitive role, as we have noted, is given normatively. It specifies the correct use of a sentence or expression. To say it is primary is to say that understanding is constituted by grasp of correct use; and this is different from saying that it is constituted by the brute facts of behaviour and physiological process. Why, it might be asked, introduce such a notion at all? Why have an intermediate level, of assertoric and inferential ability, between the brute facts and the hermeneutic level of semantic content? If we are allowing that a grasp of normative principles constitutes understanding, why not simply say that what constitutes understanding is grasp of semantic content—the semantic rules which guide correct practice? On this minimalist view the theory of semantic content is all we need; there is no further meaningful dispute between realist and anti-realist conceptions of meaning as to the status of that theory.

Once we have eliminated ET from our version of anti-realism do we still have a real dispute about the nature of meaning at all—whether or not it is properly called a dispute about realism? We are certainly manœuvring in a very tight space; but there is still a real issue at stake. It turns on the sense in which grasp of semantic content *explains* correct use. As a first approximation: the realist thinks that grasp of a sentence's correctness condition *underlies* and thereby explains grasp of its assertion conditions and its inferential power; whereas the EM theorist, on the contrary, thinks it is simply *constituted* by grasp of assertion conditions and inferential power. But this can only be a first approximation, because the EM theorist in some sense must also agree that grasp of assertion conditions and inferential power is explained by grasp of semantic content, that is correctness condition. The difference in cognitive role between *S* and *It is assertible that S*, and hence their different contribution to the cognitive role of complex sentences in which they appear, turned on our possession of a distinction between justified assertibility and objective correctness. But grasping inferential power is a matter of grasping what can be relied upon to preserve objective correctness. It therefore requires a grasp of correctness conditions.

So both EM theorist and realist agree that grasp of semantic content is genuinely explanatory. What then is the difference between them? From the EM theorist's perspective it is, that while he accepts an empirical sense in which grasp of use is explained by grasp of semantic content, he rejects the metaphysical picture which, he alleges, the realist associates with it. The picture will be considered further in Section X. But it might immediately be countered that a more obvious problem arises for the EM theorist—if correct assertoric and inferential dispositions are what constitute grasp of a sentence's correctness-condition, how can they be guided by it?

These are essentially the terms of the rule-following problem: if mastery of proper practice constitutes grasp of a rule, how can grasp of the rule explain that practice? How, for example, can my understanding of a formula explain my expansion of the series it determines? (In what sense does it determine it?).

When I say that I wrote these numbers down because they are in accordance with the formula for the series I have certainly given an explanation of why I wrote them. I grasp the formula and I thereby see what it requires in particular cases. Similarly with 'I stopped because I saw the light was red and I know one should stop when the light is red'. Or 'I inferred *q* because I saw that *p* and *p* implies *q*'. In each case there is a grasp of a norm and of what it requires in a particular case: these are normative explanations. They explain, we say, by reference to the agent's *recognition* of the application of a norm to a particular case.

The temptation at this point is to succumb to a relational model of that recognition. Normativity or rationality is transmuted into knowledge of logical or semantic or moral objects, known by semantic, logical, or moral intuition.

Certainly the formula represents the series. I am able to tell whether a number belongs to the series because I grasp what the formula represents. Similarly the sentence represents a set of possible worlds. I am able to tell whether a world belongs to the set because I grasp what the sentence represents. But what does 'because I can tell what it represents' mean in these cases? My practice responds to an objective requirement, practical, theoretical, or semantic. There is a powerful tendency to see that as the tracking of an entity—a 'rule-object', or 'pure meaning'—which I intuit and which tells me how to go on. This is the metaphysical explanation of use. (The temptation is strengthened by the 'Now I can go on' experience. Is an infinitary feat of imagination or intuition rolled into an instant, or do I suddenly discern the rule-object?)

In this metaphysical explanation my cognitive or practical dispositions are thought of as having a certain kind of categorical base—a state of relational awareness of a rule. But no such state could do the explanatory work required of it. There is no epiphany in which a self-interpreting entity reveals its meaning. No entity to which I could stand in the relation of awareness—physical, mental, or abstract—could do that. (The existence or otherwise of mental or abstract objects is not the central issue.) We are looking for something on the hermeneutic level when we have gone beyond the hermeneutic level. We come to the limits of interpretation with the ability. Its base is not, and could not be, hermeneutically intelligible.

A possible response to this line of thought is scepticism about objectivity as such. This is not the response the anti-realist relies on; it would knock out any philosophical account of understanding and inference, realist or anti-realist, because any such account is inherently normative. The point rather is that an answer which avoids scepticism, if it is possible at all, requires one to appreciate the primacy of cognitive role: training in what is correct, and corrigibility in one's practice, perhaps sensitivity to the speech-community's ideal consensus, are all the materials that suffice for normativity. A corrigible and converging practice is all that normativity requires and the most it can get.

Semantic content cannot transcend practice, but on this view, as against the rule-sceptic's, it can be immanent in it. We assert 'He understands the correctness condition of *S*' when we believe that his dispositions are sufficiently tuned to correct practice and that mistakes in his performance are explicable in a way which does not impugn his competence and is autonomously correctible. Grasp of the correctness condition is the 'default' explanation—a statement having the form of explanation which it is correct to give by default when practice is broadly in line with competence and no substantial deviant explanation is forced. However it does not *underlie* competence: it is not the categorical base grounding the dispositions which constitute competence. Rather, it is another way of characterizing competence.

The anti-realist gets his argument from a non-sceptical response to rule-scepticism. We are not here considering the very real and difficult question of how such a non-sceptical response can be made to stick. The point we are stressing is that any response which *can* be made to stick must also vindicate an empirical level at which practice is explained by rules.

In the special case of semantic rules framed in terms of truth-conditions there will be further points to note. Where a sentence has a truth-condition there is a picture of a state of affairs which corresponds to it. The picture of the state of affairs is not itself a picture of assertion conditions and inferential powers. Constructive imagination plays an essential empirical role. If I try to explain to you what it is to be afraid, I don't give you an account of assertion conditions for an ascription of fear, and predictions licensed by such an ascription; I say 'It's what you'd feel if you saw your daughter wandering towards a precipice'. *This* psychological reality should not be denied. But the essential point will be that the content of pictures is entirely exhausted by their control of assertion conditions and inferential roles.

These issues must all figure prominently on the EM theorist's agenda; but they are not our topic here. We are outlining the EM theorist's general stance. He recognizes that a person's dispositions can of course be explained by reference to his grasp of a rule; what he rejects is a philosophical mis-interpretation to which such an explanation very naturally gives rise. This misinterpretation pictures the rule-follower as tracking a self-interpreting entity which guides his behaviour; it is at the heart of the realist conception of meaning. On this realist view, grasp of truth-conditions is philosophically primitive: it *grounds* the thinker's assertoric and inferential dispositions and is not constituted by them. In the epistemic conception of meaning, on the other hand, there is no such primitive ground. In that sense the dispositions are *not* explained. The primitive level is that of cognitive role, not that of semantic content. However, recognizing these points does not entail replacing one metaphysical picture of the role of truth and truth-conditions by another equally metaphysical one such as ET. Truth can play an independent empirical role in the theory of semantic content. And that theory can play an empirical role in providing a semantic interpretation of our assertoric and inferential dis-positions. The task of the EM theorist is to get a really clear view of this dialectical relationship between cognitive role and semantic content. In particular, he must of course explain in some detail and in specific cases how cognitive role determines semantic content. Our concern in this discussion however is with the general implications of his position for the epistemology of logic, and the sense in which those implications involve a rejection of philosophical realism. We approach these issues through a closer look at the EM theorist's treatment of the constants, and his relation to semantic 'holism'.

VI

The EM theorist takes assertion condition and inferential power as equally primitive components of cognitive role. In contrast, the intuitionistic anti-realist, as described by Michael Dummett, holds that inferential power must in some sense be grounded in assertion conditions—just as the realist holds that it must in some sense be grounded in truth-conditions. Both the realist and the Dummettian anti-realist think that an independent notion of content, given before inferential power, determines or explains, and in doing so justifies, inferential power. Both agree that the phenomena of meaning are to be explained in terms of a single key concept, that of the conditions under which a sentence makes a correct assertion. But where the realist identifies these conditions with conditions of truth, the anti-realist as portrayed by Dummett identifies them with conditions for warranted assertion.

Dummett compares philosophers who assume that the theory of meaning 'has some one key concept', be it that of truth or of verification, with Wittgenstein. Wittgenstein, he suggests, may be interpreted as rejecting the idea that there must be one key concept; or perhaps alternatively, he may be interpreted as holding that the key concept lies not 'on the side of the *grounds* for an utterance ... but on the side of its *consequences*', that is, the appropriate responses of hearers, and the commitments the speaker enters into by uttering it.[3]

Of course those who hold, perhaps against Wittgenstein, that meaning is to be characterized by one key concept are not denying that sentences have a variety of features of use; but they consider that there should be some 'uniform pattern of derivation' whereby these other features of the meaning of a sentence can be derived from its meaning as determined in terms of the key concept. A main strength of their approach, Dummett holds, is that it opens up a framework within which the meaning of sentences can be described compositionally, as a function of the meaning of their constituent expressions—the meaning of these being thought of in turn contextually, as their contribution to sentence meaning.

The idea that there is a 'key concept' for the theory of meaning—viz. the notion of a sentence's condition of correctness—and the identification of correctness with warranted or justified assertion, are two basic elements in the Dummettian anti-realist's thinking. Other ingredients are the epistemic conception of truth, the idea that deduction stands in need of a certain kind of justification, an opposition to 'holism' about meaning, and endorsement of intuitionistic semantics and rejection of classical logic.

But if our arguments hitherto are accepted, this syndrome will seem to have a central flaw: it does not distinguish perspicuously between the levels of cognitive role and semantic content. Certainly there is important common ground between the EM theorist, and the positions developed by Dummett and Wright. For both the latter have accepted unequivocally the appropriateness of casting semantic theory in truth-conditional terms, while both continue to argue, against the minimalist, that a more full-blooded level of theory is required, at which the insight that meaning is use receives due recognition. Up to that point their line of thought coincides with the EM theorist's. But Dummett and Wright think of this full-blooded theory as giving directly epistemic readings to semantic concepts—truth as assertibility, or satisfaction clauses in terms of criteria of application.

By contrast, the EM theorist brings the distinction between objective correctness and warranted assertion into centre stage. Semantic theory, the theory of semantic content, does indeed require a key concept, and it is indeed the notion of a correctness condition that is required. But that concept must be distinguished from the notion of justified assertion, for the reasons canvassed in Sections IV and V. The notion of justified, as against correct, assertion does not and cannot enter directly at this level. Whereas on the level at which it does enter, it enters jointly with the notion of inferential power. (Compare Brandom, Kremer.) At that level, it will not be true that inferential power is 'justified' in terms of conditions of assertibility. But since assertion conditions and inferential power jointly determine semantic content, it will not be true that an epistemic justification of deductive principles, as against a semantic validation, can be provided at the level of semantic content either.

The difference between the two approaches comes out most clearly in relation to the doctrine of assertion-functionality. A cluster of issues centres on that doctrine; in particular, Dummett's account of the sense in which a justification of deduction is required is closely associated with it. We shall examine the arguments to assertion-functionality more closely in this section. The EM theorist's position has interesting points in common with what Dummett has called 'holism'. In the next section, Section VII, we shall consider what the common points are and where they differ.

It we are given ET, the argument to assertion-functionality is obvious. For if truth[4] is assertibility, then truth-functional connectives are assertion-functional connectives—the truth-functionality of the constants reduces to their assertion-functionality. But what gives ET? There could be a variety of sources.

One would flow from a conflation of correctness and justified assertion. For if the theory of meaning has a 'key concept' and if justified assertion is that key concept, then truth must be either marginalized, as irrelevant to meaning, or it must be identified with justified assertion. But as we noted at the outset, it is a platitude that understanding the meaning of a (factual) sentence is understanding what makes it true—and that forces the second option.

We have considered at length the EM theorist's response to this. But a more direct argument to ET is quite simply that verification-transcendent truth is unintelligible. At one level this is an old idea in philosophy which can be traced to various perennial metaphysical or epistemological sources. But Dummett has given the idea a new setting by connecting it with the Wittgensteinian idea that a grasp of any conceptual content is fully 'manifested' in its use. The suggestion is that epistemic constraints on truth follow from this idea, because grasp of verification-transcendent truth cannot be manifested or acquired. However, the doctrine that understanding is constituted by a set of assertoric and inferential abilities (appropriately linked to action) can be made to yield an epistemic conception of truth only if very strong assumptions about what constitutes grasp of a concept or a sentence-content are fed in. It has to be argued, in particular, that *only* the ability to recognize a truth-condition as obtaining when one is directly presented with it can constitute grasp of a truth-condition. There might well be scope for the critic of realism to hold that the *realist* is committed to this very strong claim, because of his conception of truth-conditions and of their relation to meaning on the one hand and evidence on the other; and thus to force realism towards an untenable reductivist position. But there is no ground for the anti-realist himself to endorse it.[5]

However, while ET does not follow from 'meaning is use' we have recognized that EM does. If there is an argument from EM to assertion-functionality we will have to accept it too. Is there such an argument?

There are outlines of it in Dummett's writings. If sentence-meaning is fixed by assertion conditions then that applies to complex sentences too. Dummett's anti-realist wants to implement this approach in a way which recognizes that sentence and constituent meaning are related contextually and compositionally. It then seems to follow that

> *We no longer explain the sense of a statement by stipulating its truth-value in terms of the truth-values of its constituents, but by stipulating when it may be asserted in terms of the conditions under which its constituents may be asserted.*[6]
> (Italics in the original)

When this is applied to the particular case of the logical constants, we are led to reject classical logic. This particular argument is quite independent of ET, and hence it seems to apply even to the EM theorist who rejects ET.

My understanding of a complex sentence must be related uniformly to my understanding of its constituents. That is indisputable. But in itself such compositionality says nothing about the *direction* in which understanding flows—it remains an open possibility that when operators which form new complex sentences are introduced into a language, the new rules governing their use may interact with existing rules, in such fashion as to modify the cognitive role of all sentences in the initial language. There may be that much truth in 'holism'; but it must still be true that cognitive roles of complex and constituent are held together in a determinate linguistic structure. The language-user's grasp of the assertion conditions for a complex sentence must be uniformly related to his understanding of its constituents. Otherwise he might understand the constituents, understand the operator, and still have an imperfect grasp of the complex sentence's cognitive role.

This much the EM theorist must accept. But it does not force him to attempt an assertion-functional account of the connectives. He is free to appeal to the truth-conditions of constituent sentences in giving an account of the cognitive role of complex sentences which the connectives are used to construct, because he holds that those truth-conditions crystallize the assertoric and inferential dispositions which constitute cognitive role. So long, therefore, as an account of how the cognitive role of constituent sentences determines their truth-conditions is available in principle, constituent truth-conditions can be appealed to in an account of the assertion conditions of the complex sentence. Let us carry this thought through for negation, implication, and disjunction.

Suppose I am given the standard rule

'Not-p' is true iff 'p' is not true.

Then I can infer that

'Not-p' is assertible iff it is assertible that 'p' is not true.

So I grasp the assertion conditions of a negation and the contribution made by the constituent sentence in it—via grasping the truth-condition of the constituent sentence. Similarly for the conditional. Given the rule

'If p then q' is true iff if 'p' is true, 'q' is true (iff the inference from 'p' to 'q' preserves truth)

I can infer that

'If p then q' is assertible iff there is evidence warranting the assertion that if 'p' is true, 'q' is true (warranting acceptance that the inference from 'p' to 'q' preserves truth).

Once again, given that we have an account of the truth-conditions of antecedent and consequent, as determined by their cognitive role, there is no obstacle to appealing to their truth-conditions in giving an account of the assertion conditions of the conditional.

What about disjunction? The standard rule here is

'p or q' is true iff 'p' is true or 'q' is true.

If I know the rule I can infer

'p or q' is assertible iff there is evidence warranting the assertion that 'p' is true or 'q' is true.

Contrast the 'intuitionistic' clause for disjunction.

'p or q' is assertible iff there is evidence warranting the assertion that 'p' is true or there is evidence warranting the assertion that 'q' is true.

Here the assertion conditions for a disjunction are determined directly in terms of assertion conditions for its disjuncts. The result flies counter to the facts of use. There may be evidence that a disjunction holds without specific evidence being available for a particular disjunct. (If the criminal has been seen entering the house, we are justified in inferring that he is in one of the rooms.) Similar points could be made about intuitionistic negation and the intuitionistic conditional. The EM theorist grounds his position on an appeal to the insight that meaning is use. So he is unlikely to endorse an account of the constants which flies in the face of use. This is not a global sanctification of existing conceptual practice—it is not being denied that philosophical reflection as such may and does alter use (for example about the nature and limits of responsibility). Use may turn out to be out of harmony with itself and open to 'immanent critique'. But the EM theorist holds that sentences have assertion conditions only in the context of an inferential practice which embodies principles of inference determining what states of evidence justify assertion of a sentence. And he sees no scope for a purely philosophical critique of that practice.[7]

Given an understanding of 'p', I have an understanding of 'not-p'—so long as I can recognize the conditions which warrant denial of 'p' (that is assertion that 'p' is not true). The truth-condition for 'not-p' is determined by the truth-condition of '*p*'. But that does not hold for its assertion condition; I cannot, from the assertion condition of a given sentence, mechanically derive the assertion condition for its denial; and hence neither can I derive the condition for assertion of its negation. But there is nothing in the principle of compositionality which requires that *semantics* for the negation operator should themselves equip me with the ability to recognize when denial of any arbitrary sentence *p* is justified. A semantic theory for English tells me that the correct way to negate an English sentence '*p*' is by saying *It is not the case that p*. It registers the semantic complexity of negations by delivering truth-conditions for negations as a function of truth-conditions of the sentences negated. In doing so it enshrines the substantive principle that negation of *p* is justified just if denial of *p* is. But it has no mission to tell me any more than that.

Of course on the EM theorist's view, we must still supply an account of my understanding of what negation is, that is, of the *cognitive role* of 'It is not the case that ...', and this will have to proceed in terms of my assertoric and inferential dispositions in relation to negations. We return to this in Section IX. But it remains perfectly open for the EM theorist to hold that those dispositions are such as to fix the semantic value of 'It is not the case that ...' in terms of its classical truth-table.

The same goes for implication and disjunction. The standard clauses tell me that the way to express these relations is by sentences of the form *If p then q* and *p or q*; and they register the semantic complexity of such sentences by yielding their truth-conditions from the truth-conditions of their constituents. In doing so, they enshrine substantive principles of truth, which must be traced back at the level of cognitive role to our actual assertoric and inferential dispositions. However, recognizing this complexity is all that semantic theory is asked to do. There is no requirement that a semantic account of the corresponding connectives should by itself give me the power of telling when arbitrary pairs of sentences, '*p*' and '*q*', can be justifiably held to stand in relations of inferability or disjunction.

VII

Our conclusion is that the principle of compositionality does not require the EM theorist to give an assertion-functional account of the constants. We have taken for granted standard semantic clauses in giving an account of the compositionality of cognitive role; but so long as the classical principles of truth which they embody are determined by the actual assertoric and inferential use of language-users, there can be no objection.

This is not to ignore the epistemological question, of what justifies us in accepting the inferential principles which are in fact enshrined in use. The question is legitimate and it requires an answer. We shall approach it in Sections VIII and IX, where it will be argued that certain principles can be said to be 'self-justifying', or 'justified but groundless' inasmuch as they enter into determining the cognitive role of the connectives; their status is, in a sense to be explained, 'weakly a priori'. That may sound much like what Dummett has referred to as 'linguistic holism'.[8]

On a 'molecular' view of language, Dummett holds, there is a sense in which one can envisage a justification of deductive rules of inference. They are justified

> precisely by ... the fact ... that they remain faithful to the individual contents
> of the sentences which occur in any deduction carried out in accordance with
> them.[9]

In a realist context, their faithfulness is demonstrated by a semantic validation which establishes that the rules of inference preserve truth in all models. But in an anti-realist context, where the central semantic concept is that of assertibility, the notion of 'faithfulness' is implemented by requiring that the introduction of a constant should extend the language conservatively. That is, it should not give a warrant for asserting sentences which are free of that constant and for which, prior to the constant's introduction, no warrant could have been obtained. The constants and their associated proof-theoretic rules should be conservative relative to assertibility.

The 'holist' does not ask for any such justification of deduction. He holds that our forms of deductive inference are part of the linguistic practice which shapes the meaning of each sentence and is therefore uninterested in a requirement of conservative extension.

With this the EM theorist agrees. He agrees in particular that sentences cannot have cognitive roles outside the context of spontaneous inferential dispositions: those dispositions are partially constitutive of the cognitive roles. He further agrees that such dispositions, or the inferential principles which express them, are in no sense justified by 'faithfulness' to an antecedently or independently determined content.

However Dummett's contrast between molecularist and holist is stated in a framework which makes no distinction between the level of cognitive role and semantic content, and takes assertibility as the central directly *semantic* concept. Thus the challenge as presented by Dummett is either to present a compositional semantics in terms of that central concept of assertibility, or with the holist, to reject the possibility of compositional semantics. It is here that the common ground between Dummett's holist and the EM theorist comes to an end. For the EM theorist distinguishes between the theory of semantic content, whose key concept is truth, and the theory of cognitive role, where the central concepts are those of assertibility and inferential power. Having made this distinction he can show how the assertion conditions of compound sentences formed by means of the connectives are grasped compositionally, as we saw in the last section.

'On a holistic view,' according to Dummett,

> no model for the individual content of a sentence can be given: we cannot
> grasp the representative power of any one sentence save by a complete grasp
> of the linguistic propensities underlying our use of the entire language; and

when we have such a grasp of the whole, there is no way in which this can be systematised so as to give us a clear view of the contribution of any particular part of the apparatus.[10]

The EM theorist will not agree that 'no model for the individual content of a sentence can be given'. When we are considering the 'representative power' of a sentence we are considering it at the level of semantic content. The sentence as representation is precisely meaning seen from the aspect of semantic content, and the semantics of a language can be systematically described. A systematic theory of semantic content provides a focused picture of the vertebral structure by which the cognitive roles of sentences in a language are linked.

It also provides the materials for a semantic validation of deduction. However, the EM theorist again agrees with the holist that such validation in no sense constitutes a philosophical justification of deduction. He makes no claim to provide a semantic 'justification' of deduction in assertibilist terms, by requiring that extensions effected by introducing a new operator should be conservative relative to assertibility. He is satisfied with the simple requirement that deduction should indefeasibly preserve truth.

It is not only deductive principles which on his view shape cognitive role. The *whole* fabric of spontaneous inferential dispositions shapes our understanding of the sentences of a language, and that includes inductive as well as deductive dispositions. Consider the simple case of a language in which assertion of universal sentences is warranted only by exhaustive enumeration of instances, or by a deductive proof that all instances are true. Suppose we introduce the rule of enumerative induction. That makes a difference to the cognitive role of the word 'all'; nor is the new rule conservative in relation to assertibility. It becomes, for example, justified to assert 'Margaret Thatcher is mortal' even though she is still alive.

The standard rules of natural deduction do not exhaust the possible ways in which disjunctions and conditionals can get into our fabric of belief. Existential and universal sentences are introduced via inductive generalization and inference to the best hypothesis (with its dependence on analogical reasoning), and these generate whole new stocks of disjunctions and conditionals. Such inductive reasoning expands the stock of accepted general sentences as banks create money. Unless the EM theorist is wedded to positivism he must take account of this theoretical expansion in his account of the cognitive roles of a whole range of specific concepts, as well as of structural words like 'all'.

VIII

If the position we have described is coherent it has important implications for issues which lie at the heart of philosophy; bringing together epistemology, metaphysics and the theory of meaning. They bear on the epistemological critique of naturalism, a more or less central crux of philosophy since Kant.

According to Kant naturalism entails that no proposition having genuine cognitive content is a priori. But that conclusion makes knowledge impossible; and Kant is thereby led to the rejection of naturalism in favour of transcendental idealism.

On the epistemic conception of meaning, we begin to see the possibility of a genuinely naturalistic response to Kant. The response will be that there is a suppressed premiss in the argument to the impossibility of knowledge: it is the 'realism' which the epistemic conception of meaning rejects. We shall be discussing just what is rejected in Section X, and the appropriateness of calling it realism; a less commital term for the position rejected would be 'the Classical Pre-understanding of Meaning'. I call it a 'pre-understanding' because it is in no sense a conscious assumption of classical epistemology (that is, roughly, from Descartes to Kant and nineteenth-century idealism). Nor could one imaginatively 'reconstruct' the classical epistemologist as recognizing it when formulated: its significance can be recognized only when alternatives come to be clearly stated. It is also true—as with any philosophical thesis which is a candidate for deflationary dissolution—that the very attempt to pin it down explicitly tends to dispel it into thin air. But we can put the point negatively: when the epistemic conception of meaning sinks in, naturalism can no longer appear to create an epistemological impasse. The unstated pre-understanding is a knot to be untied.

Many questions are raised by this line of thought; not least, whether it really constitutes an *alternative* to idealism. If it does not, naturalism has not been genuinely rescued from its Kantian critics. Of course the question is much too big to be addressed in the space of this essay! We shall focus here on a single issue—the Kantian doctrine of the synthetic a priori. The line of thought we are considering turns on distinguishing what is good in that doctrine from what is bad. That in turn requires us to distinguish a weak and a strong sense of a priori. A proposition is strongly a priori if a strongly a priori justification is available for it, and weakly a priori if only a weakly a priori justification is available. A justification is strongly a priori if (1) we are justified in holding that no train of experience would *overturn*[11] it, and (2) it is a priori in the weak sense. In the weak sense, a justification is a priori if it is 'prior to', or 'independent of' empirical investigation. It is, one may say, groundless—not conditional on any empirical ground. But it need not be empirically indefeasible; that is, the prospect of its overturn by future empirical inquiry (however indirect or theoretically mediated) need not be ruled out.

Let *empiricism* be the epistemological thesis that no real proposition, no proposition with genuine cognitive content, is strongly a priori.[12] The empiricist can accept that there is a class of merely apparent, or verbal propositions, which convey no information (other than pragmatically about the meanings of words), and which are strongly a priori; minimally, the corresponding conditionals of the class of merely apparent inferences, in which the conclusion is literally asserted in the premisses. Whether these are more than an uninteresting limiting case will depend on one's views on such matters as the nature of definition and the existence of synonymy. For those who are unpersuaded by Quine's famous polemic against synonymy the class of merely apparent propositions will be larger than for those who are; but in either case most of logic and mathematics will have to count as real. In combination with empiricism, this produces radical empiricism about logic and maths, of which Mill, from whom I have borrowed the terms 'real', and 'merely apparent', or 'verbal', is the founding figure.

Mill would agree with Kant that naturalism must entail that no real proposition is a priori; where they would disagree is on whether the result is scepticism or a radically empiricist reconstruction of knowledge. But at this point the distinction between strong and weak a priori is relevant. Naturalism does indeed imply that are are no *strongly* a priori real propositions. All assertions are empirically defeasible—none can be insulated from empirical inquiry. But does naturalism rule out the weak a priori? Well—how could the spontaneous impression that a rule of reasoning is correct *make* it correct? The question is insistently posed by Mill, and his answer is that it cannot do so. But for the EM theorist that negative conclusion is too strong—it does not follow, as Mill thought, from naturalism alone. A further distinction is required between what makes a principle correct—its truth-condition—and what justifies acceptance of it. We shall return to it: its import is that naturalism only entails the *defeasibility* of all our claims to justified belief. It is not naturalism, but realism, which makes it unintelligible that a spontaneous impression of correctness should justify us in holding a principle correct.

In this respect, the position of the EM theorist can be compared with that of the Fregean as well as the Millian realist. Both the latter hold that logic is a science, both hold its basic laws to be the classical laws of truth. The Millian holds the laws to be a posteriori; while the Fregean holds them to be strongly a priori.[13] Where the epistemic conception differs from both is in holding that there can and must be weakly a priori principles. Spontaneous principles of reasoning enter into the constitution of meaning, and the very possibility of language—because a common assertoric practice presupposes a spontaneously shared inferential practice.

Are there sentences which express weakly a priori principles? If there are, is that because they can in some sense be said to be 'true by virtue of their meaning'? If so, in what sense? We shall discuss these questions with special reference to the logical constants; but it should not be assumed that our answers are applicable to principles of logic alone—similar points could be made about certain principles in geometry or arithmetic, perhaps also to framework principles in scientific inquiry such as determinism or assumptions of conservation and continuity.

IX

Before considering the questions directly I should like to take account of a programme pursued by Christopher Peacocke: I believe it has a number of points in common with the argument of this essay. The programme has been developed by Peacocke with great subtlety and care in a series of detailed studies.[14] In his paper 'Understanding Logical Constants', he is concerned with the logical constants and raises in a precise and illuminating way all of the issues which concern us. Yet on the fundamental epistemological questions which we have just raised, and on the interrelated question of the nature of realism, the relationship between Peacocke's position and that of the 'EM theorist' as developed here is I think not altogether easy to define. By focusing on what is, at least to me, an area of unclarity we shall be led to a sharper statement of those issues themselves. Let us first spell out some common points.

I have distinguished between cognitive role and semantic content as two aspects of meaning, taking cognitive role to be fixed by assertoric and inferential dispositions. Peacocke similarly remarks that

> There are two dimensions to the propositional content of a given sentence or of a given mental state. On the one hand, there is a dimension which carries information about such matters as the conditions which may lead a thinker to accept such a content, and its consequences in thought once accepted. On the other hand, there is the truth-condition of the content. . . .[15]

The grounds which justify a person in accepting a content, and the commitments he enters into by accepting it, are called by Peacocke its 'acceptance conditions'; as he points out, a

> question then arises about the relation between these two dimensions of content: what, in general, is the relation between a content's acceptance conditions and its truth condition?[16]

Peacocke's general answer is that the contents of thought are constituted by their 'acceptance conditions'; he puts forward the conjecture that acceptance conditions determine truth-conditions and his programme consists in developing analyses which confirm the conjecture in detail for particular types of contents.

His starting point is Dummett's 'manifestationism', that is to say, the requirement that every feature of meaning be manifestable in use. The term 'manifestation' is not a happy one; it gives the requirement an epistemological slant whereas the point at issue is constitutive—but it is in fact the constitutive thesis that Peacocke starts from.[17] If this thesis is granted, then an account of acceptance conditions or cognitive role must appeal to the cognitive and perceptual powers, and assertoric and inferential dispositions that we *actually* have. It must not appeal to the dispositions of an idealized thinker whose cognitive and perceptual powers exceed our own. Peacocke too makes this a fundamental constraint.

Peacocke regards himself as a realist; but what he means is a rejection of the verificationist view of truth. ('By a realist, I mean merely a theorist who allows that a sentence or content can be true though unverifiable by us.'[18]). This is of course a legitimate and familiar use of the term. On the other hand, it is also true that there are philosophies which at some level can be said to involve a rejection of realism but which would nevertheless also hold 'that a sentence or content can be true though unverifiable by us'. In this essay I am reserving the terms realism and anti-realism for that level; we have yet to see what acceptance or rejection of realism at that level involves. Terminology apart then, there is a further point of similarity here, for the EM theorist is a realist in Peacocke's sense—he rejects ET; but he endorses EM on the basis of the insight that meaning is use. Peacocke summarizes his position as 'manifestationism without verificationism';[19] so he too must hold that while EM (or a related position) does, ET does not, follow from the doctrine that meaning is use.

We have then two broadly contrasted approaches, each of which stems from a reading of the Wittgensteinian analyses of understanding and of rule-following. One takes the epistemic conception of meaning to be the upshot of these, rejecting the epistemic conception of truth as an extraneous intrusion. On this approach it is a central requirement that any working out of the epistemic conception must refer only to the *actual* capacities of language-users. On the other approach (Dummett, Wright, Tennant) it is the epistemic conception of truth which is central, the epistemic conception of meaning being a corollary. In this other approach the requirement that only actual powers of language-users may be appealed to is perhaps less prominent—this reflects an unclarity as to just what epistemic constraint is to be placed on the notion of truth. It sometimes seems that appeal may be made to verifying powers of idealized agents, counterfactually located, etc. Our concern is with the implications of the first approach.

Peacocke's account of the logical constants[20] aims to show how acceptance conditions determine truth-conditions in the special case of sentences formed by means of the corresponding logical connectives. Our inferential dispositions are also expressed in our spontaneous modal impressions—impressions of what follows from what, of what is incompatible with what; certain of the principles which thus spontaneously impress us as valid, enter into the sense and determine the semantic value (Fregean *bedeutung*) of the connectives. Understanding of these connectives, Peacocke holds, is partly *constituted* by a sense or impression of particular inferences or particular laws of truth involving them as 'primitively obvious'.

Peacocke does not hold that all deductive inferences are primitively obvious, or that only primitively obvious principles enter into the sense-constituting determination of a connective's semantic value; his discussion makes many points which we cannot do justice to here. We shall consider only some aspects of his treatment of conjunction and negation; these already raise the issues about the nature of realism and the apriority of logic which concern us.

In the simple case of conjunction, Peacocke holds that understanding is partly constituted by finding the introduction and elimination rules primitively obvious.[21] The semantic value of the conjunction operator is then that unique truth-function which ensures that those rules do indeed preserve truth. The case of negation is more complex. Here Peacocke considers that

> What is primitively obvious to anyone who understands negation is just that ¬A is incompatible with A. [Unless] the ordinary user of negation ... appreciates that A and ¬A cannot both be true, then he does not understand ¬.[22]

He notes that 'it takes further reflection to realize that ¬A is also the weakest condition incompatible with A'.²³ It requires one to go beyond the primitively obvious incompatibility 'in accepting that in any case in which A is not true, ¬A is true'. Given these two principles (and the principle that if ¬A is not true, A is true) a semantic value—the classical truth-function—will be assignable to 'not'. So in this case the appeal is directly to laws of truth; these determine the connective's semantic value, which validate the connective's introduction and elimination rules.

Before we consider the epistemological underpinnings of Peacocke's approach let me return again to the distinction between validation and justification which has been a main theme of this essay. What validates S is what makes it true or in the case of a rule of inference valid. What justifies S is what justifies belief in it. The two must indeed be linked—but it is on the question of how that link is made that the difference between realism and anti-realism emerges.

One ingredient of the 'realism' at stake here is what I will call the Realist Epistemological Principle. The general idea is that a thinker has a justified belief that S only if he stands in an appropriate epistemic relation to S's validating condition. What is appropriate? A paradigm of appropriateness is the relation of direct awareness. Of course a Realist will want to allow that acquaintance with data, or symptoms, from which sound inference permits a conclusion that the validating condition holds, is also appropriate. But his underlying conception, giving priority in the way that it does to a sentence's truth-condition, gives him chronic trouble in explaining how any such inferences can be *known* to be sound; so the Principle always tends to slide inexorably towards the limiting case, in which the *only* adequate relation is the paradigm of direct awareness.

Peacocke, as we have seen, holds that understanding conjunction and negation is partly *constituted* by finding certain logical principles primitively obvious or compelling. What is the significance of 'constituted'? Can we, in particular, conclude that the thinker has a priori justification for accepting those principles? The realist position of which I have made an initial sketch would resist this notion. For how can an impression of a logical principle as obvious or compelling constitute the appropriate epistemic relation to its validating condition? This, we saw, was Mill's question.

Obviously a great deal turns on what we mean when we say that finding instances of a particular principle obvious is partially constitutive of under-standing a connective, such as '&'. Peacocke explains it thus:

> To say that it is so partially constitutive is to make the following conjunctive claim: that no one understands '&' unless he finds these instances primitively obvious, and that the explanation of this fact is to be traced to what is involved in understanding conjunction.²⁴

But this explanation in turn at least requires a further gloss. There is a sense in which the Realist can accept that the conjunctive claim applies to various logical principles, and therefore, on the account given so far, accept that finding those principles obvious is 'partially constitutive' of understanding the relevant connective. Assuming a broadly common psychology among language-users, all will be disposed to the same spontaneous modal impressions; we shall therefore not count someone as understanding a particular connective unless he shares those impressions of obviousness, and of course the fact that he evinces a particular impression about the relevant sentences trivially traces back to what he understands by those sentences. But the realist will not accept that this in itself provides a basis for holding a principle which is partially constitutive of understanding to be a priori. For him it would be quite irrelevant to that epistemological claim. An epistemological claim about a sentence requires some account of the thinker's mode of access to that sentence's validating condition.

However, perhaps more should be read into the second conjunct, which says that the way in which understanding in certain cases depends on having certain impressions of obviousness is to be explained in terms of what understanding in these cases involves.

Compare an analogous claim about the word 'blue'. No one understands 'blue' unless he finds the sentence 'It's blue', said of a cloudless daytime sky (in normal viewing conditions, assuming he hasn't taken vision-distorting drugs, etc.) obvious—just on the basis of looking. And the explanation of this fact is to be traced back to what is involved in understanding the concept blue. Willingness to assert 'It's blue', just on the basis of looking and registering a sensation of blue is partially constitutive of understanding 'blue'.

What the EM theorist understands by this is that that sensory state on its own, that is in its own right in the absence of overturning collateral information, warrants the statement—even though the statement is a statement about one's physical environment. This is at the level of cognitive role. He must of course also have an account of the statement's truth-condition. The semantic account of 'blue' will treat the predicate as satisfiable by physical objects; it dovetails into a theory of nature in which blueness is considered an intrinsic property of physical objects, and subjective appearances of blue are thought of as (normally) resulting from the instantiation of this property in the objective visual field.[25] A causal account of how one *knows* that a thing is blue (as against being justified in thinking it blue) can then be fitted into that context.

Compare the realist view. Once again the realist could agree that a thinker finds 'It's blue' a primitively obvious response to certain states of experience, that explanation of this is to be traced to what is involved in understanding 'blue', and hence, that the primitive response is in a certain sense 'partially constitutive' of understanding 'blue'. Where the assertion 'It's blue' is not prompted by just these stimulus conditions, there are grounds for doubting that the speaker means that it's blue. But what the realist does not accept is that the statement 'It's blue' can be justified by a sensory state alone. All that that state on its own justifies is something like 'I have a sensation of blue'. The truth-condition of the latter statement is immediately given in a way that the truth-condition of the former is not. So for the realist, my epistemic relation to the former's truth-condition cannot be such as to provide immediate warrant for its assertion. The typical problem for the realist is then to give an account of what justifies us in asserting statements which transcend immediate experience; his answer can at best make my warrant for saying 'It's blue' go via an implausibly roundabout route (involving inference to an overall hypothesis explaining my sensations, etc.).

On the EM view, the justifying relation between sensory state and statement expresses a rule but the statement is defeasible. It can be defeated by enlargements of my information state which warrant assertion that lighting conditions are not normal, that my senses are malfunctioning, and so on. Nor need there be any 'paradigm' situation in which it is indefeasible. At the limit, a theory could emerge which would strictly provide no truth-condition for 'It's blue', because it neither deployed the predicate 'blue' nor provided any remotely natural reduction for the supposed property of blueness. In that information state we would say that no sensory state strictly justifies 'It's blue'—the justifying relation, in that information state, would be systematically defeated.

Let us now go back to the epistemology of logic. Conjunction is not a good example for us, because it might well be held that the introduction and elimination rules are 'merely apparent inferences', in which the conclusion is literally asserted in the premises. This would have been Mill's view; he held that assertion of a conjunction is nothing but assertion of its conjuncts. Such a view requires an account of conjunctions in subordinate scope; but if one accepts it, the contrast between realist and EM theorist does not emerge.

With negation however the case is otherwise. A Millian ultra-empiricist would have to consider the law of contradiction to be a real proposition and hence straightforwardly a posteriori. The EM theorist, on the other hand, while not denying that it is a real and not merely verbal or apparent proposition, holds it to be weakly a priori. There is a primitive impression that A and $\neg A$ are incompatible. That impression warrants assertion of the principle $\neg(A \mathbin{\&} \neg A)$. To say that a principle is weakly a priori is just to say that I am justified in asserting it by such a modal impression of its validity.

It is important that the modal impression is spontaneous: it does not result from but is presupposed by training. (And that it's authentic—a lot of filling-in about our practice with logical and mathematical intuition is needed here.) In general, paradigm assertion conditions for complex sentences formed by logical connectives are learnt in elementary cases, and certain deductive principles involving them are then simply found obvious. Consider the learning of 'not': perhaps a child asks where its teddy is, and is told 'In the kitchen'. If it looks in the kitchen and fails to find its teddy it learns to come back saying 'It's not'. If it is taken to the kitchen and its teddy is found it learns to withdraw the negation.

When the child learns such basic moves with negation, it spontaneously finds certain inferential principles obvious. They are not inferred from assertoric use, nor from experience, nor learnt by direct training. Having grasped the conditions for negation in various kinds of simply decidable case, the child finds its evident that the assertion S is incompatible with the assertion $\neg S$; in effect, that acceptance of a pool of assumptions which warrant assertion of both S

and $\neg S$ is forbidden. And further, it finds it evident that *negation* of a given assumption within such a pool is warranted by any state of information which contains the others; and this underlies its grasp of negations in more theoretical, non-decidable cases. The reasoning principles are not taught as 'add-on' features of the meaning of 'not'; but this does not mean that the corresponding inferential dispositions require justification, or that they could receive it. An inference principle linking assertions can be primitively constitutive of meaning, just as a criterial relation between a perceptual state and an assertion can be constitutive of meaning.

The EM theorist differs in this from the Millian empiricist; but we have not committed him to claiming more than that such an inference principle is weakly a priori. He can accept the general argument from naturalism to the defeasibility of all real propositions. To drive the point home, take the extreme case. Imagine that scientists discover certain ultra-elementary particles, hegelons, which are governed by bizarre principles whose interpretation causes much controversy. An up-to-the-minute ultra-empiricist, Mill II, proposes that overall consider- ations of theoretical simplicity are best served by allowing that in certain situations hegelons can be described as both having and not having a particular property; and he develops an alternative to classical logic which suitably blocks the derivation of false sentences from these descriptions (for example by placing restrictions on disjunctive syllogism). On this basis he regards the unrestricted law of negation as a posteriori and false.

It is, no doubt, wildly implausible that any such proposal could meet all the complex and hard-to-spell-out canons by which we are guided, when we judge the explanatory quality of theories—naturalness, simplicity, and the like. We literally cannot imagine what gains of simplicity, let alone of naturalness, it could secure. But is it strictly incoherent or unintelligible? Can it be ruled out in advance? Can we point out to Mill II, that since he does not appreciate that A and $\neg A$ cannot both be true, he does not understand 'not'?

Not on the EM theorist's view. He does claim to be able, as we have just seen, to give a philosophical basis for the view that the law of contradiction is *weakly* a priori; but he has found no ground for holding it *strongly* a priori. He therefore has no way of *ruling out* the possibility that our primitive incompatibility reaction may be overridden, even in this case, by sufficiently weighty theoretical circumstances. In contrast, a Millian realist cannot accept that the impression of incompatibility—which of course he shares with everyone else—can give an a priori warrant to a factual claim about real incompatibility. His problem is then to explain on what basis we can have reason for accepting the law of contradiction. It is not just that, as in the case of 'blue', any reason he can provide goes by an implausibly roundabout route. The difficulty is now deeper: it is impossible to see how a theory could be arrived at in the first place, unless some real principles are a priori. Thus for realism the choice is forced between scepticism and a Platonistic or Kantian rejection of naturalism.

So much for the epistemological differences between EM theorist and realist. Reading sections 6 and 7 of Peacocke's 'Understanding Logical Constants: A Realist's Account', in which closely related issues are raised, my initial impression is that Peacocke's position is that of the EM theorist, rather than that of the realist.[26] Yet, on the other hand, if principles of logic which are not 'merely apparent' are only *weakly* a priori, as the EM theorist holds, it would be too strong to say that a person does not understand negation 'unless he appreciates that A and $\neg A$ cannot both be true'. Certainly he must have the primitive impression of incompatibility—it is a central feature of the role of negation in our thinking. Consider however someone who does have that primitive impression, who shares with us our spontaneous inferential practice, but on philosophical grounds accepts that he might be forced to override the impression—or on complex physical grounds actually holds that he should override it. It would be quite unconvincing to assert that he has simply failed to *understand* negation. That would be unconvincing on any sensible view of interpretation, but the EM theorist, furthermore, must accept that such a person might be right in his view. His own conception of meaning gives him no way of constructing impenetrable armour even around the law of contradiction.[27]

If there is indeed this difference between the EM theorist and Peacocke, the tenor of Peacocke's remarks on the relation between the justification of logical principles and their semantic validation becomes harder to follow. Of course he recognizes, just as Dummett does, that semantic validation could not in the nature of the case provide an outright justification of logic which relies on no logic; that is not at issue. However he gives semantic validation a greater role in the justification of logical principles than the EM theorist would accept. Consider the following:

> learning certain of the primitive laws *is* part of coming to understand some of the constants; but those laws also receive a *justification* from a non-proof-theoretic semantics. On the other hand, what makes the assignments given in the semantics correct is their *validation* of certain primitive and limiting principles. Without some such principles, we would have no source for the semantics; without the semantics, we would have, it seems, no *justification* for the principles.[28] (Last three emphases mine.)

In what sense do the semantics which validate those primitive laws justify them? The realist has a clear answer. The semantics form part of a philosophical justification, in which proof-theoretic principles are justified in terms of the classical laws of truth—the fundamental laws of the science of logic. Our justification for accepting proof-theoretic principles is to be supplied from our knowledge of these laws; the laws correspond to a domain of empirical or trans-empirical fact.

The Fregean and the Millian Realist must each give an account of our knowledge of these laws which accords with the Realist Epistemological Principle. This works in an orderly, if epistemologically incredible or even unintelligible, way for the Fregean realist. For the Millian, on the other hand, there is a disharmony: between the acknowledged fact that we do have spontaneous impressions of the validity of Bivalence and Exclusion, which in fact ground our acceptance of their validity—and the fact that such impressions are quite unconnected with the only grounds which could give us a genuine warrant for accepting these laws. The grounds, for the Millian, would have to be inductive. He might still hope, *within* the context of scientific theory, to be able to show how our spontaneous impressions of validity stand in the right epistemic relation to the facts for them to constitute knowledge; but that story would be a posteriori.

If neither of these is Peacocke's position, what is? How are the principles which express our primitive impressions of validity *justified* by a semantics which appeals to the classical laws of truth?

If 'justified' is being used epistemically, the answer is that they are not. We find certain proof-theoretic principles primitively obvious; that primitive impression alone gives us warrant for accepting them. But whereas the warrant for accepting 'It's blue' is provided by a sensory input, nothing provides a warrant for accepting the logical principle other than an impression of the validity of that principle itself. In that sense these logical principles are self-justifying. They are not analytic or verbal propositions 'empty of content', and they are not strongly a priori. They too fall within the remit of standard scientific canons of simplicity and predictive adequacy—in that they are indirectly vindicated by the efficiency, in these terms, of our total pattern of beliefs. This is the truth in empiricism about logic; but it has nothing to do with semantic validation.

X

Is the EM theorist a realist or does he reject realism? He does not reject realism in Peacocke's sense. Realism in that sense is not a metaphysical position but the rejection of a metaphysical position. Nor does he reject scientific realism. There are realisms with a small 'r'; but there is a systematic metaphysical position which, it seems to me, has a fair claim to be described as Realist, with a capital 'R'. This the EM theorist does reject: he is an anti-Realist, because he opposes that metaphysical conception. But he does not put another metaphysical conception in its place, as does the ET theorist.

We have come across all the themes in the Realist syndrome already. The most basic is

(1) Metaphysical Realism: correctness is always and everywhere truth as correspondence to fact—truth as fit. The notion of truth proper— correspondence with the facts—is extended from its proper domain to all cases which can be appraised as correct/incorrect; any genuinely assertible content must correspond or fail to correspond to what is the case. Objectivity of assertion always requires a domain of reality to which assertion aims to correspond.

Then there is

(2) The Classical Pre-understanding of Meaning: understanding an asser- toric sentence is grasping what must be the case for it to be true—where

this ability is conceived of as being free-standing: independent of a grasp of principles of evidence, rather than constituted by them.

Corresponding to the metaphysical and meaning-theoretic strands is an epistemological one:

(3) The Realist Epistemological Principle: I am justified in holding a statement to be true only by virtue of standing in the right epistemic relation to its truth-condition.

This is not the place to explore in full the connections between the three strands. But one route may be sketched.

The truth of the sentence 'Grass is green' involves correspondence with the fact that grass is green. But apparently it also involves further 'facts', such as that 'grass' denotes grass, 'green' denotes (the set of) green things, and so forth. Are there such facts? Undoubtedly these latter assertions are correct, so given metaphysical realism, there must be facts to which they correspond. The problem then is to explain what constitutes these facts. 'Grass' means grass; that is, English speakers mean grass by 'grass', intend it to have that denotation (and believe each other to have that intention, etc.). But what makes it true that by 'grass' I mean, or intend, grass? At this point meaning-realism is extremely tempting; must it not be the fact that I am tracking a meaning, or a rule, a mental or abstract entity which lays down its own application? To this realist temptation meaning-scepticism provides the realist recoil. Wittgenstein's discussion of rule-following seeks to find a way out of the dichotomy.

Meaning-realism generates the classical pre-understanding of meaning. For understanding a sentence is then just grasping the meaning-entity which it represents—it is the state which underlies assertoric and inferential dispositions, and provides me with a potential vantage point for wholesale philosophical questioning of rules of evidence. Hence in turn the Realist Epistemological Principle: the understanding of a truth-condition now floats free of any constituting framework of epistemic dispositions; it provides on the contrary an ontological yardstick against which epistemological rules must be measured. Their justification must be their soundness; they must be 'faithful' to the meanings of sentences which appear in them as premises or conclusions. Insofar as an epistemological rule is correct it must have a validating condition—something in the world which makes it correct.

If, in contrast, we reject the idea that normative statements (semantic, moral, or modal) correspond to domains of fact we have two choices. Either we reject the idea that they can be said to be objectively correct or incorrect altogether, or we reject metaphysical realism: we hold that normative assertions can indeed be objectively correct or incorrect (though Bivalence need not be ubiquitous); but cannot be said to be true or false—at least if these predicates are understood narrowly in correspondence terms. '"Grass" denotes grass', 'Killing is wrong', will be correct but not true.

This is not the place to argue for the latter option, which seems to me to be the right one. But we must briefly consider its consequences for the status of principles of inference, the case we are discussing.

Once again the key lies in distinguishing sharply between justification and validation. An inference principle may be presented at the normative level of justification. For example *reductio*: 'Where A & $\neg A$ is deducible from a pool of assumptions, negation of any given assumption is warranted in any information state which warrants assertion of all the others'. That normative principle corresponds to no fact—it can be said to be correct but cannot be said to be true. Yet there is a fact which can be said to validate it—namely, that it is never a fact that A & $\neg A$. It provides an internal validation of the normative principle because principles of inference should be truth-preserving. But it is not what gives me ground for accepting the principle; for that I *have* no ground.

The realist thinks I can have reason to accept the normative principle only by knowing the fact. The fact might be conceived, as by the Platonist or Fregean, to be a fact of 'ultra-physics', or as by the Millian, simply as a fact of physics.[29] The EM theorist's quarrel with the Millian is not about empiricism (at least in its weak form) but about realism—about the existence of a form of justification which is not internal validation: groundless justification as it might be called.

Of course groundless justification and internal validation are not totally out of relation to each other. Internal validation has epistemic force just because a belief which has an a priori warrant may *not* be internally validated—it may be internally undermined. Thus consider the assertion that two straight lines never intersect twice. We learn the meaning of 'straight' ostensively, both directly and by learning to judge ostensively which of a pair of lines or edges is straighter or less crooked. When we grasp this part of the use of 'straight', we have the primitive modal impression that biangles cannot be. That intuition survives critical (non-empirical) reflection; we count on it, in the absence of offsetting empirical evidence, as warranting the assertion that two straight lines cannot meet twice. Having that modal impression is partially constitutive of understanding 'straight'. Yet if we subsequently acquire indirect theoretical reasons for affirming the possibility of biangles, the assertion that straight lines cannot meet twice is withdrawn.[30] A belief which has groundless justification is eventually undermined on internal grounds.

Justification can spread through the fabric of beliefs only if the fabric has a priori strands; but the strands need only be weakly a priori. Does rejection of Realism permit one—paradoxically—to concede that much to Kant, without conceding idealism? If the epistemic conception of meaning can be bedded down with common sense, if it really shrinks to a truism and is not a metaphysical thesis among other theses, the answer will be 'Yes'.

Notes

1. J. Skorupski, 'Anti-Realism: Cognitive Role and Semantic Content', in J. Butterfield (ed.), *Language, Mind and Logic*, and 'Critical Review of Wright, *Realism*,

Meaning and Truth', *Philosophical Quarterly* 38. Dummett's and Wright's views are best studied in their collections of essays, including the respective introductions.

2. Just how these themes are to be related to any of the schools I refer to— the Vienna Circle, mathematical intuitionism, pragmatism, or the late Wittgenstein, are fascinating historical questions which cannot be pursued here. The conception of meaning as use occurs in Wittgenstein's conversations with Schlick and others (B. McGuinness (ed.), *Ludwig Wittgenstein and the Vienna Circle*), and in Schlick's published writings (M. Schlick, 'Meaning and Verification', *The Philosophical Review* (1936)). In the *Investigations* Wittgenstein's statement is not unqualified: 'For a *large* class of cases—though not for all—in which we employ the word "meaning" it can be defined thus: the meaning of a word is its use in the language' (*Philosophical Investigations*, para. 143).

It can at least be said that the position I describe, that of the 'EM theorist', has affinities with important themes in the later Wittgenstein. But one might also cite Carnap, 'Truth and Confirmation', in H. Feigl and W. Sellars (eds), *Readings in Philosophical Analysis*—where Carnap invokes Tarski's semantic theory of truth to distinguish between truth and confirmation—and one might also refer to the pragmatist aspects of Quine. Obviously however there are many points on which these philosophers would diverge.

Putnam has been an important influence on this debate—see Putnam, *Meaning and the Moral Sciences*, and some of the essays in Putnam, *Realism and Reason*. (But Putnam would be sceptical, e.g. about the possibility of a systematic theory of cognitive roles—cf. Putnam, *Realism and Reason*, pp. xvi–xvii.) Finally, I should mention that the ideas developed here seem to have a number of close similarities to those of John Pollock, particularly in his *Contemporary Theories of Knowledge*.

3. Dummett, *Frege: Philosophy of Language*, pp. 360–2.

4. For the remainder of this section, to conform with Dummett's discussion, I shall use the notion of truth broadly, i.e., as objective correctness.

5. For further development of these points see Skorupski, 'Critical Review of Wright, *Realism, Meaning and Truth*'.

6. Dummett, *Truth and Other Enigmas*, pp. 17–18.

7. In using the standard clauses to infer an account of the assertion conditions of negations, implications, and disjunctions, we rely on the principles of truth which they themselves express together with principles of Assertibility and Equivalence:

> *Assertibility*: 'S' is assertible if and only if 'It is assertible that S' is assertible.
> *Equivalence*: 'S' is assertible if and only if '"S" is true' is assertible.

Note also the Principles of Bivalence and Exclusion:

> *Bivalence*: (i) if 'S' is not true then 'not-S' is true; (ii) if 'not-S' is not true then 'S' is true.
> *Exclusion*: (i) if 'S' is true then 'not-S' is not true; (ii) if 'not-S' is true then 'S' is not true.

I shall refer to Equivalence, Bivalence, and Exclusion as the Classical Laws of Truth. The EM theorist has no philosophical quarrel with them (at least for the narrow case of strict truth—they would fail if truth were broadly read as correctness). Thus in the case of factual sentences assessable for strict truth-value, he has no objection to the standard rule for negation, which enshrines Exclusion (ii) and Bivalence (i). Similarly, he is happy to let his statement of assertion conditions for a disjunction leave open the possibility that a disjunction may be assertible where neither disjunct is.

8. Dummett, *Elements of Intuitionism*, pp. 363 ff.; 'The Philosophical Basis of Intuitionistic Logic', in *Truth and Other Enigmas*, pp. 218–20; 'The Justification of Deduction', in *Truth and Other Enigmas*, pp. 300–4. Tennant, *Anti-Realism and Logic*, ch. 6 provides a useful survey and commentary.

9. Dummett, 'The Justification of Deduction', p. 303.

10. Ibid., p. 309.

11. A justification for S is overturned when new empirical data enlarge or delete from the beliefs which are included in the justifying information state, in such a way that the resulting information state no longer justifies S. It is in contrast *invalidated* if on examination it turns out to make a faulty application of epistemic rules. The epistemic possibility that a justification could be invalidated would not by itself defeat its claim to be strongly a priori. ('Information' is here understood to include states of feeling and experience as well as states of belief—see p. 155.)

12. The thesis covers factual propositions, not norms. Corresponding to the distinction between weak and strong a priori, there is strong and weak empiricism. Strong empiricism holds that no real proposition is weakly a priori. In stigmatizing this as incoherent the Kantian critic is on unassailable ground.

13. For an account of Mill's views and a comparison with Frege see my *John Stuart Mill*, chs. 1–5.

14. Peacocke, *Thoughts: An Essay on Content*; 'What Determines Truth Conditions?', in J. McDowell and P. Pettit (eds.), *Subject, Thought and Context*; 'Understanding Logical Constants', in *Proceedings of the British Academy* 63; 'The Limits of Intelligibility', in *Philosophical Review* 97.

15. Peacocke, 'What Determines Truth Conditions?', p. 181.

16. Ibid.

17. In 'The Limits of Intelligibility' he prefers 'The Discrimination Principle' to the term 'manifestationism', as being 'less loaded', and adds that it 'involves no commitment to behaviourism' (pp. 468, 470).

18. Peacocke, 'Understanding Logical Constants', p. 153.

19. Peacocke, *Thoughts*, p. 207.

20. Peacocke, 'Understanding Logical Constants'.

21. Ibid., p. 154.

22. Ibid., p. 163.

23. Ibid., p. 163.

24. Ibid., p. 15.

25. Semantically, 'blue' is simple, 'sensation of blue', or 'looks blue', complex. It is the composition rules for the latter, complex, phrases which underwrite analytic truths: as that x is a sensation of blue iff x is a sensation of the kind which would be caused in a normal perceiver of our kind, in circumstances normal for that kind of perceiver, by a suitably presented perceptible blue object. (Note that 'normal' is not effectively decidable, and that the biconditional does not entail the existence of blue objects.)

26. Consider in particular principles (1)–(4) in section 6 (p. 16), and Peacocke's discussion of them.

27. Mill II, like Mill, could accept that 'A and $\neg$A cannot both be true' if 'cannot' is understood physically, not metaphysically. And the immediate issue at stake in our discussion is epistemological—viz., can the principle be claimed to be strongly a priori. But if we cannot claim it to be so, the onus on anyone who holds it to be metaphysically necessary is to explain how that can be.

28. Peacocke, 'Understand Logical Constants', p. 166.

29. 'Ultra-physics': Wittgenstein's comments on logic as 'a kind of ultra-physics'

(*Remarks on the Foundation of Mathematics*, I.8) are quoted by Peacocke, 'Understanding Logical Constants', p. 179. In the *Investigations*, Wittgenstein quotes Ramsey as having emphasized that logic is a 'normative science' (para. 81). In that latter context Wittgenstein is raising questions about how far our linguistic practice can be taken to be rule-guided; but Ramsey's remark would most naturally be used to make the point that logic is neither physics nor ultra-physics: it states rules of reason. Or rather, on the view developed here, it would be best to say that in the perspective of justification it articulates epistemic norms, while in the perspective of validation it expresses 'physical' laws.

30. The same distinction can be made for induction itself, as by Strawson in *Introduction to Logical Theory* (1963 edn.). Strawson distinguishes two propositions, '[The universe is such that] induction will continue to be successful' and 'Induction is rational (reasonable)'; holding the second to be analytic, the first to be 'contingent' (p. 261). On the present approach, the second proposition could not be said to be analytic—that would be a claim at the level of semantic content, rather than of cognitive role. However that leaves open the question whether at the level of cognitive role it could be said to be a priori. Could it not, or something corresponding to it, be regarded as partly constitutive of understanding 'All'?

6

Proof and Truth

Christopher Peacocke

How does a proof succeed in establishing the truth of its conclusion? Why are the steps of the proof justified? And how are truth, proof, and justification related to the meaning of the sentence proved? I will be addressing some aspects of these perennially intriguing questions.

John Skorupski's essay provides a springboard from which to plunge into the issues. He holds these theses:

(i) The meaning of a sentence is given by its assertion conditions *and its inferential power* (p. 134, emphasis in original).

(ii) Truth cannot be identified with assertibility (pp. 134–9).

(iii) Our grasp of a sentence's truth-condition is constituted by our assertoric and inferential dispositions (p. 134).

(iv) Inferential power is not grounded in grasp of anything else (pp. 143–4).

(v) Inferential practice is in a sense 'self-justifying' (pp. 147–8, 158–9): there is 'no scope for a purely philosophical critique' of an inferential practice (p. 146).

(vi) If we accept Theses (i)–(iv), we will indeed not think deduction in need of justification.

It is only with thesis (ii), that truth cannot be identified with any concept of (warranted or warrantable) assertibility, that I agree unreservedly. I begin my discussion with some types of justification which Skorupski seems to overlook.

1. A Real Obligation

The first type of justification can be introduced by mentioning two gaps in Skorupski's account. The two gaps are at the places where one would expect a general theory of concepts and theories of particular concepts. One would have to be a curmudgeon to complain that Skorupski should have filled these gaps by writing a different essay. But I do want to argue that plausible ways

This is the text, as submitted to the editors in October 1988, of a revised version of the comments read at the St. Andrews conference.

of filling these gaps force us to alter the Skorupskian structure which surrounds them. Let me explain, and then go on to discuss some wider issues arising from the explanation.

Skorupski says that truth-conditions are 'constituted by' assertoric and inferential role. So presumably he is committed to the correctness of something of this form: a sentence has as its truth-condition the content that p because the content that p stands in such-and-such relations to the assertoric and inferential role of the given sentence. If we applied this at the level of the component concepts of a content, we would equally say: a word expresses a certain concept because that concept stands in such-and-such relations to the assertoric and inferential role of sentences containing the word.

These statements of Skorupski's position contain phrases of the form 'the content meeting so-and-so condition' and 'the concept meeting so-and-so condition'. In so using these phrases, we incur two obligations: to explain why the commitments to *existence* and to *uniqueness* implicit in these phrases are fulfilled. These obligations are real. Let us take existence. It is possible for a theorist to believe there is a concept or content meeting a certain condition when in fact there is no such content or concept. Roderick Chisholm believes he understands a notion of personal identity on which, even in a perfectly symmetrical case of fission of a person, the pre-fission person is identical with one and not the other of the post-fission persons.[1] He can hardly substantiate his claim that there is such a notion of identity merely by saying 'I mean that notion of identity on which just one of the resulting persons may be identical with the original, even when all else is perfectly symmetrical'. For one reason or another, many of us will say that there is no such notion of identity. In doing so, we will have to appeal to a general theory which states constraints on the nature, existence, and identity of concepts. For example, if we believe that some form or other of Dummett's manifestability requirement is right, then this is the point at which it would be written in and justified. A general theory will also need to consider the correct form for specifying genuine concepts of whatever category, and to justify the implicit semantical apparatus it employs. The same points hold *pari passu* for uniqueness. This then is the first gap: if we say meanings are determined by inferential roles, we have to show how the roles determine the meanings.

The second gap, in the area of theories of particular concepts, is this. Skorupski does not give us a theory, in accord with his own principles, of any particular concept. This is because he gives us no account, for any particular expression, of *how* its truth-condition or contribution to truth-conditions is constituted by its assertoric and inferential role. For Skorupski, meaning is given by assertoric and inferential role. But he also says that 'I grasp the assertion conditions of a negation and the contribution made by the constituent sentence in it—via grasping the truth-condition of the constituent sentence' (p. 146). There is nothing illegitimate about this in principle. But its acceptability as a candidate theory is totally dependent upon our ability to say in turn what it is to grasp the truth-condition of the embedded sentence. We know that

Skorupski holds that it is determined somehow by knowledge of the assertoric and inferential role of the embedded sentence. But again, until we are told how, we do not have a theory we can begin to assess in the case of any particular concept.

Perhaps Skorupski's view is that what I am requesting is trivially supplied: any combination of assertion-conditions and inferential role, subject only to consistency, determines an appropriate contribution to truth-conditions. But I do not think this is true.

Consider the following imaginary operator $Qx \ldots x \ldots$, of the same category as the quantifiers, and which is stipulated to have the following inferential role. Q has the same introduction rule as the existential quantifier: from $F(t)$, one can legitimately infer $QxF(x)$, subject to the usual restriction on variables. But Q does not have the same elimination rule as the existential quantifier. In fact, it has no elimination rules at all. There will be derived rules for Q, but they are derived from the introduction rule for Q and the rules for other operators. This is a specification of an inferential role for Q; but I suggest that we have no idea what Q might mean.

From a classical point of view we can elaborate our bafflement as follows. $QxF(x)$ can mean something no stronger than existential quantification, since it can be inferred from any single instance. Yet it cannot mean exactly the same as existential quantification, since the corresponding elimination rule is said not to be valid for Q. And it cannot be that $QxF(x)$ means something which is true when some object is F and also in some other cases. For if that were so we would be able to infer from the holding of one of those other cases that $QxF(x)$—yet this was not amongst the introduction rules given in the specification of inferential role. From a classical standpoint, this exhausts the cases.

From a more constructivist, proof-theoretic semantics, we could also explain our bafflement. If the introduction rules given are exhaustive of the canonical ways of establishing $QxF(x)$, we would expect there to be a rule for Q analogous to existential elimination. For in that case, whenever $QxF(x)$ is established, there must be some establishable $F(t)$ from which it is derivable. So if C is derivable from an arbitrary instance $F(t)$, it will be validly derivable from $QxF(x)$; that is, some analogue of existential elimination should be valid. But it is said not to be valid. Yet if that elimination rule is not generally valid, then there should be some other canonical means of establishing $QxF(x)$ beyond the existential-like introduction rule. But according to the specification of Q's inferential role, there are no such further rules.

It does not explain what is defective about Q simply to say that is has no elimination rules. For if we were to provide it with an elimination rule like that for existential elimination, but with the proviso that the conclusion be shorter than a certain finite length, that would hardly remove our puzzlement. Since there is no corresponding restriction in the introduction rule, the problem of saying what Q might mean remains.

In the theoretical framework which I myself favour, Q's defect is as follows.[2] For any genuine concept, there must be an account of what it is for a thinker to possess that concept. A correct account of this can be said to be the concept's *possession condition*. But it is also required that there exist for this possession condition what I call a *Determination Theory*: this is a theory which says how a semantic value (at the level of Fregean reference) is determined for the concept from the given possession condition, given the way the world is. It is this second requirement which Q fails. We can presumably take it that the possession condition for the alleged concept expressed by Q is that there be some specified sort of mastery of Q's proposed inference rules. Our difficulties in saying what Q could possibly mean are precisely that it is impossible to give a Determination Theory for Q. Classical semantic values for Q which validate the introduction rule (and no other underived introduction rules) also validate the analogue of existential elimination, which however is said not to be valid for Q. Though the general theoretical framework alluded to here is elaborated in a classical fashion, there are of course constructivist versions of the requirement that a Determination Theory exist. Indeed the demand that the introduction and elimination rules be in harmony, in Prawitz's sense, a requirement which in effect we were arguing is violated by Q, is itself such a constructivist version.[3]

In any case, quite apart from these theoretically more loaded arguments, I suggest that intuitively Q has not been supplied with a meaning, and that correspondingly no content has been fixed by the given inferential role for alleged sentences containing it. Q is one example amongst many with which one might develop the point.

If this is right so far, then there is one minimal kind of justification for principles of logic which is inescapably needed. That is the sort of justification which consists in showing that the principles endorsed (and the principles rejected) which essentially involve a certain constant are consistent with the assignment to that constant of a unique concept. If we hold some additional thesis to the effect that the concepts must be fixed by certain principles in which the constants occur, then the principles must determine a unique concept, by the standard of whatever substantive theory of concepts we endorse.

Justifications of the kind motivated by these first considerations are very much minimal justifications. In particular, nothing in this requirement explicitly requires some distinctions within the class of valid principles, between those which need one kind of justification and those which need another. Correlative with this minimal notion of justification, we have also a minimal notion of error. The intelligibility of justification is always correlative with the intelligibility of a notion of error, since error consists in the failure to hold of the condition which justification aims to establish. So the corresponding notion of error here is that of there being no concept, or no unique concept, having the properties determined by the principles endorsed and the principles rejected. This minimal notion of justification must of course also make us qualify any sense in which logical principles can be said to be self-justifying, and make us disagree with the claim that there is 'no scope for a purely philosophical critique of [an inferential] practice' (p. 146).

2. Two Kinds of Principle

Once we acknowledge the need for a general theory of concepts, the door is open to a more substantial notion of justification. It is open to a theory of a given concept to draw a distinction, within the class of principles containing the concept, between those principles I shall call *sense-determining* ('s-d') and those which I will call *sense-resultant* ('s-r'). It is arguable that such a distinction can be made for all concepts, and for a wide variety of liaisons and transitions involving them. But since our concern here is with logical principles, I will initially confine the discussion to them. In addition, I want at this point in my response to be as non-committal as possible on the form and nature of substantive theories of particular concepts. So instead of trying to define 's-d' and 's-r' outright, I will try to elucidate what it is for a philosophical theory of concepts to *treat* a principle as s-d or as s-r.

A theory treats a principle Π as s-d for a particular logical constant provided that two conditions are met: (i) according to the theory, understanding the logical constant requires some specified kind of non-inferential acceptance of (certain) instances of the principle Π; and (ii) according to the same theory, a certain semantical property of the constant is crucial to the validity or otherwise of principles in which it occurs, and according to the theory what makes it the case that the constant has that semantical property is (at least in part) that it has some specified relation to the given principle Π. Thus, intuitively, a theory treats a principle as s-d for a constant if it says that the semantics for the constant is crucial to the validity of inferences containing it, and that the semantics in turn is correct in part because of its relations to that principle, which has a special status amongst those accepted by the understander. A theory treats a principle as s-r for a given constant, on the other hand, if: (i) it does not treat it as s-d and (ii) on the theory's conception of validity, the validity of the principle follows from the semantical property assigned to the constant in virtue of its relations to those principles which it *does* treat as s-d for the constant. We can give some simple illustrations. Suppose we have a theory of the constants of classical propositional logic which says that a certain non-inferential acceptance of the classical introduction and elimination rules is required for understanding the material conditional. Suppose it says also that a valid (propositional) argument is one which is truth-preserving under all assignments of truth-values to the non-logical constituents, and that what makes it the case that the material conditional expresses the truth-function it does is that it is the truth-function which makes the introduction and elimination rules truth-preserving under all assignments. According to this simple little theory, then, *modus ponens* and the rule of conditional proof will be s-d. Peirce's law $((p \supset q) \supset p) \supset p$, on the other hand, is s-r according to this theory. We could equally give simple examples of each sort of principle for a constructivist theory of the sense of the constants. For instance, on one sort of constructivist theory, the contribution made to proof-conditions by a given constant is the relevant semantical property, which might be regarded as fixed by certain introduction and/or elimination rules whose instances must be non-inferentially accepted. This too will result in a non-vacuous distinction on that theory between s-d and s-r principles containing the constant.

To say that a principle is s-r is not to say that it is valid solely in virtue of the meaning of expressions in it. Logic will be used in deriving its validity from the semantical properties of the logical constants. So to accept a non-empty s-d/s-r distinction is not immediately to block the Quinean view that a logical truth is true partly in virtue of the way the world is, viz. the holding of its disquotational truth-condition. On one other point of clarification, I should also note that the s-d/s-r distinction should not be identified with Dummett's distinction between direct (canonical) methods of establishing something and indirect (non-canonical) methods, even as restricted to logical principles.[4] The s-d/s-r distinction rather generalizes Dummett's. Dummett's distinction is formulated for the special case of a constructivist theory of meaning which is built from proof-conditions, but the s-d/s-r distinction is available to non-constructive theorists of meaning too.

If use of the s-d/s-r distinction is legitimate, then there is a second kind of justification of logical principles going beyond the minimal sort previously canvassed, and which is available to verificationist and anti-verificationist alike. Skorupski writes:

> ... the intuitionistic anti-realist, as described by Michael Dummett, holds that inferential power must in some sense be grounded in assertion-conditions—just as the realist holds that it must in some sense be grounded in truth conditions. Both the realist and the Dummettian anti-realist think that an independent notion of content, given before inferential power, determines or explains, and in doing so justifies, inferential power (pp. 142–3).

Skorupski characterizes the realist, in particular, as rejecting the view that the truth-condition of a sentence containing logical vocabulary is derivative and constructed in some way from its inferential role: 'the realist thinks that grasp of a sentence's correctness condition *underlies* and thereby explains grasp of its assertion conditions and its inferential power' (p. 140, emphasis in original). Because Skorupski is using the label 'realist' for this doctrine about explanation, I will avoid use of the term and just talk of 'anti-verificationists' (and sometimes 'anti-constructivists'). The important point is that an anti-verificationist can consistently (and in my view correctly) endorse this second notion of justification which is available for s-r logical principles whilst rejecting the notion of explanation which Skorupski pins on his realist. In outline, this anti-verificationist's position could run as follows.

This anti-verificationist will say that a certain sort of non-inferential acceptance of what he will count as *s-d* logical principles is to be *written in* to a correct account of understanding of certain of the logical constants they contain. If he says this, then in the relevant sense he will be bound to agree that acceptance of these s-d principles is not explained by his grasp of their truth-conditions. Indeed they cannot be so explained on this anti-verificationist's theory: a good account of grasp of the contribution of the logical constants in question to the truth-conditions of sentences containing them is grounded in primitive non-inferential acceptance of the s-d principles, rather than the other way about. Now suppose this anti-verificationist meets two further conditions. He holds that not all valid logical principles are s-d; and he holds that the uniform semantic value of a given logical constant is fixed by a certain relation to the s-d principles in which it occurs. He will then put to use a good notion of justification for the remaining s-r logical principles containing the constant. They can be shown to be valid, on his conception of validity, on the basis of the semantic value of the constant fixed by the s-d principles.[5]

I have formulated this point for the anti-verificationist; but structurally exactly the same points could be made on behalf of a Dummett-style intuitionist, in favour of a notion of justification for the principles which *he* counts as s-r. Skorupski seems to me to misrepresent Dummett's views when he writes that the Dummettian anti-realist thinks that an independent notion of content, given before inferential power, determines or explains inferential power. Dummett's position seems to me rather that certain s-r inferential principles are justified by, and answerable to, their relations to certain s-d principles which are not themselves so answerable or justifiable. These s-d principles will, on a proof-theoretic constructivist semantics, have the status of definitional specifications of how (for instance) a conjunctive sentence is canonically established. I do not seen how such a theorist can rightly be accused of using a notion of content 'given before inferential power'. Inferential power is precisely what he is using to individuate content.[6]

3. Against Deductive Conservatism: A Responsible Opposition

I now broaden the discussion beyond John Skorupski's paper to consider more generally the relation between the meaning of logical constants and rules of inference. In recent years, several writers have argued that anti-verificationists cannot give an acceptable account of this relation. Dummett has in effect argued that anti-verificationists will be committed to the implausible view that the introduction of a new logical constant alters the meaning of sentences in the old, unextended language.[7] Tennant argues that the anti-verificationist's classical rules of inference fail a basic requirement of justification, that of being 'responsible to some notion of sentential content, molecularly composed from the meaning of its constituents'.[8] Skorupski, who unlike the preceding two writers is an anti-verificationist, implies that the anti-verificationist must be in at least partial agreement with radical holists to the extent that rules of inference for a new logical constant do not need justification relative to the fragment they extend. 'Our forms of deductive inference are part of the linguistic practice which shapes the meaning of each sentence' (p. 148). I believe the anti-verificationist can give answers to these criticisms, and without being a radical holist. First, though, we need to consider more closely what is involved in a meaning being determined by a set of inference rules.

It is important at the outset to draw a distinction between a general criterion for such meaning-determination and the further elaborations it may receive in the presence of additional theses about meaning. Such further elaborations may be acceptable given a thesis that meaning is determined by assertibility-conditions, or by some thesis of molecularity. But it would be a mistake to take such further elaborations as a statement about what it is for the relevant meaning-determination to hold. The elaboration is rather dependent upon the conjunction of the claim of meaning-determination together with the additional theses about meaning.

The general thesis that the meaning of a logical constant is determined by a certain set of inference rules, stated independently of commitment to any of the additional theses about meaning in question here, is this:

> The given rules of inference, together with an account of how the contribution to truth-conditions made by a logical constant is determined from those rules of inference, fixes the correct contribution to the truth-conditions of sentences containing the constant.

I will call this 'the General Requirement'. The General Requirement is neutral as between additional theses about meaning, because the notion of truth it employs may or may not be subject to constructivist requirements, and may or may not be subject to molecularity requirements.

It is far from clear that the anti-constructivist has to fail the General Requirement. The accounts outlined for individual logical constants in my 'Understanding Logical Constants'[9] are the beginnings of one attempt to show how the General Requirement may be met by a classical theorist. With some oversimplification, we can say that those accounts make the semantic value of a logical constant that function which makes certain rules of inference necessarily truth-preserving. This is only the beginning of an attempt, for a good philosophical theory must also motivate this account's use of the classical notion of being truth-preserving (under-an-assignment). I discuss this more below too.

In *Elements of Intuitionism* Dummett gives two requirements for a given set of inference rules to determine a range of meanings for the logical constants:

> First, the condition for the correctness of an assertion made by means of a sentence containing a logical constant must always coincide with the existence of a deduction, by means of those rules of inference, to that sentence from correct premisses none of which contains any of the logical constants in question. Secondly, there must not be any deduction from premisses of the same kind, via sentences involving the logical constants, to a conclusion also containing no logical constant whose assertion would not itself be correct. This second requirement is, in effect, the requirement that the addition of the logical constants to that fragment of the language which lacks them is a conservative extension of the fragment (with respect to the property of being correctly assertible).[10]

Dummett's first requirement here results in the General Requirement as elaborated in a theory on which the meaning of a sentential constituent is given by its contribution to proof-conditions, and on which truth is provability.[11]

The status of Dummett's second requirement is more complex. Suppose we read it as imposing a requirement of proof-theoretic conservative extension. It would then be the requirement for any new set of logical constants that their rules of inference not extend the derivability relation on sentences of the unextended language. So read, Dummett's second requirement is an elaboration of what is involved in fulfilment of the General Thesis, an elaboration relying upon two additional theses. One is the thesis that meaning is given in terms of proof-conditions, and the other is the thesis that the introduction of new logical constants does not alter the meaning of sentences already in the language. Given these two theses, Dummett's second thesis, read proof-theoretically, is compulsory. For if the new rules expand the deducibility relation within the unextended language, and meaning is given by proof-conditions, either some of the new rules are invalid, or some of the meanings of expressions in the unextended fragment have altered. This consideration in favour of the compulsoriness of the requirement depends upon acceptance of both this form of molecularity and of the constructivist theory of meaning. It will carry no weight for the anti-constructivist.

This, though, is hardly the end of the matter. The question arises whether there may not be some analogue of Dummett's second requirement which can apply even to the anti-constructivist. In particular, the most interesting and theoretically crucial case to consider is that of the molecular anti-constructivist. If we can show that there is a substantive requirement on rules of inferences for the molecular anti-constructivist, a requirement met by the classical inference rules, then the criticisms of anti-constructivism mentioned at the start of this section will lapse.

It will not come as news that it is to a form of molecular anti-constructivism that I am drawn. The task of developing this position is at least threefold. First, we have to give a sharp formulation of the appropriate anti-constructivist analogue of Dummett's second requirement. Second, we have to give a philosophically satisfying account of how this requirement can be met even in cases in which Dummett's second requirement fails. Third, we need answers to the objections raised by some of the above writers to particular inferences which are classically endorsed.

In formulating the requirement for the molecular anti-constructivist, we need to draw a distinction between the property of being *deductively* conservative and the property of being *semantically* conservative. Suppose Σ is a set of rules for a new logical constant, and that L is a system of deduction for a language not containing the new logical constant. Then

> Σ is deductively conservative over L iff for any sentences $A_1, \ldots, A_n, B$ of L, $A_1, \ldots, A_n \vdash_{L+\Sigma} B$ only if $A_1, \ldots, A_n \vdash_L B$;

and

> Σ is semantically conservative over L iff for any sentences $A_1, \ldots, A_n, B$ of L, $A_1, \ldots, A_n \vdash_{L+\Sigma} B$ only if $A_1, \ldots, A_n \vDash B$ (where as usual $\vDash$ is the relation of semantic consequence).

This distinction is a natural version for inference rules of the distinction between deductive and semantic conservativeness of one theory relative to another.[12] The requirement we are looking for is of course stronger than merely that a set of rules Σ involving a new logical constant be semantically conservative over the system to which they are added. That is just the requirement of soundness, and will be accepted by everyone for their own favoured notion of semantic consequence. The requirement that the molecular anti-constructivist will endorse is that of semantic conservativeness, under the further condition that the semantics used in the notion of consequence be ratifiable as appropriate for the unextended system, independently of any acceptance of the new set Σ of inference rules.[13] Ratifying a semantics as appropriate is a philosophical matter, not a purely technical one.

The addition of second-order quantifiers to a first-order language for arithmetic is a relatively well-understood case in which the molecular anti-constructivist will say that his requirement has some bite. We will fix on the case in which we have a recursive set of axioms for the first-order arithmetic. The second-order enrichment will lead to the derivability of some first-order sentences of arithmetic which were not previously derivable, such as the Gödel sentence for the first-order axiomatization. The molecular anti-constructivist will regard this as unproblematic, provided he can give an account, meeting the philosophical requirement just formulated, of the semantics on which the previously underivable sentence is a semantic consequence of the axioms for first-order arithmetic.

Here an objector may protest. 'There must already be something wrong here! For we have the completeness theorem for the relation of first-order derivability. So we know that for any recursive first-order axiomatization R of arithmetic, a first-order sentence S is derivable from R if and only if it is a semantic consequence of R. Hence in the arithmetical case you are discussing, semantic conservativeness implies deductive conservativeness.' However, the range of models required for the completeness theorem to hold has to include non-standard models of arithmetic. They will, for instance, include models in which the actually true but underivable Gödel sentence for R is evaluated as false. If we restrict our attention to standard models for a first-order language for arithmetic, the completeness theorem will not hold.

The burden of the molecular anti-constructivist's position will be precisely that he can give a reason for saying that even for the unextended language without second-order vocabulary, only standard models should be used in the definition of the relation of semantic consequence. Here the molecular anti-constructivist can appeal to the account of understanding of classical universal quantification over natural numbers which I offered in *Thoughts*, the so-called commitment account.[14] The commitment account makes two claims. It claims (a) that what makes it the case that someone is judging a content of the form 'All natural numbers are F' is that he thereby incurs this infinite family of commitments: to $F(0)$, to $F(1)$, to $F(2)$, ... That someone has incurred this family rather than some other will be evidenced by the circumstances in which he is prepared to withdraw his judgement. The commitment account also claims

(b) that a content of the form 'All natural numbers have property F' is true just in case all its commitments are fulfilled. The commitment account makes it relatively unproblematic that a first-order universal quantification should, though true, be unprovable from a particular recursive set of axioms. On the commitment account, what gives the universal quantification its truth-condition is not the set of ways it can be proved, but the commitments incurred in judging it. The commitments of a first-order quantification may all be fulfilled, and hence the quantification may be true, even though it is not provable from the first-order axioms a subject is employing. Suppose the molecular anti-constructivist does endorse the commitment account. Then he will have a motivation for favouring a notion of a model of the first-order arithmetical axioms which excludes from the domains of his favoured models the presence of the non-standard elements characteristic of non-standard models.

In this arithmetical example, it seems quite inappropriate to level the charge that in violating deductive conservativeness by adding second-order quantifiers, our molecular anti-constructivist is altering the meaning of the first-order quantifiers. On the contrary, this anti-constructivist is offering an account of the meaning of the first-order quantifiers which explains how, on the meaning already grasped at the first-order level, a first-order sentence may be true but underivable using the given first-order resources.

This development of the molecular anti-constructivist's position also points up a further complex pattern of agreement and disagreement between John Skorupski and me. Given the preceding discusion, I am of course at one with him in rejecting any requirement of deductive conservativeness. But, if I have understood his position correctly, we differ over the requirements the semantics must satisfy. Skorupski is happy to say that grasp of meaning is grasp of correctness conditions, and for him correctness conditions are constituted by assertoric and inferential dispositions (p. 140). But there is nothing in his position to rule out, and some hints that he would permit, this possibility: that the appropriateness of a semantics for a fragment of a language not containing a new logical constant be determined in part by inference rules for the new connective. I have been trying to say how the molecular anti-constructivist disallows this possibility.

A very different critic, Tennant, writing from a constructivist standpoint, argues that rules of inference are justified only if they satisfy a principle of inherited warrant.[15] If we take the meaning of a logical constant to be given by its introduction rules, the principle of inherited warrant requires of a valid inference that there is an effective method of turning warrants for the assertion of its premisses into warrants for the assertion of its conclusion.[16] Tennant argues that if this principle is correct, such classical laws as $(P \supset Q) \vee (Q \supset P)$ are not justified: for we do not always have an effective method which will either produce a warrant for asserting $P \supset Q$ or produce a warrant for asserting $Q \supset P$.

What will be the anti-constructivist's attitude to the principle of inherited warrant? The anti-constructivist cannot take conformity to the principle as sufficient for the validity of an argument. The inference 'P, so it's verifiable that

P' conforms to the principle. But for an anti-constructivist, it will not be truth-preserving under an assignment to *P* which is true but unverifiable.[17] Tennant's argument, though, relies only on the necessity for validity of conformity to the principle of inherited warrant. So will the anti-constructivist agree at least that it is a necessary condition for validity? The anti-constructivist will readily agree that there is *a* sense in which any valid argument will meet the principle of inherited warrant. Presumably, if we have an initial warrant for a set Σ of premises, and have a valid derivation of *B* from Σ, then the initial warrant and the derivation jointly constitute a warrant for *B*. But this of course is an acknowledgement by the anti-constructivist of the necessity of the principle of inherited warrant only on his favoured anti-constructivist semantics for *B* and for the sentences in Σ. So the crucial question is not the principle of inherited warrant, but rather whether those anti-constructivist semantics are philosophically justifiable. If they are not, then the anti-constructivist is in trouble anyway; while if they are justifiable, he will have good reason for acknowledging one form of the principle of inherited warrant. So let us look very briefly at one way in which the anti-constructivist might defend his semantics. Since Tennant mentions it, we will fix on the classical law $(P \supset Q) \vee (Q \supset P)$.

It is well-known that $(P \supset Q) \vee (Q \supset P)$ is not derivable in a natural deduction system using only the rules for $\supset$ and $\vee$.[18] Addition of the classical rules for negation permits its derivation. The derivability of $(P \supset Q) \vee (Q \supset P)$ is justified, then, if the classical rules for negation are justified. From the standpoint of the molecular anti-constructivist, this is another case in which an extension—that formed by adding the negation rules to those for $\supset$ and $\vee$—is deductively non-conservative but semantically conservative. The philosophical issue then turns on what makes the classical, rather than the intuitionistic, notion of semantic consequence appropriate.

What is in question here is not whether we can give a description of the practices of a community for which the intuitionistic semantics is appropriate. The molecular anti-constructivist should not be in the business of denying that such descriptions are possible (at least for the language of arithmetic[19]). In fact Tennant provides vivid descriptions of such practices.[20] The question is rather whether we can describe a practice for which the classical semantics is appropriate and equally justified. One way is as follows.

It is hard to conceive of the use of any sentences without the use of some negation device which can be applied to them, even if only in thought. There are many pressures to have such a device in the language. Let us take it that we do have such a device in the language. (This involves no loss of generality, since the present considerations can be applied equally at the level of thought.) In 'Understanding Logical Constants', I argued that classical negation can be introduced over a primitive incompatibility relation, written '*A*|*B*' for '*A* and *B* are incompatible'.[21] Classical negation is the weakest unary operator *O* for which the rule *P*|*OP* holds generally. Suppose a thinker uses an incompatibility relation in his thought. Then the claim that an operator *O* used by the thinker should indeed be given as its semantic value the weakest operation which validates the rule $P|OP$ is certified by the fact that there is no proposition stronger than P which he treats as primitively incompatible with OP.

If O is the weakest operator for which $P|OP$ holds generally, the classical introduction and elimination rules are valid for it. Take the introduction rule first. Suppose that for an operator O for which $P|OP$ holds generally, the analogue of negation introduction fails, that is that this inference is not valid:

$$\frac{\begin{array}{c}[A]\\ \vdots \\ OA\end{array}}{OA.}$$

(Square brackets indicate discharged premisses.) This would imply that from the fact if A holds, incompatible propositions (A, OA) hold, we cannot infer this: that OA holds. This is inconsistent with OA being the weakest proposition incompatible with A. So negation introduction is validated for O. As for the analogue of the classical negation elimination rule, suppose we had a case in which this inference fails:

$$\frac{OOA}{A.}$$

In this case we would have that OOA is true and A not true. Since OOA is incompatible with OA, OA must be not true in the given case. But if A and OA are both not true, OA is not the weakest proposition incompatible with A, for being the weakest entails that OA is true in any case in which A is not. Since by hypothesis OA is the weakest such proposition, there can be no case in which the analogue of classical negation elimination fails.

The constructivist may protest: '*I* accept that $P|\sim P$ quite generally; and nor in a sense do I think that anything stronger than P is incompatible with $\sim P$. So how can your considerations justify the classical assignments of truth-values in the propositional calculus?' But what the intuitionist means by the incompatibility of P with Q is that a contradiction is derivable from the set $\{P, Q\}$. The practice of a clearly classical community will manifest no such immediate commitment to the derivability of such a contradiction from the incompatibility of P and Q. For the classicists, such incompatibility means only that there is no model in which both P and Q are true. Even in the restricted languages in which incompatibility does imply the existence of such a derivation, the implication will be regarded as a substantive thesis (a completeness theorem). Suppose we do have a community which manifests no such commitment to the existence of a derivation from the incompatibility of two propositions. If the constructivist insists on taking their incompatibility relation as involving such a commitment, then the requirement that grasp of content be suitably manifestable, on which he often so strongly insists elsewhere, will here apply against his own position. It will be the constructivist, not his opponent, who in his semantics will be making a gratuitous, and apparently incommunicable, contribution to the meanings justifiably ascribable.[22]

4. Gödel's Theorem: A Problem for Constructivists

I now give an argument for the superiority of a theory of understanding which entails an anti-constructivist semantics, an argument which concerns the constructivist's favourite domain, that of proof procedures. The argument turns on difficulties the constructivist has in giving a satisfactory philo-sophical account of Gödel's undecidability results. This may seem like a technical issue, but it is not. It is one which goes to the heart of the difference between a constructivist and his opponent, viz. the issue of whether a content is to be individuated by specified means of establishing it, or rather is to be individuated by what has to be the case for it to be true, without any mention in that individuation of means of establishing the content in question.

As is well known, Gödel's theorem applies to a suitable formalization I of intuitionistic arithmetic. Let $Pf(x, y)$ be that open sentence of the system I which says that the number x is the proof of a formula with Gödel number y. Gödel showed us how to find a number g such that g is the Gödel number of the formula $\forall n \sim Pf(n, \mathbf{g})$, where $\mathbf{g}$ is the numeral for g. The predicate $\sim Pf(x, \mathbf{g})$ is primitive recursive and so Gödel's famous reasoning goes through unprob-lematically for the intuitionistic formalization. Part of the Gödel argument applied to this case is that if I is consistent, then for any natural number n, the sentence $\sim Pf(\mathbf{n}, \mathbf{g})$ is provable in I. Yet the sentence $\forall n \sim Pf(n, \mathbf{g})$ is not provable in I if I is consistent. This reasoning is normally, and it seems to me quite reasonably, taken as a demonstration that $\forall n \sim Pf(n, \mathbf{g})$ is, though unprovable in I, true.

I am going to argue that the philosophical account which makes this a reasonable attitude also underwrites an anti-constructivist semantics. That is, the reasonable attitude is unavailable to the constructivist. So the question I want to concentrate on is this: under what conception of meaning is the Gödel sentence $\forall n \sim Pf(n, \mathbf{g})$ true?

On the commitment account of universal quantification over the natural numbers, this question has a straightforward answer. Suppose that the axioms of a formal arithmetical system are true. In that case, if for any n the sentence $\sim Pf(\mathbf{n}, \mathbf{g})$ is provable, then for any n the sentence $\sim Pf(\mathbf{n}, \mathbf{g})$ is true. So all the commitments of the sentence $\forall n \sim Pf(n, \mathbf{g})$ are fulfilled. But according to the second part of the commitment account (Section 3 above), a universal numerical quantification is true if and only if all its commitments are fulfilled. So on the commitment account, $\forall n \sim Pf(n, \mathbf{g})$ is a true sentence.

The reasoning in this straightforward answer is unavailable to the constructivist. The reasoning relies on the commitment account, which allows for the possibility, incompatible with any constructivism deserving of the name, that a universally quantified arithmetical sentence be true though unestablishable.

How might the constructivist who wishes to hold to the truth of the Gödel sentence respond to this challenge? This constructivist needs an answer which meets three requirements:

(i) he must give a constructivist specification of the meaning of the universal quantifier ('the meaning requirement');

(ii) he must give an argument to establish that the Gödel sentence is true ('the establishability requirement'); and

(iii) he must show that the argument he gives in meeting the establishability requirement (ii) is faithful to the meaning-specification he gives in meeting the meaning requirement (i). We can call this third requirement 'the fidelity requirement'.

The usual informal semantical explanation of universal quantification given by intuitionists is that a proof of a universal quantification $\forall n F(n)$ is any method which applied to an arbitrary number n yields a proof that $F(n)$, together with a proof that it does. By itself, this does not obviously meet the meaning requirement (i), since it does not exclude the possibility that one of the proofs mentioned in the proof-condition is non-constructive; nor does it exclude the possibility that one of those proofs relies on principles which can be justified only on a classical conception of meaning; nor does it rule out impredicativity in the specification of proof-conditions. The usual informal explanation could be sharpened up by requiring that a (canonical) proof of $\forall n F(n)$, where $F(\ )$ is quantifier-free, is a proof in Primitive Recursive Arithmetic of $F(n)$, for suitably chosen free variable 'n'. But by this standard, the Gödel sentence $\forall n \sim Pf(n, g)$ is definitely not provable by any means, direct or indirect. It could not be counted as true by an intuitionist who adopts that demanding standard.

Can an intuitionist relax the standards a little, still retain a definitely constructivist account of meaning, and count the Gödel sentence as true? Crispin Wright has proposed that essentially Gödel's own reasoning can be enlisted to the service of the intuitionist as follows.[23] 'Take some recursively axiomatized intuitionistic formalization I of arithmetic, and consider an arbitrary natural number n. Suppose, for *reductio*, that $Pf(n, g)$. The relation $Pf(x, y)$ is primitive recursive, and we can take it that all primitive recursive relations are representable in I. It follows that $Pf(n, g)$ is probable in I. Then, by decoding the Gödel numbering, we have that the formula whose Gödel number is g is provable in I, that is, that $\forall n \sim Pf(n, g)$ is provable in I. But then I would be inconsistent. So given that I is true, we have reduced to absurdity the supposition that $Pf(n, g)$. By the intuitionist's semantical account of negation, we then have a demonstration that $\sim Pf(n, g)$. The whole of the preceding proof can then be taken as a method which, applied to an arbitrary number n, yields a demonstration that $\sim Pf(n, g)$. Hence, by the intuitionist's intuitive semantics for universal quantification, we have an intuitionistic proof that $\forall n \sim Pf(n, g)$, under the supposition of the consistency of I.'

The anti-constructivist should happily agree that Wright's demonstration does give a method which, applied to each natural number n, yields a demonstration that $\sim Pf(n, g)$. (The anti-constructivist should not quarrel with the assumption of consistency of the formalization, which he equally makes for his own system.) The problem for the intuitionist who defends his position via the Wright demonstration is rather in meeting the meaning and fidelity requirements (i) and (iii) above.

How might this intuitionist meet the meaning requirement? Perhaps he might say that a proof of $\forall nF(n)$, where $F(\ )$ is quantifier-free, is a proof that for all natural numbers n, $F(\boldsymbol{n})$ is provable in Primitive Recursive Arithmetic. The Wright demonstration would certainly meet the fidelity requirement with respect to this semantical proposal. The anti-constructivist who endorses the commitment account should also agree that this proposed semantics at least gives a sufficient condition for being a proof of a universal quantification of the sort in question. But again, the question is whether the intuitionist has a right to it. The intuitionist aims to individuate sense by proof-conditions. Given this aim, to try to specify what a proof of a universal quantification is by helping oneself to a phrase of the form 'proof that for any natural number . . .' is circular.

To clarify the complaint, it should be added that this charge of circularity against the intuitionist does not preclude the use of universal quantification elsewhere in the _____ of 'A proof of $\forall nF(n)$ is _____', provided it is not embedded in the phrase 'proof that'. Further, in accordance with more general views I hold on the individuation of sense, I agree that it is legitimate to quantify over a newly individuated sense in a clause which aims to individuate that very sense by means of its contribution to proof-conditions.[24] But it is hard to see how acknowledging this point helps the intuitionist here. The point might lead to the formulation 'Universal quantification over natural numbers is a second-level concept $Qn \ldots n \ldots$ such that a proof that $QnF(n)$ is a proof that Qn (it is provable in Primitive Recursive Arithmetic that $F(\boldsymbol{n})$'. But that condition is hardly uniquely individuating of universal quantification.

Alternatively the intuitionist may say that a proof of $\forall nF(n)$ is a constructive method which, applied to each natural number n, yields a proof of $F(\boldsymbol{n})$. But we need a statement of what 'constructive' means. We presume, when issues in the theory of meaning are not at stake, that what distinguishes a constructivist is the semantical clauses he accepts for various constructions. Our hold on the idea of constructivism begins to slip if these semantical clauses themselves contain the notion of constructive proof eliminably. (We do not get a positive theory of meaning just by rejecting proofs which use the law of the excluded middle or double-negation elimination.) If all and only constructivist notions were properly manifestable in use, perhaps we could obtain some independent constraints on such notions. But the burden of the commitment account, and of other arguments in *Thoughts*, is that that biconditional fails.

At this point, our intuitionist may say that we should simply rest content with an intuitive recognition that the Wright demonstration is a suitable method, which applied to an arbitrary natural number n, yields a proof that $\sim Pf(n, g)$. But if he rests content with that response, he will never allay the suspicion that the proof can be ratified as sound only by an anti-constructivist account of content. The anti-constructivist will say that we find it acceptable because it employs means which we can see to be sound for the kind of meaning which is possessed by the numerical quantifier over natural numbers. But what this kind is, the anti-constructivist will say, is given precisely by the commitment account.

An apparently different response to the anti-constructivist's challenge is given by Dummett.[25] Dummett is partly concerned to rebut the charge that Gödel's results give a counter-example to doctrines that say that meaning is use. That is not a charge I would make: the commitment account, though anti-constructivist, certainly says in terms of use what it is for an expression to have the meaning of the universal quantifier. What is of interest here in Dummett's discussion is his positive account of the way he says the intuitionist should react to Gödel's results.

One of Dummett's points is that the notion of provability is indefinitely extensible. What he means by this is that for any definite characterization of provability, there is a natural extension of it which yields a more inclusive notion of provability. Anti-constructivists should agree that the notion of provability is indefinitely extensible in this sense. Dummett continues by saying that when meanings are given in terms of the methods of proof we possess,

the very meanings of our mathematical statements are always subject to shift.[26]

The meanings, he writes, 'must, at any given stage in the development of mathematics, be specific',[27] but as the notion of a canonical proof changes over time, the meanings of mathematical statements are 'subject to fluctuation'.[28]

Does this response meet the challenge? The crucial issue concerns the meaning of the universal quantifier in the days before we had any conception of Gödel's theorem. Is it possible to give a meaning to the universal quantifier over natural numbers such that on that old meaning—not on some new, shifted meaning—we are rationally required to accept Gödel's argument as conclusively establishing the truth of $\forall n \sim Pf(n, g)$? If we accept the claims of the commitment account, we can give a theory of understanding and truth which underwrites the view that it is possible to grasp such a meaning. But the response that there is a shift of meaning does not.

In the earlier paper, 'The Philosophical Significance of Gödel's Theorem', Dummett describes the step from the truth of all of $\sim Pf(0, g)$, $\sim Pf(1, g)$, $\sim Pf(2, g), \ldots$ to the truth of $\forall n \sim Pf(n, g)$ as 'quite evident'.[29] On the commitment theory of universal quantification, the step is indeed quite evident. But is that also the case for an intuitionist theory? Suppose we follow Dummett's later approach and restrict at a given time the methods of canonical proof to a precisely specified class and then explain truth in terms of provability using those methods. In that case the step will be invalid: we cannot move from

$$\forall n \ \text{True}('\sim Pf(\textbf{\textit{n}}, \textbf{\textit{g}})')$$

to

$$\text{True}('\forall n \sim Pf(n, \textbf{\textit{g}})').$$

Alternatively the intuitionist may say that the schematic principle that one can move from

$$\forall n \ \text{True}('F(\textbf{\textit{n}})')$$

to

$$\text{True}(`\forall n F(n)\text{'})$$

is to be adopted as extending the intuitionist's concept of truth. But here we then go through an argument of the form we had above. Is the given extension justified on the basis of what was previously meant by the universal quantifier, or not? If it is justified, we have yet to be given the account of how the justification runs. If it is not justified, the constructivist is doing less well than the anti-constructivist who endorses and exploits the commitment account.

The discussion of the preceding paragraph can be reproduced *pari passu* in response to someone who defends the intuitionist's view by saying 'The correctness of an extension of any system of arithmetic by the omega-rule is evidently valid'. This time the argument would be applied to rules for object-language sentences rather than to the metalinguistic truth-predicate.

The general argument of this section has its seeds in the considerations of the immediately preceding Section 3 of this essay. It is essentially a development by contraposition. The preceding section endorsed the conditional that if we hold a proof-condition theory of meaning, then deductive conservatism is compulsory. Here we have been arguing in effect that Gödel's results show that deductive conservatism is implausible, and have been drawing by contraposition the negative conclusion about proof-conditional theories of meaning.

The argument of this section also prompts a reflection about indefinitely extensible concepts more generally. The natural extension of any definite characterization of a given indefinitely extensible concept always strikes us as justified, as something which is not a matter for mere decision. In the case of the indefinitely extensible concept of proof, we have tried to underwrite this impression of justification—at least for arithmetical universal quantifications— by appeal to the commitment account of understanding. The question then opened for further investigation is this: is it true of all indefinitely extensible concepts that there is a theory which plays a role analogous to the commitment account in the present treatment of Gödelian cases, and which succeeds in justifying one extension rather than another?

5. Rule-Following and Justification

Do the various notions of justification above and the considerations involving them require a non-sceptical response to Kripke's challenge about rule-following?[30] If not, why not? And if so, what non-sceptical solution will mesh with the arguments above?

The answers to these questions vary for the several types of justification we considered. But we should first clarify the questions themselves by saying what a sceptical solution is. Suppose a thinker has applied a concept in a number of cases. A sceptical solution is one according to which no non-trivial property of those previous applications, be the property individual, social, or of any other relational kind, makes an application of the concept correct (or makes it incorrect) in a new case. Rather, according to sceptical accounts, the correctness or otherwise of an application in the new case is some complex function of the thinker's and others' reactions to the new case.

This way of characterizing a sceptical solution takes as definitive the negative claims in the sceptic's challenge, rather than the positive features of the sceptical solution Kripke outlines. That solution employs assertibility-conditions which require a kind of social agreement. But we should not take the presence of social elements in a solution as sufficient for it to be sceptical. A theorist may have social elements in his solution because he accepts, for instance, Burge's anti-individualistic arguments.[31] This does not necessarily make his solution sceptical in our sense. Equally, a solution framed using assertibility-conditions is not necessarily sceptical. A theorist may have Dummettian reasons for a formulation in terms of assertibility-conditions, while not being sceptical in our sense about rule-following.[32] Nor is the combination of assertibility-conditions and social elements enough for scepticism, since we can conceive of a consistent theorist falling under the label 'non-sceptical Burgean Dummettian'.

To endorse a sceptical solution certainly seems consistent with acknowledging the obligation discussed in Section 1 above, the obligation to offer an account of understanding for which an adequate Determination Theory exists. Even if the correctness of applications in a new case is a function of a thinker's and others' reactions to that case, it is consistent to require that the range of that function exhibit a certain pattern if the putative concept is to be genuine. It seems that the sceptic can legitimately object to the alleged quantifier Q of Section 1 without abandoning the sceptical nature of his solution.

It also seems that some sceptics can accept a non-vacuous distinction between sense-determining and sense-resultant principles. Consider the case of addition. One of these sceptics may say that the rule for conjunction introduction is sense-determining (s-d): the semantic value of '&' is, he argues, fixed in part by the fact that his favoured condition on communal acceptance of it is met. This is consistent with his acknowledging that an inference such as

$$\frac{(A \vee B) \, \& \, (A \vee C)}{A \, \& \, (B \vee C)}$$

is sense-resultant (s-r), something determined as true in part because of the semantic value fixed for '&' and '∨' in the sense-determining cases.[33] (This is of course not the most radical kind of scepticism.) This moderate scepticism would maintain an analogous position about the sense of 'plus'. As we noted in Section 2, the s-d/s-r distinction applies outside the logical constants too. We said generally that a theory treats a sentence s as s-d for a particular expression in it if (i) according to the theory, understanding the expression requires some specified kind of non-inferential acceptance of s, and (ii) still according to the theory, a certain semantical property of the expression is crucial to the truth or falsity of the sentences in which the expression occurs, and what makes it the case that the expression has that semantical property is (in part) that it has some specified relation to the given sentence *s*. So, one of our moderate sceptics might take '7 + 1 = 8' as s-d for '+', while also taking '11 + 13 = 24' as s-r for '+', its truth resulting in part from the semantic value of '+' determined by the favoured kind of acceptance of other sentences containing '+', including '7 + 1 = 8'.

When, however, we turn to the above discussion of Gödel's theorem and the commitment account, this relative independence from stances on rule-following disappears. If the arguments of the previous Section 4 are to be sound, the Gödel sentence must be s-r for universal quantification over natural numbers, rather than s-d. If the sentence were s-d, that would indeed not rule out our finding its informal demonstration compelling. But if it were s-d, it would be a mistake to look for something present in our previous uses of its constituent vocabulary from which we can soundly argue that it is true, rather than false. The argument of Section 4 presumes that this would not be a mistake.

The commitment account is also naturally elaborated in a non-sceptical theory. Since the theory in which it is naturally elaborated is of a type which can be made plausible for other logical constants too, I will devote the remainder of this section to this general type. The upshot is that although some of the earlier points about justification are consistent with sceptical theories, it is a non-sceptical account that I will be endorsing.

Someone who understands 'and' finds this transition primitively compelling:

$$\frac{\text{John is in London and Peter is in Paris}}{\text{John is in London.}}$$

In saying the transition is found primitively compelling I do not mean merely that it is not accepted on the basis of an inference currently made. A transition made because the subject has remembered it, having perhaps heard it endorsed by someone he trusts, would meet that condition. What I mean by 'primitively compelling' is rather that the subject finds it compelling, and does not need to take its acceptability as answerable to anything else in order to be credited with the concepts expressed in it. More particularly, a thinker who understands 'and' finds the transition compelling because it is of a certain form, viz.

$$\frac{A \text{ and } B}{A.}$$

Similar remarks holds for inferences of the forms

$$\frac{A \text{ and } B}{B} \quad \text{and} \quad \frac{A \qquad B}{A \text{ and } B.}$$

On the non-sceptical solution I advocate, the semantics for conjunction is determined from these forms which causally explain what the thinker finds primitively compelling. In the classical case, the semantic value of 'and' is that truth-function which makes inferences of the three displayed forms always truth-preserving—that is the classical truth-function for conjunction. An intuitionist could equally adapt this approach to his own ends. For the intuitionist, this non-sceptical conception would be developed by saying that the contribution made to meaning-giving proof-conditions, or assertibility-conditions, by 'and' will be that a sentence containing 'and' can be established by, and has consequences given by, the forms above.

This non-sceptical approach sustains a notion of normativity in both the classical and the intuitionistic cases. In both cases, the way in which the semantics is determined from the forms guarantees that the principles which are found primitively compelling are indeed *correct* on the semantics determined. On the semantics determined, transitions of the displayed forms are valid on the notion of validity endorsed by the semantical conception in question.

The commitment account fits squarely into this non-sceptical approach. One who understands the universal quantifier over natural numbers finds it compelling that, given the supposition that every number is, if even, the sum of two primes, then 17 is, if even, the sum of two primes. He finds it compelling because the transition is of the form

$$\frac{\text{Every number is } F}{n \text{ is } F}$$

where n is a canonical numeral for a natural number. The semantic value of 'every number' is determined from this form. The form captures the commitments of an arbitrary universal numerical quantification, and the commitment account of Section 3 said how the contribution of the quantifier to truth conditions is fixed from these commitments.

I make three observations about this general non-sceptical approach. First, a form which is instantiated in surveyable transitions and causally influences a thinker can also be instantiated in unsurveyable transitions. We can hardly say that what causally influences the thinker is that a transition is of a certain form and is surveyable, without being committed to the claim that the form is causally influential.[34] So on this theory, 'and' has a semantical value in unsurveyable cases as well as surveyable ones.

The second observation is this: to say that the transition is found primitively compelling because of its form is not to say that the thinker has to conceptualize that form. The thinker does not have to conceptualize it. The form can be causally influential at the level of a subpersonal psychology. Indeed if one is to generalize the present non-sceptical approach to other cases, it is crucial that the form is *not* conceptualized by the thinker. Otherwise, one would simply be trading in a problem about possession of the concept of conjunction for one about possession of the concept of a certain form.

The third observation is that probably nothing at all is found primitively compelling in all circumstances. This non-sceptical approach will have to make use of, for instance, the idea that what matters is what is found primitively compelling in the normal circumstances in which content-involving personal-level psychology gets a grip.[35]

I have been discussing issues of justification and of responsibility to meaning, and arguing the need for Determination Theories and for grounding our treatment of all these issues in positive accounts of grasp of logical concepts. But issues of justification and responsibility are not unique to logical notions; they arise for all concepts. The particular proposals developed here, and their mention of form, are no doubt appropriate only for theories of grasp of logical and broadly mathematical notions. For other concepts, positive accounts of mastery must be built from different materials. Yet we should also be interested in the structural features common to all concepts. One of our goals should be the formulation of a general theory of concepts, a theory in which we can display something like the present account of logical notions as an instance of a general type common to all concepts. Without this, our understanding of logical concepts, or of any other concepts, will remain incomplete.

Appendix

The later parts of John Skorupski's paper became available after completion of the material above. I cannot deal here with all the points he makes in his later sections, but I will very briefly address the queries he raises in his Section IX about my own position.

Skorupski implies, rightly, that I endorse neither Mill's ultra-empiricism about logical principles, nor the view that logical principles express the laws of 'a domain of ... transempirical fact'. But if I occupy neither of those positions, he asks, 'How are the principles which express our primitive impressions of validity *justified* by a semantics which appeals to the laws of truth?' (p. 159, emphasis in original).

I answer that we should recall the spurious quantifier Q. Q is spurious because no account is possible of its contribution to truth-conditions, given the laws which are said to be valid and the laws which are said to be invalid for it. The reasoning which supports the conclusion that Q is spurious relies neither on Mill's empiricism nor on the assumption that logical principles express the laws of 'a domain of transempirical fact' (nor on the alternation of these two views). When we show that the principles found primitively compelling which involve a given operator determine a semantic value, we show that the operator does not suffer from the same defects as Q. Once we have shown that the operator possesses a semantic value, we are then under the obligation to demonstrate that the semantic value determined is one which makes the logical principles in question truth-preserving under all relevant assignments. Such a demonstration will consist of metalinguistic reasoning involving the predicate 's is true under interpretation I'. It seems reasonable to describe such a vindication of an operator and its laws as a justification by means of a semantics, a justification which relies on various principles about truth-in-an-interpretation.

On this position, an impression, however primitively compelling, of the validity of a linguistic form is never sufficient for its being so. For such impressions could exist for principles involving Q, or indeed for Arthur Prior's *tonk*.[36] Even when the impression is present for a meaningful operator, any sound argument from such impressions to the validity of a principle will not appeal solely to the account of understanding (the possession condition) for the operator. Any such argument has to proceed through the appropriate Determination Theory, applied to the possession condition, in order to establish that, on the determined semantic value for the operator, the principle in question is valid.

Skorupski also tentatively suggests that his position and mine in 'Understanding Logical Constants' diverge over whether any principles are what he calls strongly a priori. By saying that a proposition is strongly a priori, he means roughly that experience could not justify us in rejecting it. Skorupski's view is that 'naturalism does indeed imply that there are no *strongly* a priori real propositions' (p. 151). A logical principle is, he says, only weakly a priori— that is, we are rationally justified in accepting it 'prior to', or 'independent of' empirical investigation (p. 150). There is then a divergence from my own views, Skorupski holds, because I (Peacocke) say that a person does not understand negation 'unless he appreciates that A and $\sim A$ cannot both be true'. It seems I must hold some principles to be strongly a priori.

Actually, it is an interesting question whether the claims of 'Understanding Logical Constants' can be stated entirely without reliance on modal notions. But since coyness is hardly going to advance discussion here, let me acknowledge in any case that I do think logical principles are strongly a priori. Skorupski by contrast says that a proposal that certain physical particles both have and do not have a certain property is not 'strictly incoherent or unintelligible' (p. 157). I disagree. If for some operator O, a theorist consciously allows that both A and OA may be simultaneously true, I do not know with what right we could interpret O in his mouth as negation. What would make it negation? To say that this question does not need answering would not sit well with Skorupski's view that meaning is given by assertion-conditions and inferential power.

Skorupski argues from naturalism to the conclusion that there are no strongly a priori propositions. He does not define 'naturalism' in the present paper, but elsewhere he writes that

> Naturalism begins with the elementary or primitive notion that we are simply and straightforwardly a part of the world we know ... perception, cognition, motivation, action and so on are purely empirical, causal processes.[37]

I enthusiastically endorse this moderate naturalism. My problem lies in seeing how it entails that no real proposition is strongly a priori, that is that every real proposition is one which experience could justify us in rejecting. What does follow from the naturalism, I agree, is a certain kind of fallibilism. For propositions knowledge of which requires some causal influence of the world on us, we can always conceive that earlier stages of the causal chain were not of the right kind. It seems that we could always be wrong about some matter of fact where a claim to knowledge of it requires such a causal influence. This fallibilism is entirely consistent with the necessity of $\sim(A \& \sim A)$, for any proposition A, and is consistent too with the view that experience could never justify us in rejecting something of the form $\sim(A \& \sim A)$. For, first, a model of knowledge of logical truths as beliefs causally explained by the facts they state seems wrong. Second, and more important, consider the case in which a thinker *does* in fact infer a logical truth, (say $A \vee \sim A$), from his causally acquired belief that A. Maybe the fallibilism allows us to conclude that he might be wrong about A, and that it might be that $\sim A$ is true.[38] It does not follow that he might be wrong about $(A \vee \sim A)$, for 'might be wrong about' is not closed under logical implication. The conclusion that he might be wrong about it would require the additional premiss that it could be false that $(A \vee \sim A)$. This premiss would be additional to the naturalism, rather than something entailed by it. A naturalist could, and in my view should, deny the additional premiss.

So far I have been considering a moderate naturalism. But there is a more radical variety. The more radical variety adds to the moderate version the further thesis that all truths supervene on descriptive truths about the actual world. There is also a relativized version: to be a radical naturalist about truths of a given kind is to hold that all truths of that kind supervene on descriptive truths about the actual world. Hume, on the usual reading of him, was a radical naturalist about truths involving the relation of causation (as it is in the world). Is Skorupski's claim about naturalism and the strong a priori true if we construe it as concerning radical naturalism?

There is indeed a problem for a radical naturalist in claiming that experience could not justify rejection of certain propositions. There is a problem, because there is a problem for him about the meaning of *any* modal claim. The radical naturalist must either abandon modal discourse altogether, or believe that it is possible to do for it what Hume tried to do for talk about causation as it is in the world. There has been some work in this latter direction.[39] It is no easy task, and this Appendix is no place for a detailed discussion of it. But suppose it could be done. Then just as a Humean should not object to, but should endorse, the claim that heat causes expansion, so the radical naturalist who offers a positive treatment of necessity will say that certain propositions are necessary. May not propositions of the form $\sim(A \& \sim A)$ be amongst them? I do not think that John Skorupski has shown that they cannot be. If they can, then even the radical naturalist can coherently accept that they are strongly a priori.[40]

Notes

1. Chisholm, 'Identity Through Time', and 'Reply to Strawson's Comments' in H. Keifer and M. Munitz (eds.), *Language, Belief and Metaphysics.*

2. I discuss this framework in more detail in 'What Are Concepts?', in P. French, T. Uehling Jr., and H. Wettstein (eds.), *Contemporary Perspectives in the Philosophy of Language II, Midwest Studies in Philosophy* 14.

3. For extended discussion of the notion of harmony, see N. Tennant, *Anti-Realism and Logic: Truth as Eternal.*

4. See Dummett, 'The Justification of Deduction', in *Truth and Other Enigmas* and *Frege: Philosophy of Language.*

5. Not all such valid principles need be logical consequences of the s-d principles. The philosophical account of how the semantic value of a constant is fixed may capture other cases too. See for instance the treatment of what are called 'limiting principles' in my 'Understanding Logical Constants: A Realist's Account' in *Proceedings of the British Academy* 63.

6. Skorupski's other criticism of intuitionistic semantics is that standard introduction rules do not exhaust the possible ways in which disjunctions and conditionals can get into our fabric of belief. He notes that induction generates wholly new habits of inference, and says that because this is so, we cannot require that extensions effected by introducing 'All', with associated inductive rules, be conservative (p. 149). One would expect, though, that a Dummettian intuitionist would require conservative extension only for rules acceptance of which is logically required given the meanings determined by the canonical introduction and/or elimination rules. Rules of inductive inference do not meet this condition. If they were to, it would be much easier to despatch the inductive sceptic than it actually is.

7. Dummett, *Elements of Intuitionism*, pp. 364 ff.

8. *Anti-Realism and Logic: Truth as Eternal*, p. 146.

9. 'Understanding Logical Constants'.

10. *Elements of Intuitionism*, pp. 363–4.

11. That it goes beyond the General Requirement in a book devoted to intuitionism is of course not a criticism.

12. See H. Field, *Science Without Numbers*, esp. p. 115 (fn. 30) and S. Shapiro, 'Conservativeness and Incompleteness', *Journal of Philosophy* 80, pp. 521–31, esp. p. 525. The distinction is in fact employed in some passages of Dummett's 'The Justification of Deduction'. If what I say below is correct, the distinction is of greater philosophical relevance than it is accorded in that discussion.

13. This is a slight overstatement. A reasonable molecular anti-constructivist can consistently recognize local holisms. If the 'new' logical constant is one whose sense must be grasped (at least in thought) in order to possess the concepts expressed in the unextended fragment, the 'further condition' of this sentence of the text should not be imposed with respect to it.

14. See *Thoughts: An Essay on Content*, in particular the chapter on universal quantification.

15. *Anti-Realism and Logic*, pp. 81–2.

16. Tennant gives a formal development of the principle in his ibid., 'Version 5', p. 103.

17. It seems to me that Tennant's valuable and stimulating discussion also begs the question against the anti-constructivist when he answers his own question as to the effect of introducing a new connective by saying 'For our answer there is nowhere to turn to but to an inspection of the assertibility conditions governing assertions of the new form' (ibid., p. 79). In general, recognition of a wider range of ways of manifesting grasp of classical meanings than those discussed by Tennant generates the possibility of a correspondingly wider range of philosophical accounts of the justification of inferences.

18. There are various ways to see this, of which the simplest is to note that the intuitionistic rules for $\supset$ and $\vee$ are the same, and yet $(P \supset Q) \vee (Q \supset P)$ is not intuitionistically derivable.

19. Though for some complications, see the next section.

20. *Anti-Realism and Logic*, passim.

21. Here I was partly influenced by G. Harman's discussion in the 'The Meaning of Logical Constants', in E. LePore (ed.), *Truth and Interpretation: Perspectives on the Philosophy of Donald Davidson*. For more on the relations between some of the positions and notions in the present part of the paper, and Harman's views, see the Appendix of 'Understanding Logical Constants'.

22. In 'The Limits of Intelligibility: A Post-Verificationist Proposal', *Philosophical Review* 97, I argue that what is right in manifestation requirements can be stated without the commitment to behaviourism, verificationism, or to the rejection of local holisms. The Discrimination Principle developed and defended there would apply against the constructivist interpretation of a classical incompatibility relation.

23. In discussion and correspondence.

24. For more on this, see the discussion of what I call 'the A(C) form' in 'What are Concepts?'

25. See 'The Philosophical Significance of Gödel's Theorem' in *Truth and Other Enigmas*, and the discussion in *Elements of Intuitionism* at pp. 401–3.

26. *Elements of Intuitionism*, p. 401.

27. Ibid., p. 403.

28. Ibid.

29. *Truth and Other Enigmas*, p. 193.

30. S. Kripke, *Wittgenstein on Rules and Private Language*.

31. In T. Burge, 'Individualism and the Mental', P. French, T. Uehling Jr., and H. Wettstein (eds.), *Midwest Studies in Philosophy* 4, and many other writings.

32. Dummett's reasons are summarized in 'What is a Theory of Meaning? (II)', in G. Evans and J. McDowell (eds.), *Truth and Meaning*.

33. This point was emphasized to me by John Campbell.

34. More cautiously, we may prefer to say that the form differentially explains the thinker's finding the transition primitively compelling, in the sense of 'differential explanation' given in chapter 2 of my *Holistic Explanation*.

35. For more on all three points in the partially comparable case of understanding arithmetical concepts, see my 'Content and Norms in a Natural World', in E. LePore and E. Villaneuva (eds.), *Information-Theoretic Semantics and Epistemology*.

36. See A. Prior, 'The Runabout Inference-Ticket', *Analysis* 21, pp. 38–9.

37. See his 'Anti-realism: Cognitive Role and Semantic Content', in J. Butterfield (ed.), *Language, Mind and Logic*.

38. In fact even this needs qualification when we consider the necessary a posteriori. A chemist's procedures employed in discovering that water is H_2O are fallible, and rely on his causal interaction with the world. It does not follow that it is metaphysically possible that water is not H_2O. Similar qualifications are in order at several points in the text above.

39. See S. Blackburn's 'Morals and Modals', in G. Macdonald and C. Wright (eds.), *Fact, Science and Morality*.

40. In the five years since this reply was written, I have thought more about the relations between the a priori and possession conditions. The interested reader will find more in my paper 'How Are A Priori Truths Possible?', *European Journal of Philosophy* 1, and may find it fruitful to compare those views with John Skorupski's.

III

REALISM AND SCEPTICISM

7

Realism and Scepticism

Michael Williams[1]

I

It is a longstanding philosophical opinion that metaphysical realism is an essential ingredient in the case for scepticism.[2] However, as I see things, the source of scepticism lies in realist commitments of another sort entirely, commitments carried by a doctrine I call 'epistemological realism'. This is what I want to explain.[3]

II

Realism seems to open the way to scepticism because it seems to make it impossible to account for the necessary truth-conduciveness of epistemic justification.[4]

The primitive realist intuition is that the world is objective, meaning that how things are is independent of how we think, or even under certain conditions would think, they are. The obvious way to unpack this intuition is in terms of a certain view of truth, the view that, as Putnam says, truth is a radically non-epistemic notion.[5] This is the absolute minimum that must be involved in any conception of truth as 'correspondence'. We may have a lot to say about what this belief–world relation consists in. Or we may have very little, being content to see the content of the idea that truth is correspondence as exhausted by the thought that, for any given language, the extension of its truth-predicate is fixed by an appropriate 'disquotation' schema. But however truth *is* to be further explicated, if at all, realists must agree that it is *not* to be explicated in terms of any epistemic concepts. Not merely can we not identify truth with current justifiability, we cannot even identify it with ideal justifiability, assertibility at the limit of inquiry or anything like that. Any such account of truth will compromise the world's objectivity.

If this is right, any realist, whatever the details of his or her realism, is committed to viewing truth as epistemically unconstrained. The problem is to explain why this does not play into the sceptic's hands by decoupling justification and truth altogether. If truth is not to be analysed in epistemic terms, and is thus epistemically unconstrained, there can be no internal or conceptual connection between a proposition's or theory's being justified and its being true, no matter how strict or refined our standards of justification become. But we cannot establish an empirical connection between the conditions under which we take beliefs to be justified and the conditions under which they are true unless, *per impossible*, we have a way of grasping facts that is independent of whatever beliefs we happen to find credible. This seems to mean that we cannot establish any connection between justification and truth. Yet it is surely an essential feature of *epistemic* justification that justifying a belief makes it more likely to be true, which is all that is meant by the claim that epistemic justification is necessarily truth-conducive. So it seems that, once we become realists, we will be unable to show that what we call 'justification' really deserves the name, and hence unable to understand how our usual epistemic procedures are capable of yielding knowledge. We will become sceptics.

There are, of course, trivial connections between justification and truth that any realist is entitled to assert. For example, to justify a claim that p is automatically to justify a claim that 'p' is true: this much is guaranteed by the disquotation schema. Or again, if justifying a proposition or belief involves showing that it is likely to be true then, trivially, to justify p is to show that p is likely to be true. But such trivial connections provide no automatic links between the truth of our beliefs or theories and whatever *specific factors* we take to be relevant to their justification. The problem for the realist is to show how justification is truth-conducive, given that it ought to be; and this problem cannot be solved simply by pointing out that it is a conceptual truth that epistemic justification is truth-conducive. The necessary truth-conduciveness of epistemic justification *sets* the realist's problem: by itself it does not solve it.

We can bring the problem into sharper focus by exploring the traditional opposition between foundational theories of knowledge and coherence theories of truth. We might wonder how anyone could ever have thought there could be a dilemma with an epistemological theory as one horn and a metaphysical or semantic theory as the other. The need to account for the truth-conduciveness of epistemic justification gives the answer: either we explain knowledge in terms that connect directly with correspondence, hence with truth as the realist understands it, or we abandon realism and take truth to be some kind of epistemic notion. If neither strategy works, it will look as if we cannot account for the truth-conduciveness of justification at all and the result will be scepticism.

Traditional foundational theories of knowledge take the first option. They do more than postulate epistemologically basic beliefs, from which the credibility of all other beliefs is supposed ultimately to derive, they offer a distinctive account of how those beliefs come to constitute knowledge. As Schlick put it in his classic paper 'The Foundation of Knowledge', such beliefs involve a kind of 'pointing to reality', so that merely having such a belief ensures, or creates a strong logical presumption in favour of, its truth.[6] Any theory of this kind rests, in the end, on the idea of verification by confrontation. Certain facts, objects or properties are thought of as simply 'given'. Beliefs that record or refer to them can thus simply be seen to be true: the very way in which we form or understand the propositions involved in basic beliefs ensures that those propositions will be true so that, at the level of basic belief, the gap between believing with justification and believing truly becomes vanishingly small. This seemed to Schlick the only way of holding on to the notion of truth as correspondence. If truth is correspondence with reality, it must be possible at some points to grasp this correspondence directly, without inferential or even conceptual mediation.

To reject the idea of verification by confrontation, or so it seems, is to settle for some kind of coherence theory of justification. As Davidson puts it,

> What distinguishes a coherence theory is simply the claim that nothing can count as a reason for holding a belief except another belief. Its partisans reject as unintelligible the request for a ground or source of justification of another ilk.[7]

But now the pressure is in the other direction. If we do not explain knowledge and justification in terms that invoke the notion of correspondence, how are we to avoid explaining truth in terms of coherence. The necessary truth-conduciveness of justification seems to demand that we go one way or the other. As Blanshard once put it, in defence of the coherence theory of truth, 'If you place the nature of truth in one sort of character and its test in something quite different, you are pretty certain, sooner or later, to find the two falling apart.'[8]

This charge has considerable intuitive force. We cannot analyse truth and justification in wholly disparate terms without decoupling them entirely. The trouble is, we cannot usefully, or even coherently, analyse them in the same terms either. So whatever we do, it seems that scepticism is just around the corner.

The problems facing foundational theories of knowledge, which postulate some kind of 'direct' grasping of facts, are twofold. First, they seem vulnerable to a fatal dilemma. We need only ask whether or not this direct grasping of reality is supposed to be a cognitive state with propositional content or not. If it is not, it can have no impact on verification, since the 'knowledge' involved will have no content that could count for or against anything we believe. But if it is, all we have been given is another sort of belief.[9] Beliefs of this kind may still be thought of as privileged, in the sense that other less basic beliefs must, in the end, be accommodated to them. Nevertheless, justification has become a matter of accommodating some beliefs to others and so, in this weak sense, a matter of coherence. We have not shown how such a conception of justification can be combined with a realist conception of truth.

The second major problem is that, even if we could find a way between the horns of this dilemma, we would make little progress, if any, towards avoiding scepticism with respect to knowledge of the objective world. For the facts that we might grasp 'directly' are not plausibly taken to include facts about the objective world. At this level, the gap between believing with justification and believing truly is simply too wide. Experiential facts are therefore the only serious candidates, in which case we still face the problem of explaining how coherence among our privileged representations provides a basis for knowledge of the objective world. The standard sceptical thought-experiments, in which the world is very different from the way we take it to be without that difference being reflected in experience, suggest that this problem has no solution.

But though we cannot explain the necessary truth-conduciveness of justification by postulating beliefs that constitute knowledge in virtue of our direct grasp of 'given' facts, we fare no better if we move in the other direction and try to explain truth in epistemic terms.

First of all, epistemic accounts of truth arguably concede the sceptic's point. For since all such accounts of truth make how things objectively are depend on how, in certain circumstances, we would think they are, they appear, to realists anyway, to sacrifice the objectivity of our knowledge of the world.

Of course, this is not conclusive, since advocates of such theories of truth will charge the realist with wanting more from the concept of objectivity than can coherently be demanded. The core of the concept of objectivity, they will argue, is the idea of evidence-transcendent truth, and we retain this idea so long as we do not identify truth with justifiability according to our current standards. It is not necessary that truth be a radically non-epistemic notion.

The problem with this reply, however, is that, to the extent that the epistemic theorist of truth is successful in capturing the realist's intuitions about objectivity, he appears no better able than his opponent to explain the necessary truth-conduciveness of justification, and so no less vulnerable to scepticism. Consider, for the sake of argument, the neo-Peircean view of truth currently advocated by Putnam, according to which truth consists in ideal verifiability.[10] Such a view supposedly avoids some of the pitfalls of realism while allowing truth to remain evidence-transcendent, in the sense that, no matter how refined our standards become, it will always make sense to say of any belief that, though fully justified so far as we can see, it may not be true. But this weak form of evidence-transcendence, which of course realism also allows for, seems to give the sceptic his room to manœuvre, for he can challenge us to explain how justification according to us is connected with ideal justification, why assertibility now or coherence with current beliefs should be taken as any indication of ideal assertibility or coherence with whatever we would find ourselves believing at the limit of inquiry. Since the neo-Peircean view of truth is designed to allow for at least a weak form of evidence-transcendence, nothing we say that involves reference to specific factors relevant to justification will have any logical connection with truth, even though truth is now supposed to be understood in epistemic terms.

I think this is all true and shows, not only that such epistemic accounts of truth yield no advantages when it comes to dealing with the threat of scepticism, but that they offer only illusory alternatives to realistic accounts. For what are we supposed to understand by *ideal* justification, verification, assertibility, etc.? Since the neo-Peircean explication of truth is designed to decouple truth from anything *we* might be inclined to cite as relevant to justification, thus doing justice to one of the realist's central intuitions, we can give no further explication of this key notion in epistemic terms. As soon as we try to be specific about what ideal justification involves, we will be able to say of any belief that, even if it meets those standards, it might still not be true, which is to say *not* ideally justified. So to the extent that we understand anything by 'ideal justification', we do so in virtue of a prior grasp of the notion of truth. Ideally justified or verified beliefs are beliefs formed under conditions in which all relevant sources of error are either absent or have been allowed for, which is as much as to say under conditions in which there are no obstacles to discovering the truth. We cannot give an informative analysis of truth in terms of ideal verification because that notion is either empty or understood in terms of truth. This means, incidentally, that Putnam is wrong to differentiate himself from the meta-physical realist on the grounds that such a realist must hold that even beliefs in an ideally justified system of beliefs could all be false.[11] There may well be a close connection between truth and ideal justifiability, but not because truth is an epistemic notion in disguise.[12]

If this is right, we have no real alternative to some kind of realistic under-standing of truth. Equally, if we reject the idea of verification by confrontation, as it seems we must, we have no alternative to adopting some kind of coherence theory of justification. But if we explain truth and justification in wholly disparate terms—one as a relation between beliefs and the world and the other as a relation between beliefs and other beliefs—we have no hope of accounting for the necessary truth-conduciveness of justification, hence no way of explain-ing how knowledge is possible. Realism, it seems, leads inevitably to scepticism.

III

We need answers to two questions. First, why should we expect to be able to explain, in some fully general way, how 'justification' is necessarily 'truth'-conducive? And second, why should failure to come up with such an explanation be thought to lead to scepticism? Perhaps it just seems obvious that some such explanation should be forthcoming and that, if none can be provided, we will be unable to see how knowledge (taken to presuppose justification) is possible. But if it does, it shouldn't.

Recall Blanshard's claim, which goes to the heart of the matter, that if we place the nature of truth in 'one sort of character' and its test in 'something quite different', the two are bound to fall apart sooner or later. We can respond that this argument simply assumes that there is one essential something (correspondence) that constitutes truth and another essential something (coherence) that constitutes justification. If it is wrong to think of either truth or justification this way, it will be misguided to demand some fully general connection between 'justification' and 'truth'. No sceptical conclusion will follow from failure to provide one.

I think that this charge of misplaced essentialism, is correct. However, it is not easy to make it stick. The trouble is that the sceptical problem in question does not, on the face of it, depend on any rich theoretical conceptions of either truth or justification.

On the side of truth, the argument that realism threatens to decouple truth and justification appears to depend only on the realist's negative point that truth is a radically non-epistemic notion. No positive account of truth seems to be required.

Of course, realists generally do have positive ideas about what truth is, not just a view about what it is not. But perhaps all this means is that different versions of realism all resolve into two components. All share a certain *negative core*, the thesis that truth, not being any kind of epistemic concept, is evidentially unconstrained. Where they differ is in their *positive* or *theoretical supplements*. If this is right, we can treat realism's negative core, without theoretical supplement, as a kind of minimal realism. And it is far from obvious that minimal realism, though all the realism the sceptic appears to need, amounts to an unacceptably 'essentialist' view of truth.[13]

The reply is that minimal realism is a lot less minimal than it looks. An account of minimal realism in terms of realism's negative core obscures the crucial distinction between minimal (but none the less genuine) realists and deflationists. What matters is not just *whether* we have little or nothing positive to say about the nature of truth but *why*.

Suppose we combined a generally anti-reductionist attitude towards semantic concepts with the thought that, of all such concepts, truth is the most fundamental. We would then take truth as primitive, as a non-epistemic property of beliefs or belief–world relation that is simply not further analysable. This would be an example of minimal but genuine realism. But we might be suspicious of the very idea of truth as a property of beliefs. If so, our view of truth would be deflationary. Since neither has much positive to say about the nature of truth, the minimal realist and the deflationist are easily confounded. However, there is all the difference in the world between thinking that the nature of truth cannot be further explained and doubting whether there is any such things as 'the nature of truth'.

As a possible route to minimal but genuine realism, consider Davidson's approach to the theory of truth. One way in which Davidson's realism is minimal is that his account of truth, although he considers it a correspondence theory, makes no use of the notion of correspondence to fact. Rather,

> The semantic concept of truth ... deserves to be called a correspondence theory because of the part played by the concept of satisfaction; for clearly what has been done is that the property of being true has been explained, and non-trivially, in terms of a relation between language and something else.[14]

However, we are neither to regard the concept of satisfaction, or reference, as absolutely fundamental nor to aim at a reductive analysis. This is because 'words have no function save as they play a role in sentences'. Thus,

> If the name 'Kilimanjaro' refers to Kilimanjaro, then no doubt there is *some* relation between English (or Swahili) speakers, the word, and the mountain. But it is inconceivable that one should be able to explain this relation without

first explaining the role of the word in sentences; and if this is so, there is no chance of explaining reference directly in non-linguistic terms.[15]

A Tarski-style theory of truth for any language must be understood in terms of a distinction between

> explanation *within* the theory and explanation *of* the theory. Within the theory, the conditions of truth of a sentence are specified by adverting to postulated structure and semantic concepts like that of satisfaction or reference. But when it comes to interpreting the theory as a whole, it is the notion of truth, as applied to closed sentences, which must be connected with human ends and activities.[16]

Not only will the connection not go by way of the notion of correspondence to fact, there will be no reduction of any kind to non-semantic (for example behaviouristic) terms: '[a] general and pre-analytic notion of truth is presupposed by the theory'.[17]

Given this general approach, it is not surprising to find Davidson rejecting *epistemic* analyses by claiming that

> Truth is beautifully transparent compared to belief and coherence and I take it as primitive. Truth, as applied to utterances of sentences, shows the disquotational feature enshrined in Tarski's Convention T, and that is sufficient to fix its domain of application. Relative to a language or speaker, of course, so there is more to truth than Convention T; there is whatever carries over from language or speaker to speaker. What Convention T ... reveal(s) is that the truth of an utterance depends on just two things: what the words mean, and how the world is arranged. There is no further relativism to a conceptual scheme, a way of viewing things, a perspective.[18]

These remarks show a clear commitment to what I have called realism's negative core: truth is not any kind of warranted assertibility, not even assertibility by the standards of our Peircean descendants. At the same time, however, they reject a purely disquotational view of truth: there is more to truth than Convention T. Since, as we have seen, we should not expect to give a reductive or even an illuminating analysis of the general, pre-analytic notion of truth, we must see truth as a primitive, non-epistemic property of utterances (or beliefs). We end up with minimal but genuine realism.

No one drawn to a purely disquotational view of truth will be much moved by Davidson's reasons for rejecting it. As Stephen Leeds points out,

> It is not surprising that we should have a use for a predicate *P* with the property that '"---" is *P*' and '---' are always interdeducible. For we frequently find ourselves in a position to assert each sentence in a certain infinite set *z* (e.g. when all the members of *z* share a common form); lacking the means to formulate infinite conjunctions, we find it convenient to have a single sentence which is warranted precisely when each member of *z* is warranted. A predicate *P* with the property described allows us to construct such a sentence: $(x)(x \in z \rightarrow P(x))$. Truth is a notion we might reasonably want to have on hand, for expressing semantic ascent and descent, infinite conjunction and disjunction.[19]

On a view like this, 'what carries over from language to language' is the utility, for each language, of its own disquotation device, which means that we cannot go straight from the fact that something carries over from language to language to the conclusion that there is 'more to truth than Convention T'. As Leeds notes,

> to explain the utility of disquotation, we need say nothing about the relations between language and the world, we do not have to give a natural definition— indeed any definition—of 'true in L' for arbitrary L.[20]

This way of refusing to define truth does not amount to taking truth as a 'primitive' property of beliefs (or anything else).

So I think it is fair to say that minimal realism is not all that minimal. But does a deflationary approach to truth dispose of the sceptical problem we are concerned with? This much we can say: Davidson's view—or the view I have used his remarks to illustrate—tolerates Blanshard's traditional formulation of the problem in a way that Leeds' does not. If we treat truth as a primitive, non-epistemic property of beliefs, then we are well on the way to placing the nature of truth in 'one sort of character' and its test in 'something quite different', even if we do not think that the character of truth lends itself to further analysis. By contrast, if we opt for a view like Leeds', we do not place the 'nature' of truth in any sort of character, so the problem of forging an essential connection between disparate natures lapses. Or so we might argue.

To argue this way is to assume that, if we resist attributing a nature to truth, then any problem connected with truth-conduciveness will lapse automatically. After all, what could deflationists suppose justification to be necessarily conducive to? But here the sceptic can reply that his challenge does not depend on any particular understanding of 'true'. His intention is to ask a certain very general question about knowledge or justification: why, with respect to the various propositions $p, q, r \ldots$ that we happen to believe, is p's being confirmed (according to our standards) any indication that p, why is q's being confirmed any indication that q, why is r's being confirmed any indication that r, and so on? The challenge to explain the necessary truth-conduciveness of justification is simply a compact way of achieving the right level of generality. In other words, it is not clear that, in the sceptic's questions, 'true' has to amount to more than a pure disquotationalist like Leeds allows.

We might respond that, although a purely disquotational view of truth allows us to *formulate* a sceptical question, the question lacks bite once we give up understanding the need to explain truth-conduciveness of epistemic justification in terms of connecting disparate essences. But why? On the metaphysical side, the sceptic invokes no more than realism's negative core, the thought that truth is epistemically unconstrained, and this thought too finds a natural expression on the most purely disquotational view of truth, in that Convention T tells us that 'p' is true if and only if p, not if and only if p is suitably justified. But since the sceptic can continue to remind us that, having rejected the idea of verification by confrontation, we have made justification always a matter of coherence, of accommodating beliefs to other beliefs, he seems to have all he needs. Our beliefs that snow is white, that grass is green, that bananas are yellow, and so on, may fit together beautifully: but why does this make it likely that snow is white, that grass is green and that bananas are yellow? Or, using the truth-predicate as a handy way of putting the question in its properly general form, why does a belief's fitting in with other beliefs make it likely to be true?

It will not do to reply that our beliefs include epistemic beliefs, for example beliefs having to do with the reliability of observational evidence. The sceptic will just remind us that we have no warrant for these beliefs except their capacity for fitting in with beliefs whose epistemic status has already come to seem problematic. The argument is still with us: justification can only be understood in terms of coherence but, once it is so understood, we cannot see why any so-called justification procedures should be truth-conducive.

If this is right, deflating the notion of truth will not automatically defuse scepticism. Neither will inflating the notion of truth make sceptical problems more acute. Still, something important has emerged from our detour through the deflationary approach to truth. The capacity of the sceptical problems concerning the truth-conduciveness of justification to survive deflation of the notion of truth indicates that the more-than-negatively realist conception of truth as a sentence– or belief–world relationship was never that important for getting the problem off the ground. It seems, rather, that in the sceptical argument the truth-predicate functions as Leeds says it functions generally: as a handy device for achieving a certain kind of generality. This focuses our attention where it should be focused: on the peculiar generality of the sceptic's questions and, something that will prove to be intimately connected with it, the precise way in which justification is supposed to be a matter of 'coherence'.

The result was to be expected. Why suppose that the question of how to understand truth has any particular connection with the problem of scepticism? Scepticism is an epistemological thesis having to do with knowledge or justification, and there is no arguing for an epistemological conclusion without an epistemological premiss. But the simple claim that truth is a radically non-epistemic notion carries no commitments as to what is involved in knowledge or justification and, consequently, implies nothing about how or whether either is possible.[21] This said, we can turn to the epistemological side of our sceptical problem.

IV

On examination, the 'realist' element in the argument linking realism with scepticism seems vanishingly small. And, at first sight, the argument's epistemological commitments seem equally modest.

Certainly, no rich, theoretical conception of coherence is involved. As we saw, Davidson, who is insistent that combining a coherence theory of justification with a realistic conception of truth, takes the core of the coherence theory to be 'simply the claim that nothing can count as a reason for holding a belief except another belief', the force of this claim lying in its 'reject[ing] as unintelligible the request for a ground or source of justification of another ilk'.[22] By this standard—and, if the standard is correct, for the purposes of the sceptic's argument—any theory of knowledge or justification will count as a coherence theory that rejects the idea of verification through bringing beliefs into confrontation with reality. Thus we can apply the same pattern of analysis to epistemological coherentism that we applied earlier to metaphysical realism. We can identify the negative core of coherentism as its rejection of the idea of verification by confrontation. Richer forms of coherentism will result from adding distinctive theoretical supplement, more detailed accounts of coherence.

In light of this, the sceptic can claim with some plausibility that his 'coherentism' is hardly controversial. He rejects verification by confrontation but has nothing positive to say about what, if anything, is essential to epistemic justification. Since, as we have seen, his argument also survives deflation of the notion of truth, the charge that it rests an overly essentialist view of truth or justification will not stick.

However, our tentative analysis of realism into negative core and theoretical supplement proved misleading because it glossed over the distinction between minimally realistic and deflationary views of truth. So we must ask whether this pattern of analysis is comparably misleading when applied to the coherence theory of justification. It is: the negative core of the coherence theory does not distinguish coherence theories of justification from contextualist theories.

Whatever else they say about coherence, coherence theories treat justification holistically. An individual belief derives its credibility from its place in a coherent total belief-system, and the factors that determine coherence—typically such things as comprehensiveness and explanatory integration—even if they supervene on relations between particular beliefs in a system, have to do with the character of the system as a whole. I take holism to be essential to coherence theories properly so called. And just as the conception of truth as a property of beliefs or a belief–world relation is an addition to the negative thesis that truth is not an epistemic notion, so this holistic conception of justification is an addition to thesis that nothing can justify a belief except another belief.

In fact, this thesis is too weak to capture even what Davidson himself understands by a coherence theory. This is apparent from his understanding of what must be done to answer the sceptic, which is to argue that 'most of the beliefs in a coherent total set of beliefs are true'.[23] If we can show that 'there is a presumption in favour of the truth of a belief that coheres with a significant mass of belief', we can conclude that 'every belief in a coherent total set is justified in the light of this presumption'.[24] Davidson thinks of his coherence theory as 'mild' for much the same reason that he thinks of his correspondence theory of truth as 'unassuming': he does not think that much needs to be said about what coherence involves. Coherence theorists typically offer elaborate accounts of the factors relevant to coherence because they concede their critics' point that, if there were no more to coherence than consistency, it would be possible to believe, with justification, anything whatsoever. Davidson is different: because he thinks that *any* system of beliefs must contain an overwhelming preponderance of truths (and so must largely overlap any other system), he feels no need for a fine-grained specification of the criteria for coherence. But all this means is that his theory is mild compared with other holistic theories. It amounts to a minimal but genuine coherence theory of justification, analogous to his minimal but genuinely realistic theory of truth.

It is precisely in virtue of their holistic character that coherence theories invite sceptical challenges. In our earlier discussion of truth, we saw that the sceptical argument did not presuppose any positive form of realism, however minimal. What did appear to be crucial, however, was the legitimacy of asking questions about justification at a very high level of generality or abstraction. This is where coherence theories of justification make their contribution: for by analysing justification in terms of features belonging to our system of beliefs as a whole, they offer a way of making sense of the sceptic's characteristically global requests for justification and, more importantly still, reinforce the thought that we have a useful notion of 'our system of beliefs' or 'our knowledge of the world', such that we might reasonably be expected to offer some kind of defence of its epistemological status.

Contextualist theories, by contrast, though they share with coherence theories the negative thesis that nothing can justify a belief except another belief, have no use for such notions as 'our total view' or 'our system of beliefs'. In other words, they are distinguished by their rejection of the radical holism that is definitive of coherence theories proper. This is not to say that contextualists understand the way credibility attaches to beliefs atomistically. It may well be that, in specific contexts of inquiry, beliefs are evaluated or sustained on the basis of their systematic connections with other beliefs: justification may be, so to speak, locally or contextually holistic. But this local or contextual holism needs to be kept distinct from the strong holism, characteristic of coherence theories of justification, according to which a belief owes its credibility to its being embedded in a suitably coherent 'total view'[25] or (global) system of beliefs.

I think we can see right away that this contrast may have implications for our sceptical problem. A coherence theory of justification makes it seem perfectly proper to seize on any random 'belief' or set of beliefs and ask 'Justifiable or not?' This simply means: 'Can the belief or beliefs in question be embedded in a suitably coherent total view?' However, on a contextualist view of justification, the propriety of such questions is much less obvious. For a contextualist, there is no straightforward matter of fact as to whether a given belief or proposition, abstractly viewed, is or is not 'justified'. For a contextualist, questions of justification arise only in the face of specific difficulties, hence only in contexts of inquiry where *not* everything is open to question. The contextualist agrees with the coherentist that nothing can justify a belief except another belief. However, he does not see that a fully general account of how 'getting some beliefs to fit in with others' favours truth is either possible or required. Everything depends on the beliefs in question and the kind of fit. The characteristic generality of sceptical demands for justification begins to look suspicious.

So, although our sceptical problem survives deflation of the notion of truth, it is not at all clear that it survives contextualization of the notion of justification. The problem demands that justification be understood in a way that allows us to make sense of demands for justification imposed at an unusually high level of generality and in abstraction from all specific, directed forms of inquiry. Even when sceptical attention is focused on more restricted kinds of beliefs, the kinds are very broad and have no clear relations to more ordinary divisions by subject-matter. 'Beliefs about the past' is not co-extensive with 'history' nor 'beliefs about the external word' with 'physics'. Sceptical argument requires a conception of justification that makes such classifications seem reasonable. This is what is right about the claim that the sceptical challenge to connect coherence with truth rests on an essentialist conception of justification. 'Justified beliefs' must constitute a theoretically coherent kind. On a contextualist view of justification they do not. The same goes for true beliefs on a deflationary view of truth.

But how exactly does a contextualist view of justification work to undermine or defuse our sceptical problem? The most obvious suggestion appeals to a contrast between local and global demands for justification. For a contextualist, only local demands are admissible and, with this restriction in place, there is no longer any problem about combining a realistic account of truth, of any degree of strength indeed, with a rejection of the idea of verification by confrontation. Challenged on the truth of a given belief, I can appeal to my own experience, to the testimony of others, to whatever tests, experiments or investigations I or other people have carried out, and so on. Should the evidential value—the truth-conduciveness—of whatever I cite itself come under suspicion, we have a further matter for empirical investigation. How reliable an observer am I in the relevant circumstances? Is my friend's testimony generally trustworthy? How accurate are these instruments? How often does this test produce false positives? And so on. So long as questions about evidential value remain at this level of specificity, we will feel no temptation to suppose that we can justify a given belief by appeal to something other than further beliefs. Neither will we be tempted to reconstrue truth in epistemic terms or to feel that the evidential value, the truth-conduciveness, of a given justifying move must have some kind of a priori basis. A problem arises only if we admit the sceptic's demands for some kind of global account of the truth-conduciveness of 'the test of coherence', precisely what a contextualist view of justification says we need not do.

However, a blunt appeal to the contrast between local and global demands for justification does not go to the heart of the matter.[26] It leaves too many questions hanging to be a satisfying explanation of how the sceptic goes wrong.

For one, at what point do demands for justification become too general? How local must they be to remain admissible? Lacking an index of improper generality that is independent of our becoming vulnerable to scepticism, we have a dismissal of sceptical questions but no real account of what is wrong with them.

For another, how does a contextualist view of justification go beyond a point any sceptic will readily concede: that to get on with various ordinary, more specific forms of inquiry, we have to rely on all sorts of assumptions? No one denies that, for everyday practical (and even theoretical) purposes, we have to ignore fundamental epistemological questions. But this does not mean either that such questions are badly posed or that sceptical answers to them are incorrect.

And finally, sceptical questions can be very general without being global. Even the challenge to connect coherence with truth concedes, for the sake of argument, that we know what we believe and how our beliefs hang together. So it does not violate the contextualist stricture on attempts to validate everything we believe, all at once. The sceptical problem that results from failure to meet this challenge is not therefore going to be defused by ruling out global demands for justification. We must look beyond the simple local/global distinction for the anti-sceptical potential in a contextualist understanding of verification.

V

The most significant feature of the contextualist understanding of justification is that it is anti-realist, or anyway non-realist, with respect to the typical objects of epistemological theorizing—knowledge, justified belief and the like. In this way, it is opposed both to foundationalist and coherence theories of the traditional kind, which are committed to what I call 'epistemological realism'. This is not, I must stress, realism with respect to what we claim to know, but *realism with respect to the objects of epistemological inquiry*.[27]

We can begin with foundationalist accounts of justification, where commitment to epistemological realism is most immediately visible. The doctrine of the given, which contextualists and coherence theorists agree in rejecting, does not capture all that is distinctive about foundationalism. Rather, the root idea of foundationalism lies in the doctrine of epistemological priority. Beliefs are seen as partitioned into broad epistemological classes arranged in an epistemological hierarchy, an 'order of reasons' that cuts across ordinary subject-matter divisions. This hierarchy is not seen by the foundationalist as imposed for the purpose of carrying out some particular, restricted theoretical project. Rather, he takes it to capture the fundamental, underlying, and fully objective structure of empirical justification, a structure that determines what kinds of belief can, in the last analysis, be taken to provide warrant for others. On this view, beliefs stand in definite and objective epistemological relations, independently of how they are embedded in particular, specific contexts of inquiry. Foundationalism is therefore not just a doctrine about the formal structure of empirical inference: it embodies a definite realism with respect to relations of justification.[28] Beliefs, we might say, stand in *natural* epistemological relations, and the classes they fall into, depending on their place in the order of reasons, constitute *natural epistemological kinds.*

As I see it, then, the most significant feature of a contextualist understanding of justification is not that it tries to place 'global' epistemological questions under interdict, but that it amounts to a decisive rejection of epistemological realism. For a contextualist, a belief has no intrinsic epistemological character or status. Accordingly, there are no invariant epistemological relations or natural epistemological kinds. If this is right, there is nothing compelling about the ways beliefs get classified for the purposes of sceptical arguments. Of course we *can* partition our beliefs into, say, those having to do with the external world and those having to do only with 'experience'. However, unless this partition corresponds to some fundamental and objective epistemological asymmetry, failure to show in some fully general way how the latter can serve to ground the former will have no special significance. It will not imply that we never know anything about the external world.

We noticed earlier that sceptical arguments classify beliefs in ways that cut across ordinary subject-matter divisions. They do so because the principles of classification are epistemological through and through. Beliefs are sorted according to their potential for certainty, to whether they can be justified immediately or only inferentially, and so on. This kind of sorting stands or falls with epistemological realism. If there are no natural epistemological kinds, there is no reason even to try to sort beliefs this way. So when a sceptic raises questions about beliefs about the past, beliefs about the external world or, at the limit of abstraction, justified beliefs, a contextualist will be unmoved: not because the sceptic's questions are too general or because his negative verdict is a priori unacceptable, but because he has failed to identify a coherent object of assessment.

This answers our questions about the contextualist reply to scepticism. The first question was 'How general is too general?' In particular, is there a criterion for improper generality in epistemological questions independent of their tendency to suggest sceptical answers? However, we can sidestep all such questions, for the issue is not generality as such, but the peculiar kind of generality achieved by reliance on a purely epistemological classification of beliefs.[29] The contextualist's objection is not to the generality of the sceptic's questions but to their implicit reference to natural epistemological kinds.

The second question was: how is contextualism different from the uncontroversial point that, to get on with ordinary, specific investigations, we have to make all kinds of assumptions? I think we can now see that this 'uncontroversial' point is tendentious. As Wittgenstein remarks,

> It isn't that the situation is like this: we just can't investigate everything, and for that reason we are forced to rest content with assumption. If I want the door to turn, the hinges must stay put.

Exempting some things from doubt, in a particular context, reflects neither practical incapacities nor epistemological insouciance: it is rather a function of the direction of inquiry. The idea that, in giving an inquiry a definite direction, we are making assumptions which, theoretically speaking, ought to be justified, even if present interests and practical limitations deter us from making the effort, derives its force entirely from the picture of an underlying structure of empirical knowledge, present in and presupposed by all particular attempts at investigation. Abandon that picture and we see that loosening the hinges does not yield a more rigorous approach to our original topic: rather it amounts to *changing the subject*. To entertain doubts about the reality of the past is not to insist on a more rigorous approach to history, as perhaps to advocate formal proof is to insist on a more rigorous approach to mathematics. Entertaining such doubts leads to a wholly different set of problems, epistemological rather than historical, failure to solve which in no way impugns the legitimacy of historical research.

This leads to the third objection, which was that the sceptic need not try to question everything we believe. As we might put it now, his examination of our knowledge of the world has its own hinges: contextualism thus cannot amount to an objection to scepticism, because the sceptic creates a context in which his highly general questions make perfectly good sense. That, however, is the point: he *creates* a context; whereas, for his conclusions to have the significance he wants them to have, his questions have to be responsive to objective epistemological constraints, not to self-imposed limitations. The contextualist thinks that, to the extent it succeeds at all, the sceptic's approach to classifying beliefs is completely artificial. The sceptic claims to be investigating the presuppositions of all ordinary inquiries and arguments when in fact he is only inventing a conundrum.

VI

The relevance of this line of criticism to the sceptical problem we have been most concerned with may not be immediately obvious. Can it be used to defuse the demand that we connect coherence with truth?

Epistemological realism is less immediately visible in coherence theories of justification. We might be tempted to conclude that it is not present at all, certainly not in a theory as mild as Davidson's. For a hallmark of coherence theories is their rejection of any general doctrine of epistemic priority. How, then, can they be committed to such things as natural epistemological kinds?

However, here we must remember that even a coherence theorist is committed to thinking that, in talking of 'justified beliefs', he identifies some clear object for analysis and assessment. So his epistemological classifications may be less fine-grained than or in some other way different from those of the foundationalist. But this does not mean that he escapes epistemological realism.

One dimension of the coherentist's realistic understanding of justification has to do with the factors that determine coherence, understood holistically. Coherence theorists usually concede that there is more to coherence than logical consistency: our beliefs must not just be compatible with one another, they must 'hang together'. However this idea of explanatory coherence, as it is generally called, is far from easy to grasp. Explanation seems to be a paradigm of a context-sensitive or interest-relative relation, which is why attempts at purely formal accounts of it have met with little success. Whether some particular facts can be taken to be a good explanation of a given fact seems to depend crucially on what particular questions are on the table. But the coherentist's notion of explanation cannot be like this. The explanatory relations that contribute to coherence must be seen as context-independent, as holding between our various beliefs in virtue of their content alone. Like the foundationalist's hierarchical relations, they are taken to be fully objective. Only taken this way can they contribute to the 'coherence' of our 'total view'.

Seen this way, the foundationalist and coherence theorist agree that there is an objective structure of empirical knowledge while differing as to its character. The foundationalist appeals to an epistemological hierarchy, while the coherence theorist focuses on more complex explanatory inter-relations between beliefs. However, I think it would be a mistake to represent the coherence theorist as unqualifiedly hostile to the doctrine of epistemological priority. I think that coherentists are as committed to this doctrine as foundationalists. True, for coherentists, rational change of belief is not a matter of accommodating our beliefs to certain privileged beliefs. Rather we make overall revisions in the light of the factors that determine coherence. But such a view does not so much eliminate epistemic privilege as relocate it: in general criteria as opposed to particular factual beliefs.[30] Even for the coherence theorist, the regress of justification has to stop somewhere and, for him, it stops with the criteria of coherence. Coherence theorists are committed to a criterial conception of justification.

But this is not all. There is a way in which the coherence theorist is committed, not just to a variant of the foundationalist's epistemological realism, but to the very same doctrine. If there is to be a serious sceptical question about the relation between coherence and truth, we must allow that it is possible for us to know what, in general, we believe, and how our beliefs cohere, even if we do not know that any of them are true. In this sense, then, even for a coherence theorist, knowledge of our beliefs is epistemologically prior to knowledge of the world. And this priority must be objective, if failure to solve the sceptical problem is to amount to a negative assessment of our knowledge of the world. Even Davidson's mild coherence theory, which avoids reliance on the notion of explanatory coherence, carries this commitment.

If we reject epistemological realism, we will be unmoved by the demand that we connect 'justification' with truth. We will hold that this demand seems pressing to coherence theorists proper only because they have already mistakenly construed justification holistically and criterially. We will be dubious about the need for any general account of the relation between the factors relevant to justification and truth because we will be dubious about the very notion of 'the factors relevant to justification'. We will see no reason to think of 'justified belief' or 'empirical knowledge' as objects of uniform theoretical analysis. Accordingly, we will be reluctant to concede that the sceptic, in his insistence that we assess the totality of our knowledge, or our knowledge of the world, has picked out anything for assessment. The fact that there is some fairly stable linguistic usage with respect to terms like 'know' proves nothing: think of Bacon on 'heat' or Grice and Strawson on 'analytic–synthetic'.[31] Stable linguistic contrasts do not guarantee the existence of natural or theoretically significant kinds: Bacon's 'hot' things includes fires and spices. What takes us from a merely nominal to a natural or theoretical kind is the idea of an underlying structure. In epistemology, the study of 'knowledge', the idea of such a structure is fleshed out by the foundationalist's epistemic hierarchy or the coherentist's criteria of 'global' coherence.

Highlighting the coherentist's critical conception of justification is perhaps the way to throw into sharpest relief the differences between coherentism and contextualism. To reject epistemological realism is to become dubious about the idea of purely epistemological questions, questions about justification that are to be raised and answered in the absence of all background, factual information. A contextualist never thinks of justifying a belief or statement as simply a matter of showing that it satisfies some set of purely epistemic criteria. This view is typical of the genuine coherentist and it is this view that, by treating questions of justication as detachable from all background factual beliefs, makes it seem possible to call into question the legitimacy of all our beliefs, or all our beliefs about the world, all at once.

For an anti-realist about the objects of epistemological inquiry, there will be no question of identifying the factors relevant to justification in abstraction from all specific subject-matters and contexts of inquiry. But we have already seen that, so long as questions about justification remain relatively local and specific, there is no problem in principle about how to explain the evidential value of whatever we cite in support of a belief that has come into question: generally, the explanation will be straightforwardly empirical and will treat evidence as a reliable indicator of the truth of whatever it is cited as evidence for. What makes this kind of explanation legitimate is the contextualist's rejection of the coherentist's criterial conception of justification.

So the contextualist conception of justification, while receptive to the view that nothing can justify a belief except another belief, is hostile to questions about the credibility of our beliefs taken as a whole and, as a result, sees no need for anything like a completely general relation between coherence and correspondence, still less one that can be shown to hold a priori. Whether or not this hostility is in the end well-founded, the point remains that (metaphysical) realism does not threaten us with scepticism when combined only with what I initially identified as minimal negative coherentism, the thesis that nothing can justify a belief except another belief. The key ingredient in sceptical argument is *epistemological* realism.

VII

In conclusion, let me return briefly to some questions about truth. I argued earlier that adopting a deflationary attitude towards truth does not necessarily put any serious obstacles in the sceptic's way. His question about the relation of justification to truth can be posed without reliance on any particular account of what, if anything, truth consists in. He simply asks why, for any belief that *p*, *p*'s being confirmed according to our standards makes it likely that *p*? Whether such questions are legitimate, I have argued, turns on the acceptability of epistemological rather than metaphysical realism. No matter what we say about metaphysical realism, epistemological realism creates the logical space for sceptical problems.

So suppose, conversely, we reject epistemological realism while holding on to metaphysical realism, minimal or otherwise. Are we equally open to sceptical challenge?

I think not, for a reason implicit in an argument already given: epistemological problems cannot be erected on a purely metaphysical basis. But this general consideration may fail to carry conviction in this particular case. In fact, we might well suppose that combining a contextualist view of justification with a realist view of truth raises the sceptical problem about the relation between truth and justification in an even more acute form. For if justification strategies vary with context, but truth remains always the same, a context-insensitive property of beliefs, or belief–world relation, won't it be miraculous if these heterogeneous procedures all tend to produce truth. It will certainly take some explaining.[32]

Plausible as it seems at first, I do not find this line of argument convincing. It is crucial to remember that the contextualist does not just insist that justification procedures are diverse and context sensitive: he insists that questions about justification and answers to them are always local and specific; and he denies that justification is ever a matter of satisfying purely epistemic criteria. Accordingly, he feels under no compulsion to show, in some general way, how satisfying diverse collections of such criteria will tend always to ensure the presence of some non-epistemic relation between our beliefs and the world. Questions about the truth-conduciveness of justification procedures will have to be asked case and case and, when they are so asked, they will be answerable empirically.

By way of illustration, suppose we have adopted a rich, theoretical form of realism, conceiving truth in terms of a causal-physical relation of reference; and suppose we now ask about the value of some particular kind of evidence, for example why the readings given by a particular piece of apparatus should be taken as reliable indicators of the truth of certain statements about the occurrence of a given kind of physical event: then in this and similar contexts, we will be able to connect evidence with truth, understood in causal terms, provided we are allowed to appeal to knowledge of the relevant causal relations. We will run into a serious sceptical problem only if the appeal to such knowledge is ruled out of court. Such a ruling will in turn depend on the legitimacy of following the traditional sceptical procedure and collecting our beliefs into broad, context-independent epistemological classes and insisting that we assess the epistemic standing of all the beliefs in some such class all at once. But we have now come right back to what I have been calling epistemological realism. We no longer have even a prima-facie sceptical problem resting on metaphysical realism alone.

I conclude that epistemological realism is the crucial presupposition of sceptical questions, indeed that metaphysical realism has no particular connection with any sceptical problems or answers to them. This is not to say that we might as well be metaphysical realists. On the contrary, once the question of how we should understand truth has been disconnected from the project of responding to scepticism, there are no reasons for not being a deflationist. But that is another argument entirely.

Notes

1. I want to thank Edward Craig for his comments on the version of this essay read at the St Andrews conference. They forced me to clarify what is perhaps its central point: my account of the significance of rejecting epistemological realism. Thanks also to Arthur Fine for penetrating criticisms of any early draft.

2. For example, Colin McGinn writes that realism 'inevitably introduces the possibility of a sceptical challenge'. According to Barry Stroud, the source of the sceptical problem about our knowledge of the external world lies in our 'conception of an objective world or in our desire, expressed in terms of that conception, to gain a certain kind of understanding of our relation to the world'. Thomas Nagel states flatly that 'Scepticism . . . is only a problem because of the realist claims of objectivity'. See McGinn, 'An A Priori Argument for Realism', *Journal of Philosophy* 76, p. 115; Stroud, *The Significance of Philosophical Scepticism*, p. 82; Nagel, *The View from Nowhere*, p. 71. I must stress that Stroud is far from thinking that scepticism is forced on us by realism alone. See n. 14 below.

3. Arthur Fine has suggested to me that it is important to distinguish the question of whether realism allows us to raise the problem of scepticism from the question of whether realism leads to scepticism as a position. I am inclined to regard this as a distinction without a difference. Like Stroud, I suspect that, once the sceptic is allowed to ask his questions in the way he wants to ask them, there is no avoiding his answers. That is why I think that it is important to defend a distinction between direct answers to scepticism, which take the questions more or less at face value, and indirect, which try to find fault with the questions themselves.

4. I owe this way of formulating the problem to Lawrence Bonjour. See his *The Structure of Empirical Knowledge*, p. 8.

5. Hilary Putnam, 'Realism and Reason', in *Meaning and the Moral Sciences*, p. 125. Not everyone would agree that realism has to involve a thesis about truth. Michael Devitt takes realism to be the view that the world of common-sense physical objects—or, in the case of scientific realism, the world of entities postulated by the theoretical physicist—really exists. The world is neither a fiction nor a construction, especially not a construction out of anything mental. Realism is thus opposed to idealism and, as a metaphysical or ontological thesis, is to be sharply distinguished from all epistemological or semantic theses. It is especially to be distinguished from any thesis about the nature of truth, notably the mis-named 'realist' view that truth consists in correspondence with reality. Questions about realism and questions about the nature of truth are to be settled independently. Thus Devitt.

One obvious difficulty with such a view is that it makes it even less clear than it otherwise might be what form a debate on the question of realism might take. The other is that any such attempt to identify realism with commitment to a certain body of *truths*, rather than a view about truth, is bound to misfire. For we have to add the proviso that these truths be accepted at 'face value' and explaining how and why this is so will inevitably reinvolve us with questions about what the truth of the propositions of common sense and science should be understood to consist in. For Devitt's views see *Realism and Truth*.

6. Moritz Schlick, 'The Foundation of Knowledge', *Erkenntnis* (1934) reprinted in A. J. Ayer (ed.), *Logical Positivism*.

7. Donald Davidson, 'A Coherence Theory of Truth and Knowledge', in Ernest LePore (ed.), *Truth and Interpretation: Perspectives on the Philosophy of Donald Davidson*, pp. 310–12 (quotation p. 310). Further reference to this article given by 'CTTK' and page number.

8. Brand Blanshard, *The Nature of Thought*, vol. 2, p. 268. It has been claimed, e.g. by Bonjour, *The Structure of Empirical Knowledge*, p. 25, that the absolute idealists, the main historical proponents of the coherence theory of knowledge, 'tended at times to conflate (or confuse) coherence theories of *justification* with coherence theories of *truth*'. And, at first sight, a tendency to argue for a coherence theory of truth by arguing against foundational theories of knowledge suggests such a tendency. However, such a procedure will seem entirely natural to a philosopher convinced that justification and truth simply cannot be analysed in wholly disparate terms and, with such a conviction in the background, need not imply confusion.

9. I have argued against foundationalist appeals to notions like knowledge by acquaintance in *Groundless Belief*, ch. 2. See also Donald Davidson, CTTK, pp. 310–12. On the obscurity attaching to the idea of a basic belief see also Bonjour, *The Structure of Empirical Knowledge*, ch. 2.

10. See, for example, Putnam, *Reason, Truth and History*, ch. 3, esp. pp. 54–6.

11. 'Realism and Reason' in *Meaning and the Moral Sciences*, p. 125.

12. Though I will not try to develop it in detail, I think that a similar argument could be offered against the more properly Peircean identification of truth with assertibility at the limit of inquiry. To the extent that we understand this mathematical metaphor at all, we do so in terms of a prior grasp of the notion of truth, as that on which long-run inquiry ought to converge. I want to thank Chris Hookway, who I am sure would not agree with any of this, for insisting that I distinguish between Putnam and Peirce.

13. Not everyone would agree. Michael Friedman argues that only an account of truth based on a causal-physical theory of reference can really allow for a sceptical challenge to our knowledge of the world. Thus only such an account of truth can make room for a genuine project of self-justifications. His thought is that the main alternative approach to reference—the sort of charity-based theory favoured by Davidson, according to which referents are to be assigned to terms so as to maximize the number of true belief on the part of whoever's speech is being interpreted—precludes the possibility of anyone's beliefs being largely false, thus preventing the sceptic's argument from getting off the ground. However, it seems to me unnecessary to set the sceptical problem to insist that global falsity in our beliefs be a genuine possibility. All that matters initially is that global falsity not be ruled evidently impossible, a condition even minimal realism clearly meets. If there are deep connections between belief, meaning, and truth— connections that stand in the way of global falsity—we may be able to exploit them to show where the sceptic's argument goes wrong. At least, we do not want to make

pre-emptive concessions that would bar us from so doing. But the existence of such connections will need to be argued for. Realism's negative core—the thesis that truth is a radically non-epistemic concept—neither evidently precludes nor evidently favours the existence of such connections. So it seems to me that minimal realism offers just enough for the sceptic's purposes. If we ought to adopt a richer version of realism, we need a reason other than the alleged desirability of making room for a sceptical challenge to our knowledge of the world. See Michael Friedman, 'Truth and Confirmation', in Hilary Kornblith (ed.), *Naturalising Epistemology*. I criticize Friedman's ideas about truth and confirmation in 'Do We Epistemologists Need a Theory of Truth?', *Philosophical Topics* 14. However, though I think Friedman misunderstands the need for the principle of charity, I do not think that Davidson's ideas about reference can be used to combat scepticism. See my 'Scepticism and Charity', *Ratio* (forthcoming).

14. Donald Davidson, *Inquiries into Truth and Interpretation*, p. 48.

15. Davidson, *Inquiries*, p. 220.

16. Ibid., pp. 221–2.

17. Ibid., p. 223.

18. CTTK, pp. 308–9.

19. Stephen Leeds, 'Theories of Reference and Truth', *Erkenntnis* 13 (p. 121). For further defence of the deflationary approach to truth, see Paul Horwich, 'Three Forms of Realism', *Synthese* 51; Arthur Fine, 'The Natural Ontological Attitude', in J. Leplin (ed.), *Scientific Realism*; 'And Not Anti-Realism Either', *Nous* (1986), pp. 51–65; 'Unnatural Attitudes: Realist and Instrumentalist Attachments to Science', *Mind* (1986); and my own 'Do We Epistemologists Need a Theory of Truth?'.

20. Leeds, 'Theories of Reference and Truth', p. 122.

21. Theoretically supplemented forms of realism may be able to link realism directly with scepticism, but only if the supplementation is explicitly epistemological. A characterization of truth in terms of a physicalistically acceptable notion of reference will be as non-committal epistemologically as the most deflationary account. On the other hand, someone like McGinn ('An A Priori Argument for Realism'), who follows Dummett and explains realism in terms of willingness to admit the possibility of recognition-transcendent facts, may well be able to link realism directly with scepticism, but only because of the substantive epistemological commitments carried by his account of the conditions under which facts in various categories can be recognized.

22. Davidson, CTTK, p. 310.

23. Ibid., p. 308.

24. Ibid.

25. See, for example, Gilbert Harman, *Thought*, ch. 10. There is, however, a long-standing ambiguity in the tradition of coherentist epistemology: sometimes coherence is treated as a relation between a candidate belief and a given body of beliefs and sometimes as a property of the system of beliefs as a whole. For a discussion of some problems facing 'global' coherentism see my 'Coherence, Justification and Truth', *Review of Metaphysics* (1980).

26. I am grateful to Edward Craig for forcing me to be clearer about this.

27. For further discussion of epistemological realism, especially in relation to foundationalism, see my 'Epistemological Realism and the Basis of Scepticism', *Mind* (1988).

28. To see what the debate between foundational and coherence theories looks like when they are treated as purely formal accounts of the structure of inference, see Gilbert Harman, *Change in View*.

29. No one has done more than Barry Stroud to bring out the importance and

distinctive character of the element of generality in the sceptic's questions and I have learned a lot from his writings. When Stroud says that the source of scepticism lies in 'our conception of an objective world or our desire, expressed in terms of that conception, to gain a certain kind of understanding of our relation to the world' (*The Significance of Philosophical Scepticism*, p. 82), he is indicating that it is not realism alone that leads to scepticism, but realism set in the context of the quest for 'a certain kind of understanding of our relation to the world': roughly an understanding of how knowledge in general is possible. Scepticism is the product of the interaction between the sceptic's insistence that we explain the possibility of knowledge, or knowledge of the world, in a completely general way and his insistence that the knowledge whose possibility is to be explained be objective. A recent paper of Stroud's that I have found especially illuminating is 'Understanding Human Knowledge in General' (forthcoming). I am particularly indebted to Stroud in my brief remarks about 'externalism' in the theory of knowledge, which appear later in this essay. Where Stroud and I differ, is over the question of what theoretical presuppositions, if any, are packed into the idea of such a general assessment of knowledge. My epistemological non-realism lead me to think that what the sceptic or traditional epistemologist wants to assess is not really there: that terms like 'empirical knowledge', 'justified belief' and so on do not pick out natural or theoretically coherent kinds of belief. Or rather, to make them do so, we have to take on a lot of theoretical baggage, making the case for scepticism much less intuitive, hence much more open to theoretical rebuttal, than it initially seems.

30. From classical times, sceptics have exploited two apparent regresses: the familiar regress of justification and the 'problem of the criterion', the regress of justification applied to epistemic standards. Foundationalists halt the first regress by finding basic beliefs. Since these are intrinsically credible—i.e. credible without validation by a criterion—they halt the second regress as well. Coherence theorists halt the second regress by postulating fundamental criteria of justification. Since these apply holistically, they can tolerate circular inferential relations between beliefs, and so have no neeed to find a definite stopping place for the first regress. Foundationalism and coherentism offer mirror-image responses to the two classical regresses.

I should add that the Pyrrhonian sceptics, though they make these regress problems central to the epistemological aspect of their position, do not use them in quite the way that 'the sceptic' uses them in contemporary discussions. For a detailed discussion of the differences between ancient and modern attitudes to sceptical arguments, see my 'Scepticism without Theory', *Review of Metaphysics* (1988).

31. H. P. Grice and P. F. Strawson, 'In Defence of a Dogma', *Philosophical Review* (1956). They infer from the fact that people can be trained to use the terms 'analytic' and 'synthetic' in a way that allows application to new cases that the terms mark a significant distinction. Defenders of Quine reply that one could say the same about the witch/non-witch distinction.

32. The need to respond to this objection was brought home to me by Arthur Fine. He does not, however, agree with my response.

8

Understanding Scepticism

Edward Craig

I

To be asked to write about Realism and Scepticism is rather like being given the classic military order to go and do something somewhere: a great deal is left to one's initiative. Recent work on realism and anti-realism has brought to the limelight a number of doctrines, in some cases closely related, in others less closely. But it has had little tendency to hone the word 'realism' itself down to a sharp semantic point. As for scepticism, it is true that one continually hears philosophers speak of 'the sceptic' in ways which suggest that they take those words to identify some view precise enough for conclusive discussion. If so, they make an assumption which does not so much define scepticism as deserve it.

As regards the distinction between realism and anti-realism, I should imagine that any reader at all familiar with the bibliography will agree that it appears in a number of versions, variously related but by no means all equivalent. Realism (to concentrate on one of the partners) has been defined as the doctrine that takes reality to be independent of what we think about it, that refuses to define the concept of truth in epistemic terms, that allows the possibility of recognition-transcendent facts. It has been stated as the view that no reductive analysis (of the class of propositions to which the realism in question applies) is possible, and as the unrestricted acceptance of the Law of Excluded Middle. It also has a prominent form in the theory of meaning: meaning is to be explained in terms of truth conditions rather than conditions of verification or assertibility. And at least one writer has suggested defining realist positions in terms of their vulnerability to scepticism.[1]

Faced with this jungle, I am grateful to have a path which I can follow for a bit before plunging off on my own. Michael Williams' interest centres on the second item of the preceding list: the realist will not have truth defined in epistemic terms. And in addition he focuses on another realism not comfortably classifiable in any of the above ways: his epistemological realism. I shall focus there too, and leave all the other things which 'realism' can nowadays mean, and their various relations to scepticism, for another occasion.

So much, or little, for 'realism'; what of 'scepticism'? Finding an uncontroversial formulation is not easy. A popular first shot is likely to be that a sceptic is someone who holds that we do not know anything about X, where X is some area of which we take ourselves to know a good deal. But the apparent univocality of that shatters on the dispute about the analysis of 'knows'; the way that dispute is decided may significantly affect what scepticism, so formulated, really comes to and hence what tactics are appropriate for establishing or refuting it. One obviously important watershed here is the divide between internalist and externalist analyses, for it is clear that if scepticism be formulated as we have just suggested, and the concept of knowledge analysed externalistically, the sceptic will have much greater difficulty in maintaining his case. To be as brief as I dare: an externalistic analysis of 'S knows that p' will add to the conditions that p be true and that the subject believe it, some further requirement which—and this is the crucial point—will merely need to hold, whether S is aware that it holds or not. It might be that the belief that p must have been caused by the fact that p, or acquired by some method very likely to issue in a true belief, but there is no need for the subject to have any awareness that this is the case. Faced with such an analysis, one who expresses his scepticism as 'We don't know whether X' will have to argue that these beliefs are not caused by the facts believed in, or were not acquired by a method liable to lead to truth—which will involve him in a dogmatic (if negative) claim of a sort that conflicts awkwardly with his own scepticism.

One response would be to say point blank that if externalism holds scepticism falls, realism or not, and that seems to be what those are saying who suggest that the sceptic needs an internalist analysis of knowledge. But now we get a sight of the difficulty of finding a definitive statement of scepticism. For someone may agree that (given the externalist analysis) it is perfectly possible that we know that we have hands, but then say that this doesn't help much, because we *can't tell whether we know or not*: we can't distinguish the situation in which we do from that in which the demon is on the loose and we don't.

Is this still scepticism? Nomenclature aside for the moment, it does something to reveal what was bothering us about the original claim to knowledge: there is nothing in our state of awareness to distinguish the situation we believe in from a range of other situations all of which strike us as purest fantasy. Whether this is still scepticism or not may be a question with no determinate answer; perhaps it depends on what we are antecedently keen to believe, and that may change. I do not believe that any positive propositions of theology are known to be true, or even to be the slightest bit likely. In the time of Berkeley, when in many people's ears the expression 'Sceptic and Atheist' sounded like one word, I would have been a sceptic; now, when I am bleating with a large flock, I would be called a sceptic only in religious circles—in the eyes of other disbelievers I have merely noticed something that is pretty obvious once you think about it. What I am suggesting by this example is that whether the position earlier under discussion is scepticism or not depends on what we expected our state of awareness to do for us.

What these expectations may in turn depend on is not a matter I can attempt to discuss in what is only the introduction to a standard-length essay. Of the possibility that they are the outcome of an historically conditioned picture of ourselves, now widely in retreat, I have written elsewhere.[2] There may also be a more lasting reason in the phenomenology of consciousness. Perceptual states, especially visual states, have the feel of putting us in contact with objects. There they are—we see them! It is the naïve realist's only argument. With difficulty, we can bring ourselves to believe that there may be something misleading about our perception of colours, but as to the very existence of the objects, surely perception gives us a *guarantee* of their presence? The claim that our state of awareness cannot distinguish between the presence of a table and the presence of Descartes' demon conflicts with that very natural, indeed almost compulsive view of what consciousness can achieve.

In view of such considerations I do not want to approach Williams' paper, much less the topic, with any too rigid or narrow conception of scepticism in mind. If we do, we risk finding the sceptic too easy to refute and the whole issue too easily dismissed. Scepticism needs understanding, not proof or refutation.

II

Whether contextualism, Williams' epistemological anti-realism, offers us any defence against scepticism may well depend crucially on what we take scepticism to be, or, as I would prefer to say, on what claims we find sufficiently disruptive of our picture of ourselves as rational, cognitive beings to regard as sceptical. Let us for the moment allow contextualism all the room it wants: let what counts as the justification of a belief be no fixed quantity, but everywhere dependent on the context in which the belief is being considered, on the nature of the current inquiry and on the purposes for which we are conducting it. Suppose, if you like, that this is true for every belief, of whatever content. Now consider the following claim:

(*S*) Even if some belief you hold is as justified as can be, justified that is in every context in which you have considered or ever will consider it, even in any context in which you ever could consider it, it might still be false.

Whatever the powers of contextualism may be, one thing it surely cannot do is refute (*S*). It is empowered to tell us that it is only those contexts, of which (*S*) speaks, that determine what counts as justification at all, and that there is no question formulable in abstraction from such contexts as to whether a certain belief is or is not justified. But all of that is compatible with (*S*), which happily takes over the notion that justificational demands are functions of context, and then asks what the fact that our belief that *p* satisfies the justificational demands of all its (humanly possible) contexts has to do with its truth. If Descartes' demon is operating, it will be said, then a whole bagful of beliefs actually are false in spite of the fact that any investigation we can conduct, in any context, will pronounce them to be justified.

What contextualism about justification may do is block the inference from (S) to the conclusion that the belief in question is not justified; and contextualism about knowledge may block the inference to the conclusion that it is not known. This they may do by saying that whether beliefs are justified or known is to be decided afresh, indeed formulated afresh, according to the context in which the question arises. Contexts have their own cognitive fixed points, so to speak, and it is in relation to these that matters of justification and knowledge are properly to be judged. The sceptic may have invented a context in which a lot of beliefs turn out unknown and unjustified which turn out justified and known in virtually any other context. Well, good for him, but let us not go on about it too much, because his is only one context out of a multitude of others and has no unique status, especially not that of the final court in which claims to 'real' justification and 'real' knowledge are allowed or, more often, disallowed.

That view makes sense, but is there any reason to adopt it other than that it gets rid of scepticism for us? And in any case, how much scepticism does it actually get rid of? For a start, there is a danger that it will turn out two-edged. If no special status is to be allowed to the sceptic's favourite contexts (in which justification and/or knowledge claims fail), why allow any to those others in which they (frequently) succeed? These are just other contexts. Admittedly, they are distinguished by their greater frequency in practical thought and by the comparative ease with which the mind operates within them; but that is just another verbal variation on the theme which sceptics have got used to playing just as well as anyone else: the greater psychological comfort, perhaps even compulsion, which attaches to the common-sense position. If we have got rid of scepticism at the cost of denying that beliefs ever are simply and unelliptically justified or known, hasn't the sceptic won after all? I for one wouldn't be surprised to see a smile on his face: he has been paid pretty well to go away.

Unless we know exactly who he is, it isn't easy even to be sure that he has gone away, well-paid or not. Let the question whether we have seen any reason, other than the supposed defeat of the sceptic, to adopt contextualism, be kept in abeyance for the moment. What contextualism tells us is something about the semantics of the terms 'justification' and 'knowledge'—and no doubt it can effortlessly be extended to take in near relatives like 'has good reason' and 'has the right to be sure'. That will balk anyone who insists on putting his views in such forms as: we don't know that there is a physical world, none of our beliefs about the mental states of others is justified, and so on. But that scepticism has to be expressed in some such way as this is a presupposition of much discussion for which I see no clear reason. What of the person who just suggests that (S) is true, and stops? Has he not said just as much to disrupt our picture of our cognitive prowess as if we had allowed him to say 'Ultimately, none of our beliefs is justified'—instead of dismissing him with the contextualist line that talk of 'ultimate justification' is just a conceptual mistake? We may have thought that if only we were careful enough in the use of our cognitive equipment we could reach a point at which our beliefs were just bound to be true. Not so, if (S) holds: we could make all the effort of which we are capable and end up completely off beam. And contextualism will not refute (S); our best chance of bringing (S) down rests in the concept of being on and off beam, in other words of truth and falsity. But whether we can achieve anything along those lines without giving up realism as Williams understands it, that is to say the doctrine that truth is not to be defined in epistemic terms, must be doubtful at the very least. There I have nothing to add to what he has already said.

It seems then that the defeat which contextualism inflicts on the sceptic may not be so crushing after all. But leaving that aside, what reason has been or can be given for accepting it, other than the alleged damage to scepticism? In Williams' mind the epistemological realist, to whose view the contextualist has the acceptable alternative, has saddled himself with an identifiable implausibility. The realist holds that what constitutes the justification of a belief is independent of context, of human interests and purposes. He holds that beliefs are classifiable in certain very general ways, for instance as beliefs about the past, or beliefs about the physical world, or beliefs about our experiences, and his epistemological realism expresses itself in the idea that there is some objective order of justificational argument which these classifications embody. So that the response to a demand for justification must take the form of showing how beliefs of one class can be grounded on those of some other, and the discovery that they cannot therefore amounts to a demonstration of scepticism. Not so, says the contextualist, for these classifications and their hierarchical ordering have no objective status. They are conventions, options, whims; you can take them or leave them, and if you want to leave the ones which entail scepticism, go ahead and leave them. If it makes you ill don't eat it; let the people at the next table eat it if they want to.

This line of thought has two features which make me uncomfortable. One is that it seems to misrepresent the way in which scepticism—or some influential forms of it—arise. The second is that it implies a degree of independence between these investigative contexts: you can accept some and reject others, in particular you can accept the normal ones and reject those that lead to scepticism, with never a word said, somewhat as you can love plums and not like greengages, and there's an end of the matter. This has for me too much in common with the old idea, often brought against Hume, that scepticism is achieved by subjecting beliefs to arbitrarily severe tests which they then demonstrably fail. But if these tests are *arbitrarily* severe the sceptic ought to be in much the same position as the person who first defines 'doctor' as 'someone who can cure any known ailment within two minutes' and then announces that there are no doctors.[3] Whatever we may say about scepticism it is not in this sort of way merely fatuous. We need to explain its attraction as well as its repulsion, and this method does not promise to do so.

We shall return to that point. I would first like to elaborate on my remark that the contextualist's story seems to misrepresent something about the way in which scepticism arises. It makes it sound, namely, as if some philosophers began by making certain assumptions about the structure of justification: beliefs about other minds need to be grounded on beliefs about physical occurrences, beliefs about physical occurrences need to be grounded in beliefs about experiences, and such like. But whereas something like this is certainly recognizable in much sceptical thought, it doesn't appear to be so much an assumption as an outcome of prior considerations.[4]

They are all too familiar. Experience soon teaches us that we can be misled. So when we are keen on being right we begin to take account of the kinds of circumstance under which the beliefs that are suggested to us can turn out false after all. The strategy helps: we are not fooled quite so often. After a while, when the idea of keeping an eye open for ways in which our investigations might be going wrong has become a valued part of good practice, someone introduces a disturbing thought: suppose that there were a demon . . . etc. Well, if there were, a great deal of what we believe would of course be false. But shouldn't we therefore—remembering what we take to be good practice when we think of a way in which we might be going wrong—just turn aside for a moment to check up that we aren't going wrong in that way? Then the awful point strikes us: unlike the ones we are used to dealing with, in this case there is no way to check.

How are we to react? We could react sceptically, by admitting that all the threatened beliefs were unknown or unjustified. (That would be a natural extension of the usual strategy: if you can't rule the disturbing hypothesis out be careful—for all you know maybe your belief is not true.) Or we could respond with an attempt at foundationalism: are there any beliefs that would not be false if the demon were in action, and can they be used as a basis for showing that he is not after all? (That would also be a natural extension of the usual strategy: if we suspect that we are confronted by an illusion we resort to beliefs which it would not affect and see whether they enable us to settle our suspicion one way or the other.) If we do that we will, as I think is now widely agreed, finish with scepticism again. That is not to say that scepticism is inevitable: a third possibility is to say that we can, after all, check up on the demon: check that there is a table in front of you. Good. Now, if there were any such demon there would not be a table; but there is, so there is no demon. Back to normal business.

Williams, if I have understood him correctly, would stress the third and last option, saying that in choosing it we are accepting what the demon-fantasy demonstrates, namely the logical independence of reality and experience, but refusing to treat that independence asymmetrically for epistemological purposes and commit ourselves to judging claims about the physical world on their grounding in beliefs about experience. We might also describe it as just refusing to take the Cartesian hypothesis seriously, as just waving it aside. I have a good deal of sympathy for the view that we *can* do this: there is nothing about the idea of the demon, or of a brain in a vat, which prevents us. But if the implication is that we can simply do it, with no nagging questions left over, then I differ.

Two questions, in particular, nag. If we can just dismiss the Cartesian demon without any kind of hindrance, why is the sceptic who uses him not felt to be in the same position as the person we mentioned earlier who arbitrarily misdefines 'doctor' and then says that there are no doctors? Could it be because the sceptic does not actually say that he is defining the word 'know' (or 'justified') when he introduces the demon, but just does so implicitly by demanding that the hypothesis of the demon be met? That seems thin. If it were the right explanation then the 'doctor sceptic' should be able to make the same effect merely by avoiding an explicit definition, and perhaps saying instead: 'Find me someone who can cure every known illness in two minutes. You agree you can't? Right, so there aren't any doctors.' That might momentarily stun the audience, but not so as to give rise to any lasting puzzlement or debate.

Whatever the answer be to that first question, one feels that the second must somehow be related. Suppose that we do summarily dismiss the demon and his ilk. Where is the discontinuity between that case and those we normally encounter? For unless we can locate some discontinuity and show why it invites this reaction we shall still be in the position of rejecting the sceptic's favourite hypotheses without any rationale other than that taking them seriously leads to scepticism.

It will be noticed that I have shifted attention from epistemological realism to the question of the severity of the tests to which a well known sceptical tactic subjects claims to knowledge and justification. Are such tests admissible? If not, on what grounds are they to be rejected? Might it be that the question of their admissibility has no determinate answer at all? I am aware that Michael Williams has said in as many words that this is not the point: it is on epistemological realism that scepticism is founded:

> The challenge is not to the strictness of the sceptic's standards but to his epistemological realism.[5]

But that cannot be the whole story. Epistemological realism by itself will not produce scepticism—not if it is just the doctrine that whether a particular belief is justified is a straightforward matter of fact. That leaves it open to us so to arrange the justificational demands on any proposition that, as a straightforward matter of fact, they are often fulfilled. To generate scepticism, epistemological realism must include at least some view about epistemological classifications and hierarchical ordering. But again, not every such view will deliver scepticism, if by that we mean scepticism about one of the major areas of discourse. We might, for instance, use physical object statements as the bottom level, and then no general scepticism about them could emerge from our hierarchical ordering. Once we get to the idea that it has to be statements about experiences on which the justificational structure rests, then of course things will begin to happen, but I would not wish to pack all of that into the meaning of 'epistemological realism'—and neither I think would Williams, since he convicts a coherence theory of truth of epistemological realism as well.[6] In that case, however, it seems that the crux is indeed the strictness of the sceptic's standards for justification or knowledge and not, or not just, his epistemological realism. For it is surely the strictness of those standards, embodied in the demand that we confront the logical possibility of the demon, that makes statements about experience the bottom line—they at least are something which would still be true even if the demon were working.

One further point about the characterization of epistemological realism. Williams sometimes appears to contrast the view that whether or not a belief is justified is a 'straightforward matter of fact' with the view that what constitutes justification depends on our interests and purposes.[7] But the essential underlying idea, if I am not mistaken, is not that of a matter of fact, but rather that what constitutes justification *varies* with our interests and purposes. What I can digest may vary with the state of my health, but whether I can *now* digest *this* is as straightforward a matter of fact as any. And we should notice too that even if there is only one, invariant, standard, and even if it is so strict that 'the concept of knowledge ... demands that we consider every logical possibility of error'[8] we may still be able to derive this concept from our interests. Admittedly, it may be hard to see how the formation of such a concept could have anything to do with advancing our interests, especially if we add the ill-understood word 'practical', but that is a point that deserves further inquiry and should not be ruled out *ab initio* by our terminology.

I persist in thinking, therefore, that an understanding of the role of the traditional 'sceptical possibilities'—demons and so on—is vital to an understanding of the debate about scepticism, and this whether realism (in the form: truth is not an epistemic notion) is central to it or not. In developing this thought I shall not be as far from contextualism as some of my remarks so far may have suggested. What we need, however, is not contextualism itself but insight into the motivations that pull us towards it, and those that push us away from it.

III

In the rest of the paper I shall develop a hypothesis about the nature of these motivations and how they arise. I shall often speak as if my hypothesis were concerned specifically with the concept of knowledge and the verb 'to know', but this detail is inessential. Indeed, concentration on it may even do harm by suggesting that what I have to say can touch only the scepticism which is expressed by saying that certain things are not known—whereas I hope to have made it clear that I would regard such a restriction as seriously damaging. Briefly, the central idea is that any community advanced enough to have a language will need a concept which marks reliable sources of information, and it is the conditions of work attaching to this post which generate both the compulsion and repulsion of scepticism. Whether or not the word 'knows' is the present post-holder is not of vital importance; the point is that the post exists, and someone who thinks that 'knows' does *not* occupy it ought to feel that homing in on the word 'knowledge' is not the best way to understand the debate about scepticism.

Because they are in general better guides to action, we want true beliefs rather than false ones. Consider someone who wants a true belief on some matter, we may say schematically on the question whether *p*. He has his own equipment, powers of perception and inference, for attaining belief. But it will often be to his advantage if he can make use of beliefs already attained by other members of his social group, that is to say, if he can use them as informants. (The one up the tree can see the predator; those on the ground can't, but badly need to know where it is.) So it becomes imperative to assess informants: whose belief is it best to take over? At a slightly more sophisticated stage we will also sometimes feel the need to assess our own beliefs, but I shall not need to use the point in what follows—scepticism is not as dependent on the first-person standpoint as some writers imply.

We may start by considering a principle which has work to do in the formation of the vast majority of our concepts if not absolutely all. I shall call it the principle of objectivization, and as the name implies it has some kinship with the notion of an objective viewpoint as brought to prominence by Thomas Nagel and Bernard Williams, amongst others. But it concentrates on the purposes of the concept-user rather than the items to which concepts are applied, and its effect is not just that of adapting our thought to the idea of an objective, observer-neutral world.

A creature has a certain need and desires its satisfaction. What it wants is something which, there and then, will satisfy the need; and unless it is the sort of thing which just comes completely unbidden, the creature must be able to register it as such so as to be able to orientate its behaviour towards it, and it must have the necessary motor-capacities to do so. It needs this situation as a whole—if it all obtains, the creature succeeds, if any of it is missing, the creature fails and the need persists. So if all we are thinking of is the fulfilment of this need here and now, it has no cause to distinguish the various aspects: the presence of food, its own capacity to be nourished by that food, its own capacity to detect the food and reach it. But with the slightest hint of intelligence this primitive holism starts to fragment. The creature must distinguish between food, here, now, provided it makes the right movement, and food here, soon, provided it waits very quietly for a bit and then makes the right movement. It must distinguish these from food, there, soon, provided it can get there; and cases in which it can get there from ones in which it cannot. Helpful again, as life grows more varied, will be the capacity to distinguish cases in which it simply cannot get there from those in which it cannot get there because of some temporary hindrance, either in the environment or in itself. These are differences in the situation which require different strategies, and the creature which can respond to each of them appropriately will be more likely to prosper.

That creature was an individualist. If we place it in a social group the possibilities expand again. What it cannot reach perhaps a maturer individual can—which suggests a way of getting at food that would otherwise be inaccessible. Others may be better than it at recognizing food; so far as they seem trustworthy, follow their recommendations. Others may be able to use substances as food which it cannot; see that they get it. (That will be encouraged by altruism, if it has any, but it can and will arise without it; it is not necessarily for the sake of the horse that we give it the oats instead of eating them ourselves.)

What we see here are the natural forces driving thought away from the totally subjectivist stance, the pure 'here and now for me as I am here and now'. They induce the thought of the satisfaction of a need at other times and other places—whether that be the present need or a similar need expected for the future, the thought of recognitional and behavioural capacities other than those I have here and now, and hence of an object which in the right circumstances can satisfy such needs whilst coming nowhere near to meeting the wholly subjectivized conditions from which our thought-experiment began.

We can now apply these ideas to the situation of the inquirer and the concept of a good informant. We begin by considering it at its most subjective. I am seeking information as to whether or not *p*, and hence want an informant who is satisfactory for my purposes, here and now, with my present beliefs and capacities for receiving information. As well as having the right answer to my question, he should meet at least these four conditions:

(1) He should be accessible to me here and now.
(2) He should be recognizable by me as someone likely to be right about *p*.
(3) He should be as likely to be right about *p* as my concerns require.
(4) Channels of communication between us should be open.

All of these depend to some extent on my present state or relationship to the potential informant, and all will be affected by the process of objectivization. But in this context I shall discuss only (3), for this is the one relevant to an understanding of scepticism.

Our inquirer is looking for a good informant as to whether *p*, in certain specific circumstances for certain specific purposes; let us suppose him to have found a likely candidate. His interest in the candidate's competence cannot be limited to performance in the actual world; it must extend to various possible worlds as well. For since he is human, his ignorance is not limited to the question whether *p*, but extends to a vast number of other propositions. If he is ignorant of the truth about *q* he will hope to find an informant who will give him the truth about *p* whether *q* is true or not, which is as much as to say, since *q* cannot turn out both true and false, that the informant should be right about *p* not just under the actual but also under certain merely possible circumstances.

Our inquirer's interest, however, will not stretch to all worlds which he takes to be theoretically possible, but only a selection of them. Some he will exclude because he has already come to believe that, although possible and even antecedently quite probable, they are not actual: he can see that the potential informant is wearing a red shirt, and so excludes those worlds in which he is wearing a blue shirt as merely possible and non-actual. Some he will exclude as too improbable to need taking into account. If the candidate would fail (hold the wrong belief as to whether *p*) in some world *W*, he will not allow that to influence him if he rates the likelihood of *W*'s being the actual world low enough. How low, will depend on a number of factors. One is the urgency of forming a belief as to whether *p*: sometimes the penalty for not forming a belief at all is as great or greater than that for forming a false one. If my train leaves in five minutes I had better come to a decision about whether the station is this way or that way. Guessing will be better than not deciding, and anyone with a better than evens chance of telling me the right answer will be welcome. Another issue is the relative pay-off of being right and being wrong: if being wrong will not matter too much, but being right will be very advantageous, I may be satisfied with an informant whose views have a lower probability of being true than I would be if being wrong would turn out very damaging.[9] A further element is my personal attitude to risk. I may positively enjoy it, and so be prepared to take risks which I would not take if I enjoyed it less; one type of risk-taking is being somewhat less demanding in the choice of informant. Or the converse: my natural inclination may be towards security.

This is to take the concept of the good informant at its most subjective, so to speak in its me-here-now shape. This version is ripe for objectivization. We shall have an interest in judging that someone is/would be a good informant as to whether *p* under circumstances which, since they are multifaceted and variable, we are not in a position to specify in advance. In addition, I shall be concerned that others should make judgements as to who is a good informant. That may be because I have enough altruism to hope that their enterprises, hence also their enterprises of belief-acquisition, will succeed. But if I lack that much altruism, I shall still want them to make assessments of informants, because that may turn out to be useful to me. I shall not suppose, however, that in making such assessments they have my particular circumstances in mind: if they tell me whom to ask about the times of trains to London, I shall not expect them to take into account how important it is to me to get the right answer, what I shall lose if I do not arrive on time. (I may not yet know that myself; or perhaps it isn't even on my own behalf that I am trying to find out, but for someone else whose exact concern with the information is unknown to me.)

All this is going to edge us towards the idea of someone who is a good informant as to whether *p* whatever the particular circumstances of the inquirer, whatever rewards and penalties hang over him and whatever his attitude to them. That means someone who is very likely to be right—for he must be acceptable even to the most demanding. Our recommender will not in general know of the concerns for which the informant and his information are needed, so there will be an important role for an assessment at a high enough standard for him responsibly to make his recommendation whilst knowing nothing of them: a level which he may reasonably take to be high enough to satisfy all practical purposes. So of the worlds that he feels he cannot quite definitely exclude, he will feel obliged to include in his assessment even those that he regards as very improbable. Moreover, he will be moved to take a pretty careful look at those which he 'can quite definitely exclude'—is that really as many as we think? These thoughts take us further down the road of objectivization. Knowledge, so the hypothesis goes, lies at the end of it.

But we must not slip into saying that for knowledge, given that the concept grows by objectivization in the way just envisaged, 'absolute' objectivization is called for, meaning by that the demand that the informant be certain to have the right answer in any possible world, including those 'sceptical worlds' of demons and brains in vats. That would explain how and why the concept of knowledge brings scepticism in its train; but it is not within a mile of being warranted by anything we have established so far. Objectivization is fuelled, on our hypothesis, by practical pressures very widely felt; and as a fairly uncontentious matter of observation the pressure to take account of those ways of going wrong that are embodied in the standard sceptical fantasies is not one of them. If there is a real job for such an absolute concept to do, it has not yet been shown.

Someone who once thought that there was such a job, and furthermore that 'know' was the word that did it, was Peter Unger. (I use the past tense because—significantly—he has since retracted and put forward a different view.[10]) He described a whole category of what he called 'absolute terms'. Being flat, he said, means being perfectly flat—not *at all* bumpy—a standard which, for all we know, no real surface achieves, but which in all practical contexts is relaxed in accordance with the degree of flatness needed for whatever purposes are under consideration—a rugby pitch, a lawn, a billiard table. A necessary condition of knowing, he then argued, is being certain. And 'certain' is an absolute term: being certain is being absolutely certain, as being flat is being absolutely flat, and being a vacuum is being absolutely empty. So we should consider 'know' in the same light; we may and do relax the standard, but the standard calls for the truth of the belief to be (absolutely) certain, so it is truly satisfied only by a belief whose truth would survive even the worst efforts of the demon. At most hardly any surfaces are flat, and hardly any of the regions we declare to be vacua actually are such; so in respect of both these terms we say a lot of things which are false, but they are actually close enough to being true for their falsity to have no adverse practical effects, given the purpose we have in mind. Our claims to knowledge, Unger holds, are in the same position. The sceptic is therefore right, though the point that he typically insists on, that we do not *know* anything, makes no significant practical difference.

Here I would like to make just one point, the connection of which with the central concern of this paper will be obvious: Unger's view can explain the existence of sceptics, but can it explain why scepticism should have met with such resistance? Consider the term 'vacuum', to which 'knowledge' is alleged to be analogous. What would be the likely response to the suggestion that scarcely any of the things we refer to as 'a vacuum' actually is such? Surely that it is quite true: 'vacuum' picks out an ideal state to which the best of our vacua are good approximations—and that what approximations count as good depends on which purposes the so-called vacuum is to serve. But a debate, with each of two or more parties warmly advocating their own view, one would not expect; and it is not in fact found. 'Are there nearly as many vacua as we think?' is not an issue, and this is reflected in the fact that many would prefer to reformulate the question: 'Are there nearly as many vacua as we commonly *say* there are?'—with the implication that we are perfectly well aware that we do not really think what, if our words are taken quite literally, we often say. If 'knowledge' were analogous to 'vacuum' the debate about scepticism would be very different; most likely it would not exist at all. Not only can one not see how an absolute concept of knowledge could have arisen; there is positive reason to think that it has not. If it had, of course, scepticism would be not merely comprehensible, but true—which was just what Unger then thought.

Unger saw this problem, or one very close to it. He observed[11] that when pressed to be accurate we are inclined to say that we never did believe that (many of) the various surfaces which we called 'flat' really were flat, only that they were flat enough for our then current purposes; but that in the case of 'know' we feel, even if we are convinced and finish up complete sceptics, that previously we really did believe that we knew (most of) the things we verbally claimed to know. Having pointed this out Unger honestly admitted that he could give no explanation, which must therefore 'remain a further question'. The answer, I believe, lies in giving up the thesis that 'know' is an absolute term—and then we shall have to take a more complex, and less partisan, view of the phenomenon of scepticism than Unger then recommended.

It seems then that there is no reason to continue the unpromising search for practical factors that might push objectivization of the concept of knowledge to its theoretical limit. So we should go on to ask another highly pertinent question: are there any such factors which would cause objectivization to stop at any definite and specifiable point?

The reply most immediately suggested by the foregoing is that the concept will simply be open-ended: it will make room for any degree of caution in its application, provided there are purposes and circumstances to which that degree of caution is appropriate. But there is more to be said than that. We have already agreed that the relevant level of caution will be high—the practical requirement of objectivization will put a fairly stringent lower bound on it. May there not be practical requirements that put some upper bound on it as well? If so, do they perhaps shield the concept from confrontation with the possibilities traditionally used for generating scepticism?

We have to say at once that there may well be some such factors. For a start, we have already observed that there are many 'possibilities', including the now standard sceptical scenarios, which are just not treated as such in ordinary (meaning: non-philosophical) practice. Not that they are considered and jettisoned; they are not properly placed in the class of possibilities mentioned earlier which are rejected as sufficiently improbable not to bother about. Rather, they are just not considered, the very thought of them is something strange and new, and the great majority of human beings never encounter it at all. Now if standard practice thus excludes them, will they not also be excluded from any role in determining the applicability of the standard concept of which, presumably, standard practice is constitutive?

Further, can it not be argued that this is more than just a descriptive point? Such extreme possibilities are not worth considering for the powerfully practical reason that their realization would make no noticeable difference to us. Maybe our beliefs would be false were the demon, or Berkeley's God, in action. But then if the demon, or Berkeley's God, is in action, acting on them will have, so far as I am concerned, just the effect I wanted. There can be no practical advantage in trying to distinguish between two situations which will be, so far as we can tell, indistinguishable. And few enterprises are in this respect neutral; where there is no advantage to be gained, there is nearly always disadvantage in pursuing them. Had we unlimited time and capacities, then perhaps; since we do not, their pursuit mostly distracts us from what is more urgent.

There may be some truth in that thought when it is applied to certain sceptical hypotheses, such as for instance the postulate of a demon absolutely consistent in his deceptions now and henceforth. But the more disturbing hypotheses, practically speaking, are ones that propose some sudden change, a demon whose powers or intentions are wearing out, a deity bored with the present order or disgusted by our smugness. Here we are threatened by practical consequences enough, but still such possibilities play no real part in our thinking, no matter how important it may be to us to acquire true beliefs.

For an explanation of this, however, we can look to another point: no practical purpose can be served by a test which every informant must fail. We do have to find someone who satisfies the test, for otherwise no informant, no belief, no action, no success. And no success, no survival. Let it be granted that there are compelling practical reasons for wishing to avoid falsehood, especially if it might fall at an important junction in our whole system of beliefs from which it could infect many of the others. But if action needs belief, having false beliefs is no worse than not having any beliefs at all, so no practical motives could lead us to prefer the latter state to the former and impose tests that would expunge all belief before admitting a single falsehood. On the contrary, what they recommend is the rejection of the tests. It looks as if all practical factors will push us towards a concept immunized by its own limiting conditions against the sceptic's threat; and if the concept of knowledge is vulnerable to scepticism, no pragmatic account of its origins will be able to explain how it got that way.

This must surely be the wrong way to argue, however. We have said that in everyday practice the idea of applying such tests as the standard sceptical fantasies just doesn't come into anyone's head. It follows that the opportunity to lay down the practice of rejecting this kind of test, either for the reason of its unsatisfiability or any other, equally just does not occur. We may conjecture about what would happen to an attempt to introduce such tests into everyday thinking—it isn't very hard—but that is not to say that everyday practice is already determinate on the point. It has after all no practical need to be determinate. A decision isn't called for; no one raises the question, no one even entertains it, let alone seriously considers allowing such a test to affect the formation of his beliefs. We must not be misled: there are, in a sense, factors which cause objectification to stop short of the sceptical fantasies: it is bound to stop short of considerations which are never considered. But that does not mean that the concept so formed acquires as it were a 'hard boundary' at this point. On the contrary, the operative fact is precisely that *nothing* happens here, so we neither have a definite boundary nor the definite absence of one.

Here we find ourselves arriving at the realism debate from another direction. One way of being an anti-realist, we recall, is to abjure the application of the

Law of Excluded Middle to the affected area. In this sense, I am here proposing an anti-realist approach to questions about conceptual boundaries, and that of the concept of knowledge in particular. The number of Lady Macbeth's children is determined by Shakespeare, so that if he omitted to think (or perhaps to document) any thoughts on that matter then no propositions about it have truth-values, and *a fortiori* neither 'Lady M. had *n* children' nor 'Lady M. did not have *n* children' is true. In somewhat the same way, the boundaries of concepts are determined by our practice, and if our practice includes nothing that settles a certain question about concept-application then it has no answer. That is what I am suggesting about the question before us.

The resultant area of indeterminacy hosts the controversy about scepticism. On the one hand, the genesis of the concept through the process of objectivization pushes us on towards acceptance of ever severer tests and so finally over the edge and into the arms of the sceptic; on the other, we are held back by the perception that the edge marks the end of any contact with the practical requirements which are the concept's ancestry. In much the same way, in a related area, the impetus of objectivization pushes us towards the thought of a state of affairs which is in principle beyond our powers to recognize; and pragmatism causes us a bad conscience if we give way.

Though I may appear to have implied the contrary, none of this yet explains the factual existence of a debate about scepticism; what it concerns is rather the opportunity for such a debate, and the difficulties of bringing it to any definite conclusion, should any philosopher find motive to start it up. He will then find in everyday practice, I have argued, a tendency which he can extrapolate without doing anything which the concept of itself forbids; and this extrapolation will lead to scepticism. His opponents, on the other hand, can find in the normal rationale of everyday practice a reason for crying halt to the extrapolation before an irremediable scepticism is reached. Their perception that some non-arbitrary boundary has been crossed is no illusion; and no more than the radical sceptic do they do anything which the ordinary concept of knowledge disallows.

We cannot just leave things there, however. If the question whether a knowledge claim has to face up to the demon or not were in just the same boat as those about Lady Macbeth's offspring one would expect the fact to have become clear by now, and that should have put an end to at least this corner of the debate. We may infer that it is not, and we would be right. What it takes to settle issues about the biographies of fictional persons is easily agreed; but what features of linguistic practice settle, and fail to settle, issues about the applicability of a concept is altogether less well understood, and probably less clear-cut in itself.

It has of course recently been suggested—and indeed has ignited one flourishing area of realist/anti-realist debate—that strictly speaking nothing about linguistic practice can settle anything about how a word is to be applied in future cases. I shall not jump into that crucible, but simply say that insofar as past practice can dictate to future it must do so by virtue of the similarity between the cases in question. That launches us out on to thin ice. Very often items are so naturally and uncontroversially perceived as similar that one can scarcely imagine it otherwise—were it not so, we could neither speak nor think. But most items we speak about are complex, and it is bound to happen that they are alike in some features, unlike in others. That opens up the possibility that the way we employ some term in other cases may not indicate how these similarities and dissimilarities are to be weighted when it comes to deciding whether it applies to the present case or not.

Should the introduction of Descartes' demon affect claims to knowledge? The stage seems perfectly set for an interminable dispute, interminable, that is, if we think that it must terminate in a clear win for one side or the other. Looked at in one way, the hypothesis of the demon is continuous with our normal approach to gathering information, indeed with an essential feature of our normal approach. Once he has got used to the idea that he can be mistaken, any information-gatherer with a distaste for error will be on the lookout for ways in which he could have gone wrong; and if he thinks of one he will try, by reflection or further observation or both, to exclude it. The hypothesis of the demon is another idea about how he could have gone wrong. Provided we are not to have resort to theories of meaning which tell us that the hypothesis of the demon is not really an idea at all, that should be uncontroversial. Notice that I did not say that it was *just* another idea about how he could have gone wrong. That 'just' would have wrecked everything by implying, quite spuriously, that there is nothing to be said on the other side and so *of course* we must be prepared to test knowledge-claims against this and other radical hypotheses.

Quite the contrary, there is plenty to be said on the other side. The practice of keeping an eye open for sources of error had a point. And the point was not just avoidance of the false but the maximization of truth amongst our beliefs—otherwise we might equally well have tried to stop believing anything. The label 'knowledge' distinguished well-tested from half- or untested opinions, which made it a helpful flag. But confronting claims to knowledge with the idea that our beliefs may be induced by the demon can have no such function, which means a massive discontinuity between the instruments of sceptical doubt and the resoluble caution which is firmly entrenched practice.

Which feature is to predominate? The continuity, which implies that the sceptic is just doing what normal practice really requires of us, if only we had noticed? Or the discontinuity, which implies that (as Williams puts it) he has merely changed the subject? (Let us for now shelve the question whether what he has in that case changed it to might still deserve to be called scepticism.) People can and do have their preferences. But until someone exhibits features of the uncontroversial part of our linguistic practice which clearly favour one above the other I have to say that I see no objective basis for a decision—nor any reason to think that there ought to be one.

Does realism lead to scepticism? Does scepticism need realism? That was where we started, and we can end by saying at least this: thinking that scepticism is true, or for that matter that it is false, calls for a certain kind of realism, the view that the family of concepts used to express sceptical positions have real boundaries in certain crucial places. But I know of no general argument for thinking that they must, and in the absence of one I favour the view that they do not.[12]

Notes

1. See C. McGinn, 'An A Priori Argument for Realism', *Journal of Philosophy* 76, p. 115.

2. E. J. Craig, *The Mind of God and the Works of Man*, esp. chs. 1 and 2.

3. I borrow the example from Paul Edwards, 'Bertrand Russell's Doubts about Induction'.

4. Williams is well aware of this line of objection; see his paper 'Epistemological Realism and the Basis of Scepticism', *Mind* 97.

5. Ibid., p. 428.

6. See his essay in this volume, especially Section VI, pp. 207–9.

7. 'Epistemological Realism and the Basis of Scepticism', pp. 419, 420.

8. Ibid., p. 428.

9. The limiting case is that of Pascal's wager, in which we are invited to adopt a belief on game-theoretical grounds without learning anything that raises in the slightest its chances of being true.

10. See P. Unger, *Philosophical Relativity*. This new view is not so far from the one I shall arrive at. The fact that I use different reasons from Unger does not mean that I disapprove of his.

11. Unger, *Ignorance—a Case for Scepticism*, p. 89.

12. Much of Section III of this article has since been incorporated into E. J. Craig, *Knowledge and the State of Nature*, esp. chs. X and XII.

IV

REALISM, VALUE, AND SECONDARY QUALITIES

9

Objectivity and Moral Realism: On the Significance of the Phenomenology of Moral Experience

Michael Smith

1. Mackie's Error Theory

In chapter 1 of *Ethics: Inventing Right and Wrong* (hereafter 'E') John Mackie makes two claims: firstly, that we ordinarily conceive of values as 'objectively prescriptive' features of the world, and, secondly, that, as a matter of fact, the world contains no such features.[1] Central to Mackie's discussion is thus the relationship between a conceptual claim and an ontological claim. It is *because* our concept of value is the concept of an objective and prescriptive feature of the world, and thus a part of our ontology, that we can make the ontological claim that nothing *like that* figures in our ontology. Mackie thus adopts an 'error theory' about moral value. Our moral thought embodies a commitment to evaluative realism but, in being so committed, we are in error.

In 'Values and Secondary Qualities' (hereafter 'VASQ') John McDowell offers a potentially devastating critique of Mackie's error theory.[2] He argues that Mackie ascribes to common sense a conception of the objectivity of values that makes the idea of an objectively prescriptive value incoherent, and obviously so—no surprise, according to McDowell, that there is nothing *like that* in our ontology. McDowell thinks that we should therefore be suspicious of Mackie's claim that common sense has such a conception of value; better to think that, according to common sense, values are objective in a rather different sense. Embracing this alternative conception of the objectivity of values enables us to see not only that the idea that there exist objectively prescriptive values is coherent but also, according to McDowell, that the claim that there do exist such values is plausibly true.

McDowell may be right to criticize Mackie's own version of the conceptual claim. However the analogy with secondary qualities is itself potentially misleading. Once we correct the analogy in the appropriate way—a way suggested by Mackie himself—we see that there is no straightforward move from McDowell's own version of the conceptual claim to the conclusion that there do exist objectively prescriptive values. An error theory may be on the horizon yet. So, at any rate, I will argue.[3]

2. McDowell's Rejection of the Error Theory

McDowell agrees with Mackie's 'phenomenological thesis' that when we have moral experience we seem to be confronted with objectively prescriptive features of the world (VASQ, p. 110). However, according to McDowell, Mackie goes on to argue that there are no such features only because he mistakenly thinks that, in order to be objective, values would have to be objective in one of the senses in which primary qualities are objective: that is, 'objective' in a sense that contrasts with the sense in which secondary qualities are 'subjective'. McDowell explains the distinction as follows:

> A secondary quality is a property the ascription of which to an object is not adequately understood except as true, if it is true, in virtue of the object's disposition to present a certain sort of perceptual appearance: specifically, an appearance characterizable by using a word for the property itself to say how the object perceptually appears. Thus an object's being red is understood as obtaining in virtue of the object's being such as (in certain circumstances) to look, precisely, red. (VASQ, pp. 111–12)

Such a conception of secondary qualities may rightfully count them as subjective because, according to it, our concept of a secondary quality just is the concept of a disposition to produce certain subjective states—in this case, perceptual appearances. We could put the point by saying that our concept of a secondary quality is the concept of a property having an 'internal relation' to perceptual appearances.[4] McDowell claims that this feature of secondary quality concepts contrasts with a feature of our primary quality concepts:

> In the natural contrast, a primary quality would be objective in the sense that what it is for something to have it can be adequately understood otherwise than in terms of dispositions to give rise to subjective states. (VASQ, p. 113)

Thus, according to McDowell, since we can understand what it is for something to have primary qualities in terms other than what it is for them to present certain perceptual appearances—in the theoretical terms dictated by geometry, or physics, for instance—so our conception of what it is for something to have such properties does not tie their presence or absence constitutively to the possibility of their presenting a certain sort of perceptual appearance.[5] We could put the point by saying that our concept of a primary quality *is not* the concept of a property enjoying the 'internal relation' to perceptual appearances enjoyed by the secondaries. Such a conception of primary qualities may therefore rightfully count them as objective, by contrast with the earlier account of secondary qualities.

Let's now return to Mackie's idea that values are 'objectively prescriptive' features of the world. McDowell agrees with Mackie that if our concept of value were the concept of a property that is objective in the primary quality sense just described then it would be impossible for evaluative thought to have 'the internal relation to "attitudes" or the will that would be needed for it to count as evaluative' (VASQ, p. 110), and hence there could be no objectively *prescriptive* values.[6] However, for reasons that should now be apparent, he expresses a certain incredulity at Mackie's suggestion that the fact that there are no objectively prescriptive values in this sense is any sort of *discovery* (VASQ, p. 113). For the sense in which we are to suppose that values are objective is defined in a way that *contrasts with* the idea that the concept of the relevant property bears an internal relation to a subjective state. What it would be to conceive of a value as objective is thus, *inter alia*, to conceive of the denial of what it would be to conceive of it as prescriptive. Thus if Mackie were right that we conceive of value as an objectively prescriptive feature of the world, in the primary quality sense of 'objectivity', then what he tries to pass off as an empirical discovery about the world is really something that we can trace to an incoherence in our evaluative thought; indeed, an incoherence that lies very close to the surface.

For his part McDowell thinks the implausibility of the idea that ordinary moral thought is guilty of so grotesque an incoherence constitutes a *reductio* of Mackie's version of the conceptual claim. He thus suggests that we conceive of value as a property that is objective in a different sense, a sense in which we conceive primary and secondary qualities to be alike with respect to objectivity: that is, 'objective' in the sense of being 'there to be experienced' (VASQ, pp. 113–14). For once we see that there is no obstacle to supposing that there really are secondary qualities, properties that really are there to be experienced which we conceive in terms of a relation to our perceptual states, we see that there is no obstacle to there really being values, properties that are there to be experienced which we conceive in terms of a relationship to the will. That is, we see that there is no obstacle to there really being values, objectively prescriptive features of the world. On this account of the matter, ordinary moral thought is not to be convicted of the kind of error of which Mackie convicts it. Ordinary moral experience may yet be veridical. How plausible is McDowell's response to Mackie?

The suggestion is that we ordinarily conceive of values as objective in the sense of being 'there to be experienced'. But what does McDowell say in support of his claim that *that* is part of our conception of value? And, even if we grant him that, why does he think that it is so clear that values, so conceived, really are there to be experienced? It will be helpful if we first consider these questions in the case of colour, and then compare and contrast the case of value. What does McDowell say in support of his claim that we conceive of colour as a property that is there to be experienced? And even if we grant him that, why does he think that it is so clear that colours really are there to be experienced? I begin by considering the second question first.

3. McDowell on the Objectivity of Colour

Let's digress for a moment. In *The Nature of Morality* (hereafter 'TNOM') Gil Harman suggests that, in these terms, we have reason to believe that a property really is there to be experienced only if we need to posit an object's having such a property in order to give a satisfying explanation of our experiences.[7] Mackie too endorses this explanatory test for whether something really is a property of an object.[8] Mackie and Harman differ, however, over the proper status of colours, given the explanatory test. Mackie thinks that colours fail the explanatory test. Harman thinks that they pass. Who is right?

There is strong prima-facie reason to think that colours fail the explanatory test. For, as Harman points out, in order to explain our experiences, it seems that we need make no mention of the colours of objects. It suffices that we appeal to the 'physical characteristics of surfaces, the properties of light, and the neurophysiological psychology of observers' (TNOM, p. 22). Indeed, it is for this very reason that Mackie thinks colours fail the explanatory test. Why, then, does Harman think that colours none the less pass the test? Harman thinks that colours pass the test because they will covertly have been mentioned in giving such explanations; for, in his view, 'facts about colour are . . . reducible to facts about physical characteristics of perceived objects, facts about light, and facts about the psychology and perceptual apparatus of perceivers' (TNOM, p. 14).

However a little reflection reveals this move to be wholly illegitimate. What entitles Harman to believe that we can give such a reduction at this stage of the argument? After all, such a reduction itself *presupposes* that we are entitled to think of colours as properties that really are there to be experienced in the first place, otherwise there would be nothing there to reduce. But then we have to ask what our reason is for presupposing that, given that the explanatory test suggests otherwise.[9]

It is important to see the inadequacy of the explanatory test to this task in the present context, because at one point McDowell seems to suggest, in the spirit of Harman, that, properly applied, it is the explanatory test that delivers the result that secondary qualities, conceived of as dispositions to elicit certain experiences, are properties of objects that are there to be experienced. Here is what he says:

> A 'virtus dormitiva' objection would tell against the idea that one might mount a satisfying explanation of an object's looking red on its being such as to look red. The weight of the explanation would fall through the disposition to its structural ground. Still, however optimistic we are about the prospects for explaining colour experience on the basis of surface textures, it would be obviously wrong to suppose that someone who gave such an explanation could in consistency deny that the object was such as to look red. The right explanatory test is not whether something pulls its own weight in the favoured explanation (it may fail to do so without thereby being explained away), but whether the explainer can consistently deny its reality. (VASQ, pp. 117–18)

McDowell is right that if we have reason to think that colours are dispositions of objects—if that is our *concept* of colour—then the fact that we need mention only the ground of the disposition, not the disposition itself, in our explanations, does nothing to undermine the claim that the object really has the disposition.[10] This is why, when he imagines someone conducting the explanatory test, he says that they will not consistently be able to deny the reality of colours. But if we are to take seriously his suggestion that this is meant to be an interpretation of how properly to conduct an *explanatory test* for whether a property really is there to be experienced, then the remark seems altogether irrelevant. For the reality of colours seems then to have been determined prior to administering the explanatory test by whatever gave the tester the conviction that our concept of colour is the concept of such a disposition, a disposition that objects possess.

Another way of putting the same point is this. Someone who denies that colours are properties of objects need not deny that objects *have* these dispositions, all he has to deny is that colours *are* such dispositions (that our concept of colour is the concept of such a disposition). In the case of both values and secondary qualities, John Mackie denied precisely this.[11]

The upshot is that, even if we do conceive of colour as a property that is there to be experienced, this conjoined with the explanatory test will not clearly yield the result that colours really are there to be experienced. If we had reason to believe that we conceive of colours as there to be experienced because, contrary to Mackie, we conceive of them as dispositions, then that would certainly help yield the result that colours really are there to be experienced. But that in turn that just makes us wonder why anyone should think that we conceive of colour as such a disposition. It is time to go back to the first question. What does McDowell say in support of his claim that we conceive of colour as a property that is there to be experienced?

What we have just seen is that, in order to argue for the claim that colours are there to be experienced it will not be enough for McDowell to argue that we conceive of colours as being there to be experienced. He needs to argue for something else besides, perhaps for the claim that our concept of colour is the concept of a certain kind of disposition, perhaps for the claim that the explanatory test is not the only test for whether a property really is there to be experienced. What does he have to say as regards these matters?

As far as I can see, the only remark of relevance is the following, made in passing:

> Secondary-quality experience presents itself as perceptual awareness of proper-
> ties genuinely possessed by the objects that confront one. And there is no
> general obstacle to taking that appearance at face value. (VASQ, p. 112)

Talk of how secondary quality experience 'presents itself' is talk about the phenomenology of such experience. As I understand it, McDowell is therefore claiming that the phenomenology of secondary quality experience is *representational*. Now this certainly seems plausible. For if we were asked to make an unreflective judgement about our secondary quality experience, we would certainly describe it in apparently representational terms. That is, we would say that such experience is the *experience of coloured objects*. And this in turn certainly suggests that we conceive of colours as there to be experienced. For it is a necessary condition of such descriptions being apt that we have such a conception of colours. Thus, to the extent that facts about our use of language are useful 'surrogates' for talk about the phenomenology of our experience, McDowell seems to be right that the phenomenology of secondary quality experience supports the idea that we conceive of colour as a property that is there to be experienced (VASQ, p. 110 and fn. 2).[12]

I will have more to say about this 'phenomenological' argument presently. For the moment, however, I want to concentrate on a different point: the way the argument just given interacts with the ideas of giving a dispositional analysis of colour concepts and coming up with a different test for whether a property really is there to be experienced.

Remember we just saw that in order to argue for the conclusion that colours really are there to be experienced McDowell has to do more than simply argue for the claim that we conceive of colours as properties that are there to be experienced. For when we conjoin that claim with, say, the explanatory test, colours seem not to turn out to be properties that are there to be experienced. However the argument just given suggests a different test for whether colours really are there to be experienced.

Suppose we concede the phenomenological claim that colours seem to be there to be experienced. Then, in order to show that colours really are there to be experienced, we need simply to be able to draw the is/seems distinction for them and show that they satisfy the 'is': that is, show that objects do not *merely seem* to be coloured. Enter the dispositional analysis. For it is precisely the role of the 'in normal perceivers' and 'in certain conditions' clauses of the analysis to explain the various ways in which we might be mistaken about the colours an object has on the basis of our experience, and hence to allow us to draw the distinction between an object's really being coloured and merely seeming to be so. Indeed, it would seem to be this McDowell has in mind when he says that 'there is no general obstacle' to taking the 'appearance' of representation in secondary quality experience 'at face value' (VASQ, p. 112 and fn. 8). There is no general obstacle because the dispositional analysis provides us with the materials to take the appearance at face value: that is, make the is/seems distinction.

Unfortunately, however, there is an obstacle. For even if we grant McDowell that the phenomenology of colour experience gives us reason to think that our concept of colour is the concept of a property that is there to be experienced, and concede he is right that if we can make an is/seems distinction then we can take this appearance at face value, and concede he is right that if we could give a dispositional analysis of our colour concepts then that would give us a way of making an is/seems distinction, we must not let him simply assume that giving a dispositional analysis of our colour concepts would be an appropriate way of making an is/seems distinction for colours. After all, if we could give a dispositional analysis of our shape concepts then that would enable us to make the is/seems distinction for shapes. However, as McDowell himself emphasizes, it would be totally inappropriate to analyse our shape concepts dispositionally, for shape concepts 'can be adequately understood otherwise than in terms of dispositions to give rise to subjective states' (VASQ, p. 113). Thus we make the is/seems distinction for shapes in non-experiential terms, in terms of our geometrical concept of shape. McDowell therefore has to provide a further *argument* for the claim that it would be appropriate to give a dispositional analysis of our colour concepts.

McDowell seems to recognize this, for he does provide an argument of sorts for the dispositional analysis. However the argument he provides does not really help. For what he says is that the phenomenology of colour experience presents objects to us not merely as being coloured, but also as possessed of 'qualities that could not be adequately conceived except in terms of how their possessors would look' (VASQ, p. 113). Thus, according to McDowell, 'colours figure in perceptual experience ... as essentially phenomenal qualities of objects', *as* dispositions to look certain ways (VASQ, p. 113). However this is likely to convince no one. The phenomenology is being asked to do too much.

Recall McDowell's suggestion that we can read the fact that we conceive of colours as properties that are there to be experienced off from the phenomenology of our colour experience. As I have said, this claim has some plausibility, for we would certainly unreflectively describe our colour experience in representational terms as the experience of coloured objects. However the further claim that we can read the fact that we conceive of colours as dispositions to produce certain experiences off from the phenomenology of our colour experience is surely quite simply incredible. For we have no disposition whatsoever unreflectively to describe our colour experience in these terms at all. The idea of colour as a disposition is thus, in the very best sense of the word, a 'philosopher's' idea.

Of course, McDowell may agree with this. For he may think that colours figure in experience as being however the correct analysis of colour concepts says they are—adding, *sotto voce*, that according to the correct analysis colours are dispositions. But then all the work is being done by the additional claim, the claim for which we want to see an argument, an argument McDowell simply fails to provide.

Can we provide an argument on McDowell's behalf? We can certainly sketch an argument. Note that there are all sorts of platitudes about colour, platitudes like 'Things don't usually look the colour they are in the dark', 'If you want to see what colour something really is, take it into the daylight', 'If your eyes aren't working properly, you might not be able to tell what colour things are', and so on. Indeed, the phenomenological claim made earlier is another platitude about colour: 'Objects that we see seem all to be coloured'. And then there are platitudes about the nature of colours, and the relations between them, 'There's no such thing as transparent matt white', 'Red is more similar to orange than to blue', and the like. And there are also platitudes about the sense specific nature of colours, as when we say 'Blind people don't really know what colours are like', 'A normal person can tell an object is red just by looking at it, but not just by touching it or smelling it', and the like. These platitudes about colour play a certain crucial role in our coming to master colour vocabulary. For we master colour vocabulary precisely *by* coming to treat remarks like these *as* platitudinous. Of course, to say that they are platitudinous is not to say that we couldn't be argued into giving one or another of them up, perhaps by being made to see that one or another is in tension with other platitudes. But it is to say that we will give them up only with the greatest reluctance. For to give up on these platitudes wholesale would be to give up on talking about *colours* altogether.

If an account along these lines of what it is to have mastery of colour terms is right, then, it seems to me, a certain natural picture emerges of what would be involved in giving a dispositional analysis of our colour concepts. It would be to argue that the dispositional analysis *best encapsulates*, or is the *best systematization of*, our platitudes about colour.[13]

Arguing convincingly that this is so would, of course, be an enormous task. Doing so would require that we see implicit in the platitudes about colour just mentioned the idea that there is a privileged kind of perceiver, and a privileged set of conditions in which that person perceives, such that the colour experiences had by that perceiver in those conditions represent the colours of objects as they are. I do not myself think that this task is impossible, however I do not intend to attempt the task here.[14] For I am not so interested in whether a dispositional analysis of colour concepts is correct. What interests me is rather the plausibility of the strategy just outlined as a response to the original problem.

Remember, the problem was to argue for the following pair of claims: 'Our concept of value is the concept of a property of objects that is there to be experienced' and 'Objects really have such properties'. The detour via colour has served its purpose if it has shown us a coherent and non-question-begging way of arguing for these claims. For whether or not, in the case of colour, we can support the crucial premiss that our concept of colour is properly to be given a dispositional analysis, we may plausibly be able to argue for the corresponding premiss in the case of value. Let's therefore consider the argument by analogy for the claim that values are properties of objects that are there to be experienced.[15]

4. Are Values Objective in McDowell's Sense?

The argument is to proceed in two stages. In the first stage we are to argue that our concept of value is the concept of a property that is there to be experienced. The argument for this is to be phenomenological. We are to argue that evaluative experience presents itself to us as the experience of properties genuinely possessed by the objects that confront us. This phenomenological argument is to yield the conclusion that objects *seem* to have evaluative properties. In the second stage we are to argue for the is/seems distinction by showing that, according to the best systematization of our platitudes about value, values are dispositions to elicit certain attitudes in us under certain conditions: that is, our concept of value is the concept of such a disposition. Let's consider the two stages in turn.

Many think that this argument is doomed from the start. Thus, for instance, Chris Hookway has recently remarked that unlike the case with colours, it 'does not seem obvious' to him at all that 'we would all agree that we experience values as "there to be experienced"'.[16] And I am sure that he is right, at least in the sense that there are those who reject the claim—he cites Simon Blackburn. However I suspect that Hookway's pessimism is somewhat premature. In order to see why, let's remind ourselves what it means to think of a property as being there to be experienced.

To say that we conceive of a property as being there to be experienced is, you will recall, to say that that property may figure in the representational content of an experience (Section 3). Now we have seen that to say that the phenomenology of our experience supports this conclusion about a property is to make a rather minimal claim. It is to say merely that we would unreflectively describe our experiences as experiences of that property: that is, in apparently representational terms. The crucial question is therefore whether we would unreflectively use moral concepts in the 'predicate position' in describing our evaluative experiences. If we would then it seems that we do have reason to believe that we conceive of values as being there to be experienced.

Put like this, however, it is not at all clear that, despite what they may say about the 'phenomenology' of moral experience, philosophers do not all agree that we do experience values as being there to be experienced. For who denies that we would unreflectively describe the experience we have when, say, we witness a wilful murder in apparently representational terms: that is, as the experience of a wrong act? Even Blackburn agrees, for he himself admits that moral discourse has a 'realist-seeming *grammar*'.[17]

Now no doubt Blackburn would protest at this point. For he has urged that since the realist-seeming grammar of moral discourse can be explained without supposing that there are, nor even that we believe that there are, any values, so that grammar cannot properly be used in an argument for the existence of values.[18] But this is to put the cart before the horse. The most natural explanation of the realist-seeming grammar is surely here, as it is elsewhere, that the realist-seeming grammar reflects the way we take things to be—perhaps even, if we are lucky, the way things are. *If we can make this most natural explanation out*—that is, if we can make sense of the claim that there are values, perhaps even make sense of the claim in such a way as to make it come out true—then what reason do we have *not* to suppose that there are values?

Of course, there may be some principled reason why the preferred explanation of the realist-seeming grammar of an area of discourse cannot be made out in a particular case. Blackburn himself offers several arguments for just this conclusion in the case of values.[19] But such arguments presuppose, rather than undermine, the legitimacy of *preferring* the more natural explanation of the realist-seeming grammar, the explanation that takes the realist-seeming grammar at face value. Consequently, if the more natural explanation can be made out, as McDowell claims it can in the case of values, then we will have a vindication of the realist-seeming grammar that ought to be acceptable to Blackburn on his own terms.[20]

It seems, then, that the claim that we conceive of value as a property that is there to be experienced finds support from the realist-seeming grammar of the discourse we use in describing our evaluative experience. I want now to argue that we can find additional reasons for accepting this conclusion. For the fact that values may figure in the representational content of experience manifests itself more directly in the phenomenology of evaluative experience.

In order to see what I have in mind here, contrast the experiences we have when we are disposed, on the basis of experience, to judge that something is red, and the experiences we have when we are disposed, on the basis of experience, to judge that something is nauseating.[21] The contrast is illuminating because, as I understand it, though we clearly hold that being red is part of the representational content of our experiences of red objects, we are less comfortable, indeed, perhaps not disposed at all to hold that being nauseating is part of the representational content of our experiences of the nauseating (though, as we shall see, that we are not so disposed at all is not essential for the point that I am making). Moreover, and this is important, we take this to be so despite the fact that we unreflectively describe our experiences of the nauseating in apparently representational terms—that is, *as* experiences of the nauseating—and thus despite the realist-seeming grammar. We need to ask why there is this difference and whether moral experience is, in the relevant respect, more like the experience of red or the experience of the nauseating.

What is it like to experience something as red? It is commonplace that when we experience something as red the colour seems to be, as we say, 'out there, on the object'. This appearance shows up in the nature of our experience in the fact that our attention is drawn away from our own bodies, and indeed away from the intrinsic character of our experience itself altogether, and is focused instead on the object of our experience. The relevant point is best seen by contrasting the experience of the nauseating, for in experiences of the nauseating our attention is very much focused on an aspect of our own inner life. To the extent that we focus on the object at all, we fix on it merely as cause of what is inwardly experientially salient: that is, merely as cause of the easily identifiable combination of an uncomfortable feeling in the stomach, and a kind of giddiness located behind the eyes. When we experience something as nauseating our attention is thus very much focused on something that is 'in here, in my body'.

Why is there this difference in facts about where our attention is focused? Why do giddiness and feelings of nausea not play a role in experiences of the nauseating analogous to the role played by visual sensations in experiences of colours? Here is a suggestion.

Facts about the focus of our attention are not themselves primitive. They may be explained. For it is significant that we have rich resources in our practice of colour ascription for correcting our experiential evidence as to whether some object is red. Is there a red light shining on it? Would I get a better look at it if I took it out into the daylight? Are my eyes functioning properly? And so on. This should come as no surprise. They are, after all, just the platitudes about colour mentioned earlier that allow us to provide for the is/seems distinction. And the fact that we can make an is/seems distinction for colours is thus reflected in the *nature* of our colour experience. It reflects itself in the fact that we experience colours as properties whose existence is not merely constituted by our colour experiences. This, we might say, is what it is to have our attention focused 'out there' rather than 'in here' on features of our own experience.

Contrast the experience of the nauseating. It is significant that there is no rich set of resources in our practice of calling things 'nauseating' for correcting our experiential evidence as to whether something really is nauseating. And, because this is so, experiences of the nauseating present themselves as experiences of something whose existence is largely constituted by our feelings of nausea. We might say that this is what it is to have our attention focused 'in here' on features of our own experience rather than 'out there' on the object.

It should now be apparent why it does not matter for the purposes of this argument whether in the end we would say that the nauseating may figure in the representational content of an experience or not. For what we have said suggests that there will be a spectrum of cases between the clearly representational in this sense, the experience of colour, say, and the clearly non-representational in this sense, say, the experience of pain.[22] It is not important where the nauseating figures on this spectrum. What is important is rather that focusing in the difference between the red and the nauseating enables us to see that there is such a spectrum, and what it is about an experience that determines where it figures on the spectrum: the richness or paucity of the associated platitudes that allow us to adopt a critical perspective on our experience so making for an is/seems distinction.[23]

Consider now evaluative experience. If we do not conceive of values as being there to be experienced, if they cannot figure in the representational content of our experience, then we should surely expect this to reflect itself in the phenomenology of our evaluative experience. The question thus becomes whether evaluative experience is more like the experience of red or the experience of the nauseating.

Suppose we judge a wilful murder to be wrong on the basis of experience. Where is our attention focused? If evaluative experience were like experience of the nauseating, then we would expect our attention to be focused partially outward, partially inward, much as with the experience of the nauseating: outwardly on the features of the murder that make us, now inwardly, feel so disapproving (or whatever) towards it. But this is surely phenomenologically quite false. Our attention need not be focused at all on an aspect of our own inner life. Indeeed, there may be no *feelings* of disapproval to focus on. Rather, when we judge a wilful murder to be wrong, our attention may be wholly focused, as it were, 'out there' on features of the murder itself.

If the suggestion made above is correct then we should be able both to confirm and explain the fact that this is where our attention is focused by reference to the platitudes associated with mastery of moral terms. And, indeed, we can. For there exists in our evaluative practices a rich set of resources for correcting our unreflective judgements about the value of objects, and thus of discounting or redirecting our consequent attitudes of approval and disapproval. For example: 'In making moral judgements it is important to consider the matter from perspectives other than your own', 'If you disagree with someone in your moral judgements then at least one of you is making a mistake', 'Being taken in by an ideology is a sure-fire way of making mistaken value judgements', 'It's sometimes useful to check your value judgements with those you admire', 'Depression can make you blind to the value of things', and so we could go on.

Indeed, I doubt that Hume himself would have disagreed with this. In order to see why, consider once again the much quoted passage from which the 'wilful murder' example is taken:

> Take any action allowed to be vicious: wilful murder, for instance. Examine it in all lights, and see if you can find that matter of fact or real existence which you call vice. In whichever way you take it, you find only certain passions, motives, volitions and thoughts. There is no other matter of fact in the case ... the vice entirely escapes you, as long as you consider the object. You never can find it until you turn your reflexion into your own breast, and find a sentiment of disapprobation, which arises in you, towards this action. ... So that when you pronounce any action or character to be vicious, you mean nothing, but that from the constitution of your own nature you have a feeling or sentiment of blame from contemplation of it.[24]

For one remarkable, yet little mentioned, feature of this passage is that Hume is precisely trying to focus our attention away from where it is naturally focused when we judge a wilful murder to be wrong: that is, away from the murder itself, and on to an otherwise quite unnoticed 'calm passion' he supposes to arise in us. Hume did not fail to notice this aspect of the phenomenology of evaluative experience, the aspect that undermines a conception of moral experience as non-representational. He did notice it, and tried quite literally to explain it away. In this respect Hume seems to have been more aware of the phenomenological barrier to denying that we conceive of value as being there to be experienced than are his contemporary followers.

Let us recap. We have been concerned so far with the first stage of the argument for the existence of values, the claim that we experience values as being there to be experienced. We have seen that this claim finds support from the realist-seeming grammar of our unreflective descriptions of our evaluative experience and from the fact that the phenomenology of the experience of value seems more like the phenomenology of an experience with representational content than an experience without such content. It is time to consider the second stage of the argument.

In the second stage we are to argue that there really are values by providing for this is/seems distinction and by showing that values fall on the side of the 'is'. We are to do so by arguing that, according to the correct analysis of evaluative concepts, values are dispositions to elicit certain attitudes in us under suitable conditions. The task is once again the enormous one of showing that the dispositional analysis best encapsulates, or provides the best systemization of, our platitudes about value.

Now I do not want to underestimate the difficulty of this task. Rather I want to join with others in emphasizing two related problems we face in undertaking it, for two serious sources of disanalogy now present themselves.

First, whereas the platitudes governing colour terms suggest that the 'privileged' conditions in which a 'privileged' perceiver's colour experiences represent objects as being the colours that they are are conditions in which, at the very least, the perceiver has *causal contact* with a coloured *object*, the platitudes governing values suggest no such thing. For it seems entirely consistent with the platitudes governing colour terms that we could decide what is right and wrong without being in causal contact with any right or wrong *acts*; for we merely have to think about the non-moral features an action may have in order to decide whether an act with those features would be right or wrong.[25]

Now I do not think that this is devastating for McDowell's argument by analogy. Rather, what it does is undermine any serious sense in which we can talk of 'moral perception'—perception is, after all, a *causal* process—and thus any serious sense in which we can model moral knowledge on perceptual knowledge. This does not undermine the force of the argument by analogy, however, for to say of an act that it is wrong may still be to say of it that it has a certain non-moral feature, and that reflection upon that non-moral feature elicits a certain attitude in us under suitable conditions. Such an analysis allows that we may decide whether actions are right or wrong by merely reflecting upon their non-moral features. The argument by analogy may thus be disconnected from a perceptual model of moral knowledge.

There is, however, a second and potentially more worrying feature of disanalogy.[26] For whereas the platitudes governing colour ascriptions may seem to suggest a quasi-statistical conception of what a 'privileged' condition and a 'privileged' perceiver are, the platitudes governing values suggest no such thing. Indeed, there seems to be a problem in getting the requisite distance from our moral vocabulary itself in explaining what a 'suitable' condition is, or who 'we' are, in such a way as to make true the claim that an act with some non-moral feature is valuable just in case reflection upon that non-moral feature elicits a certain attitude in 'us' under 'suitable' conditions. Is there any answer that could plausibly hope to give the truth conditions of ascriptions of value except the answer that 'we' are those who accept the correct moral principles and that conditions are 'suitable' when we can apply these principles without error? If not, then the idea that we have given any kind of *analysis* of value is simply a sham. We have come full circle.

I do not want to attempt a solution to this problem just yet. Rather I want to digress for a moment. For it is important to notice that there is yet another sense in which we might think that values are objective, a sense quite different from the sense in which values would turn out to be objective even if this argument were to go through. I have in mind the idea that moral requirements are objective in the sense of being requirements of reason. There is good reason to believe that John Mackie supposed values to be objective in just this sense. Surprisingly, by focusing on the idea that values are objective in this sense we come across a traditional answer to the question of how to specify the 'suitable' conditions and 'us' clauses in the dispositional analysis.

5. Mackie on the Objectivity of Value

John Mackie certainly talked of values as being like primary qualities. However, it is significant that alongside such talk we find a different, perhaps incompatible, way of explicating the idea of the objectivity of value. Here are some examples:

> A categorical imperative ... would express a reason for acting which was unconditional in the sense of not being contingent upon any present desire of the agent. ... Kant himself held that moral judgements are categorical imperatives ... and it can plausibly be maintained at least that many moral judgements contain a categorically imperative element. So far as ethics is concerned, my thesis that there are no objective values is specifically the denial that any such categorical imperative element is objectively valid. The objective values which I am denying would be action-guiding absolutely, not contingently (in the way indicated) upon the agent's desires and inclinations. (E, p. 29)

> Another way of trying to clarify this issue is to refer to moral reasoning or moral arguments. ... Let us suppose that we could make explicit the reasoning that supports some evaluative conclusion, where this conclusion has some action-guiding form that is not contingent on desires or purposes or chosen ends. Then what I am saying is that somewhere in the input to this argument—*perhaps in one or more of the premisses, perhaps in some part of the form of the argument*—there will be something which cannot be objectively validated—*some premiss which is not capable of being simply true, or some form of argument which is not valid as a matter of general logic*, whose authority or cogency is not objective, but is constituted by our choosing or deciding to think in a certain way. (E, pp. 29–30—my emphasis)

For these passages suggest that when Mackie claimed that, according to common sense, values are objectively prescriptive he had in mind the sense of 'objectivity' that we associate with *rationalism*. But what exactly is that sense?

The characteristic rationalist thesis is that moral norms, if there are any, reduce to norms of practical reason. Thus, according to the rationalist, just as fully rational creatures either believe that q when they believe that p and that $p \to q$ or give up believing p or $p \to q$ (that is, conform their beliefs to *modus ponens* and *modus tollens*), and desire to Ψ when they desire to Φ and believe that they can Φ by Ψ-ing (that is, conform their desires to the principle of means–ends, Kant's hypothetical imperative), so, for example, if they are morally required to Ψ when someone is in pain and they can relieve his pain by Ψ-ing, fully rational creatures form the desire to Ψ when they believe that someone is in pain and they can relieve his pain by Ψ-ing (that is, conform their desires to the principle of limited altruism).[27] If morality requires some limited form of altruism then, according to the rationalist, the principle of limited altruism is a principle of reason on all fours with *modus ponens* and *modus tollens* and the principle of means–ends. According to the rationalist moral judgements are thus objective in this sense: they are expressive of reasons for action that are binding on rational creatures as such.[28]

Note how different this sense of the objectivity of value is from the idea that moral values are objective in the sense in which primary qualities are objective, the sense that contrasts with the sense in which secondary qualities are supposed to be subjective. For the rationalist says nothing to make us think that we can have a conception of what a moral value is other than as a disposition to elicit certain subjective states. This will be important in what follows (Section 6).

Moreover, note how different this sense of the objectivity of value is from the sense in which primary and secondary qualities are alike objective, 'objective' in the sense of being 'there to be experienced'. For the rationalist says nothing to make us think that value is there to be experienced. For all he tells us moral experience may not be representational. Indeed, moral judgements may not properly be thought of as ascriptions of properties to objects, they may rather have the semantic form of, say, imperatives: indeed, *categorical* imperatives.

Mackie thought that the objectivity of moral judgements in this sense, the rationalist's sense, was part of our *common-sense* conception of moral value. Is that plausible? I believe that it is, for, as I see it, rationalism is simply an attempt to articulate much that is platitudinous about moral practice.

Consider, for example, the phenomenology of moral choice. Think of what it is like to act on one desire, rather than another, in the context of some moral conflict. Does it seem that we are simply being, as it were, led around by the strongest desire? No. It seems that we choose to act on one desire rather than another for reasons; that we come to desire to act in one way rather than another because we think that acting in that way is more appropriate, the course of action supported by the best reasons. Acting in that way is not more appropriate, not supported by the best reasons, simply because that is what *we* happen to desire to do.[29]

The rationalist offers us a plausible way of making sense of this aspect of the phenomenology. He suggests that when we come to desire to act in one way rather than another we do sometimes do so for reasons. To take the schematic example just mentioned, he suggests that we may form the desire to Ψ because of our appreciation of the reasons: that is, because we believe that someone is in pain and we can relieve his pain by Ψ-ing. The transition from these beliefs to the desire to Ψ is, he suggests, a rational transition on a par with forming the belief that q on the basis of the beliefs that p and that $p \rightarrow q$.

The rational appropriateness of desiring to relieve pain is not a matter of our simply finding ourselves, contingently, desiring to relieve pain.

Rationalism enables us to make good sense of other platitudinous features of moral practice as well. For example, as we have already seen, it is a platitude that if *A* claims that Φ-ing is worthwhile, and *B* claims otherwise, then, when the value in question is moral value, at most one is right. Argument ensues: 'What are your reasons for believing that Φ-ing is worthwhile? Display them to me so that I too can see the value in Φ-ing.' If such reasons are not forthcoming then *A*'s assumption isn't just that he hasn't been given reason to believe that Φ-ing is worthwhile, he will assume that *B*'s belief is ungrounded; that in having such a belief he is mistaken or in some other way in error. Contrast the case where the disagreement in question does not concern something of moral value, but concerns a mere matter of taste: say, whether ice-cream is good to eat. In this case we are quite happy to resolve the apparent conflict by making it *merely* apparent, thereby preserving the cognitive integrity of each agent. Eating ice-cream may be good from the point of view of *A* but not from the point of view of *B*. Both may be right. However finding such hidden relativities and making both right seems never to be the appropriate way of resolving an apparent conflict when the value in question is moral value. As the point is sometimes put, moral disagreement is *disagreement*, not mere *difference*.[30]

Rationalism enables us to give substantive content to these platitudes about moral disagreement. For to say that when *A* claims that Φ-ing is worthwhile and *B* claims otherwise at most one is right is, according to the rationalist, merely to insist that at most one of *A*'s and *B*'s claims reduces to a norm of reason. And to say that at least one of *A* and *B* is making a mistake or is in some other way in error is merely to acknowledge that the beliefs of at least one of *A* and *B* are contrary to a norm of reason, merely to insist that at least one is being, in some way, irrational.

I am not saying that the rationalist's explanation of these platitudes is compulsory. But it is certainly a coherent explanation, one that seems to me to be very difficult to resist once we begin to take seriously the cognitive implications of moral choice and moral disagreement.

In summary, there is good reason to believe that when John Mackie said that values are objectively prescriptive he had it in mind that they are objective in the sense in which the rationalists claim moral judgements to be objective: 'objective' in the sense of being expressive of reasons for action that are binding on rational creatures as such.[31] Moreover, it is plausible to think, as Mackie did, that it is part of our common-sense conception of value that moral judgements are objective in just that sense. For rationalism enables us to make sense of much that is platitudinous about moral judgement and practice.

6. Mackie's Error Theory Again

Let us return to the substantive issue. What we have just seen is that we can give a phenomenological argument for the claim that values are objective in the sense of being expressive of reasons that are binding on rational creatures as such. And what we saw earlier is that we can give a different phenomenological argument for the claim that values are objective in McDowell's sense, the sense of being there to be experienced. That suggests that both claims to the objectivity of values can be found in ordinary moral thought: that is, both claims find support in our platitudes about value.

Now recall the role of our platitudes about value in coming up with an analysis of our evaluative concepts. The question that immediately arises is whether a single analysis could capture both kinds of platitude; that is, whether ordinary moral thought is, in this respect, coherent. I want to suggest that it may well be. Indeed, I want to suggest that the idea of the objectivity of moral judgement in the rationalist's sense gives us a way of completing the dispositional analysis, and thus filling out the idea of the objectivity of value in McDowell's sense.

Remember, according to the dispositional analysis an act with a certain non-moral feature is valuable just in case reflection upon that non-moral feature would elicit a certain attitude in 'us' under 'suitable' conditions (Section 4). And recall that we faced a problem in completing the account, for we have yet to give some sort of plausible and non-circular gloss on who 'we' are, or what makes conditions 'suitable'. But now the rationalist appears to have offered us an answer. For remember that his is a *reductive* theory. In his view, the 'us' in whom attitudes are supposed to be elicited is thus simply all rational creatures—no circularity there—and the 'suitable' conditions in which to take the attitudes elicited in us to be indicative of value are simply those conditions in which our evaluative reasoning, and hence our desires, are controlled by the particular norms of practical rationality to which moral norms reduce, the categorical requirements of reason—no circularity there either. So, if the rationalist is right, then we can have it that our conception of value is *both* the concept of a property that is there to be experienced, *and*, given that the idea is that rational creatures will not differ in the attitudes that are elicited in them in the appropriate conditions, our concept of value is also the concept of a property which, when ascribed to an act, say, is expressive of reasons for action that are binding on rational creatures as such. It thus seems that we can give a single dispositional analysis of our concept of value that has some claim to capturing the platitudes about value that support the objectivity of value in both McDowell's and Mackie's senses.

Once we see that this is so, however, we are bound to ask the final, crucial question. If this is our conception of value, are there any values so conceived? Is our moral experience veridical?

As is perhaps already evident, this turns, in part, on whether the rationalist is right that there are norms of practical reason to which we can reduce the norms of morality. If there are such norms, it follows that there are non-moral features of acts that elicit certain attitudes in us when our thinking is in accordance with such norms, and so there are values. But if, as John Mackie thought, the rationalist is wrong, then we may well have to face up to the fact that none of our evaluative concepts are instantiated. And that, of course, is just identical with the conclusion that John Mackie reached in the first place.

Of course, since the arguments for and against rationalism are conducted on a priori grounds, so it follows that the error, if error there be in our ordinary moral thought, is not empirically discoverable. To that extent John Mackie was wrong. But it should not be thought that, for that reason, the error would amount to some sort of surface incoherence, the kind of incoherence McDowell thought there would have to be if we were to take seriously Mackie's idea that values are objectively prescriptive. For the very fact that the debate between the rationalists and the anti-rationalists has remained moot for so long indicates that any problem that may exist with the idea of norms of practical reason to which we can reduce moral norms lies rather deep beneath the surface of ordinary thought about such matters. The error may well be discoverable a priori, but it may be unobvious for all that.

If the argument in this final section has been on the right track then it seems to me that, for all that John McDowell tells us, John Mackie may well have been right to convict ordinary moral thought and experience of a pervasive error. Indeed, in reaching this conclusion, my suspicion is that John Mackie displayed a greater sensitivity to the phenomenology of moral experience than many of us may have thought he did. For he appreciated, as so many of us now don't, the extent to which ordinary moral talk presupposes a conception of value as built upon a secure rational foundation. If we want to resist the Error Theory then it seems to me that we have no choice but to tackle head on the widespread assumption that no plausible account can be given of how morality could be erected on that basis.[32,33]

Notes

1. John Mackie, *Ethics: Inventing Right and Wrong.*

2. John McDowell, 'Values and Secondary Qualities', in T. Honderich (ed.), *Morality and Objectivity.*

3. In VASQ McDowell tells us that Mackie's response to the position McDowell adopts 'used to be, in effect, that it simply conceded his point' (p. 121). He goes on to ask whether Mackie is right to claim that the position he outlines 'is at best a notational variant ... of [Mackie's] own position?' In essence my aim is to defend Mackie's contention that, for all McDowell says, it may well be.

4. Let me enter a caveat here. I am prepared to go along with McDowell's talk of our concept of redness being the concept of a disposition of an object to look red. However, insofar as I do, I want it to be understood as not prejudging whether our concept of a disposition of an object to look red is itself the concept of a property of an object that causes it to look red. Leaving this question open allows us to entertain the possibility that secondary qualities are identical with their categorical bases. On this matter see Gareth Evans, 'Things Without the Mind', in Zak van Straaten (ed.), *Philosophical Subjects: Essays presented to P. F. Strawson*, esp. p. 95; Martin Davies and Lloyd Hymberstone, 'Two Notions of Necessity', in *Philosophical Studies* (1980); Colin McGinn, *The Subjective View*, p. 14, fn. 13.

5. Compare Evans, 'Things Without the Mind', part III; McGinn, *The Subjective View*, ch. 7.

6. Note McDowell's assumption that it is sufficient, in order to capture the prescriptivity of value, that we define our evaluative concepts in terms of a relation to the will. Unfortunately matters are more complex. Not just any old definition of value in terms of the will will do, at least not if the 'prescriptivity' of value requires a necessary connection of some sort between judging a course of action to be right and being motivated accordingly. See, e.g., David Lewis' explanation of why his own definition of value in terms of a relation to the will fails to provide for that sort of connection in his 'Dispositional Theories of Value', *Proceedings of the Aristotelian Society*, Supplementary Volume 1989, pp. 114–16. However, in my 'Dispositional Theories of Value', *Proceedings of the Aristotelian Society*, Supplementary Volume LXII, I argue that that sort of connection can be captured by a definition of value in terms of a relation to the will provided we make certain further assumptions.

7. Gilbert Harman, *The Nature of Morality*, ch. 1.

8. John Mackie, *Problems from Locke*, pp. 17–18.

9. Harman's own response to this problem seems to get him into more trouble. For when he comes to justify his belief that colours are properties of objects that are there to be reduced, as he realizes he must, he does so by insisting that colours really pass the explanatory test after all. Here is what he says:

> we will still sometimes refer to the actual colours of objects in explaining colour perception, if only for the sake of simplicity. ... It may be that the reference to the actual colour of the object in an explanation ... can be replaced with talk about the physical characteristics of the surface. But that would greatly complicate what is a simple and easily understood explanation. That is why, even after we come to be able to give explanations without referring to the actual colours of objects, we will still assume that objects have actual colours and that therefore facts about the actual colours of objects are somehow reducible to facts about physical characteristics of surfaces and so forth, even though we will (probably) not be able to specify the reduction in any but the vaguest way. (TNOM, p. 22)

Thus, says Harman, we will believe that colours are there to be reduced because we will still invoke colours in giving ordinary explanations; that is, because colours still pass the explanatory test. But I thought the problem was supposed to be that colours seem to fail the explanatory test!

10. Indeed, it seems to me that we should then quite rightly insist that the 'virtus dormitiva' objection is misplaced; that colours do causally explain our experiences. For relevant considerations see Frank Jackson and Philip Pettit's comments on what they call 'programme explanations', as against 'process explanations', in their 'Functionalism and Broad Content', *Mind* 97.

11. For Mackie's discussion of the dispositional theory of value see *Hume's Moral Theory*, pp. 73–4.

12. Indeed it seems to me that McDowell's point here closely resembles Crispin Wright's idea, in his contribution to this volume, that it is the syntactic potentialities of the sentences that we use in an area of discourse that gives support to the idea that the sentences in that area of discourse are truth-assessable.

13. The account of what it is to give an analysis proposed here is supposed to be reminiscent of David Lewis on the analysis of mental state concepts: see his 'How to Define Theoretical Terms' and 'An Argument for the Identity Theory' in his *Philosophical Papers*, Vol. I; 'Psychophysical and Theoretical Identifications', in *Australasian Journal of Philosophy* (1973). It should be evident from this account of what it is to give an analysis why the phenomenology of colour experience, what it is like to have

such experience, gives the experiencer no special insight into the proper analysis of colour concepts. For someone who has colour experience need not even have contemplated, let alone gone through, the laborious process of trying to give system to our platitudes about 'colour.

14. John Campbell and Mark Johnston argue against such an analysis in their contributions to this volume. See my reply to Campbell in 'Colour, Transparency, Mind-Independence', this volume.

15. It is, I hope, clear from what has been said why I do not think that someone impressed by the idea of an argument by analogy for realism about values has any need to deny many of the substantial disanalogies between values and secondary qualities. For some suggested disanalogies see Simon Blackburn, 'Errors and the Phenomenology of Value', in T. Honderich (ed.), *Morality and Objectivity*, pp. 13–15. For a response to some of these see section II of Crispin Wright's, 'Moral Values, Projection and Secondary Qualities', in *Proceedings of the Aristotelian Society*, Supplementary Volume LXII. However, as we will see in the next section, certain disanalogies are more worrying than others.

16. Christopher Hookway, 'Two Conceptions of Moral Realism', in *Proceedings of the Aristotelian Society*, Supplementary Volume (1986), p. 190.

17. Blackburn, 'Errors and the Phenomenology of Value', p. 5. Compare once again Crispin Wright's idea, in his contribution to this volume, that Blackburn should himself agree that the syntactic potentialities of the sentences that we use in moral discourse give support to the idea that such discourse is truth-assessable.

18. Blackburn, 'Errors and the Phenomenology of Value', p. 5.

19. Simon Blackburn, *Spreading the Word*, pp. 182–8.

20. McDowell's theory seems tailor-made to answer those who argue that it is impossible to take the realist-seeming grammar of moral discourse at face value. For certainly the most popular argument given for this conclusion is that the realist-seeming grammar is inconsistent with the prescriptivity of value. I discuss this argument further in my 'Dispositional Theories of Value'.

21. Simon Blackburn first led me to think about the significance of contrasts like this. More recently Steve Stich and Mark Johnston have stressed their importance. Blackburn's example was the funny, Stich's was the yummy. The example of the nauseating used in the text comes from Johnston, and the substance of what follows owes much to discussions with him. (I am not sure whether he agrees with my conclusions.)

22. It might be objected that contrary to what I say here the experience of pain is representational, for it represents part of the subject's body as being a certain way. This is why I have said that the experience of pain is not representational 'in the relevant sense'. For, in these terms, an experience is representational in the relevant sense only if the way it represents something as being is not wholly constituted by our experience of its being that way—such is not the case with the experience of pain.

23. I suspect that the existence of such a spectrum helps explain why secondary qualities are not all on a par. Why, for instance, is there a difference in our modal judgements about the *colours* objects would possess if our perceptual apparatus were to change as against the *tastes* objects would have if our perceptual apparatus were to change? Why do tastes seem more 'mind-dependent' than colours? My suggestion is that colours and tastes differ in this respect because of the differences in the associated corrective platitudes.

24. David Hume, in L. A. Selby-Bigge (ed.), *Treatise of Human Nature*, pp. 468–9.

25. Compare Simon Blackburn's objection to the idea that values are analogous to

secondary qualities in his 'How to be an Ethical Antirealist', in P. French, T. Uehling, Jr., and H. Wettstein (eds.), *Midwest Studies in Philosophy* (1987), p. 365. McDowell is not unaware of the point: see VASQ, pp. 118–20.

26. Here I follow a line of argument presented most forcefully in Wright, 'Moral Values, Projection and Secondary Qualities'.

27. I am here simply assuming that rationalists will endorse such a principle of limited altruism. The precise content of the principle is, of course, not important for present purposes. What is important is rather its form and status. For a discussion of these matters see my 'Reason and Desire', *Proceedings of the Aristotelian Society* (1987–8).

28. As Tom Nagel puts it, moral requirements are 'inescapable'. See his *The Possibility of Altruism*, ch. 1.

29. I discuss this matter further in 'Dispositional Theories of Value'.

30. See McGinn, *The Subjective View*, p. 152.

31. Tom Nagel discusses this aspect of Mackie's concern in his *The View From Nowhere*, p. 144.

32. In this connection it is worthwhile considering Mackie's own reason for rejecting rationalism. That reason, you will recall, is that the norms of reason to which the rationalist seeks to reduce moral norms—the principle of limited altruism, for instance—are not 'valid as a matter of general logic' (E, p. 30). As he puts it later: 'Disagreement on questions in history or biology or cosmology does not show that there are no objective issues in these fields for investigators to disagree about. But such scientific disagreement results from speculative inferences or explanatory hypotheses based on inadequate evidence, and it is hardly plausible to interpret moral disagreement in the same way. Disagreement about moral code seems to reflect different people's adherence to and participation in different ways of life' (E, p. 36). This objection should not impress us however. For note that we could similarly object to any principle of *inductive* logic that underwrites the validity of some scientific inference that it does not satisfy the standards of *deductive* logic. For a good discussion of this point see Paul Edwards, 'Russell's Doubts about Induction', J. O. Urmson, 'Some Questions Concerning Validity', and Wesley Salmon, 'Rejoinder to Barker and Kyburg', all in R. Swinburne (ed.), *The Justification of Induction*. I discuss the prospects for rationalism in *The Moral Problem*.

33. I would like to thank Simon Blackburn, John Campbell, Jonathan Dancy, Robert Gay, Mark Johnston, Mark Kalderon, David Lewis, Steve Stich, Jay Wallace, and Crispin Wright for many helpful comments.

10

A Simple View of Colour

John Campbell

I

Physics tells us what is objectively there. It has no place for the colours of things. So colours are not objectively there. Hence, if there is such a thing at all, colour is mind-dependent. This argument forms the background to disputes over whether common sense makes a mistake about colours. It is assumed that the view of colour as mind-independent has been refuted by science. The issue, then, is whether the view of colour as mind-independent is somehow implicit in the phenomenology of colour vision. I want to look at the background argument which controls this dispute.

We can see this argument at work in the dispute between Mackie, who presses the charge of error in the phenomenology, and McDowell, who resists the charge. They take the issue to be the characterization of colour experience. For Mackie's Locke, 'colours as we see them are totally different ... from the powers to produce such sensations'.[1] Further, if we take the appearances at face value, we will not take colours to be microphysical properties of things: they do not appear as microphysical properties. Still, if we take the appearances at face value, we will take it that we are seeing the properties of objects in virtue of which they have the potential to produce experiences of colour. The perception reveals the whole character of the property to us. Since it is not just a power to produce experiences in us, there is a sense in which this property is mind-independent; and according to Mackie, the mistake of common sense is to suppose that there are any such non-physical mind-independent properties. McDowell, on the other hand, insists that vision presents colours as dispositions to produce experiences of colour. After all, he asks, '[w]hat would one expect it to be like to experience something's being such as to look red'—that is, as having the dispositional property—'if not to experience the thing in question (in the right circumstances) as looking, precisely, red?'[2] For Mackie and McDowell, the legitimacy of our ordinary talk about colours turns on this issue about phenomenology. They agree that we do have colour experiences, and that objects have the powers to produce these experiences in virtue of their microphysical structures. They agree there is no more going on than that.

The only issue between them is whether this is enough to vindicate the phenomenology. The question is whether it seems that there is more to colour than dispositions to produce experiences of colour, whether it seems that colour is mind-independent.

I shall take the view of colours as mind-dependent to find clearest expression in the thesis that they are powers of objects to produce experiences in us. I shall not be concerned with more rarefied theses of mind-dependence, which might be applied to properties quite generally.

The view of colours as mind-independent must acknowledge some role for colours in colour-perception. I shall equate this view with the thesis that they are to be thought of as the grounds of the dispositions of objects to produce experiences of colour. This is not a kind of physicalism about colours. To suppose that it must be is to assume an identification of the physical and the objective which the thesis may question. It may instead be that the characters of the colours are simply transparent to us. Of course, we often have to consider cases in which the character of a property is not transparent to us; but there may also be cases in which transparency holds.

The background argument with which we began needs elaboration. It does not as it stands provide a convincing argument for the assumption that colours are mind-dependent. A simpler view of colours thus remains in play. On this view, redness, for example, is not a disposition to produce experiences in us. It is, rather, the ground of such a disposition. But that is not because redness is a microphysical property—the real nature of the property is, rather, transparent to us. This view of colours would be available even to someone who rejected the atomic theory of matter: someone who held that matter is continuous and that there are no microphysical properties. The view of colours as mind-independent does not depend upon the atomic theory. Nevertheless, without there being a commitment to any thesis of property identity, someone who holds this simple view may acknowledge that colours are supervenient upon physical properties, if only in the minimal sense that two possible worlds which share all their physical characteristics cannot be differently coloured. It is usually supposed that if common sense accepts this position, it is mistaken: to defend common sense is to clear it of the charge of accepting the view. But we shall see that we do not have any reason to abandon this Simple View.

II

The central line of objection to the Simple View depends upon a particular conception of what is required for a property to be mind-independent. This attack depends on supposing that a mind-independent property must be one that figures in an 'absolute', or 'objective' description of the world. The defining feature of such a description of reality is that understanding it does not require one to exploit anything idiosyncratic about one's own position in the world.

Colours, conceived as the Simple View conceives them, cannot figure in any such description. The Simple View acknowledges that to understand ascriptions of colour, one must have, or have had, experiences of colour. There is no other way of grasping what a particular colour-property *is*. The character of the property is, though, transparent to this way of grasping it.

This is a forceful line of argument for the mind-dependence of colours. But it proves too much. If it were correct, it could be extended to show more than that colours are mind-dependent. We could also use it to show that *particularity*—a physical thing's being the *particular* thing that it is—is mind-dependent. It is much easier to see what is going wrong when we apply the above line of thought to the case of physical things. So I shall spend most of this section on this case, returning at the end of it to draw the comparison with colour.

The possibility of massive duplication shows that the subject can never fade out of the picture in singular reference. There is no 'absolute' or 'objective' conception which refers to particulars. The point needs some glossing, though. The possibility of massive duplication makes it vivid that we use spatio-temporal locations to differentiate things—that is what makes the difference between identifying particulars, and identifying types. But we can identify spatio-temporal locations only by appeal to their relations to things. How then does the apparatus of singular reference get off the ground? The possibility of massive duplication rules out its being by purely qualitative singling-out. One answer is that one uses one's own location, as what ultimately anchors one's singular reference to *this* sector of the world rather than to a duplicate. Yet this cannot be right. One cannot locate all other objects by reference to oneself, for one's own location is itself identified by appeal to the objects one perceives. One is not oneself somehow a uniquely firmly anchored spatial thing. In fact, the conclusion is correct, that the subject can never fade entirely out of the picture in singular reference, but not because one has always to identify things by appeal to one's own location. The point is rather that the demonstratives we need to get reference to physical things off the ground invariably *introduce* the subject: his identifications of objects always provide a frame of reference by which the subject can triangulate his own location, or else they depend upon a range of identifications of objects by references to which the subject can triangulate his own location.

One might conclude from this that particularity is mind-dependent. One might conclude that what makes a physical thing the *particular* thing that it is, is, ultimately, its relation to a mind. If we want to resist this conclusion, we have to explain how particularity can be mind-independent even though there is no 'absolute' or 'objective' way of identifying particulars.

The mind-independence of particularity is what explains a modal datum. Intuitively, it would seem that I can make sense of the idea that all the things around me might have existed, and might continue to exist, even if I simply had not been around to think about any of them. But in thinking this thought, I am, of course, using the fact that I am demonstratively linked to those things: for the thought I have is a thought about *those very* objects. This also, however, provides rooms for the thought of my own location with respect to them: so what makes it possible for me to abstract away from that? At this point one might appeal to the existence of other thinkers than oneself, who can identify those very objects whether or not I am around. But we surely want to underwrite the possibility that many of the particular things around us might have existed even if there had been no sentient beings. It is here that it can seem so appealing to invoke ways of identifying those particulars from *no* point of view. Yet there is no such way of identifying a particular thing.

We have to abandon the notion of an 'absolute' or 'objective' description of reality, which identifies particular things. We need another tack. We have to appreciate how fundamental in our thinking is our grasp of a simple theory of perception. This theory provides us with the idea that our perceptions are caused by a pair of factors: by the way things are in the environment, and by one's meeting the enabling conditions of perception—being in the right place at the right time, suitably receptive, and so on. The problem about the mind-independence of particularity is the result of operating as if we had a range of thoughts relating to what is there anyway, which we can as it happens employ in a simple theory of perception. Operating in this way, we naturally have some difficulty in explaining how it is that we find it intelligible that things are thus and so anyway. The correct response is to acknowledge that *what makes it the case* that our thoughts concern what is there anyway, is that they are embedded in a simple theory of perception. This embedment is internal to those thoughts: it is what constitutes them as being the thoughts they are.

Simple predicates of physical things are themselves explained in terms internal to this theory. The *stability* of predications of enduring objects, and the framework of expectations into which they fit, make sense only in the context of this simple theory.

This simple theory, being so fundamental, has an autonomous role to play in controlling our grasp of modal truth. It is this simple theory that makes it intelligible to us that our perceptions concern a world of objects which are there independently of us. The independence of the particulars is grasped once the subject understands that perception of them requires not just their existence, but the meeting of these further, enabling conditions of perception. The existence and character of the particulars is quite independent of whether these further conditions are met.

Of course the theory is *corrigible*, and it is always open to us to make new discoveries about the essential character of the world. The fact remains that our grasp of modal truth, including our conception of what sorts of things there are, is controlled by our developing grasp of this theory.

This point about spatial thinking marks a contrast between it and thought of abstract objects. For abstract objects in general, it is plausible that there is a canonical level of singular thought which controls our grasp of modal truth. Thus for numbers we have the numerals: modal truths about numbers are ultimately responsible to what is transparently conceptually possible at the level of thought expressible using numerals. The reason why it is not essential to any number that it be the number of the planets is that it is transparently conceptually possible that 9, for example, should not be the number of planets. The reason why 9 is essentially greater than 7 is that it is transparently conceptually necessary that 9 is greater than 7. As Quine once put it, making sense of modality here means 'adopting a frankly inequalitarian attitude towards the various ways of specifying the number'.³ In the spatial case, however, there is no level of singular thought which can play this role. The position of a number in the number series individuates it, and is essential to it, if anything is, and that is precisely what the numerals capture. In contrast, what individuates a physical thing is its location at a time: and that is the very paradigm of a contingent property. How is it that individuation and essence can come apart like this? The reason for the asymmetry is the role which is played by a simple theory of perception in the spatial case, in controlling our grasp of modal truth. This simple theory has no parallel in the case of abstract objects.

What holds for spatial things here, holds for their properties. The mind-independence of a property of physical things is just a different issue to whether it can figure in an 'absolute' or 'objective' conception of reality: it has to do rather with the embedment of the property in a simple theory of perception.

We can put the point by asking how we are to explain the modal datum for colours, that objects might have been coloured exactly as they are even had there been no sentient life. The proponent of the dispositional analysis takes it that in explaining this datum we have to appeal to an 'absolute' or 'objective' conception of the world, which can only be a physical characterization of it. And there is also an appeal to the global supervenience of colour on the physical, so that the datum is explained as amounting to the fact that the world might have had just the physical structure it actually does even had there been no sentient life: and that structure is one which has the power to produce particular colour-experiences in us, as we actually are. On this approach, the modal datum would simply not be intelligible to someone who rejected the atomic theory, taking matter to be continuous. But there is an alternative way of explaining the modal datum. The alternative is to point out that the experience of a colour is characteristically the joint upshot of the operation of a pair of factors: the object's having that colour, on the one hand, and on the other, the satisfaction of a whole range of enabling conditions of perception: for example, that the lighting is standard, the percipient is appropriately situated and oriented, and so on. All the modal datum comes to is that this pair of factors is genuinely distinct. Whether the object has the colour is one thing, and whether anybody is in a position to see it—indeed, whether anybody is there at all—is another. Grasping this point does not require an acquaintance with the atomic theory of matter. At this point, though, it may be said that colours, conceived as the Simple View conceives them, can play no role in the causation of perception.

III

One line of argument against the Simple View is that on it, colours become epiphenomena. We can put the point in terms of the intuitive notion of an 'explanatory space'. The suggestion is that common sense and science are jostling for the same 'explanatory space'. They are attempting to give causal explanations of the same phenomenon: perception of colour. One explanation we might give of colour perception is in terms of wavelengths and physiology. But on this view, to suppose both explanations are correct would be to suppose that the colour-experience is causally overdetermined. The only reasonable alternative is to take the colours to be epiphenomena.

The dispositional analysis is an attempt to resist this conclusion while hanging on to the idea that the two ways of explaining colour perception can be driven, in an easily understood way, into a single 'explanatory space'. On the dispositional theory, the relation between the two accounts is analogous to that between an explanation of the dissolution of salt in terms of its solubility, and an account of the underlying chemistry of salt and water. These two accounts do not compete; rather, the explanation of dissolution by solubility merely holds open the place for the scientific account. So too, on the dispositional analysis, the explanation of colour perception in terms of colour does not compete with the scientific account, but more modestly, just holds open the place for it.

The obvious response to this whole line of thought is to question whether talk of colours and talk of wavelengths really do occupy the same 'explanatory space'. We have, on the one hand, the causal explanation of colour perception by colour, and on the other, the explanation of visual processes by wavelength. The obvious model for the relation between the two accounts is the relation between the following two types of causal explanation: the explanation of one psychological state by appeal to others—the explanation of a desire by appeal to a further belief and desire, for instance—and the explanation of one neural state by appeal to others. There is surely some connection between these two types of explanation, but it is not easy to characterize, and it is not evident that we should think of them as occupying a single 'explanatory space'.

Another line of attack on the role of colour in causal explanation comes from Locke. In some moods, he held that causal explanation must be mechanistic. The transmission of motion by impulse is inherently intelligible, and all other phenomena are rendered intelligible by being shown to be merely complex cases of the operation of impulse. An attempt at causal explanation which did not reduce the phenomena to contact phenomena would, on this view, have failed to render them intelligible. So it would not explain. If we think of colours on the simple view, as the grounds of dispositions to produce experiences of them, we must acknowledge that they have no role to play in this type of explanation. They have no role in mechanistic science. This criticism, though, is not devastating. There is a wide range of causal explanations which are not themselves given at the level of basic physics—in zoology, in economics, in meteorology, and by common sense, for instance. And we have abandoned the view that basic physics must be mechanistic.

The obvious model is, again, causation in the mental. Many philosophers would want to view psychological explanations as causal, while acknowledging that they are not given at the level of basic physics. There is, of course, a problem about how psychological explanation is related to description of the world in terms of physical law. The very same problem arises for the simple view of colour properties as non-dispositional causes of our perceptions. The problem is how causation at this level is related to descriptions of the phenomena in terms of basic physics. But the problem here is no worse than in the case of causation in the mental, and it can surely receive a parallel solution.

Just to illustrate, a simple, familiar solution in the case of the mental would be to hold that mental events are physical events, and that the nomological character of causation shows up at the level of description of these events as physical. Just so, one might hold that a thing's being red is a physical event, an experience of redness is a physical event, and that the nomological character of the causation between them shows up at the level of physical description.

It is sometimes charged that this view allows for a systematic relation between explanations at the level of the supervening properties—psychological properties of colours—and genuinely causal explanations, but that it does not show how explanations at the level of the supervening properties can themselves be causal explanations. Another way to put the point is to ask how there can be more than one 'explanatory space', if all causation is physical causation.

This is a problem for all causal explanations given by the special sciences and common sense. We are certainly not in the habit of proceeding as if the only causal explanations are those given in terms of basic physics. Nor does it seem that any causal explanation not given in terms of basic physics must be one which appeals to properties which are dispositions, or properties which are functionally defined. Suppose, for example, that a round peg fails to enter a round hole. We explain this by saying the peg and board are made of a rigid material, and that the diameter of the peg is greater than that of the hole. This is not explanation in terms of basic physics, but it is causal explanation. And there is no reason to suppose that the roundness and size of the peg are anything other than categorical properties of it. Equally, when we explain an experience of redness by appeal to the redness of the object seen, this may be causal explanation though it is not at the level of basic physics, and even if the redness is not a disposition or a functionally defined property of the object.

There are many models which might be given for the relation between the two 'explanatory spaces'. Here is one. A thing's possession of a higher-level property can be related to a range of physical properties like this: in each nearby possible world in which the thing has the higher-level property, it also has some one or another of that range of physical properties. Suppose now that we causally explain someone's having an experience of redness, by appeal to the redness of the object seen. In each nearby world in which the object seen is still red, it has one or another of a range of microphysical properties. In each such nearby world, the particular structure the object has in that world initiates a causal sequence ending, so far as we are concerned, in a physical event which is also an experience of redness. So the explanation in terms of redness adds modal data to a description of the physical sequence. It says that in nearby worlds in which the physical character of the thing was varied but its redness maintained, an experience of redness was still the upshot. This is, of course, only a sketch. But there seems to be no difficulty of principle about providing such a picture of the relation between the 'explanatory spaces'.[4]

IV

One source of resistance to the Simple View is suspicion of the idea that colours can have any substantive role in causal explanation, suspicion grounded on their lack of what we might call 'wide cosmological role'. The argument is that even if the causal relevance of colours stretches somewhat beyond the explanation of perception, it certainly is not possible to state laws concerning colour which have the sweeping generality of laws concerning mass. As it stands, this line of argument is quite unconvincing. The special sciences make copious reference to properties which do not have a wide cosmological role, but they are none the less engaged in causal explanation.

We might in particular remark that we appeal to the colours of things not just in explaining particular perceptions of them, but also in explaining the evolution of the mechanisms of colour vision. The reason why our visual system was selected for just was, in part, its utility in identifying the colours of things. That is the point of the system. Of course, it is rarely helpful to know the colour of a thing simply for its own sake: an interest in colour is typically serving some further end of the organism. But it is precisely the identification of *colour* that has this instrumental value. There is, then, a rich role for the appeal to colours, conceived as the Simple View conceives them, in explaining the development of the mechanisms of colour vision.

It might be noted further that, even in explaining the perceptions of a single individual, there is a certain richness in the structure of our appeal to colours. It is not just that we explain an individual perception of redness by the redness of the thing perceived. We also explain the relations between our experiences by the relations between the colours of the things seen. For example, the similarity between two experiences of redness may be causally explained by the similarity in colour of the objects seen. The similarity and difference between an experience of light red and an experience of dark red are explained by the similarity and difference of the colours seen: by the fact that the objects seen have the same hue combined with varying quantities of white and black. And so on.

There is, though, a further question lying behind this suspicion about the Simple View. The challenge is the more extreme one, not merely that colours simply lack wide cosmological role, but that the attempt to use colours in framing causal hypotheses yields only pseudo-hypotheses.

We can begin by putting the point as a sceptical problem. On the dispositional analysis, there is no question but that objects have the colours we ordinarily take them to have. Looking red in ordinary circumstances just is being red, so there is no room for doubt about whether something that ordinarily seems to be red is red. It might be charged against the Simple View, though, that precisely because it rejects the identification of redness with the power to produce experiences of redness, it has to regard the sceptical question as posing a real problem. The problem is exacerbated by the fact that colours lack 'wide cosmological role'. We can bring this out by contrasting the case of shapes. Suppose someone asks whether objects really have the shapes we ordinarily take them to have, on the strength of their appearances. For example, suppose he asks whether bicycle wheels, though they look circular, might not in fact be triangular. The question can be dealt with by attempting to ride the bicycle: for ordinary motion, only circular wheels will do. Triangular wheels would give a very different effect. In contrast, consider the case in which someone asks whether this bicycle, though it looks white, really is white. Here there is no such auxiliary test we can use. Colour has no effect on the motion of the bicycle. The dispositionalist may hold that rejecting the dispositional analysis gives one a quite unreal sceptical problem, which one is forced to take seriously: do things have the colours they ordinarily seem to?

The proponent of the Simple View cannot evade the problem by saying that he takes whiteness to be whatever is the ground of the disposition to produce experiences of whiteness. That would indeed finesse the sceptical question—but it would also yield a view on which ordinary colour vision leaves us in the dark as to *which* property whiteness is. On this view, colours are hypothesized causes of our perceptions, rather than properties with which ordinary observation directly acquaints us.

As I have explained the Simple View, though, it holds that the characters of ordinary colour properties are transparent to us, and that ordinary colour vision is enough for us to know *which* property blueness is, for example. The charge is that on the Simple View, the ordinary percipient is left in the position of knowing which property blueness is, without having any guarantee that that property is the usual cause of his, or anyone's, perceptions of blueness.

The sceptical problem might be pursued by constructing an alternative explanation of ordinary colour perceptions, and asking whether the Simple View has the resources to rule it out. For example, it might be proposed that we live in an environment in which blueness is the ordinary cause of our perceptions of redness, greenness the ordinary cause of our perceptions of yellowness, and so on. To complete the construction of the alternative explanation, we should have to include stipulations about how the relations between the colours affect the relations between experiences of them. For instance, it might be said that one object's being bluer than another is the usual reason why an experience of it is an experience as of a redder object than is the experience of the second thing. And so forth. The dispositional analysis can rule out the proposal as absurd. We have yet to see whether the Simple View can do so.

The line of objection certainly ought to be pressed by someone who holds an error theory about ordinary colour vision. Someone like that takes the Simple View to be implicit in the phenomenology, but insists that the Simple View is entirely mistaken: nothing like colour figures in the causal explanation of perception, only the microphysical properties of things. If it is not only intelligible, but true, that our ordinary explanations of colour experience are altogether wrong, then it is legitimate to invite the proponent of the Simple View to consider various alternatives to his own preferred line of explanation, including deviant coloration.

At this stage, though, the objection to the Simple View need no longer be put in terms of scepticism. The problem can be reformulated as an attempt to construct what is sometimes called a 'switching objection' to the causal hypotheses offered by the Simple View, with the intention of showing them to be pseudo-hypotheses.[5]

It may help to make the strategy clearer if I first give an example of a 'switching objection' from a quite different area, and then show how a problem of that form is here facing the Simple View. The example I have in mind is the objection raised by Strawson's Kant to Cartesian dualism. The Cartesian assumes that one is immediately acquainted with one's own enduring soul. The objection is that whatever constitutes this 'immediate acquaintance', it is equally consistent with a whole series of hypotheses, for example: (i) that there is a sequence of momentary souls, each of which transmits its psychological states to the next in the sequence, as motion might be transmitted along a series of elastic balls, and (ii) that at any one time, one's body is connected up to a thousand qualitatively indistinguishable souls, all of which speak simultaneously through the same mouth.[6] This is not at all a sceptical problem. The strategy is rather to discredit the Cartesian by showing that the conceptual materials he introduces enable us to generate a variety of incompatible hypotheses, all of which must be acknowledged, by his own standards, to be equally legitimate.

The suspicion is that a parallel strategy can be used to discredit the causal hypotheses offered by the Simple View. Given the conceptual materials it introduces, the argument runs, it is possible to introduce a whole variety of causal hypotheses, all of which must be acknowledged, by the standards of the Simple View, to be equally legitimate. And, this line of thought concludes, that shows that these causal hypotheses are merely pseudo-hypotheses. We have already seen the kinds of alternative hypotheses that might be introduced, in which perceptions are said to be caused by quite unexpected colours, and the relations among the perceptions explained by quite unexpected relations among the colours of the objects seen.

This whole line of objection rests on the supposition that perceptions have their contents, as experience of this or that property, quite independently of which properties of things in the environment they are responses to. That assumption is questionable.

Again, the analogy with particulars is instructive. Recall the thesis that what makes a thing the particular thing that it is, is its relation to a mind. Consider how a proponent of this view might go about constructing a 'switching' objection to the assumption that particularity is mind-independent. The argument would be that, on that assumption, the course of one's experiences is consistent with a wide range of hypotheses as to *which* things are causing one's perceptions. The point could be stated as being, in the first instance, a sceptical problem: how can I be sure the very things I take to be causing my perceptions are causing them, rather than it being some range of qualitatively indistinguishable duplicates? There is obviously a variety of individual rival hypotheses that could be stated here. The 'switching' objection then is that by the standards of the view of particularity as mind-independent, all of these hypotheses have to be viewed as on a par with each other, and with the ordinary supposition that the things which seem to be causing my experiences are causing them. The only way out, the objection runs, is to suppose that particulars are individuated precisely by their relations to minds: that what *makes* a thing the *particular* thing it is, is the way it is related to the minds which apprehend it, so that there is no possibility of those minds being wrong about which particular thing it is.

This line of argument is not persuasive, and it seems evident that what has gone wrong is the supposition that one's experiences of things have their contents, as experiences of those *particular* things, independently of the question of which things they are responses to. That is what makes it possible for the question to arise, whether the experiences really are brought about by the things they are experiences of. But this is a mistake: the experience's being an experience of *that* thing is made so by its being brought about by that thing. So even though particularity is mind-independent, there is no possibility of the experiences being in general brought about by things other than the things they are experiences of. The answer to the 'switching' point is not that particularity is mind-dependent, but that experience is particular-dependent.

A parallel response can be made to the use of a 'switching' argument to show that colour is mind-dependent: namely, that what constitutes experiences being experiences of the particular colours they are is their being responses to just those features of the environment. Of course, it is not that illusion is impossible. It is rather than an experience's being an experience of a particular depends upon the subject's being able to use his colour vision to track that particular colour. So there is no possibility of setting up alternative causal hypotheses to explain colour vision: they simply bring with them changes in the characterization of the experiences to be explained.

V

Colour predicates seem to be in some sense 'observational'. I want to end by sketching a way of bringing this out. The point I want to make is that in the case of 'observational' predicates, there seems to be an epistemic dimension in the way the phrase 'looks φ' operates. In some cases, part of the effect of saying that a thing looks, for instance, round to someone is to say that if that person took the appearances at face value, without engaging in any reasoning, he would think that the thing is round. The phrase is connected to what one would judge without reflection. This certainly seems to hold for a whole range of 'looks φ' predications, such as 'looks old', 'looks expensive', 'looks efficient', and so on. But in the case of 'observational' predicates, there seems to be an epistemic aspect to the phrase 'looks φ'. It is possible for something to look old to a person who is in fact very bad at judging how old things are—someone whose unreflective judgements of age never constitute knowledge. In contrast, consider the phrase 'looks round'. Someone to whom a thing looks round must be someone who has the ability to tell whether things are round, unreflectively, on the strength of perception alone. It is not that such a person must be immune to illusion. Rather, the point is that without the capacity to tell, on occasion, unreflectively, that a perceived object is round, there is no basis for supporting that things ever look round to the subject. A parallel point seems to hold for colour predicates. Someone to whom things sometimes look green is someone who has a capacity to track greenness.

This line of thought can be pressed further, to resolve a dilemma over the characterization of colour experience. On the one hand, one may feel reluctantly compelled to acknowledge the possibility of inverted spectra—systematic differences between the qualitative characters of different people's colour experiences which do not show up in verbal or other behaviour. On the other hand, recoiling from this possibility, one may, in effect, deny the qualia and insist that if two percipients agree extensionally when they discriminate and group objects by colour, then their experiences just are the same, and there is no further question about qualitative similarity or difference. The Simple View allows a different approach. On it, we can say that the qualitative character of a colour-experience is inherited from the qualitative character of the colour. It depends upon which colour-tracking capacity is being exercised in having the experience. So if you and I are tracking the same colours, our colour-experiences are qualitatively identical. This view does not allow for the hypothesis of spectrum inversion; nor does it deny the qualitative character of colour vision.[7]

Notes

1. J. L. Mackie, *Problems from Locke*, p. 14.

2. J. McDowell, 'Values and Secondary Qualities', in T. Honderich (ed.), *Morality and Objectivity*, p. 112.

3. W. V. Quine, 'Reply to Professor Marcus', in *The Ways of Paradox*, p. 184.

4. This adapts the account of 'programme explanation' given in F. Jackson and P. Pettit, 'Functionalism and Broad Content', *Mind* 97, pp. 381–400, and 'Structural Explanation in Social Theory', in D. Charles and K. Lennon (eds.), *Reduction, Explanation and Realism*.

5. For a helpful taxonomy of such arguments, see C. Peacocke, 'The Limits of Intelligibility', *Philosophical Review* 97.

6. P. F. Strawson, *The Bounds of Sense*, p. 168.

7. I am indebted to Bill Brewer, Justin Broackes, Quassim Cassam, David Charles, Bill Child, Adrian Cussins, Philippa Foot, Elizabeth Fricker, Michael Smith, and Timothy Williamson. My focus on these issues was changed by Barry Stroud's John Locke lectures in 1987.

11

Colour, Transparency, Mind-Independence

Michael Smith

John Campbell proposes a simple view of colour.[1] He claims that colours are: (i) 'mind-independent' properties of objects (p. 258), (ii) 'the grounds of the dispositions of objects to produce experiences of colour' (p. 258), and (iii) properties whose 'real nature is . . . transparent to us' in colour experience (p. 258). I want to focus on three issues raised by Campbell's proposal.

1. The Simple View of Colour

Campbell admits that (iii) would be inconsistent with (i) if we were to embrace the ordinary idea that a mind-independent feature of reality is one that would be mentioned in an 'absolute' or 'objective' description of the world, a description we could understand after abstracting away entirely from our own points of view. But his response is to deny that mind-independence requires any such thing. What, then, does Campbell say mind-independence does require?

In fact he makes two suggestions. First, he tells us:

> The view of colours as mind-independent must acknowledge some role for colours in colour-perception. I shall equate this view with the thesis that they are to be thought of as the grounds of the dispositions of objects to produce experiences of colour. (p. 258)

On this construal, (i) entails (ii). An argument for (i) would therefore have to be, *inter alia*, an argument for (ii).

Elsewhere, however, he makes a rather different suggestion:

> We have to abandon the notion of an 'absolute' or 'objective' description of reality. . . . We need another tack. We have to appreciate how fundamental in our thinking is our grasp of a simple theory of perception. This theory provides us with the idea that our perceptions are caused by a pair of factors: by the way things are in the environment, and by one's meeting the enabling conditions of perception—being in the right place at the right time, suitably receptive, and so on. (p. 260)

> The mind-independence of a property of physical things is just a different issue to whether it can figure in an 'absolute' or 'objective' conception of reality: it has to do rather with the embedment of the property in a simple theory of perception. (p. 261)

But what does the 'embedment' of colour 'in a simple theory of perception' amount to? Does it amount to the same as the claim that colour is the ground of the disposition of objects to look coloured?

Campbell's stated view is that it amounts to no more, and no less, than the claim that the perception of a coloured object requires two distinct elements: a coloured object, on the one hand, and a perceiver who meets the enabling conditions of perception, on the other, in a causal relation (p. 261). According to this second suggestion, then, the mind-independence of colour is clinched once we acknowledge that colour is a property of objects that plays a causal role in perception. And now the problem should be clear. For if colour can play a causal role in the perception of coloured objects without being the ground of the disposition of objects to look coloured, then Campbell's second suggestion is weaker than his first. The question will then be whether Campbell can consistently maintain, not now both (i) and (iii), but both (ii) and (iii). Does this problem really loom?

In claiming that colours are the ground of the disposition of objects to look coloured Campbell casts himself as someone who rejects the view that colours are identical with such dispositions themselves. In order to see that Campbell's second suggestion is indeed weaker than his first, it thus suffices that we see why someone who accepts such a dispositional conception of colour may yet accept the claim that colours play a causal role in perception. (This is not yet to admit that we know exactly what it means to say that colours are the 'grounds' of such dispositions. We will raise this question again presently.)

In fact the reason is stated by Campbell himself. According to the dispositionalist, colour is a higher-order property of objects, related in a certain systematic way to the lower-order properties that figure in the 'grounding' explanation of colour experience (pp. 262–3). The dispositionalist can therefore agree with Campbell that what makes an explanation in terms of, say redness, a genuine causal explanation of an experience of redness is the fact that it 'adds modal data to a description of the physical sequence':

> It says that in nearby worlds in which the physical character of the thing was varied but its redness maintained, an experience of redness was still the upshot. (p. 263)

But if the dispositionalist can, in this way, agree that colours play a causal role in perception while denying that colours are identical with the properties that ground the disposition of objects to look coloured, then he can agree with Campbell that colour is mind-independent in his second sense, and yet deny that it is mind-independent in his first. (Note that this account of the 'explanatoriness' of the explanation of colour experience in terms of colour suggests one way in which we might explain what it is for a property to be the ground of the disposition of objects to look coloured: 'a property is the ground of that disposition just in case it figures in the appropriate lowest level explanation of colour experience: i.e. the explanation in terms of fundamental physics'.)

We are now in a position to draw together the threads of the discussion thus far. Let's agree that Campbell has successfully argued that colours may play a causal role in the perception of coloured objects even though they are not properties that would be mentioned in an explanation of colour experience at the level of fundamental physics. As such, he has successfully maintained (i), interpreted in accordance with his second suggestion. But if he is to argue for the simple view of colour, he needs to do more. He needs to provide a further argument for (ii), the claim that colours are the ground of the disposition of objects to look coloured. And in doing so he needs to give an account of what he means by the claim that colours 'ground' that disposition, an account consistent with (iii), the claim that the nature of colour is transparent to us in colour experience. (He certainly cannot have in mind the idea just mentioned, that colours figure in the lowest level explanation of colour experience, for that is straightforwardly inconsistent with (iii).) But does Campbell give such an account?

Campbell does not explicitly give an account of what it is for a property to ground such a disposition. However he does offer some hints:

> Suppose ... that a round peg fails to enter a round hole. We explain this by saying the peg and board are made of a rigid material, and that the diameter of the peg is greater than that of the hole. This is not explanation in terms of basic physics, but it is causal explanation. And there is no reason to suppose that the roundness and size of the peg are anything other than categorical properties of it. (p. 263)

Let us first make sure that we understand the hint and then see how it might be exploited.

Campbell is certainly right that being round and a certain size may figure in a causal explanation despite the fact that the roundness and size of the peg and board are not features that figure in explanations at the level of fundamental physics. In order to see that he is right it suffices to note that we can account for the 'explanatoriness' of this causal explanation in the same way that we accounted for the 'explanatoriness' of the causal explanation of colour experience in terms of colours: that is in nearby worlds in which the materials remain rigid and the peg and hole remain constant in shape and size, there is some distribution of atomic particles constituting peg and board that prevents the matter that constitutes the peg from occupying the region of space that constitutes the hole.

Moreover, Campbell is certainly right that we ordinarily classify shape and size as 'categorical' properties of objects, by which I take it he means that we reject out of hand the idea that being a certain shape or size is merely a matter of appearing a certain shape or size to us.[2] We reject that idea out of hand because there exists a particular canonical method for determining the shape and size of an object: namely, by (correctly) measuring its various sides and angles. This guarantees the independence of facts about shape and size from facts about the appearance objects present to us. There is, of course, no denying that objects do appear to be certain shapes and sizes to us. But that must be understood as, in Crispin Wright's phrase, 'merely a deep fact of experience':

> For bluntly, it is not *a priori* true ... that our (best) judgements of ... shape, made on the basis of predominantly visual observations, usually 'pan out' when appraised in accordance with more refined techniques, where such are appropriate. ... It is not *a priori* that the world in which we actually live allows reliable perceptual appraisal of ... shape—is not, for example, a world in which the paths travelled by photons are subject to grossly distorting influences.[3]

Objects of various shapes and sizes are, then, *de facto*, disposed to appear those shapes and sizes to us under certain conditions. But their being so shaped and sized is what *grounds* the disposition to appear those ways to us. Being so shaped and sized is what *explains* the appearances, and explains the appearances at a *lower* level than the mere having of those dispositions themselves explains the appearances.

Here, then, we have a model for an account of what it is for colours to 'ground' the disposition of objects to look coloured. The idea is to be that colour, just like shape and size, is an ordinary 'categorical' property of an object. That is, though colour is a *higher*-order property than the properties mentioned in the explanation of colour experience at the level of fundamental physics, colour is a *lower*-order property than the disposition of objects to look coloured. Just as with shape and size experience, the explanation of colour experience in terms of the disposition of objects to look coloured supervenes on an explanation of colour experience in terms of a categorical colour property.

This is all well and good, as far as it goes. The problem is, however, that Campbell offers us no reason to think that colour *is* a categorical property of objects, as opposed to, say, a dispositional property. (Remember, all he has argued so far is that colours may figure in causal explanations. But that doesn't tell us whether colours are categorical or dispositional.) And indeed, once we have a closer look at the model, we might wonder whether such reasons could be given at all.

Remember, what vindicates our ordinary classification of shape and size as categorical properties is the fact that we can canonically determine the shape and size of an object by (correctly) measuring its various sides and angles. It is this that guarantees the independence of facts about shape and size from facts about shape and size appearances. But what is the analogue of this kind of canonical method in the case of colour? More to the point, what is the analogue if the 'real nature' of colour is supposed to be 'transparent' to us in colour experience: that is, if ordinary perception is supposed to be enough to know *which* properties are referred to by our colour terms;[4] if ordinary perception is supposed, in this way, to reveal everything there is to know about the *nature* of colour? There simply is no analogue. Facts about colour thus seem not to be independent of facts about colour appearances in the way required to make the model work.

And this gives rise to a related problem. For if the categoricity of shape and size is really to provide a model for the categoricity of colour, then it had better be readily intelligible to us how the distribution of properties at the level of fundamental physics *could* constitute such a coloured object, much as it is readily intelligible to us how such a distribution constitutes an object of a certain shape and size. But it is our independent grip on what it is for objects to be a certain shape and size—the fact that we have available a canonical method for determining shape and size, of the kind described—that helps to make the latter constitution claim readily intelligible to us. For we can form a picture of ourselves determining the shape and size of an object by the canonical method, by (correctly) measuring its sides and angles, and we can then, as it were, imagine decomposing that very object, so sized and shaped, into its constituent parts. But if the 'real nature' of colour is supposed to be 'transparent' to us in experience then, when our project is to understand how a certain distribution of properties at the level of fundamental physics could *constitute* such a coloured object, this sort of intelligibility simply eludes us. We cannot even *begin* to understand the constitution claim.[5]

It might be thought that Campbell's discussion of the 'switching' objection suggests a reply to this line of objection (pp. 266–7). There he concedes that facts about colour are not independent of facts about colour experience. But, he argues, that is not because facts about colour are *constituted* by facts about colour experience. Rather it is because what makes an experience an experience of the particular colour of which it is an experience is the fact that *that* colour is the normal cause of such experiences. And this, he claims, is straightforwardly consistent with the simple view of colour as a categorical property. For the particular categorical colour properties that are the normal causes of our colour experiences *determine* which colours our experiences are experiences of.

However this reply seems to me not to engage with the objection at all. The objection is that we have no understanding of what it would be for colour to be a categorical property of objects in the spirit of the simple view. For that would require that we have some independent grip on what it is for an object to be coloured, an independent grip that simply isn't to be had if we are also to imagine, as the simple view demands, that the 'real nature' of colour is 'transparent' to us in colour experience. Campbell's response to the 'switching' objection *presupposes* that we understand what it is for colour to be a categorical property, it doesn't *provide* us with such an understanding.

In the end, then, it seems to me that the simple view of colour is dubiously coherent. Certainly Campbell's own hints as to how we might reconcile the claim that the nature of colour is transparent to us in experience with the claim that colour is the ground of the disposition of objects to look coloured leave the matter wide open.

2. The Transparency Thesis

So far I have been uncritical of the claim that the 'real nature' of colour is 'transparent' to us in colour experience. But surely this claim requires some attention for, at least as we should ordinarily understand it, the claim seems simply false.

Now no doubt there are properties whose real nature seems to be transparent to us in experience. Pain is the obvious example. According to many, at least, a painful experience is both necessary and sufficient for knowledge of which property pain is. However, in the case of pain, such transparency comes as part of a package deal.[6] Not only does a painful experience give us knowledge of which property pain is, we also know that something felt as pain *is* a pain and that something not felt as pain *is not* a pain. Transparency explains these consequences. For once we know which property pain is we know that there is nothing for a pain to do but to manifest itself in experience. There is nothing for an unexperienced pain to be. And nor is there any room for a state that masquerades as pain.

Can the same be said of colours? Is an object that appears to be a certain colour that colour? Is an object that does not appear to be a certain colour not that colour? No. Neither of these consequences follows. There is, after all, the genuine possibility of colour illusion and unperceived colour. But if this is right then it seems that there is something about colour that *is not* manifest to us in colour experience: namely, what it is about colour that makes colour illusion and unperceived colour possible. This is not manifest to us in colour experience because colour experience merely gives us the 'experience' side of the equation, and what we want is an account of why the 'experience' side of the equation may yet be an unreliable indicator of an object's colour. (Note the disanalogy with pain.)

Someone who wants to maintain the transparency thesis in the case of colour thus faces a challenge. He needs to explain why colours and pains are disanalogous, in the respects just mentioned, despite the fact that the transparency thesis holds for both. If the transparency thesis holds for both then why can pains not exist unperceived when colours can? I see no way of answering this challenge. It thus seems to me that we should reject the transparency thesis for colours.[7]

As I understand it, it is thoughts like these that lead the dispositionalist to embrace the dispositional theory and reject the transparency thesis. The dispositionalist agrees that colour experience is required in order to know what colour is. And he agrees that colour experience is the canonical way of determining what colours objects are. (So far colours and pains are on a par.) But he thinks that claims like these exhaust what can plausibly be maintained by someone who says that the real nature of colour is transparent to us in colour experience. And he thinks this because he sees no other way of explaining the possibility of colour illusion and unperceived colour. Thus he offers us the dispositional theory and rejects the transparency thesis. The mere having of colour experience is not enough to know what property colour is—that is that colour is a certain sort of disposition—for that is a distinctively *philosophical* claim made for *philosophical* reasons.[8]

3. Mind-Independence

Campbell hopes his discussion will have the salutory effect of forcing us to rewrite the distinction between mind-independence and mind-dependence. He wants us to abandon the ordinary idea that a mind-independent feature of reality is one that would be mentioned in a description of reality that we could understand after abstracting away entirely from our own points of view. He wants us to think, instead, that a mind-independent feature of an object is a feature that is causally independent of our minds, a feature that can cause us to have certain perceptual experiences. I want to close with some remarks about this aspiration.

Campbell's reason for rejecting the ordinary idea is that it entails that *particularity*—an object's being the particular thing that it is—is a mind-*dependent* feature of reality. And this, he claims, is simply wrong (p. 259). An object's being the particular thing that it is is a mind-independent feature of reality if anything is. Thus he is led to rewrite the distinction.

Let me say up front that I find Campbell's discussion of our concept of particularity both fascinating and illuminating. However there is something very odd about the conclusion he would have us draw from it. It's a bit like this: troubled by the fact that, by ordinary standards, I am indeed a philistine, I recommend that we redefine 'philistine' to mean 'person who eats dirt'. If we adopt the recommendation, then it turns out that I am not a philistine. But how, exactly, does that recommendation, even if we adopt it, engage with what troubles me? Surely the underlying problem is that I satisfy the ordinary standards for being a philistine, where 'philistine' has its normal meaning. Redefining the *word* 'philistine' will not help me solve *that* problem. Similarly, it seems to me, Campbell's proposed redefinition of the terms 'mind-independence' and 'mind-dependence' will not help solve the puzzle with our concept of particularity that he has quite rightly brought to our attention. That requires a different kind of response.

Of course, Campbell might have in mind a different point. He might think that the ordinary way of making the distinction between mind-dependence and mind-independence is *uninteresting*. But again, that just seems to me to be wrong. What is interesting about the ordinary distinction is that it tells us something about the *availability* of a concept. It tells us that the concept of colour is *unavailable* to someone who is incapable of visual experience. And it tells us that the concepts of being round, and a certain size, for example, are. That *is* an interesting conclusion. Now, if Campbell is right, it follows that the concept of particularity is *unavailable* to someone who is not situated in the context of other objects with which he causally interacts. If Campbell is right about this, then surely that is an interesting conclusion to have reached about our concept of particularity.

At this point we should make it explicit that the ordinary distinction between mind-dependence and mind-independence invites us to think of this distinction as a matter of *degree*. Perhaps certain concepts can be understood after a little abstraction away from our own points of view, but not after a great deal of abstraction. Others may remain intelligible even after a good deal of abstraction. A proper understanding of the distinction would thus require us to be more precise about the *dimensions* along which we are measuring the degree of abstraction-away-from-our-own-points-of-view. But this is, of course, no objection to the distinction—or, at any rate, it isn't yet. Rather it is a plea for us to ensure that we know what we are talking about when we use the distinction. (If no account of the dimensions could be given then that would, of course, be a fatal objection to the distinction. But that doesn't seem to be Campbell's concern.)

The upshot is, I think, this. We can afford to be ecumenical with the ideas of mind-dependence and mind-independence. We can have different distinctions for different purposes. Campbell's distinction enables us to sort concepts into two groups: those that apply to perceptible properties of objects and the rest. The ordinary distinction enables us to sort concepts along a spectrum: at one end we find those that can be understood even after we have wholly abstracted away from our own points of view and at the other we find those that can only be understood from our own points of view.[9] These distinctions can happily co-exist. They enable us to make different distinctions, distinctions appropriate for solving different problems.[10]

Notes

1. John Campbell, 'A Simple View of Colour', this volume. Unless otherwise stated, all page references are to this paper.

2. Campbell may have in mind the stronger claim that no functional characterization of shape and size would be appropriate. However I see no argument for that claim in his essay (by which I do not mean to imply that I believe the claim to be false). The whole issue of 'categorical' versus 'dispositional' properties seems to me drastically in need of sorting out. For a useful discussion of the issue, see Gareth Evans, 'Things Without the Mind' and Peter Strawson, 'Reply to Evans', both in Zak van Straaten (ed.), *Philosophical Subjects: Essays presented to P. F. Strawson*.

3. Crispin Wright, 'Moral Values, Projection and Secondary Qualities', in *Proceedings of the Aristotelian Society*, Supplementary Volume LXII, p. 20.

4. I take this interpretation of the transparency claim from Campbell's discussion of the 'switching' objection (p. 266). Note that his discussion of that objection (pp. 266–7) reveals that, as he understands it, the transparency claim tells us merely that *which* property colour it is manifest to us in colour experience, it does not tell us that *whether* objects have certain colours is manifest to us in colour experience. I consider the plausibility of this distinction in Section 2.

5. See also n. 7 below.

6. Here I consider the plausibility of the distinction described in n. 4.

7. As perhaps the discussion makes clear, since I am attracted to the idea that the nature of pain is transparent to us in pain experience, I find it hard to see how a certain distribution of properties at the level of fundamental physics could *constitute* a pain (or, for that matter, a painful experience). I therefore find unhelpful Campbell's various

appeals to an analogy with positions on the mind–body problem (p. 262). For the positions he appeals to assume the coherence of such constitution claims.

8. See my earlier contribution to this volume, pp. 241–2.

9. Importantly, the existence of the spectrum does not commit us to the view that there are concepts occupying each of the end points. Thus Philip Pettit has recently argued that the moral of the rule-following considerations is that *none* of our concepts can be understood if we abstract away from our points of view *entirely* ('The Reality of Rule-Following', *Mind* (1990)). We have at least to retain the inclination to 'go on in the same way' given a suitable crop of initial instances, the inclination that is so crucial to our being able to learn a language at all. As he points out: 'This means . . . that . . . all the properties with which we engage fit a condition which many think of as a mark of secondary properties only' (p. 18). That is, they are all, to *some* degree, mind-dependent.

10. I would like to thank John A. Burgess, John Campbell, Adrian Cussins, Lloyd Humberstone, Robert Pargetter, and Crispin Wright for useful discussions and suggestions.

12

What the Non-Cognitivist Helps Us to See the Naturalist Must Help Us to Explain

Peter Railton

Suppose that one were not inclined toward non-cognitivism about discourse in general. What characteristic features of moral discourse might make one think non-cognitivism peculiarly appropriate to *it*?

Various features present themselves as candidates, and we will briefly consider two, the seeming oddness of 'moral facts' and the persistence of moral disagreement, before coming to a third, the normative character of moral judgement, which will occupy most of our attention.

It is quite unclear what 'the normative character of moral judgement' consists in, and so our discussion of normativity will begin by considering two familiar conceptions of the normativity of moral evaluation: a Kantian conception based upon the idea of categorical reasons and a non-cognitivist, attitudinal account.[1] These two conceptions will be compared, and my argumentative strategy will run as follows. First we will discuss how a non-cognitivist might argue, against the Kantian, that one can accommodate the normative character of moral judgement without appealing to categorical reasons. Then we will examine a counter-argument meant to show that a purely attitudinal account cannot satisfactorily replace the Kantian conception, for if the *grounds* of the attitudes are left out of account, the distinctive normative force of moral evaluation will be lost. But this criticism will then be seen to be a costly one for the Kantian to make, since it may apply to his own account as well. The upshot will be that both non-cognitivism and Kantianism need supplementation by an appeal to the grounds of moral judgement. We will then consider whether the supplementation itself might not form the basis for a naturalistic cognitivist's approach to normativity.

The aim of this dialectic will not be to attempt to establish the superiority of naturalistic cognitivism over either the Kantian or the non-cognitivist alternative, but rather to explore some of the issues that arise for each competitor and some of the resources that each might have available to contend with these issues. Still, if at the end of our discussion the naturalistic cognitivist does not emerge at some very great disadvantage with regard to accommodating normativity, this will hardly be a neutral result, since philosophers have often held that non-cognitivism enjoys a real, perhaps decisive, advantage over naturalistic cognitivism precisely in the area of accommodating normativity. In any event, my remarks will be very preliminary. In this area of philosophy as elsewhere it is impossible to make reasonable assessments of the plausibility of claims unless they are considered as parts of large and well-articulated views, held up for comparison with other large and well-articulated views. And that is the farthest thing from what I will attempt here.

1. Moral Facts

Anyone who would be cognitivist about ethics, but not a sceptic, must explain how we are able to gain epistemic and semantic access to the purported realm of moral facts. Those who have defended non-cognitivism have often emphasized how daunting problems of access can be for some familiar objectivist approaches to ethics. Moreover, by dispensing with a realm of moral facts for the interpretation of moral discourse, non-cognitivism has avoided these metaphysical and epistemological worries.

Of course, it remains for the non-cognitivist to reconstruct in his own terms the objective or cognitive character of moral discourse, and no entirely satisfactory reconstruction of this kind has yet been given. But this difficulty might be thought more than offset by the gain non-cognitivism achieves in explaining away the problematic idea of moral facts. Surely, for example, the decline of non-subjectivist value-based ethical non-naturalism in this century has had much to do with the difficulty of making sense of *sui generis* value properties, or of the means by which we obtain purported knowledge of, or reference to, objective value.

However, cognitivists who are ethical naturalists need not experience this embarrassment. If, for example, moral facts are identified with—or otherwise reducible to—natural facts, then there is no special mystery about what sort of things they are, or how we come to have knowledge of them, refer to them, and so on.[2] But then the choice of non-cognitivism over such a naturalism could not rest upon the mysteriousness of moral facts.

Similarly, the choice of non-cognitivism over such a naturalism could not rest upon any alleged ontological excesses of cognitivism. If moral facts are identical with—or otherwise reducible to—natural facts, then cognitivism may be possible without worrisome ontological expansion.

Such a naturalism could have the advantage not only of permitting an explanation of epistemic and semantic access to moral facts, but also of affording a straightforward explanation of the cognitivity of moral discourse.

2. Moral Disagreement

Well, perhaps it would afford a straightforward explanation—but such an explanation might be difficult to defend in light of actual moral practice. For another feature of moral discourse that non-cognitivism has helped make especially visible is the intractability of many moral disputes. This intractability seems hard to reconcile with the idea that, say, 'morally right' picks out some definite natural property. For then could we not simply apply the methods of empirical science to the resolution of our moral disagreements? Yet moral dispute strikes us as quite unlike disputes in the empirical sciences.

The non-cognitivist, for his part, has a ready answer. Genuine moral disagreement involves at bottom disagreement in attitude, and therefore is not resoluble by empirical investigation. Individuals who happen to share a number of attitudes may find that they can remove certain disagreements among themselves through empirical investigation. But where attitudes fundamentally differ, disagreement can persist even in the face of full empirical investigation—beyond a certain point, the effect of scientific investigation upon disputants can at best be a matter of causal influence rather than rational resolution.

Yet we must proceed carefully if we are to see just how the phenomenon of moral disagreement might bear upon a naturalistic cognitivism. To begin with, we must not beg the question by assuming a ready-made fact/value distinction. Nor should we begin with a controversial position in epistemology from which the naturalist is likely to dissent. For the naturalist in ethics can be a naturalist in epistemology, too, and might hold a causal theory of evidence, or believe that we must analyse the notion of epistemic warrant in terms of the causal explanation of belief rather than by appeal to some method of 'rational resolution'. Of course, such an epistemology typically requires that the naturalist be able to say what it is for a causal mechanism to be reliable, and this in the present case would require some account of the truth-conditions of moral discourse. But it would beg the question against naturalistic cognitivism simply to say that no such truth-conditions exist in the moral case. What we need, if we are to assess the force of an argument from moral disagreement, is a way of characterizing the phenomenon of moral disagreement that does not *assume* naturalistic cognitivism to be false.

Presumably, 'the phenomenon of moral disagreement' refers not to a philosophical thesis about the impossibility of rational resolution in ethics but to the actual character and extent of moral disagreement. It is for various reasons easy to overstate the extent and depth of moral disagreement. Points of moral disagreement tend to make for social conflict, which is more conspicuous than humdrum social peace. And though we sometimes call virtually any social norms 'moral', this does not mean that we really consider these norms to be serious competitors for moral standing in our communities. If, in any area of inquiry, including empirical science, we were to survey not only all serious competitors, but also all views which cannot be refuted, or whose proponents could not be convinced on non-question-begging grounds to share our view, we would find that area riven with deep and irremediable disagreement.

The real issue here is that a satisfactory account of morality should explain why we see the amount and kind of moral disagreement we do within the range of views with some claim to be serious competitors. Similarly, an epistemologist should not be saddled with the task of accommodating every sort of belief that has been called knowledge. Neither the epistemologist nor the moral theorist need put himself forward as giving an account of that element of the meaning of evaluative terms that is common to all their actual uses. When a naturalist in either ethics or epistemology claims that a given evaluative property is identical with some natural property, he is engaged in something like the task the logical empiricists called 'reconstruction': showing how certain central features and functions of an area of discourse can be captured by an account in terms of less problematic notions. Such a naturalistic reconstruction—like the empiricist reconstructions of such notions as physical object, natural law, causation, justified belief, or explanation—is likely not to capture all features and functions of the original discourse, and so it typically will be at odds with some elements of the commonly understood meanings of terms in that discourse. But whether any given reconstruction is happily viewed as an 'error theory' will depend upon what goes by the board. Indeed, the point of reconstruction may precisely be to vindicate the main characteristics of the original discourse.

In the case of naturalism in ethics, the reconstruction might aim to accomplish the following: to preserve the cognitivity of moral discourse; to indicate why moral evaluation has emerged as a distinctive and also socially significant mode of assessment; to give some account of why we—and those who disagree with us but whose views we none the less take seriously— make the sorts of moral evaluations we do; and to give an account of why moral agreement and disagreement have exhibited certain characteristic patterns.[3]

For example, a naturalistic cognitivist can offer the following sort of explanation of the extent and persistence of observed moral disagreement. First, the category of moral evaluation as found in ordinary language is hardly a determinate one, encompassing as it sometimes does elements of religion, etiquette, prudence, and so on. It perhaps can be said that moral evaluation has begun to emerge as a distinctive category of assessment only within the last century or so (one may of course regard this as a great cultural misfortune), and in common discourse, its emergence is hardly complete.

Second, across societies, within societies over time, and also within societies at a given time, we find wide variation in the circumstances under which people live and in their opinions about the world (concerning, for example, the existence of God, the effectiveness of retributive punishment, the character of 'human nature', etc.). These differences do much to explain variation in moral judgement. Indeed, as individuals come to occupy similar circumstances, and to agree in their opinions on general as well as particular facts, their moral judgements also tend to converge. To call such convergence a 'merely causal-psychological' phenomenon, again, would involve taking a position on a controversial issue in epistemology, a position that could hardly be expected to be neutral.

Third, and equally important in the explanation of persistent moral disagreement, is the existence within and across societies of significant conflicts of interest and differences in social role or group identity. Many of the striking evaluative disagreements in society follow these lines of social conflict and differentiation. Here we may also return to the second point, above, for along these lines also lie many of the striking disagreements in non-moral belief to be found within society.

Finally, moral judgements typically concern complex interpersonal phenomena where relevant particular and general facts are difficult to ascertain and where multiple dimensions of assessment may be at work, giving rise to problems of comparison. Indeed, when we look at those areas of social science where complexity is great and competing interests are deeply involved—for example, in debates over the causes of poverty or the conditions for sustained economic growth—we find a situation strongly reminiscent of moral dispute: protracted disagreements among a fairly limited number of competing schools, each of which becomes more elaborate with time but none of which seems capable of persuading all others.

Appeal to similar considerations could help to explain why in some areas of morality there is, by contrast, significant moral *agreement*: where beliefs and experiences are very much alike, where almost all parties have both interconnected interests and significant potential for reciprocal harm or benefit, where important interests can be protected by mutually-recognized norms, and so on. Examples would include the keeping of promises, truth-telling, and strictures against theft and assault.

In order to carry out his reconstruction, the naturalist need not claim there to be some heretofore undetected consensus on the nature of the right or the good underlying our moral discourse, a consensus which points univocally toward his own reconstruction. He may, for example, attempt a reconstruction of moral discourse which would permit us to see how the claims made within that discourse might be persistently controversial in certain areas, or might change over time, even though the discourse is interpreted as making cognitive claims about something genuine.

One can complain against any such reconstruction that it has merely changed the subject. This charge will be more compelling to the extent that one can show elements of the meaning of moral terms as they function in ordinary discourse to be sharply at odds with the naturalistic reconstruction. The charge will be less compelling to the extent that central features or functions of ordinary discourse can be captured by the reconstruction.

3. Normativity

Perhaps the naturalistic cognitivist is not in worse shape than the non-cognitivist to explain epistemic and semantic access in ethics, or to account for the character of moral agreement and disagreement. The naturalistic cognitivist might even be thought in some respects to have an easier time with moral dispute than the non-cognitivist, since he has no special difficulty in accounting for the uses of assertion, negation, inference, claims of relevance, and other cognitive features of moral argumentation.

But there is a third feature of moral discourse which the non-cognitivist has helped us to see and which does threaten to pose special difficulties for the naturalistic cognitivist—the so-called normativity of moral evaluation.

Now this problem would be easier to discuss were there clear agreement about what the normativity of moral evaluation consists in. But there is not. One hears talk of 'action-guidingness' and 'standard-setting', of the 'binding-ness' or 'authority' of moral judgement, of the 'magnetism' of the moral vocabulary, of morality as a system of 'categorical imperatives', and so on. These are not either entirely clear or clearly equivalent ideas. So we will have to begin somewhat impressionistically before moving on to a more careful account.

Let us restrict attention initially to so-called 'thin' moral judgements, judgements of moral rightness, value, or obligation, for that is where the discussion of normativity has had its greatest development.

What I will call the traditional conception of normativity can be introduced as follows. One cannot, it is claimed, appropriately be said to be under a moral obligation unless one has some sort of reason or motive to go along with the obligation. Whence, otherwise, the force of the obligation? This claim seems to figure in Hume's effort to find an 'interested obligation' to be moral and also in Hobbesian and neo-Hobbesian attempts to show the advantages of being moral.

But a strand of moral philosophy running back at least as far as Hutcheson and Kant holds—not without considerable support from common-sense morality—that there are reasons or motives for being moral that are qualitatively distinct from considerations of personal interest or prudence.[4] On such views it may still make sense to ask whether interest lies on the side of moral conduct, and it may even be thought that the answer to this question is, necessarily, positive. But none the less the normative standing of moral assessment, on such views, is importantly independent of personal interest or prudence. For if prudence were all that were needed to establish the normativity of morality, then a powerful tyrant with a highly effective apparatus for detection and repression could do the job. The reason or motive for moral conduct, on this view, has to be of the right sort if it is to account for the special authority of morality as opposed to mere prudence.

Here is a place where autonomy can naturally enter—the effective tyrant provides normative governance 'from without', which reaches no further than his repressive apparatus. Moral norms, by contrast, are thought not to owe their scope and authority to the threat of punishment alone. Thus emerges, for example in Rousseau's complaint against Hobbes, the idea that moral authority is autonomous—a genuinely moral agent is regulated by norms he gives himself as a rational, social being. The notion of autonomy has suffered various twists as it has moved from Rousseau to Kant to modern Kantianism, and though my sympathies lie with the original, I will try for now to avoid sectarianism. Instead, I wish to focus on a way in which the idea of autonomy leads easily to the idea of categoricalness, and to consider how the latter idea could be used to account for the special authority of morality.[5]

One understanding of an autonomous reason for action is the notion of a reason that all rational beings possess simply in virtue of possessing practical reason. For such a reason would not be a mere product of external circumstances or contingent desire, and would instead come 'from within' in a way that is tightly bound to the very feature of us that makes us capable of rational action and self-regulation. Such a reason would be categorical in this sense: it would be a requirement of practical reason, independent of any particular end or desire that an agent might have. The normativity of morality, on this view, comes from the fact that what we experience as its commands are in fact non-hypothetical requirements of this sort. Thus the tyrant, and worries about his arbitrariness and jurisdiction, drop from view when discussing the normative standing of morality.

This conception of categoricalness fits the widely-reported feature of the phenomenology of moral experience that the 'ought' of a moral judgement has a force that is non-hypothetical—that is, independent of the individual's particular ends or desires, whether these are understood manifestly or dispositionally. Categoricalness in this sense also seems to capture quite directly another feature of moral judgement, its 'inescapability'. One cannot, for example, claim exemption from the application of moral judgement—or its implications for one's actions—on the ground that one lacks any desire to be moral.

4. A Non-Cognitivist Response

An important line of criticism of this traditional approach to the normativity of morality is that categorical reasons of the sort it requires simply do not exist—practical rationality does not provide us with ends that are in this way wholly independent of desire, manifest or dispositional. But without entering into that discussion, let us consider how the non-cognitivist has allowed us to see that invocation of categorical reasons may simply not be necessary in order to capture the non-hypothetical character of moral judgement. The phenomenology of moral experience does indeed reveal that a certain non-hypothetical force attaches to moral judgements. But this force is not linked to *being under a moral obligation* as such, rather, it is linked to *making or accepting a moral judgement*. When a purported moral obligation is present, for example not to discriminate on racial grounds, those who do not recognize or accept this obligation feel no special 'force', except perhaps to the extent that they sense, and are moved by, the threat of the negative opinion of others or the operation of law. If I judge that racial discrimination is wrong, then, on the non-cognitivist account, this judgement is the expression of a negative attitude on my part toward such discrimination. And this affords a straightforward explanation of why I feel a certain force in connection with this 'ought'—for I do have a negative attitude toward what it urges against. What about those other than me? Here the non-cognitivist will say that part of why my attitude can be termed a moral attitude is that it involves a kind of urging that others also disapprove of or refrain from racial discrimination and a readiness to condemn or punish them if they do not. This urging and readiness put a kind of pressure upon others in my community either to share my attitude or to defend themselves. Moreover, another part of why my attitude can be termed a moral attitude is that this urging and readiness are not conditioned by my sense of the particular desires or inclinations of agents who would discriminate, including myself. As a result, the judgements that express this attitude are non-hypothetical.

Moreover, if the attitude against discrimination is fully internalized, it will function in an autonomous way psychologically. I may, for example, experience disapproval of racial discrimination even when circumstances make it expedient for me to practise or tolerate it. Circumstances may of course create incentives strong enough to sway my behaviour, but if the attitude has been internalized then this behaviour will lead me to feel a defensiveness and dissonance about the behaviour that are the psychological form of normative conflict.

We can have, act on, express, and be influenced by internalized, non-hypothetical attitudes without genuine categoricalness, that is, we can have the psychological (and, when the story is filled out, sociological) equivalent of categoricalness in a world devoid of Kantian categorical reasons. Although it follows from the fact that I make a sincere judgement against discrimination that *I* will 'automatically' have a reason not to discriminate—namely, discrimination would involve acting against my own negative attitude toward such behaviour—there is no invocation here of reasons that all rational persons automatically possess. Moreover, the non-cognitivist can point out that in a community people typically will be influenced by the attitudes of others, and will tend to seek the approval of others. These sources—as well as existing attitudes on the part of others that resemble the attitudes underlying my disapproval of discrimination—will give other members of the community as well some reason to act in accord with my judgement. Such reasons will not, however, be necessary or universal concomitants of rationality, and the traditionalist may here register the objection that the non-cognitivist's attitudinal account therefore cannot capture categoricalness after all. But the non-cognitivist may reply that there is no need to explain the normative force of our moral judgements on those who have no tendency to accept them and who recognize no significant community with us. For that is not a force we observe in moral practice.

The non-cognitivist's attitudinal account obviously needs considerable development in order to produce conviction about its adequacy to our moral experience. The objections to it that I will consider below indicate some of the directions such development might take. But they also have a further purpose, namely, of bringing the dialectic between the non-cognitivist and the traditionalist to a point where I can begin to draw a moral of some relevance to cognitivist naturalism.

5. An Objection to the Attitudinal Account of Normativity

The first objection I will mention concerns the plurality and diversity of attitudes that we find within individuals, even when we consider only non-hypothetical attitudes urged upon others. Many of these attitudes concern flatly descriptive matters or questions of taste or good manners, and so on, and thus would not be counted as *moral*. What is needed is some way of characterizing a class of attitudes and expressions that captures both the distinctiveness of moral evaluation and the peculiar importance we typically attach to it.

Here the non-cognitivist may choose among several lines. On the first, she allows that moral judgements have descriptive as well as expressive content. This line, however, diminishes the sense that there is a genuine difference between non-cognitivism and a cognitivism that recognizes (as it must) that moral language has non-cognitive functions as well.[6] On the second line, the non-cognitivist retains a wholly expressivist account of the meaning of moral judgements, but marks off moral attitudes by appeal to the specific emotions they engage or the particular social functions they serve—the sorts of practices into which they enter and the roles they play within those practices, for example with regard to the application of certain kinds of sanctions. This second line involves a distinction like the one Moore makes between the meaning of 'good' and the grounds of judgements of goodness: even if some naturalistic account of good-making features is correct, it does not follow, according to Moore, that good itself is a natural property.[7] Similarly, on this second line, even if a naturalistic account of the features of the world to which moral attitudes are responsive is possible, it does not follow that it is even part of the meaning of moral judgements to describe these features. This line is more protective of the distinctive claims of non-cognitivism as a theory of the meaning of moral discourse, but it must in consequence rest considerable weight upon the analytic/synthetic distinction, especially if the features of the world to which moral attitudes are responsive function very centrally in shaping the evolution of moral discourse and practice.[8]

Perhaps neither of these lines is wholly satisfactory. But I am less concerned at this point to assess their plausibility than to draw attention to the fact that, on both lines, the specific normative nature of moral assessment is accommodated by looking beyond the non-hypothetical character of attitudes distinguished as moral attitudes to their characteristic *ground* or *function*. If we were to ask the further question 'Why do moral attitudes have a special standing or importance in comparison to other non-hypothetical attitudes?', then presumably the answer on both lines would point to the conspicuous importance to social life of this characteristic ground or function. Let us keep these observations in mind as we move on to a second objection to attitudinalism.

6. A Second Objection to the Attitudinal Account of Normativity

From the standpoint of the traditional conception of normativity, attitudinal accounts seem disappointingly weak, incapable of capturing the 'inescapability' of moral assessment. For although the non-cognitivist may say that my attitude toward, say, racial discrimination is non-hypothetical in the sense that it does not involve any qualification concerning particular ends, still, at a higher order, must not the non-cognitivist claim that my moral assessment of discrimination *is* in a sense hypothetical, dependent as it is upon my having this particular attitude toward discrimination? For all the non-cognitivist has said, I could lack this attitude without ceasing to be rational. It may look as if moral 'oughts', on the non-cognitivist's account of normativity, are going to turn out to be optional or escapable in a way that goes against some of the features of moral experience that inspired the traditional account.

But once more, the non-cognitivist will reply that the features of moral experience in question can be accommodated without categoricalness. She has her own resources for explaining why, for example, I reject the suggestion that the wrongness of discrimination depends in any way upon my particular attitude toward it. She might say that the sort of attitude I have toward discrimination simply is one that is hostile to any such suggestion. Or, perhaps, she might give a more general account according to which it is among the characteristic features of distinctly moral attitudes that individuals holding them possess higher-order attitudes concerning the relevance or irrelevance of certain possible changes in their first-order attitudes.

It may seem that these replies are open to a reiteration of the original objection: there remains, at bottom, an appeal to attitudes a rational agent might happen to lack. Indeed wouldn't any appeal merely to further features of my attitudes show a misunderstanding of the objection being raised? Given all the possible reasons why one might have an unconditional attitude with regard to a given object of evaluation, whether an attitude is appropriately seen as moral must depend in part upon what accounts for its unconditional character, not merely upon its bald unconditionalness. One might for example argue that the harm done by discrimination to those who suffer its effects, and the loss of mutual respect it engenders within the community, would not disappear if my personal preferences were to change, and therefore the wrongness of discrimination is independent of my personal preferences. This would afford a way of saying that it is the character of discrimination itself, not some fact about the unconditional character of my attitudes, that is the basis for the independence of its moral status from my particular attitudes.

This, to me compelling, view of things is not, however, something the non-cognitivist need deny outright. For the attitudes to which she appeals are attitudes *toward* states of affairs. Thus my disapproval of discrimination can be put down to racism's horrible costs, and my angry rejection of the suggestion that the moral status of discrimination depends upon my attitudes can be put down to the independence of these costs from my attitude toward discrimination. For non-cognitivism is a view about the *content* of moral judgements, not about the *ground* of moral judgement or about right-making features.

Such a reply seems correct as far as it goes. Once again, however, the non-cognitivist has been led to a reply that requires a distinction between content in a narrow sense and meaning in a broader sense that encompasses the properties a term must track if it is to have its characteristic role and force, that is, the properties which contribute most centrally to explaining the use of the term. Unless this distinction turns out to be quite powerful and important—and certainly philosophy in this century has done much to question its capacity to illuminate linguistic meaning—the special point of non-cognitivism is, again, at risk.[9]

7. A Reply to Defenders of the Traditional Conception

Although the critic of non-cognitivism who is also a defender of the traditional conception of normativity may feel that he has successfully pushed non-cognitivism into a corner, the non-cognitivist can now turn tables and point out that the claim that categoricalness captures the distinctive force of moral assessment is itself vulnerable to a similar line of criticism. Let us grant that there may exist categorical reasons in the sense used above, namely, reasons that are not hypothetical upon the agent's possession—even in a dispositional sense—of any particular end, but which exist for him in virtue of his practical rationality as such.

Consider the following argument, which, the non-cognitivist might plausibly contend, brings us as close to a categorical reason as she ever expected to come. While there could, perhaps, be practically rational beings who lacked desires, it is difficult to conceive how there could be practically rational beings without ends of any sort, whether or not these are psychologically realized in deliberation as desires. Having an end in this sense is an empirical feature of an agent, yet it has a tight connection with a normative feature—the possession of a reason for acting. Indeed, if anything is clear about what sorts of reasons agents have, this much seems to be: other things equal, when an agent currently has an end he therefore has a prima facie reason to choose actions which promise the realization of this end. He may also, of course, have contrary reasons, and it certainly need not be assumed that an end always furnishes a prima facie reason for the agent actively to aim at the end, since a more indirect approach might be better.

Now the point is that this prima facie connection between the factual and the normative—the possession of ends and the possession of reasons—does not depend at all upon the particular content or character of ends of the agent. All that matters is *that* he has ends. Because the connection is not contingent upon the agent's particular ends, the higher-order reason it supplies is in an important sense categorical. One might say that categoricalness is required to avoid regress. Moreover, this reason is autonomous in the sense that it depends upon no external sanctions or 'pathological' desires, and appears to follow merely from the nature of practical reason. An agent would lack practical reason could he not see that his having a certain end at a given time furnishes a prima facie reason at that time for action to promote it.

Now the non-cognitivist need not claim that this argument is sound, only that it is about as credible as other arguments that have been floated for the existence of categorical reasons. Indeed, something like this argument, when allied to a desire-based conception of ends, may help explain the sense of uncontroversiality attending the idea that whatever else practical reason may involve, synchronic instrumental rationality is at least part of it.

Defenders of the traditional conception of normativity will no doubt wish to carry this argument a step further. By appeal to something like a symmetry principle, perhaps as a generalization of diachronic instrumental rationality, they will seek to include the ends of all rational beings as well as the agent himself. Such a step seems more problematic than the steps taken thus far, though for the non-cognitivist's dialectical purposes it is important only that it is a further step, one which does not appear to call the first step into question.[10]

Interestingly, if for argumentative purposes the further step of generalization is granted, then what results is the existence of *multiple* categorical reasons for a given agent: a categorical reason to attend to his own present ends, whatever they may be, and a categorical reason to attend to the ends of all rational beings as such.[11] But now we find that those who would defend an approach to normativity based upon categorical reasons are presented with a difficulty very similar to the first problem they raised against non-cognitivism: how to capture the distinctive normative force or status of morality, as compared to other non-hypothetical norms, such as those of prudence.[12] To be sure, it is natural to associate symmetrical categorical reasons with morality. And it typically has been assumed that the authority of morality is such that its claims not only extend to all rational beings, but also enjoy the status of potentially overriding competing reasons. But neither this symmetry nor this overriding authority follow from categoricalness as such.

The non-cognitivist thus may claim that one must go beyond categoricalness to account for the peculiar force of moral assessment. The obvious place to go is really the same place the non-cognitivist went in her own responses to like criticism. Consider a case in which my categorical reason to attend to my own ends or intentions points me in one direction—say, the direction of racial discrimination—while a symmetric consideration of ends points me in the opposite direction. What would be the basis for calling the latter consideration 'moral' or giving it deliberative priority? The answer could not be the categorical character of the reasons that stand behind it—for we may say that categorical reasons stand behind both—though it could be the symmetry and encompassingness of the perspective from which the latter consideration of ends takes place. This answer seems plausible because it locates the special force of moral reasons (among categorical reasons) in the impartial comprehensiveness of their grounds, which extend beyond the agent's own ends to the ends of all rational beings as such.

So, the non-cognitivist may conclude, the defender of the traditional conception is in the same boat as she, for both are led to go beyond their initial notions—of attitude or categoricalness—and to adduce the characteristic grounds of moral attitudes or reasons in order to explain the peculiar authority of moral assessment.

8. The Naturalistic Cognitivist Rejoins the Argument

At this point the naturalistic cognitivist I have in mind may take advantage of the state of the dialectic between the non-cognitivist and the defender of categorical reasons, for the boat aboard which these two have now found themselves is the very one on which he shipped as soon as he distinguished the normativity of moral assessment from the problem of showing it to be advantageous to be moral. In what sense might the naturalistic cognitivist be at a special disadvantage with regard to giving an account of normativity?

What sort of naturalistic cognitivist *have* I in mind? I will be considering a non-subjectivist naturalist according to whom an act or practice is better from a moral point of view to the extent that it contributes to aggregate well-being impartially considered. Of course, if this claim is to be genuinely naturalistic, then the notion of well-being that figures in it must be given a naturalistic account. I will suppose for the sake of discussion that this account is an informed desire theory.[13] The naturalistic position thus characterized does not as yet contain a theory of moral rightness or obligation,[14] but before discussing such matters, let us pause and notice a few things about the naturalistic position as a standard of assessment.

First, it permits assessment that is non-hypothetical with regard to the agent's own desires. Suppose that I perform act *A* in a circumstance in which I could instead have performed act *B*. Then whether I have done what is better from a moral point of view will depend upon the relative contribution of *A* in comparison to *B* to aggregate well-being, a matter not ordinarily settled entirely by the contribution of *A* or *B* to the satisfaction of my own desires. I might most desire to do *A*, but, according to the standard, it might be morally better to do *B*.

Second, although contribution to well-being does not encompass everything that people have found significant in moral assessment, a standard based upon such contribution does capture something that has been widely held to be a significant part of morality. On some moral theories, such as utilitarianism, it is the very heart of moral assessment. On others, such as orthodox Kantianism, it emerges as something like a necessary consequence of the groundwork of duty. On still others, such as a Rossian deontology in which beneficence figures as a prima facie duty, it is one component of assessment among others. Although certain theories of practical reason that are occasionally called moral theories by their proponents, such as non-universal moral egoism, do not accept this standard as even one component of moral assessment, such theories, unless they implicitly involve some sort of universalism, appear to lack the distinctive character of morality. Moreover, many of the assessments of common-sense morality, especially as it has evolved in its secular form, can be explained by considering the tendencies of various types of action, motive, and so on to contribute to aggregate well-being.

Third, the naturalistic standard described above provides a ground for moral assessment that would enable us to understand why moral considerations have a certain importance in social life. If someone asks, 'Why should this standard be important in regulating our conduct toward one another?', the answer can be given, 'Because well-being, and the alleviation of suffering, are important.' If the question returns, 'But who is to say that such ends are important?', the answer can be given, 'It is not thanks to my attitudes or theories that it matters significantly to a person whether her well-being is enhanced or suffering decreased.' The importance of well-being is not circularly dependent upon adopting a moral point of view of the sort the standard itself involves, since well-being, and freedom from suffering, are *non*-moral goods of the first order. As a result, it is not hard to see how community evaluation of individual action or character could have come to take general effects on well-being into account, and why, as the scope of community has enlarged, the range of those affected who are taken into account has become more universal. Nor is it difficult to see how the internalization of norms and attitudes conducive to the well-being of others—perhaps especially including internalization of prohibitions on the infliction of suffering—could have become an important part of the socialization of individuals.

These initial observations about the standard of moral value sketched above are, of course, very much underdeveloped. But perhaps they will suffice to suggest how this standard could have a number of those features that seemed needed in our earlier discussion in order to account for the peculiar force of moral assessment: it is non-hypothetical; it is symmetric rather than agent-centred; it is connected with some of the basic characteristics of moral evaluation as actually practised and is appropriately distinct from merely prudential evaluation; and it points to phenomena of other-than-moral importance and thus helps contribute to an explanation of how moral assessment itself could have come to be important.

Nothing we have said so far has tended to show the Kantian or non-cognitivist conceptions of normativity to be ultimately incorrect, since we have argued only that they stand in need of supplementation. But perhaps, if we were to look more directly at the sorts of features that supplementation involves—symmetry, descriptive content, functional role in the community, the 'reaction basis' of moral attitudes—we would find that these features are doing the bulk of the real work in capturing what is distinctive in moral assessment. If so, and if these supplementary features can furnish key ingredients of a naturalistic account of normativity, then we might question how great is the inherent disadvantage of naturalism, in comparison with its competitors, in capturing normativity.

9. Naturalism in Another Area of Normative Assessment

We might find it profitable at this point to compare naturalism in ethics with naturalism in a different domain, epistemology. The epistemic naturalist that I have in mind is someone who claims that a belief is better warranted in proportion as the belief-forming mechanism of which it is a product is reliable. This standard, like the standard of moral value discussed above, is non-hypothetical and distinct from prudence. Moreover, it, too, has obvious connections with prevailing norms of belief-formation. Further, it possesses a non-epistemic importance which is not difficult to understand. Many of the desiderata of traditional epistemology—such as concern over the certainty and the stability of beliefs—can be seen to be motivated in part by a concern about reliability in belief-formation. And given the practical importance of reliability in virtually every sphere of life, we can see how norms and attitudes conducive to reliability—or at least tending against the most immediately evident sorts of unreliability—could come to play a significant role in our social existence. If anyone were to ask, 'Why should epistemic warrant, understood in terms of reliability, be important in the regulation of thought?', the answer could be given, 'Because being right rather than wrong is important in the conduct of life.' Importance, here, as in the moral case, is not circularly dependent upon adoption of the normative point of view in question, for one need not be occupying the epistemic point of view in order to care about not being mistaken.

So much by way of parallel with the case of naturalism in ethics. In epistemology, in contrast to the ethical case, the issue 'Can a naturalistic account capture normativity?' has been slow to emerge in the philosophical literature. Instead, epistemic naturalism has been confronted with a thousand specific criticisms as opponents have generated counter-examples meant to show that particular naturalistic accounts yield verdicts contrary to various familiar epistemic judgements. General criticism of epistemic naturalism has spent considerably more time on the issue of *epistemic* externalism than *normative* externalism.

I suspect that the principal reasons for the relative absence of a debate over normativity in epistemology are two: first, it simply is less controversial that concern about reliability is at the heart of epistemic evaluation than that concern about (e.g.) well-being is at the heart of moral assessment; second, for any agent, it virtually always is the case that at least some of his goals will be aided by reliability in belief, so that he reliably will have some reason to be epistemically justified, whereas the existence of a reason to be moral in the naturalist's sense may be more problematic. Yet both of these reasons are matters of degree.

If these are matters of degree, and if reliability and well-being can both be analysed naturalistically, then, absent some further distinction, the tenability of the projects of epistemic and moral naturalism should differ only as a matter of degree. Therefore those philosophers who have expressed profound puzzlement at the very idea that a natural property could play a normative role in ethics, but who have expressed no similar wonderment in the epistemic case—and, rather, have gone straight ahead with the standard philosophical business of developing counter-examples—should ask themselves whether there is here a genuine difference in kind, after all.

Comparison of the moral with the epistemic case may be of use for another reason as well: epistemic naturalism affords an example of standards that are non-hypothetical but also not backed by categorical reasons.[15]

One might, however, argue against this last claim as follows. A categorical reason exists for following epistemic norms in belief-formation because belief is a matter of *believing true*, and, since epistemic norms 'aim at' truth, being in good epistemic standing is our best (purported) access to truth.

Such an argument surely captures something about belief, but it seems unlikely to yield the desired categorical reason. First, at least some philosophers have denied that belief is always believing true; others have denied that epistemic norms aim, or aim exclusively, at truth. Second, the argument at most establishes that some tension arises whenever a believer *thinks*, of a belief she holds, that it would be proscribed by epistemic norms. But a believer can avoid this sort of thought by means other than better conformity to epistemic norms. And third, if the issue is the bare psychological possibility of belief in the face of actual recognition that one is unjustified by epistemic norms, then it should be pointed out that people sometimes do hold beliefs 'against all odds'.

The argument for categorical reasons to follow epistemic norms seems to me unavailing. Yet epistemic standards can still be non-hypothetical. The standard of reliability, for example, makes no essential reference to the ends of epistemic agents. Moreover, non-categorical epistemic reasons—reasons connected with our interest in forming beliefs reliably—are typically strong enough to explain the centrality of (non-hypothetical) epistemic standards in our social practice. The parallel, of course, is with our ethical naturalist's effort to show that the non-categorical reasons we have for paying attention to a non-hypothetical moral standard—reasons connected with our interest in how acts and practices affect well-being—are typically strong enough to account for the centrality of moral assessment in our practices, and to indicate thereby how the impression of categorical reasons might have arisen.

10. The Force of Moral Obligation

But is there not a special characteristic of the moral case, a characteristic that furnished the entry point for our discussion of normativity? And so we are finally led back to the question of obligation.

On the naturalistic view sketched here, what becomes of the idea that there is something odd about accepting a judgement that X has an obligation to do A if one at the same time believes that X has no reason or motive to do A?—something must stand behind the talk of obligation, and yet our naturalist has thus far been silent about both obligation and its sanction.

We must, however, be clear about what is being sought. Strictly speaking, nothing could at once genuinely *oblige* and be resistible. But there is no prospect of anything like this sort of 'must' in the case of morality—even categorical reasons are not irresistible. The most that can be said is that to act contrary to obligation—or contrary to categorical reasons—is to be vulnerable to a certain kind of criticism and to incur certain costs.

The question becomes: what criticism, and what costs? Suppose we say that the person who acts against duty acts against good reasons. But what sort of reasons are these? Surely they are not merely prudential—duty can presumably extend where sheer self-interest does not. Suppose, then, that the reasons must themselves be moral in character. Yet even an externalist has no difficulty finding a tight link between obligation and *moral* reasons. If a moral reason is the sort of reason that emerges from a moral point of view—for example a reason that would exist for an impartial, benevolent observer—then we can expect that whenever a genuine obligation exists, so will a moral reason for carrying it out.

What anti-externalists must be seeking, it would seem, is a kind of criticism or cost that will reliably be present whenever obligations are violated, but which has normative force for the agent independent of the moral point of view. The obvious candidate is a criticism of irrationality. On a non-categorical view of things, the ground for a criticism of irrationality would apparently have to be hypothetical, and this would introduce a contingency into the sanction of obligation of the sort the anti-externalist thinks it essential to avoid. For, as the anti-externalist points out, it is contrary to common-sense morality to permit agents to escape the scope of moral obligation by the simple expedient of failing to satisfy certain hypothetical conditions.

Yet our externalist naturalist can rebut the charge of unwanted contingency (and the associated counter-intuitive avoidability of obligation) in something like the following way. The sort of naturalism sketched above begins with the notion of that which is better or worse from a moral point of view, not with the concept of moral obligation, and so it remains to be said how obligation might come into the picture. A position that is open to our naturalist is to insist that moral obligation is a social creature, a notion which does not sensibly apply apart from developed patterns of behaviour. In order that agents be under obligations to one another—as opposed to possessing the capacity or inclination to act in ways which do more or less good—there must be a backdrop of social institutions, expectations, and sanctions, as indeed there is in core cases of obligation such as keeping promises and telling the truth. From a fundamental moral point of view, we can, of course, abstract from any particular set of obligations and ask what sorts of behaviours it would be better or worse for us to teach, to expect of one another, and to hold one another accountable for failing to perform through such means as punishment, blame, and the internalization of guilt. But such matters about the appropriate domain of moral obligation are not themselves questions of moral obligation.

If we see obligation as involving a backdrop of institutions, expectations, and sanctions, we can also see how it could almost always be the case that when an individual genuinely is under an obligation, he will have a reason—based upon both external sanctions and internalized motives and sanctions—for carrying it out. For any assignment of duties, there will be some motivational gaps and exceptions, since particular individuals may have failed fully to internalize a recognized moral standard and may also be clever or lucky enough to evade any external sanction. But the fact of moral experience we are trying to accommodate—the regular accompaniment of recognized obligation by some reason or motive to carry the obligation out—is widely recognized as possessing gaps and exceptions, too.

A fairly reliable connection between obligation and reason or motive can be secured, and gross linguistic anomaly avoided, though not as a deep fact at the foundation of morality of the sort that the Kantian account of normativity envisaged. Instead, this connection finds its place as a feature of psychologically possible moral practices in which obligation plays a role.

11. A More General Account

Still, it might be thought, isn't there need at the deepest level for a perfectly general connection between moral evaluation of any sort and agents' reasons or motives for action? Both the non-cognitivist and the Kantian conceptions of normativity may have needed supplementation by some account of the *ground* of moral evaluation, but both also included prior to supplementation an essential *motivational* component, either an attitude on the part of the evaluator or a reason on the part of the agent.[16] To suggest as I have done that the naturalist can capture the ground of moral evaluation would appear to leave such a motivational component out of account—except rather indirectly, in the case of particular categories of assessment such as obligation.

Actually, we have already looked briefly at the stuff of a quite general motivational account. Our naturalist has tied moral evaluation to the assessment of the tendencies of various sorts of behaviour to contribute to the non-moral good of those affected. It is not difficult to imagine functional explanations of why practices that assess such tendencies might arise and be sustained within social groups, along with a tendency to celebrate those who substantially contribute to the well-being of others in the group and to sanction or shun those who do significant harm. Through the teaching of contributory behaviour, and through the operation of individual desire not to be shunned or devalued, contributory norms are internalized and come to play an important role in regulating social interaction and judgement. At the same time, however, it would simply be unavailing in general to attempt to teach or sanction norms of behaviour with which the individual would characteristically have little reason or motive to comply. Thus there may arise a quite general connection between the sort of assessment that is the ground of moral evaluation and the sorts of things that we find reason or motive to do, and find moreover to bear a peculiarly compelling sort of social value. As social conceptions of the relevant group have expanded historically to include not only members of family or tribe or religion, but all those potentially affected, this social value and the associated internalized norms have emerged as distinctively moral.

Even so, our naturalist must admit that such considerations establish at best a quite general, contingent connection between evaluation in terms of his substantive moral standard, on the one hand, and motivation, on the other. No guarantee is afforded that moral evaluation in his sense will always be accompanied by appropriate motivation, and the naturalist must admit that this is the sort of thing that non-cognitivist and Kantian approaches to normativity sought to prevent.[17] He may however reply that we should be wary of attempting to establish in moral theory a connection with motivation stronger than anything we encounter in actual moral experience. We must, after all, make appropriate space for the often-impressive lack of motivation accompanying moral evaluation and for the fact that people we rather uncontroversially call rational do not always appear to find in moral evaluation regulative reasons.

The naturalist can point to the widespread tendency of individuals to see their own attitudes and conduct as morally acceptable, one result of which is that moral self-assessment—and willingness to accept others' evaluations of oneself—is largely restrained within the boundaries of what individuals find themselves with reason or motive to do. The naturalist can further point to the widespread reluctance of individuals, at least among acquaintances and when tempers are cool, to make moral evaluations of others in the absence of any substantial reason or motive for them to act accordingly. It would appear possible to account for these and related facts by postulating a nomological rather than semantic connection between moral evaluation and motivation.

The social valorization of moral assessment, the extensive internalization of moral norms, the importance to individual self-esteem of maintaining a conception of what one does as fundamentally defensible or worthy in the eyes of others, the ineffectuality and interpersonal costliness of passing negative judgements of any sort in the absence of incentives or other grounds to expect behavioural change—these and other social-psychological characteristics of moral assessment may suffice to account for the facts of moral experience. Indeed, many of these characteristics are found in other highly valenced areas of social judgement where the standard seems more plainly external, for example; evaluations of the relative magnitude of one's contribution to the efforts, achievements, or failures of those groups—families, teams, departments, neighbourhoods, and so on—membership of which makes some significant contribution to one's identity.

It is part of the naturalist's ambition to understand how evaluation based upon moral grounds—where 'moral' is understood in his sense—has come to be so highly valued as a dimension of social assessment and so important to individual self-conceptions.[18] The naturalist's understanding would provide, as a matter of social-psychological fact rather than conceptual necessity, an explanation of the connection between moral assessment and motivation that has made non-naturalist and non-cognitivist views so plausible.[19]

Notes

1. Although our focus will be upon certain areas of moral discourse proper—judgements of moral rightness, obligation, or value—questions about the normativity of

value judgements certainly can arise in connection with non-moral value as well. Although there are significant parallels in the moral and non-moral cases, I would claim that the connection between an agent's non-moral good and his motives (or other reasons for action) is importantly different, and tighter, than the connection in matters of moral value in general. For some discussion of the normativity of judgements of intrinsic value within a cognitivist framework, see Peter Railton, 'Facts and Values', *Philosophical Topics* 14, and 'Naturalism and Prescriptivity', *Social Philosophy and Policy* 7.

2. Note that merely declaring that the moral supervenes upon the natural would not suffice to remove epistemic or semantic mystery—indeed, it would create a mystery of its own. Supervenience is, one might say, a descriptive category, and what is wanted is an explanatory account: *why*—in virtue of what features or relations—does the moral supervene in this way upon the natural?

3. For some discussion of such uses of a naturalistic account of moral evaluation see Peter Railton, 'Moral Realism', *Philosophical Review* 95.

4. The distinction made here differs from at least one established usage of the terms 'internalism' and 'externalism', as, for example, in William K. Frankena, 'Obligation and Motivation in Recent Moral Philosophy', in A. I. Melden (ed.), *Essays in Moral Philosophy*. There internalism is concerned specifically with the existence of *motives* for agents, as opposed to other sorts of reasons for action that might carry justificatory force. Thus, in Frankena's scheme, Kant is an externalist, since on his view obligation can exist when motive is not present. But in the present discussion, Kant is on the internalist side, for his view grounds obligation in reasons the agent necessarily has. Internalists in the present discussion—the non-cognitivist and those holding some form of the traditional conception—have in common the idea that (at least part of) the *normativity* of morality resides in a non-contingent link between moral evaluation and reasons or motives.

5. In what follows I will be discussing a thesis about autonomy as applied to reasons, ignoring for now the question of autonomy in motives.

6. I suppose the distinctiveness of non-cognitivism-cum-descriptive-meaning might be defended on the ground that it is the attitudinal character of moral language that is constant across cultural or historical changes in descriptive content. But it may be problematic to say of a system of non-hypothetical attitudes attaching, for example, to injunctions that place military glory or masculine honour above all else, that the injunctions are none the less appropriately deemed a morality in other than an 'inverted commas' sense.

7. G. E. Moore, *Principia Ethica*, p. 9.

8. It is, of course, part of the claim of the sort of naturalistic cognitivism under consideration in this paper that certain natural properties do indeed play a central role in the evolution of morality. For some discussion, see Railton, 'Moral Realism'.

9. As before, the non-cognitivist has the option of saying that moral language has (necessary) descriptive as well as non-descriptive content, but without further argument it may seem that this position sacrifices the distinctive interest of non-cognitivism as an alternative to a cognitivist position which includes a recognition of the non-cognitive force of moral language.

10. The obvious thing for the defender of categorical reasons to do at this point is to deny that the first step can be taken on its own, independently of the second. A person's own ends, on this view, could not offer him a *reason* for action unless normative principles have entered that would already suffice to guarantee generalization. If this argument could be made without simply begging the question against alternative

conceptions of normativity, then the non-cognitivist's argument would be disarmed, though the conclusion she seeks to reach concerning the need to capture the distinctive character of moral reasons may be accessible to her through other routes.

11. Kant of course would have thought that ultimately these categorical reasons could not come into conflict. But in order to secure this result—given that an agent's own happiness is, according to Kant, a necessary end for him—a universal teleology must be postulated.

12. The issue here is not the status of any particular prudential reason, which may indeed depend hypothetically upon a certain desire, but the status of a class of reasons whose ground lies in the ends—contingent or necessary as the case may be—of the agent.

13. For an example of the sort of theory I have in mind, see Railton, 'Moral Realism' and 'Facts and Values'.

14. Indeed, it does not as yet contain a theory of *moral value*, according to one common philosophical usage of that expression. For moral value, in this usage, is attributed only to such things as motives and traits of character, often but not always in proportion to their general tendencies. The notion of 'better from a moral point of view' that I have in mind could apply as well to individual acts (even in the narrow sense which does not comprise motives) and to social practices. I feel somewhat free to use 'moral value' in this broader way because ordinary language is not decisive about the term's scope.

15. Is it merely confused on my part to compare the epistemic and the moral cases, since the former belongs to theoretical reason and the latter to practical reason? Unhappy as I am with this distinction, let me attempt to situate the present discussion with respect to it. Suppose that one were to insist that epistemology proper belongs to theoretical rationality, for this reason: epistemology itself does not tell us anything about what we ought to believe, or how our choices should respond to evidence; instead, it tells us only such things as how much epistemic probability a hypothesis has, or, whether a given belief constitutes knowledge. Then my comparison here would not be with epistemology proper but with what might be called 'epistemic norms of belief-formation', for example, norms of belief-formation according to which agents should insofar as possible conform their degrees of belief—as expressed in choice behaviour, betting, etc.—to epistemic probability. Surely such 'epistemic norms of belief-formation' are practical in the sense that morality is.

16. Here and below I will use the word 'motivational' in a way that is meant to encompass both reasons for action and motives.

17. A *subjectivist* naturalism would be able to affirm a necessary connection between motivation (of some sort) and evaluation. Throughout I have been interested in non-subjectivist forms of naturalism because I find these the most plausible, but I certainly have done nothing to defend this judgement in the present essay. Note, again, that the issue here is distinct from externalism v. internalism in at least one familiar sense, since it concerns (non-moral) reasons as well as motives.

18. Such an explanation would require the naturalist to make good on his claim to be able to account for many of the most significant features of distinctively moral assessment in terms of relations to an empirically grounded, epistemically respectable conception of well-being. For otherwise the possibility exists that we could not connect actual moral practice to the naturalist's standard, and as a result the motivational apparatus associated with actual moral practice could be disconnected from any ground that would, on critical reflection, have the requisite non-moral value. For example, it might turn out that actual moral practice really is—as some have suggested—no more than an arbitrary repressive scheme with no connection to the conditions under which

humans actually would flourish. If so, then on critical reflection morality might lose any normative force for us. By contrast, if the naturalist is correct in locating the grounds of a significant component of moral practice in effects upon well-being, and if he is right in assuming that well-being is of the first non-moral importance, then the normativity of morality in this sense—survival of critical reflection—is not thus threatened.

19. I am grateful to David Copp, William Frankena, and David Velleman for comments on an earlier paper on the justification of morality. I am also indebted to my colleagues Paul Boghossian, Richard Brandt, Stephen Darwall, Allan Gibbard, Donald Regan, Nicholas White, and Crispin Wright for helpful conversations on these and related matters.

13

Cognitivism, Naturalism, and Normativity: A Reply to Peter Railton

David Wiggins

I

Peter Railton is concerned with the normative character of moral judgements and the challenge that they present to naturalistic and/or cognitivist accounts or reconstructions of ethics. I shall begin my reply by saying a word or two about what naturalism is, then try to say something about what normativeness/normativity amounts to in moral judgements, then touch on the difficulty that normativity may be thought to make for naturalism as such and for cognitivism as such.

II

What is naturalism, and what is its relation to cognitivism (which I take to be the idea that judgements of morality are susceptible of truth and knowledge)? Often Railton writes as if he thinks that naturalism in ethics *coincides* with cognitivism in ethics. He disjoins and conjoins the labels freely. I think myself that this is a mistake. But even if it were not a mistake it would still be a pity to proceed in this way. For our best chance of making anything stick in this area of controversy is surely to have a careful inventory of the theoretical possibilities and then refrain from foreclosing upon questions of their mutual coincidence.

In ethics there are at least two things that go under the name of naturalism. The first is explanatory or Humean naturalism. This is a position that Hume himself never envisaged as going with cognitivism. But it might do so, and I shall submit that explanatory naturalism stands in no general relation to cognitivism. The second sort of naturalism is the naturalism that enraged Moore. This is necessarily a cognitivist option. But I cannot see that this kind of naturalism is coextensive with cognitivism as such. (Certainly, Moore, who was a cognitivist would have denied that they were coextensive.) The philosophical interests of the first and second sorts of naturalism are prima facie distinct. The first by definition must, and the second can, see man as 'part of nature'. But the first kind of naturalism is purely speculative and the second is more practical or operational in its outlook. The two views can of course be combined. But they need not be.

III

Hume attempted (he said) to apply the experimental method of reasoning to moral subjects. In the *Treatise* he searched for principles in the moral sphere that would be like the principles that Newton found in the sphere of natural science. Hume hoped that in moral science, as in natural science, wherever some 'principle [had] been found to have a great force and energy in one instance', it would be possible to 'ascribe to it a like energy in all similar instances' and thereby find a system in a multitude of moral (social and psychological) phenomena. Man looks (to man) very special and peculiar; and human morality is certainly a singular creation. But perhaps the moral scientist can show how it is possible for fidelity, justice, veracity, integrity, and many other estimable and useful qualities and principles to arise from simpler virtues such as 'humanity, benevolence, friendship, public spirit, and other social virtues of that stamp', virtues which have themselves arisen from some explanatorily basic endowment of nature. In Hume's theory the basic endowment is fellow-feeling, or the spark of friendship for human kind, beyond which it is needless (according to Hume) to push our researches.[1]

Obviously a theorist of this persuasion might want to offer some 'philosophical analysis' of moral predicates and thereby represent them as coextensive with naturalistic predicates (in a special scientific or scientistic sense of 'naturalistic' that I shall explain in a moment (Section IV)). Perhaps that is what evolutionary and utilitarian moralists saw themselves as attempting, along with the reduction of moral problems to a certain sort of calculation. But such an analysis is in no way essential to the Humean type of naturalism or to the attempt to introduce the 'experimental method' into the moral sciences. And Hume for one did not want to do this. He seems to have been happy to see moral judgements (i) as irreducible and *sui generis* ('[Taste and morals] gild and stain . . . natural objects with the colours borrowed from internal sentiment' and thereby 'raise in a manner *a new creation*', he writes [my italics], in the first appendix to the *Inquiry into the Principles of Morals*); and (ii) as comparable in certain important respects with judgements of colour, these being conceived as Locke conceived them.

A naturalist of the Humean kind will not think he needs to offer any reduction of moral language. Most likely, he will see this language not only as *sui generis* in its content but also as cognitive in its aspiration.[2] But this would-be cognitive content is not the cue for the Humean naturalist to try to arrive at the operational criterion of right and wrong that interests the other sort of naturalist. Hume does not take the cognitivist aspiration seriously enough, and other Humean naturalists who take it seriously may not see moral philosophy instrumentally or operationally enough, to feel any need to look for such a criterion. And in any case it is open to a Humean naturalist to deviate in another direction from Hume and Hume's comparison of values and colours. He may incline in the direction of twentieth-century emotivism and see sentences that involve moral predicates as lacking proper declarative purport or intent.

IV

These distinct theoretical possibilities all flow from the Humean way of being a naturalist. This position is equally hospitable, I judge, to cognitivism and to extreme anti-cognitivism. In whichever further direction explanatory naturalism is developed, it need not see valuational predicates as fit to be reduced to naturalistic predicates or as properly coextensive with naturalistic predicates in the sense of 'naturalistic' that corresponds to the naturalism of the *second* kind, to which I now come. This second, more practical way is the way of the naturalist who provoked Moore's indignation. Especially it is the way of the philosopher who wants ethics to be more scientific, and whose principal contention amounts (in Moore's characterization) to the claim that Good is identical with some property belonging to the class of properties that are either *natural* or *metaphysical.* Following the best clue we are given in *Principia Ethica* (see especially p. 40) and the confirming evidence of the new preface that Moore drafted for *Principia* and never published (see Casimir Lewy's masterly resumé and interpretation),[3] we may say that Moore meant the following by these terms (which were for him terms of art): a *natural* (or *naturalistic*) property is a property with which it is the business of the natural sciences or of psychology to deal, or which can be completely defined in the terms of these.[4] It is a property that can be defined, one might say, in terms that pull their weight within these sciences. And a *metaphysical* property is a property that stands to some supersensible object in the same relation in which natural properties stand to natural objects. These are special senses of 'natural' and 'metaphysical', but they surely have a philosophical point and usefulness, and they could be refined to any requisite degree.

I know no other way than this to make dialectical sense of *Principia Ethica,* or to make sense of what one ought to mean by the naturalism that Moore attacked. What Moore thought, you will remember, is that anyone who identified Good with a natural or metaphysical property was committing the naturalistic fallacy. Later[5] he came to see that he had never proved that this identification was a fallacy—or a *formal* oversight or blunder. Nevertheless one might insist that he always did have a real argument, for what it was worth, against the identification. As applied against the naturalistic suggestion that is mentioned in Railton's paper, this argument runs as follows (cp. *Principia,* p. 44, section 27 *ad fin*): an act or practice may well 'contribute to aggregate well being [or happiness], where this includes the alleviation of suffering', but, even allowing that it does contribute in that way, it must still be an *open question* whether the act or practice is good (is, as Railton puts it, better from the moral point of view).

Moore was driven by a strong animus against all proposals of this kind, which he saw as crude, as scientistic and, in some cases (for example the case of Professor Tyndall's unforgettable recommendation to us to 'conform to the laws of matter'), as idiotic. But for the case of naturalistic proposals that are not idiotic (as Railton's is not), we can surely see (whether or not we share Moore's particular animus) that it is indeed bound to be problematic (to say the least) whether proposals of this sort can represent moral judgements as having the right kind of content to enjoy normativity. (I understand Railton's evident concern on this point.) Another thing we can see, however, is that Moore would have greatly improved his deployment of the open question argument if he could have given *a reason* why one would expect there to be this problem for reductive naturalism. If he had done so—adverting perhaps (however alien this proposal may seem to *Principia*) to the difference between conceptualizing our experience in a manner that is conditioned by the ethical as such and conceptualizing it in the scientific manner—he might have turned what has probably struck everybody as an inappropriately inductive seeming consideration into an argument of genuinely explanatory power.[6]

V

But this is to anticipate, albeit in the interests of keeping Moore's open question argument alive, points that belong later. I shall come back to normativity in the proper place. Let me finish first with naturalism and the relation of naturalism and cognitivism.

Against the particular sort of naturalism that Moore attacked, the charge of 'scientism' seems to me to stick. But the charge of scientism would be utterly unconvincing if it were levelled against the very attempt to find a Humean naturalistic and/or latter day Humean explanation of the emergence and development of morality. Because a Humean explanation of these things has no need to deny the *sui generis* character of moral and other evaluative categorizations or even to subject their content to reductive analysis, it is simply not in the nature of Humean naturalism to lay itself open to any convincing use of the open question objection. Nor of course could scientism have been Moore's charge against absolutely every theory that saw the propositions of morality as candidates for knowledge and as fit to be asserted in the dimensions of genuine truth and falsehood. After all, Moore's own theory was of this kind.

To those schooled on certain other reconstructions of G. E. Moore, these may seem strange points to emphasize. But so long as we remember the definition of 'natural' on p. 40 of *Principia* (later emphasized by Moore himself and by Lewy) and we see the non-natural as simply the logical complement of the natural in Moore's special, technical sense of 'natural', there can surely be indefinitely many distinguishable cognitivist theories that are not naturalistic in Moore's sense—including Moore's own. That is another advantage of the interpretation. If such theories speak of non-natural properties, that may sound odd. But, whatever Moore's own language or example may have suggested, such properties may well be very ordinary (non-queer) indeed. The difficulty of non-naturalistic (second sense) cognitivist theories, insofar as they have a difficulty, lies neither in their naturalism (for even if they are in Hume's sense they need not be naturalistic in Moore's sense) nor in their interest in non-natural properties as such. Nor does it seem to me, moving now to my second topic, that they need face any special problem about normativity. But what is normativity?

VI

Railton says all sorts of interesting things about normativity, and about the advantages and disadvantages of cognitive and non-cognitive approaches to it. But in reading his essay I felt at some points that I was in danger of confusing his question about normativity with his answer to the question. So let me now encourage him to say some more about what the question itself is, but try to do this by saying a word or two about what I thought the question was before his essay arrived.

Well, insofar as I had a clear belief about this, I suppose I believed that the problem was put succinctly and correctly by Wittgenstein:

> Supposing that I could play tennis and one of you saw me playing and said 'Well, you play pretty badly' and suppose I answered 'I know, I'm playing badly but I don't want to play any better', all the other man could say would be 'Ah, then that's all right'. But suppose I had told one of you a preposterous lie and he came up to me and said 'You're behaving a like a beast' and then I were to say 'I know I behave badly, but then I don't want to behave any better', could he then say 'Ah, then that's all right'? Certainly not; he would say 'Well, you ought to want to behave better'.[7]

Wittgenstein goes on to comment that, like other ethical judgements, 'you ought to want to behave better' is an absolute judgement, whereas 'you play pretty badly' is a relative judgement. If Wittgenstein had wanted to reproduce the doctrine of Kant, he could have called the latter a hypothetical imperative, an imperative whose purported force is avowedly conditional upon the agent's having at some time some inclination (to play tennis properly), and he could have contrasted it with a categorical imperative, whose purported force is not conditional on anything at all.[8] A categorical imperative is addressed to (and it announces itself as binding on) anyone at all who can understand it, however his will is disposed.

So is this all right so far? Railton's naturalist, who is a naturalist in the second of the two senses I distinguished, has to say how a judgement whose content is reconstructed as tantamount to the naturalistic claim that this act produces (say) the largest aggregate of well being (as, for example quasi-scientifically specified) can still, even in reconstructed form (this being represented as the reconstructed form of the very same judgement), make a claim upon an agent (or his will) that is not conditional on anything. One who affirms the original or unreconstructed judgement is committed to see himself as having a reason to do the act and a reason that is a reason regardless of any other reasons he may be afforded by conflicting ends or inclinations, whether past, present, or future. No doubt the unreconstructed judgement can also come charged with the idea of a suitable retribution upon anyone who should transgress its requirements. It sustains and is sustained by such ideas. The question is how any of this—that sort of reason for that action, or the idea of that sort of retribution—can attach to a judgement that relates to purely naturalistic properties (in the second sense of 'naturalistic'). Of course there is no problem at all here if predicates that stand for moral properties are already naturalistic! But, if we remember the Moorean definition of 'naturalistic', doesn't the fact that moral predicates have this power suggest that prior to reconstruction they are not naturalistic? And surely the power to import this 'objective prescriptivity', as Mackie would call it, is not something that can be *painted on to* a naturalistic predicate. Some might say this, but they could scarcely be naturalists or cognitivists. It is something that must accrue to the *content*, and, according to any naturalistic cognitivism, it must accrue to the naturalistic content. Can it do this?

VII

Now if that is the problem, it is important—and important for everyone, not excluding the non-cognitivists—not to exaggerate the quality or quantity of the normativity phenomenon itself. Surely Wittgenstein, whose own view was that, by being non-relative and absolute (categorical), the propositions of ethics cannot be statements of fact, does exaggerate it when he writes (a page later on):

> The right road is the road which leads to an arbitrarily predetermined end and it is quite clear to us all that there is no sense in talking about the right road apart from such a predetermined goal. Now let us see what we could possibly mean by the expression '*the* absolutely right road'. I think it would be the road which everybody on seeing it would, *with logical necessity*, have to go, or be ashamed for not going. And similarly the *absolute good*, if it is a describable state of affairs, would be one which *everybody*, independent of his tastes and inclinations, would *necessarily* bring about or feel guilty for not bringing about. (All these italics are in the original)[9]

If a philosopher sets up the problem in this way and requires that each and everybody who sees the absolutely right road should with logical necessity either take the road or be ashamed, then he is pretty well bound to arrive at the same conclusion as Wittgenstein did, namely that such a state of affairs as this being the right road is a chimera, because 'no state of affairs has in itself what [Wittgenstein] would like to call the coercive power of an absolute judge'.[10]

Could normativity amount to less than this? Perhaps it would suffice to say that a moral judgement, '*A* is the [absolutely] right road' (say) or (more plainly) '*A* is what I/he/she has to do' can be normative by virtue of being categorical, and that it can be categorical if, as a result of its being what it is and its saying what it says, its simple acceptance will give anyone who accepts it a reason for doing *A* that is not sensitive to what he desires or is inclined to do or will desire or will be inclined to do. *Pace* Kant, this need not necessarily be a reason that can under all circumstances outweigh all others. (That is a further claim, which Kant would make.) What it is above all is a reason not conditioned by inclination that would still be a reason of that unconditional sort even where it was overwhelmed by some other reason. And the exigency of this demand that the judgement places upon the agent who accepts it is part of its *content*, which must, for a cognitivist, mean its *declarative* content.

VIII

If this is the phenomenon to be explained or accommodated, then it will be best to distinguish its impact upon different forms of cognitivism. But let me begin on this task by offering one part of an explanation of the phenomenon which is both open to the Humean naturalist who is not a cognitivist but respects the *sui generis* content of moral discourse and open equally to the cognitivist who is a neo-Humean (non-Moorean) naturalist but disinclined by the strength of his respect for the cognitive aspirations of that discourse to follow Hume in his denial that moral judgement can ever attain to proper truth.[11] I would stress, however, that what I shall offer is by way of a supplement to Hume's own account of the motivational charms of the explanatorily basic virtues and the artificial virtues (in Hume's sense of 'artificial'), not a replacement for it.[12] I would also stress that I do not seek to offer any argument for the claim that a virtuous motivation (either of Humean benevolence or of benevolence artificially redirected) is *rationally mandatory*. (I doubt that one can settle a properly non-question-begging sense of 'rational' to fix the sense of the question as a genuinely open question that one can then try to close by argument.) All that will be offered (or needs to be offered) is an explanation of how the perception of the right sort of 'non-natural' fact (in Lewy's and Moore's sense of 'natural') can give the perceiver a certain sort of reason (and motive) for a certain sort of act.

Suppose that, like most people in most places, I find myself in the midst of a social morality—not on the margins of society, and not systematically disadvantaged by the workings and practices of that morality. Suppose then—for this is already entailed by my ordinary participation—that I have already been caught up in the shared sentiments and responses that are presupposed to my having grasped the sense of the moral and political language that my membership in the social morality commits me to learn to express myself in.[13] Then, presumptively but only presumptively, the link must already be in place between the affirmation of a judgement and some determination of the will. Otherwise I could not have grasped the sense of the distinctively moral and political language that sustains the practices in which I participate.

This is simply the beginning of the explanation of my having a reason that is not sensitive to inclination. No doubt, under the conditions so far described, I am inside morality, and some link of commitment holds between my moral judgement and my will, unless I opt out and I sever the link. But, even when the element of exaggeration is reduced in Wittgenstein's (and Hume's) accounts of the universality and strength of the phenomenon that is to be accounted for, the explanation of the linkage is so far still incomplete. What we have to go on to confront are such things as the apparent contingency of the fact that it is these practices rather than some other practices I find myself in the midst of, and the consequential contingency of the fact that it is this rather than that I find I am expected here to do in the circumstance C. Is it not accidental—cannot just anyone come to suspect that it is accidental—that these are the sentiments I had to be able to experience in order even to grasp a social morality I could be in the midst of? Surely my need there then to experience those sentiments in order to grasp the sense and point of all sorts of distinctly moral categorizations does not irrevocably commit me to *continue* in this way of feeling. Now that I am a moral being of some sort, why should I not replace them by others?

Perceiving that there seem to be alternatives to the practices that exist where I am, suppose I seek out the reason why these are the ones that exist here. Suppose I then discover what (if anything) suits the actual social morality I am in the midst of to me and creatures like me and discover what (if anything) suits us and our animal natures to it (or what suits our second or acquired natures to it). It may then seem that any of three different reactions will be available. I can seek to escape altogether, by outright rejection of the whole set-up. Call this option (1). On the other hand, staying within the set-up, there are the options of piecemeal criticism (2) and simple acceptance (3).

It is important that on a correct view of the problem we are trying to solve, it is not necessary to argue against the rationality of option (1). Still less is it necessary to argue against the rationality of (2). It is consistent with everything I have said in order to solve the given problem that these reactions should be reasonable. What is theoretically needed is only to explain the reasonableness of simple acceptance, or option (3), in the cases where it is reasonable—and then to show that there *are* such cases.

Faced with the idea of apparent alternatives and faced with a Humean explanation of why I confront the particular practices I do confront, I may accept these practices because I find that no alternatives come to life for me. Even if I cannot muster a further or vindicatory explanation for them,[14] I may reflect that my own life is rooted in these practices and scarcely meaningful to me outside them. And what is more, this may be the most reasonable kind of reflection for me to pursue (especially where I sensibly resolve to hold my mind open to any criticisms that others may in due course urge against these practices). Of course, if the social order that sustains and is sustained by these practices is manifestly unjust, this may not be a reasonable reaction. But if matters are not as bad as that—if there is some semblance of a 'proportion between people' the preservation of which preserves my society better than any alternative that comes to light in the process of criticism[15]—then why is it not reasonable to choose option (3), leaving intact the presumptive link between judgement and will? (Remember that I am not attempting to demonstrate here the *un*reasonableness of all other options.)

So far, the Humean explanation of normativity is not a distinctively cognitivist one (though I have tried to ensure at each point that the explanation should be consistent with cognitivism). What a self-announced cognitivist must now add is some mention of the possibility that one who is participating in a practice may succeed in showing that the practice exists because it is *good* to behave thus and so. There has to be the possibility that the reason why we think it obligatory to *A* is that it *really is* obligatory to *A*. What the cognitivist then adds to the story is the possibility of objective vindication. Never mind here exactly how a cognitivist might attempt this; but note that in the neo-Humean picture, this vindication *presupposes* the passions. It does not call them into being *ex nihilo*. Note also that in the neo-Humean picture the passions need not be required to hold themselves in abeyance pending the production of an objective vindication. Objective validation accrues, if it accrues at all, to a going practice.

IX

It is possible then, whether objective vindication is available or not, to be reasonably confirmed in option (3). When one is so confirmed, one will often find oneself confronted with the obligatoriness of an act for which one has no inclination whatever (except insofar as the obligatoriness itself is going to lend one an inclination) or the obligatoriness of an act for which there is some powerful counter-inclination. But even then, by virtue of one's identification with the practices one is involved in, so soon as the obligatoriness of the act appears, this can still afford one a reason for doing the act. (Which is not to say that one may not also have a reason *not* to do the act.) No doubt the obligation will appear in this case as a constraint, or as something coming as if from outside oneself. Or as Kant describes the case in his terms:

> If the will [413] is not of itself in complete accord with reason (the actual case of men), then the actions which are recognised as objectively necessary are subjectively contingent, and the determination of such a will according to objective laws is constraint.

But on all descriptions—the Humean, the neo-Humean, and the Kantian, despite their many differences—it is perfectly possible for the constraint to be a constraint that is not conditional on any inclination past, present, or future, and a constraint that the agent accepts as not conditional on any inclination past, present, or future, and that it is reasonable for him to accept on these terms.

X

There is little chance of this sort of answer to the problem being seen as any answer at all unless (even at risk of repetition) I emphasize four points.

First, on a proper view of the phenomenon itself that is to be explained, the connection we have to explain (viz., between the affirmation of a judgement and some constraint on the will that is not itself conditional upon inclination) is only a presumptive and normal connection.

Second, in our picture, what affirmation of a judgement provides is a reason for the will to see itself as unconditionally constrained to act in some other way, and a good reason. We do not say that this reason is always a better reason than any other reason there might be for acting in another way that excludes the obligatory act. But then, on any ordinary view of the relation between morality and practical reason, this is surely an advantage. If (say) my whole life will be affected for the bad by keeping the promise to meet you at a certain time and place, it would surely be insane for me to keep the promise, even if I could not warn you in advance. Of course a promise is a promise for all that. But how I must *recognize* that fact here is by making full subsequent amends to you, not by faulting some only 'prima facie' obligation that you who turned up for our appointment (apparently wrongly?) supposed flowed from my promise.

The third point to be made is this. It may be objected that, if I simply accept the social morality I find myself in the midst of, and if I accept it because of some attachment I have to the welfare of the larger enterprise in which I see myself as belonging, and I accept it because I can see that my life is rooted there and could not be rooted anywhere else, then it is only my *inclinations*, or my lack of contrary inclinations, that retain me. It may then be said that the obligatoriness that attaches in this account to a required act is not a categorical obligatoriness. It is merely conditional or hypothetical. But that would be an error, and a *non-sequitur*. The *content* of the judgement that *A* is what I ought to do carries no reference whatever to my inclinations: and it gives one who accepts it and is fully engaged in his or her moral practices in the way I have described a reason to do *A* that is not itself conditional upon past, present, or future desires or inclinations. In Hume's picture of the rational possibility of an artificial virtue, I can do *A because it is just*, say. Of course inclinations enter somewhere in the account of what makes the engagement possible that makes it possible for the agent to be furnished with this sort of reason. But the reason itself that he has is as unconditional as the obligatoriness from which it arises. Surely the objector wilfully *mislocates* inclinations in the Humean aetiology of my having a reason to do *A*.

The fourth and final point I must note is that I have been content here to explain what gives agents a reason for an act without attending very much to the question whether they *ought* to find this a reason, that is, logically ought. But that is only what is to be expected from a Humean naturalist.[16] No doubt, if psychological egoism were true, then it would be necessary to argue from a standing start for the validity or reasonableness of the non-egoistic considerations that I say count with people as giving them a reason. But, as Hume showed, there is nothing to suggest that psychological egoism is true, and much to suggest that it is false. More damaging to the account would be to say absolutely nothing about what can give one a reason to accord a motivationally overwhelming *importance* to a categorical judgement accepted as categorical. But again we must be suitably impressed by the considerations that actually work to that effect. 'Only a worm would do [or fail to do that]', we may reflect. And the reflection is a powerful one. It lends extra strength—and it is possible to understand within a framework such as Hume's (or Aristotle's) how and why it lends extra strength—to a reason that already possesses all the force of all the considerations that backed the unconditional requirements not to do that [or not to fail to do that].

XI

So much for one account of normativity that is open to a Humean and open also to a cognitivist of Humean formation, who may or may not keep in reserve his further claim that vindicating explanations are possible for some of our moral and political beliefs. But can the reductive naturalist, the naturalist who provoked G. E. Moore's indignation, participate in this kind of explanation? It might seem that he ought to be able to do so because he may have explanatory aspirations comparable to Hume's, *as well as* reductive aspirations and aspirations to put ethics on a more effective or operational basis. The chief questions that then arise are (1) whether his denial of the *sui generis* character of moral predicates will permit him to catch that which is distinctive in ideas like that of obligatoriness (here I echo the open question argument); and (2) whether, in his own very special reductive terms, this naturalist can make as intelligible as a Humean can the attachment that a human agent may feel for the practices in which he sees the significance of his life as rooted. Is it consistent with the reductive remit to offer the sort of explanation that the Humean naturalist can offer of what the ordinary person can have a reason to do?

I have real doubts under both heads. When the naturalist reconstructs moral predicates, I suspect he loses hold of moral properties altogether. What I feel most certain of however is that these are problems not for cognitivism as such (its difficulties lie elsewhere, such as they are) but (at worst) for the naturalistic version of cognitivism that we must explain by using Moore's extremely special (though well enough definable) sense of 'natural'.

Notes

1. 'It is sufficient that this is experienced to be a principle in human nature', he says, at *Inquiry into the Principles of Morals* V. Part II, footnote, (178). A sociobiologist would scarcely be content to stop there. And no doubt he would have other reservations about Hume's construction. See, e.g. J. L. Mackie, *Persons and Values*, Essay XVII.

2. This was Hume's position, I believe. For an attempt to vindicate the cognitive aspiration against the claim that it involves an error, see my *Needs, Values, Truth*, pp. 103–8, 185–211. For my own view of the impact upon the cognitive aspiration of the question of the origin of morality see ibid. pp. 67–8, 195–200, 351–60.

3. Casimir Lewy, 'G. E. Moore and the Naturalistic Fallacy', *Proceedings of the British Academy* L, pp. 251–62. See also Aurel Kolnai, 'The Ghost of the Naturalistic Fallacy', *Philosophy* 55.

4. On this view, Moore's discussion in *Principia* of what exists/has existed/will exist in time is to be seen as an (erroneous and unfortunate) further elucidation of the idea of the 'subject matter of the natural sciences'.

5. See Lewy, 'G. E. Moore and the Naturalistic Fallacy', fn. 3.

6. *Needs, Values, Truth* p. 134. It is possible that the open question argument appears empty or captious when it is directed against Peter Railton's particular proposal. But, if that is how things appear, it will be salutary to notice how breezily that proposal overlooks the claim of a more deontological or normative conception of goodness and badness in acts. The proposal simply ignores the powerful idea that there are some acts one must have no part in, unless somehow forced to do so. (It is arguable that Moore himself relaxed his grip on the full potency of the open question argument when he concluded later in *Principia* that it is obligatory for us to produce the most probable maximum of intrinsic good. Could an act not promise this without itself being good, or obligatory?)

7. Wittgenstein, 'Lecture on Ethics', *Philosophical Review* (1965).

8. See Kant, *Foundations of the Metaphysics of Morals* (trans L. J. Beck). [414]: The categorical imperative would be one which presented an action as of itself objectively necessary without regard to any other end.

9. Wittgenstein, 'Lecture on Ethics'.

10. Even Hume seems sometimes to exaggerate the problem—if we read his account of it from the same distance at which we need to be in order to understand his delimitation of the province of 'real existence and matter of fact':

> We must also point out that connexion betwixt the relation [on which moral judgements are based] and the will and must prove that this connexion is so necessary that *in every well-disposed mind* it must take its place and have its influence. (My italics, Treatise III.3.1)

Either this description is truistic (a mind is well-disposed if and only if its will is suitably inclined) or it is too strong to speak here of every well disposed mind. 'We are stealing', the starving multitude may say, meaning by that just the same as might be meant by 'You are stealing', uttered by the outraged managers of the supermarket chain they had no alternative but to descend upon. Is the starving multitude by definition ill-disposed? Or if it is, then ought Hume to have chosen to make his point by reference to the 'well-disposed'? Well it all depends, I suppose, on how strong the claim is that Hume wants to make. (Perhaps *that* is not clear.)

11. Of course this naturalist takes those cognitive aspirations far more seriously than Hume himself thought possible. See again *Needs, Values, Truth*, ch. 5.

12. I assume that Hume's account of the distinction between natural and artificial virtues and of the motivational possibility of the artificial virtues is only improved if we replace the *Treatise*'s concern with self-love by the *Inquiry*'s emphasis on fellow-feeling and humanity. I also assume (contrary to what Kant must have believed) that Hume's explanation of how we may be attached to something as artificial as justice can be made to explain our attachment to justice as an attachment to justice *as justice*, justice being

considered now in a manner strictly at variance with Hume's official doctrine of the objects of moral approval and disapproval—viz. that they can only be the durable principles or qualities of the mind—and as a property of moral beauty in practices or observances themselves (as at *Treatise*, pp. 484, 500).

13. *Needs, Values, Truth*, pp. 117–20 and ch. 5; Hume, 'Of the Standard of Taste' see passage quoted in *Needs, Values, Truth*, p. 198; John McDowell, 'Values and Secondary Qualities', in Ted Honderich (ed.), *Morality and Objectivity*.

14. For vindicatory explanations, see *Needs, Values, Truth*, pp. 150, 156, 354.

15. Dante's *De Monarchia* definition of justice as *proportio hominis ad hominem quae servata servat hominum societatem*. For the attempt to arrive at a needs-involving account of justice in this kind of way, see *Needs, Values, Truth*, ch. 1.

16. I do not mean to deny that a Humean can attempt a critical, properly normative account of rationality—only to stress that such an account must begin with people and their reasons as they actually are, and with the ends that they actually have. Cp. *Needs, Values, Truth*, p. 122. It cannot begin in the void.

14

Reply to David Wiggins

Peter Railton

I hope in this reply briefly to explore some differences and similarities in the views of David Wiggins and myself, and, in so doing, to locate the sort of naturalism I am exploring more clearly on the philosophical landscape.

1. Naturalism (and Cognitivism)

Wiggins takes the fact that I 'disjoin and/or conjoin' the labels 'naturalism' and 'cognitivism' to be evidence that I think the two views coincide. I would not ordinarily expect disjoining and conjoining to give this impression, so I certainly join Wiggins in insisting that they are distinct.[1]

One can be a cognitivist without being a naturalist (as, for example, the Intuitionists were) or a naturalist without being a cognitivist (as, for example, some contemporary expressivists are). In the essay under discussion, my interest lay in exploring a specifically *naturalistic* cognitivism. David Wiggins' remarks indicate to me that I need to say more about what the view I have in mind amounts to.

As Wiggins points out, there are several ways in which one might be a naturalist. He draws special attention to two, 'Humean or explanatory naturalism' and naturalism of the kind 'that enraged Moore' (p. 301).[2] I believe I understand his distinction, but would like to suggest a slightly different, though related, way of dividing things up. A *methodological naturalist* is someone who adopts an a posteriori, explanatory approach to an area of human practice or discourse, such as epistemology, semantics, or ethics. This fits what Wiggins says about Hume. A *substantive naturalist* is someone who proposes a semantic interpretation of the concepts in some area of practice or discourse in terms of properties or relations that would 'pull their weight' within empirical science.[3] This fits with what Wiggins says about enraging Moore, for certainly the naturalists who enraged Moore were substantive naturalists in this sense. Like Wiggins' two naturalisms, methodological and substantive naturalism need not go together. A methodological naturalist might be led to a view of the discourse he studies that is not substantively naturalistic. This appears to be Wiggins' image of Hume on morality. Similarly, a substantive naturalist might put forward his semantic interpretation on wholly a priori grounds. That is what happens in so-called Analytic Naturalism, the target of Moore's attacks.

Wiggins expresses interest in a 'careful inventory of the theoretical possibilities'. Unfortunately, however, when Wiggins considers possible combinations of his two sorts of naturalism, he notices only Analytic Naturalism:

> Obviously a theorist of [the Humean] persuasion might want to offer some 'philosophical analysis' of moral predicates and thereby represent them as coextensive with naturalistic predicates. (p. 302)[4]

A position that Wiggins has failed to inventory is substantive naturalism defended on methodologically naturalistic grounds, as part of an explanatory theory of what is going on in the area of discourse or practice under study rather than as a piece of 'philosophical analysis'. The result of such an explanatory theory in ethics might be, for example, a synthetic claim identifying a moral property with some complex natural property.[5] It is this overlooked sort of naturalism that I had in mind.

Now Wiggins writes that even if Moore never established that substantive naturalism involves an outright fallacy, nevertheless 'one might insist that he always did have a real argument', the open question argument (p. 303). But the open question argument engages directly only those substantive naturalists who defend their accounts of moral discourse as a 'philosophical analysis', since the open question test applies only to (purported) analytic truths. Moore himself is at pains to make this clear, going so far as to say at one point that his argument can be summarized in the (peculiar) claim that all truths about good are synthetic.[6]

Of course, something like the open question test can be used to generate evidence for or against any a posteriori account that claims to preserve significant continuity with existing linguistic usage, but this is quite different from the outright refutation it is supposed to provide of analytic definitions of 'good'.[7]

The sort of naturalist I wish to consider is at heart a methodological rather than substantive naturalist, and therefore sets himself the task of searching for an a posteriori account of the origin, nature, and function of moral discourse and practice. He does not commit himself in advance to substantive naturalism—or to cognitivism, for that matter. If the best a posteriori account of moral discourse attributes expressive rather than cognitive meaning to moral expressions, my sort of naturalist would end up arguing that what Wiggins aptly calls the 'cognitive aspiration' of moral discourse cannot be vindicated. Certainly non-cognitivism does provide significant insight into the nature and function of moral discourse and practice, and that was the starting point for my original discussion. The possibility I sought to explore is one in which methodological naturalism might lead—via a synthetic identity claim—to an a posteriori vindication of the cognitive aspiration of moral discourse, without thereby rendering moral judgements systematically false, as they are according to 'error theories'.

2. Reductionism

Is the naturalism I have in mind reductionist? In principle, it need not be. One could, for example, hold that in the best a posteriori account of moral properties they emerge as irreducible natural properties—supervenient upon the non-moral to be sure, but able to 'pull their weight' in the sciences in their own right. That is, moral properties might simultaneously be natural and *sui generis*.[8] However, my naturalist finds such a position unsatisfactory for various reasons, and instead entertains a reductionist hypothesis, a synthetic identification of the property of moral value with a complex non-moral property. He does so because he believes the identification can contribute to our understanding of morality and its place in our world—including such matters as semantic and epistemic access to moral properties—while preserving important features of the normative role of moral value.

Now I recognize that there is a specialized usage of 'realist', according to which only the believer in *sui generis*, irreducible properties of kind K is a K-realist. In this sense, my naturalist is not a moral realist. However, it seems to me that whether any given reduction should be viewed as eliminative depends upon the purported nature of the thing reduced and the actual character of the reduction base. Thus, the existence of micro-reductions of macroscopic properties in chemistry or thermodynamics in itself casts no doubt upon the reality of the macroscopic properties. The identification of salt crystals with matrices of NaCl, for example, hardly prompts irrealist or anti-realist reflexes about salt. Quite the contrary, this reduction vindicates the common-sense view that salt is a definite and distinctive form of matter, plentiful in the oceans, soluble in water, effective as a preservative, corrosive to ferrous metals, and so on. Indeed, *failure* to discover a plausible reduction—as in cases like phlogiston, caloric fluid, and vital force—has been an important source of eliminativist thoughts.[9] Some reductions explain away the reduced phenomenon, but others simply explain it—and thereby show it to be well-founded.

A successful, vindicative, identificatory reduction of moral value could help the case for moral realism if it could provide a foundation for moral value that removes some of the mystery surrounding this notion while at the same time providing support for many of its central characteristics. For example, a reductive identification might indicate how moral value could be, on the one hand, a property to which we have epistemic and semantic access, and, on the other, a property which, through identifiable psychological processes, could engage people motivationally in the ways characteristic of moral properties. Similarly, a reductive identification might help us to understand how certain patterns of moral disagreement could persist, despite the cognitive character of moral discourse, and to understand as well the supervenience of the moral upon the non-moral to which Moore drew notice. Demystification of moral value—and of moral epistemology, language, 'normative force', and supervenience—would point toward eliminativism only if moral value were somehow (as some appear to believe) essentially elusive and mysterious.

I should hasten to add that an interest in reduction need not reflect a commitment to Metaphysical Naturalism—the view that the world contains only natural properties. It can be informative to find a reduction basis for a range of properties *R* within a range of properties *S*, even without any claim to the effect that *S* is utterly comprehensive. A reduction of *R* to *S* could none the less tell us about the place of *R* in the world, and would be of special interest if there existed a well-developed theory of properties of kind *S*, or if properties of kind *S* were less problematic in some way than those of kind *R* seemed (before the reduction) to be.

For example, some are interested in the reduction of the psychological to the physical because they are committed to Physicalism. Yet one might wish to remain open-minded about whether all properties—including, say, those of mathematics—are physical properties, while at the same time being interested in determining whether, and to what extent, psychological properties can be reduced to physical properties. One's interest might derive from a desire to understand the place of psychological phenomena in nature, or to account for seemingly asymmetric supervenience of the psychological upon the physical. Moreover, a reduction of the psychological, if possible, could make a signal contribution to theory development, because physically-oriented theories are in a number of respects better developed than psychology, and more amenable to experimentation. Physiology, for example, is more directly linked than psychology to powerful underlying theories in biochemistry, molecular biology, and genetics.

Such talk of theory development in ethics may strike some as simply wrong-headed, and Wiggins indeed appears sympathetic to a view he attributes to Moore, that reductive naturalism is 'crude [and] scientistic' (p. 304). Scientism, I suppose, is the view that all genuine phenomena are within the scope of the scientific method, and that no other means can issue in any legitimate form of knowing. But a naturalist interested in reduction in ethics need not believe that there is such a thing as 'the scientific method' (certainly the history and sociology of science give us reason for doubting this) or that all truths in ethics are accessible to us through some mechanical, fact-gathering, 'value-neutral' procedure.

We will return to the charge of scientism shortly. But first, let me expand a bit on my naturalist's view of things.

My naturalist believes that the natural and social sciences have drawn a broad—in some ways detailed, in other ways quite general—picture of the world and our situation in it. This picture situates humans in nature, and incorporates various mechanisms by which they come to interact with each other and the world, including mechanisms that afford humans the wherewithal to represent the world (where 'represent' is understood in some suitably thin sense) and to act upon and communicate these representations. The picture also involves various explanations—not only biological, but also social and historical—of how humans and their beliefs and practices have evolved, and how it has been possible for us to effect changes in ourselves, in one another, and in our circumstances. The naturalist asks: where in this picture of behaviour, language, knowledge, and the world might morality fit?

Here is one possibility. Anthropologists assure us that humans have long regulated and co-ordinated their social behaviour by means of internalized norms of discourse and conduct (where 'norms', also, is understood in some suitably thin sense). These norms include those of language, custom, 'saving face', law, religion, and so on. Recognizably moral norms have emerged (perhaps, as yet, only partially) within this constellation of social regulative forms, distinguished in part by their tendency toward generalized sympathy and impartiality in assessment, and in part by the absence of appeals to authority—wordly or other-worldly—to silence requests for justification. Of course, as societies and individuals have changed, so has opinion about what is morally good or right. My naturalist is interested in asking to what extent the emergence of distinctively moral assessment, as well as the variation in moral opinion, can be understood as an evolving response to certain empirically-accessible properties within a setting of changing non-moral beliefs and social circumstances. His thought is that appeal to these properties might contribute to the explanation both of the range of substantive moral judgements actually made and of the special sort of motivational force that moral judgements typically have had. Such an explanatory enterprise, if reasonably successful, would provide support for his claim that these particular properties figure in an account of the *content* of moral judgements.[10]

There are, of course, competing accounts of what is going on in moral discourse and of why it has emerged and evolved as it has—error theories, non-cognitivism, non-naturalism, and so on. My naturalist believes that the choice among these accounts should be made on the basis of a posteriori merits, and cannot be settled by a simple a priori conceptual test such as the open question argument. As a result, my naturalist is interested in how these competing accounts could be fit into explanatory theories of moral practice, semantics, and epistemology, and into more comprehensive theories of society, language, and knowledge. Does his interest in the comparative virtues of these accounts of morality, understood as components of an enterprise in which empirical explanation plays a central role, make his approach scientistic? If it does, where is the sting?

Perhaps the sting is meant to come not with the label 'scientism' as such, but with an adjective Wiggins uses in its company: 'crude'. Typically, even vindicative reductions are in some measure deflationary, if only of a pre-theoretical presumption of the *sui generis* character of the area of discourse in question. The reduction of water to H_2O, for example, denies water the special status it has been accorded as one of the few basic, irreducible elements of the universe. Similarly, any reduction of good will deny it the elemental status Moore claimed it to have. But I find nothing crude in the reduction of water to H_2O, and fail to see why a reduction of good must be any worse in this regard. No doubt all proposed reductions of good, mine included, are too crude as they stand.[11] The point of offering them despite their crudity is to provide a basis for further development and refinement of our understanding of the phenomena in question. If one takes the attitude that all substantive naturalistic proposals are—because preliminary and crude—

beneath consideration, a chance to see where theory development might lead will be lost.

Wiggins associates yet another set of adjectives with 'scientism', listing as a distinguishing feature of his second, Moore-enraging sort of naturalism that it is 'operationalist', interested in 'the reduction of moral problems to a certain sort of calculation' by means of an 'instrumentally' useful criterion of moral value (pp. 302–3). Historically, some naturalists have indeed been interested in operationalization of moral judgement, partly for the quite respectable reason that they felt a 'purely speculative' (p. 302) approach to morality would give aid and comfort to a not-very-savoury social *status quo*.[12] But, contrary to Wiggins' suggestion, the substantive naturalist who follows a naturalistic method must view as open questions how and to what extent moral knowledge might be attainable by actual persons, and with what implications for moral deliberation.

If these are open questions, then why is my naturalist so concerned to advance a particular reduction? One reason for pursuing the definiteness involved in hypothesizing a given reduction is that it is difficult to assess the adequacy of a cognitivist account of moral discourse which, like some contemporary anti-reductionist accounts, says little that is definite about the substantive content of that discourse. A more definite account is more readily subject to criticism, contributing to the location—and, where possible, remedying—of difficulties. Moreover, as I attempted to indicate, it may be precisely in the content of moral evaluation that we find an answer to some basic questions about the normativity of moral judgement—morality may be viewed as having the normative status it does in part because it has the content it does. In saying this, I believe I am in agreement with Wiggins, who urges that the naturalistic cognitivist must show how the normativity of moral evaluation 'accrues to' its content (p. 306).[13]

3. Normativity

Let us consider how it might come about that normativity accrues to substantive naturalistic content. Since Wiggins introduces his discussion of normativity by considering the phenomenon of obligation, let us try starting there as well. Wiggins quotes Wittgenstein:

> Supposing that I could play tennis and one of you saw me playing and said 'Well, you play pretty badly' and suppose I answer 'I know, I'm playing badly but I don't want to play any better', all the other man could say would be 'Ah, then, that's all right'. But suppose I had told one of you a preposterous lie and he came up to me and said 'You're behaving like a beast' and then I were to say 'I know I behave badly, but then I don't want to behave any better', could he then say 'Ah, then that's all right'? Certainly not; he would say 'Well, you ought to want to behave better'.[14]

As a description, this seems plausible enough. It may be tempting to think that the explanation of the difference in normative force between a judgement that one is playing poor tennis and a judgement that one is behaving like a beast must reside in the difference between that which is incumbent upon an individual only hypothetically—in this case, dependent upon the contingent goal of playing tennis well—that which is imperative in an absolute sense, independent of inclination. As Wittgenstein says in the second passage quoted by Wiggins:

> The right road is the road which leads to an arbitrarily predetermined end and it is quite clear to us all that there is no sense in talking about the right road apart from such a predetermined goal. Now let us see what we could possibly mean by the expression '*the* absolutely right road'. It think it would be the road which everybody on seeing it would, *with logical necessity*, have to go, or be ashamed for not going. And similarly the *absolute good*, if it is a describable state of affairs, would be one which *everybody*, independent of his tastes and inclinations, would *necessarily* bring about or feel guilty for not bringing about.[15]

Wiggins argues that in order to account for the normativity of moral judgement, the naturalist who would avoid scepticism about morality must show how his reduction of moral judgements preserves the fact that one who affirms a moral judgement

> (a) is committed to see himself as having a reason to . . . act that is a reason regardless of any other reasons he may be afforded by conflicting ends or inclinations. (p. 306)

And, moreover, as Wiggins notes, a reduction must account for the fact that moral judgements

> (b) No doubt . . . can also come charged with the idea of a suitable retribution upon anyone who should transgress its requirements. (p. 306)

How might features (a) and (b) accrue to the content of moral judgement if that content is given naturalistically?

Return to Wittgenstein's example about tennis and lying. Very roughly, my naturalist would say that the difference between playing tennis poorly and lying is grounded in the fact that how well or ill one plays tennis seldom matters much to the well-being of others, whereas lying, and beastliness generally, usually do. Moreover, lying, unlike tennis, is something that affects the most common and important sorts of relations among individuals, and partly for this reason, lying is something that individuals are both tempted to do in order to advance their own goals and liable to sanction for—at a minimum, by loss of the benefits of trust.

The naturalist seeks to reconstruct moral discourse in such a way that the notion of 'morally wrong' tracks behaviours with the features just associated with lying, while 'morally permitted' tracks behaviours with characteristics closer to playing tennis poorly.[16] Then, as in the case of 'water' tracking H_2O, the naturalist will say that these features properly figure in an account of the content of 'morally wrong' and 'morally permitted'—though not necessarily in the intentions of those using the moral vocabulary.

Can we use these features to explain why characteristics (a) and (b) 'accrue to' moral judgements? Surely these features do help to explain why there has developed around lying a social practice that condemns non-trivial lying, independent of the inclinations of those who would lie, and that deems it suitable to apply sanctions to those who lie. Similarly, these features help explain why no such practice has developed around playing tennis poorly.[17]

On this account, the reason that we have for not lying—and for participating in social sanctions against lying—ultimately resides in the various sorts of harm that lying typically effects. This tendency to produce harm is in general a sufficiently weighty concern to account for the importance we attach to truthfulness. By contrast, where there exist identifiable classes of cases in which lies are regarded as *typically* harmless—perhaps even less harmful than unrelenting truth-telling—such as 'white lies', we do not find similar opprobrium attaching to lying.

The harm arising from lying affords an *objective* reason, one that does not much depend upon the agent's particular inclinations or interests. The defender of the view that moral judgements express *absolute* or *categorical* reasons will not find such an account sufficient, for he wishes to find something like the connection that Kant had in mind when he spoke of objective necessity, or that Wittgenstein apparently had in mind when he spoke of 'logical necessity'.

But on Wiggins' account, like mine, the views of Kant and Wittgenstein exaggerate the force of moral judgement. For example, it seems to me no mark against the *correctness* of my judging that an individual has behaved badly from a moral point of view that this person can agree with my judgement without either shame or irrationality. Perhaps he is someone who feels no force from considerations unconnected to his own interests, or those of kith and kin. Perhaps the objective reasons for not lying fail to motivate him, so that they are not reasons *for him* in a way that his ignoring them would give rise to irrationality on his part. He lacks human fellow-feeling, not reasoning or deliberating capacities. 'I agree with you that morality demands I should sometimes sacrifice the interests of my own people in order to respect the interests of my enemies, and I say, so much the worse for morality', he remarks without shame, apology, or—as far as I can see—misuse of language or irrationality.

Of course, most people are not like this. They are not wholly unmoved by the suffering of others, even their enemies, or by the prospect of alienating themselves from others through deception. Nor are they entirely without interest in defending their conduct from a disinterested perspective. Nor do they find compensating benefits to offset fully the likelihood of ostracism or punishment for immoral behaviour. These facts about most people most of the time are central to the explanation of why morality has emerged as a persistent and important phenomenon in human societies.

At a general level, then, there are regular connections between judgements of moral obligation (for example) and facts about human motivation. Were these facts about motivation radically different, the very idea of moral obligation would never have taken hold. None of this requires endorsement of Kant's idea of a categorical imperative, or Wittgenstein's idea of 'the coercive power of an absolute judge'. That, I think, is fortunate. If the normative force of morality did depend upon such notions, we would be on a short road to scepticism.

It might be objected that my naturalist is already a sceptic, that in a post-Kantian world the idea that moral reasons, if they exist, must be both independent of inclination and able to exert a necessary effect upon the will, is seen to be part of the concept of moral judgement. Then my naturalist must say that *this* notion of the absoluteness of morality will go by the board in his reduction of moral assessment, in much the same way that the elementhood of water did. The objection could then be restated: such revisionism is tantamount to eliminativism.

I take it that the objection is not very plausible in the case of water and H_2O. How plausible is it in the moral case? In the first place, it is hardly clear that the rather singular Kantian conception of absoluteness is essential to our common-sense understanding of moral judgement. Second, it seems rash to speak of eliminativism when the revisionist story preserves much of the connection between moral evaluation and specific, central human concerns and practices, and captures as well many of our actual moral judgements. And third, the revisionist story is of a kind that, I believe, brings into view a compelling picture of how moral assessment is to receive what Wiggins calls 'objective vindication' (p. 309), to which we now briefly turn.

4. Vindication

Wiggins wishes to locate the normative force of moral judgement in the developed sentiments an agent must possess in order that he be genuinely 'in the midst of' going social practices 'in which he sees the significance of his life as rooted' (p. 308). If these social practices include some obligations, such that certain acts that are required of an agent regardless of his inclinations, then once he is fully a part of these practices he will 'often find [him]self confronted with the obligatoriness of an act for which [he] has no inclination whatever (except insofar as the obligatoriness itself is going to lend [him] an inclination)' (p. 309).

This much is uncontroversial, in my naturalist's view. But it clearly does not capture the whole of the normativity of morality. For the description given thus far is a perfectly generic account of obligatoriness, which could apply to social requirements of an immoral or morally indifferent character, so long as they reproduce themselves in part through individual internalization of norms involving 'oughtiness'. Wiggins apparently agrees, since he holds that the reasonableness of an individual's going along with prevalent norms depends not only upon whether the individual is 'rooted' in the system of norms, but also upon whether the social arrangements that underlie them are or are not 'manifestly unjust' (p. 308).

Now the question that immediately arises is whether this additional, substantive condition also is tied to the developed sentiments of the socially-situated agent being judged (as distinct from the speaker). If it is, then an unwanted relativism may be built into the account of the normativity of morality: agents rooted in the norms of caste societies, slave-holding societies, or societies founded upon religious intolerance would come to have, by virtue of their embeddedness in these social practices and their developed sentiments, obligations to uphold these practices even in the face of contrary personal inclination—for example an empathetic inclination to treat a personally-known social 'inferior' or heretic as an equal. If, alternatively, the additional, substantive condition is not tied to the developed sentiments of socially-situated agents, then relativism may be avoidable, but the resulting view be externalist, lessening the contrast with my naturalist's.[18]

Wiggins adds another condition that must be met if his account of normativity is to point, as he hopes it will, in a distinctively cognitivist direction. It must be possible that 'one who is participating in a practice may succeed in showing that the practice exists because it is *good* to behave thus and so' (p. 309).

Now I am not convinced that the prospect of every sort of *cognitivism* depends upon the possibility of such a demonstration, for cognitivism is a thesis about the liability of moral judgements to truth *or* falsity, and can be held by an error theorist. None the less, the prospect of the sort of naturalistic vindication of our moral practices that I have been considering surely does depend upon meeting Wiggins' condition. For part of my naturalist's thinking is the idea that some explanations are justifications, and my naturalist follows this idea in investigating the possibility of a *vindicative* reduction of moral assessment.

In the case of epistemic naturalism, this idea of vindicative explanation expresses itself roughly as follows: if our beliefs can be explained as the result of a reliable mechanism, then that explanation can also contribute a central ingredient in their (reliabilist) epistemic justification. In the case of ethical naturalism, the idea of vindicative explanation may take the following form: if (for example) we can explain our judgements of moral goodness as tracking features of individual conduct and social practice that contribute to well-being, impartially assessed, then this explanation can also supply a central ingredient in their moral justification. This would be a case of showing that a norm-invoking practice exists and is sustained 'because it is *good* to behave thus and so'. Contrast an explanation of our moral judgements that would have them tracking arbitrary social conventions unconnected with—or even opposed to—human well-being, and sustained by our unwillingness to entertain genuine alternatives.

I therefore find myself eager, like Wiggins, to meet this further, explanatory condition. So I think Wiggins and I may be in some agreement about what a satisfactory, vindicative account of the normativity of morality of the kind we have in mind would involve: giving a methodologically naturalistic account of how social practices could come to have the features of moral obligation (features (a) and (b), above); showing that these practices are not at odds with what is morally good or just; and providing an explanation of how these practices arose and are sustained in which their being morally good or right plays a genuine role.[19]

Where Wiggins and I do seem to disagree, in a way that puzzles me and makes me fear I am simply missing something, is that, while I believe an appropriate naturalistic reduction can furnish essential ingredients for this sort of vindicative account of morality, Wiggins appears to think that reduction stands in the way of vindication and that treating moral properties as *sui generis* somehow helps.[20] In particular, he concludes his discussion by remarking that treating moral properties as *sui generis* helps to explain the notion of obligation and to promote movement along the road to 'objective vindication'.

Yet a reductionist of my sort can say everything Wiggins says about how obligation is realized in social practices through the internalization of norms. And a reductionist of my sort can say everything Wiggins says about the ways individuals draw meaning and significance from the social practices with which they identify, in such a way that they may have grounds for action in accord with internalized norms but contrary to personal inclination. Of course, my sort of reductionist cannot capture Kant's or Wittgenstein's idea of obligation without some deflation. But Wiggins, too, is deflationary in this regard (pp. 306–7)—as I think any sensible account must be.

Puzzled as I am, I wonder whether there might be a particular misunderstanding at work here. My sort of naturalist reduces moral properties to complex social-psychological phenomena, not to extra-human Nature. At least since Durkheim there has been a naturalistic way of understanding how social phenomena may bring into being in individuals a notion of obligatoriness that will present itself to them as objective and independent of their personal inclinations, even though it is grounded not in Nature—or Reason—but rather in the developed motivational structure and beliefs of those very individuals. Such is the real character, for example, of the sacred. Mention of naturalistic accounts of the sacred may suggest reduction of the non-vindicative sort, for such accounts make no appeal to real divinity in order to explain the nature of the sacred.

However, the sort of reduction my naturalist has in mind for moral properties is vindicative. When we learn that the business of making moral judgements, and of acting upon them in the face of personal inclination, is grounded in a set of practices that have developed in response to the enhancement of human well-being in a social setting, our response is not likely to be 'Well, so the whole thing is a sham, a load of prejudice.' If we look for reasons to take morality seriously beyond mere fear of disapproval or attachment to existing ways of life—both of which could be present for a set of arbitrary or even pernicious social practices—then a content-based connection of morality with well-being can help supply the sought-for rationale.

Depending upon its character, a naturalistic reduction can either demean or redeem a category of social assessment. I suppose that treating a category as *sui generis* or irreducible might be taken as a mark of respect for it *as a category*, but surely it is neutral—at best[21]—with regard to the question whether we should take the category seriously in the conduct of our lives.

I therefore fail to see the (advertised) advantage in accommodating the normativity of morality that Wiggins imputes to his anti-reductionist, non-naturalist approach.

Notes

1. For a discussion of a number of distinct dimensions of possible 'moral realism'—including cognitivism and naturalism—see section II of Peter Railton, 'Moral Realism', *Philosophical Review* 95, pp. 163–207.

2. Unattributed page references in the text refer to David Wiggins' 'Cognitivism, Naturalism, and Normativity: A Reply to Peter Railton', in this volume.

3. This phrase is used by Wiggins in his reconstruction of the distinction Moore wished to draw between natural and non-natural properties. My discussion of two forms of naturalism draws upon Peter Railton, 'Naturalism and Prescriptivity', *Social Philosophy and Policy* 7.

4. Why 'coextensive'? Moore certainly allows that 'good' be coextensive with a naturalistic predicate. I assume that Wiggins here has in mind Moore's view that such coextension could not be guaranteed by any *definition* or *analysis*. See G. E. Moore, *Principia Ethica*, p. 9.

5. Alternatively, the identification could be expressed as a 'reforming definition' of the sort that figures in theory construction, and that is explicitly defended—and revisable—a posteriori. Let us use for the purposes of this discussion not Moore's own definition of 'natural property', but the one Wiggins believes best captures Moore's concerns in *Principia*:

> a *natural* (or *naturalistic*) property is a property with which it is the business of the natural sciences or psychology to deal, or which can be completely defined in terms of these. (p. 303)

6. *Principia*, p. 7. (The claim is peculiar because it implies that a statement such as 'Good is what it is, and not another thing' must be either synthetic or false.)

7. I say 'supposed to provide' because it seems to me that an analysis of a complex concept like 'good' could not be decisively refuted by the sort of direct inspection of concepts that Moore appears to assume when he deploys the open question argument.

8. Something like this possibility is, I take it, the position being explored by Richard W. Miller in 'Ways of Moral Learning', *Philosophical Review* 94, and by Nicholas Sturgeon in 'Moral Explanations', in D. Copp and D. Zimmerman (eds.), *Morality, Reason, and Truth*.

9. I simplify here greatly, for the sake of having ready examples.

10. Wide content, that is, not narrow. No claim is being made here about what an individual speaker must have in his head in order to be competent with the moral vocabulary.

11. I certainly would want to insist that a reduction of moral value is only part of a general theory of morality, and that incorporating such diverse categories of moral assessment as obligation and character requires considerable complexity. I believe that moral value, as understood herein, can play a fundamental role in an explication of obligation and character, but it is not intended in any way to supplant these concepts (compare Wiggins' remarks at p. 312, n. 6). For further discussion, see Peter Railton, 'How Thinking About Character and Utilitarianism Might Lead Us to Rethink the

Character of Utilitarianism', in P. French, T. Uehling Jr., and H. Wettstein (eds.), *Midwest Studies in Philosophy* 13.

12. Compare here the reformist ambitions of Mill with the complacent attitude toward existing moral practice of Moore.

13. Later, Wiggins insists that 'the exigency of this demand that the (moral) judgement places upon the agent who accepts it is part of its *content*, which must, for a cognitivist, mean its *declarative* content' (p. 307). As long as exigency 'accrues to' moral judgements nomologically, *in virtue of* their content, why is it further necessary that the exigency be *part of* their declarative content?

14. Ludwig Wittgenstein, 'Lecture on Ethics', *Philosophical Review* 74, esp. p. 5.

15. Ibid., p. 7.

16. Compare these two cases of the home handyman at work. (1) You look across your fence and see your neighbour sloppily retouching the paint on his car's fender. 'You're doing a pretty bad job,' you note, helpfully. 'I know—I just can't be bothered to do a good job of this,' is the response. And there matters can rest. (2) You look across your fence and see your neighbour sloppily repairing the brakes of his car. 'You're doing a pretty bad job,' you observe. 'I know. I just can't be bothered to do a good job of this,' is again the response. But matters do not rest there—a car with faulty brakes is a menace and your neighbour ought to see to it that a proper job is done. Should we explain the difference between cases (1) and (2) by noting that the domain of car repair is divided into two areas, one governed by merely hypothetical imperatives and the other governed by categorical imperatives? Or isn't the difference—and related differences in, for example, the laws governing car ownership—better explained by noting the greater harm potential of faulty brakes than sloppy paint? How different are these two cases from the pair Wittgenstein considers?

17. In a related way, these features help explain why such norms of conduct as those requiring chastity before marriage or forbidding divorce no longer seem to be central to morality, since views about the harm done by intercourse before marriage or by divorce, as opposed to the harm done by trying to prevent all such behaviour, have changed.

18. There is another way for Wiggins to avoid relativism. He can simply say that the content of *our* use of such terms as 'unjust' and 'wrong' is fixed by our practices, and so the practices of a caste system, or slavery, or religious persecution will not count as just or right. The difficulty here is that this dims any prospect for objective vindication, for the fixing is merely indexical. Would the normativity of morality survive this sort of limitation? Moreover, limited in this way, moral discourse would capture at most judgement internalism, not existence internalism.

19. Does the existence of an identificatory reduction of, say, moral goodness strip that concept of any explanatory role? I cannot see why this should be so. Does the existence of an identificatory reduction of water to H_2O make it no longer explanatory to say 'The radiator was filled with water' in response to a question about why it cracked during a freeze?

20. A further difference, which I will not explore here, is that Wiggins wishes to view moral properties as akin to secondary qualities. In this instance, too, I find myself puzzled at the claim that such treatment helps toward the development of an account of morality that would vindicate its cognitivity. One reason for puzzlement: moral assessments in many areas—perhaps most obviously, in social and political matters—must, if they are to have any title to be taken seriously as claims of objective knowledge, take into account a large number of factors. In such cases (among others), it seems to me problematic to view the moral properties as involving a distinctive, judgement-guiding phenomenology.

21. To whatever extent treating a realm of discourse as *sui generis* becomes a substitute for attributing definite content to it or tracing its relations to other areas of substantive inquiry, then such treatment may make objective vindication more, rather than less, difficult. This will be so especially if reservations about the idea that moral properties are manifest in first-person experience (see previous note) cannot be overcome.

15

A Neglected Position?

David Wiggins

I

Peter Railton has brought about a real clarification of his original essay. The position he holds to have been overlooked is 'substantive ethical naturalism' as 'defended on methodologically naturalist grounds'. Inasmuch as this position is methodologically naturalistic, it arises (as does Railton's general outlook) from an a posteriori (benign in principle) explanatory approach to morality and its practices. Insofar as the neglected position also qualifies as *substantive naturalism* (that is, insofar as it turns out that substantive naturalism is the approach that methodological naturalism decides, against my counsel, to recommend towards moral discourse), what it proposes for moral discourse is 'an interpretation' of moral, normative and valuational concepts. This interpretation is to be 'semantical'. But it is to be given in terms of properties or relations that pull their weight within an empirical science. The semantic interpretation offered by substantive naturalism is to be part of an explanatory theory of 'what is going on' in the area of moral discourse, and such a doubly naturalistic account of morals will have to rest at some point on a synthetic claim *identifying* the moral property by which this or that predicate is interpreted with some complex natural property.

II

Let us begin with the fact that, in the first instance, substantive naturalism represents a semantic interpretation of moral terms. What I say to this is that, if it is really interpretation that naturalism represents itself as offering, then the versions or readings it offers can only be correct if they can be given in some way that makes them recognizable. They can only be correct if those who engage in moral discourse are prepared to see these interpretations as faithful to their own declarative intentions. This is not to deny however that so soon as the interpretive aim has been achieved, with or without some element of sorting or straightening out, the substantive naturalist is at liberty to decide whether to go further and advance the synthetic claim that the moral property imported by his interpretation is none other than some complex natural property. If he is right, then it may indeed turn out that justice (say) is such and such a complex natural property (in Moore's sense of 'natural').

Railton holds that such identifications as this will contribute to our understanding of morality. They can contribute to the philosophical understanding of 'our semantic and epistemic access to moral properties', and they can help us to understand our moral motivation to morality. That is not all. The interest of such philosophical identifications is not only speculative. The identification can have practical import.

That, in brief, is Railton's methodologically motivated substantive (non-analytic) naturalism. There are still some things I find obscure. But in this reprise I will only try to explain the reasons that one who takes the line I take in my reply to his first essay will have for continuing to doubt whether substantive naturalism can escape Moore's objections to naturalism. Once they are put on to a proper basis, Moore's objections will reach further (I shall argue) than 'definitional naturalism'.

I do have to confess, however, that I now see that one effect of pressing these objections in the way I shall press them is to raise a question I can hardly hope to resolve about the relationship between (1) uncontroversially scientific aspirations, (2) social scientific aspirations, (3) the aspirations proper to human interpretive understanding. There is a slide here that Railton will probably claim introduces no discontinuity. What I claim is that, however smooth the transition appears, it carries us from one sort of thing to a qualitatively different sort of thing. My tentative suggestion is that we are carried from aspirations that do not require engagement to aspirations that must however coolly require it. (I should add that the difference is not in my view a difference in respect of cognitivity, but in respect of *what sort of thing* is cognized.) But I note that there might be other accounts of what the slide is between. Someone might think I was right about there being a slide and wrong in my account of its nature. Whatever it amounts to, it is this qualitative difference, not the a posteriority as such of naturalistic identifications, that is drawn to our notice by the open question argument and stands in the way of the substantive naturalist's succeeding in his programme.

III

What is a natural property? Railton expresses himself content with the idea (which he attributes to me at one point but which I derive from Moore's *Principia*, p. 40) that a natural property is a property that pulls its weight within a natural science. (Or, as Railton will prefer to say, pulls its weight within some empirical science.) On this view, every natural property *either* has some specification or other under which it can figure (and figure essentially[1]) in a natural science *or else* can be defined in terms of properties that have some specification or other under which they figure (and figure essentially) in such a science.

According to any minimally adequate view of the sense and reference of property-words,[2] we now have to be ready for the possibility that a given natural property presented by one predicate may have indefinitely many other specifications (be introduced by indefinitely many other predicates). And what we have to remember is that these other specifications of the property will not need to exhibit its satisfaction of Moore's criterion for being natural. It follows that often we shall be unable to tell straight off from the predicate under which some property is first presented to us whether the property is a natural or a non-natural one. A property is only non-natural *tout court* if *no* predicate that presents it either pulls its weight in an experimental science or is definable in terms of such. Of course, it is this point that makes Railton's substantive naturalism a starter. I do not deny that it is a starter. The live question is, how far will it get?

IV

Consider then the substantive naturalist's synthetic identity claim: such and such a value property V is the same as the natural property X. All we have agreed so far is that what this must amount to is that the property V is to be a property discernible by an interest in the ethical or the aesthetic as such and the property X is to be a property that counts as natural by the criterion stated in Section III *sup*. What more can be said about the difference between the interest in the ethical or aesthetic and the interest in the natural?

If a philosopher like Moore were to be persuaded by the account that I offered in the first reply to Railton of the proper working of the open question argument and that I would still back against '$V = X$', then he would have to describe in his own Moorean way the difference between the ethical or aesthetic interest in value and the theoretical cum explanatory interest in the prediction and control of natural or social processes. But putting the matter in my own way, I should say that, in the case of an ethical or aesthetic interest, the only way to characterize that kind of interest is by reference to the proper response to the value in question. In its original or pure form, the proper response, whatever else it is, will be a response of engagement. More specifically, this will not be the response of merely believing item x to have value V but the response of *finding* V in x. In the second place, this response will be keyed not to the question whether everyone reacts in such and such a way to item x *qua* possessed of V but to the question whether one is oneself to concur in this reaction. In the third place, if a value has *qua* moral or aesthetic to have some connection with feeling (the particular feeling depending on the particular value), then, in the cases where feeling connects with will, finding the value in x must have some however indirect connection with the will. On the other hand, none of this, neither the point about the response being one of engagement nor any point about the however indirect connection with the will, has to hold of the purely empirical interest that descries this or that natural property.

That interest is concerned with prediction and retrodiction or with the possible connections of the property with other properties annexed to other interests of this character.

V

Where Railton envisages the naturalist's saying that $V = X$, my own first claim is that V must have been presented to us under a predicate with the right kind of sense to express a valuational interest; and my second claim is that the Fregean semantics that make it a question whether the property V might, as Railton claims, be the same as the property imported by a predicate that figures essentially in an empirical science (or is definable by means of such) will also carry with them another implication. This is that there must correspond to the property V (as to any putative property) some particular function from objects to truth-values. Call this the V-function.

Putting the two points together, what we shall be led to expect is that the V-function will give expression to the particular determination of the ethical or aesthetic interest that gives a point to the ascription of V to things; and then that this function will be such that the inverse image of the True under it (that is the 'extension' of V) comprises just those items that answer to that particular interest; finally, that if $V = X$ then the X-function from objects to truth-values must match the V-function exactly. Not only then must the X-function turn out to project this interest faithfully across a circumscribed set of putative cases that happen at any time to be actual. It must project it non-accidentally faithfully into the future and across any other cases that could arise. Can it do so? Surely if substantive naturalism means what it says when it *identifies* V and X, then it is committed (and Railton does not demur, it seems) to attempt very much the same sort of things as an old-fashioned reduction is.

VI

I do not question that, across a fixed number of cases, the function for X could mimic the function for V, and place exactly the same items in its inverse image of the True as the V-function places in its inverse image of the True. (At worst I suppose it would always be possible to specify the required extension by using disjunctions of natural properties.) But the thing I emphasize is that the function for X must *also* be able to mimic the function for V in indefinitely many new cases, it being inevitable that some of them present novel and not necessarily marginal problems of decision or discrimination.[3] In order to mimic the V-function across the open ocean of new cases, surely the X-function has somehow to catch on to the point of the attribution of V. It has to capture and make its own the interest that discerns that value. How else is it to go on indefinitely, generating the same extension as the function for V generates? Can it do this consistently with the claim that the property X is one that can *also* be introduced—as *ex hypothesi* it actually was when the identity was announced—by a predicate that pulls its weight in an empirical science or is definable in such terms? These interests seem quite different. (Cf. Section II above.)

VII

The natural interest could I suppose try to *join forces* somehow with the interest that gives us the property V. But, if Railton proposes that, then we have to ask how this will affect the strictly empiricistic title of the science or sciences within which the property X pulls its weight. Where the two ways of thinking are *combined*, what we should really anticipate is the humanization of social science, the abandonment of all ideals of reduction, and then the consequential replacement of a clinical or scientific ideal of understanding by a different, more participative (however coolly participative) ideal.

There is everything to be said (I happen to think) for such a change. I suppose I think that this is one of the things suggested by the study of what makes radical interpretation possible. The question is whether such a combination of ways of thinking could count as a science of the natural in *Moore*'s sense of 'natural'. When the social scientist embraces *this* ideal in his study of morality, what he embraces will have to be a first-order concern with the full gamut of valuational considerations that will actually weigh with real live moral agents. Or that is where he must begin. (There will be no presumption at all in favour of the considerations the games theorist finds to be rational, for instance.) But if it is this open-ended host of considerations that make the running, then the inquiry that results will be interestingly dissimilar to any modern social science. In honour of Hume, we might call it a *moral* science. The first task of such a science must be to anatomize the unreconstructed character of what we have got in morality and explain how that evolved. There will be a presumption, as there is in Hume, against consequentialism. This new inquiry may supplement morality with speculations that will organize our practices and sentiments and enable us to understand them better. It can interest us in the question whether there are alternatives to our actual practices. But always it begins from the inside; and when it redescribes, it does not reduce. If this inquiry is to be continuous with moral philosophy, then, where it departs from the phenomenology of our practices, well, the presumption is that it will have failed. For the link with interpretation will have been severed.

VIII

Here it may be instructive to mention once again Hume's explanatory treatment of the artificial virtues. According to Hume's speculations, what explains the charm of these virtues involves long-term utility, the happiness produced and misery prevented by the cultivation by everybody of certain classes of practices. If the Humean explanation stopped there, however, then we should be short of an explanation of the duty to heed the requirements of these virtues even when the infraction will promote utility or when (whatever else anybody else may do) the infraction cannot damage the general tendency to conformity. But in Hume the duty does not lapse there and the explanation does not stop there. His next move, after the utility of the practice argument, is to point to *the moral beauty of the observance*—that is the beauty that we are so constituted that we attribute to conformity to a general practice which we see as promotive of happiness or preventive of misery. This is a fact about us. It is not necessarily inexplicable, but it is not in itself something that Hume represents to us as an antecedently demonstrably rational requirement flowing from self-love, or from benevolence, or from anything else. (Insofar as there is a question of its rationality, that rationality supervenes on the fact about us.) Hume is offering an account of how we do actually go on within a practice that has established itself. Do such Humean explanations obey the canons of explanation proper to Railton's methodological naturalism? Is not the sense in which they are definitely naturalistic a much less demanding one than the sense in which Railton's approved explanations would be?

IX

To sum up. Consider the explanation one might try to give of the function from objects to truth-values associated with the property X. Either one explains the principle this works on in value-involving terms, or one does not. If one imports value-involving terms, then it remains to be shown that the function is indeed the one corresponding to a natural property in Moore's sense. On the other hand, if one specifies the principle in natural terms proper to the explanation, prediction and control of natural or social processes, then what can assure us that the function is faithful to the valuational interest that discerns V? Following through on Moore's open question argument, one will take leave to question whether the function can ever be better than non-accidentally faithful to it in any particular case.

I have not proved that $V \neq X$. I have only tried to measure the distance across which it would be necessary to stretch the natural or stretch the non-natural to make them meet; and expressed the doubt whether anything in moral philosophy had better depend on such an identity's obtaining.

X

A substantive naturalist who does not want to give up his position will wish to question the terms in which I conducted my side of the debate. He may try to offer a less constructivist account of properties than the one I have arrived at by adaptation from Frege (see note 3). I do not know how that would go.

Or, more promisingly perhaps, he may go back to look again at the Moorean test for the distinction of the natural and the non-natural. I only note that if he chooses to do this and he wants to create conviction, he will need to detach Moore's proposal (which seems to me and seems to Railton, in spite of important differences in our understanding of it, potentially robust and satisfactory) from some of the other, much stranger, things that Moore says about the distinction of natural and non-natural. It will be important that the anti-naturalist who explains himself by the use of Moore's original distinction is not committed to thinking that a thing's possession of a non-natural property cannot be temporally qualified or cannot constitutively involve this or that material modification. On a proper understanding of the non-natural properties, they will not necessarily be queer at all. *A fortiori* they will stand in no need of any salvage operation by the substantive naturalist.

XI

In place of vindication by reduction or vindication by identification with natural properties, what I suppose value properties or putative value properties might stand in need of is simply vindication. In my original answer to Railton, I did not enter at all into the question of their vindication. This was because I was focusing there—contrary to Railton's impression of my reply—on what could be equally well said by a cognitivist and by Hume himself, who was not a cognitivist. For that reason I did not engage with the task of vindicating categorical obligations either. But since Railton has mentioned vindication, let me now say briefly but in my way what such vindication would involve. What it involves is highly substantial.[4] A value property or an obligation is vindicated if certain straightforward positive beliefs or convictions essentially involving it are vindicated. P's belief or conviction is vindicated if its existence is explained in a way that conforms to the following schema: (1) Item x has value V. Or it would be wrong not to do A. [Explainer shows this—in full moral depth.] (2) There is nothing else to think but that x has value V or that it would be wrong not to do A. [Explainer claims to have left no room for any other serious view.] (3) So no wonder person P finds value V in x or finds that he must ϕ!

If this is right, then a vindicatory explanation is an explanation that is already engaged with the moral and that employs moral terms unabashedly. In the work of explanation, it may supplement the moral but it need not reduce it. In a sense, moral science has here *swallowed* social science. Contrast an explanation that begins by trying to show that it would be wrong not to do A by demonstrating the connection of that act with something about human well-being as naturalistically specified. I think it is no accident that it is well-being that Railton seeks to connect with the obligatoriness of some act. For well-being may seem to promise to pull its weight in a social theory. But if that is the place from which the would-be vindicator proceeds, he cannot help but leave himself open to the retort: 'To do A may promote human well-being as naturalistically specified. But it is an open question—indeed doubly open—whether it is indeed obligatory.' First doubt: is the naturalistic version of well-being something we fully recognize as the proper object of all our striving? Secondly, can one here get from statements about it to statements of right and wrong? Contrast Hume's way: one goes directly from the object as it affects one to the moral judgement—and *sometimes* there is no room (in Hume's view, at least) for any other judgement about that object.[5]

Notes

1. 'Figure essentially' in a manner analogous to Quine's sense. See *Mathematical Logic, ad init.*

2. For the Fregean background, see the citations of doctrines of Frege (and the repair I propose to them) in my 'The Sense and Reference of Predicates', *Philosophical Quarterly*, 34. I ignore here the reservations I express there about properties, which I distinguish in that place from concepts. Here, in deference to common philosophical usage, I state Frege's doctrine of concepts as a doctrine of properties.

3. I think that Frege would have been within his rights to insist that the only *basis* on which one could assert that whatever lay in the extension of *V* lay in the extension of *X* and vice versa would have, *on the strict and exigent reading of the quantifier*, to be some consideration that had already addressed just these problems—no less.

4. Cf. my *Needs, Values, Truth*, pp. 153, 200, 348.

5. Cf. Hume, *Treatise*, p. 608.

16

Can There Be a Logic of Attitudes?

Bob Hale

1. Expressive Theories, Geach's Problem and Quasi-Realism

Can we be non-revisionist about morals without embracing moral realism? Can we see our moral talk and thought as philosophically quite in order, but devoid of commitment to any realm of distinctively moral facts or states of affairs. One way to pursue that goal is to argue that moral utterances are not, as their surface form invites us to suppose, genuine assertions, in the market for truth, but have some other role or function, such as to express attitudes of approval and disapproval and to encourage their formation in others. The epistemological and ontological attractions[1] of an expressive theory—no distinctively moral facts, and so no problem of explaining our epistemic access to such facts—are too obvious to require elaboration. Its advantage over naturalism—the reductionist option here—and crude subjectivism (construing moral utterances as self-ascriptions of pro- or con-attitudes) may seem scarcely less so; where each of these positions has trouble making room for moral disagreement, the expressive theorist locates it in clashes of attitude. The general approach is familiar enough, but has never won widespread acceptance. Lately, however, it has received a fresh lease of life as one component in the programme Simon Blackburn has labelled *quasi-realism*.[2] Briefly and somewhat pro-visionally, the *q*-realist sees us, when we moralize, as engaged in a *projection* of natural features of ourselves on to the world. We talk *as if* there were moral facts and falsehoods—we make free use of evaluative predicates, we embed sentences formed with them in contexts which seem to call for completion by items capable of truth-value, etc. *Q*-realism seeks to rehabilitate an expressive theory of such talk, whilst at the same time, and in contrast with error theories, aiming to make out that our continued employment of truth-idioms is perfectly respectable, and need not be seen as in any sort of tension with its projective origin.

Any sort of expressive theory, and so the *q*-realist programme, must confront and surmount some serious obstacles. Prominent among them is a difficulty rightly emphasized by Professor Geach, centred on what he labels the 'Frege point'.[3] Sentences of the kind which, when affirmed on their own, the expressive theorist wishes to construe as serving in an essentially expressive, non-fact-stating role, may occur, without change of meaning, in non-assertive contexts such as conditionals and disjunctions,[4] where they can scarcely be taken to express the attitudes they allegedly express when affirmed on their own. We happily affirm that if lying is wrong, getting others to lie is also wrong, without thereby expressing or endorsing the attitude of disapproval towards lying, or getting others to lie, which we should, according to the expressive theorist, be taken to express or endorse when we affirm the components in isolation. Crucially, compounds in which evaluative predications occur unasserted can combine with others to furnish premises for intuitively valid inferences, such as:

(1) If lying is wrong, so is getting little brother to lie
(2) Lying is wrong

---

(3) It is wrong to get little brother to lie

This constitutes an obstacle, but not, I think, a decisive refutation of any kind of expressive theory. It is an indisputable fact that we use sentences like 'lying is wrong' not only on their own but as 'unasserted' components of, for example, conditionals and disjunctions. And the capacity of sentences of both sorts to figure together in valid inferential transitions such as that on display imposes an important constraint on any attempt the expressive theorist may make to accommodate that fact; negatively, and minimally, it debars him from offering wholly disconnected accounts of the semantic role of asserted and unasserted components. If it were true that the expressive theorist is obliged to give wholly disconnected accounts of the semantic roles of asserted and unasserted components, or again, if it were true, not just that inferences like that just cited are valid, but that the sense in which they are so is the usual one (that is, that it is impossible for their premises to be true without their conclusion being so as well), then—but, it seems to me, only then—Geach's point would be decisive. But it is not clear that either condition is satisfied.

To take the first point first: the expressive theorist holds that when I affirm that lying is wrong, I do no more than express disapproval of lying. Since, when I assert the conditional (1), I am *not* expressing that attitude, it might seem to follow that he must admit that, on his account, the semantic roles of the sentence are wholly distinct. But it does not follow. What does follow is that the expressive theorist must discern some complexity in the speech act of expressing an attitude, paralleling the complexity we can discern in ordinary assertive utterances. There we can say that the speaker both expresses a certain proposition and registers a commitment to its truth. When he asserts a conditional with the same sentence as antecedent, he expresses the same proposition, but registers no such commitment to its truth. As I have been using the words, expressing an attitude is a speech act co-ordinate with assertion, rather than with the neutral act of expressing a proposition. So 'expressing disapproval of lying' is ill-suited to hit off what is common to normal utterances of (1) and (2). Rather than risk confusion by employing that phrase in different senses, I shall say that when a man (sincerely) affirms 'Lying is wrong', he both *presents* a certain attitude (disapproval of lying) and registers commitment to it. Someone affirming (1) presents the same attitude, but registers no commitment to it, and so does not, in our sense, express disapproval of lying.[5]

As for the second point: it is just not obvious that the *only* sense in which we can hold it to be inconsistent to endorse the premises of our inference but reject its conclusion is one which requires us to think of them as bearers of truth-value, because inconsistency consists in the impossibility of joint truth. There may be available some decent notion of attitudinal inconsistency in terms of which the validity of moral *modus ponens* can be understood.

What Geach's points do incontrovertibly reveal is that the expressive theorist has some serious explaining to do. Given that one who sincerely affirms (1) is not thereby expressing the attitudes which he could, supposedly, be expressing, were he to affirm its components separately, what is the semantic role of those components? How *are* they to be understood, if not as conveying truths or falsehoods about matters evaluative? That is the first thing he must explain. And unless he is, quite implausibly, to reject as misleading the strong appearance of validity attaching to inferences such as (1), (2)/(3), he must explain it in a way that leaves room for—or, better, paves the way for—a further explanation, of what makes for the validity of such inferences, if not the impossibility of joint truth of premises and falsehood of conclusion. At the very least, he must accomplish the first explanatory task without convicting such inferences of simple equivocation.

Blackburn has done much to persuade us that Geach's problem may not be insurmountable and, more generally, that the *q*-realist programme is a good one. I remain, however, unpersuaded. In what follows I try to make clear why. I shall find it convenient to organize my misgivings around a dilemma that seems to confront the *q*-realist. This concerns the interpretation of what are, in surface form anyway, conditionals with evaluative components—both purely evaluative conditions like (1), and 'mixed' conditionals like 'If Bill stole the money, he should be punished'. Roughly, the proposed dilemma is this: either such compounds are to be construed, as surface form suggests, as involving a dominant conditional operator, or they are, rather, to be understood as expressive of some attitude towards the truth of an appropriately specified proposition. The first construal promises to ease the problem of doing justice to the intuitive validity of moral *modus ponens* and the like, but (arguably) fails to provide for the kind of expressive interpretation *q*-realism calls for. Taking evaluative conditionals the other way accords well enough with the expressivist thesis, but it is then far from clear that we can get a satisfactory account of intuitively valid inferences involving them.

That is, I ought to stress, no more than a preliminary and tentative formulation of the suggested dilemma. My main aim in the body of this essay will be to elaborate and sharpen a line of objection corresponding to it, and to explore the prospects for an effective *q*-realist rejoinder. To this end I shall consider in some detail two treatments of these issues by Blackburn—in his book *Spreading the Word*, and in a later paper 'Attitudes and Contents'[6]—

principally because some of the difficulties they severally confront may be seen as illustrating the envisaged dilemma's two halves. But I shall not seek to confine my discussion of Blackburn's defence(s) of *q*-realism to what is strictly required by my main argumentative strategy. For whilst his earlier defence has already received some critical attention, there are, I believe, some further difficulties attending his more recent approach which deserve notice. Even if it should prove that the *q*-realist can either blunt one of the horns of my proposed dilemma, or steer a course between them, there is, I shall argue, an issue about how much of our seemingly realist moral talk and thought he can hope to rehabilitate (that is, under some suitably disinfected (re-)interpretation). Here it will be important to distinguish two versions of the *q*-realist programme. The *q*-realist whose aims were briefly sketched a few paragraphs back could be of a relatively modest sort: he will have accomplished all he set out to do, if he manages to explain how we can respectably and intelligibly talk and think as if there were moral truths and falsehoods—presenting our attitudinal commitments in propositional style, with all that that entails, by way of propositional embeddings—although there are in reality (as he conceives it) no such things. There is, on his account, no notion of truth applicable to moral judgements—or better, since he will surely wish to make room for our practice of endorsing moral judgements by the use of truth-idioms—there is no substantial notion of truth for those judgements, nothing that goes beyond a thin, merely disquotational use of phrases like 'That's true'.

Blackburn remarks, somewhat prophetically to my mind, that there is room for argument concerning 'the extent to which [expressive theories] can explain the appearance that we are making judgements with genuine truth-conditions. Ultimately it is the attempt to explain this which introduces the need for a wider theory of truth. ... We should realize that expressive theories, like reductive theories, may be uncertain about how much they need to explain.'[7] For Blackburn, as I read him, defence of the modest position is but the first stage of an altogether more ambitious programme. In part, this more ambitious programme is so because its scope goes well beyond morals—encompasses, for example, treatment along projectivist lines of causality, counterfactuals and modalities in general. But even in the field of morals, this more ambitious *q*-realist looks for more—most importantly, he looks to construct a substantial (but non-realist) notion of truth which really is applicable to moral judgements. I am sceptical, for reasons some of which I have sketched elsewhere and others which will occupy us in the sequel,[8] about this more ambitious project, but even if that scepticism is well-founded, it leaves wide open the question whether modest *q*-realism about morals is a defensible option.

So the plan of this essay is as follows: I shall first sketch Blackburn's earlier defence in sufficient detail to make plausible the contention that it runs foul of the second half of my proposed dilemma. I shall then turn to consideration of his more recent defence. This I shall discuss in rather more detail. The first part of my discussion will be directed towards disentangling a modest from a more ambitious *q*-realist enterprise, and arguing that the *q*-realist had better be modest in his aims. I shall then turn to further difficulties which seem to me to indicate that, if he adheres to this more recent approach, even the modest *q*-realist will be impaled on the first horn of the dilemma. By this stage it will, if all goes well, be clear that if the (modest) *q*-realist is to remain in play, he must do something to blunt the second horn. In my closing sections, I shall expound a line of thought directed to that end, and consider whether it can accomplish what the *q*-realist requires.

2. *Spreading the Word*, Conditionals and Higher-Order Attitudes

The fact that one who affirms (1) above does not thereby express either disapproval of lying or disapproval of getting others to lie does not, of course, mean that it would be a mistake to regard (1) as a whole as serving to express an attitude, rather than as stating some sort of fact. It is clear enough that we may disapprove, for moral, aesthetic or other reasons, of combinations of things of which we do not separately disapprove, and it is plausible to view certain conditionals as voicing this sort of disapproval—for example 'If you're going to drink, you'd better not drive' (I don't mind you drinking, nor do I mind you driving, but I do mind you doing both). A simple suggestion would construe (1) along these lines, as expressing disapproval for combining refraining from lying yourself with getting little brother to do it for you. This suggestion captures something wanted—endorsement of (1) will be consistent with refusal to endorse (2)—but it is too simple. If argument is needed, consider the following—admittedly somewhat bizarre, but clearly conceivable—case. You think there's nothing wrong with lying, nor with getting others to lie. But you also think that, other people's attitudes to these things being as they mostly are, it is generally prudent to get others to do your lying for you. So you refrain from lying, but not from getting others to lie. Suppose now that I'm well aware of your position. Does my endorsement of (1) commit me, *by itself*, to disapproval of your actions? Surely not—though of course, if I also endorse (2) I shall, or at least should, disapprove. But what I find objectionable, just insofar as I endorse (1), is not refraining from lying but getting others to do so, but thinking that while lying is wrong, getting others to lie is (morally) acceptable. There is, in the case as described, no reason to suppose that you merit disapproval on that score.

If that is right, we might do better to see (1) as serving to express a higher-order attitude—disapproval for a certain combination of attitudes (disapproval of lying and tolerance (= lack of disapproval) of getting others to lie). Combining that higher-order attitude with disapproval of lying (that is, endorsement of (2)) and tolerance of getting others to lie (that is, refusal to endorse (3)) lands you in some sort of attitudinal inconsistency—you both disapprove of a certain combination of attitudes and yourself combine those very attitudes.

That is not quite Blackburn's proposal in *Spreading the Word*, though not much separates the two. The theory there sketched[9] has two parts—an informal account, consonant with the general expressivist stance, of 'what we are up to when we use the conditional form with evaluative components', supplemented by a 'semantic theory'. The basic idea in the former is that it can be important to us, in thinking out and expressing our commitments, not just to voice our attitudes towards (types of) actions, but also to criticize or endorse dispositions to couple together different such (first-order) attitudes. The evaluative conditional comes into play as the natural device for endorsing certain combinations of attitude rather than others. In particular, the suggestion goes, someone who affirms (1) endorses (voices approval for) coupling disapproval for lying with the same attitude towards getting little brother to lie.

The accompanying semantic theory may strike purists as somewhat oddly so described, since it provides none of the model-theoretic apparatus under-pinning a definition of truth—or, in the present case, some surrogate for truth—characteristic of what usually goes by the name. What we get instead is a sketch of a language—E_{ex}—in which evaluative commitments are conveyed, not, as in ordinary English, by sentences which give the appearance of propounding truths or falsehoods, but by sentences whose expressive character is fully explicit. The point, in part at least, is, as I understand it, this. To the extent that our use of declarative sentences, deploying, for example, evaluative predicates such as 'is wrong', in voicing our evaluative commitments, along with our readiness to embed them in, for example, conditionals, tempts us to think that those commitments are in the market for truth, it is philosophically misleading. So it ought to be possible to describe what it would be like for speakers to do transparently what, on the *q*-realist's view of the matter, they do in potentially misleading fashion when they employ truth-like idioms to voice their commitments. We could then view the sentences of E_{ex} as displaying the deep structure, or underlying logical form, of simple and compound evaluative sentences of ordinary English.

Transparently expressive English has a couple of operators—H! and B!—which are applied to gerundival phrases descriptive of actions to form sentences. Thus simple sentences expressive of approval and disapproval, such as 'Giving money to WoW is good', 'Lying is wrong' go over into 'H!(giving money to WoW)', 'B!(lying)'. They might be informally read as 'Hooray for giving etc.', 'Boo to lying'. To provide for the expression of complex, higher-order attitudes, two further devices are introduced. If, speaking E_{ex}, I wish to express disapproval of disapproval of, for example, mixed race marriage, I can't just iterate B!; 'B!B!(mixed marrying)' is just ill-formed, since B! is not a sentential operator, but operates upon gerundives, as remarked. B! needs to be applied, not to a sentence expressing disapproval of mixed marrying, but to an expression which denotes the attitude which such a sentence expresses. To get an expression of this sort, Blackburn puts the sentence expressive of the attitude in question inside bars, thus: /B!(mixed marrying)/. I can now express my higher-order attitude by: B!(/B!(mixed marrying)/). The other new device is a binary operator on attitude descriptions; Blackburn writes the semi-colon between such descriptions to stand for the coupling of the attitudes described, or the involvement of one by/with the other.

With both devices in play, the premises and conclusion of our instance of moral *modus ponens* look like this:

(4) H!(/B!lying/;/B!getting little brother to lie/)
(5) B!(lying)

---

(6) B!(getting little brother to lie)

Glossing the premises as expressing, respectively, 'approval of making (disapproval of getting little brother to lie) follow upon (disapproval of lying)' and 'disapproval of lying', Blackburn contends:

> Anyone holding this pair must hold the consequential disapproval: he is committed to disapproving of getting little brother to lie, for if he does not, his attitudes clash.[10]

The distinctive *q*-realist thought is then that, since anyone endorsing the attitudes expressed by the premises but refusing to endorse that expressed by the conclusion is involved in inconsistency, it will be entirely natural for us to avail ourselves of a more familiar way of signalling that fact—we

> invent a predicate answering to the attitude, and treat commitments as if they were judgements, and then use all the natural devices for debating truth. If this is right, then our use of indirect contexts does not prove that an expressive theory of morality is wrong; it merely proves us to have adopted a form of expression adequate to our needs. *This is what is meant by 'projecting' attitudes onto the world.*[11]

Two minor worries about the theory on offer are as follows. Firstly, it is just not clear that approval of making one attitude 'follow upon' another excludes toleration of holding the second attitude without subscribing to the first. The gap is, perhaps, most easily perceived if we consider simple attitudes: I may surely approve of giving money to WoW without thinking it intolerable not to do so. Because of this, it does not appear that approval of *x*-ing and intolerance of not-*x*-ing are related, as Blackburn's claim seems to require them to be, in the same way as the modalities 'L' and '-M-'. But if not, there does not have to be any clash of attitudes in one who endorses (4) and (5) but not (6).

There may, secondly, be some question concerning the *q*-realist's right to avail himself of Blackburn's gloss on /*x*/; /*y*/ as 'making *y* follow upon *x*'. This doubtless smooths the way to the thought that endorsing (4) and (5) but not (6) involves some sort of inconsistency. But the object of (this part of) the exercise is—is it not?—to *explain* what we are 'up to' employing conditionals with (non-truth-bearing) evaluative components, and the obvious worry is that this informal reading of ';', redolent as it is of the notion of conditionality, may smuggle in by the back door just what is to be explained. What does 'making disapproval of *y*-ing follow upon disapproval of *x*-ing' mean, if not something like 'ensuring that *if* you disapprove of *x*-ing, *then* you also disapprove of *y*-ing'?

Neither worry need detain us long. I see no reason why the *q*-realist should not simply concede that the ordinary notion of approval is not quite what's wanted—that he needs a somewhat stronger notion, which stands to toleration as necessity stands to possibility—but get what he wants, either directly, by stipulating that H!x is to be understood as expressing an attitude of insistence upon x, or indirectly, by taking toleration (T!x) as primitive, and defining H!x as expressing refusal to tolerate failure to x (that is, H!$x =_{df} \neg$T! $\neg x$). B!x might then also be defined, in the obvious way, as refusal to tolerate x (that is B!$x =_{df} \neg$T!x). There is more than one way to allay the second worry. We might stick to an austere reading of 'x; y' as simply 'combining x with y', and get what we want by representing (1), by obvious analogy with the truth-functional conditional, as

(4a) B!(/B!lying/;/$\neg$B!getting little brother to lie/)

—that is as expressing disapproval for combining disapproval for lying with lack of disapproval for getting little brother to do it. Coupling this with (5) and rejection of (6) would give a clash that involves combining attitudes ((5), (6)) of whose combination you expressly disapprove ((4a)). Alternatively, the richer reading of ';' might be defended, on the ground that while the conditional form is essentially involved, the components of the conditional are descriptive, not evaluative, so that its employment here is unproblematic.[12]

There is, however, a more fundamental ground for dissatisfaction. This emerges if we ask: just what is wrong, on the present account, with endorsing the premises of an instance of moral *modus ponens*, but refusing to endorse the conclusion? The answer we get, briefly, is that doing so involves you in a 'clash of attitudes'. In a little more detail: asserting (1) amounts to expressing approval for (or maybe better, insistence upon) ensuring that if you disapprove of lying, you also disapprove of getting little brother to lie. So if you also assert (2) and reject (3), your combined attitudes (disapproval of lying and toleration of getting little brother to lie) are in conflict with that insistence. Or on the variant account suggested, we would see (1) as voicing disapproval for combining disapproval of lying with lack of disapproval of getting little brother to lie. The fault, in endorsing (1) and (2), but rejecting (3), would then consist in holding a combination of attitudes of which you expressly disapprove. Faults these doubtless are, and no doubt we might naturally describe one who commits them as involved in some sort of inconsistency; but they seem to be *moral* faults, not logical ones. But as Wright has urged[13] the failing of one who endorses the premises of our sample inference but refuses to endorse its conclusion is not, or at least not merely, a moral failing, but a *logical* one. The kind of account on offer fails to do justice to this point, and thereby impales itself on the second horn of my dilemma.

Can the *q*-realist do better? I want now to consider Blackburn's more recent treatment of these issues.

3. Attitudes and Contents

In matters of syntax, at least, the theory of AC diverges sharply from that of StW. In E$_{ex}$, the operators H! and B! are applied to *descriptions*—gerundival phrases like 'lying', 'getting others to lie', etc.—and so are not, properly speaking, iterable. In the new theory, H! is retained, and the toleration operator T! is added. But now they behave as regular sentence-forming operators on *sentences*. Compounds so formed, such as H!p, T!(p & q), and the like, are allowed all the sentential embeddings that plain p can undergo. The syntax thus provides for iteration and for sentences expressing higher-order attitudes, such as H!(B!p → B!q) corresponding, roughly, to the earlier form H!(/B!x/; /B!y/); though, as we shall see, Blackburn now prefers, with conditionals with attitudinal components to hand, to construe evaluative conditionals like Geach's as involving no higher than first-degree attitudes.

We have, then, in place of E_{ex}, something that looks very much like the formal languages of familiar intensional extensions of the language of standard first-order logic, with attitude operators supplanting the more familiar intensional operators. The thought is that we can adapt techniques already to hand for, for example, deontic logic to produce a generalized logic of attitudes which does justice, *inter alia*, to our sense that one who refuses to accept inferences such as (1), (2)/(3) is illogical, not just depraved. The particular approach to deontic logic Blackburn favours is Hintikka's method of model sets.[14] In essence, this formalizes the intuitive idea that a set of obligations is consistent if there is a possible situation in which all obligations in the set are fulfilled. Bringing in permissions complicates things a little. Roughly, the idea is that a set of obligations and permissions is consistent if there is a system of 'deontically perfect' possible worlds (connected by an accessibility relation) such that each permission is enacted at some world and each obligation is fulfilled at every world. (Hintikka prefers, of course, to put all this in terms of sets of sentences, and systems of such; talk of possible worlds is just convenient shorthand.)

The basic idea underlying Hintikka's way of defining deontic consistency is not, Blackburn observes, peculiarly applicable to statements of obligation and permission; rather, it has application to any kind of statement whose role is, in a quite broad sense, action-guiding, and so, he proposes, to statements expressive of attitude such as H!p, T!q, etc. are now being understood to represent. We can—the thought is—get a formal logic of attitudes by adapting deontic logic (Hintikka style). But Blackburn grants that it is not enough to provide a logic that is formally workable—it needs to be shown that it admits of a coherent interpretation when H!A and T!A are understood as fundamentally expressive in character, rather than descriptive. So he offers, also, an informal interpretation which tells us how to make sense of formulae like ¬T!p, p ∨ H!q, etc., when T!p and H!q are construed as expressive.

> *The system AC*   Let L be a set of sentences, possibly containing some of the forms H!A, T!A.

Then Blackburn defines[15] a *next approximation to the ideal*, L* of L as a set of sentences constructed by following these rules:

  (1) If H!A ∈ L, then H!A ∈ L*
  (2) If H!A ∈ L, then A ∈ L*

(3) If T!$A \in$ L, then a set L* containing A is to be added to the set of next approximations for L

(4) If L* is a next approximation to the ideal relative to some set of sentences L, then, if $A \in$ L*, $A \in$ subsequent approximations to the ideal L**, L***, . . .

Rules (1) and (2) stipulate, in effect, that whilst a goal may go unrealized in the actual world (that is we may have H!A but $\neg A$), it must be fulfilled in all approximations to the ideal (relative to our initial attitude set), and must remain in force as a goal in those approximations. Rule (3) sees realization of a toleration as compatible with perfection, but not required for it. If the point of these rules is thus reasonably clear and straightforward, that of the fourth is rather less so. The following remark explains the general idea behind the rule, but hints also that a further restriction on reiteration from one ideal to another might be needed:

> If L* is already a next approximation to the ideal and contains a sentence A, then except where A derived from realization of a toleration, it must transfer to further approximations to the ideal L**. . . . Here the idea is that once we are following out what is so in the progressive approximations to a perfect world, any realized ideal remains realized. The denizens of paradise do not move.[16]

The intention is that when these rules, together with semantic tableau rules for ordinary sentential operators, are applied to an initial set of sentences L, they will generate a partially ordered set of sets of sentences (next ideals). An ideal is said to be *final* when further applications of the rules produces no new sentences. If L, or any next ideal, contains ordinary branching compounds, then there will be more than one *route* to a set of final ideals. What matters for the consistency of L is that there should be at least one set of final ideals providing for the realization, separately, of each of the T!A in or implied by L, compatibly with realization of all the H!B in or implied by L. Thus Blackburn defines:

> A set of sentences L is *unsatisfiable* iff each route to a set of final ideals from L terminates in at least one set of sentences containing both A and $\neg A$, for some A.[17]

So much for the logic. Can it be given an expressive interpretation? If H! and T! are taken as forming compounds expressive of attitude towards the (possible) states of affairs represented by the sentences they embed, there is an obvious worry about the legitimacy or intelligibility of more complex sentences in which such compounds figure as proper subformulae: how, given that H!A functions expressively, not descriptively, are we to interpret embeddings under ordinary sentential operators, like $\neg$H!p, $p \rightarrow$ H!q, . . . and iterations like T!H!p?

As far as negation goes, Blackburn's proposal[18] is that we can assign intelligible content to compounds in which negation dominates attitude operators by construing them as equivalent to other compounds, expressive of opposed attitudes, in which negation has its scope reduced to some proper subformula whose interpretation raises no problem, since what's negated is a genuine proposition, in the market for truth. Thus $\neg T! p$ is taken as expressing the same attitude as $H! \neg p$, and $\neg H! p$, similarly, as equivalent to $T! \neg p$. The prospects for generalizing this strategy to yield interpretations of other problematic compounds do not, however, look good. At least some conditionals, such as the Geach conditional 'if lying is wrong, so is getting others to lie', appear to have irreducibly evaluative constituents, and so to require formalization involving attitudinal compounds within the scope of a conditional operator. And it is anything but clear how the strategy could help with iterations.[19] Blackburn follows a quite different course, seeking to exploit the way binary compounds are standardly treated in tableaux methods. One who affirms $p \ \& \ H! q$ registers non-branching or conjunctive commitment—he commits himself both to accepting that p and to approving of, or endorsing, its being the case that q. One who affirms $p \lor H! q$ registers a branching or disjunctive commitment—it is the commitment, as Blackburn puts it,

> of one who is ... *tied to a tree*. That is, tied to (*either* accepting that p, or endorsing q), where the brackets show that this is not the same as (being tied to accepting that p) or (being tied to endorsing q). Rather, the commitment is to accepting the one branch should the other prove untenable.[20]

The proposal, as I understand it, is that we can characterize the sense of compounds whose components may be evaluative, not in terms of their truth conditions, but in terms of the inferential commitment involved in endorsing them. This makes, Blackburn now thinks, for a simpler and improved treatment of conditionals like (1). Discarding the higher-order attitude construal, he now sees someone asserting this as voicing an essentially disjunctive commitment— that of being 'tied to the tree of (either assenting to "lying yourself is not wrong" or to "getting your little brother to lie is wrong")'. If Geach's conditional can be construed as of the form $H! p \to H! q$ then we have, it seems, an agreeably simple resolution of our central problem—the failings of one who endorses (1) and (2) but rejects (3) is indeed a *logical* failing, for moral *modus ponens* is just what it appears to be, viz., a special case of *modus ponens*.

4. Ideals

That is, I hope, a fair summary of the distinctive features of Blackburn's latest defence of the q-realist programme for morals. My principal misgivings about it concern the interpretaton of the proposed logic of attitudes. These I shall come to shortly. I begin with some comments upon the logic itself and upon what strikes me as a fairly clearly undesirable feature of it.

Brief reflection on rules (1)–(3) reveals that they confer S4-like properties upon AC. Thus let $L = \{H! p, T! \neg H! p\}$. Then by rules (1) and (3) we have $L^* = \{H! p, \neg H! p\}$. Since there are no alternative routes to the ideal from L, $\vdash_{AC} H! p \to H! H! p$. It is easily verified that rules (1)–(3) suffice[21] to establish $T! T! p \to T! p$, the analogue of the alternative characteristic S4 thesis. We have also analogues of the principle $Lp \to (L(p \to q) \to Lq)$ of L-distribution and of the Rule of Necessitation. What we do not get—and of course do not want, since our ideals may go unrealized—is an analogue of the Law of Necessity; the accessibility relation for AC-structures, as characterized by Blackburn's rules, is not reflexive. Nor is it symmetric. Just as well, for if it were, we should have the S5-like thesis $T!p \rightarrow H!T!p$. Some sort of intuitive case might be made for it—if you tolerate p, should you not applaud toleration of p?—but given our rules are stated, its presence would be disastrous. For we would then have: $\{T!p, T!\neg p\} \Rightarrow \{H!T!p, T!\neg p\} = 0 \Rightarrow \{T!p, \neg p\} = 0 \Rightarrow \{p, \neg p\}.$[14] That is, indifference—not minding whether p or not—would be inconsistent, and we would have the clearly unacceptable thesis $T!p \rightarrow H!p$.

Well, we don't get this unwanted result, but we do get something which is, to my way of thinking, very nearly as bad, and the like of which is not a thesis even in S5, namely: $\vdash_{AC} H!T!p \rightarrow H!p$, That is, $\{H!T!p, T!\neg p\}$ is demonstrably inconsistent by AC rules. For $\{H!T!p, T!\neg p\}$ gives $\{T!p, \neg p\}$ (by rules (2) and (3)), from which we have $\{p, \neg p\}$ (by rules (3), (4)). This seems to say that we should approve of/insist upon toleration of p only if we approve of/insist upon p itself. But consider: might I not think it desirable that I should not mind you not laughing at my feeble jokes $(H!T!\neg p)$, yet not mind if you do $(T!p)$. Or again, you might want to insist upon toleration of National Front rallies, without insisting that they take place. These seem to be consistent positions, but AC says they are not.

The obvious ploy at this juncture, since the final step requires use of the unrestricted reiteration rule (4), would be to restrict that rule along the lines Blackburn suggested might, in any case, be desirable—that is to allow reiteration of A from $L^{* \cdots *}$ to $L^{* \cdots **}$ only when A does not derive from a T!-formula. But whilst that would certainly block unwanted derivations of inconsistency like this one, it will also block some that are wanted. Thus Blackburn wants $H!(H!p \rightarrow p)$ as a theorem, and is surely right to do so; but $\{T! \neg(H!p \rightarrow p)\}$ cannot be reduced to inconsistency with only the restricted version of (4) to hand.

The difficulty just disclosed seems to have its source in an important divergence which we have already remarked between the strong attitude operator H! and the usual necessity operator. What is necessarily true is true *simpliciter*, but what should be true in an ideal world may very well fail to be so in the actual world, and, at least on Blackburn's approach, may also fail to be true in worlds 'closer' to the ideal than ours, but still falling short of it. In his account, it is only in final ideals that all relevant formulae of the type $H!A$ are realized. Under AC rules, $H!A$ at $L^{* \cdots *}$ only ever gets realized at the next ideal $L^{* \cdots **}$. Formally, this means that getting closure in certain cases where, intuitively, we should get it requires reiterating A into subsequent ideals, once it has got into a next ideal. Thus the need for (unrestricted) rule (4).

Since the usual strong deontic operator is like H! rather than the necessity operator in the relevant respect, and since AC is explicitly modelled upon Hintikka's system of deontic logic, we might expect to find a parallel difficulty there. Interestingly, we do not. AC diverges from Hintikka's system at this very point. Hintikka has no rule analogous to AC's rule (4); what he has is a quite different rule which says, in effect, that in any alternative to the actual world which is a candidate for deontic perfection, all relevant obligations are fulfilled.[22] The strict analogue of his rule for AC would be:

(4') For any L* from L, if H!$A \in$ L* then $A \in$ L*

With (4') replacing the troublesome rule (4), we no longer get {H!T!p, T!$\neg p$} coming out inconsistent, but the amended rules are strong enough to validate H!(H!$p \rightarrow p$). Indeed, so far as I have been able to see, the switch will give us everything we might want without giving us anything we definitely would not want. In short, it appears that the way to resolve this particular difficulty is to drop (4) in favour of (4').

If the ill is thus so easily cured, why labour the point? Well, the real importance of the difficulty lies not so much in getting the rules right, as in getting clear about the philosophy behind them. Reflection on the intuitive justification for (4') as opposed to (4) should lead us to make a distinction that is very much to our present purpose. The thought behind Hintikka's rule, I take it, is that whilst we can have Op holding but p false in L (some set of sentences representing a deontically flawed world, such as ours), we should not have this situation in (any) L*, since L* is supposed to be/represent a deontically 'perfect' alternative to L. There is, in Hintikka's system, no gradual approximation to deontic 'perfection'; rather, if reachable from L at all, it is reachable in a single step. By contrast, the idea of gradual approximation to the ideal is very much part of the philosophical picture underlying AC, as is clear from some of the informal explanations quoted above. It is true that Hintikka's system provides for *sequences* of deontic alternatives, but this should not be allowed to obscure the difference just pointed out: the need to bring in sequences of deontic alternatives arises, in his system, not because some alternative, L* say, may be less than deontically perfect, but simply because it may include unexercised permissions—consideration of further alternatives is then required to check for consistency, that is to verify that any such permissions could be exercised without violating any of the relevant obligations. But a world L** that differs from L* only in that some permission is exercised in the former but not in the latter is not thereby closer to perfection; we do not, in the interests of making the world a better place, have to do everything that is permitted. It remains the case that each L* · · * in the system is deontically 'perfect', in the purely technical sense that it contains no relevant unfulfilled obligations ('full' or 'complete' might be less misleading than the rather irrelevantly suggestive 'perfect').

There are at least three reasons why it matters cleanly to separate the two notions of ideal in play here. One is that talk of successively closer approximation to the ideal is misleadingly suggestive of the project, adumbrated in StW, of constructing a q-realist notion of truth applicable to evaluations. The idea, it may be recalled, is that a notion of truth for evaluative statements can be built up in terms of the notion of belonging to the limiting set of attitudes which results from 'taking all possible opportunities for improvement'.[23] One obvious difficulty with this conception concerns the—clearly very substantial—

presupposition that there is a unique best set of attitudes on which any series of improvements on any imperfect set converges. I can see little to encourage belief that this presupposition is fulfilled; but even if the prospects for this more ambitious q-realist project are better than I think, it is important to observe that there neither is nor need be any involvement with it, insofar as our aim is simply to work out a logic of attitudes. Then we are concerned just with how to check sets of attitudes (or sentences expressing them) for consistency; there is absolutely no reason to think that the process of doing that will generate sets of attitudes that are ideal in the sense of resulting from making all possible improvements. Certainly any set of attitudes constituting an ideal in that sense must be consistent, but there is no reason to think that there cannot be consistent sets of attitudes that are, in that sense, less than ideal. Getting to the ideal, in that sense, from our present set of attitudes may involve both discarding altogether attitudes we now have and acquiring new attitudes.

Reflection on the last point discloses a further reason. Let L be a consistent set of sentences (including some of the form H!A, and perhaps also of the form T!A). Let us say that L* is an ideal^A wrt L if L* results from making all possible improvements on L (so ideals^A are limit ideals in the sense of StW); and say that L* is an ideal^R wrt L if all relevant H!A are realized in L* (that is roughly, all H!A in or implied by L—so ideals^R correspond to Hintikka's deontically perfect worlds, but are perfect only in the special sense explained). Now consider AC's rule (1), which says we are to reiterate any H!$A \in$ L into any L* from L. This rule would be surely indefensible, if the L*$\cdots$* were taken to be ideals^A—for it surely can be the case that, as things are in some less than perfect world, H!A is a good or at least acceptable goal to have, but that in some ideal^A wrt that world, it is not. Taking the L*$\cdots$* to be ideals^R, however, the rule is quite sensible—a set of attitudes may turn out to be consistent, even if it could be improved by eliminating some attitudes and adding others.

A third reason why it matters to distinguish the two sorts of ideal, and to appreciate the independence of the task of circumscribing an appropriate notion of consistency for attitudes from the project of constructing a notion of moral truth, is afforded by a nasty looking dilemma posed by Wright. In the course of arguing that irrealist efforts to make good an expressive, or any other kind of non-assertoric, account of seemingly fact-stating moral and other (for example modal) types of utterances are misdirected, he says this:

> The goal of the quasi-realist is to explain how *all* the features of some problematic region of discourse which might inspire a realist construal of it can be harmonised with projectivism. But if this programme goes through, providing inter alia—as Blackburn himself anticipates—an account of what appear to be ascriptions of truth and falsity to statements in the region, then we shall wind up—running the connection between truth and assertion in the opposite direction—with a rehabilitation of the notion that such statements rank as genuine assertions, with truth-conditions, after all. Blackburn's quasi-realist thus confronts a rather obvious dilemma. Either his programme fails—in which case he does not after all explain how the projectivism which inspires it can satisfactorily account for all the linguistic practices in question—or it

succeeds, in which case it makes good all the things which the projectivist started out wanting to deny: that the discourse in question is genuinely assertoric, aimed at truth, and so on.[24]

The dilemma, Wright claims, is fatal unless the projectivist can make out that the notion of truth so rehabilitated is suitably irrealist. But if he can, then the route that proceeds through the idea—eventually scrapped—that the problematic statements are not genuinely assertoric but expressive must surely constitute at best an unnecessary detour. The proper focus of disputes between the realist with respect to a given class of statements is not, Wright contends, on whether those statements are genuinely assertoric or have rather some other, for example expressive, role, but on *what* notion of truth has application to them—the thought being that the tight connection between assertion and truth need not involve a distinctively *realist* notion of truth.

Whether or not that is the best direction for the irrealist to take, it might be thought that Wright's dilemma at least reveals that projectivism, and hence *q*-realism, is a blind alley. But that thought may, it seems to me, pay insufficient heed to the distinction I drew between modest and more ambitious sorts of *q*-realism. The former indeed seeks to 'rehabilitate' the notion of truth—to construct, as Blackburn has it, a conception of truth applicable to moral judgements—and so must confront the dilemma head on. But must a *q*-realist reinstate the notion of truth at all? The central thought of the last few pages—that we can effect a clean break between the task of making out a decent notion of logical inconsistency for sets of attitudes, and so a notion of validity for inferences involving evaluative components, and the project of constructing a notion of truth applicable to evaluative judgements—suggests not. The modest *q*-realist, if he is to be described as rehabilitating the notion of truth at all, will surely want to insist that this means nothing more than explaining how we can defensibly speak *as if* moral judgements were true or false, when in fact they are not. By his lights, moral statements are expressive and retain that character right through his explanation of those of our linguistic practices—including our inferential practices—that might suggest otherwise; the expressive theory is, for him, a permanent fixture, and not the throw-away ladder it appears to have to be for his more ambitious counterpart. In consequence, he need not engage Wright's dilemma, and his position may yet be playable.[25]

5. Problems of Interpretation

There may, then, still be room for a theory which sees our evaluative talk as expressive of attitude, syntactic appearances to the contrary notwithstanding. This modest *q*-realist theory will claim that by casting our expressions of attitude in propositional style, we secure the advantages of thinking and arguing about our commitments as we think and argue about matters of fact. And once presented in that style, it is only to be expected that we should be found endorsing the attitudes expressed using truth-idioms and ascribing attitudes to others using propositional attitude constructions—that is, that we should speak as if there are evaluative truths and falsehoods, fit objects of knowledge and belief, etc., when in reality there are not. And this theory could, it seems, avail itself of the characterization of consistency and validity embodied in (our revised version of) Blackburn's logic of attitudes. Or at least, it could do so, if that admits of satisfactory interpretation in expressive terms. There is, as I shall now try to show, a serious difficulty here.

It is clear enough how an expressive interpretation is to be secured for formulae like $\neg H!p$. They are to be understood as notational variants on equivalent formulae with dominant attitude operators. The difficulty concerns rather those formulae in which things like $H!p$ lie within the scope of binary connectives, such as $p \rightarrow H!q$, which Blackburn now wishes to regard as an appropriate formalization of mixed conditionals like 'if Bill stole the money, he should be punished'. If '$\rightarrow$' is understood as the ordinary truth-functional conditional, then the formula simply makes no sense, unless the components are interpreted as items capable of truth-value.

Doubtless it would be possible to supply a descriptive reading for $H!q$, analogous to the sort of descriptive reading deontic logicians usually have in mind for formulae such as Op and Pq, wherein these are construed as reports of which norms are in force within a certain community of agents. But the possibility of securing sense for $p \rightarrow H!q$ in this way can be of no interest here, since it would entirely fail to provide for an *expressive* interpretation of the formula. In other words, so long as the binary connectives of AC are read as the familiar truth-functions, this latest approach must fail to do justice to the idea that evaluative statements are expressive, not descriptive, and so must get stuck on the first horn of my original dilemma.

One way to avoid this problem would be to generalize the treatment proposed for negations of attitude formulae, that is: construe formulae like $p \rightarrow H!q$ as elliptical for others in which some attitude operator is principal.[26] Provided inner occurrences of attitude formulae are always read descriptively, we could then retain a truth-functional interpretation of the connectives. Indeed, I think this is, in effect, the only option. If I am right about this, then the q-realist will have to accept that inferences such as (1), (2)/(3), and that from (7) and

    (8) Bill stole the money

to

    (9) He should be punished

cannot, after all, be properly regarded as proceeding *modo ponente*.

It might be thought that Blackburn's interpretation of conditionals and disjunctions by way of the notion of being 'tied to a tree' provides the way past the difficulty that now threatens. For isn't the effect of that precisely to secure an expressive meaning for, for example, $p \rightarrow H!q$ which still allows us to see the conditional as the dominant operator, and so allows us to see these inferences as proceeding by *modus ponens*? Well, perhaps it appears to—but the appearance is deceptive. The essential point, as I see it, is this. Let it be agreed that by interpreting $p \rightarrow H!q$ in the tree-tying way, we get an expressive interpretation—what is expressed is a commitment to either denying p or insisting on q. The crucial question is whether the commitment distributes across the disjunction. Blackburn, as we have already seen, insists that it does not. We have a single disjunctive commitment, not a disjunction of commitments. Someone who affirms $p \vee H!q$, he says, need not be committed to affirming p or committed to endorsing q; he is committed to (either affirming p or endorsing q). I think it is clear that that is the answer Blackburn has to give, if his expressive interpretation is to be credible. But it is fatal to the claim that $p \rightarrow H!q$ can figure as the major premiss for a step of *modus ponens*, or—what comes to the same thing—that the usual tableau rule for conditionals can be applied to it. For to pass from $\ldots, p \rightarrow H!q, \ldots$ to a pair of alternatives $\ldots, \neg p, \ldots$ and $\ldots, H!q, \ldots$ is precisely to treat the commitment as distributive. For it is tantamount to saying that if—in the actual world, say—you are committed to (either denying p or endorsing q) then—in the actual world— either you are committed to denying p or you are committed to endorsing q. To put the point slightly differently, if $p \rightarrow H!q$ registers a *non*-distributive commitment to (either denying p or endorsing q), then it has to be reckoned a possibility that this commitment goes unrealized in the actual (morally imperfect) world, just as any other evaluative commitment may go unrealized. The upshot is that, so far from facilitating the treatment of the evaluative inferences which concern us as straightforward instances of *modus ponens*, the proposed interpretation of conditionals and disjunctions in terms of being tree-tied actually debars us from so treating them.[27] In short, Blackburn's latest defence looks set to impale itself on one or other horn of my original dilemma: if formulae like $p \rightarrow H!q$ are read as ordinary (for example truth-functional) conditionals, their evaluative components demand a descriptive reading, and we lose our grip on the expressivist thesis; if the tree-tying interpretation is invoked to secure the construal as expressive of an essentially disjunctive commitment, a fatal gap opens up between the proposed logic and the preferred interpretation—in effect, when that interpretation is in play, it is no longer justifiable to treat such formulae as the logic treats them (that is as truth-functional conditionals).

6. Consistency, Norms, and Beliefs

The q-realist's prospects ought by now to seem bleak. But it would be premature to conclude that his position is hopeless. For there remains at least one possibility to be investigated. He should accept that, if he is to sustain a thoroughgoing expressive interpretation of moral discourse, he must be able to locate, for each moral statement, a non-cognitive attitude which it primarily serves to express. If the notational apparatus deployed in our discussion thus far is retained, and the connectives are interpreted truth-functionally, that will mean finding, for each such statement, a representation of its logical form in which some attitude operator is principal. And that in turn will mean finally abandoning any hope of exhibiting inferences such as those we have been discussing as straightforward instances of *modus ponens*; but if I am right, that hope is vain in any case. But it is not yet clear that it must mean giving up all hope of exhibiting them as (corresponding to) formally valid inferences of some sort. One pitfall, we know, has to be avoided: failure to accept their conclusions must constitute a *logical* and not merely a moral shortcoming. But AC embodies a clear, and clearly logical, conception of consistency which does not require us to think of statements of the forms H!A and T!A as themselves true or false. The possibility still to be explored is that we may, whilst observing the constraint upon formalization of moral statements adumbrated above, be able to exhibit intuitively valid moral inferences as valid in a sense directly definable in terms of that notion of consistency, or perhaps some well-motivated adaptation of it.

If compounds with evaluative constituents are to be represented as involving dominant attitude operators, pure evaluative conditionals like (1) should be seen, as on the StW approach, as expressive of higher-order attitude. In contrast with that earlier approach, however, we are now construing evaluative attitudes as *propositional* attitudes. This suggests taking (1) to exemplify the form H!(B!p → B!q) or, equivalently, B!(B!p & T!$\neg q$). Under either formulation of its major premiss, the inference (1), (2)/(3), though no longer, of course, an instance of *modus ponens*, is easily seen to be AC-valid: that is, we get a closing tree-structure for the set {H!(B!p → B!q), B!p, $\neg$B!q}. AC has no rules for B!, but we could easily add some; alternatively, we can handle B!-formulae by treating B!A as abbreviating H!$\neg A$. Taking the latter course, $\neg$B!q boils down to T!q, so that our next ideal includes {q, H!$\neg p$ → H!$\neg q$, H!$\neg p$} (by rules (3), (2), and (1)). This splits into {q, T!p, H!$\neg p$} and {q, H!$\neg q$, H!$\neg p$}. The first alternative generates the closed ideal {p, $\neg p$} (by rules (3) and (2)), while the second gives the closed ideal {q, $\neg q$, $\neg p$} (by rule (4′)).

So far, so good. But we have yet to consider how to handle mixed conditionals, such as (7). On the present approach, we are to replace Blackburn's preferred representation of its form (that is p → H!q) by one in which an attitude operator dominates. The obvious candidates are H!(p → H!q) (equivalently B!(p & $\neg$H!q)) and H!(p → q) (or B!(p & $\neg q$)). The former sees (7) as expressive of a higher-order attitude of sorts (approval for approving Bill's punishment, if he stole), while the latter construes it more simply, as expressive of approval for the truth of the conditional 'if Bill stole . . . , he is punished'. I see no grounds for insisting upon the former—the present approach does not specifically enjoin *higher-order* treatment in every case; what it requires is a dominant attitude operator, and so higher-order construal in those cases where representation of the components themselves has to involve attitude operators. The real question concerns not the choice between these two ways of representing (7), but the adequacy of either. For it is easy to verify that neither {H!(p → q), p, T!$\neg q$} nor {H!(p → H!q), p, T!$\neg q$} comes out inconsistent in AC (whether amended along the lines suggested above, or not). That is, the immediate effect of representing (7) with dominant H! is that we can no longer disclose any inconsistency in the set representing the premises and negation of the conclusion of the intuitively valid inference (7), (8)/(9). No such problem arises on Blackburn's preferred representation of (7); the set $\{p \rightarrow \text{H}!q, p, \text{T}! \neg q\}$ is easily seen to be AC-inconsistent. The initial set splits into $\{\neg p, p, \text{T}! \neg q\}$ and $\{\text{H}!q, \text{T}! \neg q\}$; the first alternative closes immediately, and the second at the next ideal $\{\neg q, q\}$ (by rules (2) and (3)). The crucial difference, of course, is that the $\neg p$ branch from $p \rightarrow \text{H}!q$ is generated before the T!-rule is applied, so we get closure on that branch in virtue of the presence of p in the initial set. When $p \rightarrow \text{H}!q$ is replaced by $\text{H}!(p \rightarrow q)$ (or by $\text{H}!(p \rightarrow \text{H}!q)$), however, the $\neg p$ branch does not get generated until the next ideal, but the p of the initial set can not be reiterated into that set, so one alternative fails to close. Since the difficulty seems certain to recur on any dominant attitude operator formulation of (7), it is tempting to conclude that the present approach must fail to deliver the goods.

Tempting perhaps, but the point merits closer scrutiny. If it seems obvious that we *ought* to be able to locate an inconsistency in the conjunction of (7), (8), and $\neg$(9), *when these are construed expressively*, that is surely because we are supposing these sentences to be affirmed by a single subject, who may be presumed to have not only the normative attitudes expressed by (7) and $\neg$(9), but also the *belief* expressible by (8). Certainly if a man believes (whether truly or not) that Bill did *not* take the money, his endorsement (7) and $\neg$(9) does not suffice to convict him of *inconsistency*. The worst that could be said of him is that he is guilty of a false belief, and that, were he brought to recognize its falsehood, he would be required to revise his normative attitudes—that is cease to endorse at least one of (7) and $\neg$(9). It might then be said that his normative attitudes are unstable, because co-tenable only so long as he retains his false belief. But that is, plainly, not to say that his total set of attitudes is inconsistent. Of course, it could be said (where he believes falsely that $\neg$(8)) that his normative attitudes are inconsistent with the *facts*, but that falling is equally present in one who simply holds (consistent) beliefs some of which are false; in neither case is the failing a specifically *logical* one.

This suggests that, if we are to interpret AC as a logic of attitudes, we ought to think of the initial sets of sentences to which its rules are applied, not as purporting to depict a collection of normative/evaluative attitudes held in certain circumstances but, as characterizing the combined moral attitudes *and beliefs* of some single (possible) subject. The consistency-question we are concerned with, in other words, is not whether, *given that the facts are thus and so*, it is consistent to adopt such and such a collection of normative attitudes: but whether, *given that the subject has such and such beliefs about how things are*, he can consistently hold those normative attitudes. That is, when we start off considering some such set as $\{p \rightarrow \text{H}!q, p, \text{T}! \neg q\}$, it has to be understood that the sentences devoid of attitude operators represent the (germane) factual beliefs of some possible subject who also subscribes to the normative attitudes expressible by the remaining sentences. In short, and first appearances to the contrary notwithstanding, it is not just the member sentences with explicit attitude operators that are representative of attitudes: all are, the only difference being that those representing the subject's beliefs, or other cognitive attitudes, are not expressly marked as such.

This bears upon the significance of the tree-structures generated by the AC rules, and particularly that of open trees. Consider, for example, the tree we get for $\{H!(p \rightarrow q), p, T! \neg q\}$—the premisses and negated conclusion of (7), (8)/(9) on the simpler of my suggested renderings of the major premiss:

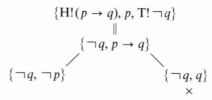

The failure of the formal inference $H!(p \rightarrow q)$, $p/H!q$ will be totally unsurprising, since it exactly matches the failure, in standard deontic logics, of $O(p \rightarrow q)$, p/Oq (as contrasted with $p \rightarrow Oq$, p/Oq, which is of course straightforwardly valid, and which matches Blackburn's preferred formalization of our English inference). But, unless I am badly mistaken, the thought of the preceding paragraph calls into question the significance of that parallel. In a normal tableau in this style, a terminal open set of sentences establishes the consistency of the initial set, by depicting a possible situation in which all the members of the latter would be true together. And it is easy to suppose that that is precisely what the open set that terminates the left path in our tree does. Or rather (since we are no longer viewing the initial sentences as candidates for truth) that it establishes the consistency of the combination of attitudes represented by the initial set, by disclosing a situation in which they would all be realized. But that is not quite right. For whilst the left path remains open, one of its terminal set of sentences is the contradictory of a (non-evaluative) sentence in the initial set. What it shows, strictly, is that the *normative* attitudes of the initial set are consistent (= realizable) *provided that the subject's belief that* p *is false*—or, perhaps, *provided that the subject believes that* ¬p. Whichever of these provisos we might finally decide is the right one, we cannot, or so it seems to me, avoid this conclusion: that a sufficiently reflective subject who endorses (7) and (8) but rejects (9) will be able to see that his normative attitudes are jointly realizable only at the cost of his factual belief. He should recognize—should he not?—that something is amiss, and that he is logically obliged either to revise his belief or jettison one of his normative attitudes.

That suggests that it may yet be possible to construe (7) with dominant H!, as I have argued we should, and still do justice to our sense of logical impropriety attaching to the joint affirmation of (7) and (8) coupled with rejection of (9); the q-realist may, that is, still have the resources to blunt the first horn of my original dilemma. But what we have is no more than a suggestion; whether what it envisages is a real way forward, and not merely another blind alley, is another question, and one that is, I fear, too large and difficult to tackle here. There is, however, one problem that will certainly have to be faced; by way of a (somewhat inconclusive) conclusion, I shall venture a few thoughts about it.

It is clear that if anything worthwhile is to be made of this latest suggestion, we shall need to circumscribe an extended notion of consistency; we need a notion which takes seriously the thought that combinations of norms and beliefs can be inconsistent in a way that essentially involves both the norms and the beliefs figuring in the combination. Putting together a consistent set of normative attitudes with a consistent set of beliefs may—so the suggestion has it—result in a mixed set which is, as a whole, inconsistent. But in what sense? How exactly is the notion to be defined? We know what it is for a set of beliefs to be consistent—that is so just when it is possible for all the beliefs in the set to be true together. And we have a notion of consistency applicable to sets of normative attitudes—the notion which underlies AC, according to which, roughly, a set of normative attitudes is consistent if there is a system of possible worlds (meeting certain constraints) which realizes it. And now it might seem natural to define the extended notion we require by simply amalgamating these two notions: to say, roughly, that a mixed set of normative attitudes and beliefs is consistent iff there is a system of possible worlds which realizes all the normative attitudes and is such that every belief in the set is true at each world.

But, however natural that extension of the notion of consistency might seem, it has to be recognized that it has, pretty immediately, what appear to be totally unacceptable consequences. To pick out the worst of many, it becomes inconsistent both to believe that $\neg p$ but hold that it ought to be otherwise (the tree for $\{\neg p, \text{H!}p\}$ is open, but its only terminal set contains p), and to believe that p but not hold that it ought to be so (the tree for $\{p, \neg\text{H!}p\}$ is open, but its only terminal set contains $\neg p$). For entirely parallel reasons, it becomes inconsistent to find it tolerable that p whilst believing that $\neg p$, and to believe that p but find that intolerable. If the suggestion is not to be scrapped, we must, it seems, accomplish one of two things: we must either pin down an appropriately weaker notion of consistency for mixtures of belief and normative attitude, or we must somehow argue that the consequences of adopting this one are, contrary to first appearances, ones that we can live with. The former course requires, in effect, some non-arbitrary restriction on the range of a subject's beliefs which need to be held true conjointly with satisfaction of his normative attitudes, if his total norm-belief set is to be deemed consistent. The latter calls, essentially, for an explanation. For one who tries this route must, surely, emphasize that it need not be irrational or illogical to retain a combination of belief and normative attitude which is inconsistent in this sense—that is, which is such that not all his normative attitudes can be realized so long as all his beliefs are true. That is, he will want to hold that inconsistency, in this sense, does not always enjoin revision of one's beliefs or norms. But he will also want to hold that it sometimes does so. So he will need to explain what makes the difference—what makes it irrational for me to refuse to endorse Bill's punishment, when I believe that he stole and contend that if he stole, he should be punished, but not irrational for me to condemn lying, while recognizing that people tell lies.

It is important not to mislocate the problem just disclosed. It would be a relatively straightforward matter to put things formally right, as it were, by adding to AC what might be termed a 'fixity' operator, to be prefixed to precisely those non-evaluative sentences representing beliefs which are to be held constant—treated as fixedly true—through the search for a consistent realization of the subject's total attitude set. The obvious extra rule would then stipulate that each formula governed by this operator is to be reiterated into all next ideals. Equally obviously, this makes no advance on the real problem, which is to specify which non-evaluative sentences, among those expressing the subject's beliefs, are to be formalized as fixed. No question but that this will be a highly context-dependent matter—that is beliefs that are to be held fixed in some evaluative contexts will be 'movable' in others. It ought, nevertheless, to be possible, if the proposed logic of attitudes is to have significant application, to provide a general account of the criteria by which it is to be determined, in context, which beliefs are to be held fixed and which not.[28]

Neither course is transparently hopeless. Indeed, since it plainly is irrational to believe that Bill stole and that if he did so, he should be punished, and yet refuse to endorse punishing him, and is, equally plainly, not irrational to condemn lying, whilst acknowledging that people tell lies, there has, surely, to be an explanation for this difference. And assuming that explanation of the required sort is generally available, it is not implausible to suppose, further, that it will supply materials in terms of which a non-arbitrary restriction of the kind envisaged by the first course might be framed. That is, of course, no more than a promissory note. There is no reason to suppose that redeeming it will prove an easy or straightforward task. It is finally worth stressing, however, that—so far anyway—no clear reason has emerged for thinking either that the problem just aired distinctively afflicts the q-realist, or that it is one which he is especially ill-placed to address.[29]

Notes

1. For a fuller statement, see Simon Blackburn, *Spreading the Word*, ch. 5 and especially pp. 167–71.

2. See Blackburn, *Spreading the Word*, ch. 6.

3. P. T. Geach, 'Assertion', *Philosophical Review* 74.

4. Conditionals and disjunctions are not, of course, the only contexts in which evaluative or normative sentences can figure in positions where we expect to find candidates for truth, and which must, therefore, be viewed as problematic by the expressive theorist. There is no sense of impropriety attaching to the description of someone as knowing, or believing, that lying is wrong, that one ought to keep one's promises, etc., or in the embedding of such sentences in such contexts as 'It is true that . . .'. But I doubt that these other problematic contexts raise any essentially new problems for the expressivist. Once we have taken the step of expressing our attitudes in propositional style, it is only to be expected that the sentences thus employed should—in sharp contrast with, e.g., imperatives—enjoy the full range of propositional embeddings, and that we should thus ascribe to someone the attitude of disapproval for lying by saying that he believes that lying is wrong, use the form 'He knows that

lying is wrong' to both ascribe that attitude and register our agreement in attitude, and use devices of truth-ascription to endorse attitudes.

5. That is, *expressing* an attitude is presenting it committedly. Presenting an attitude is to be thought of as an *abstraction* from the total speech act of expressing that attitude, much as expressing a proposition may be viewed as an abstraction from the total act of assertion. There need, of course, be no additional (overt or covert) performance that transforms presentation of an attitude into its expression—committed presentation can be just presentation accompanied by no indications of non-commitment.

6. Simon Blackburn, 'Attitudes and Contents', *Ethics* 98.

7. Blackburn, *Spreading the Word*, p. 170.

8. For some of the reasons, see Bob Hale, 'The Compleat Projectivist', *Philosophical Quarterly* 36, pp. 75–6. For others, see the discussion of Wright's dilemma in Section 4 of this paper.

9. See Blackburn, *Spreading the Word*, pp. 189–96.

10. Ibid., p. 195.

11. Ibid.

12. As Simon Blackburn was quick to point out, in correspondence on an earlier version of this essay.

13. See Crispin Wright, 'Realism, Anti-Realism, Irrealism and Quasi-Realism', in P. French, T. Uehling Jr., and H. Wettstein (eds.), *Midwest Studies in Philosophy* 12, p. 33.

14. See e.g. Jaakko Hintikka, 'Some Main Problems of Deontic Logic', in Risto Hilpinen (ed.), *Deontic Logic: Introductory and Systematic Readings*, pp. 59–104, or 'Deontic Logic and its Philosophical Morals', in J. Hintikka (ed.), *Models for Modalities*, pp. 184–214.

15. This comes more or less verbatim from Blackburn, *Spreading the Word*. For a number of reasons, I do not think (1)–(4) constitute an acceptable definiens for the open sentence 'L* is a next approximation to the ideal of L'. In particular, the bound occurrences of 'L*' in (3) and (4) prevent these clauses from imposing conditions upon L* in the definiendum. But it is sufficiently clear what is intended. I ought to point out that Blackburn's definition assumes (as he makes clear) that L and the various L*··* meet certain further, fairly obvious and standard, conditions in regard to formulae with standard logical operators dominant (e.g. A & B ∈ L*··* only if A, B ∈ L*··*, etc.).

16. Blackburn, 'Attitudes and Contents', pp. 514–15.

17. Ibid.

18. Ibid. G. H. von Wright makes a strikingly similar proposal, in the course of arguing for the possibility of a *prescriptive* interpretation of deontic formulae; see his 'Norms, Truth and Logic' in his *Practical Reason: Philosophical Papers, Vol. I*, pp. 130–209. Of particular interest, in view of its obvious parallel with the main claim I defend in section 5, is von Wright's contention that to secure a prescriptive interpretation for mixed norm-formulae, such as $p \rightarrow Oq$, it is necessary to construe them as elliptical for formulae with dominant deontic operators, such as $O(p \rightarrow Oq)$, in which any inner norm-formulae are accorded a descriptive reading (see esp. pp. 151–2). More generally, von Wright argues that norm-formulae of higher order, including iterations like POp, can be given a prescriptive interpretation, but that this requires interpreting embedded norm-formulae descriptively (cf. p. 135).

19. It might be supposed that iterations could be handled by appeal to appropriate reductive equivalences, such as $H!H!p \leftrightarrow H!p$, $T!T!p \leftrightarrow T!p$, etc. This will not do, for several reasons. For one thing, whilst AC sanctions some of the required reductions, such as those cited above, it would need to validate the full range of reduction principles, including the S5-like $H!T!p \leftrightarrow T!p$ and $T!H!p \leftrightarrow H!p$, if iterations are to be generally

interpreted in this way. It does not do so. More importantly, it is quite unclear how AC could be strengthened to get all the required reduction principles as theorems, whilst retaining any sort of fidelity to its intended interpretation. Getting the S5-like principles will require a symmetric, as well as transitive, accessibility relation among ideals, but then we shall also get the unwanted analogue of the Law of Necessitation, i.e. H!$p \rightarrow p$, which is quite unacceptable if H!p expresses a normative attitude. I ought to stress that Blackburn himself shows no tendency to follow the line criticized here. Nor, however, does he offer any alternative treatment of iteration; there is thus an important gap in his proposed expressive interpretation of AC at this very point.

20. Blackburn, 'Attitudes and Contents', p. 512.
21. Assuming interchange of $\neg$H! and T!$-$, etc. is allowed.
22. See Hintikka, 'Some Main Problems', p. 71, the rule in question is (C. O)$_{rest}$.
23. Blackburn, *Spreading the Word*, p. 198.
24. Wright, 'Realism, Anti-Realism', p. 35.
25. Blackburn has indicated (in correspondence) that he is happy to see expressivism as a 'throw-away ladder', and so sees no particular threat to his (more ambitious variety of) q-realism in the second half of Wright's dilemma. I continue to find this puzzling, for what I take to be essentially the same reason as Wright. If the thought is that, from some more enlightened (q-realist) vantage point, we can somehow see that the expressive theory is actually incorrect (as distinct, perhaps, from only incompletely capturing the truth about moral thought and talk), then I cannot see how any more can be claimed for the play with expressivism than that, by disclosing some essential features that the expressive theory ignores or mishandles, we can get into position to form a better account. It might be a useful expository device, but how could it be any more than that—how could flirtation with the expressive theory form an essential stage in the route to the q-realist truth about morals?—unless we are being offered, as I take it we are not, some sort of *genetic* theory of the evolution of the notion of moral truth. Quite apart from this general worry, it seems to me that Blackburn ought not to be content to discard quite so much of the expressivist starting point. For the notion of moral truth he wants is something along these lines:

> a moral statement is true if the attitude it expresses belongs to the limiting set of attitudes that results from taking all possible opportunities for improvement, etc.

and that involves retaining the idea that moral statements are expressive of attitude.

If that is right, then however precisely Blackburn's ambitious q-realism differs from the more modest position I have sketched, it ought not to be by ditching the idea that moral utterances are expressive, not descriptive. It may now seem that the better line (i.e. for the ambitious q-realist) would be that what is to be thrown out is not that idea, but the further notion standardly harnessed to it, that moral utterances are not, precisely because of their expressive character, in the running for truth. I have two worries about this suggestion.

First, if we take this line, then the contrast between *expressive* and *descriptive* needs to be retained, but that between *expressive* and *apt for truth-value* must go. So some sort of distinction needs to be made between a statement's being descriptive and its being apt for truth-value. But since any sort of descriptive statement is, *eo ipso*, a candidate for truth, we shall need to distinguish, it seems, some different notions of truth here—descriptive statements will be apt for truth of a kind to which expressive statements, though also in the running for truth (of some other kind), cannot attain. But now it looks—doesn't it?—as though the appropriate distinction here would be just between realist and non-realist truth. But if, as now seems on the cards, proper understanding of the expressivist claim involves *prior* appreciation of some such distinction, doesn't that mean that Wright was right after all in claiming that the proper focus of disputes between realists and their opponents is on what notion of truth has application to e.g. moral statements?

Second, the proposed *q*-realist treatment of the Geach problem (StW or AC version) must now seem needlessly roundabout. For if he needs in any case to make room (right from the outset) for a good sense in which moral utterances can be true or false, why shouldn't he dispose of the problem directly: we have a problem if we suppose that expressives are not true or false, but want to acknowledge the possibility of their figuring in unasserted contexts where, so it appears, only items apt for truth-value can go; but now we are in a position to just reject the presupposition about the incapacity of expressives to be true or false, so the problem doesn't get going. That is, the kind of response to Geach's problem which Blackburn advocates best subserves a modest, rather than ambitious, *q*-realism.

26. See n. 18.

27. The argument given here met with considerable resistance in the conference discussion. In particular, Christopher Peacocke argued that there is no reason why Blackburn shouldn't be seen, in offering his 'tree-tying' account, as fixing a special, expressive, sense of e.g. '$p \to$ H!q' by laying down inference rules for it. Blackburn himself sought to resist my argument by claiming that '$p \to$ H!q' could be expressive in virtue of there being a *background* commitment on the part of one who asserts it, but still be properly treated by the ordinary tableau rule for conditionals. Probably these should be seen as alternative ways of elucidating and defending Blackburn's position, for the following reason, among others. It is agreed on all sides that if '$p \to$ H!q' is an ordinary truth-functional conditional, it is well-formed only if 'H!q' is read descriptively. Peacocke's proposal is that an alternative, appropriately expressive, type of conditional can be (completely) characterized by specifying its logical powers—by giving the inference rules governing it. Blackburn's proposal can, and may well have been intended to, retain the ordinary truth-functional conditional (and so have 'H!q' read descriptively), whilst securing an expressive interpretation by reference to the commitment which its assertor has but does not make explicit.

To take Peacocke's proposal first: there is nothing necessarily amiss with the idea that we can specify the sense of a type of statement (or logical connective) by giving the inference rules for it (at least, so I shall grant for the sake of argument—there are, of course, well-known problems here (Tonk, etc.)). But if it is granted, as it is, that for the expressive interpretation, the conditional cannot be truth-functional, then specifying the inference rules in this case ought to *distinguish* the special, expressive form of conditional allegedly introduced from the ordinary truth-functional variety. Yet that the proposal manifestly fails to do, since the only inference rule proposed is just the usual tableau rule for the truth-functional conditional, Hence if a special expressive sense of conditionals is to be introduced in this way, it has to be conceded that it has not been completely specified. The crucial question is then: how is the meaning specification to be completed? And the trouble is that Blackburn wants '$p \to$ H!q', etc., to have just the inferential liaisons of the ordinary truth-functional conditional. But then the proposal collapses.

A crucial question for Blackburn's proposal is: of what character is the background commitment in the presence of which '$p \to$ H!q' functions expressively? If no specially expressive sense of $\to$ is being invoked (which we may assume, since the proposal is otherwise redundant), the background commitment *must* be evaluative, if the proposal is to capture the idea that a *moral* attitude is expressed in this oblique fashion. But now, granting that a sentence may be expressive, in a certain range of uses/circumstances, without being *explicitly* so, I have two objections:

(a) The object of the exercise was—wasn't it?—at least in part, to provide a formalism in which the (allegedly) expressive character of ordinary evaluative remarks is rendered *fully explicit*. The present proposal just gives up on that aim.

(b) (more importantly) Granted that a sentence may function expressively without there being any indication in its vocabulary or syntax that it is doing so, should it not be at least possible to produce an *equivalent* sentence which fully explicitly does the same thing. Compare the case of non-explicitly performative sentences like 'I'll do it'. On occasion, saying this constitutes the making of a promise. Though it is, quite properly, often left to be understood from context that a promise is being given, it must be at least possible to make explicit the character of the speech act—i.e. to give an explicitly performative version of it. But an explicitly expressive version of '$p \rightarrow H!q$' (i.e. a version which does not rely upon the audience's knowledge of the speaker's background commitment for its recognition as expressive) is going to be either '$H!(p \rightarrow H!q)$' or something not relevantly different, having a dominant attitude operator. For this there will be no allowable distribution move, i.e. no allowable move from . . . $H!(p \rightarrow H!q)$ . . . to the alternatives . . . $\neg p$ . . . and . . . $H!q$. . . . Since $H!(p \rightarrow H!q)$ just gives full-dress expression to the same commitment as, in context, $p \rightarrow H!q$ expresses, the move is no more legitimate for the latter.

I am indebted to Harold Noonan for helpful discussion of these matters.

28. The idea of introducing a fixity operator was put to me in correspondence by Blackburn. I had independently begun to think along somewhat similar lines, but could see no generally adequate way to explain when, in his terms, a belief should count as fixed. I need hardly say that the paragraph to which this note is appended is not meant to suggest that he is in any danger of failing to appreciate the need for such an explanation. His proposal was that we should 'call a belief *fixed* if, *for some evaluative purpose in hand* it is immovable'. I think I have some feeling for the idea this is getting at, but would like to see it spelled out more fully, preferably without reliance on the equally problematic notion of a belief's being (im)movable. It is, of course, a familiar enough thought that moral judgements are typically made against a background of factual beliefs. If I thought that foxes would die of boredom if they weren't chased, that they derived great pleasure from giving the hounds a good run around, and that there was anyway a negligible chance of their being caught, I might well take a different view about the morality of foxhunting. The opposed beliefs, those which I actually have, are presumably fixed (for me)—immovable for the evaluative purpose of reaching a view on the morality of foxhunting. But another of my beliefs is that people do actually hunt foxes: does that count as fixed here? If unwanted inconsistency is to be avoided, it had better not. But now what makes the difference? It is tempting to think one could explain it in terms of the potential role of fixed beliefs as reasons for the moral judgement made: the belief that being pursued by a pack of bloodthirsty hounds is, to put it mildly, no fun for the fox is, maybe, one reason I have for disapproving; but the belief that people hunt foxes could scarcely figure as a reason for disapproving of their doing so. The snag is that someone who, irrationally, accepts that Bill stole the money, and that if he stole, he should be punished, but refuses to agree that he should be punished, precisely does not treat the belief that Bill stole as a reason for thinking that he should be punished. That is, tying the notion of fixity to the beliefs which the relevant moral subject would recognize as affording reasons for particular moral judgements looks as though it won't

justify treating as fixed the beliefs that have to be so treated, if the subject is to be convicted of illogicality.

29. I am grateful to John Haldane and Crispin Wright for inviting me to contribute a paper to the conference. Special thanks are due to Simon Blackburn and Crispin Wright for a three-cornered discussion which provided much of the stimulus for writing this paper. I thank them, and my colleague John Benson, for helpful comments on earlier drafts.

17

Realism, Quasi, or Queasy?

Simon Blackburn

I

I have often introduced the position I call quasi-realism by a kind of flow chart. We start with a division. On the one hand there is theorizing about some area of our commitments (moral, aesthetic, conditional, causal, or whatever) by seeing them in terms of beliefs, answering to facts or possessed of truth-conditions. We may say that this is the realist path, at this choice point, leaving it open whether later on there is room for anti-realist theorizing within this option. On the other hand there is theorizing about the same commitments by seeing them as something different: expressions of attitude, or of other dispositions, or of modes of acceptance of propositions, or of preparedness to adjust other beliefs in various ways, and so on. One voicing such a commitment is certainly expressing a facet of his cognitive or conative make-up, but it is one best theorized about in contrast with the more ordinary case of strict belief. In this scenario the word 'commitment' is of course intended to be entirely neutral. It is the word for whatever it is that might turn out to be best thought of as belief, or might turn out to be best theorized about as something else. Someone might be annoyed at this blanket use of the term: is it permissible to use it so that beliefs may turn out to be a proper subset of commitments? That will be decided by finding whether the division between attitudes and the rest on the one hand, and beliefs, can be sustained, so we should accept the term provisionally, in order to conduct just that enquiry.

I do not regret introducing the issues in this way, but it can cause confusion, and I now think we can do without it (although what we get when we do may not be as different as some critics would wish). The reason is this. Following down the anti-realist path immediately leads to a further choice point. What view should the anti-realist take of the way commitments *seem* pretty homogeneous—the way in which causal or moral or modal commitments seem just like other beliefs, admitting of truth or falsehood and capable of sustaining propositional attitudes and logical embeddings that might seem to be the exclusive preserve of sentences that express objects of belief? One response would be that of the *error theorist*, who regrets the phenomena, seeing them as

365

the illogical result of ignorance of the true status of these commitments. We are betrayed, according to him, into both forms of thought and linguistic expressions of them (I shall call these the *propositional surface* of the discourse) that are improper. A logically perfect language would, in this view, pay proper attention to the permissible expressions of dispositions, conative states, and the rest, and the result would be something very different from surface English.

How different? That depends on how calamitous the error is supposed to be. It *might* be that only fairly recherché constructions involve error—for instance, only a tendency to put the relevant sentences into some particular embeddings, or occasionally to use certain logical laws on them. Or it might be that many aspects of our discourse show us in the grip of error, and that nothing but wholesale flight from the forms of ordinary language and thought will purge it. Call the behaviour of an expression *perfectly propositional* if in every way it actually accords with that of paradigm judgement-expressing sentences. Then the point is that while an error theorist is opposed to perfect propositionality, he has freedom in saying just how much of it is wrong.

The *quasi-realist* by contrast seeks to show that there is no essential error. According to him the ordinary forms of thought do not depend upon metaphysical errors, and can be sustained in full understanding of the expressive starting point. Similarly the language we use to conduct our thought is perfectly in order. We can *earn* our right to use the logic and the propositional forms we do, from the anti-realist starting point. Seen like this, a quasi-realist may or may not regard the forms in question as perfectly propositional. He could be receptive to signs, embedded in normal discourse, that we do not always think and speak as if the sentences in question were just like others. But he is opposed to the revisions of ordinary discourse urged by the error theorist, and of course to any attempt to press the surface aspects of the discourse into the service of realism.

Experience teaches me that this position is apt to seem paradoxical to people, and its tenability can be doubted. It can of course be doubted whether it is successful in its own terms—whether the reconstruction of a logic and of a reading for the propositional contexts is adequate. I shall say more about that later. But the immediate puzzle I want to address is different. The trouble is that the overall package is easily charged with incoherence. The charge is that it starts by depending on a contrast—that between attitudes and so forth on the one hand, and beliefs on the other. But it typically ends by assimilating them so closely that, it may be charged, the original contrast seems to evaporate. We understand the contrast at the beginning, so a critic might say, by thinking of beliefs, as opposed to attitudes, as capable of negation and disjunction, as sustaining truth, falsity, and probability, and as objects of doubt and denial. But the forms of thought and language that embody these capabilities of belief are precisely the ones that the quasi-realist claims to earn for his attitudes. So in that case the original contrast collapses, and with it any coherent position. We cannot say 'such-and-such commitments are not beliefs; they are other states that properly sustain the appearance of being beliefs', if properly sustaining that appearance is all that there is to *being* a belief—all that there is to mark off beliefs from attitudes and the rest in the first place.

We cannot say this, but we can say something just as interesting, by dropping the first clause of the conjunction. We could say: attitudes (and the rest) properly sustain the appearance of being beliefs, so they are beliefs. They belong to the subset of beliefs that are also attitudes (dispositions, inference tickets, or whatever). We would not say things like 'conditionals are not propositions; they are commitments of a different sort, held by those who have corresponding conditional probabilities'. We would say 'conditionals are propositions; they are the subset of propositions belief in which is (functionally and logically) equivalent to having certain conditional probabilities'. We would not say 'modal commitments are not propositions; they are commitments of a different sort, assent to which is equivalent to voicing an imaginative block of a certain kind'. We would say 'they are propositions; they belong to the subset of propositions assent to which is functionally and logically equivalent to voicing an imaginative block of a certain kind'.

The point is that showing *how there can be* propositions of this kind is just the difficulty. The trick will be to show how this can be true. But *that* will take all the work that quasi-realism tries to carry out. Sometimes (in the theory of conditionals, for example) there is precise argument that there *cannot* be any propositions with the required assertibility conditions.[1] In other cases there is a more diffuse philosophical discomfort: an early example is the antinomy of taste: Kant's problem of how there can *be* a normative judgement of beauty, commanding the assent of others, given its non-cognitive starting point in the sensation of pleasure.

Does it matter whether we opt for a 'contrastive' story, according to which attitudes and the rest are not beliefs, however much we can earn them a right to behave like them, or an 'inclusive' story, according to which what is shown is that they are beliefs, of a special kind? In the absence of any definitive account of what makes a state of mind a belief, it is hard to see that it can matter. To focus the point a little, suppose that the quasi-realist gives us a persuasive account of why it might be legitimate to discuss the commitments in question using a truth-predicate, whose function he can explain. So we hear ourselves saying, with a good conscience, that moral/modal/conditional commitments are sometimes true. Are they ('really') true, or is this a convenient expansion of the term? This is the question that in *Spreading the Word* I said I did not greatly commend: it seems to depend upon a finer discrimination of the real sense of the term 'true' than any we ought to claim.[2]

The choice is not uninteresting. But my present point is that it is before getting to this choice that most of the work has to be done. Both the contrastive and inclusive options require the same scene setting. In each case propositional behaviour needs description, explanation, and sometimes defence. For this reason I reject Crispin Wright's suggestion, endorsed by Bob Hale, that quasi-realism would be at best a detour, leading us back to the real task, which is to work our way into a satisfactory conception of truth for the area in question.[3] By my lights, this is itself subject to a dilemma. Either it is simply restating the way the quasi-realist conceives of the task, which is that of earning propositional forms of thought in a way that recognizes the challenge of scepticism, like that voiced in Kant's antithesis. Or it is a way of ducking the issue—for example, of taking assertoric forms simply for granted, and mounting a much more restricted debate about some aspect of truth in the area (for instance, what to make of the fact that in a particular area the views of cognitively competent judges may not converge). But my instinct is to start, with Kant, as far back as possible: how *can there be* such a thing as moral/conditional/modal, etc. judgement? If we do not start this far back, we will always be vulnerable to the error theorist, saying that even if we do have an assertoric discourse, we should not: the familiar charge that ethical, aesthetic, modal thought is a fraud.

II

So far I have defended the coherence of quasi-realism against any expansion of the term 'belief'. An equal threat comes from expansion of the term 'realism'. Is there always a coherent realism to be 'anti'? Or might the term be best regarded as sufficiently innocuous that anyone, except perhaps the sceptic or error theorist, should be regarded as a realist? It is important here to insist on a Carnapian distinction between what I shall call 'immanent' and 'external' versions of realism. Immanent realism is the position that the forms of ordinary discourse in the area form the only data, and themselves impose realism ('You believe that we have duties to our children? Then you are a realist about duties! You believe that judges need to think about the right verdict? Then you are a legal realist?'). External realism would be a conjunction of the view that (a) there is a further external, metaphysical issue over whether the right theory of the area is realistic, and (b) the answer to this issue is that it is. Immanent realism entails the denial of (a); quasi-realism agrees with (a), but denies (b).

For completeness we ought to notice immanent anti-realism. This would be the largely unoccupied position that while no external questions arise, the internal forms of the practice compel us *not* to think in terms of fact, truth, or ontological commitment. An example of this position is the view that our actual logical practice with conditionals shows that they are not fully fledged propositions; another possible example would be the (unlikely) view that we actually use a non-bivalent logic in mathematical argument, and that this too has constructivist implications for the philosophy of mathematics. But the position is uncomfortable, if only because it seems at least implicitly to acknowledge external questions, even if it then confines the evidence on which they are to be answered to first-order usage. In contrast, the more common view that we *ought* to modify practice in such areas is a typical externalist norm, arising from reflection from outside on what the area is for and how thought in it ought to be conducted, and as such it is clearly committed to obtaining evidence other than actual use.

To understand the immanent/external distinction, picture the case of mathematics. Here we have a first-order discipline that happily quantifies over abstract objects. Let us accept that there is no reduction that preserves its content while avoiding the quantification. According to the immanent realist, this settles it: we have no alternative but realism about numbers and sets, and must admit them to our ontology forthwith. According to the externalist, whether realist or not, there is a further metaphysical battle still to be joined. The best theory about the area might indeed demand this ontological commitment—the realist says that it does. But it might not—we might be able to see what we are up to in accepting the commitments of first-order discourse without being realists about the entities in question. This space is the one that quasi-realism inhabits. Perhaps using mathematics is to be thought of instrumentally, and wielding the instrument is not to be thought of as describing a world of abstract objects, or indeed describing anything at all; perhaps there are other ways of seeing what we are doing.

In the case of mathematics denying that there is this space is fairly unattractive. It means supposing that commitment to the first-order practice entails commitment to realism, whereas to the unprejudiced eye it is one thing to accept a practice, and quite another to advance any particular theory of it.

III

Although as I have said immanent anti-realism seems theoretically possible, in the phrase 'immanent realism' it is the first word that does nearly all the work. That is, the difficult task is to show whether the right place from which to theorize about the discourse is entirely from within, so that no external questions are to be asked. Once that point is gained, the word 'realism' will not count for much, any more than the word 'belief' or 'truth'. Once we hear ourselves saying 'there are duties/causes/conditional facts/colours/sets (etc.)' then, given that we are convinced that no external questions can be posed, we will not be increasing the stakes much by saying that 'there are really duties/causes . . .' or 'it is true that there are . . .'. These just tag along with the propositional surface. So the interesting question becomes that of whether there is an external standpoint from which to theorize about the area.

The idea that there is not is apt to seem extraordinarily unadventurous: a refusal to seek explanations where, on the face of it, explanations may be had. It is not however quite right to see the position as one of passive acquiescence in all the forms and commitments of a given discourse, if passivity means lack of interest in *any* kind of scepticism, or *any* kind of theory about the area. For as John McDowell has rightly urged, there may certainly be purely *internal* sources of pressure, that might exercise the theorist and even lead to scepticism or to change in the direction urged by an error theorist.[4] Thus in the case of ethics, a sufficiently pessimistic view of the endemic conflicts, or tainted conceptual links of moral concepts such as those of rights and obligations, might itself lead to scepticism about there being such a thing as moral truth at all. And this pessimism could have a purely *moral* source: it might come from despair at the myth-tainted origins of our thought, or sadness at the fragmented contemporary scene, rather than scepticism arising from an alleged second-order, philosophical position. It comes, as we might put it, from despair at what we find as we walk around our moral boat, rather than any external vision of what a moral boat is in the first place. But it might also lead to despair about the very possibility of a seaworthy moral boat (I take it this is Alasdair Macintyre's view of our current position, and Bernard Williams' position with regard to morality, if not with regard to ethics[5]).

An external theorist does not of course deny that this is a possible predicament. The commitments of the area turn out to have their own problems; if this erodes confidence in them, they may wither away. His position is that this is not the *only* philosophical problem we face (if it were, it would be hard to see how there is space for, say, a philosophy of arithmetic, since the first-order practice scarcely encourages internally generated scepticism). He is distinctive in thinking that even if we are happy to accept the practice, there is still space for realist versus anti-realist theorizing.

Quasi-realism must acknowledge, and indeed absorb, one element that will also belong to the purely immanent position. Consider that the bid to *earn* a conception of truth in the area cannot proceed without stressing the *merits* of the area—without the kind of first-order boost of confidence that comes from walking round our boat, and finding it reasonably in order. Thus suppose the challenge comes: whether we conceive of the existence of moral properties as made acceptable by the story of the last section, or whether we go through a more elaborate process of looking first at attitudes, and only secondly at their propositional forms, the upshot is the same. The materials on hand are simply too thin to sustain the practice: it is made to appear (for instance) no better than the way in which predication and talk of truth and properties can be grafted on to the purely subjective pleasures of the wine-taster or ice-cream connoisseur.

In the ethical case an answer to this challenge must respect its autonomy: it takes a value to make a value. There is no purely external 'proof' that the education of sensibilities is a good thing. Any defence has to presuppose some value, if only that the meeting of human needs is a good thing. Without some common ground, there is no progress. Similarly of course with wine-tasting: there is no arguing someone into caring about the pleasures of the palate, but once she cares somewhat, she may be helped to care more. In particular of course there is no external support from other virtues, such as that of rationality. The ethical boat floats; it does not sit perched upon that rock.

But now the immanent theorist may press his advantage. Consider two features of truth. It should be unique, and it should stand at a sufficient distance from our actual opinions for us to entertain the thought that our actual opinions may not be true. These are features that the quasi-realist will need to earn. But surely what is required is, again, an essentially first-order ethical inquiry. To take the second point first: what is wrong with someone who cannot entertain the thought that her opinions might not be true? Absence of self-criticism and doubt and incapacity to see room for improvement—essentially *moral* faults that only an improvement in character will cure. And consider the first: thinking in terms of anything other than unique truth would be *either* losing confidence in the entire area (disaffection and alienation), or losing sight of the need to work through to the correctness of one ethical stance and the inferiority of others—a numbing relativism that, again, requires an essentially moral counter.

It begins to look as if the 'earning' a right to propositional discourse is not, as it was billed, a second-order theoretical task, but is instead a purely first-order exercise in inspecting the boat and finding it good. Similarly, a cure for scepticism about the features plumed by wine-tasters will be given only by sympathetic immersion in the practice. There is no external justification on offer. The Macintyrean predicament is now the only one.

It is ironic that this now seems to be an objection to a projective, quasi-realist strategy. For one of the strengths of the position has been to insist on recognizing when second-order issues are actually first-order ones in disguise. On the issue of the mind-dependency of values, for example, one of its merits has been its ability to treat a thought such as 'if we had nourished different sentiments, kicking dogs would have been right' not as a statement of second-order dependencies, but as a first-order moral view, whose repugnancy is easily seen (naturally, by an exercise of first-order, ethical imagination). Yet it now seems, dangerously, that this strategy can be extended until it blocks out the space the theory needs, leaving the field in the hands of immanent realism after all.

I said above that the externalist seeks evidence for or against a realist theory from an area other than the actual first-order practice about which he wants a theory. What other kind of evidence could there be? Provided the area in question is local, the answer is obvious: we can have evidence from its surroundings, or in other words from other things we think, for example about explanation, truth, fact, reality, and our knowledge of it. Thus a realist has an obligation to make us comfortable with knowledge of the area of reality he sees us as describing; he has to make us comfortable too with the utility we find in describing it (both aspects are highly visible when we think of a realist theory of possible worlds). Making us comfortable is not a task that is easily circumscribed, notably because many realists are comfortable with things, such as advanced epistemological powers that offend others. Equally anti-realism must make good its explanations of the discourse and the role it plays in our lives, whilst avoiding the view that it exists *because* it describes a genuine aspect of reality.

Clearly this introduces a background problem: which are the aspects of reality that are to be taken as genuine? What is a proper base from which to conduct this theorizing? Quasi-realism is often charged with 'scientism' at this point, or in other words with confining genuine reality to an ontology and set of features delineated by some favoured fundamental science, such as physics.[6] A better basis, it is then suggested, will include much more: why should it not include the properties and features that, on the face of it, we know about as we indulge the area in question—moral, aesthetic, causal, and modal features, for example? In *Spreading the Word* I adopted a fairly cavalier attitude to this problem, taking it for granted that if you can reach a good explanation of an area from a more economical baseline, that will be preferable to one that needs to cite more—more aspects of reality, more ways in which they matter, and more epistemological powers to know about them.

Perhaps it was wrong to take this for granted. There is, I suppose, an attitude that smells 'scientism' in any attempt to make the human world fit comfortably into the scientific, and such an attitude allows its victims to turn their backs on the problem. I have met philosophers who profess blank incomprehension at any such project. Who knows what they think Hume, Kant, Ramsey, Wittgenstein, and the others were doing? But there is a more respectable attitude that needs addressing. For an opponent might concede the desirability of bringing what we say about ethics and the rest into some working relationship with a scientific world view. But he might suppose that this can be done in a different way, and one that makes no room for the quasi-realist starting point.

IV

In a sensitive passage John McDowell allows that there is a legitimate question of 'placing', as I called it, ethics or humour, a question of 'how ethics or humour relate to the scientifically useful truth about the world and our dealings with it'. But, he continues

> we do not need to suppose that such 'placing' functions by allowing us to make sense of a range of subjective responses to a world that contains nothing valuable, or funny-responses that we can then see as projected on to that world so as to generate the familiar appearances. What we 'place' need not be the sort of sentiments that can be regarded as parents of apparent features: it may be pairs of sentiments and features reciprocally related—siblings rather than parents and children.[7]

I shall return to the sibling metaphor later. For the present let us discard an ambiguity in the first sentence, an ambiguity between, as it were, starting and stopping point. Consider the scientific investigation of colour discrimination. Does this function by allowing us to make sense of a range of subjective responses to a world that contains nothing coloured? Well, it does not *draw upon* colours in its description of the different wavelengths and types of reflection of light, sensitivities of our cones, or the neural functions that aggregate their information. But it need not *end up* denying that roses are red: that is only one way, and in my view a bad way, of expressing the endpoint. The explanation steers clear of any such issue. Similarly, I should say, the placing of our propensity for ethics or humour into a working relationship with the scientific world view, whilst it must not draw upon the existence of values, obligations, and the rest, need not anticipate ending up saying that there are none of them. On the contrary, it is the point of quasi-realism to enable us to say, with a good conscience, that there are lots.

There is however another very serious point in McDowell's response. He lines up the options so that a projectivist 'placing' of ethics and humour differs from the preferable 'sibling' placing in a crucial and damaging respect. This is that the projectivist execution of this 'placing' task is undermined 'if we cannot home in on the subjective state whose projection is supposed to result in the seeming feature of reality in question without the aid of the concept of that feature, the concept that was to be explained'.[8] And it seems plausible that this is often so: our best understanding of what it is to find something comic may be just that: we have no independent fix on amusement as a reaction that is (as it were) antecedently fixed, ready for use in an explanatory story about how its projection started us off thinking that things are comic. And similarly for ethics, where it is often remarked that the 'attitudes' needed by the quasi-realist tend to remain damagingly undifferentiated from other things (likes, dislikes, aversions, and so on) unless located by an ethical vocabulary.

The 'sibling' story, by contrast, allows us to 'work from within', making use of ethical or comic judgements as we seek to understand our propensity to make them:

> the no-priority view allows, then, that it might be possible to do something recognizable as earning truth by focusing on the funny itself ... this contrasts with a constraint that seems to be implicit in a serious projectivism, according to which the idea of a superior discernment has to be made clear without exploiting exercises of the way of thinking which is to be explained as projective, so that it is available for use in certifying some such exercises as (quasi-realistically) true.[9]

McDowell suggests that I have been casual about this problem because I presume that if we are not realists of an unsatisfactory (intuitionist) sort, then we just have to be projectivists, thereby ignoring the 'no priority' view.

Let us call the alleged problem for projectivism, the problem of the contaminated response. Now it ought to be doubtful that the way out of this problem, in the context of the 'placing' operation that all sides agree to be legitimate, is to give explanatory rights to moral or comic *features*. Again, consider the parallel with colours: it is always noticed that one of the problems in front of a philosophy of colour is that the experienced response is just that of seeing or seeming to see something *as some definite colour*. Now it may not be clear whether this is a problem for the view that we can well be described as projecting colours on to the world. But what is surely more clear is that the problem opens no door to a *different* rapprochement between the human world and the scientific world—one that cites this very feature of things (that they are coloured) in a story explaining our perceptual and cognitive powers. Certainly, one might want to think hard about colour as a rapprochement proceeds: one is not going to do a good job if the nature of colour discrimination is badly described or underdescribed in the first place. But (unless we are proceeding in terms of a reduction) this will not be to invoke colours as features explanatory of our practices. How could colour come in at *that* point, to do any work?[10]

There are certainly *other* points at which we must work from within, making use of and trusting ethical (or comic) judgement as we do so. Notably, whenever we are in the first-order business of assessing the truth of some particular verdict. As I said, it takes a value to make a value: there is no proving the virtue of this or the vice of that without standing on some other element of the moral boat (this is the point of the metaphor of the boat). But this is not the context of the 'placing' operation: this is the exercise of first-order theory, not the attempt to understand our right to use such theory, given a starting sympathy with the scientific world view. I return to this conflation later.

Meanwhile, how serious in its own terms is the problem of the contaminated response? Surely if there is a point at which the contamination cannot be understood, in ways that respect the point of the 'placing' inquiry, it is equally serious for everybody. When someone gestures at a starting point for under-standing ethical responses, in terms perhaps of the need for social devices for putting pressure on choice and action, he is not committed to saying that this is the last word, that no historical deposit has shaped the idiosyncratic ways in which we currently think and feel. But if the story is to help, he is committed to supposing that no unintelligible sea-changes (for instance, as one might suppose the emergence of the propositional surface to be) have occurred as the journey proceeds. The point of the story is to do some naturalized psychology, so there is to be nothing unnatural about the transformations that have brought us where we are. Similarly there will be something we do not understand about ourselves if the reaction of amusement, equalling the finding of something funny, stands as a solitary peculiarity, with no smooth natural history embedding it in other responses to the world. By this standard, and in this context, appeal to the features we talk of will represent defeat. In answer to the question (say) why people are disposed to find things comical, the reply that often they just are blocks off the 'placing' operation rather than advancing it. And so does the view that we find things good (or beautiful, or red) because they are so.[11]

Quasi-realism focuses, indeed, upon the emergence of the propositional surface of our practice. It takes seriously the worry that this might itself be just the kind of sea-change that blocks a naturalistic understanding of what we are doing. And it seeks to disarm that fear. Seen like this, it is hard to see quite how the opposition arises, given that the 'placing' operation is in order in the first place.

V

I now turn to introduce another twist, that also threatens to be hostile to quasi-realism. Consider the case of chairs. We know that there is no single physical kind, definable without reference to humans and their activities and postures that is co-extensive with the class of chairs. Do chairs then share a feature? They presumably share a dispositional feature, although it is hard to define it. What is more certainly true is that there is something in the overall system, of us-discriminating-chairs, that results in some things getting the verdict, and others not. There had better not be anything physically inexplicable in that overall system, and I see no reason to suppose that there is. Here is a wild sketch. One could imagine robotic discriminations starting to approximate to ours pretty well, if the robot contained, for instance, a sensitivity to physical shapes and sizes, to stress in some of its parts, and perhaps if it contained a capacity to test whether something was strong enough to support it, or a memory to tell whether it had been made in one of a number of ways (fortunately, with the arrival of neural networks, the absence of precise necessary and sufficient conditions for being a chair is not a principled obstacle to such a robot—it need have no programme definable on other features for its discriminations to be explicable, and to approximate arbitrarily closely to our own).

Do norms, 'correctness', and correspondingly the phenomenon of illusion get a place in such a picture, or are they forever excluded? Imagine a community of robots, capable of signalling whether something is a chair to one another; imagine that various kinds of consequence follow on signalling a chair when one is not present; imagine that some situations are apt to prompt such signalling (for example confrontation with what is actually only a chair facade). Enough of these embellishments and we begin the emergence of a similar approximation to verdicts of correctness and incorrectness. Of course, I am not trying to solve one of the central problems of philosophy *en passant*, but just suggesting that if there is some principled objection to regarding such devices as making judgements at all, it is not to be found here.

Now such a sketch is apt to encourage a relaxed attitude to properties. If beforehand we were inclined to say that 'being a chair' is not a real property, on the grounds that the corresponding predicate plays no part in physics, we might now reconsider. If physics can tolerate and explain a system in which some things are discriminated as chairs, and others not, then what is the *point* in denying that the things that *are* so discriminated share a property? Properties are abstractions from predicates; predicates come from judgements; judgements from discriminations.

One suggestion we can now sidestep would be that in the story outlined chairs indeed share a property—a dispositional one, of getting the verdict from the discriminators. It is important to what follows to see that there is something right about this, and something not. The right part is that in the explanation this is all that is going on: the discriminator, sensitive to a number of other aspects of its situation (not all of which need even seem to be properties of the object it is classifying), is eventually prompted to give its verdict. Chairs are things which typically prompt and (unlike chair facades) sustain such verdicts. The wrong part, in my view, would be putting the disposition into the 'content' of the judgement, as if the discriminator were therefore centrally concerned with whether the object is disposed to have some effect on members of some defined group. That is simply not how it works. The way it works has already been sketched, and in that story none of the aspects that, together, issue in a verdict need be ones that require any such concern or awareness. The robot was sensitive to such things as shape of the object or stress in its own parts when it conformed itself to it. It was not sensitive to whether the object was disposed to create some verdict in itself or its fellow robots. For this reason it would be wrong to suggest that the monadic predicate ('is a chair') be replaced by a more overtly relational one ('is such as to gain the "chair" verdict'). While the relational one suggests the fundamental metaphysics, it pays by suggesting the wrong cognitive sensitivity, and wrong resultant way of thought.

Consider again the similar example of colour vision. From Galileo onwards philosophers have been tempted to interpret the scientific data on colour vision as showing that there are really no such properties (notice that this can be combined with an error theory, according to which colour discourse ought not to survive these discoveries unchanged, or with the view that the implication is purely one for theorists, leaving vulgar discourse untouched).[12] But we can sketch a story with similar ingredients. Physically explicable systems, responsive to such things as (definite and even apparently arbitrary functions of) the different energy levels of light at different wavelengths come to discriminate as we do. Groups of them go in for a normatively governed discourse typing objects by using this response. No error in that—so where is the error in saying that red things form a kind, sharing the property of being red? It is a kind that is, in an obvious sense, anthropocentric. Certainly creatures with differently tuned receptors, or stimulated by different functions of the output of the same receptors, would be unable to share the discriminations, or understand the classification of surfaces to which they lead. They would not be able to see the lasso we cast round the world. But we are not talking of our own dispositions: as in the case of chairs, it would be unhappy to see the judgements issued as properly relational. Creatures *use* their responses to classify surfaces: they do not *think of* their responses and their relation to the surfaces causing them.[13]

If so much is true of chairs and colours, perhaps it can be extended to ethical properties. Once more we have an explicable system, by the standards of the sketches we have been allowing. Creatures have needs and must act; they need discourse for pondering and communicating pressures designed to encourage and forestall certain kinds of action; the discourse that issues type things as good or bad, right or wrong. There is nothing inexplicable here. So if the stories above succeeded in putting the property of being a chair or being red into what I called a working relationship with the scientific world view, surely this story succeeds in putting ethical properties into a similar one. And if there should be no temptation to scepticism about chairs and colours, once we sketch the story, neither should there be about goodness and rightness.

Finally if we veer away from giving the predicates an overtly relational form, as mistaking the cognition involved, in those cases, so we should in this. We thus avoid any refutable subjectivist analysis, in which the disposition of a thing to cause a reaction in some group becomes part of the 'truth-condition' of the judgement. As well as mistaking the property to which we are sensitive in doing ethics, as in the case of chairs and colours, such analyses (I would claim) always confront a dilemma. Either the group (or the conditions which elicit its response: 'ideal conditions', for instance) is defined in ethical terms (so that a good thing is a thing disposed to elicit a certain reaction from good people, or from ordinary people in ideal conditions) in which case no gain is made, or it is not, in which case it misrepresents the property that interests us: whichever group you mention, in caring whether something is good I need not at all be caring whether it actually elicits approval from *that* group. But if chairs and colours were naturalized without incurring a relational reduction, so should ethics and the others be.[14]

We might see the view I have sketched as fundamentally sympathetic to the 'secondary properties' line on ethics advocated by David Wiggins and John McDowell, although they show more sympathy towards a dispositional analysis. In any event, it is the best way I can express the fundamental elements of that position, although it concedes more to the request for naturalistic (scientific) explanation than they might wish. This concession is only a strength: if the position incorporates no fundamental hostility to the scientific world view, it is good to have that visible. And in this sketch two more aspects become apparent. First, it is not going to be sufficient to refute it, to cite disanalogies between actual moral discrimination and the detailed mechanisms of secondary property perception. It is easy to describe such disanalogies, but perhaps at this level of abstraction they need not matter.[15] The mechanism whereby the existence of a property rides on the back, as it were, of a discriminatory practice, is sufficiently abstract to cover many different forms of practice. Second, just because no relational reduction is in the offing, the cognitive surface of a practice might take a variety of forms. It might, for instance, allow us to think in terms of a distance between our actual discriminations and ideal ones, if it makes room for standards of better and worse discrimination. So even if there is little scope for such a distinction in the case of some secondary properties, and considerable scope in the case of ethics, this need not undermine the model.

There is however no prospect of this story helping the metaphor whereby ethical properties and ethical sensibilities are 'siblings' or 'made for each other'. We still get at best a one-way dependency, of property on sensibility. Of course, on everyone's picture, there may be no limit to the capacities for critical thought embedded in the practice. So the operation of a sensibility might come to change (for better or worse) the discriminations it effects. On this story one might say that a tuning or changing of the sensibilities does change the property.[16] But one would not see by any such means a naturalized dependency the other way round.[17]

VI

Does the naturalization of a property along the lines of the last section give us a plausible rival to quasi-realism? Each answer can seem uncomfortable. If it does, then it seems to do so more by *reminding* us of the cognitive surface of our practices, than by earning them, as the quasi-realist promised. True, one kind of scepticism may have been disarmed, by pointing up the parallel with chairs and colours. But others remain, as we can see by reflecting on the very promiscuity of the move. Not only ethical properties, but those predicated in any practice at all (properties of humour, aesthetics, taste, etc.) are explicable in the same way. Can we so easily remain deaf to the doubt whether, in some of these areas, we have a practice that is concerned with *truth*? On the other hand, saying that the story is not a rival to quasi-realism entails pointing to the difference—unless one wants to extend the term to cover judgement about chairs and colours.

Two features of the colour case contrast interestingly with the areas I have talked about. One is that in the case of colour the sensitivity is 'sub doxastic'; brought about by mechanisms quite outside our control. The receptors and the information they yield are hard-wired: it is not up to us to alter the way we see a surface in a given light and surroundings. Except possibly at the margins there is no learning, no social variation, and no argument in the face of diversity. There is, on the other hand, a thriving scientific study of the nature of the receptors and information processing in the brain. In the case of ethical responses this is reversed: the sensitivity is brought about by devices that we actively control, and there is no scientific study of relevant special receptors. The other difference is that hard information is at the disposal of any needs or plans we happen to have. It is easy to imagine why it was evolutionarily successful to be good at surfaces and boundaries, but now that we (better: our brains) are so good at it, we can use the ability how we wish. Neither feature fits in the case of ethical or modal judgement. There is no evidence of hard-wiring, but only of learning, variation, and argument. And more importantly, the discriminations are not normally at the service of a great diversity of needs and projects, but connected fairly rigidly to their conative point, which is to put pressures and boundaries on thought and action.

These differences show that we have to start further back: we have to start by acknowledging the functional end of the commitments—the things that make an error theory so tempting. For if a commitment is well seen as a culturally variable, brutely contingent expression of a disposition to put pressure on ourselves and others, *everyone*, not merely the freshman relativist, ought to feel uncomfortable at its also claiming a title to objective, independent truth. It will not be enough to say that we have the practice of so dignifying it. This will only appear part of the error, or the confidence trick.

So quasi-realism is still in place. The starting point is to acknowledge that we have some *non-descriptive functional location* for the commitments of an area. Having one means needing to be able to understand why these commitments should emerge to fill other cognitive functions than describing the way of the world. They may enable us, for example, to organize our reactions to descriptions that we do have, to chart inferences amongst them, or to express our own dispositions and encourage dispositions to organization and reaction on the part of others. Insofar as these are things *we* do well or badly, they will need to be objects of conscious cognition: learning, variation, and argument will set in, and will be the motors driving us towards the propositional surface of discourse.

A final point about the dialectical position may be in order. Quasi-realism asks for only a world with natural features, and us with an explicable repertoire of desires and needs. Imagine now a group of theorists allowing themselves only the same naturalistic tool-kit. See the quasi-realist as only one of these, following an individual line in his rational reconstruction of the practice. Now suppose for a moment that the story is ineradicably flawed. What then happens? Do not just think: well, then we see that ethical (etc.) judgements are real judgements, that there are ethical properties, that realism triumphs. For that (so far as the story yet goes) means helping yourself to things that are not in the naturalistic tool-kit. All the failure could mean is that we face a dilemma: redeploy the ingredients to find another natural 'placing' of ethics, or agree with the error theorist that something like a Boo-Hooray language is all that there *ought* to be. In other words, if at some point we prove to have jumped ship, going in for a discourse whose cognitive surface is quite inexplicable quasi-realistically, this may not so much be the failure of quasi-realism, as the failure of ethics to be what it seems to be. It will be bad for everyone if a Boo-Hooray language is as far as we *ought* to have got, with the only legitimate ingredients.

VI

I now turn to the more technical criticism of some of my suggestions, skilfully and fairly developed by Bob Hale, in his essay in this volume. If this section is short, it is partly because in his own discussion Hale not only presents pertinent problems, but also to some extent my reactions to them, and modifications that have ensued at least partly from thinking about his work. There are only a few additional points that I feel able to make.

(1) As Hale notices, the system sketched in *Spreading the Word* was modified in a later paper, 'Attitudes and Contents', and the following remarks may be better understood if that paper is familiar.[18] In that paper I sought both to buttress and to some extent to generalize the theory of *Spreading the Word*. To take the first aim: critics, including Hale himself, had doubted whether that system contained the seeds of a genuine *logic*. It seemed as though a person who, for instance, failed to make an inference according to *modus ponens*, when the premises contain ethical commitments, suffered some kind of flaw, but it was not clear why it would be a specifically logical flaw. What was needed was a better account of how mismanagement of commitments expressing attitude could amount to failure of logic, but, of course, without invoking a *semantic* mark of inconsistency, in terms of failure of possible truth. For that would be to help myself to a semantic notion that, at this stage of the game, is still unavailable. But there was also a need for more generality or system. It had always been evident that the problem quasi-realism faced with conditionals must be part of a more systematic problem, arising just as much in connection with negation and disjunction (and eventually quantification, tenses, and so on). It would be little good to manage even a moderately convincing story about conditionals, if these others then floored us.

In that later paper then I hoped that both aims could be pursued by turning from the discursive approach of *Spreading the Word* to a more syntactic treatment, and seeking a general criterion for the inconsistency of a joint set of attitudes and beliefs: a criterion for the impossibility of joint satisfaction of a set containing expressions of both. This would be genuine inconsistency or failure of possibility of satisfaction, thereby furthering the first aim. And insofar as it achieved generality, it might afford the basis of a more adequate treatment of the varieties of inference possible, although as with most semantics the propositional and first-order constructions hold the limelight. To see how it might develop I presented a small modification of a standard deontic logic. The philosophical interest of this was that the expressions of attitude H!p and B!p (hooray for p!; Boo to p!) could be interpreted as they occurred in disjunctions and negations: the latter by 'driving' external negations inwards, and the former by thinking of the inferential powers attaching to disjunction—brought out in this case by a standard tree treatment. The trick was to see (with for example the late Stig Kanger) how the elements on which the logic operated did not have to be thought of as themselves 'propositional' for a notion of inconsistency to be in place. This is possible because the broad idea is that we break open an original set by imagining the ideals realized; if their realization in what Hintikka calls a 'Kingdom of Ends' is impossible, then the original set was inconsistent. 'Realization' gives a mapping from attitude to situation, enabling standard logic to get a foothold.

The idea is simple enough if we consider only endorsements and the reverse: someone is assessed for consistency if they are recommending states by imagining the recommended states realized. An original set of commitments generates an 'ideal' set, in which recommendations are imagined carried out. Things become more tricky with permissions or expressions of toleration, and it is when we chase the situations relevant to an assessment of these that there is room for error. Hale is right to recognize a problem in the logic I presented, caused by one modification of Hintikka's axioms. Hale diagnoses the problem as arising from an unconscious conflation between the logical enterprise of following through the implications of some mixed set of beliefs and attitudes, which is what the logic ought to be codifying, and the very different business of thinking of *improvements* of such a set, as we lurch towards an opinion on ethical truth. But I think my unconscious is innocent of such a criminal conflation. What caused me to tinker was a general liking for a tableau method, or in other words a transparent *step wise* procedure for getting to the final sets of sentences that are tested for consistency. With Hintikka's system this is done all at once: to take a trivial case H!H!H!p gives as an ideal the set {H!H!H!p, H!H!p, H!p, p} (all the states commended are imagined realized). However, I may have misled my unconscious by terminology. For while it is natural to call the sets obtained by realizing obligations (or hooray attitudes) further approximations to an ideal, there is no particular rationale for calling sequences got by further exercises of permissions that: they amount to the production of further tolerable alternatives, and that is all.

If this is the only divergence then all I am doing is providing an ordered sequence of sets whose last member *ought* to be the Hintikka set, obtained by him in one swoop. So the difference in strength ought to be curable, and so far as I can see it is. As we have it the difficulty for my system is that we *either* allow unrestricted axiom (4) (if L* is a next approximation to the ideal relative to some set of sentences L, then, if A ∈ L*, A ∈ subsequent approximations to the ideal, L**, L***, etc.) and meet the undesirable result that T!H!p yields H!p, *or* we restrict (4) as I suggested, and fail to get H!(H!p → p). Hintikka avoids both alternatives, because in his system in any alternative to the actual world which is a candidate for deontic perfection, all relevant obligations are fulfilled. So if we think of tolerations as modelled by introducing sets of worlds that are candidates for deontic perfection, we can I think get the same result by making a more subtle modification of (4): where what is derived from wide scope T! itself contains wide scope H! everything in the set is to iterate to the next approximation—otherwise not. More formally:

(4″) If L* is a next approximation relative to some set of sentences L, then if L* contains H!(X) then a subsequent approximation L** contains X and all the other sentences of L*.

Certainly this blocks the unwanted result that Hale cites. Everything stops where it should, at {T!p, ¬p}. But it gets the wanted result: T!(H!p & ¬p) leads to {H!p & ¬p} and thence to {p & ¬p}.

The rationale for this apparently cumbersome rule is that what you are held to when you tolerate something is treated differently if it includes a H! . . . ; this may fairly be taken as realized in assessing you for inconsistency. And so far as I can see this will give the same strength of system as Hintikka's.

(2) It is natural to read the 'H! . . .' of such a logic as meaning 'in an ideal world . . .'. But ideals come in different packages. It would be good if the prison system were more humane; in saying this I do not expect to be met with the reply that it would not, for it would only be good if there were no criminals and no prisons in the first place. For some evaluative purposes we can take something as fixed (human nature, for instance), whereas in another less practical context we might wish it away. We might imagine, then, a set of beliefs and attitudes with members flagged (e.g. p_F) according to whether they are taken as fixed for the purpose in hand. Hale raises the interesting issue of the kind of 'inconsistency' that arises if one's ideals can only be realized at the expense of some belief that, for the evaluative purpose in hand, ought to be taken as fixed. If its being taken as fixed implies its iterating through to the later sets of sentences on which we test for consistency, then from H!p and ¬p_F we would obtain a final set, {H!p, p, ¬p}. Do we want this? We could shy away from calling the vice one of inconsistency, and think of another word (impracticality?): we would then not allow p itself to iterate through, but signal the vice perhaps by allowing p_F to iterate, with the result that if a final set contains p_F and ¬p, the initial set was impractical. The same kind of wrinkle will emerge especially with tolerations: frequently something is tolerable only because something else, that would have been much better, has not been realized. We might thus need to make a distinction between a fixed toleration and a *faut de mieux* toleration, and again define different iteration paths.

Hale gives a slight impression that it is a problem for the logic that this phenomenon emerges. On the contrary, I see it as an advance: the exercise highlights a potential flaw in a set of commitments, and one that might easily go unremarked in an unsystematic development.

(3) Hale is quite right to point out that the background to any such logic is not exactly the 'Fregean' universe of pure propositions. Assessing a set for consistency is conceived as imagining the commitments involved as belonging to a particular subject, and then working out whether such a subject contravenes logical norms. This is not by any means unique to this enterprise. In subjective probability theory probabilities are treated as betting rates of agents who need to abide by the norm that a dutch book cannot be made against them, and it is on this basis that the 'logical' laws of probability are established. Probability offers sufficient structure for it to be relatively clear what is wanted from a representation theorem showing that coherent betting rates can be interpreted as probabilities. In the case of value, the logic ought to offer a similar propositional representation of attitudes, and the need is to show that we do not have a picture which allows disobedience to classical logical laws when this is done. In other words, if the propositional representation 'this is good' and 'this is bad' must be inconsistent, then an attitude *for p* and an attitude *against p* have to generate incoherence analogously to the incoherence of offering both high and low odds on p. This is what is gained by a model in which evaluations are opened out by imagining their realization (Hintikka's 'Kingdom of Ends') and seeing whether the resulting world is consistent.

It would be intriguing to follow Hale's suggestion that against this background it might be better to consider only sets in which belief is represented as explicitly as attitude is, so that instead of evaluating $\{H!p, p\}$ you would evaluate $\{H!p, B!p\}$. So far as I can see this could be done, but unless some clear advantages emerge, it is relatively clumsy. Eventually, just as you imagine the ideals realized, you would need to imagine the beliefs true. We should also remember that in subjective probability theory there is no need to introduce a stage in which we represent beliefs explicitly, although the background interpretation proceeds in terms of belief, change of belief, learning new information, and so on. All in all, then, I am not convinced of the need for the complication, but I am also not convinced that I might not become so.[19]

Notes

1. David Lewis, 'Probability of Conditionals and Conditional Probability', *Philosophical Review* 85. Lewis also attempts to show that there could not be a subset of beliefs that also function as values or desires ('besires') because decision theory would then put inconsistent constraints on them. His paper, 'Desire as Belief', *Mind* 97, p. 323 is however countered by Huw Price, 'Defending Desire-as-Belief', *Mind* 98, p. 119.

2. *Spreading the Word*, p. 257.

3. Crispin Wright, 'Review of *Spreading the Word*', *Mind* 94, pp. 318–9, and Bob Hale, 'Can There Be a Logic of Attitudes?' (this volume, pp. 350–1). Subsequent references to these writers are to their papers in this volume.

4. John McDowell, *Projection and Truth in Ethics*, Lindley Lecture, section 3.

5. Alasdair Macintyre, *After Virtue*; Bernard Williams, *Ethics and the Limits of Philosophy*.

6. See, for example, McDowell, *Projection and Truth in Ethics*, p. 12.

7. Ibid.

8. Ibid., p. 6.

9. Ibid., p. 9.

10. John Campbell, in 'A Simple View of Colour' (this volume) argues that we can appeal to colours in explaining the evolution of colour vision: 'the reason why our visual system was selected for just was, in part, its utility in identifying the colours of things'. I cannot imagine a context in which this is a good thing to say. Although as we shall see I can defend one of the main tenets of his simple theory (the avoidance of dispositional reductions) and although we should be permissive about explanations couched in terms of all kinds of different predicates, surely this particular specimen comes from a very impoverished part of explanatory space.

11. I discuss the need for allowing considerable *variation* of the responses classed as ethical in connection with a similar objection raised by Nicholas Sturgeon, in my 'Just Causes' (*Philosophical Studies*, 1991).

12. For a recent defence of this view, see P. A. Boghossian and J. D. Velleman, 'Colour as a Secondary Quality', *Mind* 98, p. 81.

13. At this point I take it I am in sympathy with Campbell's Simple Theory.

14. Similarly, someone wondering whether e.g. patriotism is a value, is not wondering whether we actually desire/desire to desire it: no naturalistic reduction of content is needed at this point. This would be part of my response to David Lewis, 'Dispositional Theories of Value', *Aristotelian Society, Supplementary Volume* LXII.

15. See my 'Error and the Phenomenology of Value', in Ted Honderich (ed.), *Ethics and Objectivity*.

16. I express reservations about this way of putting it in 'How to be an Ethical Anti-Realist', in P. French, T. Uehling Jr., and H. Wettstein (eds.), *Midwest Studies in Philosophy* 12.

17. Would a quasi-realist always be hostile to explanatory stories starting with the citation of an ethical fact: 'because the system was unjust, the peasants revolted', and so on? Not necessarily: we can cite supervening propositions in causal explanations (for it not to have been unjust, it would have had to be different in other ways, and then the peasants would not have revolted). But of course in the context of the 'placing' operation, use of ethical predicates is banned. I discuss this further in 'Just Causes'.

18. 'Attitudes and Contents', *Ethics* 98.

19. My agnosticism here is connected with similar worries about the difficulty a 'Ramsey test' approach to conditionals has with examples that force a strict split between supposing something about the world, and imagining adding the belief to an antecedent stock of belief: the stock example is 'if Thatcher is a master criminal, nobody will ever believe it'.

18

Postscript

Bob Hale

Simon Blackburn's subtle and wide-ranging contribution calls, I need hardly say, for a much fuller response than is possible here. Space permits only brief comments on those parts of it which bear most directly on the difficulties raised in my essay.

I sought to confront the *q*-realist with two dilemmas. The main dilemma concerns the construction of a logic of attitudes and runs as follows: *either* such a logic will treat what appear as conditionals with evaluative components as being of the logical form their surface structure suggests (that is as having a dominant conditional operator)—in which case, whilst there is then no special problem about seeing inferences such as moral *modus ponens* as logically valid, the expressive construal of moral utterances is lost—*or* it will treat such compounds as implicitly involving a dominant attitudinal operator—in which case, whilst this keeps faith with the expressive construal Blackburn apparently intends, there remains a substantial problem over how we may see such inferences as *logically* valid. The subsidiary dilemma is that first posed by Crispin Wright: *either* the *q*-realist attempt to earn for moral utterances the right to what Blackburn now calls 'propositional surface' will succeed, *or* it will not. If *not*, the project fails to provide a satisfactory anti-realist treatment of this region of discourse; but if it *does* succeed, it re-instates the notions of truth, assertion, etc., for statements in the region, with the effect that the *q*-realist winds up denying the very contrast—moral utterances as expressions of attitude rather than genuinely assertoric—in terms of which his projectivist construal gets off the ground.

My interest in the subsidiary dilemma was that it seemed to me to provide a strong ground for thinking that if any *q*-realist treatment of evaluative discourse could succeed, it would have to be what I called a modest one. I have to acknowledge, however, that I did not make it crystal clear what this amounts to; as we shall see, a key issue concerns just what that position involves, and where it is to be located. Before I turn to that question, it is worth stressing that the main dilemma is in no way conditional upon the effectiveness of the subsidiary one. That is, even if I were wrong in thinking that the latter leaves room for at best a modest version of *q*-realism, it would still be necessary to negotiate a path between its horns. In his essay, Blackburn concentrates on the subsidiary dilemma and says very little—so far as I can see—that directly bears upon the main one. My claim was that a satisfactory representation of the logical form of compounds with evaluative components, if it is to allow of an expressive interpretation, would have to treat them as involving a dominant attitudinal operator. It is not clear whether Blackburn accepts this, but I can find no counter-argument in his essay. (My note 27, along with the text to which it relates, tries to explain why his tree-tied construal of conditionals and disjunctions does not provide a way out.) If the claim stands, it would seem to be essential (though not of course sufficient)—if the q-realist enterprise is to succeed—that we can circumscribe an appropriate notion of consistency for mixed sets of attitudes that avoids the problem aired in the last few pages of my essay, perhaps by exploiting the plausible idea that in assessing such combinations of belief and moral attitude, certain beliefs need to be held 'fixed' (see p. 358 and n. 28, and Blackburn's paper p. 381). Blackburn is fairly sanguine here, and chides me for seeing a difficulty where there is really nothing but an advance. Well, maybe. But notice that if we go this way, just which combinations come out inconsistent will depend, *inter alia*, on which beliefs are treated as fixed. Remembering that our concern centred on how, if at all, flouting moral *modus ponens* and the like could be exhibited as a logical—as opposed to merely moral—failing, it is evidently important to be clear about what criteria are involved in settling questions of fixity. Until it is clear that such questions do not essentially involve evaluative judgement, we cannot be sure that an expressivist *logic* of attitudes is after all possible.

Let us turn now to the subsidiary dilemma. It is agreed on all sides that we cast our moral and other evaluative commitments in propositional style. That is, we record them using declarative sentences which are, as such, syntactically suited to figure as components of conditionals and disjunctions, or as content-specifying clauses governed by verbs of propositional attitude such as 'know' and 'believe', and of course as fillings for 'p' in truth-idioms such as 'it is true (false) that p'. It is, I take it, definitive of any q-realist position that there need be nothing improper in all this. Blackburn concedes this much to Wright's dilemma: the q-realist 'cannot say "such and such commitments are not beliefs; they are other states that properly sustain the appearance of being beliefs", if properly sustaining the appearance is all that there is to *being* a belief'. Instead, since the q-realist holds that, for example, moral commitments do properly sustain the appearance, he will say that they *are* beliefs, 'but that they belong to the subset of beliefs which are also attitudes (dispositions, inference-tickets, or whatever)'. One might expect, in view of this, that Blackburn would have little time for the distinction I sought to draw between modest and ambitious q-realist. So it is somewhat surprising that he proceeds to acknowledge that there is still a question about whether we should go for a '*contrastive* story', according to which moral attitudes are *not* beliefs, however much we can earn them the right to behave like them, and an '*inclusive* story', which holds that earning them that right shows that they are beliefs, of a special sort. He goes on to explain that the choice between these stories is the choice between modest and ambitious *q*-realist, as he understands it. I do not think this is the right way to look at the matter. Let me try to explain why not.

Blackburn contends that the question whether moral commitments are 'really' true 'seems to depend upon a finer discrimination of the real sense of the term "true" than any we ought to claim' (his essay, p. 367). And he would, presumably, take a similarly dim view of the question whether such commitments 'really' are beliefs. In view of this, it is hard to see how he can regard modest *q*-realism, identified with adoption of a contrastive story, as an option worthy taking seriously; for it would seem that—unless (contrary to his suggestion) we *can* draw some relevant distinctions within the class of commitments that properly sustain the appearance of being beliefs—the only way to run a contrastive story would have to involve denying that moral commitments do *properly* sustain that appearance, which would amount to an error theory, in John Mackie's sense. It now seems to me, however, that identifying the modest–ambitious distinction—at least as I intended it—with that between contrastive and inclusive stories mislocates the issue. There *is* room for an interestingly modest version of *q*-realism, but it belongs *within* an inclusive story. The reason for this is quite simply that the modest *q*-realist will want to agree that there is *a* sense of belief in which moral commitments qualify as beliefs, just as he will want to agree that there is a use of 'true' in which such commitments can be said to be true. But he will not take the fact that we say—with no sense of linguistic impropriety—things like 'It's true that lying is wrong' and 'He believes that political assassinations are sometimes justified' as evidence that the expressive construal of moral discourse is wrong; instead he will take it as showing that 'it is true that . . .' and 'he believes that . . .' do not provide test contexts for discriminating seriously assertoric from merely expressive discourse, and that there are some beliefs (viz., evaluative ones) the holding of which just consists in subscribing to certain (evaluative) attitudes. Just as he holds that the notion of truth applicable to moral statements to be a thin, merely disquotational one, the applicability of which is quite consistent with viewing such statements as fundamentally expressive in character, rather than substantially assertoric, so he will hold that moral commitments are beliefs only in a correspondingly dilute sense which, like the notion of truth applicable to them, demands no more than that they may properly be voiced in propositional style. If this is how modest *q*-realist should be understood and located, then the real issue concerns whether there is room for a version of the position that exceeds the bounds of modesty. That would have to involve, it seems, either denying, after all, that moral statements are expressive rather than substantially assertoric, or maintaining that there is some substantial notion of truth applicable to them. If we really cannot make further discriminations of this sort *within* the broad class of commitments which 'properly sustain the appearance of being beliefs', then there would seem to be no scope for ambitious *q*-realism. But if—contrary to Blackburn's suggestions—we can do so, and if, in particular, we can identify some thicker notion of truth in terms of which moral statements can be appraised, then we can articulate a more ambitious *q*-realism, but I see no reason to suppose it can slide past Wright's original dilemma.

All this supposes, of course, that there is a philosophically significant contrast to be made out between statements that are merely expressive and those that are substantially assertoric; and further that this contrast is not to be made out in terms of the capacity, or otherwise, of commitments of some given sort to appear in propositional clothing. Some things Blackburn says give the impression that he is sceptical on both counts. But there surely is a significant contrast to be made—roughly in terms of different directions of fit: if the world is out of line with my moral attitudes, that is a reason for me to change the world, whereas if it does not accord with my non-moral beliefs, it is the beliefs that need adjustment. How in detail this contrast should be developed is too large and difficult a question for treatment here. The point I want to make here is just that, if I am right about how the modest–ambitious contrast needs to be made out, then it is at least very much open to question whether Blackburn has rescued ambitious q-realism from Wright's dilemma—as opposed to retreating into the modest position, as I understand it.

To end on a point of complete agreement. Blackburn conjectures that his new AC rule:

(4″) If L* is a next approximation relative to some set of sequences L, then if L* contains H!(X), then a subsequent approximation L** contains X and all the other sentences of L*

could replace my adaptation of Hintikka's original rule, that is:

(4′) For any L* from L, if $H!(X) \in L*$ then $A \in L*$

to yield a system of the same deductive power. This is of course quite correct, as can be seen by reflecting that the crucial question is whether (assuming rules (1)–(3)) $L* = \{\Delta, H!(X)\}$ closes with (4″) iff it closes with (4′). Applying the latter rule expands L* to $\{\Delta, H!(X), X\}$, while applying the former yields $L** = \{\Delta, X\}$. But applying rule (1) to L* ensures that this L** contains H!(X). Hence the original L* must close either way or neither.

Bibliography

Aquinas, T. *De Entia et Essentia*, trans. by A. Maurer, C.S.B. as *On Being and Essence* (Toronto: P.I.M.S., 1968).
———— *De Potentia*, trans. by L. Shapcote as *On the Power of God*, 3 vols. (London, 1932–4).
———— *De Veritate*, trans. by R. Mulligan, J. McGlynn, and R. Schmidt as *On Truth*, 3 vols. (Chicago: Regnery, 1952–4).
———— *Scriptum Super Libros Sententiarum* (Commentary on the Sentences of Peter Lombard) as yet this work remains untranslated.
———— *Sententia libri Peri Hermeneias*, trans. as *Aristotle's On Interpretation with Commentary by St Thomas and Cajetan* by J. T. Oesterle (Milwaukee, 1962).
———— *Summa Contra Gentiles*, trans. by the English Dominican Fathers, 5 vols. (London, 1924).
———— *Summa Theologiae*, 60 vols. by various translators (London, 1964–76).
Aristotle, *De Interpretatione*, trans. (with the *Categories*) by J. L. Ackrill (Oxford, 1963).
Bealer, G. *Quality and Concept* (Oxford, 1982).
Belnap, N. 'Tonk, Plonk and Plink', *Analysis* 23 (1962).
Bennett, J. *Locke, Berkeley, Hume, Central Themes* (Oxford, 1971).
Blackburn, S. *Spreading the Word* (Oxford, 1984).
———— 'Error and the Phenomenology of Value', in T. Honderich (ed.), *Morality and Objectivity* (London, 1985).
———— 'Morals and Modals', in G. Macdonald and C. Wright (eds.), *Fact, Science and Morality* (Oxford, 1986).
———— 'How to be an Ethical Antirealist', in P. French, T. Uehling Jr., and H. Wettstein (eds.), *Midwest Studies in Philosophy* 12 (Minneapolis, 1987).
———— 'Attitudes and Contents', *Ethics* 98 (1988).
———— 'Just Causes', *Philosophical Studies* (1991).
Blanshard, B. *The Nature of Thought* (London, 1939).
Boghossian, P. 'The Rule Following Considerations', *Mind* 98 (1989).
Boghossian, P. and Velleman, J. D. 'Colour as a Secondary Quality', *Mind* 98 (1989).
Bonjour, L. *The Structure of Empirical Knowledge* (Cambridge, Mass., 1985).
Brandom, R. 'Truth and Assertibility', *Journal of Philosophy* 73 (1976).
Burge, T. 'Individualism and the Mental', in P. French, T. Uehling Jr., and H. Wettstein (eds.), *Midwest Studies in Philosophy* 4 (Minneapolis, 1979).
Carnap, R. 'Truth and Confirmation', in H. Feigl and W. Sellars (eds.), *Readings in Philosophical Analysis* (New York, 1949), a translation, with adaptations, of 'Warheit und Bewahrung', *Actes du Congres International de Philosophie Scientifique* (1936).
Charles, D. and Lennon, K. (eds.), *Reduction, Explanation and Realism* (Oxford, 1992).

Chisholm, R. 'Identity Through Time', in H. Keifer and M. Munitz (eds.), *Language, Belief and Metaphysics* (Albany, New York, 1970).
—— 'Reply to Strawson's Comments', in H. Keifer and M. Muntz (eds.), *Language, Belief and Metaphysics* (Albany, New York, 1970).
—— 'Theory of Knowledge in America', *The Foundations of Knowing* (Brighton, 1982).
Craig, E. J. *The Mind of God and the Works of Man* (Oxford, 1987).
—— *Knowledge and the State of Nature* (Oxford, 1990).
Davidson, D. *Inquiries into Truth and Interpretation* (Oxford, 1984).
——'A Coherence Theory of Truth and Knowledge', in E. LePore (ed.), *Truth and Interpretation: Perspectives on the Philosophy of Donald Davidson* (Oxford, 1986).
Davies, M. and Humberstone, L. 'Two Notions of Necessity', *Philosophical Studies* (1980).
Devitt, M. *Realism and Truth* (Oxford, and Princeton, New Jersey, 1984).
Dummett, M. *Frege: Philosophy of Language* (London, 1973).
—— *Truth and Other Enigmas* (London, 1976).
—— 'The Justification of Deduction', in Dummett, *Truth and Other Enigmas* (London, 1976).
—— 'The Philosophical Basis of Intuitionistic Logic', in Dummet, *Truth and Other Enigmas* (London, 1976).
—— 'The Philosophical Significance of Gödel's Theorem', in Dummett, *Truth and Other Enigmas* (London, 1976).
—— 'What Does the Appeal to Use Do for the Theory of Meaning?', in A. Margolit (ed.), *Meaning and Use* (Dordrecht, 1976).
—— 'What is a Theory of Meaning? (II)', in G. Evans and J. McDowell (eds.), *Truth and Meaning* (Oxford, 1976).
—— 'What is a Theory of Meaning? (I)', in S. Guttenplan (ed.), *Mind and Language* (Oxford, 1977).
—— *Elements of Intuitionism* (Oxford, 1977).
—— 'Comments on Professor Prawitz's Paper', in G. H. von Wright (ed.), *Logic and Philosophy* (The Hague, 1980).
—— *The Interpretation of Frege's Philosophy* (London, 1982).
Edwards, P. 'Russell's Doubts about Induction', *Mind* 58 (1949); reprinted in R. Swinburne (ed.), *The Justification of Induction* (Oxford, 1974).
Evans, G. and McDowell, J. (eds.) *Truth and Meaning* (Oxford, 1976).
Evans, G. 'Things Without the Mind', in Zak van Straaten (ed.), *Philosophical Subjects: Essays presented to P. F. Strawson* (Oxford, 1980).
Field, H. 'Logic, Meaning and Conceptual Role', *Journal of Philosophy* 74 (1977).
—— *Science Without Numbers* (Oxford, 1980).
Fine, A. 'The Natural Ontological Attitude', in J. Leplin (ed.), *Scientific Realism* (Berkeley, 1984).
—— 'And Not Anti-Realism Either', *Nous* (1986).
—— 'Unnatural Attitudes: Realist and Instrumentalist Attachments to Science', *Mind* (1986).
Fodor, J. *Representations* (Sussex, 1981).
Frankena, W. 'Obligation and Motivation in Recent Moral Philosophy', in A. I. Melden (ed.), *Essays in Moral Philosophy* (Seattle, 1958).
Friedman, M. 'Truth and Confirmation', in H. Kornblith (ed.), *Naturalising Epistemology* (Cambridge, Mass., 1985).
Geach, P. *Mental Acts* (London, 1958).

——— 'Assertion', *Philosophical Review* 74 (1965); reprinted in P. Geach, *Logic Matters* (Oxford, 1973).

George, A. (ed.) *Reflections on Chomsky* (Oxford, 1989).

Glymour, C. 'Conceptual Scheming or Confessions of a Metaphysical Realist', *Synthese* 51 (1982).

Goodman, N. *Of Mind and Other Matters* (Cambridge, Mass., 1984).

——— 'Notes on the Well-Made World', in Goodman, *Of Mind and Other Matters*.

Grice, H. P. and Strawson, P. F. 'In Defence of a Dogma', *Philosophical Review* (1956).

Hacking, I. 'What is Logic?', *Journal of Philosophy* 76 (1979).

Haldane, J. 'Aquinas on Sense-Perception', *Philosophical Review* 92 (1983).

——— 'Brentano's Problem', *Grazer Philosophische Studien* 35 (1989).

——— 'Reid, Scholasticism and Current Philosophy of Mind', in M. Dalgarno and E. Matthews (eds.), *The Philosophy of Thomas Reid* (Dordrecht, 1989).

——— 'Chesterton's Philosophy of Education', *Philosophy* 65 (1990).

——— 'Putnam on Intentionality', *Philosophy and Phenomenological Research* 52 (1992).

Hale, R. 'The Compleat Projectivist', *Philosophical Quarterly* 36 (1986).

Harman, G. *Thought* (Princeton, New Jersey, 1973).

——— *The Nature of Morality* (Oxford, 1977).

——— 'The Meaning of Logical Constants', in E. LePore (ed.), *Truth and Interpretation: Perspectives on the Philosophy of Donald Davidson* (Oxford, 1986).

——— *Change in View* (Cambridge, Mass., 1986).

Hintikka, J. 'Some Main Problems of Deontic Logic', in R. Hilpinen (ed.), *Deontic Logic: Introductory and Systematic Readings* (Dordrecht, 1971).

——— 'Deontic Logic and its Philosophical Morals', in Hintikka, *Models for Modalities*.

——— *Models for Modalities* (Dordrecht, 1969).

Hookway, C. 'Two Conceptions of Moral Realism', *Proceedings of the Aristotelian Society*, Supplementary Volume (1986).

Horwich, P. 'Three Forms of Realism', *Synthese* 51 (1989).

Hume, D. *Enquiries Concerning the Human Understanding and Concerning the Principles of Morals*, L. A. Selby-Bigge (ed.) (Oxford, 1962).

——— *Treatise of Human Nature*, L. A. Selby-Bigge (ed.) (Oxford, 1976).

Jackson, F. and Pettit, P. 'Functionalism and Broad Content', *Mind* 97 (1988).

——— 'Structural Explanation in Social Theory', in D. Charles and K. Lennon (eds.), *Reduction, Explanation and Realism* (Oxford, 1992).

James, W. *The Meaning of Truth: A Sequel to Pragmatism* (New York, 1909).

Johnston, M. 'Human Beings', *Journal of Philosophy* 84 (1987).

——— 'The End of the Theory of Meaning', *Mind and Language* 3 (1988).

——— 'Dispositional Theories of Value', *Proceedings of the Aristotelian Society*, Supplementary Volume LXII (1989).

——— 'How to Speak of the Colors', *Philosophical Studies* 68 (1992).

——— 'Reasons and Reductionism', *Philosophical Review* 101 (1992).

——— 'Dispositions: Predication with a Grain of Salt' (forthcoming).

Kant, I. *Foundations of the Metaphysics of Morals*, trans. by L. J. Beck (Indianapolis, 1959).

Kirk, G. and Raven J. *The Presocratic Philosophers* (Cambridge, 1975).

Kolnai, A. 'The Ghost of the Naturalistic Fallacy', *Philosophy* 55 (1980–1).

Kremer, M. 'Logic and Meaning: The Philosophical Significance of the Sequent Calculus', *Mind* 97 (1988).

Kripke, S. *Wittgenstein on Rules and Private Language* (Oxford, 1982).

Leeds, S. 'Theories of Reference and Truth', *Erkenntnis* 13 (1978).

Lewis, D. 'Psychophysical and Theoretical Identifications', *Australasian Journal of Philosophy* 50 (1972).

——— 'Probability of Conditionals and Conditional Probability', *Philosophical Review* 85 (1976).

——— *Philosophical Papers*, Vol. I (Oxford, 1983).

——— 'Putnam's Paradox', *Australasian Journal of Philosophy* 62 (1984).

——— *On the Plurality of Worlds* (Oxford, 1986).

——— 'Desire as Belief', *Mind* 97 (1988).

——— 'Dispositional Theories of Value', *Proceedings of the Aristotelian Society*, Supplementary Volume LXII (1989).

Lewy, C. 'G. E. Moore and the Naturalistic Fallacy', *Proceedings of the British Academy* L (1964).

Locke, J. *An Essay Concerning Human Understanding*, A. S. Pringle-Pattison (ed.) (Oxford, 1934).

Luntley, M. *Language, Logic and Experience* (London, 1988).

McDowell, J. 'Truth Conditions, Bivalence and Verificationism', in G. Evans and J. McDowell (eds.), *Truth and Meaning* (Oxford, 1976).

——— 'Values and Secondary Qualities', in T. Honderich (ed.), *Morality and Objectivity* (London, 1985).

——— *Projection and Truth in Ethics*, Lindley Lecture (Kansas, 1987).

——— 'Scheme-Content Dualism, Experience and Subjectivity' (unpublished).

McDowell, J. and Pettit, P. (eds.) *Subject, Thought and Context* (Oxford, 1986).

McFetridge, I. *Logical Necessity and Other Essays*, J. Haldane and R. Scruton (eds.) (London, 1990).

McGinn, C. 'An A Priori Argument for Realism', *Journal of Philosophy* 76 (1979).

——— *The Subjective View* (Oxford, 1983).

McGuinness, B. (ed.) *Ludwig Wittgenstein and the Vienna Circle* (Oxford, 1979).

Macintyre, A. *After Virtue* (London, 1981).

Mackie, J. L. *Problems from Locke* (Oxford, 1976).

——— *Ethics—Inventing Right and Wrong* (Harmondsworth, 1977).

——— *Hume's Moral Theory* (London, 1980).

——— *Persons and Values* (Oxford, 1986).

Maritain, J. *The Degrees of Knowledge*, trans. by G. Phelan (London, 1959).

Miller, R. 'Ways of Moral Learning', *Philosophical Review* 94 (1985).

Moore, G. E. *Principia Ethica* (Cambridge, 1903).

Nagel, T. *The Possibility of Altruism* (Oxford and Princeton, New Jersey, 1970).

——— *The View from Nowhere* (New York, 1986).

Peacocke, C. *Holistic Explanation* (Oxford, 1979).

——— 'The Theory of Meaning in Analytic Philosophy', in G. Floistad (ed.), *Contemporary Philosophy, Vol. 1: Philosophy of Language/Philosophical Logic* (The Hague, 1981).

——— *Thoughts: An Essay on Content* (Oxford, 1986).

——— 'What Determines Truth Conditions?', in J. McDowell and P. Pettit (eds.), *Subject, Thought and Context* (Oxford, 1986).

——— 'Understanding Logical Constants: A Realist's Account', *Proceedings of the British Academy* 63 (1987).

——— 'The Limits of Intelligibility: A Post-Verificationist Proposal', *Philosophical Review* 97 (1988).

———— 'Content and Norms in a Natural World', in E. LePore and E. Villanueva (eds.), *Information-Theoretic Semantics and Epistemology* (Oxford, 1989).

————'What are Concepts?', in H. Wettstein (ed.), *Contemporary Perspectives in the Philosophy of Language II, Midwest Studies in Philosophy* 14 (Notre Dame, 1989).

———— 'How Are A Priori Truths Possible?', *European Journal of Philosophy* 1.

Pettit, P. 'The Reality of Rule-Following', *Mind* (1990).

Plato, *Euthyphro*, trans. by B. Jowett in *The Dialogues of Plato*, Vol. II (Oxford, 1892).

———— *Theaetetus*, trans. by B. Jowett in *The Dialogues of Plato* (Oxford, 1892).

Pollock, J. *The Foundations of Philosophical Semantics* (Princeton, 1984).

———— *Contemporary Theories of Knowledge* (London, 1987).

Prawitz, D. 'Intuitionistic Logic: A Philosophical Challenge', in G. H. von Wright (ed.), *Logic and Philosophy* (The Hague, 1980).

Price, H. 'Defending Desire-as-Belief', *Mind* 98 (1989).

Prior, A. 'The Runabout Inference-Ticket', *Analysis* 21 (1960).

Putnam, H. *Meaning and the Moral Sciences* (London, 1978).

———— 'Realism and Reason', in Putnam, *Meaning and the Moral Sciences* (London, 1978).

———— 'Why There Isn't a Ready-Made World', in Putnam, *Realism and Reason: Philosophical Papers, Volume 3*.

———— *Reason, Truth and History* (Cambridge, 1981).

———— *Realism and Reason: Philosophical Papers, Volume 3* (Cambridge, 1983).

———— 'Models and Reality', in *Realism and Reason: Philosophical Papers, Volume 3* (Cambridge, 1983).

———— 'Is the Causal Structure of the Physical Itself Something Physical?', in P. French, T. Uehling Jr., and H. Wettstein (eds.), *Midwest Studies in Philosophy* 9 (Minneapolis, 1984).

———— *The Many Faces of Realism* (La Salle, Ill., 1987).

———— *Representation and Reality* (Cambridge, Mass., 1988).

———— 'Model Theory and the Factuality of Semantics', in A. George (ed.), *Reflections on Chomsky* (Oxford, 1989).

———— 'James's Theory of Perception', in Putnam, *Realism with a Human Face* (Cambridge, Mass., 1990).

———— *Realism with a Human Face* (Cambridge, Mass., 1990).

Quine, W. V. O. *Mathematical Logic* (Cambridge, Mass., 1951).

———— *Philosophy of Logic* (Englewood Cliffs, New Jersey, 1970).

———— *The Roots of Reference* (La Salle, Ill., 1973).

———— 'Reply to Professor Marcus', in *The Ways of Paradox* (Cambridge, Mass., 1976).

———— 'Reply to Stroud', in P. French, T. Uehling Jr., and H. Wettstein (eds.), *Midwest Studies in Philosophy* (Minneapolis, 1981).

Railton, P. 'Moral Realism', *Philosophical Review* 95 (1986).

———— 'Facts and Values', *Philosophical Topics* 14 (1986).

———— 'Naturalism and Prescriptivity', *Social Philosophy and Policy* 7 (1989).

———— 'How Thinking About Character and Utilitarianism Might Lead us to Rethink the Character of Utilitarianism', in P. French, T. Uehling Jr., and H. Wettstein (eds.), *Midwest Studies in Philosophy* 13 (Minneapolis, 1988).

Reid, T. *An Inquiry into the Human Mind on the Principles of Common Sense*, T. Duggan (ed.) (Chicago, 1970).

Rorty, R. *Philosophy and the Mirror of Nature* (Oxford, 1980).

———— 'Pragmatism, Davidson and Truth', in E. Lepore (ed.), *Inquiries into Truth and Interpretation* (Oxford, 1986).

Russell, B. *An Inquiry into Meaning and Truth* (Baltimore, Maryland, 1965).

Salmon, W. 'Rejoinder to Barker and Kyburg', in R. Swinburne (ed.), *The Justification of Induction* (Oxford, 1974).

Schiffer, S. *Remnants of Meaning* (Cambridge, Mass., 1987).

Schlick, M. 'The Foundation of Knowledge', *Erkenntis* (1934): reprinted in A. J. Ayer (ed.), *Logical Positivism* (New York, 1959).

―――― 'Meaning and Verification', *The Philosophical Review* (1936).

Searle, J. *Intentionality* (Cambridge, 1983).

Shapiro, S. 'Conservativeness and Incompleteness', *Journal of Philosophy* 80 (1983).

Shoenfield, J. R. *Mathematical Logic* (New York, 1967).

Skorupski, J. 'Anti-realism: Cognitive Role and Semantic Content', in J. Butterfield (ed.), *Language, Mind and Logic* (Cambridge, 1986).

―――― *John Stuart Mill* (London, 1989).

―――― 'Critical Review of Wright, *Realism, Meaning and Truth*', *Philosophical Quarterly* 38 (1988).

―――― 'The Intelligibility of Scepticism', in D. Bell and N. Cooper (eds.), *The Analytic Tradition* (Oxford, 1990).

Smith, M. 'Reason and Desire', *Proceedings of the Aristotelian Society* (1987–8).

―――― 'Dispositional Theories of Value', *Proceedings of the Aristotelian Society,* Supplementary Volume LXII (1989).

―――― *The Moral Problem* (forthcoming).

Strawson, P. F. *Introduction to Logical Theory* (London, 1952).

―――― *The Bounds of Sense* (London, 1966).

―――― 'Scruton and Wright on Anti-Realism Etc.', *Proceedings of the Aristotelian Society* 77 (1976–7).

―――― 'Reply to Evans', in Zak van Straaten (ed.), *Philosophical Subjects: Essays presented to P. F. Strawson* (Oxford, 1980).

Stroud, B. *The Significance of Philosophical Scepticism* (New York, 1984).

―――― *John Locke Lectures* (1987) (unpublished).

―――― 'Understanding Human Knowledge in General' (forthcoming).

Sturgeon, N. 'Moral Explanations', in D. Copp and D. Zimmerman (eds.), *Morality, Reason, and Truth* (Totowa, 1986).

Sundholm, G. 'Proof Theory and Meaning', in D. Gabbay and F. Guenthner (eds.), *Handbook of Philosophical Logic, Vol. III, Alternatives to Classical Logic* (Dordrecht, 1986).

Swinburne, R. (ed.) *The Justification of Induction* (Oxford, 1974).

Tennant, N. *Anti-Realism and Logic: Truth as Eternal* (Oxford, 1987).

Unger, P. 'A Defense of Skepticism', *Philosophical Review* 80 (1971).

―――― *Ignorance—a Case for Scepticism* (Oxford, 1975).

―――― *Philosophical Relativity* (Oxford, 1984).

Urmson, J. O. 'Some Questions Concerning Validity', in R. Swinburne (ed.), *The Justification of Induction* (Oxford, 1974).

Van Fraassen, B. *The Scientific Image* (Oxford, 1979).

Vermazen, B. 'The Intelligibility of Massive Error', *Philosophical Quarterly* 33 (1983).

von Wright, G. H. 'Norms, Truth and Logic', *Practical Reason: Philosophical Papers Vol. 1* (Oxford, 1983).

Wiggins, D. *Needs, Values, Truth* (Oxford, 1987).

―――― 'The Sense and Reference of Predicates', *The Philosophical Quarterly* 34 (1984).

Williams, B. *Ethics and the Limits of Philosophy* (London, 1986).

Williams, M. *Groundless Belief* (Oxford, 1977).

—— 'Coherence, Justification and Truth', *Review of Metaphysics* 34 (1980).y
—— 'Do We Epistemologists Need a Theory of Truth?', *Philosophical Topics* 14 (1986).
—— 'Epistemological Realism and the Basis of Scepticism', *Mind* 97 (1988).
—— 'Scepticism without Theory', *Review of Metaphysics* 41 (1988).
—— 'Scepticism and Charity', *Ratio* (forthcoming).
Wilshire, B. (ed.) *William James: The Essential Writings* (New York, 1971).
Wittgenstein, L. *Philosophical Investigations*, 2nd edn. (Oxford, 1958).
—— *On Certainty* (Oxford, 1969).
—— *Remarks on the Foundations of Mathematics*, 3rd edn. (Oxford, 1978).
—— 'Lecture on Ethics', *Philosophical Review* 74 (1965).
Wright, C. *Frege's Conception of Numbers as Objects* (Aberdeen, 1983).
—— *Realism, Meaning and Truth* (Oxford, 1987).
—— 'Strawson on Anti-Realism', *Synthese* 40 (1979).
—— 'Truth Conditions and Criteria', in *Realism, Meaning and Truth* (Oxford, 1987).
—— 'Moral Values, Projection and Secondary Qualities', *Proceedings of the Aristotelian Society*, Supplementary Volume LXII (1988).
—— 'Realism, Anti-Realism, Irrealism, Quasi-realism' (Gareth Evans Memorial Lecture), in P. French, T. Uehling, Jr., and H. Wettstein (eds.), *Midwest Studies in Philosophy* 12 (Minneapolis, 1988).
—— 'Wittgenstein's Rule-Following Considerations and the Central Project of Theoretical Linguistics', in A. George (ed.), *Reflections on Chomsky* (Oxford, 1989).
—— *Truth and Objectivity* (Cambridge, Mass., 1992).

Index

(Note: Page ranges in boldface refer to author's article in this volume)